Financial Institutions, Financial Markets, and Money

Financial Institutions, Financial Markets, and Money

Herbert M. Kaufman
Arizona State University

Harcourt Brace Jovanovich, Inc.

New York   San Diego   Chicago   San Francisco   Atlanta
London   Sydney   Toronto

To Helen and to my parents

ISBN: 0-15-527393-0

Library of Congress Catalog Card Number: 82-82672

Printed in the United States of America

Preface

Writing a book about as complex a subject as the financial system has, I am sure, never been an easy task. However, the pace of change over the last few years has made writing this book a challenge. Describing and analyzing the financial markets and institutions in a changing environment is the primary goal of this book.

The book is intended for courses in financial markets and financial institutions. Instructors emphasizing these areas in courses in money and banking may also find the book appropriate, but it is not primarily intended for conventional money and banking courses. As a result, standard monetary theory is treated only briefly, allowing room for in-depth analysis of financial markets, financial institutions, and monetary policy. The student is assumed to have had one basic course in macroeconomic principles. The relatively small amount of mathematics in the text is at the level of simple algebra.

The organization of the book is described fully in the last section of the first chapter and, therefore, I will not repeat it here. However, I would like to highlight some aspects of the book.

Financial institutions receive careful analysis, with three chapters (Chapters 5, 6, and 7) devoted to commercial banking (including one chapter on the commercial bank as a business), a separate chapter devoted to savings and loan associations (Chapter 8), and two additional chapters on depository and non-depository institutions (Chapters 9 and 10). The latter chapter also contains a section on the new financial supermarkets such as Merrill Lynch. Because of the growing importance of international financial interactions, a separate chapter is also devoted to international exchange rate determination and international financial markets (Chapter 14). Separate chapters are also devoted to the interplay between financial intermediaries and financial markets

(Chapter 11), government-sponsored agencies (Chapter 15), and governmental regulation and financial innovation (Chapter 16). With respect to the latter chapter, interaction between regulation and innovation was substantial even before the Depository Institutions Deregulation and Monetary Control Act. The implementation of DIDMCA has further increased the necessity to understand how regulation and financial innovation interact to shape the financial system. DIDMCA is covered in detail in this chapter.

There is also considerable coverage of monetary policy in this book (Chapters 17, 18, and 19). I beleive that to understand the financial system fully the details of monetary policy must be mastered. However, some instructors may not share this view. For these instructors, the introduction to the Federal Reserve System provided in the first commercial bank chapter (Chapter 5) should suffice.

Each chapter is followed by an article taken from the financial press. The purpose of these articles is to demonstrate to the student the relevance of the material in the chapter and to enlarge on or further develop some topic covered in the chapter. All articles have been chosen with care; even when some specific details addressed in an article have changed, the article will remain relevant. A summary of the key points of the chapter, discussion questions, and suggested readings also follow each chapter.

The book is most effective when the chapters are covered in sequence. However, it is possible to change the organization after covering the first four chapters. These four chapters are the building blocks for the entire text. They introduce the financial intermediaries and markets, the flow of funds, money, and interest rates. After covering these four chapters, however, instructors can assign the chapters on the financial markets before the financial institutions chapters. In addition, the monetary policy chapters can be covered after the first commercial banking chapter.

I wish to acknowledge the help of a number of people. Throughout the preparation of this book, many useful suggestions were made by Eugene F. Drzycimski, University of Wisconsin, Oshkosh; Phillip Fincher, Louisiana Tech University; Arnold Langsen, California State University, Hayward; Morgan Lynge, University of Illinois, Urbana-Champaign; Richard Rivard, University of South Florida; Ronald L. Schillereff, President, Love Field National Bank, Dallas; Jonathan Scott, Southern Methodist University; Oscar Varela, University of New Orleans; and Daniel L. White, Georgia State University. I thank them for their help. Lynn Winkelman was expert and efficient in typing all drafts of the manuscript. Robert Watrous, the manuscript editor at Harcourt Brace Jovanovich, has shown great diligence, intelligence, and patience in copy editing the book and seeing it through production. I am also grateful to the rest of the staff at Harcourt Brace Jovanovich for their work in producing this book.

Finally, Steve Dowling, a senior editor at Harcourt Brace Jovano-vich, has overseen this book from its inception, read every draft, and made countless suggestions that have led to its improvement. His help is greatly appreciated.

I hope that instructors find this book useful in teaching a very difficult subject and that students find the time they spend with the book to be valuable.

Contents

19 The Money Supply Process and the Strategy of Monetary Policy 487

20 Inflation 511

PART 1

Finance and the Economy

Introduction to the Financial System

1

This text is about the financial system. As such, it concerns all of us because the financial system is as vital to the economy as the land, labor, and capital (productive resources) that are used to produce our goods and services. The goal of this text is to provide an understanding of the importance of the financial system and its role in the economy.

The United States has a monetary economy. This means that transactions are conducted using something that is generally acceptable as a means of payment or a medium of exchange. This distinguishes the U.S. economy—and all economies above a very primitive level—from a barter economy in which goods are traded for other goods. In a monetary economy, goods are traded for something that is called money, fundamentally altering the economic system.

Most people have engaged in barter transactions. As children, many of us may have swapped marbles or comic books, or traded baseball cards to friends for other cards that we needed to complete our collections. But what if all transactions were conducted in this way? How could the large number of transactions that take place in a modern economy be accomplished within a barter system? Clearly as soon as an economy develops any degree of complexity, it is necessary for a monetary unit to develop and one or several always do. Once money develops, the financial system has started.

The Financial System

The financial system in a modern economy is a collection of institutions and markets that interact in order to perform a number of important functions. Facilitating the borrowing and lending of funds is the most

3

Figure 1-1
The Flow of Funds from Savers to Borrowers

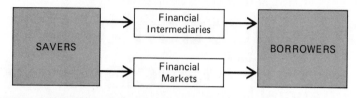

fundamental function performed by the financial system. In our economy, as in any developed economy, there are always savers and borrowers. The financial system distributes the funds saved to the borrowers. The system performs a basic service in that the borrowers are presumed to borrow for useful purposes, such as business investment in new factories. Since they pay a fee for borrowing, called the interest rate, it must be assumed that they are going to use those funds for their own benefit or at least they believe this to be the case. If not, why would borrowers be willing to pay such a fee? In a sophisticated economy, institutions and markets develop to better allocate these funds from savers to borrowers to assure a smooth flow of funds from one group to the other. Figure 1-1 depicts this process in a very simplified way; savers transmit their savings either directly through markets or indirectly through financial institutions to ultimate borrowers in the economy.[1]

Savers and Borrowers

Who are these ultimate savers and ultimate borrowers? Consumers and business, and at times even government (although this is rarer), save portions of their income. Economists define saving at its simplest level as merely not spending. Savers seek to hold their savings in forms that give them some return, that is, some reward for not spending. They may place their savings in a financial intermediary, or if they have larger amounts of funds, are more adventurous, or seek a higher return, they may directly lend those funds to ultimate borrowers through the financial markets. However, even if the funds are placed in a financial intermediary, the savings in turn will be loaned to ultimate borrowers.

---

[1]The term "ultimate" is inserted at this point to make clear that the borrowers we are referring to are not simply intermediaries but rather borrow the funds for their own use. Similarly, the term "ultimate saver" makes clear that we are referring to those individuals and organizations actually doing the saving.

Who then are the ultimate borrowers? Consumers, business, and government are also ultimate borrowers just as they were ultimate savers. If, for example, an individual does not spend a portion of her earnings from a part-time job, that individual is an ultimate saver. If the individual also borrows to purchase a car, the individual is also an ultimate borrower. Similarly, a business firm may be saving a portion of its profits, but at the same time the firm may also be financing its inventories or constructing a new factory through borrowing.

Financial Intermediaries and Markets

Figure 1-2 is an expanded version of Figure 1-1 showing the common institutions and markets that exist in our economy to transfer funds from ultimate savers to ultimate borrowers. Funds are transferred directly from savers to borrowers in the financial markets, the lower

Figure 1-2
The Flow of Funds from Savers to Borrowers: Details

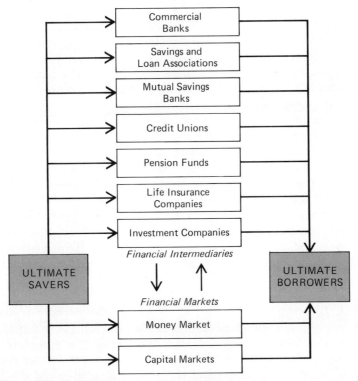

portion of Figure 1-2, or indirectly through the financial intermediaries, the upper portion of the figure. All of the intermediaries and markets listed in Figure 1-2 will come in for extensive examination in the following chapters. But it is useful at this point to discuss these institutions and markets at a very general level, beginning with the financial intermediaries.

Financial Intermediaries

The general term financial institution is used often in this book. However, of more interest is a particular type of financial institution, the financial intermediary. The financial institutions shown in Figure 1-2 are all financial intermediaries. They are called financial intermediaries because they come between ultimate savers and ultimate borrowers. They accept savings and, in return, the savers acquire claims against them. Financial intermediaries use the funds they have received from savers to make loans to ultimate borrowers, thus securing claims against these borrowers. This process is the essence of financial intermediation. In return for entrusting savings to the financial intermediary, the saver expects some return either in the form of an interest payment in the case of savings accounts or interest-earning checking accounts, or in the form of some service in the case of noninterest-earning checking accounts. The intermediaries in turn expect a fee, also in the form of an interest return, from the individuals and organizations to whom they have made loans.

Why are financial intermediaries necessary? Why can't the saver circumvent the intermediaries entirely and directly make loans to the ultimate borrower? After all, an intermediary, whether a financial one or any other middleman, does not exist out of any charitable motive. Rather, the financial intermediary is in business to make a profit. Thus, the fee that the intermediaries charge borrowers is usually considerably higher than that which they pay the saver for providing the funds with which they make the loans. Why not avoid them altogether?

The first answer to this question is that the saver can avoid intermediaries by participating directly in the financial markets listed in Figure 1-2. However, the second answer is that such participation must not be for everyone, otherwise the intermediaries would not exist. Nobody would use them. Thus they must serve some function. What do financial intermediaries do?

Risk Sharing If an individual makes a loan of all his available funds directly to another person, and that person turns out to be a bad risk who fails to repay the loan, the lender is a complete loser. His savings are gone and he has nothing to show for them. But suppose that the lender could command sufficient funds to make thousands of individual loans. If a few turned out to be bad loans and were not repaid, it would hardly make a dent in his assets. The risk of lending would have been spread over a large number of loans.

Now suppose that we are still in the situation in which a lender is only able to make one loan, and she understands very well that if that one loan proves to be a poor one, she will be wiped out. Surely the lender would need a large inducement to make the loan. That inducement would come in the form of a high return. The lender would expect to profit a great deal, if indeed the loan turns out to be a sound one, for undertaking such a risk. But consider. Suppose that a group of people said to the lender that if she would place any available funds at their disposal, they absolutely guarantee a specified rate of return on those funds. Further, suppose that the lender trusts their guarantee. She then might be willing to take considerably less return for parting with her funds.

If that group of people could gather funds from many individuals in the same way, they could make a lot of loans with those funds. Even if some loans turn out to be unsound, this is actually minimized as we shall see; the bulk of the loans they make will be good. Each individual participant (the individuals who have been induced to trust their funds to the intermediary) will not be affected materially. That is, the risk of the few bad loans has been spread over a large number of loans and a large number of depositors.

Spreading the risk also means that the intermediary, all things being equal, can charge a much lower fee than individual lenders making single loans would have to charge. This lower fee is quite important in our economy and is an important result of financial intermediation. But there is an additional element to consider. A financial intermediary possesses a degree of expertise in analyzing the merit of loans that an individual does not.

Expertise Suppose an individual decided to make a loan directly to someone wishing to buy a house. A number of questions would immediately confront the lender. Is the person credit-worthy? That is, does the borrower have the income potential and inclination to repay the debt? Is the house worth more than the loan? If it is not, then should the lender have to foreclose and sell the house to recover the loan, the full amount of the loan will not be recovered. These and a host of other questions are simply beyond the ability of most individuals to evaluate since most people have no training or experience with such matters. However, financial intermediaries can do just that.

The financial intermediaries have employees who are trained to answer such questions. Their employees also have the experience to put the answers in perspective and make a sound judgment. Even with all this, they do make a small percentage of loans that prove to be bad and are not repaid. Sometimes even the collateral, such as the house that secures a mortgage loan, may prove deficient. But an individual would clearly have much less success.

The expertise of financial intermediaries minimizes the risk that is being spread around, enabling institutions to charge lower fees for their lending. This adds to the efficiency of what we call the credit allocation process.

Efficiency and the Credit Allocation Process The use of the term **credit allocation** has thus far been avoided. Yet credit allocation is fundamentally what institutions—as well as the markets that we will discuss in this book—are engaged in. The transference of funds from ultimate savers to ultimate borrowers is called the **allocation of credit.** It is fundamentally important that credit allocation be accomplished efficiently in a highly developed economy. It was once said that "credit greases the wheels of commerce." This phrase means that credit is essential for the efficient operation of an economy. That is why a comparison between a highly developed economy such as that of the United States and a less developed economy in the third world reveals a striking disparity in the level of development of the two financial systems. The numbers and variety of U.S. financial intermediaries and the diversity of U.S. financial markets far surpass their counterparts, when these exist at all, in developing economies. With economic growth comes the need for more financial sophistication. A highly developed economy cannot exist without an advanced financial system nor would an advanced financial system evolve in an underdeveloped economy. Both are needed. Financial system development and economic development complement each other and contribute to each other's growth.

The Major Financial Intermediaries

Financial intermediaries contribute immeasurably to the efficiency of the credit allocation process. While the specific roles and details of the operation of the intermediaries will be addressed in future chapters, a brief examination of the intermediaries listed in Figure 1-2 will be useful at this stage. Table 1-1 lists the total assets of the major financial intermediaries that are discussed below.

Commercial Banks

The largest and most important of the financial intermediaries are the commercial banks. These institutions are responsible for the handling of most of the checking accounts in our economy. Checking accounts

Table 1-1
Total Assets of Major Financial
Intermediaries, Year-End 1980
(Billions of Dollars)

Commercial Banks	$1,537.0
Savings and Loan Associations	629.8
Mutual Savings Banks	171.6
Credit Unions	70.7
Pension Funds	609.3[1]
Life Insurance Companies	476.2
Investment Companies	94.5[1]

[1] 1979.

Sources: Federal Reserve *Bulletin; Monthly Statistical Review*, Securities and Exchange Commission; and *Mutual Fund Fact Book*, Investment Co. Institute.

are of great importance since they are the primary medium through which transactions are executed. In addition, commercial banks also hold substantial amounts of savings accounts.

The name "commercial bank" comes from the association of these institutions with commerce. From the earliest stages of their development, commercial banks have been associated with lending funds to businesses. In the last few decades they have greatly expanded the group to which they lend and now are major consumer lenders as well. But their primary lending is still to business and as such they are a vital link in the credit allocation process.

Savings and Loan Associations

Savings and loan associations are one of the largest financial intermediary groups. These institutions primarily offer savings deposits (often called savings and loan shares) and use the proceeds of those deposits, for the most part, to make mortgage loans for housing. In fact, they are the largest mortgage lending institution. Under legislation that became effective in 1981, savings and loan associations, along with other depository financial intermediaries,[2] can offer interest-earning checking accounts nationally. Prior to this legislation savings and loan associations, except in a few states, were prohibited from offering

---

[2] Depository financial intermediaries are commercial banks, savings and loan associations, mutual savings banks, and credit unions.

checking accounts. We will return to this and related developments in later chapters because it is one of the major factors underlying the changed competitive structure among financial intermediaries.

Mutual Savings Banks

Mutual savings banks, located primarily in the northeastern section of the United States, are similar to savings and loan associations in that their primary business is to make mortgage loans. However, a somewhat smaller percentage of their lending goes to mortgages than is true for savings and loan associations. Even though they are located in relatively few states, they are important because of the size of the states in which they operate. For example, they are very prominent in New York and Massachusetts. They are commonly called savings banks and, as the name implies, their primary form of deposits are savings accounts. Since they are a depository financial intermediary, they are permitted to offer checking accounts as well.

Credit Unions

Credit unions were, during the 1970s, one of the most rapidly growing of the financial intermediaries, though their growth slowed somewhat in the early 1980s. Despite their rapid growth, however, they remain substantially smaller than the other intermediaries mentioned thus far (see Table 1-1). A credit union is an association of individuals who have some common relationship, like employees of the same firm or members of the same profession, who hold shares—which are really savings deposits—in the credit union. The credit union uses these deposits to make loans to members for consumer purchases. As depository intermediaries, the credit unions also offer checking accounts, a fact that further reflects the growing similarity in the financial system of financial intermediaries.

Pension Funds

There are two types of pension funds, governmental and private. Both are financial intermediaries in which funds are saved by individuals for retirement. Why is the pension fund a financial intermediary? Because the pension fund uses these savings to purchase bonds (debt instruments) and equities (ownership shares in business firms) in order to generate a return which helps pension participants' savings grow. Although not as visible as some of the other institutions that have been mentioned, they are a very large financial intermediary group. Their rapid growth in recent years has already meant that they are of major importance in the credit allocation process. Furthermore, the projected future growth of pension funds ensures their continued importance in the financial system.

Life Insurance Companies

Life insurance companies at first glance do not appear to be financial intermediaries. Yet they operate as other financial intermediaries receiving the savings of individuals and using these savings to purchase debt securities, acquire equities in businesses, and make other investments. Thus, the life insurance companies are quite similar to other financial intermediaries in their basic operations. Further, the assets of life insurance companies rank them among the largest of the financial intermediary group.

Investment Companies

Investment companies, commonly known as mutual funds, pool people's savings and use the proceeds to acquire financial assets. They usually specialize in purchasing equities and debt securities. The advantage to the individual is presumed to be the investment companies' expertise in managing funds and, through the pooling of savers' funds, the ability to diversify among a large number of investments. Most individuals would not be able to afford such expertise and diversification without pooling funds with others. Mutual funds are a very popular way in which individuals invest in the stock market and in short-term high interest debt securities. Funds specializing in the latter securities are known as money market mutual funds.

Other Financial Institutions

There are other financial institutions that are not listed in Figure 1-2 because they are not technically financial intermediaries. However, these institutions share many of the characteristics of financial intermediaries. Finance companies specialize in consumer lending. Generally, however, the funds that they utilize to make loans are secured from other organizations, including financial intermediaries, rather than from ultimate savers in the economy. Casualty insurance companies also resemble financial intermediaries in the investments they make. However, their funds come through the sale of an insurance service rather than through the provision of a saving vehicle for savers in the economy. Nevertheless, the resemblance of these institutions to financial intermediaries and their importance in the financial system require that they be discussed along with financial intermediaries later in this book.

The Financial Markets

As previously mentioned, the two major components of the financial markets, the money market and the capital market, are listed in Figure 1-2 (p. 5). These markets, which are composed of numerous submarkets, are also of fundamental importance to the credit allocation process for they channel funds directly to borrowers in the economy.

The Importance of the Markets

The key role that financial intermediaries play in transferring funds from ultimate savers to ultimate borrowers was discussed above. In the money and capital markets, this transference takes place directly without the use of a financial intermediary, although financial intermediaries participate in these markets. Before proceeding, it is best to dispose of a common notion of what a market is. It is not necessarily a single place or even a formal gathering of individuals for the purpose of transacting business. In fact, most of the trading in the financial markets takes place over the telephone. Thus, it differs very much in structure from the familiar neighborhood grocery market. Nonetheless, whether enclosed in a formal structure, like the New York Stock Exchange, which actually is housed in a building on Wall Street in New York City, or composed of traders solely linked by the telephone, these markets still accomplish much the same purpose as the corner grocery, to facilitate exchange.

However, in the case of the securities markets—the general name for the money and capital markets combined—credit obligations (IOUs) of businesses and equity shares in business are exchanged for funds. The credit obligations may be sold directly to ultimate savers in the economy through brokers or to financial institutions, which in many cases are also financial intermediaries. Frequently, financial intermediaries channel funds to borrowers through the financial markets in addition to making loans directly. In Figure 1-2 an arrow running from the financial intermediaries to the financial markets illustrates this interaction between the intermediaries and markets. The financial markets are also aiding the credit allocation process by facilitating the transfer of funds available for lending to those businesses and institutions that will make use of the funds. Later in this book these markets and the specific roles that they play in the economy will be discussed in detail. However, at this point it is useful to briefly distinguish between the money and the capital markets.

The Money Market

The money market consists entirely of debt instruments. It is exclusively a market in which funds are borrowed and loaned. A debt instrument is simply a formal agreement to repay a specified sum at a given date. The instrument is offered to potential lenders in exchange for their funds. The money market is so named because of the nature of the securities traded there. These securities are short term, obligating the borrower to repay in a short period of time. The usual rule of thumb for a security to be considered a money market instrument is that it must be paid off (that is, mature) in one year or less from the date it is first issued. In fact, money market instruments run the entire gamut from securities that mature in only one day of issuance to those that must be repaid in one year and many that mature in any period in between.

Who participates as borrowers in the money market? Business firms, the government, and even financial intermediaries themselves among other groups borrow funds in this market. And who are the lenders? Individuals, business firms, sometimes governmental entities, and financial intermediaries as well participate as lenders in the money market. It may appear peculiar that the same groups can be both lenders and borrowers in the money market, but a little reflection will establish that this is not at all unusual. For example, frequently a stamp or coin collector will sell one stamp or coin in order to purchase another (a common occurrence among collectors). The collector is both a buyer and seller of stamps or coins. The collector operates on both sides of the market. It is the same with the participants in the financial markets. Sometimes a business firm is a borrower in the money market. Another firm may be a lender. Even the same business firm may be borrowing and lending at the same time in order to achieve certain financial management goals. Thus, we say that businesses appear in the money market as both borrowers and lenders. It is the same with other participants.

The Capital Market

We distinguish the capital market from the money market primarily by the fact that this market involves debt instruments that must be repaid in more than one year from the date of issuance and also by the fact that it includes, in addition to debt issues, equity issues which are not IOUs at all. Rather, equities are ownership shares in business enterprises. By acquiring shares, the purchaser acquires a piece of the business. If the business is successful, the equity holder would expect the value of his or her shares to increase; if the business is not sucessful, shares might be expected to decrease in value. In addition to a potential rise in the value of the shares, there may be additional inducements to holding equity shares, such as dividends paid out of business income. (It is equity shares that are traded on the New York Stock Exchange and other stock exchanges.)

Who are the participants in the capital markets? Not surprisingly the same answer is appropriate for the capital markets as for the money market: business, government, individuals, and financial institutions.

The use of the money and capital markets by lenders and borrowers plays a vital part in the allocation of credit in the economy. The operations of these markets will, as a consequence, be a main concern of this book.

Primary and Secondary Markets

Transactions in the money and capital markets take place not only for newly issued securities (a new issue is a security that is offered for sale for the first time), but trading also takes place in securities that are already outstanding. When securities that are already outstanding are traded, this trading is said to take place in the **secondary market,** whereas when new securities are issued, trading is said to take place in the **primary market.** Trading in the primary and the secondary markets together account for all trading in the money and capital markets. Strictly speaking, it is only when newly issued securities are put on the market that funds are transferred to ultimate borrowers. However, trading in the secondary market is vital for the credit allocation process because a broad secondary market makes security holdings more attractive. Holders know they will be able to sell securities that they hold before the security matures if this becomes necessary. Thus, the existence of the secondary market makes it easier to sell newly issued securities in the primary market.

The Financial System and the Economy

Thus far we have discussed the parts of our financial system. This brings us to a good place to glance back at Figure 1-2 (p. 5) and review. Our background discussion on the financial intermediaries and the financial markets makes mastery of this figure straightforward. Nonetheless, as simple as the figure is, it tells an interesting story about the financial system, which we will now review and examine further.

The Credit Allocation Process Once Again

From Figure 1-2 and the succeeding discussion, a simplified yet accurate view of the credit allocation process has emerged. As has been seen, the credit allocation process in our economy involves the financial intermediaries and markets transferring funds from savers to borrowers. The discussion has told a story of sophisticated and complex units in the economy interacting to achieve a desired result. Why is this so important and why has so much time been devoted to viewing the process?

If an individual was asked to explain what goals are important for the economy to achieve, that person would probably list among these goals full employment, an improved standard of living, and price stability (that is, little or no inflation). These and others are established goals of any modern economy. But unless productive activity takes place, these goals, as well as others that may be desirable, cannot be achieved.

The credit allocation process in the economy is as important to the achievement of these goals as any other vital link in the productive process. For example, it permits business the wherewithal to produce and utilize capital goods. Capital goods are goods that are used to produce other goods; they are machines and factories, or in business jargon, plant and equipment. The problem with plant and equipment is that it wears out and has to be replaced. Furthermore, for the amount of capital in an economy to increase, capital goods not only must be replaced as they wear out, but additional capital goods must be produced. Suppose that consumers spent all that they earned and did not save, and that there was also no saving by business and government. In a free enterprise economy, the purchase of consumer goods would mean that productive resources such as labor, land, and capital would be directed to produce nothing but consumer goods. If all our existing resources were utilized to produce consumer goods, what would be left over to produce the capital goods of society? The answer is that there wouldn't be any resources left over.

Since consumers do most of the saving in the economy by their decision to save, productive resources are made available to be used to produce capital goods. But it is business that decides to use such resources to produce the capital goods. How does business secure control over the resources that consumers have released from consumer goods production by their saving? Borrowing is a major way. After all, to secure control of labor and other resources in our economy, business needs the financial wherewithal. It is through the financial system that these funds are transferred to the businesses that utilize them.

Transferring funds to business is, of course, only one way in which the financial system contributes to economic progress. It has previously been noted, for example, that some consumers are also ultimate borrowers in the financial system, and we will talk more about consumer borrowing in later chapters. The explanation that has been presented above is, therefore, really a simplification of all the work that the financial system does in the economy. But it is a very important facet of that work and demonstrates the manner in which the financial system—in facilitating the allocation of credit—is an essential link in the economy. The importance of the financial system in the credit allocation process and the importance of the allocation of credit in the economy will be a recurrent theme throughout this book.

Understanding the Financial System

The purpose of this book is to give the reader a detailed understanding of the components of the financial system. By fully understanding the parts of the system, the student will be able to understand the system itself. The rest of this chapter will preview the book.

The remaining chapters of this section are in a sense the building blocks on which the book stands. Chapter 2 introduces the flow of funds in the economy. It is a detailed look at the financial interactions among the units that comprise the economy. Thus, studying the flow of funds accounts presents a picture of how these units are intertwined financially. In doing so, the flow of funds accounts further develop the relationships between saving and investment and lending and borrowing that have been introduced. The definition of money, the functions it serves, and its importance are discussed in detail in Chapter 3. The determination of the level of interest rates and the relationship among different interest rates is explored in Chapter 4. Since interest rates are the signaling devices utilized in the credit allocation process, they play a key role in the financial system.

As noted in an earlier section of this chapter, there is a coincident (economists call it simultaneous) growth of the economy and the financial system. It is simply that one sector cannot grow very much unless the other sector is also growing. Thus, the increasing development of the financial system occurs hand-in-hand with the increasing development of the economy. For example, commercial banks were among the earliest financial institutions to develop as modern economies started to emerge. Now there are many differences between those early commercial banks and what we now call commercial banks. However, there are many similarities as well, not the least being the offering of checking accounts and the granting of loans to business. In Chapters 5, 6, and 7, we will take a detailed look at commercial banking.

The development of other deposit-taking financial intermediaries, such as savings and loan associations, took place for the most part after the U.S. economy had already reached a high degree of development. In fact, although savings and loan associations have existed for many years, it is really only since World War II that they have emerged as the important institutions they are today. Mutual savings banks, while older institutions than savings and loan associations, have also experienced rapid growth in the years since World War II, and it is only in the last decade that credit unions have emerged as major financial intermediaries. Savings and loans, mutual savings banks, and credit unions will be discussed in detail in Chapters 8 and 9. In just the last ten years, many other financial intermediaries have experienced substantial growth. Chapter 10 will bring together the remaining financial intermediaries for analysis—pension funds, life insurance companies, and a number of other financial intermediaries and institutions.

Financial intermediaries have many links to the financial markets in the economy. The interaction between financial intermediaries and financial markets is of great importance to the credit allocation process. In Chapter 11 the nature and importance of this interaction will be discussed. The financial markets themselves, of course, are basic to the credit allocation process; the money market and the capital markets are crucial links between borrowers and lenders. Chapters 12 and 13 will explore these markets in detail, describing their operation and evaluating their role in the financial system.

Recently, the international financial markets have taken on increased importance for the United States. Many things have changed since the Vietnam War and the 1973 increase in oil prices. The increasing interdependence of the United States and the rest of the world has been seen most clearly in the international financial markets. These markets will be examined in Chapter 14.

The U.S. government is a vital part of our financial system and, through its activities and actions, has a profound effect on the credit allocation process. The interaction of the government and the financial markets is clearly evident in the activities of federally sponsored agencies. Chapter 15 will discuss these agencies. Through the many regulations it has issued, the government has also influenced the way in which the financial system has evolved over the years. Further, the financial system is continuously changing and adapting to meet new needs and pressures in the economy. One important result of the financial system's response to both regulatory and economic changes has been for financial intermediaries to become more competitive and similar in nature. The interaction between the financial system's evolution, governmental regulation, and changing economic needs will be examined in Chapter 16.

Although it is difficult to single out one part of government as more important than any other, the Federal Reserve System does stand out significantly with regard to the financial system. The Federal Reserve System is the U.S. central bank, and, as such, it exerts a major influence on the financial system and the economy. In Chapters 17, 18, and 19, the Federal Reserve System will be fully explored.

Inflation, a continuous rise in prices, has been a serious problem in the U.S. economy and the rest of the world since the late 1960s. Chapter 20 will analyze the inflationary process, the impact of governmental activity on the process, and governmental policy in attempting to control inflation. Since inflation is a monetary phenomena, its relationship to the financial system is significant and pervasive. Thus, a discussion of this problem is a fitting end to our study of the financial system.

THE IMPORTANCE OF SAVING,
THE U.S. PROBLEM, AND THE FORECAST

Tracking a Trend: Americans Save Far Less of Their Earnings Than Citizens Elsewhere, and the Gap Grows

Saving Rates in Key Countries:
Savings as a Percentage of After-Tax Income

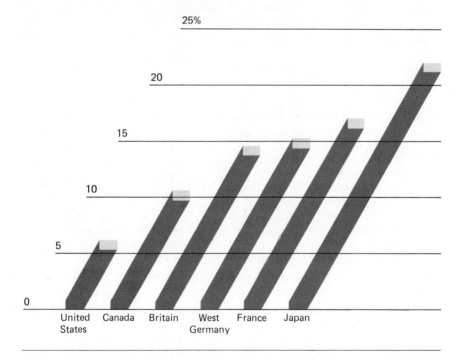

By ALFRED L. MALABRE JR.

Americans are saving far less of their money than citizens in other industrial countries.

At a time of growing uneasiness over the U.S. economic outlook, the disparity has received few headlines. Yet, it is enormous, and it has grown over the years. Many economists find the pattern deeply disturbing.

A willingness to save, of course, is fundamental to economic growth.

Paul A. Samuelson, the Nobel-laureate economist at Massachusetts Institute of Technology, has observed that "to the extent that people are willing to save—to abstain from present consumption and wait for future consumption—to that extent society can devote resources to new capital formation."

Diverse Trends

American willingness to save is low, as the accompanying chart shows, and it has been diminishing. Meanwhile, saving rates abroad have risen. The following table traces these diverse trends over the last decade. In the six major industrial countries, it pinpoints consumer saving, as a percentage of consumer disposable, or after-tax, income.

Rate of Saving

	1977	1967
United States	5.1%	7.5%
Canada	9.8	6.2
Britain	13.9	8.5
West Germany	14.0	11.3
France	16.1	15.9
Japan	21.5	18.5

It is impossible to know whether the propensity to save will continue to decline in America, or keep expanding abroad. Inevitably, much will depend on the extent to which governmental policies tend to encourage or discourage saving. And who can foresee with precision the economic plans that political leaders may be hatching?

Whatever does develop, the present disparity is significant on a number of counts. It suggests a greater *potential* for economic growth abroad than in America. "If people don't save, there can't be sufficient investment, and eventually economic growth suffers," says Martin S. Feldstein, president of the National Bureau of Economic Research, a nonprofit business-analysis organization based in New York.

Noting the remarkable rise of savings in Canada, Robert Baguley, an economist at Royal Bank of Canada in Montreal, declares: "Canadians possess the capability to increase their spending sharply." No such cushion exists in the U.S., says Paul Wachtel, an economics professor at New York University. "There is a strong argument that Americans should be saving more."

A Matter of Interest

To many analysts, the relatively low rate of saving in America suggests that the U.S. economy is particularly susceptible, in the event of brisk expansion in coming months, to interest-rate increases. By the same token, these analysts maintain that interest rates are likely to rise relatively little in countries where a large portion of income is being plowed into savings. Sharply climbing interest rates, of course, act to inhibit economic activity inasmuch as they discourage borrowing for business expansion projects, homebuilding and other endeavors.

Economic growth in America has indeed tended to lag during the last decade. This is apparent, for instance, in data showing industrial production, an economic indicator expressed in physical terms and therefore not distorted by rising prices. Since 1967, industrial production in the U.S. has risen slightly over 40%. Among the major countries, only Britain shows a smaller gain. The comparable increase in Japan is 97%. West Germany, France and Canada also show far larger gains than the U.S.

By no coincidence, capital spending in the U.S. is relatively small in terms of overall economic activity. Last year, according to a U.S. Commerce Department analysis, capital investment amounted to 17% of America's gross national product. This was a lower percentage than for any other major nation. The report shows the latest comparable rates to be 30% in Japan, 23% in France and Canada, 21% in West Germany and 19% in Britain.

International comparisons of economic data, to be sure, involve a particularly high degree of risk. It is easy to find oneself comparing oranges and apples. Different countries compile statistics in different ways. Definitions vary from country to country. Statistics involving savings are no exception.

Oranges and Apples

"These are somewhat messy statistics that should not be taken as precisely accurate," warns Gerard Villa, consulting economist of Banque Bruxelles Lambert in Brussels. He notes, for example, that in much of Western Europe "spending by self-employed small businessmen on their own businesses is counted as a part of personal savings." This would not normally be so in the U.S., he adds.

Such distinctions, however, are hardly sufficient to explain the large lag in savings in America. "This is not simply a case of comparing oranges and apples," declares Edward F. Denison, an economist at the Brookings Institution, a nonprofit business-research group based in Washington. "People really do save much higher percentages of their incomes abroad than in the U.S."

There is no single explanation for this U.S. tendency to spend or the propensity elsewhere to save. Various factors appear to be at work.

Mr. Feldstein, who also teaches economics at Harvard University, maintains that Americans have relatively extensive insurance against old age through such programs as Social Security. He finds the U.S. coverage "substantially greater" than, for example, in Japan. Not surprisingly, he says, the typical Japanese worker feels obligated to set aside a relatively large fraction of pay for the retirement years.

Big Bonuses

Mr. Denison notes that workers in some countries derive a considerable percentage of their yearly pay through annual or semiannual bonuses. In Japan, he says, bonus money recently has approximated one-quarter of annual earnings. No precise figures are available, but he estimates that the comparable U.S. rate is "far lower." Bonus money, he explains, is likelier to be put into savings than regular pay.

The sharp rise of saving in Canada apparently reflects in part governmental efforts to induce thrift. Mr. Baguley of Royal Bank of Canada mentions, for example, the advent of government-sponsored plans, set up within the last decade, that provide tax breaks on various forms of saving. One plan encourages saving for retirement and another saving for home-buying.

Tax considerations are cited by many analysts. U.S. taxation of capital gains, for instance, is deemed relatively heavy. And this, many observers claim, acts to discourage key forms of saving in America. Mr. Villa maintains that the absence of a Belgian capital-gains tax on individual savings is a major reason that his country's saving rate is up around 18%. Countries that either exempt such gains from taxation or levy less of a tax than Uncle Sam also include Australia, West Germany, Italy, Japan, the Netherlands, Britain, Sweden, France and Canada.

Proposals have recently been in the Congress to trim capital-gains taxation in the U.S. However, the Carter administration makes clear that it opposes such measures. The dispute has caused a delay in congressional consideration of President Carter's entire tax "reform" package.

Demographic factors may also work to hold the U.S. saving rate below levels elsewhere. Over the next decade, forecasters project an increase of only 470,000 among Americans aged 45 to 64, a group that tends to save a relatively high percentage of income. In the period, a 6.4 million increase is foreseen among Americans aged 25 to 44, years when only a small portion of income typically is saved. Generally, these demographic patterns are more pronounced in the U.S. than in other industrial countries.

Key Points

1. The U.S. economy is a monetary economy in which transactions are conducted using money, something generally acceptable as a medium of exchange.

2. The financial system distributes funds from ultimate savers in the economy to ultimate borrowers.

3. Financial intermediaries accept savings, and in return the savers acquire claims against the intermediaries. Financial intermediaries use the funds they have received from savers to make loans to ultimate borrowers, thus securing claims against these borrowers. Savers, borrowers, and the economy benefit from the existence of financial intermediaries because they increase the efficiency of the allocation of credit.

4. Also important to the allocation of credit in the economy are the financial markets. In the money and capital markets, funds are transferred directly to ultimate borrowers with or without the participation of financial intermediaries. Securities issued for the first time are primary market securities, while outstanding securities are secondary market securities. Trading of both the primary and secondary market securities takes place in the financial markets.

5. The efficient allocation of credit in the economy is vital to the achievement of the economic goals of the economy, such as full employment, economic growth, and price stability.

6. This book will discuss the parts that compose the financial system and their interaction. Understanding the financial system and how it works is our major goal.

Questions for Discussion

1. Explain how the financial intermediaries and financial markets are important in the allocation of credit in the economy.

2. What distinguishes a monetary economy from a barter economy?

3. What are the major financial intermediaries in the economy and what distinguishes them from each other?

4. The money and capital markets together constitute the securities market. What are the differences between the type of securities traded in the money market and the capital market? What is the difference between primary and secondary market securities?

Suggested Readings

Bagehot, Walter. *Lombard Street.* New York: Scribner, Armstrong & Co., 1873; rpt. Homewood, Ill.: Richard D. Irwin, 1962.

Burns, Joseph M. *A Treatise on Markets.* American Enterprise Institute, Studies in Economic Policy. Washington, D.C.: American Enterprise Institute, 1979.

Dougall, Herbert E., and Jack E. Gaumnitz. *Capital Markets and Institutions.* Englewood Cliffs, N.J.: Prentice-Hall, 1980.

Friedman, Milton, and Anna J. Schwartz. *A Monetary History of the United States.* Princeton: Princeton Univ. Press, 1963.

Nadler, Paul S. *Commercial Banking in the Economy.* 3rd ed. New York: Random House, 1979.

Polakoff, Murray E. et al. *Financial Institutions and Markets.* 2nd ed. Boston: Houghton Mifflin, 1981.

Ritter, Lawrence, and William Silber. *Money.* 2nd ed. New York: Basic Books, 1973.

The Flow of 2
Funds in the Economy

Having introduced the financial system in the previous chapter, we will now discuss the flow of funds accounts. The flow of funds accounts are a device by which the financial flows among sectors of the economy can be tracked. Funds flow among sectors in the purchase of goods and services, the payment to factors of production, the purchase and sale of financial assets, and so forth. The flow of funds attempts to account for all these financial flows.

It may be recalled from a previous course in economics that national income accounting is used to measure the production in the economy and the earnings derived from that production. Concepts such as gross national product (GNP), national income (NI), and personal income (PI) are among the measures developed in national income accounting. Flows of funds take place as a result of the activities measured by the national income accounts. However, many additional transactions take place in the economy resulting in flows of funds that are not included in the national income accounting measures. These also need to be understood by the financial analyst and researcher. The flow of funds accounts provide the framework and necessary statistics that enable the analyst to understand the financial interrelationships among the various sectors of the economy.

Before turning to the flow of funds accounts, however, we should briefly review national income accounting so that the important differences between this framework and the flow of funds framework can be appreciated. Furthermore, the national income accounts coupled with the flow of funds allow a more complete understanding of the saving–investment process in the economy, which is a vital element in understanding the financial system.

23

The National Income Accounts

The goal of national income accounting is to measure the production of goods and services in the economy for a period of time, usually a year, and to measure earnings out of that production for the same period of time. Further, by taking account of transfer payments, which are not generated out of the production process, and taxes, which are transferred to the government, measures of private spendable and savable income are generated.

The most familiar of the national income account measures is **gross national product** (GNP). GNP is the dollar value of all final (that is, newly produced) goods and services produced by the economy in one year. GNP can be measured in two ways. The first is by examining expenditure categories (sometimes also called the flow of product); and the second, by measuring the earnings generated by the production process. Both methods yield the same measure of GNP because the amount spent to purchase newly produced goods and services must be equal to the amount earned in the production of these goods and services.

GNP is composed of four expenditure categories—consumption (C), investment (I), government spending (G), and net exports (E). Consumption spending is the purchase of goods and services by households and individuals. Investment spending (formally called gross private domestic investment in the national income accounts) is the purchase of machines and factories by business firms and the change in business inventories. Government spending is the purchase of goods and services by federal, state, and local governments. Net exports is the difference between exports, goods and services sold abroad, and imports, goods and services bought from abroad.[1] Thus, GNP from the expenditure side can be represented in symbols as follows:

$$GNP = C + I + G + E \qquad [2\text{-}1]$$

Similarly, GNP can be measured from the earnings side. It should be clear that any amount spent on goods and services will be received as earnings as long as all possible recipients are included. For example, households and individuals receive wages and salaries, dividends on stock, and profits from unincorporated enterprises. Similarly businesses retain earnings and allocate receipts for the replacement of capital equipment that will wear out (called capital consumption allowances). Government receives taxes. Thus, if one sums all earnings generated out of the production process, GNP will be determined.

Although GNP is calculated in current prices, to facilitate year-

---

[1] For a detailed discussion of these expenditure categories, see any principles of economics textbook, for example, William J. Baumol and Alan S. Blinder, *Economics: Principles and Policy,* 2nd ed. (New York: Harcourt Brace Jovanovich, 1982).

to-year comparisons, GNP is often presented as well in terms of prices in some base year. This is referred to as real GNP and allows the analyst to judge the increase or decrease of output from one year to another with the influence of price changes removed. When inflation is rapid, such adjustment becomes particularly important for price changes can seriously distort year-to-year comparisons.

There are other measures of national income that can be derived from GNP. These include: **net national product** (NNP), which is GNP less capital consumption allowances; **national income** (NI), a measure of gross returns to factors of production; **personal income** (PI), a gross measure (since it includes personal taxes) of what households have available to spend and save, which includes transfer payments such as unemployment insurance and social security payments; and **disposable income** (DI), personal income less personal taxes. Disposable income provides a measure of what consumers have available after taxes to allocate between spending and saving. Since consumers are the largest group of ultimate savers and the largest category of spenders, this is quite important. If one divides disposable income into consumption and saving, then

$$DI = C + S_p \qquad [2\text{-}2]$$

where S_p is personal saving.

Table 2-1 presents the national income account measures for 1980. GNP is presented by major spending categories, and national income by major factor income categories. The difference between GNP and national income is due mainly to the removal, in calculating NI from GNP, of the capital consumption allowance and indirect business taxes (sales and excise taxes).[2] The largest category of factor earnings in national income is compensation of employees, which consists primarily of wage and salary income. Corporate profits are a distant second. Personal income is derived from national income by subtracting items not received by households and adding transfer payments, which are not generated out of the production process. Corporate profits, net interest, and contributions for social insurance (social security taxes) are removed from national income; and government transfer payments, personal interest income, dividends, and business transfer payments are added to arrive at personal income. But the inclusion of personal income taxes in personal income makes this a rather imprecise measure of what consumers actually have available. Subtracting income taxes from personal income yields disposable income, which can be expressed as consumption spending and personal saving as shown in equation [2-2].

---

[2] There are, in addition, a few small items that are needed to reconcile GNP and national income. See, for example, Paul A. Samuelson, *Economics*, 11th ed. (New York: McGraw-Hill, 1979) for details.

Table 2-1
The National Income Accounts, 1980
(Billions of Dollars)

Gross National Product	$2,628.8
Personal Consumption Expenditures	1,671.1
Gross Private Domestic Investment	396.8
Government Purchases of Goods and Services	534.8
Net Exports	26.1
Memo: GNP in 1972 Dollars	1,481.8
National Income	$2,121.4
Compensation of Employees	1,596.7
Proprietors Income	130.6
Rental Income of Persons	31.9
Corporate Profits	182.1
Net Interest	180.1
To arrive at Personal Income from National Income	
Subtract:	
Corporate Profits	$ 182.1
Net Interest	180.1
Contributions for Social Insurance	203.7
Wage Accruals Less Disbursements	0.0
Add:	
Government Transfer Payments	$ 283.9
Personal Interest Income	256.6
Dividends	54.4
Business Transfer Payments	10.5
Equals: Personal Income	$2,161.0
Less: Personal Taxes	338.7
Equals: Disposable Personal Income	$1,822.2
Which Equals: Consumption Spending	1,718.7
Plus: Personal Saving	103.6

Source: U.S. Department of Commerce, *Survey of Current Business,* Jan. 1981.

Furthermore, if business saving, S_b—which consists of business' retained earnings and capital consumption allowances—and taxes are added to consumption and personal saving, GNP may be expressed from the earnings side as

$$GNP = C + S_p + S_b + T \qquad [2\text{-}3]$$

Recalling that

$$GNP = C + I + G + E \qquad [2\text{-}4]$$

from the spending approach, then

$$C + I + G + E = C + S_p + S_b + T \qquad [2\text{-}5]$$

Thus for the economy total spending is equal to total income. This is always the case by definition.[3] However, if the various sectors represented in the above expression are in some way dissatisfied with their position, economic forces will be set in motion that will result in a change in economic activity over time. This can be illustrated after some manipulation of the above equations. Recognizing that C is the same on both sides of equation [2-5], it can be deleted. The result is

$$I + G + E = S_p + S_b + T \qquad [2\text{-}6]$$

which by definition is equal.

However, suppose business is dissatisfied with the existing level of I. If this is the case, the left side of equation [2-6]—although equal to the right side in an accounting sense—is not equal to the right side in terms of what business would wish to do. The level of I would be unsatisfactory to business. As a result, economic activity will change as business attempts to either increase or decrease its level of investment to achieve its desired position. For example, if business wishes to increase its level of investment, more resources may be employed and more production take place, increasing GNP. For equilibrium to hold in the economy, therefore, not only must the actual magnitudes of the equation be equal, which will always be the case, but the desired magnitudes must be equal; otherwise alterations in the level of economic activity will occur. Notice that in the above equation it is only the totals on each side of the equation that have to be equal. Individual components need not be equal either in an accounting or in a desired sense for equilibrium to exist in the economy.

What does all this have to do with the study of the financial system that is the focus of this book? Think back to Figure 1-2 on page 5. This showed that the financial system transfers funds from ultimate savers to ultimate borrowers in the economy. Notice that the right-hand side of equation [2-6] indicates the amounts that are not spent by the various sectors or, conversely, the amount that is saved. The funds represented by that foregone spending must be transferred to

---

[3] The treatment of changes in business inventories as investment ensures this equality.

those doing the spending represented on the left side of the equation. It is clear that some transfers are automatic. For example, taxes are used for government spending and much business saving for investment. However, if government spending exceeds taxes (which is a common occurrence), recourse is made to the financial markets by the government for borrowing. Similarly, investment usually exceeds business saving, and those funds borrowed by business are transferred to business through the financial system. Thus, we could say that government and business are deficit sectors in the economy—they spend more than they take in and consequently make recourse to the financial markets and institutions to secure the funds they need. Consumers are surplus sectors in the economy spending less than they take in and therefore making funds available to the deficit sectors.[4] The financial system takes these surplus funds and allocates them. None of this is absolutely clear, however, from just focusing on the national income accounts. To really understand the process, we need an accounting mechanism that goes beyond the national income accounts and fully develops the financial flows in the economy. Such a device is the **flow of funds** accounts.

The Flow of Funds Accounts

The flow of funds accounts differ substantially from the national income accounts in what they attempt to measure and in the way in which they are constructed. The purpose of the flow of funds framework is to account for all financial flows in the economy for a period of time, usually a quarter (three months) or a year. All financial flows in the economy are measured, whether they correspond to newly produced goods or services (GNP) or involve non-GNP items such as used assets. Further, all purely financial transactions, such as the transfer of financial assets, are also accounted for in the flow of funds accounts. By dividing the economy into its various sectors, we can clearly see the financial interrelationships among these sectors.

The flow of funds accounts are derived from the balance sheets and income statements of the various sectors of the economy over the period of time for which the accounts are prepared. These accounts are compiled by the Federal Reserve System. However, specialized flow of funds accounts are often constructed by financial analysts for particular purposes as will be explained below. Before turning to the actual flow of funds accounts, it is useful to work through a simplified model of the accounts.

The simplified model of the flow of funds divides the economy into four sectors. (In the actual flow of funds accounts to be examined

---

[4] Little has been said about the net export item, which is relatively small. However, international finance will be discussed later in the book.

below, the summary table that is presented disaggregates some of these sectors for a total of nine sectors. Further, data at an even finer level of disaggregation, 25 sectors, are available in the detailed flow of funds accounts provided by the Federal Reserve.) The four sectors in our simple model are the household sector, the nonfinancial business sector, the government sector, and the financial intermediary sector. Although the model is simplified, the more disaggregated actual flow of funds system discussed below can be mastered if the simple model is understood first, since it is basically the same model with more detail.

Table 2-2 uses hypothetical data to present our model.[5] The flow of funds accounts are constructed on a "uses" and "sources" of funds basis. Sources of funds are the funds received by a sector; and uses, how these funds are allocated. For every sector the uses of funds and the sources of funds must be equal; and, therefore, for the economy as a whole sources and uses of funds must balance. The division of the economy into sectors reveals the interrelationships among the sectors as funds flow from one to another. Households are surplus units because they save more than they spend, and they may place the proceeds of this surplus into financial intermediaries like commercial banks or directly into financial market instruments. On the other hand, business is a deficit sector in the economy, spending more than it saves and, therefore, taps households and financial institutions for funds through borrowing. Government has also proved to be a deficit sector many times in recent years. Our hypothetical model therefore assumes that both government and business are deficit sectors.

The first two sectors listed in Table 2-2 are the household sector and the business sector. These sectors represent the private nonfinancial part of the economy.[6] Examining the household column, for example, we can see that a distinction is made between nonfinancial and financial transactions. The nonfinancial transactions include the purchases and sales of goods, while the financial transactions involve changes in financial claims for each sector. In the first row, saving is the net sum of current income receipts less current expenditures. In the case of households, these expenditures are for consumption. For the business sector, saving would be equal to business receipts less operating expenses. Saving, what is left over, is available for investment purposes. The table shows that households saved $1,400 and business saved $100. Since this $1,500 is a source of funds, it is available for investment. In the government sector, the negative item under sources in the first row shows that the government is spending more than its income, which is derived from taxes. Financial intermediaries

---

[5] This table is based on one in the *Introduction to Flow of Funds,* Board of Governors of the Federal Reserve System, 1975, p. 3.

[6] In the actual accounts, state and local governments are included in this group.

Table 2-2
Hypothetical Flow of Funds Accounts

TRANSACTION CATEGORY	HOUSEHOLDS		BUSINESS		GOVERNMENT		FINANCIAL INTERMEDIARIES		TOTAL	
	Uses	Sources	Uses	Sources	Uses	Sources	Uses	Sources	Uses	Sources
Nonfinancial										
1. Saving		$1,400		$ 100		−$200				$1,300
2. Investment	$ 200		$1,100						$1,300	
Financial										
3. Net Financial Investment	$1,200		−$1,000		−$200				−0−	
4. Total Financial Uses and Sources of Funds (lines 5 & 6)	$1,200			$1,000		$200	$1,000	$1,000	$2,200	$2,200
5. Deposits at Financial Intermediaries	$1,000							$1,000	$1,000	$1,000
6. Loans and Securities	$ 200			$1,000		$200	$1,000		$1,200	$1,200

in the model are assumed not to save. The second row presents investment. Such items as business investment in plant and equipment as
well as household purchases of housing and durable goods are recorded in this row. (Note that in the flow of funds accounts, unlike
the national income accounts, household purchases of consumer durables are considered investment.) In the total column it is clear that
saving equals investment, the identical condition of the national income
accounts.

In the financial transactions, net financial investment (row 3) combines all financial transactions into a net figure that is the difference
between a sector's lending (its financial uses) and its borrowing (its
financial sources). For the household sector, this is positive, showing
that households lend more than they borrow. For business it is negative,
showing that this sector is a net borrower. Government is also a net
borrower necessitated by its budget deficit. The fourth row summarizes
rows 5 and 6. Financial intermediary deposits by households are clearly
a source of funds for financial intermediaries as shown in row 5. Business raises funds by securing loans and issuing securities. This can
be seen by the $1,000 source of funds in row 6. The government
also borrows through the issuance of securities. Households have acquired $200 of government and business securities as seen by the
$200 entry under the uses side of row 6, while financial intermediar-
ies—which acquired their funds from deposits of households—have
acquired securities from government and made loans to business totaling $1,000. Notice once again that if nonfinancial saving and invest-
ment are examined for each sector and net financial investment is
included, sources and uses of funds for each sector are equal. Because
net financial investment for each sector is equivalent to the sector's
financial uses and sources of funds, alternatively row 4 can be added
to rows 1 and 2 to show the equality of sources and uses for each
sector. Further, saving and investment is equal for the economy but
need not be equal for each sector, as was also shown to be true in
the discussion of national income accounting.

The model presented in Table 2-2 presents a picture of the sector
interactions that the flow of funds deals with. By accounting for these
interactions, we can see the economy as an integrated whole. By utilizing the framework of the simple model, the actual accounts become
clearer. The idea is the same although there are more sectors and
transactions categories.

The Actual Flow of Funds Accounts

Table 2-3 presents the actual summary table for the flow of funds
accounts for the year 1978. As the table shows, the sector detail is
expanded from that of the simple model presented above. There are

Table 2-3
Summary of Flow of Funds Accounts for the Year 1978
(Billions of Dollars)

Transaction Category	Households		Business		State and Local Governments		Total		Rest of the World		U.S. Government	
	U	S	U	S	U	S	U	S	U	S	U	S
1 Gross Saving		338.3		195.6	7.6			541.5		23.5		−34.9
2 Capital Consumption		181.0		172.7				353.7				
3 Net Saving (1 − 2)		157.3		22.9	7.6			187.7		23.5		−34.9
4 Gross Investment (5 + 11)	380.1		174.1		.5		554.8		12.7		−36.6	
5 Private Capital Expenditures	298.2		249.9				548.1				−2.0	
6 Consumer Durables	200.3						200.3					
7 Residential Construction	92.0		16.3				108.3					
8 Plant and Equipment	5.9		209.3				215.2					
9 Inventory Change			22.3				22.3					
10 Mineral Rights			2.0				2.0				−2.0	
11 Net Financial Investment (12 − 13)	81.9		−75.7		.5		6.7		12.7		−34.7	
12 Financial Uses	248.3		84.6		25.1		358.0		55.7		28.9	
13 Financial Sources		166.4		160.4		24.6		351.4		43.0		63.5
14 Gold and Official Foreign Exchange									1.2	.2	−2.6	
15 Treasury Currency												.5
16 Demand Deposits and Currency	18.2		5.4		−1.1		22.5		−.2		4.0	
17 Private Domestic	18.2		5.4		−1.1		22.5					
18 Foreign									−.2			
19 U.S. Government											4.0	
20 Time and Savings Accounts	105.2		2.0		8.1		115.2		1.1		.1	
21 At Commercial Banks	44.1		2.0		8.1		54.1		1.1		.1	
22 At Savings Institutions	61.1						61.1					
23 Fed Funds and Security RPs			5.5		2.0		7.5					

Table 2-3
Summary of Flow of Funds Accounts for the Year 1978
(Billions of Dollars)

		Sponsored Agency and Mtg. Pools		Monetary Authority		Commercial Banking		Private Nonbank Finance		All Sectors		Discrepancy	National Saving and Investment
Total													
U	S	U	S	U	S	U	S	U	S	U	S	U	
	18.4		1.0		.7		3.4		13.3		548.5		524.9
	6.0						2.7		3.3		359.7		359.7
	12.4		1.0		.7		.7		10.0		188.7		165.2
20.7		.5		.7		9.6		9.8		551.6		−3.1	539.0
5.6						4.2		1.4		551.8		−3.3	551.8
										200.3			200.3
−.3								−.3		108.0			108.0
5.9						4.2		1.7		221.1			221.1
										22.3			22.3
15.0		.5		.7		5.4		8.4		−.2		.2	−12.7
400.8		46.7		13.3		141.2		199.6		843.4		.2	43.0
	385.7		46.2		12.6		135.8		191.2		843.6		55.7
1.6				1.6						.2	.2		
.6				.6						.6	.5		
2.6	28.2					6.3	.3	22.0	2.3	28.9	28.2	−.7	
2.6	24.8					9.3	.3	15.5	2.3	25.1	24.8	−.3	
	−.2						.1		.3	−.2	−.2		
	3.7					−3.1		6.8		4.0	3.7	−.3	
7.8	124.2						65.0	7.8	59.2	124.2	124.2		
9.7	65.0						65.0	9.7		65.0	65.0		
−2.0	59.2							−2.0	59.2	59.2	59.2		
4.0	20.9	1.4					18.8	2.6	2.1	11.5	20.9	9.4	

(Table cont.)

Table 2-3 (cont.)
Summary of Flow of Funds Accounts for the Year 1978
(Billions of Dollars)

Transaction Category	PRIVATE DOMESTIC NONFINANCIAL SECTORS								Rest of the World		U.S. Government	
	Households		Business		State and Local Governments		Total					
	U	S	U	S	U	S	U	S	U	S	U	S
24 Money Market Fund Shares	6.9						6.9					
25 Life Insurance Reserves	12.0						12.0					.3
26 Pension Fund Reserves	65.8						65.8					6.9
27 Net Interbank Claims									5.4			
28 Corporate Equities	−6.2			2.6			−6.2	2.6	2.4	−.5		
29 Credit Market Instruments	58.0	162.6	−1.2	125.6	14.6	23.6	71.4	311.8	37.7	32.8	20.4	53.7
30 U.S. Treasury Securities	17.3		−7.1		9.8		20.0		28.2			55.1
31 Federal Agency Securities	9.7		.7		2.8		13.3				7.7	−1.3
32 State and Local Govt. Securities	3.3		.2	3.2	1.0	25.1	4.5	28.3				
33 Corporate and Foreign Bonds	−1.4			20.1			−1.4	20.1	1.6	4.0		
34 Mortgages	14.5	104.8		43.3	1.0		15.5	148.2			−.4	−.1
35 Consumer Credit		50.6	3.2				1.2	50.6				
36 Bank Loans n.e.c.		3.4		33.9				37.3		18.3		
37 Open-Market Paper	14.6		1.7	5.2			16.3	5.2	7.9	6.6		
38 Other Loans		3.8		19.9		−1.6		22.2		3.9	13.0	
39 Security Credit	1.4	1.4					1.4	1.4	0	0		
40 Trade Credit		1.4	54.9	45.5		1.0	54.9	47.9	3.4	−.3	2.7	2.4
41 Taxes Payable				3.4	1.6		1.6	3.4			3.5	
42 Equity in Noncorporate Business	−20.8			−20.8			−20.8	−20.8				
43 Miscellaneous	7.6	1.1	18.1	4.0			25.7	5.0	4.7	10.8	.7	−.3
44 Sector Discrepancies (1 − 4)	−41.8		21.4		7.0		−13.3		10.8		1.7	

Source: Board of Governors of the Federal Reserve System, *Flow of Funds Accounts, 1949–1978*, Dec. 1979.

Table 2-3 (cont.)
Summary of Flow of Funds Accounts for the Year 1978
(Billions of Dollars)

FINANCIAL SECTORS

Total		Sponsored Agency and Mtg. Pools		Monetary Authority		Com- mercial Banking		Private Nonbank Finance		All Sectors		Dis- crep- ancy	National Saving and Invest- ment
U	S	U	S	U	S	U	S	U	S	U	S	U	U
	6.9								6.9	6.9	6.9		
	11.7								11.7	12.0	12.0		
	58.9								58.9	65.8	65.8		
9.5	15.6			3.6	5.9	5.9	9.7			14.9	15.6	.7	
7.6	1.7						1.1	7.5	.5	3.7	3.7		
348.4	79.8	44.6	41.4	7.0		128.7	6.9	168.1	31.5	478.0	478.0		
6.9			.5	7.7		−6.5		5.2		55.1	55.1		
19.1	41.4	.1	41.4	−.4		7.0		12.3		40.1	40.1		
23.8						9.6		14.2		28.3	28.3		
31.3	7.5					−.3	.2	31.6	7.3	31.6	31.6		
133.9	.9	30.6				35.0		68.3	.9	149.0	149.0		
47.3						26.9		20.4		50.6	50.6		
58.4			2.8	0		58.4			2.8	58.4	58.4		
2.2	14.6	−1.2		−.4		−1.3	6.7	5.1	7.9	26.4	26.4		
25.5	12.5	14.6	0					10.9	12.5	38.6	38.6		
−1.1	−1.0					−2.9		1.8	−1.0	.4	.4		
1.3								1.3		62.3	50.0	−12.3	
	1.7						.3		1.4	5.2	5.2		
										−20.8	−20.8		
18.5	37.1	.6	4.8	.5	.5	9.1	11.9	8.2	19.9	49.6	52.6	3.0	
−2.3			.5	0		−6.3		3.5		−3.1		−3.1	−14.1

nine major sectors in the summary table.[7] The major categories are the private domestic nonfinancial sectors, the financial sectors, the rest of the world and the U.S. government. The first two categories are further divided into households, business, and state and local governments, while the financial sector is subdivided into sponsored agencies (the Federal National Mortgage Association, for example), monetary authority (the Federal Reserve System), commercial banking and the private nonbank institutions. Notice, just as in the model above, that the flow of funds is divided into sources and uses for each sector. Focusing first on rows 1–10, we see that gross saving represents the saving in the economy, which includes capital consumption allowances (depreciation). The household sector is the largest saving sector in gross terms and, eliminating the capital consumption allowances, by far the largest net saver, although there is some net saving done by business. The federal government was a net dissaver in 1978 due to its budget deficit. Consumer durables and residential construction are counted as investment; thus households are the largest nonfinancial users of funds as well, although business investment in plant and equipment is quite large. Net financial investment in row 11 confirms that households are the largest net financial investors. They allocate their financial investment among deposits and credit market instruments primarily, while doing most of their borrowing for housing and consumer purchases.

Business and the federal government show negative financial investment, indicating that they raised more funds by borrowing and issuing securities than they used to acquire securities and make loans. Business raised the most funds of any sector in this way. The financial intermediaries, the recipients of deposits primarily of households, provided large amounts of financing through their lending and securities acquisition. Similar to the simple model in Table 2-2, rows 11, 12, and 13 summarize financial activity, and the remaining rows provide detailed transaction information not provided by the aggregate transactions categories of Table 2-2.

Beginning with row 14 and running through row 40, these last categories keep track of the various types of financial items that were acquired or were utilized to raise funds. Notice, for example, households used $105.2 billion to acquire time and savings deposits in 1978, while the federal government raised $53.7 billion through credit market instruments. Rows 41–44 are relatively minor items showing, for example, that households reduced their equity in noncorporate businesses by almost $21 billion. Row 44 is the residual balancing item in the accounts, the sector discrepancy. Because each sector's sources of funds must equal each sector's uses, this sector discrepancy is utilized to ensure balance. (Similarly, the entries in the discrepancy

---

[7] In the detailed sector breakdown, these nine sectors are disaggregated to 25 sectors. These detailed accounts are available from the Federal Reserve.

column ensure that accounting relations hold across columns.) The need for such balancing items emphasizes that the accounts themselves are often best estimates, not perfect measures, of the transactions.

This summary table of the flow of funds accounts gives a detailed picture of the interactions in the economy between sectors as well as with the rest of the world. Study of these accounts gives the analyst a remarkable picture of the economy and the financial system as it functioned during the period for which the accounts were constructed.

Putting the Flow of Funds Accounts to Work

The flow of funds data are extremely useful for the financial analyst and economic researcher. By utilizing historical flow of funds numbers, analysts and researchers can track emerging trends in the economy as well as investigate changes in financial patterns through time. This type of analysis provides needed insight into the current and near future financial patterns in the economy. The quarterly and annual flow of funds data released by the Federal Reserve are an up-to-date record of what has taken place in the financial system in the very recent past. Furthermore, in addition to making use of the flow of funds data and framework provided by the Federal Reserve, financial analysts and economic forecasters often forecast flows of funds for a coming period of time. For the analyst's convenience, these flow of funds forecasts are often organized in a somewhat different format than the formal accounts that were studied above. These forecasts may focus on the overall flow of funds or be more specifically focused on the flow of funds in individual financial markets. They are then used to assess such critical issues as the likely course of future interest rates in the economy.

Many financial firms make flow of funds forecasts such as Salomon Brothers and Bankers Trust Company of New York; their forecasts are usually published annually. However, nonfinancial firms may also make similar forecasts for internal use. Morgan Guaranty Trust Company has also periodically issued a flow of funds forecast. Table 2-4 reproduces the flow of funds included in the article "Credit Markets in the Year Ahead" published by Morgan Guaranty in January, 1980.[8] Although the format of the table is different from the flow of funds tables analyzed above, similar information is contained in this table. What Morgan Guaranty has done is to present the demand for credit in the financial markets and the probable suppliers of that credit. Because this is not a formal flow of funds analysis, we do not see the precise sectors that were acquiring particular financial instruments

---

[8] *The Morgan Guaranty Survey,* Jan. 1980, pp. 3–7.

Table 2-4
The Demand for Credit and the Sources of That Credit as Presented by Morgan Guaranty Trust Company
(Billions of Dollars)

THE DEMAND FOR CREDIT

	1974	1975	1976	1977	1978	1979[1]	1980[1]
Federal Government Issues	$ 12.0	$ 85.8	$ 69.1	$ 57.6	$ 55.1	$ 39.0	$ 60.0
Federal Agency Issues	22.2	12.3	19.0	26.7	40.1	50.0	40.0
State & Local Government Issues	17.2	16.3	17.7	23.9	26.7	24.0	24.0
Corporate Bonds	21.8	30.2	28.6	31.0	27.6	30.0	40.0
Corporate Stocks	5.0	10.6	12.6	4.7	5.2	4.0	6.0
Foreign Securities	1.9	6.4	8.9	5.5	3.5	3.0	5.0
Mortgages	60.5	57.2	87.1	134.0	149.0	160.0	135.0
Other Business Credit	62.9	−13.0	18.7	55.1	80.7	110.0	75.0
Consumer Credit	9.9	9.7	25.6	40.6	50.6	45.0	30.0
All Other Credit	14.6	12.2	17.8	18.6	41.8	30.0	25.0
Total Credit Demand	$228.0	$227.7	$305.1	$397.7	$480.3	$495.0	$440.0

WHERE THE MONEY MIGHT COME FROM

	1974	1975	1976	1977	1978	1979[1]	1980[1]
Commercial Banks	$ 66.6	$ 29.4	$ 59.7	$ 87.7	$128.8	$140.0	$100.0
Savings Institutions	24.4	53.7	70.9	82.4	76.0	68.0	75.0
Insurance and Pension Sector	32.4	43.3	50.7	59.9	65.5	77.0	85.0
Other Finance	7.9	5.6	21.3	33.6	34.4	60.0	40.0
Nonfinancial Corporations	11.0	12.0	13.7	4.2	7.5	12.0	10.0
Government, including Federal Reserve	36.2	45.0	49.0	55.3	74.1	80.0	75.0
Foreign Investors	11.7	10.8	18.0	42.1	40.1	4.0	10.0
Individuals and Others	37.9	27.9	21.7	32.7	54.3	54.0	45.0
Total Credit Supply	$228.0	$227.7	$305.1	$397.7	$480.3	$495.0	$440.0

[1] Estimated. Due to rounding, components may not add to totals.

Source: Reprinted by permission of Morgan Guaranty Trust Company from the Jan. 1980 issue of *The Morgan Guaranty Survey.*

(uses of funds) and the precise sectors issuing the securities and doing the borrowing (sources of funds). The latter sectors are, however, apparent from the types of credit market instruments. Further, since the basic purpose of the Morgan Guaranty work is forecasting, the data include projections for the period being forecasted, while the actual flow of funds accounts present only data for past periods.

Morgan's table is broken into an historical section and a forecasted section. The actual flows of funds for 1974 to 1979 are given for historical interest, although 1979 was estimated since the year was not quite over when this table was compiled. The final column in the table is Morgan's forecast of credit demands and the sources of funds to satisfy these needs in 1980. This forecast is based on numerous economic factors that the forecasters believed to be likely in 1980.

Examining the table is instructive for appreciating the credit flows in the economy. Notice the large amount of credit that flows into the housing area through mortgage borrowing. Also notice that credit demands by the federal government and federal agencies have been high for most of the period covered by the table. Federal agency borrowing particularly accelerated in 1978 and 1979, and Morgan Guaranty expected substantial demand for credit from federal agencies in 1980. (The actual flow of funds accounts show that Morgan's forecast of federal agency borrowing was conservative for 1980; actual federal agency borrowing was $47.5 billion.) Other substantial credit demands come from business and consumers. Commercial banks were generally the largest suppliers of credit over the period covered in the table, with other financial intermediaries also an important factor. Individual direct participation in the markets, while substantially less than that of the financial intermediaries, nevertheless is also important. Further, since the financial intermediaries obtain a substantial portion of their funds from individuals, the individuals and others table category really understates the individuals' role in providing funds for credit demanders.

The Morgan analysts use their estimates of credit flows to forecast the likely course of interest rates. This can be appreciated from the manner in which they concluded the article in which the table appeared. "If the credit-flow estimates that go along with a mild downturn are anywhere near the mark, the economy should now be experiencing peak levels of interest rates on a cyclical basis and a declining tendency for (interest) rates should not be too far distant."[9] The interest rate forecast is necessarily hedged since it is based on a forecast of credit flows that cannot be known with certainty. Nevertheless, the quotation makes clear the usefulness of organizing the financial flows in the economy in a flow of funds framework. In this way a complicated and diverse system is integrated in a useful and usable fashion for analysis.

---

[9] "Credit Markets in the Year Ahead," p. 7.

DEBT IN THE UNITED STATES ECONOMY

Tracking a Trend: Debt Grows at Same Pace as Postwar Economy, But Spurt in Private Borrowing Worries Some

Postwar Borrowing: Diverging Patterns and Remarkable Stability

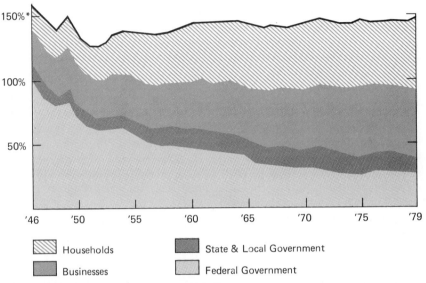

Households

Businesses

State & Local Government

Federal Government

Debt outstanding as a percentage of GNP

Sources: Federal Reserve Board and Commerce Dept.

By Alfred L. Malabre Jr.

If you're seeking an element of stability in an American economy that has changed vastly since World War II, consider the volume of debt outstanding.

Debt?

Surely debt has risen far faster than most other facets of economic activity over the postwar years? Surely it now so suffuses the economic scene that it's a major worry in the outlook?

Much depends on just what sort of debt you have in mind. The rise of private borrowing has far out-stripped the economy's postwar growth—and this does indeed generate concern among many economists. But governmental borrowing occupies a shrinking role in the total economic picture.

A Stable Big Picture

The chart [above] pinpoints these divergent trends, as well as the remarkably stable big picture. Compiled from government data by Benjamin M. Friedman, a Harvard economist, it's part of a soon-to-be-published study sponsored by the National Bureau of Economic Research, a nonprofit group based in Cambridge, Mass.

Since World War II, the chart shows, the outstanding volume of all borrowing—governmental plus private—has changed little in terms of the economy's overall size. In fact, the ratio shows a slight decline. In 1946, overall debt came to 155.9% of gross national product, the broadest economic gauge. The 1979 estimate was 145.5%.

The chart further shows that the federal government accounts for a dwindling share of all debt. In 1946, federal debt came to 103.5% of GNP, while last year's rate was only 27.1%. Meanwhile, the consumer's debt role has grown explosively. In 1946, such household debt—mainly home mortgages and installment loans—amounted to 16% of GNP. Last year's level, a record, was 53.9%. Debt outstanding among private businesses, at 29.4% of GNP in 1946, reached 52.2% last year.

The other debtor category traced in the chart represents state and local governments. In the period shown, such borrowing climbed from 7% of GNP to 12.3%. Since the late 1950s, however, state and local debt actually has dropped slightly as a percentage of GNP.

One Offsets the Other

The stability of overall debt, quite obviously, reflects the rising importance of private debt, offsetting the shrinking significance of governmental debt. The federal government, of course, borrowed heavily during World War II, while private borrowing was relatively dormant.

In the study, Mr. Friedman views debt in general as essentially a means of switching resources from "ultimate lenders, often through such financial intermediaries as thrift institutions, to ultimate borrowers." Accordingly, his compilation strips away borrowing accounted for by intermediaries to get at, as he puts it, "the economy's basic reliance on debt."

This reliance, Mr. Friedman asserts, "doesn't look excessive" in light of the remarkable stability of overall debt in relation to economic activity. Indeed, he suggests that the current worry of some analysts about debt reaching "dangerous levels" appears overdrawn, at least as far as the debt total is concerned.

The switch from governmental to private borrowing over the postwar period, however, does concern him. Federal debt, of course, is default-free, inasmuch as the federal government can print money to pay its bills. Private borrowers enjoy no such privilege, of course, and can—and occasionally do—go bankrupt.

Recalling the Twenties

The recent levels of overall debt shown in the chart, Mr. Friedman maintains, may well represent a sort of "normal" pattern. The ratio of overall debt to GNP was sharply higher during the Great Depression, when federal debt soared and the economy slumped, and briefly in World War II. But debt-to-GNP levels remarkably close to those in recent years prevailed as long ago as in the 1920s.

In 1921, for instance, overall debt came to 141.9% of GNP, within four points of last year's estimate. The breakdown for that year between governmental and private borrowing also approximated the 1979 figures. With rare exceptions, Mr. Friedman says, "the economy's reliance on debt, scaled in relation to economic activity, has shown essentially no trend for the past 60 years."

One factor in this, he remarks, is that private borrowers tend to step up their activity as governmental borrowing lags, and vice versa. He also observes that private borrowing depends to a large degree on the availability of tangible assets that can serve as collateral for loans. It's no coincidence he believes, that such assets in the postwar era have grown far faster than GNP.

Looking ahead, Mr. Friedman suspects that the big decline in federal debt is unlikely to resume. Rather, he expects a further very slow shrinkage of the sort that has gone on over the last decade or so.

Sporadic efforts to pep up the economy and beef up U.S. defenses, he predicts, will cause a continuation of the recent "era of much larger federal budget deficits." The upshot, he reckons, will be that federal debt in the 1980s will more nearly keep pace with GNP. By the same token, he doesn't anticipate any renewal of the extra-rapid rise of private borrowing that marked the 1950s and 1960s.

Other Repercussions

If private borrowing does continue to grow only very slowly in terms of GNP, Mr. Friedman anticipates repercussions elsewhere on the economic front. Corporations, he says, will probably feel compelled to turn increasingly to equity financing if they wish to sustain expansion programs. He warns that the alternative—which he regards as entirely possible—will be low rates of increase in capital investment and productivity, along the lines of recent experience.

The economist also sees a further tendency for the federal government, responding to pressures from the private sector, to guarantee business arrangements. "I expect we'll be seeing more and more Chrysler-type loan guarantees," he says.

The volume of debt channeled through such financial intermediaries as savings and loan associations and pension funds, of course, has grown sharply in the postwar era. Mr. Friedman anticipates a further move in this direction, noting that "the need for such intermediaries tends to increase along with the rise of private borrowing."

Mr. Jones and Mr. Smith

An illustration helps explain why the proliferation of such intermediaries worries many economists. Joe Jones (Mr. Friedman's "ultimate lender") deposits funds in his savings account at Busy Bank, which in turn lends to Sam Smith (Mr. Friedman's "ultimate borrower"). Mr. Smith, a prudent fellow with lots of collateral, doesn't overextend himself through the loan. But this doesn't eliminate the possibility that Busy Bank may be overextended or otherwise mismanaged.

Concern over debt, Mr. Friedman says, grows more out of this type of worry than out of questions about the credit-worthiness of all the nation's Mr. Smiths. He adds, however, that federal safeguards serving to protect and regulate financial intermediaries—for example, the Federal Deposit Insurance Corporation—should help prevent widespread financial trouble from developing.

Such safeguards didn't exist in the 1920s, before the Great Depression. Many economists believe that, if they had, the slump wouldn't have been nearly so severe.

While this change may be reassuring, it's perhaps disquieting to observe, as noted earlier, that debt-to-GNP levels in the 1920s were roughly similar to recent levels. Hyman Minsky, an economist at Washington University in St. Louis, cites this similarity as one reason that he derives scant comfort from the rela-

tively stable debt readings of recent years.

Key Points

1. The goal of national income accounting is to measure the production of goods and services in the economy and the earnings generated out of that production. It also provides measures of private spendable and savable income. National income accounting measures include gross national product, personal income, and disposable income.

2. The financial system transfers funds from those foregoing spending by saving to those borrowing the funds in order to put them to use.

3. The flow of funds accounts attempt to measure all financial flows in the economy for a period of time, usually a quarter or a year. All financial flows are included whether they correspond to newly produced goods or services, used assets, or purely financial transactions.

4. Flows of funds are derived from the balance sheets and income statements of the various sectors of the economy over the period of time for which the accounts are prepared by the Federal Reserve System. Specialized flow of funds accounts are also prepared by financial analysts for particular purposes, such as interest rate forecasting.

5. The flow of funds accounts divide the economy into various sectors such as households, business, and commercial banks. The summary table contains nine sectors, while the flow of funds detailed accounts contain twenty-five sectors. Focusing on the sources and uses of funds by each sector gives a complete picture of the financial system and the interaction between sectors.

Questions for Discussion

1. Discuss the relationship between the national income accounts and the flow of funds accounts. What is the object behind each of these accounting systems? What are the differences between these approaches?

2. Why must sector sources and uses of funds be equal in the flow of funds accounts?

3. Explain the possible usefulness of flow of funds analysis to the financial analyst.

4. What would you conclude about the financial system from an examination of the flow of funds accounts?

5. Why is the saving–investment process in the economy important?

Suggested Readings

Baumol, William J., and Alan S. Blinder. *Economics: Principles and Policies,* 2nd ed. New York: Harcourt Brace Jovanovich, 1982, pp. 130–38.

Board of Governors of the Federal Reserve System. *Introduction to Flow of Funds,* June 1980.

Polakoff, Murray E. "Institutionalization of Saving and Financial Markets," Chapter 1 in Murray Polakoff et al. *Financial Institutions and Markets,* 2nd ed. Boston: Houghton, Mifflin, 1981.

Ritter, Lawrence. "The Flow of Funds Accounts: A Framework for Financial Analysis," Chapter 2 in Murray Polakoff et al. *Financial Institutions and Markets,* 2nd ed. Boston: Houghton, Mifflin, 1981.

Samuelson, Paul A. "National Income and Product," Chapter 10 *Economics,* 11th ed. New York: McGraw-Hill, 1979.

In addition, Salomon Brothers, Bankers Trust and a number of other financial institutions publish flow of funds analyses as noted in the text. It is quite helpful to read through these forecasts as they will in the aggregate give the reader an in-depth appreciation of the usefulness of the flow of funds approach. They are usually obtainable by writing directly to the financial institution and are free of charge. The Federal Reserve *Bulletin* summarizes flow of funds information, and the detailed accounts can be obtained by writing directly to the Board of Governors of the Federal Reserve.

3

A Primer on Money

At the beginning of Chapter 1, we noted that as soon as an economy achieves any degree of complexity something develops as money. Very soon thereafter the financial system starts to take shape and develop. This chapter will examine money: what it is, how it evolves, and the role it plays in the financial system.

What Is Money?

Money is anything that is generally acceptable as a means of payment or a medium of exchange. This means that transactions can be conducted using something that is not itself desired but is accepted in exchange for goods and services because it is known that it can be used for other transactions. Simply stated, a seller of goods and services will accept money in exchange because the seller knows that others will in turn accept that money in exchange for their goods or services. It is this exchangeability that makes money valuable. A cashier at a local fast-food restaurant is content to be paid in money rather than in hamburgers—even though hamburgers have intrinsic value and money often does not—because the cashier knows that the money will allow the purchase of a wide range of items. Merchants will accept money in payment for goods and services, and so the cashier is willing to exchange labor for money.

In studying the financial system, it is important to understand early that money need not have any use in and of itself for it to be money. It need only be generally acceptable in the purchase of goods and services. Of course, nothing precludes money from having intrinsic value. A miser certainly finds money useful even without spending any of it. More to the point, many things have served as money that have intrinsic value, but it was their general acceptability as a means of payment that made them desired. For example, in Italy after World War II, cigarettes developed as money. Merchants would accept cigarettes in payment for bread, clothing, and other items. Did that mean that everybody who accepted cigarettes actually was a cigarette smoker? No. Merchants who accepted cigarettes knew that they could, in turn, buy what they needed with the cigarettes they received. Even now in what are considered advanced economies, things that we find unusual are generally accepted as money. The *New York Times* recently reported, that in Rumania, a country in Eastern Europe with a highly regulated economy, cigarettes—particularly American brands— are accepted in exchange for goods and services. Officially the monetary unit is the Rumanian *leu*. Yet taxicab drivers, bellboys at hotels, even medical doctors accept cigarettes in exchange for services. Why? In order to buy some very desirable goods, like stereos made in Western Europe, it is necessary to have these cigarettes to induce their sale. It is very difficult for private Rumanian citizens to buy these things exclusively with Rumanian currency. Thus the need for the cigarettes.

The above examples also illustrate that for something to be acceptable as money, the government need not say it is money. Throughout history there have been many instances when the government said something was money, but, since it was not generally acceptable as a means of payment, it never really functioned as money. For example, the phrase "not worth a Continental" is often discussed in history books. This phrase referred to the Continental Dollar, which was issued by the Continental Congress during the American Revolutionary War; it was supposed to be the monetary unit for the colonies fighting for their independence. Congress said it was so. However, when the war was going poorly for the colonies, most people thought the Continental Dollar would become worthless. If nobody is willing to accept money in exchange for goods and services, it loses its value as a monetary unit. There were many instances during the Revolutionary War when people presented Continental Dollars and were not sold merchandise. Indeed, when it was accepted, often it was at a penny (or less) to the dollar. Even the Revolutionary army had trouble securing supplies using the Continental as a means of payment.

It is true that in more settled times when the government of a modern developed economy says that something is money, it is usually accepted as a means of payment. On every U.S. dollar is the inscription "this note is legal tender for all debts, public and private"; and this certainly adds to the acceptability of the currency as money. However, it may be surprising to learn that the U.S. government has little directly to do with the issuance of most of the money in the economy. The largest portion of the money supply is checking accounts about which the government says nothing concerning acceptability. It is useful at this point to discuss currency in detail in order to illustrate some aspects of the above discussion.

U.S. currency itself is composed of a piece of high quality paper with a very nice picture and other designs on it. The materials are worth perhaps a fraction of a cent, even with the art work. Yet currency has been issued in denominations up to $100,000.[1] This illustrates a point that was made earlier in our study: It is not the intrinsic worth of the monetary unit that makes it money. A merchant is willing to accept a $20 bill in exchange for some item because the merchant knows someone else will in turn accept that $20 bill in exchange for goods or services the merchant wishes to purchase. U.S. currency and coin represent a type of money known as **fiat** money or **token** money, although the latter term is most often reserved for coin. It is fiat money in the sense that the government by fiat, or law, establishes it as money. It is token money because it has no intrinsic value in and of itself other than its monetary value. That is, it can't really be used for anything else. Even the metal value of U.S. coins is only a small fraction of the stated value of the coin itself. When the metal value of a coin begins to approach the coin's stated value, a base or other metal is substituted. For example, beginning in 1981 the copper content of pennies was reduced and is being replaced by zinc.

There have been periods in history when monetary units did have intrinsic value. A $20 gold piece of the nineteenth century did have $20 worth of gold in it at the gold prices then prevailing. In medieval times most money coined did have the amount of precious metal corresponding to its stated value. (This led to abuse as people often tried to gain by scraping just a little of the metal off the coin and passing it at face value. Even some kings, like Henry VIII in sixteenth-century England, were guilty of this behavior.) Money that has the same intrinsic value as its stated monetary value is known as full-bodied money. But this is very rare nowadays. Most government-issued money possesses no intrinsic value.

Furthermore, U.S. currency itself has no backing whatsoever in precious metal. There used to be a connection between currency and gold, but the last vestige of such a tie was severed in 1971. Well before that year, however, the gold backing had ceased to have any meaning to U.S. residents, who were not permitted to exchange currency for gold. The 1971 change severed the tie between dollars held abroad and gold. The fact that currency is still money even with no precious metal backing it illustrates our point: It is money because it is generally acceptable as a means of payment.

---

[1] These are not circulated and are used only for certain Treasury–Federal Reserve System transactions. In addition, currency in denominations above $100 is no longer being issued, but some $500, $1,000, $5,000 and $10,000 denomination bills are still in circulation.

As noted in Chapter 1, once something comes to the fore as the monetary unit, the economy becomes a monetary economy. In fact, that is what defines a monetary economy—an economy that uses money. The use of money separates a monetary economy from a barter economy.

Barter

A barter economy is one in which goods are traded for other goods. Corn exchanges for wheat; a cow, for a horse; and so on. An economy can only be a barter economy at a very low level of economic development. As soon as an economy starts developing, something, or somethings, come to the fore as money. What is this? What are the problems with a barter economy? The problems that are inherent in a barter economy (or even in a barter transaction) that lead to a barter economy being superseded by a monetary economy can be labeled coincidence of wants, divisibility, relative values, and specialization.

Coincidence of Wants

What are the conditions that must exist for a trade of goods to take place between two people? Both traders must want the good the other has more than the good they are willing to trade, otherwise they wouldn't trade. More technically, a double coincidence of wants must exist for a barter transaction to take place. Simply stated, a double coincidence of wants means that each person has what the other wants. In our earlier example of trading marbles or comic books, assume a child has a certain comic book that she wants to trade. For the trade to take place, it is necessary to find a friend that not only wants that comic book but has one that the child wants also.

In an economy this is much more difficult. Suppose a farmer wants wheat and has apples to trade. If the wheat farmer doesn't want apples, the apple grower is out of luck unless a third party can be found who wants apples and has what the wheat farmer wants. Then the apples can be traded for, say, corn, and then, in turn, the corn traded for the wheat. Clearly, this can get very complicated very soon. Imagine having to go through this in an advanced economy with the large variety of goods that exist. (In fact, an advanced economy simply could not exist as a barter economy.)

Divisibility and Relative Value

Continuing the example, suppose the apple grower can find somebody who has wheat and wants apples. The wheat farmer may believe that the wheat is worth more bushels of apples than the apple grower is willing to give. Who is to say? If agreement on the value of wheat in terms of apples cannot be reached, even with a double coincidence of wants, no trade can take place. There are few reference points for determining relative value. But even more complications can arise.

Suppose the farmers are not trading apples for wheat but rather a milk cow for wheat. Suppose that the amount of wheat offered in exchange for the milk cow is too little in the judgment of the cow owner. A milk cow cannot be divided into smaller units and still remain a milk cow. Therefore, because of divisibility difficulties, no trade can take place even though a double coincidence of wants exists.

Placed in a modern context, the problems become insurmountable. (In fact, the difficulties are so severe that the degree of technology suggested by the following example could not exist in a barter economy.) Suppose that an individual wishes to acquire an automobile. The individual has twenty bushels of wheat to trade. He goes down to Smiling Al's used car lot and picks out a car. Assume further that a double coincidence of wants exist—that is, for some reason Smiling Al wants wheat. Still there can be a problem. Al believes that 20 bushels of wheat is not sufficient to purchase the car. It is only worth, say, the right fender. But a right fender is not a car; it does not fulfill the same purpose. Further, even if the fender is accepted, Smiling Al is in trouble because if he continues to divide the car, it soon ceases to be a car. Even with a double coincidence of wants, divisibility and relative value raise additional problems in a barter economy.

Specialization

A barter transaction involving a car could not exist in a barter economy. The reason is that in order to produce a car, there must be specialization, and specialization to any degree at all cannot exist in a barter economy. Think about how a car is produced on the assembly line. There are people along that assembly line who simply tighten bolts. They get very good at that job. In fact, they do it better and faster than anybody else possibly could. But could such a job exist in a barter economy? The answer is obviously no. In a barter economy, the bolt tightener would have to trade that skill for everything she needed to exist—food, clothing, shelter. This would not be possible. There could be no bolt tighteners, no car finishers, no painters, and no electricians. An advanced economy has many specialized roles that add to its efficiency and simply could not exist in a barter economy. Specialization is crucial for economic growth and development—a very famous economist, Adam Smith, noted this in 1776—and as soon as an economy starts to develop, it must leave barter.

When an economy reaches the level of specialization of a modern industrial economy such as that of the United States, the ineffectiveness of barter becomes even more dramatic. For example, if the United

States suddenly reverted to a barter economy, what would a professor do? Could the professor go from farm to farm offering to tutor children in finance or monetary economics in exchange for food and clothing? (This example requires a little imagination. The fact that the subject matter of finance and monetary economics wouldn't exist in a barter economy has to be ignored to convey the image.) Clearly the professor would soon cease to be a professor. Extend this to the numerous other professions and skills, and the problem is clear.

The Monetary Economy

In a monetary economy, all these problems of a barter economy cease to exist. No longer is a double coincidence of wants necessary for a transaction to take place. All that a seller needs to do is to find someone who wants the good or service that is being offered and is willing to pay for it. The buyer need not have the specific good the seller wants. With the money from the sale, the seller can purchase other goods elsewhere. Divisibility and relative value are no longer problems either, because values are expressed in terms of money. Prices of various goods can be compared, and the buyer knows what is required to purchase a particular good. Since money is almost infinitely divisible, a particular good can cost $100 or $1.98 and the money can be divided accordingly. Finally, a high degree of specialization can take place. The bolt tightener on the assembly line is paid in money with which she can go and purchase what she needs. The bolt tightener can remain a bolt tightener, develop that skill, and add to the efficiency of the economy. Alas, so can the professor. Thus, when a particular item becomes generally acceptable as a means of payment—money— a monetary economy develops, economic growth can take place, and the financial system develops.

Before leaving this issue, however, a point does need to be clarified. Once again recall our example of trading comic books. Barter transactions may take place in a highly developed monetary economy. Does this mean that the economy can be characterized as partly a barter economy? The answer is no. For an economy to be considered a monetary economy, most and usually the overwhelming number of transactions are monetary transactions. Barter can still take place and does from time to time even in the most advanced economy. For example, in some cases in our present economy, it is not unusual for a plumber and electrician to barter their services to each other. Other kinds of barter arrangements were popular during the commune movement in the United States in the late 1960s. Many of these still operate today. The level of barter transactions relative to monetary transactions in the economy are so small, however, that the existence of some barter does not contradict anything that has been discussed above.

Other Functions of Money

By now it should be well understood that money is defined as anything generally acceptable as a means of payment. However, money usually serves other functions as well. These include the store of value function, the unit of account function, and the standard of deferred payment function.

Store of Value Although money is defined by its function as a medium of exchange, money must also serve as a store of value. It is a necessary adjunct to the exchange function because money receipts and expenditures do not coincide. Furthermore, it is simply too inconvenient to convert some assets into money every time a small transaction takes place. To the extent that people hold small sums of money to get through their daily transactions or to pay upcoming bills, they are using money as a store of value. Yet there are times when people have an incentive to minimize just how much of their funds they keep in the form of money, although these holdings cannot be eliminated entirely.

For example, in a period characterized by rapidly increasing prices, if someone placed a $100 bill into a secret compartment and took it out a year later he would have stored $100 worth of value in money for that year. But what would be the result? In a period of rapidly rising prices, $100 a year from now will purchase less than $100 today. Further, the $100 would have yielded no interest return. Thus, under some circumstances money may not be a very effective store of value.

In the above example the individual would have been better off had he put the $100 into some asset that would have yielded a return, such as a savings account that might have at least partially compensated for the loss of purchasing power. Moreover, there are a number of assets that have performed better than savings accounts in recent years in preserving value. Paintings, real estate, rare stamps, and the like are all assets in which value can be stored and which have historically done better than money in preserving purchasing power during inflationary periods. Thus, money must serve as a store of value in the sense that at any point in time some money is held to facilitate transactions, but it may be a very poor store of value. Indeed, a number of things that are not money may serve as well or better than money as stores of value.

Unit of Account Money typically serves as a unit of account as well as a store of value. What does it mean to say that money is a unit of account? Suppose that a shopper went into a supermarket and, while wheeling the shopping cart around, collected various products such as oranges, apples, cereal, and the like. The shopper then took the groceries up to the checkout clerk and placed them on the counter. Without any way of accounting for value, neither the shopper nor the clerk would know what was required for the purchase of the merchandise. But now put a price on each good; say apples cost $1, oranges $.50, and $.75 for the cereal. That totals $2.25. Suddenly the shopper knows what is required to purchase the items, and the clerk knows what to expect in return for the items. Money has served as a unit of account. Because each good has been valued in terms of money, the total value of diverse goods can be summed and expressed in terms of money. In addition, the cost of various goods can be compared. Usually the monetary unit of a country performs this function.

However, something can be a unit of account without being money. Suppose an American tourist in Britain had to see a lawyer; she might find the price of the appointment came to five guineas. The tourist might search her wallet and find only currency called pounds and coins called pence. No guineas. What does the tourist do? Actually this is not a problem; the guinea has not existed since the early part of the nineteenth century. By custom it is still used in Britain to price many things, particularly services such as those of lawyers and doctors. Yet it is no longer money. Therefore, the guinea is something that is serving as a unit of account without being money. (A guinea is worth 1.05 pounds sterling—the British currency unit.) In the United States there is also a nonmoney unit of account, although it is not as extensively used as the guinea. It is a fair bet that most people know what two bits are. Two bits are $.25. Yet we have no coin called two bits and, in fact, nothing that is equivalent to one bit. Again here is a case in which something that is not money can serve as a unit of account.[2]

While money, or more precisely the monetary unit, usually serves as a unit of account, something can serve as a unit of account and not be money. The medium of exchange function is unique to money. Other functions of money can be served by things other than money, but the medium of exchange function cannot.

Standard of Deferred Payment Money usually functions as a standard of deferred payment. This simply means that contracts are usually written in terms of money. If an art collector agrees to buy at a stipulated price a painting that an artist will complete in two

---

[2] That a bit is widely accepted as a unit of account is clear from the fact that *Webster's New Collegiate Dictionary*, 1977 edition, defines bit as "a unit of value [account] equal to ⅛ of a dollar." Like the British guinea, the bit was, in fact, at one time money. The dollar was based on the Spanish *milled* dollar, which circulated in the United States when the Spanish controlled Mexico and parts of the Southwest. The original Mexican peso, also based on the Spanish dollar, consisted of eight *reals* and the Mexican peso also circulated in the United States for a while. These *reals* were known as *bits*. Since there were eight to the "dollar," the term *bits* stuck long after *reals* stopped circulating in the United States.

months and they write a contract to this effect, money has been used as a standard of deferred payment. However, an equally legal contract could have been written in terms of wheat: a specified amount of wheat could be exchanged for the painting. Something that isn't money can be used as a standard of deferred payment in contracts. Nonetheless, money usually does serve this purpose.

The store of value, unit of account, and standard of deferred payment are all important functions of money. Though derived from the medium of exchange function of money, they facilitate exchange thereby increasing the efficiency of the exchange process.

Money in the Economy

Now that we have defined money, we can examine its composition. As was pointed out above, currency is only part of the money supply and actually the smallest portion. The major portion of the money supply is demand deposits, the formal name for noninterest-earning checking deposits. It is easy to see that demand deposits meet the definition of money. Remember that money is generally acceptable as a means of payment and demand deposits are generally acceptable in the purchase of goods and services. The reason for the phrase "generally acceptable" in the definition also becomes clear in considering demand deposits. Particular demand deposits are not universally acceptable even within the confines of the United States. If a family from Illinois vacations in California, they might have a very difficult time cashing a personal check there. Does this mean that demand deposits are not money? Not at all; demand deposits certainly are generally acceptable. The Illinois family probably pays most of their bills by check and, undoubtedly, is able to cash checks in supermarkets and at other stores in their area with proper identification. A Californian can also go into the store in his area and have no difficulty cashing his check. For the economy, then, checking accounts are indeed money.

Notice that the demand deposits themselves are money, not the blank checks. If blank checks were money, we would all immediately be rich for we can obtain just about all the blank checks that we wish. When a check is presented in payment of a bill, there is a presumption that the funds are in the demand deposit account to back up that check. If they are not, the check is not accepted in payment after the bank notifies the payee of insufficient funds.

Beginning on January 1, 1981, banks and other deposit-taking financial intermediaries nationwide were permitted to offer interest-earning checking accounts to individuals and nonprofit organizations. Most of these accounts are called **NOW accounts—Negotiable Or-**

Table 3-1
Money Supply, November 1981
(Billions of Dollars)

Currency	$122.1
Demand Deposits	235.9
Traveler's Checks	4.6
Other Checkable Deposits	75.6
Total Money Supply	$437.9[1]

[1] Due to rounding, components do not add to total.
Source: Federal Reserve *Bulletin*, Jan. 1982.

ders of Withdrawal.[3] Interest-earning checking accounts have grown rapidly since their nationwide introduction. However, demand deposit accounts on which banks are prohibited by law from paying interest still constitute the bulk of checking accounts. One reason for this is that corporations are not permitted to hold NOW accounts. That demand deposit accounts earn no explicit interest is somewhat misleading, however. Banks provide a number of services to demand deposit holders such as check clearing, monthly statements, and so forth. The extent of these services typically increases as the average size of the account increases. Service charges that banks may receive on demand deposits cover only a fraction of the costs of these services. As a result, even though banks do not pay any explicit interest on demand deposits, they do pay "implicit interest" on these accounts in the provision of services.

Table 3-1 presents the money supply of the United States as of November 1981. The breakdown is between currency (including coin), demand deposits, traveler's checks, and other checkable deposits, which are the interest-earning checking deposits. The table shows that the major portion of the money supply remains in demand deposits despite the growth of other checkable deposits.

The above discussion of the money supply illustrates the point made earlier that for something to be money the government does not have to say it is money or issue it. Demand deposits and other checkable deposits are issued by private financial intermediaries. In discussing commercial banking in Chapter 6, we will discover that in fact most demand deposits come into existence through the operation

---

[3] Some financial intermediaries in certain states have offered NOW accounts since 1972. See Chapters 8 and 9.

of the commercial banking system. The key to whether something is money is simply its general acceptability.

If currency, demand deposits, and other checkable deposits compose the money supply, what about another device that is used frequently and that appears to be generally acceptable as a means of payment, namely credit cards? Aren't credit cards also money since they seem to meet the definition? The answer is no and a little reflection will reveal the reason. Think about a credit card transaction. Suppose an individual goes into a sporting goods store, decides to purchase a tennis racket, and wants to put it on her bank credit card. What takes place in this transaction? The individual gives the cashier the credit card; it is run through a machine, and its imprint appears on a form that contains the amount of the purchase and a place for a signature. The form is nothing more than a loan agreement. When the bill comes from the bank, it must be paid either by writing the bank a check for the amount or in currency. Even if the individual decides to take advantage of the extended terms offered—only paying a part of the bill and allowing the rest to be carried forward to succeeding months—a certain portion of the bill must be paid either by a check drawn on a checking account or by currency. Although credit cards appear to be money, they are really only a quick and standard way of obtaining a loan.

Money Stock Measures and Liquid Assets

While only currency, demand deposits, and other checkable deposits are money, the Federal Reserve System regularly collects and publishes data on what are called "money stock measures and liquid assets." Not all the money stock measures, in fact, are money. The money stock itself is published. Other series that are published under the heading money stock measures and liquid assets are derived by adding other items to the money stock that are easily convertible into money. Sometimes these items are known as **near-monies.** Such items as passbook savings deposits can be converted into money simply by presenting the passbook at the financial intermediary and withdrawing the funds. Items that require a bit more trouble for conversion into money but are still relatively easy to convert are combined with money and near-monies to generate still another measure known as **liquid assets.** An example of a liquid asset that is included in this measure is a short-term U.S. government security that is easy to sell. Money stock measures and liquid assets are discussed in detail below.

Since not all money stock measures actually include money only, the terminology may appear confusing. (This is but the first example of many that will appear in this book in which the official designation of items can lead to confusion. But like the study of any subject, the terminology of the financial system must be learned in order for the subject itself to be mastered.) The rationale behind producing a number of measures of the money stock is that the money stock represents a direct claim on goods and services in the economy, and near-monies and liquid assets represent a pool of funds rapidly convertible into money for spending purposes. Thus, analysts studying the economy often find it useful to have these various series of data available. Table 3-2 presents the money stock measures and liquid assets.

The Money Supply—M1

M1 measures the money supply exclusively. It includes currency in circulation, demand deposits at commercial banks, traveler's checks of nonbank issuers, negotiable orders of withdrawal, automatic transfer service accounts, credit union sharedraft accounts, and demand deposits at mutual savings banks. Automatic transfer accounts are special passbook savings accounts. Like any passbook savings account, funds on deposit earn interest. However, in the case of these special passbook accounts, funds are automatically transferred to the depositor's demand deposit account when the need arises. If a check drawn on the depositor's demand deposit account is received by the bank for payment and insufficient funds are available in the demand deposit account to pay the check, the necessary funds are transferred from the passbook account. Until these funds are needed, however, they continue to earn interest. Since the funds in the automatic transfer accounts belong to the depositor, this arrangement differs from standard backup lines of credit frequently available for demand deposit and other checkable deposit accounts. A line of credit means that the bank will automatically loan sufficient funds to pay a check pre-

---

Table 3-2
Money Stock Measures
and Liquid Assets,
November 1981
(Billions of Dollars)

M1	$ 437.9
M2	1,824.7
M3	2,168.4
L	2,574.4[1]

[1] September 1981.

Source: Federal Reserve *Bulletin*, Jan. 1982.

sented for payment if the demand deposit balance is insufficient. It is simply an automatic loan. The nationwide spread of NOW accounts and other interest-earning checking accounts should eliminate the automatic transfer account over time.

Credit union sharedraft accounts are simply interest-earning checking accounts at credit unions. They are similar in every way to NOW accounts. Thus, M1 provides a complete measure of those things generally acceptable as means of payment. When analysts discuss the growth in the money supply or the amount of money in the economy, they are referring to M1.

Until January 1982 the Federal Reserve had reported the money supply in two different series—M1A and M1B. M1A included the major portion of the money supply, currency in circulation and demand deposits at commercial banks. The reason that M1A was compiled was that prior to the existence of interest-bearing checking accounts, it measured virtually the entire money stock. Beginning in early 1980, the Federal Reserve redefined the money stock measures to reflect changes in money, including the increasing use of interest-earning checking accounts. When the interest-earning checking accounts spread nationwide after January 1, 1981, the inclusion of these accounts in a measure of the money supply itself became even more important. Nevertheless, the Federal Reserve System believed a continuation of this series for a while would be useful for historical comparisons. However, it also published the M1B series. The M1B series is the same as M1 and was renamed M1 following the discontinuance of M1A in January 1982.

Other Money Stock Measures and Liquid Assets

There are, in addition to M1, two other measures of the money stock and one measure of liquid assets that are collected and available. These measures, M2, M3, and L, all include items that, while not money, are readily convertible into money.

M2 The M2 measure adds to M1 savings and small denomination time deposits (less than $100,000) at all deposit-taking institutions, overnight repurchase agreements (RPs) and Eurodollars, and money market mutual fund shares. In addition to money, this measure includes items that are most easily convertible into money such as passbook savings accounts. Small denomination time deposits are held for fixed maturity by depositors but can be redeemed before maturity if necessary with an interest penalty. Overnight repurchase agreements are arrangements in which a bank sells a security to another organization, often a corporation, and agrees to purchase the security back the next day. The difference between the sales price of the security and its purchase price provides the purchaser with a yield. It is a way of paying interest to a corporation for funds that are essentially demand deposits. Banks are willing to use RPs in order to maintain deposits that they might otherwise lose and to raise funds. Overnight Eurodollars are also a way of paying interest for funds to organizations that are not allowed to hold interest-earning demand deposit accounts. In this transaction, funds are placed on deposit at Caribbean branches of commercial banks where they earn a return from the banks on an overnight basis.[4]

Money market mutual funds are financial intermediaries that gather funds from shareholders and use those funds to purchase money market securities. Since many money market securities come in relatively high denominations—for example, U.S. Treasury bills have a $10,000 face value—these funds allow participation in the money market by individuals who otherwise would not be able to participate. When interest rates are high, money market mutual funds offer to the small saver a significant interest rate advantage over many other forms of holding savings. Furthermore, most money market funds allow shareholders to redeem funds by check. Usually the check must be a $500 minimum. The ability to redeem shares by check has led some economists to argue that the fund shares should be included in M1; but the Federal Reserve has not agreed with this argument in part because of the minimum check provision.

M3 The M3 measure adds to M2 large-denomination time deposits (certificates of deposit over $100,000) at all depository institutions and term repurchase agreements at commercial banks and savings and loan associations. Large certificates of deposit (CDs) are usually negotiable so that they can be sold if a holder wishes to convert them into cash before maturity. Term repurchase agreements are repurchase agreements that mature in more than one day.

L and Liquidity The Federal Reserve also compiles a data series that is essentially a measure of liquid assets in the economy, the L measure. When an asset is easily converted into money, that asset is said to be highly **liquid.** Thus, all near-monies are highly liquid. In fact, **liquidity** is defined by the ease with which an asset can be converted into money. Obviously, the most liquid of all assets is money itself since it need not be converted at all—it already is money.

However, the ease of converting something into money is not the only facet of liquidity. It must also be true that the conversion can be done without taking any substantial loss on the asset. Many assets can be converted quite easily into money if the asset holder is willing to accept a large loss—which is usually referred to as a capital loss—

---

[4] Both repurchase agreements and the Eurodollar market are quite complicated subjects which will be discussed in detail later.

on the asset. For example, a house is generally not considered a liquid asset; it usually takes some weeks or even months to sell a house and convert it into money. Yet suppose a homeowner who paid $50,000 for a house was willing to sell it for $1,000. Obviously, the house would sell virtually instantaneously and so could easily and quickly be converted into money. However, the house would still not be considered a liquid asset in the usual meaning of the term. A huge capital loss was taken in selling the house. The definition of liquidity must be restricted to refer to the degree with which an asset can be converted into money without substantial capital loss. Conversely, an asset is not very liquid or is illiquid if it cannot be converted into money easily and quickly, except with usually large capital losses. The concept of liquidity is very important, and we will have occasion to use it often throughout the book.

The L measure that the Federal Reserve publishes attempts to measure all liquid assets in the economy. It is often useful for the analyst to have some overall measure of the amount of liquidity in the economy at any point in time. The L measure adds to M3 term Eurodollars, bankers acceptances, commercial paper, short-term Treasury securities such as Treasury bills, and U.S. savings bonds. Term Eurodollars are deposits denominated in dollars held for more than one day in foreign banks or subsidiaries of major U.S. banks outside of the United States. Bankers acceptances are bank guarantees of private obligations usually used for international transactions; commercial paper consists of short-term business debt. Treasury bills are the shortest maturity U.S. treasury securities. All these items are money market instruments that are easily bought and sold.

All the money stock measures, as well as the liquid asset measure, have their uses to analysts for practical purposes which will become clear later in the book. However, the most important of the money stock measures is the actual money stock: M1 corresponds most closely to the definition of money. Therefore, at those times when it becomes necessary to discuss the actual money supply, we will use the M1 definition.[5]

---

[5] However, as the accompanying article from *The Wall Street Journal* makes clear, some economists might give a different measure more attention.

WHICH M?

Tracking a Trend: Supply of Money Supplies Is Abundant; Problem: Which 'M' Really Counts?

Will the Real Money Supply Please Stand Up?

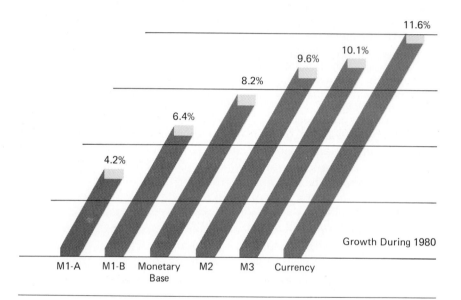

	11.6%
10.1%	
9.6%	
8.2%	
6.4%	
4.2%	

Growth During 1980

M1-A   M1-B   Monetary   M2   M3   Currency
                Base

By Alfred L. Malabre Jr.

[Note: This article appeared before the elimination of M1A and the renaming of M1B as M1 in January 1982.]

In fact, economists do occasionally agree with one another.

For instance, they agree (at least most of them do) that curbing inflation will necessitate curbing the growth of the money supply—bringing it down carefully to a pace roughly consistent with the economy's natural ability over the long term to lift the supply of goods and services that money buys. (Econo-mists place that long-term rate around 2% to 3% annually.)

It sounds straightforward, but a question arises: Just what constitutes the money supply?

Mr. Webster tells us that money is "something generally accepted as a medium of exchange, a measure of value."

A child will say that money is the change in your pocket and the bills in your wallet, the stuff represented by the chart's extreme-right bar. It rose nearly 12% last year, far faster than the economy's natural, long-term ability to expand.

When an economist talks about money, however, the picture can grow fuzzy.

A Slower Increase

A reference to the money supply may mean what the child imagines plus what's in your regular checking account at the bank—the M1-A depicted by the left-hand bar. It rose only about 4% in 1980, a fraction of the rise in currency and an increase within hailing distance of the economy's growth potential.

Or the money supply may mean M1-B, which embraces M1-A plus additional checking-type accounts including those that pay interest at all depository institutions. Its 1980 increase of more than 6% clearly seems inflationary.

Or it may mean the monetary base, which includes once again currency plus cash-type assets that banks keep on reserve to satisfy Federal Reserve Board rules. Its 1980 advance of over 8% appears still more inflationary.

The list goes on.

The money supply may also mean M2, whose reach covers M1-B plus all traditional savings-type accounts of less than $100,000 plus money-market mutual-fund shares *plus* such banking esoterica as, to quote a Federal Reserve explanation, "overnight repurchase agreements at commercial banks" and "overnight Eurodollars held by U.S. residents other than banks at Caribbean branches of member banks."

Last year's increase in M2 of nearly 10% easily dwarfs any reasonable estimate of the economy's capacity to expand.

A Still Broader Measure

The same may be said of M3's rise. This broad usage of the money supply—up more than 10% last year—encompasses M2 plus still other "repurchase agreements" plus all "large-denomination time deposits."

Even more varieties of the money supply—fewer than Howard Johnson has flavors, but too many to squeeze onto the adjoining chart—have been tracked from time to time.

Some years ago, for instance, as many as eight different M's were cited in the congressional testimony of a Federal Reserve Board chairman, Arthur F. Burns. (He was known to feel that the Fed's various money numbers had been getting excessive public attention, and some analysts saw his long list of M's as a deliberate—but unsuccessful—effort to introduce such confusion into money-watching as to kill the sport.)

Mr. Burns is long retired and the Fed's list is mercifully smaller now. But it still includes, for example, something called L. At more than $2 trillion, this Brobdingnagian measure adds to M3 the short-term liabilities of all depository institutions, nonfinancial corporations and the government. It approximates, says a Fed economist, "the volume of credit extended through financial intermediaries." L's recent rise also is sharp.

Quite obviously, the supply of money supplies is abundant. And so: Which money supply should policy makers attempt to curb to curb inflation? Which money supply should the nonexpert, who merely seeks to keep abreast, keep a newspaper eye on?

Simpler Times

Much attention once was focused on the measure represented by the chart's left-hand bar. Today dubbed M1-A, it was then known simply as M1. Its fall from grace, economists explain, can be traced to the Hydra-headed nature of money when inflation flares. M1-A by definition misses all the money that has fled in recent years of high inflation from checking accounts that pay no interest to interest-paying accounts, including lately ones that also allow checkwriting.

The upshot is that anyone—policy maker or layman—who still attempts to monitor the money supply only through M1-A would gain an impression of moderate monetary restraint when, it can be argued, monetary growth has in truth been rapid.

For a while, focus shifted to a now-defunct version of M2 that embraced various interest-paying accounts. The very recent rise of interest-paying accounts that allow checkwriting, in turn, has brought considerable attention to M1-B. This measure is deemed most important by many Fed officials and is usually what's meant nowadays when headlines talk about the money supply.

M1-B fails, however, to catch the recent precipitous growth of money-market mutual funds. To bring this into the picture, some economists now claim that M2, the version depicted and defined above, is what deserves primary attention. "It's what I mainly watch," says Sam I. Nakagama, economist of Kidder, Peabody & Co., a New York-based securities firm. (For some money-watchers, a problem with M2 and M3 is that the Fed reports them only monthly, while such gauges as M1-A, M1-B and the monetary base are available weekly.)

Notwithstanding the views of the Fed about M1-B or those of Mr. Nakagama about M2, today's consensus tends to focus on still another monetary measure—the monetary base. Precisely, the focus is on the monetary base, as adjusted weekly by the St. Louis Federal Reserve Bank to remove possible distortions because of shifting of bank deposits between savings and checking accounts.

Monetary-Base Attraction

An attraction of the monetary base, analysts assert, is that its components—bank reserves and currency—lend themselves more easily to control by Fed policy makers than, say, the wide-ranging components of M1-B or M2 or M3. Control the growth of the monetary base, it's argued, and eventually the growth of all the larger M's will be reined in as well. And, this theory holds, the Fed can indeed control the base's growth through its authority, for instance, to buy and sell securities in the open market. Fed selling acts to drain reserves from banks and Fed buying tends to supply them.

Even monetary-base watching, however, can be tricky. For example, the monetary base expanded briskly between 1930 and 1933, a time of tumbling prices when the economy was sinking toward the pit of the Great Depression. The problem was that, as business worsened in those years, the currency component of the base rose extraswiftly, reflecting such factors as an understandable wariness about the safety of bank deposits. This rise more than offset a concurrent decline in the base's bank-reserves component.

The Fed's authority to manage money, it should be noted, derives from Congress, which is empowered by the U.S. Constitution to create money. To try to bring firmer control over monetary growth, Congress recently ordered Fed officials to set and announce publicly growth targets for most of the M's every six months. The varying targets provide an indication, at least, of what the

Fed's intentions are. However, the targets are imprecise, normally covering a range of at least a couple of percentage points. Even with such latitude, the actual growth of one M or another often misses the mark.

Further Confusion

The money-supply picture can grow still more confusing when efforts are made to attach much significance to changes in the weekly monetary data. Indeed, Irwin L. Kellner, an economist at Manufacturers Hanover Trust in New York, recently proposed that the Fed stop issuing any money-supply numbers weekly. On many weeks, it does seem that some special circumstance arises that may skew the readings. Moreover, few governmental statistics are more frequently or sharply revised than money-supply figures.

An extreme illustration of weekly bewilderment developed last Friday, when the Fed released, among other things, its latest M1-B report. In the preceding fortnight, the widely followed gauge had fallen sharply, generating some concern that Fed officials, after being perhaps too lax with monetary policy, were becoming overly restrictive. But in the Friday report M1-B rose $11.4 billion. This was by far the largest one-week advance on record, and it confounded many money-watchers.

A partial explanation appears to be that the week's report incorporated the advent on a nationwide basis of so-called NOW accounts (for negotiable orders of withdrawal). These interest-paying checking accounts surely had attracted funds, for example, from savings accounts not included within M1-B.

However, some analysts say that scrutiny of the various money-supply gauges reported Friday fails to explain adequately M1-B's surge. The surge would be less perplexing, for example, had there been a large concurrent drop in M1-A, signaling a big shift of funds out of normal checking accounts to NOW accounts. But M1-A rose $1.6 billion in the report, which covered the week ended Jan. 7. Other data released Friday, for the week ended Jan. 14, seemed to shed little light on M1-B's surge. The adjusted monetary base fell $1.3 billion while bank reserves climbed about $350 million.

Fed Intentions

Some money-watchers, it should be noted, focus mainly on bank reserves. They explain that such funds, while a relatively narrow gauge, are crucial to generating growth in the broader monetary measures. It's also pointed out that such funds are most closely under the direct control of Fed policy makers and, therefore, can be highly indicative of Fed intentions.

Some experts greeted the huge increase in M1-B with dismay, suggesting that Fed policy is once again too lax. Others viewed the week's surge as an aberration, caused by special factors. Still others indicated a new skepticism about whether close money-supply watching is really worth the effort.

Paul Markowski, a New York-based economist who focuses on bank reserves, confesses that he has trouble tracking and analyzing the movements of all the M's. "When I try, I go bananas," he says, holding his palms against his temples. An analyst at New York's Merrill Lynch & Co. remarks: "Inflation killed off the Keynesian notion that big gov-

ernment is our salvation, and I'm
starting to think confusion will kill
off the idea that monetarism will
save us."

Key Points

1. Money is anything generally acceptable as a means of payment or medium of exchange. Money usually serves other functions as well: It is
   a store of value, a unit of account and a standard of deferred payment.
   These functions all derive from the use of money as a medium of exchange.

2. A monetary economy is an economy in which money is utilized in the
   vast majority of transactions. This contrasts with a barter economy in
   which the primary means of exchange is goods and services directly
   exchanging for other goods and services. Barter presents many problems not found in a monetary economy. It requires a double coincidence
   of wants, leads to difficulties because goods are not highly divisible
   (making relative value judgments troublesome), and precludes specialization.

3. The money supply is composed of currency (including coin), demand
   deposits, and other checkable deposits that earn interest. The largest
   component of the money supply is demand deposits.

4. The Federal Reserve System collects and publishes data on money stock
   measures and liquid assets. M1 measures the money in the economy
   while the other measures in general add near-monies and other liquid
   assets to the money stock. Liquidity is the ease of converting an asset
   into money without suffering a substantial capital loss. Near-monies are
   assets possessing a high degree of liquidity. The M2, M3, and L measure-
   ments provide increasingly broad measures of liquidity in the economy.

Questions for Discussion

1. What distinguishes a barter economy from a monetary economy?

2. How do the functions that money usually serves derive from the medium
   of exchange or means of payment function that defines money?

3. What role does government play in the acceptance of something as
   money?

4. Explain the difference between the various money stock measures and
   liquid assets published by the Federal Reserve System. What distinguishes M1 from these other measures? Why do you think the Federal
   Reserve publishes so many measures:

Suggested Readings

Clower, R. W. *Monetary Theory: Selected Readings.* Baltimore: Penguin, 1970.

Galbraith, John K. *Money: Whence It Came, Where It Went.* Boston: Houghton Mifflin, 1975.

Gambs, Carl M. "Money—A Changing Concept in a Changing World." Federal Reserve Bank of Kansas City *Monthly Review,* Jan. 1977, pp. 3–12.

Hafer, R. W. "The New Monetary Aggregates," Federal Reserve Bank of St. Louis *Review,* Feb. 1980, pp. 25–32.

"Money and Finance: Survey." *The Economist of London,* Part I, Nov. 29, 1980, and Part II, Jan. 17, 1981.

Nussbaum, Arthur. *A History of the Dollar.* New York: Columbia University Press, 1957.

Simpson, Thomas D. "The Redefined Monetary Aggregates." Federal Reserve *Bulletin,* Feb. 1980, pp. 97–115.

The 4
Determination
of Interest Rates

In Chapters 1 and 2 we discussed the allocation of credit in the economy and its importance. Interest rates are literally the "signals" that are given to channel credit in the economy, and to an important extent, they direct the flow of funds to and from the various sectors of the economy. In this chapter, we will discuss interest rates in detail.

It is common in economic analysis to refer to "the interest rate" as if only one existed. However, there are many interest rates that can be analyzed, depending upon which markets and which securities are being studied. The term "the interest rate" serves as a shorthand reference to the entire spectrum of interest rates much as one would use the term people to refer to a large group of persons. Such simplification is particularly useful in analyzing determinants of the level of interest rates, since rates do tend to move together. However, a number of important aspects of the study of interest rates requires delving deeper into the relationships among particular rates. Specifically, important issues are the relationship of interest rates on securities of different maturities called the term structure of interest rates and the relationship among interest rates on securities of different borrowers. We will begin our discussion with the determination of the level of interest rates.

What Is the Interest Rate?

The interest rate is the rental price of money. Money is a direct claim on goods and services so it can be exchanged directly for needed items. The medium of exchange function of money assures such exchangeability. To induce money holders to part with money and accept an asset that is not a direct claim on goods and services requires

69

some incentive. This incentive comes in the form of a rate of return on the alternative asset called the rate of interest.

Many assets can be said to yield a return. The rent on a house can be thought to be a return to the owners of the house; given the value of the house this return can be calculated. Similarly a machine utilized in a factory yields a return in additional profit that can be calculated as a rate. However, the interest rate refers exclusively to the return on financial assets. It can, however, be compared with rates of return generated on other assets for some meaningful insights. For example, if a money holder has $1,000 and has the choice of buying a security that yields 10 percent per year or a machine that can be utilized to produce $100 in profit per year, the money holder would presumably be indifferent (disregarding taxes) between the two uses of money.

Comparisons such as these are made all the time by business firms, for example, in deciding whether to invest in new plants or equipment. If prospective investment projects are expected to yield a return in additional profit that exceeds the current rate of interest, the projects will be undertaken. If not, the investment projects will be deferred or cancelled. The lower the current rate of interest, the larger the amount of investment as more investment projects are perceived as profitable by business firms. Further, it makes no difference whether a particular project is to be financed by borrowing or from generating funds internally. The business firm with funds available for the project will view the interest rate as the **opportunity cost** of the funds. Opportunity cost, an important concept in economics, is the cost of not using an asset in its next best alternative. Clearly, if the rate of interest exceeds the expected return from going ahead with an investment project, the firm is better off loaning its funds in the open market at the higher interest rate. Comparisons of alternative rates of return are also made by individual investors in deciding how to invest their money.

Thus, interest rates are key pieces of information in the economy. Interest rates can be regarded as "prices" and these prices affect decisions on the allocation of financial resources in the economy. This is analogous to the role played by other prices in the economy in allocating real resources. Furthermore, the allocation of financial resources in the economy influences the allocation of real resources in the economy since these resources are "commanded" by financial resources. In the ensuing discussion, it is useful to keep the importance of interest rates for the economy in mind.

The Level of Interest Rates

Two prominent theories are offered to explain the determination of the level of interest rates, the **liquidity preference theory** and the **loanable funds theory.** In addition, the role of price expectations in influencing the level of interest rates is important and will be considered. The liquidity preference and loanable funds theories can demonstrate why the interest rate is 9 percent rather than 5 percent or 15 percent at any particular point in time. (Recall that "the interest rate" is a general way of referring to all interest rates. It is useful to think of it as the average of all interest rates or alternatively the interest rate on a representative asset. Thus, when "the interest rate" is 15 percent, this implies that interest rates in general are relatively higher than when the interest rate is 9 percent.)

The liquidity preference and loanable funds theories can be reconciled so that the question of which theory is "correct" does not arise. However, different factors are emphasized by each theory. The liquidity preference theory, one of the major contributions of John Maynard Keynes, places heavy emphasis on the demand for money. Why people hold money and how changes in money holdings affect the interest rate are analyzed. When the demand for money at a point in time is combined with the supply of money at a point in time, the interest rate is determined. Thus, the liquidity preference model is a **stock** model in that the demand and supply of money are both given at a particular moment. The analysis proceeds by comparing the effect of changes in either the demand or supply of money or both with the position that existed prior to the changes and determining the result. Economists call analysis like this comparative statics.[1]

The loanable funds theory is a **flow** or change in stock theory. A flow theory focuses attention on a variable over a period of time. The loanable funds theory analyzes the interaction of funds available for lending over a period (which includes changes in the money supply) and the various demands for funds over the same period (which includes the demand for money). The relationship between the supply and demand for loanable funds determines the interest rate. These theories are discussed separately.

The Liquidity Preference Theory

Central to the contribution of the famous British economist John Maynard Keynes to monetary theory was the emphasis on the demand for money or, as he called it, liquidity preference. He identified three motives for holding money. The transactions motive refers to the need for money to facilitate transactions and is a direct function of income. The precautionary motive refers to the need for money to meet contingencies and also depends on income. Finally, the speculative motive (sometimes called the asset motive) refers to the holding of money as an asset in preference to other financial assets, which Keynes called

---

[1] Furthermore, the Federal Reserve System significantly affects the money supply. Thus, policy impacts on interest rates (and therefore on the economy) can easily be analyzed from a Keynesian perspective, using the liquidity preference approach.

bonds. Bonds was a general term used by Keynes to refer to interest-yielding securities. The existence of the speculative motive means that the demand for money depends in part on the interest rate. If the interest rate is high, less money is demanded because the cost of holding money is high. People would be giving up a substantial return if they held money in preference to an interest yielding financial asset. In addition, if the interest rate is high, the expectation of a possible fall in the rate means that security holders might expect to have a capital gain on their securities in addition to the high rate of return. This would also encourage money holders to switch from holding money to holding securities.

The possibility of a capital gain on securities arises because of the inverse relationship between the yield and price of a security. When the price of a security falls, the yield on the security rises, and when the price of a security rises, the interest rate falls. This inverse relationship is shown in detail in the appendix to this chapter; however, a brief numerical example may make the relationship clear. Suppose that a security is priced at $1,000 (par) and returns $100 per year. Thus, the yield on that security at par is 10 percent per year. However, once the security is outstanding, it can still be traded in the secondary market. If interest rates are rising, the security may fall to $950 in price. Since the security still pays $100 per year, its yield is now approximately 10.5 percent ($100 ÷ $950 = 10.53%). If interest rates fall, the price of the security will rise. Suppose the price increases to $1,090. Then the security is yielding about 9.2 percent ($100 ÷ $1,090 = 9.17%). While this is a simple example, the basic relationship holds for all securities.

If the interest rate is low, little inducement exists for a money holder to buy securities since the return to parting with money is low. Further, with low interest rates, there is a risk of a capital loss on the security should the interest rate rise and the security have to be sold. Therefore more money is demanded at lower interest rates. Figure 4-1 depicts the demand for money, labelled M_d, plotted against the interest rate, i. The money demand schedule shows the inverse relationship between the demand for money and the interest rate.

The money supply schedule, M_s, is also shown in Figure 4-1. It is drawn at a fixed level of money supply, M_0, for simplicity. The money supply schedule is often assumed to have some positive interest elasticity that would make the M_s schedule upward-sloping. While this possibility will be explored in a subsequent chapter, it is not necessary to assume this elasticity in the liquidity preference model.

The interaction of M_s and M_d yields the interest rate, i_e, which equates the supply and demand for money. A change in the demand for money or in the supply of money will change the interest rate. For example, in Figure 4-2A an increase in the money supply to M_s' lowers the interest rate in the model from i_e to i_e'. (If you have trouble

Figure 4-1
Liquidity Preference Approach to Interest Rate Determination

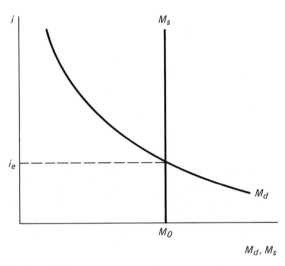

Figure 4-2
Liquidity Preference Approach—Changes in M_d and M_s

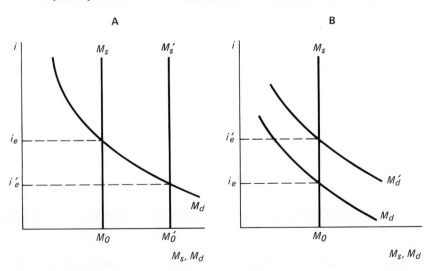

seeing how an increase in the money supply lowers the interest rate, since money supply increases may be inflationary, this means that you have come of age in the 1970s and early 1980s. The difficulties with this result will be discussed below.)

Similarly, an increase in the demand for money due to an increase in income, for example, will increase the interest rate for an unchanged money supply. This is shown in Figure 4-2B where the demand curve shifts from M_d to M_d' raising the interest rate from i_e to i_e'. The reader can easily work out the effects of reductions in the money supply and money demand on the interest rate.

The Loanable Funds Theory

The loanable funds theory focuses on the supply of loanable funds and the demand for loanable funds over a period of time such as a year. The supply of loanable funds is derived from the saving behavior of households, business, and government; changes in the supply of money; and changes in the demand for money. In the terminology of this model, a decrease in the demand for money is called dishoarding and increases the supply of loanable funds as individuals seek to buy securities. An increase in the demand for money, called hoarding in this model, would reduce the supply of loanable funds. The demand for loanable funds is composed of the demand by business, government (state, local, and federal), and households.

With regard to the supply of loanable funds, the higher the interest return, the more saving is done by households out of income because the return is greater (the opportunity cost of spending is higher). While business saving (retained earnings plus depreciation) and government saving may be unrelated to the interest rate, nonetheless, the interest sensitivity provided by household sector saving ensures that all saving taken together is positively related to the rate of interest. It may appear unrealistic to assume any positive government saving at any time since the federal government for most years after World War II has been in deficit. However, state and local governments were in surplus for much of the 1970s. Adding state and local surpluses to federal saving yields positive government saving in some years. For those years in which government saving was negative, total positive saving of business and households is offset to some degree by the negative government saving.

Increases in the supply of money and decreases in the demand for money must be added to the saving schedule to yield the supply of loanable funds depicted as S_{LF} in Figure 4-3. (Decreases in the supply of money or increases in the demand for money would be subtracted from the saving schedule to yield S_{LF}.) The S_{LF} schedule indicates the positive relationship between the quantity of loanable funds supplied and the interest rate. The positive relationship between

Figure 4-3
Supply and Demand for Loanable Funds

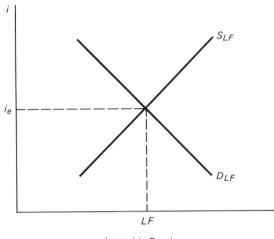

Loanable Funds

S_{LF} and the interest rate derives from the assumed relationship of saving and money demand to the interest rate. That is, the amount saved is positively related to the interest rate, while the quantity of money demanded falls as the interest rate rises, increasing the quantity of loanable funds supplied. Money supply is generally assumed to be independent of the interest rate in this model. The same assumption about money supply was made previously in discussing the liquidity preference model.

The demand for loanable funds arises from business, government,[2] and households, and from any increase in the demand for money. Business demands for funds arise from financing new investment, accounts receivable, and inventories. Business demands for funds are negatively related to the interest rate.[3] However, government deficits, federal agency activity, and state and local deficits must all be financed; it is difficult to argue that federal government or federal agency borrowing is sensitive to the level of the interest rate. But some state and local borrowing is negatively related to the interest rate, because many state and local governmental units are prohibited by local law from

---

[2] Included in government are the federally sponsored agencies that raise significant amounts of funds every year. See Chapter 15.

[3] The lower the interest rate, the more business projects become profitable and hence the larger the quantity of funds demanded.

borrowing above certain rates. Even without constraints, budgetary considerations may limit state and local borrowing at higher interest rates. This segment of government demand, therefore, is negatively related to the interest rate. The sensitivity of state and local borrowing to the interest rate ensures that overall government borrowing demand is negatively related to the interest rate. Households also demand funds for such purposes as purchasing housing, automobiles, and other consumer durables.[4] Household borrowing is also negatively related to the interest rate. Together these credit demands yield the demand for loanable funds given as D_{LF} in Figure 4-3.

The interaction of S_{LF} and D_{LF} yields the rate of interest, i_e. Any increase in the supply of loanable funds lowers the interest rate while any decrease in supply raises the rate. Similarly any increase in the demand for loanable funds raises the interest rate while any decrease lowers the rate.

Financial analysts generally find the loanable funds approach to interest rate determination attractive. In Chapter 2 it was shown how financial analysts utilize the forecasts of credit demands and supplies to forecast interest rates. That approach to forecasting interest rates derives from the loanable funds theory of interest rate determination. Later in this chapter, the segmented markets approach to the term structure of interest rates will be discussed. We will see that the loanable funds approach to interest rate determination is related to the segmented markets approach, which financial analysts tend to favor as an explanation of how interest rates on securities of different maturities are determined.

The Inflation Premium or the Fisher Effect

In discussing the liquidity preference theory, we noted that an increase in the money supply leads to a fall in the interest rate in this model. However, Irving Fisher pointed out over fifty years ago that if increases in the money supply increase inflationary expectations, the interest rate could rise rather than fall. His argument was that the rate of interest contained an inflation premium that changed as inflationary expectations changed. When the inflation premium changed, the interest rate would adjust to reflect this, although the adjustment could be slow.

Suppose that a lender wishes to receive a "real" (that is, inflation-adjusted) 3 percent return on funds that are to be loaned for a year. If there is no inflation (absolute price stability), for every $100 loaned the lender would need $3 in interest for the year to return 3 percent on the loan. However, if the rate of inflation is expected to be 10 percent for the year, the lender would be behind if he received a $3

---

[4] Alternatively, household borrowing may be netted from household saving to yield net saving. It is immaterial which course is followed.

return since the $103 total received at year's end would have less purchasing power than the original $100 loan. The lender needs a 13 percent return to yield a real return of 3 percent. This inflation premium of 10 percent in the rate of interest is known as the Fisher effect.

In symbols, the nominal rate of interest, i is equal to the real rate of interest, r, plus the expected rate of inflation, p^e. The inflation premium is an expected inflation rate that may not be realized but is the lender's best guess of future inflation at the time of the loan. Thus the nominal interest rate,[5]

$$i = r + p^e$$

Borrowers are willing to pay the nominal rate because they count on inflation (in their product prices, for example) to make the real rate they pay the same as the rate the borrower anticipates. The market combines all lender and borrower expectations—which may be quite different—and the nominal rate in the market is determined. The nominal interest rate is what we call the market interest rate.

Without going into detail on how price expectations are formed, we can see clearly that, in general, assuming a 3 percent real rate as appropriate, in most recent years interest rates have not adjusted completely to actual inflation. Figure 4-4 shows the rate of inflation as measured by the consumer price index (CPI) and the interest rate on one-year Treasury securities from 1970 to 1980. Notice that for some of the period the rate of inflation was higher than the security rate. This implies the real rate of interest was negative. However, a number of reasons may be offered to account for the failure of nominal interest rates to fully reflect *actual* inflation. Inflationary expectations may continually lag behind inflation. It may also be that nominal interest rates are slow to adjust to changes in expected inflation. Regardless of the apparent failure of nominal rates to fully reflect actual inflation, as Figure 4-4 makes clear the interest rate does track inflation fairly well. Thus, there appears to be some validity to the Fisher effect, at least during periods of significant inflation.[6]

Because of the existence of the Fisher effect, those economists— known as monetarists—who believe that changes in the money supply are the most important factors influencing actual inflation and inflationary expectations, reject the validity of the liquidity preference theory

---

[5] Actually there is a small compounding term to reflect the fact that the interest return must itself be adjusted for inflation. However, with continuous compounding this term disappears and is ignored in this analysis. Taxes are also ignored.

[6] There have been numerous studies of the Fisher effect. See, for example, William E. Gibson, "Interest Rates and Inflationary Expectations," *American Economic Review* (Dec. 1972), pp. 854–65 and "Price-Expectation Effects on Interest Rates," *Journal of Finance* (March 1970), pp. 19–34; David H. Pyle, "Observed Price Expectations and Interest Rates," *Review of Economics and Statistics* (August 1972), pp. 275–80.

Figure 4-4
Annual Rate of Change in Prices and the Rate on One-Year Treasury Securities, 1970–80

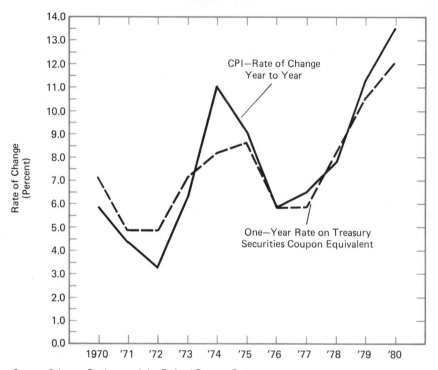

Source: Salomon Brothers and the Federal Reserve System.

over any but the shortest periods of time if money supply growth is excessive. For these economists, excessive money supply growth will intensify inflationary expectations causing the interest rate to rise rather than to fall as liquidity preference theory requires. Such monetarist views will be discussed more fully in ensuing chapters.

The Term Structure of Interest Rates

The simplification that we have used to this point in referring to "the interest rate" must now be dropped. Interest rates on different securities differ for a number of reasons. The most common factor is the term to maturity of the security, and it is this factor that is emphasized in discussions of the term structure of interest rates. However, interest rates on similar maturity securities can also differ for a number of reasons, including differing liquidity and perceived risk of default.

The following matrix in Table 4-1 is a simplified picture of interest rates on all securities. The rows represent securities of differing maturities while the columns represent the differing issuers of securities. (Only a few issuers are given for ease of presentation, but this matrix could be expanded easily.) If a weighted average of all the elements in the matrix is taken, this average could be considered to be "the interest rate" that has been employed so far in this chapter.

Each of the A's in Table 4-1 represent the interest rate on the particular maturity security issued by that particular issuer. For example, A_{11} is the interest rate on a short-term security issued by the federal government (Treasury bills), while A_{53} is the rate on a 30-year bond issued by a corporation. Reading down the columns yields a complete picture of the term structure of interest rates, the relationship between interest rates on securities of different maturities. Reading across the rows indicates the relationship of interest rates on securities of different issuers for each maturity. For example, the rate of interest on a short-term security like the Treasury bill generally differs from the rate of interest on a short-term corporate security. Since the weighted average of all rates can be thought of as "the interest rate," increases or decreases in most or all of the A's of the matrix would imply increases or decreases in "the interest rate." With this picture of interest rates in mind, we will discuss the term structure of interest rates and then explain the relationship between interest rates for similar maturity securities offered by different issuers.

There are two prevalent theories utilized to explain the term structure—the **expectations theory** and the **market segmentation theory.** The two theories really represent extremes. For example, many

Table 4-1
Interest Rate Matrix

MATURITY	ISSUERS		
	Federal Government	Federal Agencies	Corporations
1 Year	A_{11}	A_{12}	A_{13}
2–5 Years	A_{21}	A_{22}	A_{23}
10 Years	A_{31}	A_{32}	A_{33}
20 Years	A_{41}	A_{42}	A_{43}
30 Years	A_{51}	A_{52}	A_{53}

financial analysts, while favoring the market segmentation approach, do not totally discount the expectations hypothesis. We will look at each theory in turn.

The Expectations Hypothesis

The expectations hypothesis states that long-term rates are some average of expected short-term rates. Consider two securities, the first maturing in one year and the other in two years. A lender who has funds to commit for two years can invest in the one-year security knowing that when it matures the funds can be invested in a second one-year security. Alternatively, the lender can invest in a two-year security immediately. However, suppose the rate on the one-year security is 7 percent and the rate on the two-year security is 9 percent. It stands to reason that the investor will invest in the two-year security only if the one-year security in one year's time is expected to yield less than 11 percent. If the investor expects that interest rates will rise significantly and the one-year security will yield 13 percent one year hence, the one-year security will be purchased now, and the investor will expect to purchase a second one-year security a year later to yield 13 percent. This investment strategy will give the investor a 10 percent average return for the two years rather than the 9 percent that would have been received on the two-year security. Investor expectations are, of course, all different in terms of specifics; but, if all investors share this basic outlook, they will move from two-year maturities to one-year maturities, thus driving up the price of one-year securities while lowering the return, and lowering the price on two-year securities while raising the return. Movement between security maturities will cease when the yield on the two-year security is the average of the expected return on two one-year securities. When expectations change, so will the yields.

Thus the expectations theory holds that the long-term rate is the average of the current and expected short-term rates composing that maturity. In symbols for the two-year security:

$$r_{2\text{ year}} = \frac{r_{1\text{ year}} + r_{1\text{ expected year}}}{2 \text{ years}}$$

That is, the two-year rate is the average of the current one-year rate and the one-year rate expected to prevail a year hence divided by the maturity period of the longer-term security. In the example above the denominator is two years.

The simple result that the longer-term rate is an average of the current and expected short-term rates has to be modified, however. Most importantly the longer-term rate will reflect a **liquidity premium.**

The liquidity premium raises the rate on the longer-term security above the simple average result presented above. It is compensation to the purchaser of the longer-term security for the less liquid nature of that security. For example, suppose that the two-year security is bought and interest rates rise. At the end of one year the holder of the longer-term security has to sell it for some reason. As a result the security holder will experience a capita! loss. Had the one-year security been purchased instead, it would have matured and no capital loss would have resulted. Alternatively, assume that the purchaser of the two-year security can hold to maturity, but in one year's time interest rates rise more than had been originally expected. In this case no capital loss is experienced with the rise in rates (because the holder doesn't sell), but the purchaser would have been better off had he purchased the one-year security originally and then purchased another one-year security the following year. What has happened in this case is that the expectation of interest rates prevailing at the time of the original security purchase was not realized. Since the key variable at that time was the expected future rate on the one-year security and expectations may not be realized, the purchaser of the longer-term security must be compensated for the uncertainty that surrounds the expectations of future rates. Additionally, the preference for liquidity will induce investors to purchase short-term securities putting downward pressure on short-term rates. The liquidity premium will mean, when coupled with neutral expectations of constant short-term rates, that long rates would still be above short rates.

The Market Segmentation Hypothesis

The expectations hypothesis implies that the term structure is intimately tied together and kept tied by movements between securities of different maturities, which reflect attempts to bring the term structure in line with ever-changing expectations. However, another view holds that markets are in whole or in part segmented. Segmentation implies that the rate of interest on any particular category of security (or securities of a similar maturity) is determined by the supply and demand for that security. The segmented markets approach is reminiscent of the loanable funds theory of the determination of the level of interest rates.

The hypothesis stems from the observation that particular institutions have a "preferred habitat"[7] in the market they wish to operate

---

[7] Although the segmented markets hypothesis has existed for a considerable period of time, Franco Modigliani and Richard Sutch, "Innovations in Interest Rate Policy," *American Economic Review* (May 1966), pp. 178–97, first cast it in terms of the preferred habitat model that implied some movement between markets if the incentive is sufficient to move an investor from his preferred habitat.

in. For example, insurance companies have long-term obligations and prefer to acquire long-term securities, while commercial banks need liquidity in their investment portfolio and, therefore, prefer relatively short-term securities. Securities issuers may also have preferred habitats. While interest rates do tend to move together, nevertheless, differences in yields on particular maturities are accounted for by this relatively independent action in the particular markets.

The belief in the segmentation of markets led the Federal Reserve, with the assistance of the U.S. Treasury, to experiment with moving short-term and long-term rates in different directions in the early 1960s. In this action, known as "operation twist," the Federal Reserve sold short-term securities to try to raise short-term rates and bought long-term securities to lower long-term rates. The Treasury cooperated by concentrating its financing in the money markets. The motivation behind this action was to prevent dollars from flowing out of the United States and seeking higher short-term interest rates abroad while at the same time trying to stimulate interest-sensitive spending in the economy, particularly investment spending, with lower long-term rates. The success of this operation has been debated, but the fact that it was undertaken at all demonstrates at that time the belief by the Federal Reserve that at least some segmentation existed in the financial markets.

Market analysts tend to prefer the segmented markets approach. As noted previously, many market analysts focus on just such questions of supply and demand for funds in submarkets for purposes of forecasting interest rates. However, it should be pointed out that we can draw from both the expectations hypothesis and market segmentation hypothesis to arrive at reasonable explanations of the term structure relations. For example, consider institutions that operate typically in their preferred habitats but move funds to other maturity areas when the incentive is large. Clearly many institutions that normally acquire long-term securities took advantage of the very high short-term rates in early 1980 and again in 1981 in committing new funds.

Furthermore, there are often investors in the market, called **arbitrageurs,** who are willing to take advantage of interest rate differentials that may exist between markets by buying and selling securities. Arbitrageurs tend to moderate these differentials by bidding up the price of securities on which interest rates are relatively high by buying the securities and by bidding down the price of securities on which rates are relatively low by selling the securities. These actions, while they do not eliminate differentials, do tend to moderate those differentials. When the roles of arbitrageurs and institutions willing to move out of their preferred habitat are considered together, we can easily conclude that both the expectations and preferred habitat hypotheses contribute to the explanation of the term structure of interest rates.

The Term Structure and the Yield Curve

With the securities of only one issuer, say the U.S. Treasury, the rates on the various maturity securities issued by the Treasury can be depicted by the yield curve. The yield curve plots the yields against the term to maturity of the various securities. Figure 4-5 depicts possible yield curves for Treasury securities at a particular point in time. Curve I is most often regarded as the "normal shape" of the yield curve. The positive slope of this curve indicates that longer maturity securities yield higher rates of return than shorter-term securities. Curve I is regarded as normal because, since the interest rate is regarded as the rental price of money, the longer a lender is asked to part with money, the higher the return required. By acquiring a longer-term rather than a shorter-term security, the lender faces increased market risk, gives up some liquidity, and perhaps faces increased default risk if the security is issued by a nongovernmental entity.

The upward-sloping yield curve, however, can be explained in another way. In the expectations framework discussed above, the normal yield curve contains an implicit forecast of interest rates that imparts the upward slope to the curve regardless of the factors just mentioned. The upward-sloping yield curve implies that market participants expect the rate on short-term securities to be above the rate on current long-

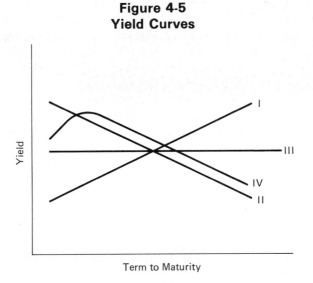

Figure 4-5
Yield Curves

Yield

Term to Maturity

term securities in the future. That is, the market expects interest rates to rise. As a result market participants tend to purchase short-term securities bidding short-term securities prices up (and therefore rates down) and to sell long-term securities bidding down the prices on these securities (and therefore these rates up). If this forecast changes, so will the slope of the yield curve.[8]

Despite the normality of Curve I, Curve II in Figure 4-5 was observed often in recent years, particularly through much of 1979, 1980, and early 1981. According to the expectations hypothesis, this negative-sloping yield curve implies that investors may expect interest rates to fall over time and attempt to lock in the expected higher rate by purchasing long-term bonds. These purchases of long-term securities place upward pressure on long-term prices and downward pressure on long-term rates. Financing during such periods tends to be concentrated in the short-term area if borrowers expect long-term rates to fall, reinforcing the negative slope to the yield curve.[9] Curves III and IV are simply variants of I and II. Curve III is a flat yield curve, implying that expectations are relatively neutral.[10] This flat curve is generally a transition position for the yield curve between I and II. Finally, Curve IV, as a variant of II, shows some uncertainty about rates in the intermediate area so that investors are essentially steering clear of intermediate term securities. Alternatively, it may reflect substantial disagreement over the likely course of future interest rates. It is most common for negative or humped curves to appear during periods in which rates are changing rapidly.

In interpreting the yield curves in the expectations framework, it is important for us to keep a number of things in mind. First, to the extent that markets are segmented, the yield curves may simply reflect the particular supply and demand for securities in each market at that point, which may not be directly related to expectations of future interest rate changes. Second, it is important to realize that expectations are continuously being revised. Thus, a negatively sloped yield curve at a point in time doesn't mean that interest rates will actually fall, only that they are expected to fall. Market participants learned this lesson repeatedly in 1980 and 1981 when negatively sloped yield curves were followed by rises, not falls, in interest rates. In the expectations theory, this means that expectations continually failed to be realized.

---

[8] Strictly speaking, the upward slope of the yield curve would have to be steeper than simply allowing for a liquidity premium for it to be interpreted as a forecast of higher short-term rates.

[9] Short-term rates tend to fluctuate more than long-term rates so that most changes in the slope of the yield curve arise due to the movement of short rates relative to long rates.

[10] Recall the discussion of the liquidity premium above. If the liquidity premium is considered in examining the yield curve, a neutral yield curve would require some upward slope.

Financial Intermediaries and the Term Structure

When financial intermediaries were introduced in Chapter 1, a facet of their intermediation function was omitted. The background that has now been developed on the term structure of interest rates allows this omission to be rectified. Almost all deposit-taking financial intermediaries intermediate along the yield curve. This means that they issue short-term obligations, such as demand deposits and most savings and time deposits, and use these to make some loans that are long term. The most dramatic examples of this type of intermediation are the savings and loan associations. Most of their lending is concentrated in long-term mortgages, while a majority of their deposits mature within one year. This yield curve intermediation can lead to difficulty when interest rates are rising rapidly.

In 1980 and 1981, the savings and loan associations were faced with large increases in the rates they had to pay on deposits as open-market interest rates rose. At the same time, many of the mortgages that they held in their portfolios yielded less than the rate they were now paying on deposits. (Most deposits are affected by a rise in deposit rates in a relatively short time, as the short-term nature of deposits allows depositors to take advantage of higher deposit rates. For example, large amounts of deposits have flowed out of low-yielding passbook accounts into higher yielding certificate accounts in recent years.) Since most mortgages held by savings and loan associations are fixed rate loans, the savings and loans had little recourse but to raise their mortgage rates on new loans—which did not affect the mortgages already in their portfolio—and to hope for a quick reversal in interest rates. The quick reversal did not come, and as a result, the savings and loan industry suffered substantial losses in 1981. The movement to widespread variable rate mortgages in which the rate can be adjusted to reflect changing open-market interest rates may alleviate this problem over time. However, the traditional intermediation along the yield curve practiced by savings and loans has hurt them severely in the interim.

Differences in Yield on Securities of Similar Maturity

The above discussion has related to the term structure of interest rates, yet securities of the same maturity can have differing yields depending on the issuer. In terms of Table 4-1 (p. 79) the focus is now on the reasons that, say, A_{11} differs from A_{13}. A number of factors can be suggested that account for these differences—among them, risk, liquidity, tax treatment, and call provisions.

Risk

In order to induce an investor to hold a more risky asset, the return on the asset must be higher to compensate for the increased risk. This general principle holds in evaluating securities of the same maturity issued by different issuers. If a security issued by one borrower is regarded as more risky than that issued by another borrower, the first security must yield more, all else being equal. Short-term commercial paper, a money market security used to obtain financing for such purposes as inventories, issued by even the most highly rated corporation yields considerably more than Treasury bills, which are regarded as the least risky of all securities. The chapter on the money market later in the book contains a number of exhibits that show how yields differ on short-term securities of the same maturity depending on the issuer. These exhibits demonstrate that, while interest rates move together and the yield spreads between the issues fluctuate, it is almost always the case that the comparable maturity rates are above the rates on Treasury securities. For example, on average in 1980, the rate on three-month Treasury bills was more than one percentage point (112 basis points) lower than that on comparable commercial paper. (There are 100 basis points in a percentage point.) Perceived differences in risk associated with different securities, as well as additional factors to be noted below, account for these yield differences.

The investor is aided in assessing the risk of a security by independent rating services. Moody's and Standard and Poor's, the two most prominent rating services, evaluate industrial bonds, municipal securities, and commercial paper. For example, corporate bonds are rated by Standard and Poor's as AAA if they are of the highest quality; a B rating indicates that the bonds are speculative. The ratings have an important impact upon the yields of securities; the yield spread between a Moody's A-rated industrial bond—Moody's third highest rating—and a Baa-rated industrial bond—one grade lower—was on average −65 basis points in 1980. An issuer of bonds would have paid more than one-half of one percentage point more for financing due to one rating grade difference. This amounts to $1.3 million annually for a $200 million issue, a rather dramatic example of the way the market charged for increased risk.

Liquidity

Liquidity is also a factor in differentiating among securities. The Treasury bill market is the largest of the money markets, and Treasury bills are the most liquid of any short-term security. The ability of the Treasury bill market to absorb large increases in supply with only small changes in price further differentiates it from even the large markets for commercial paper and short-term federal agency securities. It would be expected that additional liquidity would result in lower relative yields, because as pointed out, investors have a positive preference for liquidity. As they demonstrate their preference by bidding for the most liquid securities, the prices of these securities rise relative to those of less liquid securities.

Tax Treatment

Tax treatment can also influence yield differentials. For example, because interest on Treasury securities is exempt from state and local income taxes, their yields should reflect this. Similarly, that state and local securities are exempt from federal taxes also is most dramatically reflected in the pre-tax difference between municipals, obligations of state and local governments, and corporate and government bonds. The tax advantage for municipals can be very valuable to institutions and wealthy investors; a taxpayer in the 50 percent tax bracket will have to receive twice as much on another security to yield the same after-tax yield as on a municipal. This accounts for the fact that state and local government 30-year securities yielded on average only 73 percent of the yield on comparable U.S. government securities in 1981, as the markets reflected the tax advantage of the state and local securities in their yields.

Call Provisions

Call provisions on bonds give corporations an ability to redeem a security ahead of maturity. This means that if interest rates should drop substantially below the rate at which the securities were issued, it is likely that the call option will be exercised. Call provisions differ with regard to the length of the call protection period (the period, usually a few years, in which a bond cannot be called) and other terms. The market reflects these differences in the yields of the securities.

Convertible Bonds

There are other factors as well that can lead to differences in yields on comparable maturity securities. Bonds that are convertible into common stocks at various prices will also reflect not only current yields but the price movement of the underlying stock. The use of convertible bonds grew rapidly with the improvement of the stock market in 1980 and 1981, particularly among high technology companies. This allowed these companies to finance in the bond market generally at a rate significantly below current market interest rates on nonconvertible bonds since the market valued the convertibility provision in a positive way.

New Issue vs. Seasoned Issue Rates

Of particular interest in considering other factors that account for differing yields on similar securities is the realtionship between new and already issued securities, called **seasoned** securities, from the same issuer and for similar maturities. There is generally a positive yield spread between new issue and seasoned long-term securities having the same characteristics. Table 4-2 records the yield spread between new issue and seasoned long-term AA-rated utility bonds for the period January 1977 to December 1980. The spreads fluctuate considerably but are always positive and almost always of substantial magnitude.

Table 4-2
Yield Spreads Between New and Seasoned AA Utility Bonds,
January 1977–December 1980
(Basis Points)

1977			1979		
	January	+54		January	+17
	February	+62		February	+24
	March	+58		March	+59
	April	+61		April	+52
	May	+70		May	+74
	June	+62		June	+50
	July	+52		July	+42
	August	+57		August	+49
	September	+32		September	+67
	October	+48		October	+76
	November	+41		November	+92
	December	+42		December	+36
1978	January	+52	1980	January	+68
	February	+46		February	+139
	March	+51		March	+103
	April	+48		April	+183
	May	+48		May	+101
	June	+47		June	+137
	July	+37		July	+133
	August	+34		August	+187
	September	+27		September	+141
	October	+40		October	+168
	November	+55		November	+192
	December	+15		December	+195

Source: Salomon Brothers, *An Analytical Record of Yields and Spreads.*

A number of factors account for the yield spread between seemingly identical securities. Most important, in periods of rising interest rates, it is likely that new issues will have higher note rates attached to them and, therefore, will not sell at the same discount as seasoned issues even if the yields were equalized. Because of the different treatment of current income and capital gains for tax purposes, the seasoned issues would be favored especially if held to maturity since the favorable treatment of capital gains increases the after-tax yield on the seasoned bond. Further, if new issues have higher coupon rates, it is most likely that they would be "called" by the issuer before the lower coupon-bearing, seasoned issue. Because call provisions are reflected in the yield on securities, it would be expected that this fact would also lead to higher yields on new issues. Underwriting costs for new issues may also lead to a positive yield spread between new issues and seasoned issues.

CAPITAL GAINS AND YIELDS

Bonds: Playing for Capital Gains and Yield

The bond business is all but incomprehensible these days: tax-exempt municipals yielding 13% or 14%, high-grade utilities going for nearly 15%, and high-grade government paper offering yields approaching those of corporate issues. But as inflation-fueled interest rates keep rising, the prices of existing bonds keep falling. Thousands of investors forced to sell bonds have been horrified to find that their investments have shrunk 30% in a couple of years.

If you've been on the sidelines, consider yourself lucky. But if you also believe that inflation—and interest rates—simply must turn down in 1981, it may pay to look into the bond market not only as a source

Sorting Out the Bond Market

Security	Quality	Cost	Yield Range
CORPORATES			
Long Term Bonds			
Debt of industrial corporations, finance companies, utilities, and telephone companies. Maturities range from 10 to 40 years. Intermediates run 4 to 10 years	AAA and AA for high quality, A and BBB for medium quality	Face denomination for corporate bonds is $1,000. But new issues are often marketed above or below par to adjust to current yields. Older bonds with lower interest coupons sell at discounts	High quality industrials between 13% and 13.6%, medium quality 14.3% and 15.5%. Utilities of comparable quality around half a point more, and telephone issues often another half
Funds			
General funds mix industrial and utility issues of varying maturities. Typically, about half the securities mature in more than 20 years. High-yield funds: most maturities less than 20 years	Minimum A and often better. High-yield ratings from BB on down to issues that are unrated and very speculative	Varies. Load funds traded over the counter, no-loads purchasable at net asset value from sponsor	General funds, 12% to 13%, high-yield, 13% to 16%
Unit Trusts			
Mix of corporate issues	A or better	$1,000, plus a sales charge of 3.9%	14%

of high current income but also as an opportunity for sharp capital appreciation. Some experts, for example, believe that when the interest rate dam breaks, bonds could appreciate as much as $300 for a bond with a face value of $1,000. In 1980, more than $40 billion worth of state and local government bonds were sold. More than $38 billion

MUNICIPALS

General Obligation Bonds

Issued by states and municipalities to finance long-term capital improvements, most have first call on taxing power and have been considered extremely safe. But tax revolts, recurrent financial crises, and revelations of shaky accounting and disclosure practices have made investors wary	AAA is considered prime investment grade, and the ratings scale down from there to B in the Standard & Poor's rating system. B is considered low grade and subject to default	Face denomination for municipals is generally $5,000	Most municipals are issued serially, with portions maturing from one year after issue to 30 years and a separate yield for each maturity. Prime GOs with a five-year maturity are yielding about 7%, about 9.3% for the 30-year maturities

Revenue Bonds

Issued to finance specific projects that produce revenues to service—and eventually to retire—the bonds	Quality ranges all over the lot, largely on the judgment of the expected revenue flow	Par value usually $5,000, often serially issued	Average yields on long revenue bonds are running well above 10%. At the moment, power issues are yielding around 10.6%

Funds

Most big fund sponsors have municipal bond funds, some general funds with securities of good grade, some "high-yield" filled with speculative issues	General funds usually stick to A paper and above. High yields shade down from there	As with other funds, net asset value for no-loads, with a sales charge for broker-sponsored load funds	Yields for general funds are running between 7.7% and 8.5%. High yields between 9% and nearly 10%

Unit Trusts

Some closed-end trusts are general, some are designed for investors in a single state	Usually good quality	Usually $1,000 minimum units	Current yields are 10.7%, slightly lower for state funds that enjoy better tax benefits

GOVERNMENTS
U.S. Treasury Bonds

The Treasury funds the federal debt by issuing billions of dollars of notes and bonds with maturities to 30 years	Treasury debt is the standard of quality and safety	Minimum purchase $1,000. Notes can have par values up to $10,000	From about 13% for five-year paper down to 12.3% for 30-year bonds

Agency Bonds

U.S. government agencies and corporations issue their own debt—for example, the Federal National Mortgage Assn., the Tennessee Valley Authority, and the Federal Financing Bank. Maturities to 30 years	Agency securities generally rank just below Treasury paper	Face amounts vary. Federal Financing Bank paper starts at $10,000. Fannie Mae securities vary from $10,000 to $25,000. TVA bonds are in $1,000 denominations	Generally slightly higher than Treasury issues. A typical seven-year issue is yielding a little over 13%, 20-year maturities are averaging 12.5%

Funds

Large selection of load and no-load government funds	High-quality	In no-load funds, net asset value	Typically between 11% and 13%

Data: Merrill Lynch, Salomon Bros., Lipper Analytical Services

worth of corporate paper—much of it utility bonds—moved into investors' hands, a record. New medium-term and long-term Treasury obligations hit $23 billion. And there's no letup in sight.

A variety of choice

The variety of interest rates, maturities, discounts, and rating qualities is staggering. More than 30,000 governmental subdivisions, from the state of California down to a rural fire district badly in need of a new pumper, issue public debt of varying maturities.

Fortunately for the sanity of both investors and analysts, most of this paper never reaches the national market. The bulk of the small issues—a few million dollars—are bought up by local commercial banks, which are among the biggest institutional holders of tax-exempt paper. Much of the rest disappears permanently into the fixed-income portfolios of local investors, people whose income is substantially from dividends and interest. And those people buy close to home. "The average muni investor is parochial," says Robert E. Cline, senior vice-president of the municipal bond department at Shearson Loeb Rhoades Inc. "They're more comfortable with paper from a community they can visit and see. It's not rational, but it's understandable."

If you feel that way, there are plenty of smaller issues just about anywhere in the country. In the average month in 1980, nearly $4 billion worth of municipal bonds came to market.

But if you are looking to trade, stick with the big issues of $100 million or $200 million. The market is national, and there is enough paper around to interest the institutional buyers, who really move the market.

If you seek capital appreciation, there are rules of thumb on how prices of all bonds behave, largely a function of the complex interaction of maturities and coupon rates. Low-coupon bonds move up faster than high-coupon paper when interest rates drop. A bond with more years left in it will swing wider than paper with a shorter maturity. Obviously, when rates are very high, as they are now, 20-year bonds with low coupons are hard to find. The reasonable compromise is something with seven or eight years left that is selling at about 70% of face value.

That kind of paper, by the way, is usually protected by its low market price against call, the great bugaboo in the bond market. Most industrial and government bonds, and many municipals, have provisions for abrupt retirement by the issuer, whenever the opportunity to refund at a lower interest rate presents itself. In addition, many industrial issuers maintain a sinking fund to retire a certain percentage of the issue each year. When bond prices are depressed, call and sinking fund requirements are usually satisfied by the issuer's buying up bonds on the open market at a bargain price—which also tends to support the price for the remaining investors. But when prices rise, and rates fall, bonds get called, usually at par plus a premium equal to one year's coupon.

Sinking-fund retirement is usually by lottery in groups of 100 serial numbers. To guard against being wiped out, advises B. Daniel Evans Jr., first vice-president of E. F. Hutton & Co., don't buy bonds in groups. Scatter the numbers. Sinking-fund requirements, by the way, may be affected by recent tax legislation. So check with your accountant.

The penalty box

Call is undesirable for two reasons. First, you lose a high-yield security and have to replace it with something else in a falling-interest environment. Second, the yield you originally thought you were getting turns out to be illusory. Bond yields are figured on yield to maturity: the interest you receive over the remaining years of the bond, plus the capital appreciation if you purchased at a discount on the secondary market, plus the interest on the interest figured at the same coupon rate. The formula is incredibly complex, and it used to be figured and published in bulky "basis books." Nowadays, there are special-purpose desk calculators programmed to figure it all out when you punch in the known variables. If your bond is called before maturity, a lot of that yield suddenly disappears. Most industrials and many municipals—especially the newer issues—have call protection, a guarantee that the bond won't be called before five or 10 years, particularly if the call is to be funded by issuing new bonds at a lower interest rate.

Buying and selling bonds just to play market moves can be something of a mug's game for the amateur—the 10-bond trader in a market where the round lot is $100,000 face amount (100 corporates or 20 municipals). That's because the spread between bid and asked prices for the odd-lot trader is so high. After markups and markdowns, you can easily lose three points between purchase and sale prices even if the bond's relative price never moved. By comparison, commissions on listed stocks in odd lots usually come to no more than one point.

The experts believe that the way to play the bond market in a high-interest era is to assume that a 20% prime rate is not a sustainable level, that rates must break. The strategy then is to buy bonds for income—and the yields are indeed very attractive—and be prepared to wait until the turn comes. When it does, bond prices, which have become increasingly volatile, are likely to move up very sharply. If it takes longer rather than shorter to happen, the income, which has always been the principal attraction of long-term bonds, is still there, and if you have been reasonably prudent in the quality of bond you buy, the paper will eventually mature and pay back your principal.

More important, some specialists believe that at current coupon rates, much of the downside risk has been eliminated. Henry Arbeeny, a senior vice-president of Dean Witter Reynolds Inc., explains it this way: "Suppose you buy a New York State bond with a 10% coupon at par. If you live in New York City, you get a triple tax exemption, which means an effective after tax interest rate of about 24%. How much would the bond's price have to decline before you lose? Or buy older 8% bonds for $800. If the market goes up, they'll move up faster than the par bonds."

Traditionally, risk avoidance in its ultimate form was the bond issued by the U.S. government, its agencies, and a group of special-purpose corporations created by statute. And you paid in ultimate safety by accepting substantially lower yields. But these days, government paper is yielding almost as much as corporates, and the government market is considered among the most volatile. The reason, says Norman I. Schvey, managing director of Merrill Lynch White Weld Capital Markets Group, is the interest rate futures market, where speculation in Treasury bond futures contracts gets heavy play from the public. "And governments follow the futures market," says Schvey. "It's not unusual to see governments move three points up or down in a morning."

If you're looking for that one-time capital appreciation—the kind that became available for about a week last summer—government issues may bounce around too much to let you sleep peacefully. If you want to play it cautiously, look into some of the gimmicks that bond issuers have been devising to help hold down soaring coupon rates.

There is the "put" bond, a play on words derived from puts and calls in the stock option market. A bond put is simply the reverse of a bond call. In a call, the issuer has the right to pay off the bond before maturity under certain conditions. In a bond with a put feature, the bondholder now has the option of selling the bond back to the issuer for par value after a certain period.

The point is to insulate yourself against further catastrophic rises in long-term interest rates, which would depress the price of your bonds as their fixed coupon rate fell further behind market interest. If you worry about protection of capital and intend to trade the bonds on a relatively short-term basis, put bonds are a reasonable choice. The puts are designed to permit par redemption after four or five years, and it is a race between the bond-holder and the issuer: If prices in mid-decade fall, you get out at par; if prices rise, the issuer exercises the normal call provision, and buys you out at par.

But if you are buying new bonds to hold, in order to lock in today's record yields, and don't much care whether bond prices rise and fall like the tides, the put bonds are not much of a deal. That's because you give up a couple of points of yield to pay for the insurance the resell provision offers. As usual, there is no free lunch. One Texas mortgage bond with a put provision was brought to market in December with a 9% yield, nearly three points below the going rate.

Floaters and margining

There are also some experiments with floating-rate bonds, whose interest rate tracks current market rates through a complex formula, or tied to the price of some inflation-sensitive commodity. The drawback, of course, is that if you see an opportunity for capital gains in the bond market, floating-rate paper is not for you. If rates fluctuate, then prices will obviously remain in a very narrow range, since the price mech-anism will no longer be needed to adjust yields to current market levels.

If you really want to take a risk, on the other hand, you can take the speculator's path: buying discounted bonds on margin. On government paper, you can borrow as much as 90%, and on corporates, as much as 70%, if the discount isn't too deep. Several bond houses are setting up such "leveraged bond programs," says Michael F. Carr, research vice-president in Shearson's corporate bond department. The targets are bonds that are rated fairly low, and that the program managers expect to be up-graded the next time the rating services get around to them. So the bond will get a capital gains increase a couple of ways when interest rates turn down. If you get involved in one of these programs—and you'll need a minimum account of $25,000 to $50,000—remember two points. First, if you margin municipal bonds, the margin interest is not tax deductible under Internal Revenue Service rules. And if things go against you, you can take a terrible beating.

APPENDIX
Yields and Prices

The inverse relation between bond prices and yields can be easily explained: $1 next year is not as valuable as $1 this year. So something called present value has to be calculated to find how much $1 promised one year from now is worth today. That is, the $1 has to be appropriately discounted. If one uses a consol or perpetual bond (a bond that does not mature)[11] that pays a certain number of dollars, D, per year, it must be discounted by an interest rate i to yield a particular present value. For example, a bond paying $100 per year discounted by an interest rate of 10 percent yields a present value of $1,000, that is,

$$PV = \frac{D}{i} = \frac{\$100}{.10} = \$1,000$$

The inverse relationship between price and yield becomes clear from the PV formula. If a higher discount rate is applied, say 20 percent, then the PV is only $500 and the price of the bond must fall.

In a more complicated example, suppose that a bond has three years to maturity. The PV formula for a bond with n years to maturity is

$$PV = \frac{D_1}{(1+i)} + \frac{D_2}{(1+i)^2} + \cdots + \frac{D_n}{(1+i)^n} + \frac{P}{(1+i)^n}$$

where $D_1 \ldots D_n$ = annual interest payment

          P = the face value of the security to be redeemed at maturity

          i = the interest or discount rate with the exponents from 1, 2, 3, . . . n

If D is $50, then the coupon yield is 5 percent and the face value is $1,000:

$$PV = \frac{\$50}{(1+.05)} + \frac{\$50}{(1+.05)^2} + \frac{\$50}{(1+.05)^3} + \frac{\$1,000}{(1+.05)^3}$$

$$= \frac{\$50}{1.05} + \frac{\$50}{1.1025} + \frac{\$50}{1.1576} + \frac{\$1,000}{1.1576}$$

$$\$1,000 = \$47.61 + \$45.35 + \$43.19 + \$863.85$$

(If any three of the variables are known, for example, PV, D, and i, the fourth can easily be found.) If the interest rate rises to 10 percent, the PV falls to

$$PV = \frac{\$50}{(1+.10)} + \frac{\$50}{(1+.10)^2} + \frac{\$50}{(1+.10)^3} + \frac{\$1,000}{(1+.10)^3}$$

$$= \$45.45 + \$41.32 + \$37.56 + \$751.31$$

$$= \$875.64$$

---

[11] While such a bond does not exist in the United States, it does exist in other countries, such as Great Britain.

That is, the interest rate rises and the price falls. Thus, the inverse relation between price and yield of a security is clear.

Bond tables are available for calculations of percentage yields to maturity and present values so that the financial analyst does not have to make these calculations. Many of these tables are computerized so that the analyst can simply plug in the needed information—the interest rate, the fixed dollar payment, the par value, and the time to maturity—and the present value is determined.

Key Points

1. The interest rate is the rental price of money. There are many interest rates in the economy. When the term "the interest rate" is used by economists, they are summarizing all interest rates. Interest rates are similar to prices in the economy, signalling devices for the allocation of credit.

2. Two prevalent theories are used to explain the level of interest rates in the economy: the liquidity preference theory and the loanable funds theory. The liquidity preference theory asserts that the demand and supply of money determines the interest rate, while the loanable funds theory holds that the demand and supply of loanable funds determines the interest rate. These two theories can be reconciled.

3. The Fisher effect, or inflation premium, accounts for the impact of inflationary expectations on nominal interest rates.

4. The term structure of interest rates refers to the relation between securities of different maturities. The expectations theory asserts that the long-run interest rate is some average of short-run and expected short-run interest rates. Consideration of liquidity premiums may modify any simple average approach. The segmented markets approach concentrates on the supply and demand for securities of different maturities determining interest rates on securities of different maturities.

5. Interest rates may differ on securities of the same maturity issued by different organizations. These differences are accounted for by such factors as risk, liquidity, taxes, and callability.

Questions for Discussion

1. Compare and contrast the liquidity preference and loanable funds theories of interest rate determination. How would the conclusions of both of these theories be modified by consideration of the Fisher effect.

2. Why does the chapter call interest rates "prices?"

3. Explain the difference between a stock theory and a flow theory.

4. Are the expectations and segmented markets approaches to the term structure of interest rates irreconcilable? Why or why not?

5. Discuss risk and the role it plays in influencing the interest rates.

6. Is it useful for economists to speak of "the interest rate" when there are so many interest rates in the economy? How can this custom be explained?

7. One can calculate rates of return on any asset. What is so special about interest rates and how do they enter into economic decision making such as the decision to invest?

Suggested Readings

Bowsher, Norman N. "Rise and Fall of Interest Rates." Federal Reserve Bank of St. Louis *Review*, August/Sept. 1980, pp. 16–23.

Fair, Ray, and Burton Malkiel. "The Determination of Yield Differentials Between Debt Instruments of the Same Maturity." *Journal of Money, Credit and Banking*, Nov. 1971, pp. 733–49.

Gibson, William E. "Interest Rates and Inflationary Expectations." *American Economic Review*, Dec. 1972, pp. 854–65.

Humphrey, Thomas M. "The Interest Cost-Push Controversy." Federal Reserve Bank of Richmond *Economic Review*, Jan./Feb. 1979, pp. 3–10.

Keen, Howard, Jr. "Interest Rate Futures: A Challenge for Bankers." Federal Reserve Bank of Philadelphia *Business Review*, Nov./Dec. 1980, pp. 13–22.

Kopcke, Richard W. "Why Interest Rates Are So Low." *New England Economic Review*, July/August 1980, pp. 24–33.

Malkiel, Burton G. *The Term Structure of Interest Rates*. Princeton, N.J.: Princeton Univ. Press, 1966.

McElhattan, Rose. "The Term Structure of Interest Rates and Inflation Uncertainty." Federal Reserve Bank of San Francisco *Economic Review*, Dec. 1975, pp. 27–35.

Nelson, Charles. *The Term Structure of Interest Rates*. New York: Basic Books, 1972.

Roll, Richard. *The Behavior of Interest Rates*. New York: Basic Books, 1970.

In addition, see Murray E. Polakoff et al., *Financial Institutions and Markets*, 2nd ed. Boston: Houghton Mifflin, 1981, Section V for a series of articles on the level and structure of interest rates.

PART 2

Financial Intermediaries

The Federal Reserve System and the Structure of Commercial Banking

5

The commercial banking system is the centerpiece of the financial system. Commercial banks being the largest of the financial intermediaries, their deposit-taking and lending activities are substantial. Furthermore, since commercial banks are the largest issuers of demand and other checkable deposits, which constitute the bulk of the money supply, their role in the financial system is pivotal. This chapter and the next two chapters will explore in detail the operation of the commercial banking system and its place in the financial system. This chapter examines the history and structure of commercial banking and introduces the relationship between the commercial banking system and the Federal Reserve System. Since most demand deposits come into existence through the lending operations of the commercial banking system, the next chapter will discuss the creation of money and credit. Chapter 7 will explore the business of banking in detail.

The Development of Commercial Banks and the Federal Reserve System

When funds are deposited into a demand deposit account at a commercial bank, they are immediately available on demand. Checks can be written on the account and these checks will be honored by the bank on presentation. However, the bank does not hold on to the demand deposit until a check is written. Banks are businesses and, like any business, the goal of their operations is to make a profit. Banks must, therefore, make use of the funds deposited with them. These funds are used primarily to make loans and to purchase securities. How these funds can be used for lending and at the same time be available on demand requires an understanding of fractional reserve banking.

Fractional Reserve Banking

The first fully operational commercial bank was established in London in 1684. Like many early commercial banks, this bank had once been a goldsmith shop. By noticing that gold left with him for safekeeping generally stayed in storage (on deposit) for long periods of time, the goldsmith found that under normal circumstances he could meet withdrawal demands from new deposits of gold. Gold deposits continued to grow, due in part to the fact that the receipts the goldsmith issued to gold depositors were circulating as money; therefore, depositors did not require physical possession of their gold for transactions. The goldsmith found that as a result he could profitably loan out much of the gold on deposit, or claims to this gold in the form of receipts, without endangering his solvency. The issuance of multiple claims on a given amount of reserves (in this case gold) was the beginning of fractional reserve banking. The acceptability of bank notes (the goldsmith's receipts) as money developed rapidly as well and subsequently led to the use of deposits as money.

The principle of fractional reserve banking is still valid today. Most withdrawal demands from commercial banks are met by receipts of funds the same day. Furthermore, since commercial banks have grown over the years, it must be true that more funds have flowed into than out of commercial banks on average. Commercial banks need only keep a small percentage of funds on hand in order to meet contingencies, and they can use the remainder to make loans and buy securities. It is fractional reserve banking that allows the banking system to create money.

The commercial bank no longer decides on the proportion of deposits that are kept in reserve. The Federal Reserve System, which is the central bank in the United States, determines this requirement within limits set by the United States Congress. To understand the banking system fully, therefore, it is necessary to introduce the Federal Reserve System at this point. The Federal Reserve System will be discussed extensively in Chapters 17–19.

The Formation of the Federal Reserve System

The Federal Reserve System, popularly known as "the Fed," was founded in 1913. It came into existence as a direct outgrowth of the financial panic of 1907, which was the last in a series of financial panics that had occurred in 1873, 1893, and 1903.[1] After the 1907 panic, a commission known as the Aldrich Commission, named for its chairman, was established to recommend a solution to these recurrent financial panics. The commission's recommendations were implemented in the Federal Reserve Act of 1913, creating the Fed as the central bank in the United States. The Federal Reserve System began operations in 1914. A central bank had not existed in the United States since President Andrew Jackson scuttled the Second Bank of the United States in 1836.[2]

The Federal Reserve Act charged the Fed with "providing an elastic currency" and acting as a "lender of last resort" to the banking system. Essentially, the Fed became a bankers' bank; banks could borrow from the Fed when necessary in order to meet increases in the demand for funds by depositors. It was hoped that the creation of the Fed would eliminate the financial panics that had periodically occurred and lead to a more smoothly functioning financial system. The importance of the provision of an "elastic currency" can be appreciated by analyzing certain aspects of the demand for money and credit in the economy.

The Fed and an Elastic Currency[3]

Many times during the year there is an increased demand for money and credit in the economy. These often take place on a regular basis and are called seasonal increases in the demand for money. These seasonal increases, for example, occur at Christmas, tax payment dates, and spring agricultural planting times (because farmers need money to buy seeds and fertilizer in expectation of reaping a profit on the harvest in late summer or fall). There are also nonregular, that is, nonseasonal, temporary increases in the demand for money that occur often throughout a year. Occasionally during such times, prior to the creation of the Fed, these increased needs for money and credit could not be met by banks. The failure to meet these demands in severe cases led to financial panics.

By standing ready to lend reserves to the banking system, the Fed could ensure that banks could accommodate the needs of com-

---

[1] A financial panic is usually characterized by a widespread lack of credit in the economy and an attempt by depositors to withdraw funds from banks as a result of a loss of confidence in the banking system. The results of a panic are widespread economic disruption and bank failure.

[2] See Ross M. Robertson and Gary M. Walton, *History of the American Economy* (Harcourt Brace Jovanovich, 1979), pp. 141–48, for a brief and interesting discussion of the Second Bank of the United States.

[3] "Elastic currency" is an old term and can lead to confusion. In modern usage the words "money supply" would be substituted for "currency." An elastic money supply expands under pressure and contracts when the pressure is reduced as explained in the text.

merce under normal conditions as well as back up the banking system under abnormal conditions. As a result the money supply could expand when pressure was applied and return to normal when the pressure subsided.[4] This provision of an elastic currency was at first the main mission of the Fed. However, since its beginning, the Fed's role has expanded enormously.

Membership in the Federal Reserve System

Commercial banks that belong to the Federal Reserve System are known as **member banks.** Not all commercial banks are members of the Federal Reserve System; however, those that are members represent the majority of commercial bank assets.[5] Whether a commercial bank is a member of the Federal Reserve System or remains outside the system depends on a number of factors. One important variable that determines membership status is whether the bank has a national or state charter to operate as a bank. Because banks can secure a charter from either an agency of the federal government or the government of the state in which it operates, there is said to be a **dual banking system** in the United States.

The requirements to secure a charter differ somewhat at the state and Federal level, but they are stringent at both levels of government. The charter for a national bank is issued by the Comptroller of the Currency, a division of the United States Treasury. State bank charters are issued by the state banking authority in the state in which the bank is to operate. All national banks must be members of the Federal Reserve System and have their deposits insured by the Federal Deposit Insurance Corporation (FDIC).[6] State banks may be members of the Fed if they so choose; however, the majority of state banks are not members, although most state banks do have FDIC insurance.[7]

Table 5-1 presents the number of state and national banks, and Table 5-2 gives the breakdown in commercial bank assets between member and nonmember banks and the number of banks in each category. The tables show that the number of state banks substantially exceeds the number of national banks. But since national banks tend to be very large and most of the largest state banks are members of the Fed, the resulting breakdown of bank assets currently favors the member banks by a large amount.

---

[4] This expansion and contraction of the money supply does not mean that it does not grow over time. Such secular increases in the money supply are quite important as are cyclical (business cycle) changes.

[5] As of 1980, over 70 percent of commercial bank assets were held by Fed member banks.

[6] The FDIC was established in 1933 to insure commercial bank deposits and help to restore confidence in a banking system that was heavily shaken by the Great Depression and the resulting financial collapse of the early 1930s.

[7] Only about 2 percent of these are not insured by the FDIC and these tend to be very small, rural banks with well under 1 percent of total commercial bank assets.

Table 5-1
Commercial Banks in the United States, December 31, 1979

Type of Charter	Number of Institutions
National Banks	4,448
State Banks	10,198[1]
Total	14,646

[1] Includes 282 banks not insured by the Federal Deposit Insurance Corporation.

Source: Federal Deposit Insurance Corporation, *Annual Report*, 1979.

Reserves and the Fed

The Fed determines the percentage of deposits that must be held as reserves by its member banks, nonmember banks, and other financial intermediaries offering checkable deposits. This percentage is called the **reserve requirement.** For reserves of member banks to be eligible to meet the reserve requirement, they must be held in one of two ways. The first is vault cash; vault cash is currency and coin held by the banks to meet their daily business needs. The second way in which reserves may be held is in depository institution deposits at the Fed. These deposits account for the majority of member bank reserves and require some explanation.

All member banks maintain deposit accounts at the Fed. These are noninterest-earning accounts that are similar to demand deposit

Table 5-2
Federal Reserve Member and Nonmember Commercial Banks, December 31, 1979

Membership Status	Number of Banks	Assets of Each Group (Thousands of Dollars)
Member Banks	5,425	$1,048,737,739
Nonmember Banks	9,221	384,295,302[1]
Totals	14,646	$1,433,033,041

[1] Includes the assets of 92 nondeposit trust companies.

Source: Federal Deposit Insurance Corporation, *Annual Report*, 1979.

accounts held by the public at commercial banks. Together vault cash and depository institution deposits are called **legal reserves.** Not all legal reserves are necessarily required reserves, however. The portion of legal reserves necessary to meet the reserve requirement is known as **required reserves,** while that portion of legal reserves that exceeds required reserves is known as **excess reserves.** Despite the similarity of depository institution deposits at the Fed to demand deposits, neither these deposits nor vault cash are considered part of any measure of the money supply. The money supply measures the amount of money in circulation. Reserves are not considered to be in circulation and thus are excluded in computing the money supply.

Nonmember banks and other financial intermediaries have an option in holding required reserves. In addition to holding reserves in depository institution accounts at the Fed and in vault cash, they may maintain their reserves on a pass-through basis at Fed member banks, with the Federal Home Loan Bank System (to which most savings and loan associations belong) or at special "bankers' banks," owned primarily by depository institutions. These bankers' banks are set up by groups of depository institutions to share the costs of various common financial services and do not do business with the general public.

Reserve Requirements

The reserve requirements set by the Fed currently vary depending upon the size of the bank and whether the deposits are demand deposits, savings deposits, or time deposits. Savings deposits are passbook accounts having no fixed holding period, while time deposits are certificate accounts having a fixed maturity from date of issuance. Table 5-3 presents the reserve requirements that pertained as of April 1981 for member banks. Current legislation calls for these reserve requirements to become more uniform over time and for the same requirements to be applied to member banks, nonmember banks, and other financial intermediaries offering checkable deposits. The new reserve requirements that will apply are presented in Table 5-4. Most member banks are being phased into these reserve requirements over a three-and-a-half-year period that began November 13, 1980, while nonmember banks and financial intermediaries will have to meet these reserve requirements fully by September 1987.

Table 5-3 shows that the more a bank has in demand deposits, the larger the percentage of these deposits the bank has to keep in required reserves. The scale is graduated, however, so that no matter how large demand deposits are at a certain commercial bank, the bank only has to hold 7 percent in reserve on the first $2 million, 9.5 percent on the next $8 million, and so on. But Table 5-4 indicates that much of this scaling will be eliminated. Notice also from both Tables 5-3 and 5-4 that the reserve requirements are always higher

Table 5-3
Reserve Requirements of Federal Reserve
Member Commercial Banks, April 1981

Demand Deposits	Reserve Requirement
$ 0– 2 million	7.00%
$ 2– 10 million	9.50%
$ 10–100 million	11.75%
$100–400 million	12.75%
Over $400 million	16.25%
Time and Savings Deposits	
Savings Passbook Accounts	3.00%
Time Deposits	
$0–5 million by maturity	
30–179 days	3.00%
180 days to 4 years	2.50%
4 years or more	1.00%
Over $5 million by maturity	
30–179 days	6.00%
180 days to 4 years	2.50%
4 years or more	1.00%

Source: Federal Reserve *Bulletin*, June 1981.

Table 5-4
Reserve Requirements Fully Effective in 1987[1]

Net Transactions Accounts	
(Demand Deposits and other Checkable Deposits)	
$0–25 million	3%
Over $25 million	12%
Personal Savings and Time Deposits	0%
Nonpersonal Time Deposits by Original Maturity	
Less than four years	3%
4 years or more	0%

[1] For existing nonmember banks and nonbank financial institutions offering checkable deposits, the phase-in period ends in 1987. For existing member banks the phase-in ends in 1984. All new institutions have a two-year compliance period from the date they open for business.

Source: Federal Reserve *Bulletin*, June 1981.

on demand deposits than on time deposits. They are eliminated entirely on personal savings and time deposits under the new legislation as shown in Table 5-4.

The reason for the different treatment of checking accounts and savings and time deposit accounts is clear. Sometimes demand deposit and other checkable accounts are called transaction accounts as in Table 5-4, because funds that are going to be used shortly to pay bills are likely to be deposited in a checking account rather than a savings or time deposit account. The latter is usually reserved to hold funds that are expected to be on deposit for at least some period of time. Technically, financial institutions can require notice to be given for withdrawal of funds from any savings or time deposit account, including a passbook account. In practice, however, passbook deposits are available for withdrawal at the time requested. The differing functions usually served by checking, savings, and time deposits results in a higher turnover rate of checking deposits. As a result, historically, demand deposits have commanded a higher reserve requirement in the interest of safety and liquidity.

The percentage of reserve requirements presented in Table 5-3 are subject to change by the Federal Reserve System within rather wide ranges that have been set by the U.S. Congress.[8] In practice, because of the phase-in of the changes shown in Table 5-4, these ranges are now obsolete. However, once the transition of the Table 5-4 requirements is complete, new ranges will be applicable.[9]

Required and Excess Reserves—Further Terminology

We have seen that a bank holds a certain amount of legal reserves (vault cash plus deposits at the Fed) to meet its **reserve requirement.** The reserve requirement is sometimes also known as the **reserve requirement ratio.** The amount of reserves held to meet the reserve requirement is known as **required reserves.** Any amount of legal reserves above required reserves is **excess reserves.** The sum of a bank's required reserves plus any excess reserves is known as its **total reserves.**

An example should make this terminology clear. Suppose a bank has $2 million in demand deposits. From Table 5-3 the reserve requirement for this amount is 7 percent; therefore, the bank's required reserves are $140,000. If the bank doesn't have any time deposits,

---

[8] The ranges are 7–22 percent for demand deposits and 3–10 percent for time deposits on average for the entire category.

[9] The new ranges are 8–14 percent on transactions accounts over $25 million and 0–9 percent on nonpersonal time deposits. The Board of Governors of the Federal Reserve System also has the power under the new procedures to impose a supplemental reserve requirement of 4 percent on transactions accounts under certain conditions.

this is all it is required to hold. However, the amount that the bank has at the Fed and in vault cash totals $200,000. The $60,000 surplus is the bank's excess reserves, while the entire $200,000 are its total reserves.

The same breakdown holds for the banking system as a whole. For example, if the demand deposits in the banking system total $1 billion, required reserves are $100 million, and the banking system has total reserves of $120 million, $20 million are excess reserves. Notice that whether referring to the individual bank or to the entire banking system, total reserves must be legal reserves. It is the strictness of the definition of legal reserves that has presented a problem to the Fed of banks withdrawing from membership. Finding a remedy for this problem was part of the motivation behind the change in the law governing reserve requirements discussed above.

The Fed Membership Problem

The percentage of commercial bank assets held by member banks of the Federal Reserve System declined significantly over the period 1969–80 from about 80 percent of total bank assets to around 70 percent. The major reason for this decline was the implicit cost of being a member of the Federal Reserve System. Since reserve requirements can only be met by holding vault cash or by holding deposits at the Fed—neither of which yields any interest return—banks forego interest that could be earned on this balance. On the other hand, nonmember banks have considerably less stringent reserve requirements set by the state banking authority in the state in which they operate. Therefore a positive incentive for nonmembership existed and grew considerably in the 1970s as interest rates rose. Banks increasingly recognized the opportunity cost of membership and responded as any profit-maximizing business would if given a choice.

As pointed out previously, national banks really have no option over retaining membership in the Fed. However, nothing prevents a national bank from switching to a state charter and then withdrawing from Fed membership. While this has occurred in some cases, the major reason for the decline in Federal Reserve membership has been the withdrawal of existing state bank members and the acquisition of state rather than national charters by new banks coming into existence. For the most part, new banks chose to remain outside the Fed in the 1970s.

Even though reserve requirements vary greatly from state to state for nonmember banks, they do share some characteristics in common.[10] Most states allow their banks to keep a large percentage of their reserves in income-earning assets, usually U.S. government securities.

---

[10] Only Illinois does not impose reserve requirements on nonmember banks.

In addition, all states allow their banks to count deposits at other banks ("due froms"), called **correspondent deposits,** as part of their reserves. Since most banks keep some deposits at other banks for various reasons that are examined later in this chapter, this provision is quite favorable for the banks. In addition, vault cash is also counted by states as part of required reserves. When state reserve requirements are analyzed, the results show that in general these requirements are nonbinding on banks since banks hold securities, vault cash, and correspondent balances anyway.[11] The nonbinding nature of state reserve requirements means that banks would hold sufficient amounts of these assets voluntarily even without being required to do so. Thus, meeting state reserve requirements does not entail any sacrifice on the part of the nonmember banks. The advantage of nonmembership in the Fed is apparent. Table 5-5 shows various state reserve requirements for a representative sample of states and the manner in which these requirements can be satisfied. Notice particularly that a large portion of the sample states permit banks to hold income-earning securities to meet a portion of the reserve requirements.

The incentive for banks to leave the Federal Reserve System or for new banks not to join will be eliminated entirely once the new reserve requirement system is fully operational in 1987. Since nonmember banks as well as nonbank depository institutions will be required to meet Fed reserve requirements, the advantage of nonmembership will cease to exist. In fact the attrition in membership will likely be reversed well before 1987 since there are advantages to membership in the Federal Reserve System. Despite the incentives to leave indicated above, these advantages have induced most existing members to retain their membership.

Advantages of Fed membership include the prestige of being a national bank and a Fed member as well as more tangible benefits.[12] Tangible benefits have included most importantly, access to the large Fed check clearing network and the ability of member banks to borrow from the Fed.[13] In addition, the Fed provides securities safekeeping,

---

[11] See John Paulus, "The Burden of Federal Reserve Membership, NOW Accounts and the Payment of Interest on Reserves," Federal Reserve Board of Governors, *Staff Economic Study* (June 1977), typescript.

[12] Prestige as a benefit of membership is often overlooked, but as Benston points out, banks appear to regard it as important. George J. Benston, "Federal Reserve Membership: Consequences, Costs, Benefits and Alternatives," Study prepared for the Association of Reserve City Bankers (Sept. 1978), p. 33.

[13] Nonmember banks have been permitted in the past to borrow from the Fed only under emergency conditions when "credit is not practicably available from other sources and failure to obtain such credit would adversely affect the economy." A nonmember bank is expected, in times of need, to borrow from a larger correspondent bank or in the federal funds market in which banks borrow and lend reserves. The importance of the borrowing privilege to member banks is reflected in a survey conducted by Peter Rose: 46 percent of the member banks surveyed ranked the borrowing privilege as the most important benefit of membership. See Peter Rose, "Banker Attitudes

Table 5-5
A Representative Sample of State Reserve Requirements[1]

State	Deposits Subject to Reserve Requirements	Current Reserve Requirement Ratios	Vault Cash	Demand Balances Due From Banks	Securities[2]	Other
Arizona	T Dem-US$_d$-SL$_d$-R$_d$	10%	X	X	X	CIPC
	TS-US$_t$-SL$_t$-R$_t$	4%	X	X	X	
Arkansas	T Dem	FR	X	X		CIPC
	S	3%	X	X		
	T	{3% first $5 million, plus 5% over $5 million}				
California	T Dem-US$_d$-SL$_d$-R$_d$ -CIPC-Due From	FR	X	X		
	TS-US$_t$-SL$_t$	5%	(at least 20%)		(up to 80%)	
Florida	T Dep-US$_d$-SL$_d$ -US$_t$-SL$_t$	20%	X	X	X	
Georgia	T Dem-US$_d$-SL$_d$-R$_d$	15%	(at least 50%)		(up to 50%)	
	TS-US$_t$-SL$_t$-R$_t$	5%	X	X	X	CDs
Illinois	(No statutory reserve requirements)					
Indiana	T Dem	10%	X	X		CIPC
	TS	3%	X	X		CIPC
Iowa	T Dem	7%	X	X		
	TS	3%	X	X		
Kentucky	T Dem	7%	(at least 75%)		(up to 25%)	
	TS	3%	X	X	X	CDs

RESERVE ASSETS ELIGIBLE TO MEET REQUIREMENTS

Table 5-5 (*Continued*)

State	Deposits Subject to Reserve Requirements	Current Reserve Requirement Ratios	RESERVE ASSETS ELIGIBLE TO MEET REQUIREMENTS			
			Vault Cash	Demand Balances Due From Banks	Securities[2]	Other
Maryland	T Dem-US$_d$-SL$_d$ TS-US$_t$-SL$_t$	15% 3%	(at least two-thirds) X	X	(up to one-third) X	
Massachusetts	T Dem plus time deposits subject to withdrawal within 30 days	Boston—20% Others—15%	{at least 15%} X	{up to 80%} X	{up to 80%}	
New Jersey	T Dem TS	FR FR	X X	X X		CIPC CIPC
New York	T Dem-CIPC -Due From	Same as FR except one percentage point lower on all deposit size categories	X	X		
Ohio	TS T Dem S T	FR 7% 3% {Time deposits of $100,000 and over maturing in less than 6 months: 3% first $5 million 6% over $5 million Other time deposits: 3%}	{at least 40%} X X	X X	{up to 60%}	
Oklahoma	T Dem TS	FR FR	X X	X X		CIPC CIPC

State	Deposits	Percent	at least 50%	up to 50%	Qualifying assets
Pennsylvania	T Dem	12%			
	S	3%			
	T	{ 3% first $5 million, plus 5% over $5 million }			
Texas	T Dem	15%	X		CIPC
	TS	5%	X		Time Deposits and CIPC
Utah	T Dem	FR			
	TS	FR			
Virginia	T Dem-R_d	10%	X	X	CIPC
	TS-R_t	3%	(at least 75%)	(up to 25%)	
West Virginia	T Dem	7% { at least 20% }	X		CIPC
	TS	3%	X		CIPC
Wisconsin	Reserve Banks	20%	{ at least five-twelfths }		
	Other	12%		{ up to seven-twelfths }	
	TS				

[1] For a complete listing of all states and specific details on qualifying assets see the source cited in this table.

[2] Mostly U.S. government and related securities.

KEY TO CODING

SL_d	State and local government demand deposits
SL_t	State and local government time deposits
Due From	Demand deposits due from domestic commercial banks
R_d	Reciprocal demand deposits
R_t	Reciprocal time deposits
CIPC	Cash items in process of collection
CD	Certificate of deposit

FR	Same as reserve requirements of Federal Reserve
T Dep	Total deposits
T Dem	Total demand deposits
T	Time deposits
S	Savings deposits
US_d	U.S. government demand deposits
US_t	U.S. government time deposits

Source: R. Alton Gilbert and Jean M. Lovati, "Bank Reserve Requirements and Their Enforcement: A Comparison Across States." Federal Reserve Bank of St. Louis *Review*, March 1978, pp. 22–31.

delivery of currency and coin, and wire transfer services. Studies have also shown that the cost of Fed membership is considerably higher for smaller member banks than it is for larger member banks. These studies have emphasized the advantages larger banks have in using the free services provided by the Fed, particularly the check clearing network.[14] However, the Fed has been required by Congress to begin charging for many of these services. If the Fed charges a competitive price as it is required to do under the law, many of these advantages will be eliminated. The results of the complete adjustment in Fed membership to the new system of reserve requirements, service pricing, and access to borrowing by a broader group of financial intermediaries will take time to be seen.

Monetary Policy and the Federal Reserve System

The relationship between the Federal Reserve System, the commercial banking system, and the financial system goes beyond that discussed above. As the central bank in the United States, the Fed is responsible for fulfilling a number of functions such as providing banking services to the U.S. Treasury and approving bank mergers. However, perhaps the most important of Federal Reserve functions is the conduct of **monetary policy.** Monetary policy is the attempt by the Fed to influence the course of economic activity by affecting the reserves of the banking system. The reserve position of the banking system in turn affects the money supply, interest rates, and the economy. By making money and credit hard to obtain or expensive, the Fed tries to reduce inflationary pressures in the economy. Alternatively, by making money and credit plentiful and inexpensive, it attempts to stimulate the economy.

The conduct of monetary policy is such an important part of the Fed's activities that we will devote three chapters to it later in this book. However, before proceeding with our discussion of the commercial banking system, we must look briefly at how the Fed conducts monetary policy. The Fed has three major tools at its disposal in its conduct of monetary policy: changes in reserve requirements, discount rate changes, and open-market operations.

Reserve Requirement Changes When the Federal Reserve raises or lowers the reserve requirement, it changes the distribution between

---

Toward the Federal Reserve System: Survey Results," *Journal of Bank Research* (Summer 1977), pp. 77–84. With regard to the check clearing network, nonmembers can gain access to this network through their correspondent banks. Under new legislation all banks and financial institutions that must meet reserve requirements can borrow from the Federal Reserve. This includes nonmember banks and nonbank depository financial intermediaries.

[14] For a discussion of larger bank advantages, see the previously noted article by Paulus, and Stuart G. Hoffman, "The Burden of Fed Membership Revisited," Federal Reserve Bank of Atlanta *Economic Review* (March/April 1979), p. 23.

required and excess reserves in the banking system. An increase in reserve requirements lowers the level of excess reserves, while a decrease in reserve requirements increases excess reserves. Excess reserve availability influences the amount of bank lending in the economy. Since most demand deposits come into existence through bank lending, a change in reserve requirements may be translated into money supply changes.

The Fed has been reluctant to change reserve requirements very often, in part because such changes have rather dramatic impacts upon the reserve position of banks. Further, because of the membership problem in recent years, the Fed has decided against raising reserve requirements for fear of inducing even more banks to leave the system. However, it will be interesting to see if the universal extension of reserve requirements to depository financial institutions that eliminates the membership problem makes this tool somewhat more useful to the Fed.

Discount Rate Changes The discount rate is the rate charged for borrowing at the Fed. Allowing financial intermediary borrowing fulfills the Fed's role as "lender of last resort." Presumably, borrowing would be discouraged by a rise in the discount rate and encouraged by a fall in the rate. More borrowing leads to additional reserves in the banking system. In practice, however, the discount rate is almost always below open market rates. Therefore, financial institutions can profit by borrowing from the Fed and relending in the open market. While changes in the discount rate may lead to increases or decreases in bank borrowing, the Fed must also supervise borrowing carefully to make certain this privilege is not abused. Banks that borrow too frequently in the Fed's judgment can be denied access to the "discount window." Also in recent years the Fed has imposed a surcharge on the discount rate for too frequent borrowers.

Changes in the discount rate are considered important beyond their impact on borrowing itself. These changes may "announce" the Fed's intentions to change monetary policy or its determination to continue existing policy. This announcement can take on important meaning when combined with other evidence of its intentions because decisions on open-market operations, through which monetary policy is chiefly implemented, are not announced in advance.

Open-Market Operations Open-market operations are the purchase and sale by the Fed of primarily U.S. government securities in the money and capital markets. A purchase of securities injects reserves into the banking system as the proceeds of the purchase are deposited in bank accounts. Sales of securities drain reserves from the banking system as deposits at banks are used to pay for the securities. Thus, the banking system's ability to lend is affected through these open-market operations. Open-market operations are conducted by the Federal Reserve Bank of New York on instructions of a major committee of the Federal Reserve System called the Federal Open Market Committee. The Federal Reserve relies on open-market operations on a daily basis to manage the reserve position of banks to meet its monetary policy objectives.

The Federal Reserve System clearly has a profound impact upon the commercial banking system. Other governmental bodies, both federal and state, also affect commercial banking through law and regulation. The setting of reserve requirements for state chartered banks has already been discussed. State and federal governments have also imposed restrictions that have determined the structure of commercial banking.

Banking Structure

Whether a bank is a national bank, and therefore a Federal Reserve member, or a nonmember state bank, it must still abide by restrictions on branch bank operations imposed by the state in which the bank operates. These rules vary from state to state so that in some states banks are restricted to only one office, while in other states banks may have branches throughout the state. There are states that fall in between these extremes as well.

Under the McFadden Act passed in 1927, branching across state lines is prohibited to essentially all banks. The only exceptions are some very old organizations started in states before statehood and branches of foreign banks.[15] The Bank of California, which has branches in Oregon and Washington as well as in California, is the largest bank so "grandfathered." However, the recent spread of bank holding companies has allowed some bank organizations to pursue branching of another kind. Branching provisions within states and bank holding companies are two of a number of related issues that need to be discussed under the heading of banking structure.

Unit Banking vs. Branch Banking

Only twenty-two states and the District of Columbia allow unlimited statewide branching for banks. Branching increases the market area from which banks draw deposits and other banking business. It is not surprising, therefore, that one of the largest banks in the United States and the world, the Bank of America, is located in California, the largest state in population, and a state that has permitted statewide branching for decades. In thirteen other states limited branching allows banks to branch within the county in which the home office is located or

---

[15] Foreign banks will be discussed below.

within counties contiguous to the home county. Massachusetts is an example of a limited branching state. In the fifteen remaining states no branching is allowed; these are known as unit banking states. Texas and Illinois are the largest states that are unit banking states, although in Illinois a bank is permitted to have two small automatic branches for convenience very close to the home office. Table 5-6 lists all the states and the various forms of branching or unit banking permitted, and Figure 5-1 is a map of the United States giving the same information at a glance.

The rationale that originally lay behind branching restrictions was that a banker should be close to those served. Because this belief derived from the agrarian heritage of the United States, most of the

Table 5-6
Banking Structure by State

Unit Banking	Limited Branching	Statewide Branching
Arkansas	Alabama	Alaska
Colorado	Georgia	Arizona
Florida	Indiana	California
Illinois	Kentucky	Connecticut
Iowa	Louisiana	Delaware
Kansas	Massachusetts	Hawaii
Minnesota	Michigan	Idaho
Missouri	Mississippi	Maine
Montana	New Hampshire	Maryland
Nebraska	New Mexico	New Jersey
North Dakota	Ohio	New York
Oklahoma	Tennessee	Nevada
Texas	Wisconsin	North Carolina
West Virginia		Oregon
Wyoming		Pennsylvania
		Rhode Island
		South Carolina
		South Dakota
		Utah
		Vermont
		Virginia
		Washington
		Washington, D.C.

Source: Federal Reserve Board.

Figure 5-1
Branching Laws or Practices

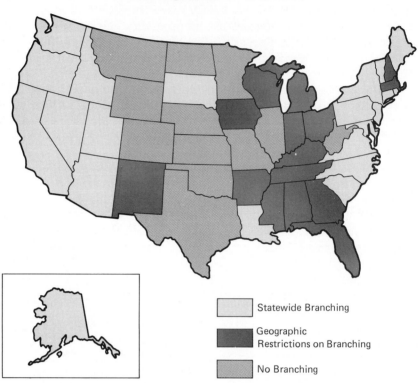

Statewide Branching

Geographic Restrictions on Branching

No Branching

Source: Reprinted by special permission from the Jan. 1981 issue of *ABA Banking Journal.* Copyright 1981 by the American Bankers Association.

unit banking states are located in the midwestern portion of the United States. However, there is a growing challenge by banks in unit bank states to this restriction. The current focus of the argument is the employment of computer terminals located away from the bank in nonbank facilities. Banks making use of these unmanned "branches" have argued (and are arguing in court cases) that these remote site facilities do not violate the unit bank provision while some states are claiming that they do. Several unit banking states have agreed to the provision of this new service.

The ban on interstate branching is also under attack. Under the McFadden Act banks are prohibited from accepting deposits across state lines. Large banks in the United States have generally been supportive of legislation that has been introduced in Congress to repeal the McFadden Act. However, this legislation has proved unsuccessful thus far, primarily because of opposition from smaller banks that apparently fear the increased competition from larger banks moving into their areas. Despite the lack of success in repealing the act, large banks have been very aggressive in expanding nationwide operations that are permitted. For example, many banks have loan production offices nationwide that essentially do all the groundwork for their parent bank's lending. Banks in different states are increasingly forming bank networks to provide their customers with banking services while away from home. Furthermore, established under the Edge Act of 1919, Edge Act Corporation Subsidiaries, which are set up by banks to deal in international financial transactions, are also commonplace and can branch across state lines. Much of the permissible nationwide activity of banks has been facilitated by the bank holding company form of organization.

Holding Companies

Since the late 1960s, a rapid expansion in bank holding companies has occurred. There are two types of bank holding companies, one-bank holding companies and multibank holding companies. As the names imply, a one-bank holding company owns or controls one bank, while a multibank holding company owns or controls two or more banks. Usually, the motivations behind the formation of a one-bank holding company differ from those behind a multibank holding company.

One-bank holding companies have traditionally been started to allow a bank to expand into other activities related to banking, such as personal finance, mortgage banking,[16] and investment management. This expansion was motivated by a desire to broaden the base of revenue sources traditionally available to a bank. In addition, it has been felt that contact with a bank by a potential customer through one of the bank's affiliated businesses would enhance the likelihood that the bank would attract the customer to its banking services also.

The multibank holding company was often organized for the purpose of circumventing state and even national branching restrictions. These holding companies allow the operation of independent banking entities in states that restrict or prohibit branch banking. Further, through the operation of banks in a number of states, federal prohibition against nationwide branching can be circumvented to some degree. It should be noted, however, that these banks in separate states must be separately incorporated in the state in which they operate and follow the regulations of that state. The formation of interstate bank holding companies was eliminated by law in 1956. However,

---

[16] Mortgage banks are nondepository institutions providing essentially a brokerage service in the mortgage market.

the seven existing interstate bank holding companies were permitted to continue operations. Despite the regulations limiting their activities, multibank holding companies do provide a number of services to their affiliated banks that would not be available if the affiliated bank was not part of the group.

Much important legislation dealing with bank holding companies has been enacted by Congress. The original legislation became law in 1933; however, the major piece of legislation was the Bank Holding Company Act of 1956. This act primarily defined a bank holding company as one owning or controlling 25 percent of the voting stock of two or more banks. It required that a bank holding company receive Federal Reserve approval for additional acquisitions, and the Act specified terms under which the Fed should consider bank holding company expansion.[17] By amendments in 1966 and 1970, Congress further tightened the requirements on bank holding companies and extended the 1956 Act to include one-bank holding companies. Also the Federal Reserve was required under the 1970 amendment to specify the nonbanking activities considered appropriate for holding companies. The Fed has continued to update and limit the kinds of permissible activities for bank holding companies so that the current list of permissible and nonpermissible activities is quite lengthy.[18]

The Fed has also been quite strict since the mid-1970s on the expansion of bank holding companies. This has slowed the increase both in the number of bank holding companies and in the growth of existing companies. One of the reasons for this increased restrictiveness is the belief that bank holding companies increase concentration in banking and reduce competition. By 1978, bank holding companies controlled about 40 percent of commercial bank deposits, up from less than 10 percent in 1965. However, studies summarized by Norman Bowsher have concluded that holding companies have not fundamentally altered commercial banking and that the net effect of holding companies has been favorable for the public. Further, the expansion of holding companies has not reduced competition in commercial banking. In fact, there is some evidence that competition has been enhanced by affiliates of holding companies moving into local banking markets.[19]

One-bank holding companies continue to flourish even though engaging in nonbank businesses has at times presented problems to the holding company. For example, the 1973–75 recession was a period of difficulty for some one-bank holding companies. Despite occasional

---

[17] See Oliver Wood, "Bank Holding Companies," in *Commercial Banking* (New York: D. Van Nostrand, 1978), for a detailed introduction to bank holding companies.

[18] See Dale S. Drum, "Nonbanking Activities of Bank Holding Companies," Federal Reserve Bank of Chicago *Economic Perspectives* (March–April 1977), pp. 12–20, for a discussion and listing of permissible and nonpermissible activities.

[19] "Have Multibank Holding Companies Affected Commercial Bank Performance?" Federal Reserve Bank of St. Louis *Review* (April 1978), pp. 8–15.

problems, however, from the point of view of economic efficiency, such financial conglomerates may be desirable. One thing seems clear, the one-bank and multibank holding companies presently are an important part of the commercial banking system. The holding companies of the larger banks are in particularly good position to take advantage of the possible repeal of the McFadden Act through their various national subsidiaries.

Correspondent Banking

Correspondent banking refers to the practice of one bank maintaining noninterest-earning deposits at another bank. The holder of these deposits is the correspondent bank while the bank making the deposit is known as the respondent. Usually, the respondent bank is a smaller bank than the correspondent. Many reasons for these correspondent relationships exist that justify the respondent banks' foregoing potential earnings.

In most states, nonmember banks can count correspondent balances toward meeting state reserve requirements (see Table 5-5 p. 111). More importantly, the correspondent bank provides a number of services to its respondents—advice, loan participation, and check clearing among them. Advice usually consists of investment and economic analysis. The larger correspondent bank usually has more expertise in such areas as portfolio management and economic analysis. The respondent can call upon this expertise and is spared the sometimes prohibitive expense of developing in-house capabilities in these areas.

The correspondent bank may allow its respondent to participate in profitable loan syndicates that it forms. The respondent, on the other hand, may not have to pass up profitable loan opportunities that exceed its own resources. It can call on its correspondent to participate in making the loan. In addition, nonmember respondents can utilize the check clearing network provided by the Fed through their correspondent banks, which are usually Fed members. However, since the Fed implemented charges for check clearing in August 1981, these charges may be passed on to the respondent.

The attractiveness to the correspondent bank of holding correspondent balances is straightforward. The correspondent bank has the explicit interest-free use of the balances, and for many large banks, correspondent balances are a substantial source of funds. While the services the correspondent provides are an implicit interest payment on correspondent balances, the arrangement is still profitable for the correspondent since the correspondent balances subsidize activities that the correspondent would undertake anyway. For example, correspondent business subsidizes the cost of maintaining large research staffs.

In summary, the correspondent relationship is a profitable one for both correspondents and respondents. Even many smaller Fed member banks keep some correspondent balances at larger banks, although generally these balances are smaller than those kept by nonmember respondents.[20] This fact provides additional evidence of the usefulness of the correspondent banking relationship. The explicit pricing of Fed services to member banks and universal reserve requirements will likely alter the correspondent relationship in yet undetermined ways.

International Banking

International banking refers to banking activities undertaken by banks outside their home countries or banking activities directed at international business inside the bank's home country. It includes U.S. banks operating outside the United States and foreign banks operating in the United States. Many of the large U.S. banks trace their foreign operations back more than a hundred years. For example, Chase Manhattan and First National City Bank (now Citibank) operated branches in Europe in the nineteenth century. Yet recent years have seen tremendous increases in American banking overseas.

Total assets of foreign branches of U.S. banks were almost $290 billion in December 1980. From 1970 to 1976, the overseas earnings of the ten largest banks in the United States grew at a 30 percent compounded annual rate. In 1970, these ten banks earned $167 million overseas—accounting for 17.5 percent of their total profits. By contrast, in 1976 overseas earnings were $825 million, over one half of the total profit of these large banks. For some banks, the contribution to total profits of overseas earnings has been even greater. Citibank received over 75 percent of its total 1978 profits from foreign operations. While the overseas earnings growth rate for the ten largest banks slowed in 1977 and 1978 to only 10 percent, the presence of U.S. banks overseas and their importance is still substantial.

The development of the Eurodollar market (Eurodollars are dollar denominated deposits held outside the United States), floating exchange rates, OPEC's position in the world, and the great upswing in international business as more and more American companies have become multinational—all have contributed to the rapid development of U.S. banks abroad. By mid-1978, it was estimated that U.S. banks had loaned over $250 billion to foreigners. Of this, $50 billion had gone to non-oil producing, less developed countries. The increased loans to less developed countries, primarily made to finance their oil imports since 1973, has increased the exposure of U.S. banks to de-

---

[20] George J. Benston, "Federal Reserve Membership: Consequences, Costs, Benefits and Alternatives," study of the Association of Reserve City Bankers (Sept. 1978), p. 36.

fault risk since the economies of many of these countries are very weak. In addition, political instability is a problem in some of these countries. As a result, U.S. banks engaged in international activities have been trying to increase the amount of lending to corporations and to reduce direct loans to governments, particularly the governments of the less developed countries.

In terms of future trends in U.S. banking overseas, expansion in Western Europe is, to a large degree, completed. The Pacific area, South Korea, Australia, Africa, and parts of South America are promising areas for further development, and many banks are actively expanding in them. Further, under changes in U.S. banking regulation effective in 1981, U.S. banks are able to conduct additional international banking operations from the United States that were previously restricted to their foreign branches.

There is increasingly more foreign banking in the United States; foreign banks with offices here greatly multiplied in the 1970s. In July 1979 over a hundred foreign banks operated in the United States—more than double the 1972 total—with 328 offices. Total U.S. assets of foreign banks in September 1980 were $131 billion compared to $24.3 billion in November 1972, a compounded growth rate of almost 25 percent. This compares to the growth of assets of domestic banks of about 10 percent compounded annually. This growth has meant that foreign banks control about 8 percent of commercial banking in the United States compared to 3 percent in 1972 and now account for approximately 20 percent of all corporate lending done in America.

Foreign banks operating in the United States have many organizational forms.[21] The major forms are:

Subsidiary bank: A subsidiary bank has its own state or national charter and is separate from its foreign bank owner; it operates as a full commercial bank, accepting deposits and making loans.

Branch: A branch is a fully functioning part of its foreign bank parent.

Agency: An agency cannot accept deposits but can make loans and provide the financing for international transactions.

Representative office: The representative office cannot accept deposits or make loans but can make contacts for its parent bank.

For a long time, foreign banks in the United States have enjoyed advantages over domestic banks. These advantages arose mainly from

---

[21] This summary of organizational forms is drawn from Gerald H. Anderson, "Current Developments in the Regulation of International Banking," *Economic Review*, Federal Reserve Bank of Cleveland (Jan. 1980), p. 3.

the lack of branching restrictions and the lack of Federal Reserve requirements. These issues, among others, were addressed by Congress in the International Banking Act passed in late 1978. While the Act partly rectifies some of the disadvantages that domestic banks face against foreign banks, it doesn't completely eliminate them, as U.S. banks are quick to point out to Congress and the public.

International Banking Act of 1978[22]

The International Banking Act specifies that foreign banks must choose a "home state" and restrict their growth to that state alone. However, existing operations in other states at the time the Act took effect can be maintained. The provisions of the Act enable a foreign bank with offices in New York and California to choose New York as the home state but continue to operate (but not expand) in California. The choice of the home state is also flexible; banks may choose a home state where they do not have sizable operations. A bank already well established in New York could choose California and build up a substantial operation in that state, for example. They can continue to expand international banking operations in other states where they are not presently located by opening subsidiaries under the rules of the Edge Act. The Edge Act of 1919, originally designed to facilitate international banking activity by domestic banks, allows any bank to open an office in another state as long as the activity of these offices is restricted to foreign lending, but Edge Act subsidiaries cannot take local deposits.

In addition, the International Banking Act extends FDIC insurance to deposits at foreign banks. In the past, lack of FDIC insurance has slowed their acquisition of retail (consumer) deposits. While branches of foreign banks were previously exempt from Fed reserve requirements, the International Banking Act grants authority to the Fed to impose reserve requirements on these banks as long as the parent bank has $1 billion or more in worldwide assets. Almost all foreign banks with U.S. offices exceed the $1 billion requirement. The imposition of reserve requirements increases the cost of funds for foreign banks and puts them on a more equal footing in lending charges with large domestic banks.[23] The Federal Reserve, as well as the Federal Deposit Insurance Corporation and the Comptroller of the Currency, was also granted additional regulatory powers over foreign bank opera-

---

[22] See John P. Segala, "A Summary of the International Banking Act of 1978," Federal Reserve Bank of Richmond *Economic Review* (Jan./Feb.) 1979, pp. 16–21, for a more complete discussion of this Act.

[23] U.S. branches of foreign banks are treated the same as domestic banks for reserve requirement purposes. Reserve requirements to bring the treatment of foreign banks in line with U.S. banks are being phased in. This process began in November 1980 and the $1 billion limitation no longer applies.

tions. The Fed, for example, is now permitted to make independent examinations of any and all foreign bank operations in the United States.

In summary, the act places foreign banks on a more competitive footing with American banks, but it does not totally remove the advantage they have in branching. The competition from foreign banks in the 1970s and 1980s is one of the reasons that large domestic banks are pressing for the repeal of the McFadden Act.

TOWARD INTERSTATE BANKING

Banking on a New Future

For sun, fun and the pleasures of offshore banking, there's no place like the Cayman Islands, the Caribbean paradise used by bankers and corporations as a tax refuge. The dowdy city of Wilmington, Del., is no match for the Caymans, but if Gov. Pierre S. du Pont IV gets his way, his state will soon become as lucrative a tax haven for the nation's largest banks. Already the nominal home of more than 100,000 U.S. companies because of favorable incorporation laws, Delaware is now wooing giant out-of-state banks by drastically revising its laws. This week du Pont is expected to sign the newly minted Financial Center Development Act, a sweeping measure that removes the ceiling on interest rates, slashes bank taxes and welcomes non-Delaware banks to the state.

Creation of a tax haven in Delaware is only the latest evolutionary step toward creation of a nationwide banking system. Federal law permits some cross-border banking if a host state approves—and as states like Delaware are discovering, out-of-state banks can be a new source of revenue for tax-hungry treasuries. Last year South Dakota lifted the usury ceiling on interest rates, and New York's Citibank promptly announced that it would move its entire multimillion-account operation to Sioux Falls. Even without a relaxation of legal barriers, the explosion of electronic banking technology is blurring geographical boundaries: setting up out-of-state subsidiaries often simply means reprograming computers. Now, with the growing expectation that nationwide banking will become a reality, some banks are even positioning themselves for more deregulation by buying stock in out-of-state banks.

The big money-center banks have actively encouraged several states to change their laws—and Delaware, for one, zealously courted out-of-town bankers, entertaining them at the exclusive Wilmington Club, with Governor du Pont and Irving Shapiro, chairman of Delaware-based Du Pont, Inc., playing host. Delaware took aim at tax laws in states like New York and came up with a package money-center bankers could hardly refuse. The ceiling on interest rates charged on most loans was removed entirely. Bank profits will now be taxed on a sliding scale: the more money a bank makes, the lower the tax rate. Bank earnings over $30 million will be taxed at only 2.7 per cent, far below the minimum 12 per cent New York State and the 13.8 per cent New York City tax rates. In fact, the new law is so skewed to giant out-of-state banks that no Delaware bank qualifies for the cut-rate tax.

Thus far, two major New York banks, Chase Manhattan and Morgan Guaranty Trust, have announced plans to move operations to Delaware. Chase will leave existing credit-card accounts in New York, but it will issue new Visa accounts and student loans in Delaware. Morgan Guaranty, which is largely a wholesale bank, with little consumer business, will book much of its new corporate and municipal lending in a new subsidiary on the Delaware River. Bank analysts say it won't be long until others follow suit. "When a state goes out of its way to offer these goodies, you can't bury your head in the sand," says Robert Cole, a spokesman for the New York State Bankers Association.

Exodus: Officials in rival states are fuming at the beggar-thy-neighbor policies. "If states keep passing laws to steal banking jobs from other states, it could have an adverse effect on the entire banking system," says Muriel Siebert, New York State Superintendent of Banks. Moving too much business away from New York could undermine the city's strength as a money center, warns Anthony M. Solomon, president of the Federal Reserve Bank of New York. Fears of a massive exodus are probably exaggerated. New business will migrate to non-money-center states mostly on paper and in the electronic recesses of computer memories. Chase Manhattan's new credit-card business will initially add only about 100 new jobs to Delaware payrolls, for example,

and will not cost any jobs in home-state New York.

Still, small-town bankers fear that they will be ovewhelmed by their big-city cousins if deregulation goes too far, and most states protect their own against the possibility. The new South Dakota law, for instance, explicitly prohibits out-of-state bankers from competing for local business. A bigger threat may be the new trend to buy stock in attractive out-of-state banks. National Detroit Corp. has already spent $62 million to purchase shares in ten bank holding companies, and Houston's aggressive Texas Commerce Bancshares has a piece of Wyoming Bancorporation. So far, banks are limited by Federal law to 4.9 per cent of another bank's stock. But that could change, especially given the growing interest in bank deregulation in Washington. If it does, the long-predicted consolidation in American banking may become a reality.

Key Points

1. Commercial banks are the largest financial intermediaries in the economy. Their lending and deposit-taking activities assure their importance in the financial system. The fact that they hold the vast majority of demand and other checkable deposits, which constitute the bulk of the money supply, adds further to their importance.

2. Fractional reserve banking is the retention of only a small fraction of commercial bank deposits in the form of reserves. The Federal Reserve System sets reserve requirements within limits set by Congress.

3. The Federal Reserve System is the central bank for the United States. Its activities now extend far beyond the original purpose at its inception in 1913 of providing an elastic currency and being a lender of last resort to the banking system. Its role in conducting monetary policy,

primarily through the use of open-market operations, makes the Fed a key factor influencing the course of economic activity.

4. Banks may be chartered by the federal government or by state governments. Whether a bank has a national or state charter, it must abide by the branching laws of the state in which it is located. Unit banking states prohibit branching, while all other states allow either limited or full state branching.

5. Banks are often owned by bank holding companies. This form of organization permits banking organizations to participate in financial activities that are prohibited to banks.

6. Correspondent banking refers to the practice of banks holding noninterest-earning deposits at other banks in exchange for services such as advice and check clearing.

7. International banking has grown dramatically in the last decade; both U.S. banking activity abroad and foreign bank activity in the U.S. have expanded substantially. The International Banking Act of 1978 and the imposition of reserve requirements on branches of foreign banks in the United States have eliminated to some degree the competitive advantages that foreign banks have enjoyed over domestic banks.

Questions for Discussion

1. Differentiate between required reserves, excess reserves, total reserves, and legal reserves.

2. Why was the discovery of fractional reserve banking important to the development of modern commercial banking?

3. The conduct of monetary policy has become an important part of the responsibilities of the Federal Reserve System. Why is monetary policy important and what are the tools the Fed has available for its conduct?

4. What is the rationale of some states for maintaining restrictions on bank branching? The McFadden Act prohibits interstate branching, but some banks have increasingly been pressing for a repeal of this law. What activities have banks or bank holding companies been able to engage in across state lines? What implications emerge from these interstate activities for the future of interstate banking even without the repeal of the McFadden Act?

5. What is the rationale behind correspondent balances?

Suggested Readings

Anderson, Gerald H. "Current Developments in the Regulation of International Banking," *Economic Review*, Federal Reserve Bank of Cleveland, Jan. 1980, pp. 1–15.

Board of Governors of the Federal Reserve System. *The Federal Reserve System: Purposes and Functions*. Washington, D.C.: FRS, Sept. 1974.

Humphrey, Thomas M. "The Classical Concept of the Lender of Last Resort." Federal Reserve Bank of Richmond *Economic Review,* Jan./Feb. 1975, pp. 2–9.

Klebamer, Benjamin J. *Commercial Banking in the United States: A History.* Hinsdale, Ill.: The Dryden Press, 1974.

Mayo, Robert P. "Utilizing the Bank Holding Company." *Economic Perspectives,* Federal Reserve Bank of Chicago, July/August 1980, pp. 3–6.

Maisel, Sherman J. *Managing the Dollar.* New York: Norton, 1973.

Nadler, Paul S. *Commercial Banking in the Economy,* 3rd ed. New York: Random House, 1979.

The Creation
of Money and Credit

he majority of demand deposits—the major portion of the money supply—come into existence through the operation of the commercial banking system. The creation of demand deposits results from the commercial banks' lending process. Therefore, the creation of both money and credit are intertwined.

The focus of this chapter is the commercial banking system. However, nonbank depository institutions have been offering checkable deposits nationwide since January 1, 1981. This potentially gives these institutions a similar ability for creating money, but the relatively small amount of checkable deposits at nonbanks at present and the restriction of these deposits to individuals and nonprofit organizations limit the impact of their activities on money creation at this point. As these institutions become a larger factor in issuing checking accounts, their similarity to commercial banks in the creation of money will grow. There is, however, no loss of generality in concentrating only on commercial banks in discussing the creation of money as we shall do here. While some of the details of the analysis would change with the inclusion of nonbanks, the fundamental process remains the same.

The Bank Lending Process and Money Creation

Primary Deposits, Derivative Deposits, and Lending

A commercial bank can make a loan only if it has excess reserves. It may acquire additional reserves, part of which may be excess, through a **primary deposit.** A primary deposit can be defined, then, as a deposit that adds to reserves of the bank when the deposit is made. Notice that reserves mean **total reserves,** which have to be allocated between required reserves to be held against the primary deposit and excess reserves. If no additional reserves are available to a bank as a result of a deposit, the deposit is known as a **derivative deposit.**

Derivative deposits arise out of the lending process. When a loan is made, a bank creates a demand deposit to enable the borrower to draw on that loan. The borrower may be a depositor of the bank, and the proceeds of the loan may be credited directly to the borrower's existing demand deposit account. Alternatively, the borrower may receive a check drawn directly on the bank itself, which will be honored on presentation for payment. A new demand deposit account may even be created in the borrower's name at the bank and the proceeds of the loan credited to this account. In any of these procedures, the deposit created is a derivative deposit.[1] In some cases the creation of a derivative deposit may even be automatic; such is the case when a bank depositor has a line of credit or overdraft privilege attached to her demand deposit account. When a check is written by the depositor that exceeds the demand deposit balance, the bank automatically pays the check by creating the additional deposit balance necessary. The depositor is then liable for the repayment of this amount just as in the case of any other loan.

The creation of a derivative deposit obviously does not add to the reserves of the bank. However, as the loan proceeds are spent by the borrower (as the derivative deposit is drawn down), the derivative deposit of one bank becomes a primary deposit for another bank. For example, suppose the loan was made so that the borrower could purchase a new car. When the purchase is made, the car dealer deposits the check in a demand deposit account at another commercial bank where the dealer's account is maintained. The car dealer's deposit is a primary deposit to that commercial bank.

The notion of a primary deposit can also be extended to the entire banking system. In the example above, although the car dealer's deposit was a primary deposit for his bank, it was not a primary deposit for the banking system as a whole. No new reserves flowed into the banking system as a result of the process; reserves that were at the lending bank were transferred to the car dealer's bank. For a deposit to be a primary deposit for the banking system, it must result in additional reserves for the entire system. An example of a primary deposit for the banking system is a deposit of cash by an individual into her demand deposit account at a commercial bank. This deposit is not only a primary deposit for the bank, since the bank's reserves are increased, but also one for the banking system because the cash had been outside

---

[1] Only a very small percentage of loans are made in cash. Consideration of such loans does not alter the analysis significantly.

the banking system and is now transformed into the banking system's reserves. The distinctions between derivative deposits, primary deposits, and primary deposits for the whole banking system are important and useful in explaining the creation of money; and we will refer to these concepts throughout the discussion that follows.

The Accounting Approach to Money Creation

A very simplified hypothetical balance sheet of a commercial bank is presented in Table 6-1. (The actual balance sheet for the entire commercial banking system will be presented and analyzed in Chapter 7.) The balance sheet gives a financial picture of a firm, in this case a bank, at a moment in time. The balance sheet in Table 6-1 satisfies the balance sheet identity that assets must equal liabilities plus capital. Further, any change in one category of the balance sheet must be matched by an equal change on the other side of the sheet or by an offsetting change on the same side of the balance sheet in order for it to continue to satisfy the identity.

The categories listed on the left side of the balance sheet are reserves and loans. Reserves include vault cash and depository institution deposits at the Fed. Assume for purposes of the following example that banks do not hold or purchase any securities. Demand deposits and capital are the only items listed on the right side of the balance sheet. No time deposits are held by the bank. The demand for loans is assumed to be sufficient so that banks can make all the loans they wish, and banks are assumed to hold no excess reserves except for transitory periods between loans. Also, no cash flows out of the banking system. Many of these assumptions will be relaxed later. For computational ease a uniform 20 percent reserve requirement on demand deposits is specified.

Our example of the money creation process begins by assuming

Table 6-1
Hypothetical Commercial Bank Balance Sheet
(Millions of Dollars)

Assets		Liabilities plus Capital	
Reserves	$1,000	D.D.	$5,000
Loans	5,000	Capital	1,000
Total	$6,000	Total	$6,000

Table 6-2
$1,000 Deposit of Cash to a Customer's Demand Deposit Account

Assets		Liabilities	
Reserves	+ $1,000	Demand Deposits	+ $1,000

that a man with $1,000 in his mattress decides to deposit it in a demand deposit account at the commercial bank in Table 6-1. It is clear from the figure that the bank is "loaned up"—that is, has no excess reserves available for lending—prior to this man's deposit. As a result of the man's action, the bank has received a primary deposit.[2] A device known as a T-account can be used to isolate the transaction. Using the T-account in Table 6-2, we see that the bank finds its reserves have increased by $1,000 and its demand deposits have increased by $1,000. Since the T-account is in balance, the bank's balance sheet will, of course, also remain in balance after this transaction.

The bank—call it Bank A—now has excess reserves of $800 since it only has to keep 20 percent in reserve against the $1,000 demand deposit. Table 6-3 reproduces the T-account in Table 6-2 as panel (A1). Since the bank has $800 in excess reserves, it will seek to lend that amount. Suppose the bank makes an auto loan to an individual, creating a derivative deposit for $800 as pictured in panel (A2). However, T-account (A2) applies only until the individual actually buys the car, issues a check for $800, and the check clears. After securing the car loan, the individual goes to Smiling John's Used Car Lot and purchases a car. Smiling John banks at another commercial bank in town called Bank B. (If John banked at Bank A, nothing but the details of the example would be altered—the end result would be the same.) John deposits the check into his demand deposit account at Bank B, as shown in panel (B1). Once the check is paid by Bank A, Bank B has $800 in reserves above what it held previously, because John's deposit was a primary deposit to Bank B.[3] At the same time, as shown in panel (A3), the $800 derivative deposit has been extinguished when Bank A cleared the check, and, in addition, $800 in reserves have

---

[2] This deposit also happens to be a primary deposit for the banking system since the cash deposit results in an increase in reserves both for the banking system and for the bank.

[3] But in this case the deposit is not a primary deposit for the banking system since the $800 in reserves was already in the banking system.

Table 6-3
The Credit Expansion Process

BANK A

(A1)

Reserves	+$1,000	Demand Deposits	+$1,000

(A2)

Reserves	$1,000	Demand Deposits	$1,000
Loans	+ 800	Demand Deposits	+ 800

(A3)

Reserves	$200	Demand Deposits	$1,000
Loans	800	Demand Deposits	$1,000

BANK B

(B1)

Reserves	+$800	Demand Deposits	+$800

(B2)

Reserves	$800	Demand Deposits	$800
Loans	+ 640	Demand Deposits	+ 640

(B3)

Reserves	$160	Demand Deposits	$800
Loans	640	Demand Deposits	$800

BANK C

(C1)

Reserves	+$640	Demand Deposits	+$640

(C2)

Reserves	$128	Demand Deposits	$640
Loans	512	Demand Deposits	$640

flowed out of Bank A to Bank B. Therefore, panel (A3) depicts the final position of Bank A, as shown by the double line under the data. Unless something else happens, Bank A cannot make any additional loans.

However, Bank B is now in a position to loan out $640 (80 percent of $800) holding the remainder as required reserves. It makes the loan by creating a derivative deposit, as indicated in panel (B2). When the loan is used and the check is cleared, Bank B is left in the final position depicted in panel (B3). Suppose the loan is made to someone to buy furniture. When the borrower pays for the furniture, the furniture seller—Flo's Antiques—deposits the check in its demand deposit account at Bank C. Bank C has received a primary deposit when the check is cleared by Bank B as shown in panel (C1). Bank C now has $512 available to be loaned out and makes this loan. Bank C's final position is shown in panel (C2). The process then continues through other banks.

In summary to this point, notice that if the final position for Banks A–C are added, the total amount of demand deposits is $2,440. The process started by a deposit of $1,000. Since the original $1,000 was in cash held outside the banking system, it was already considered part of the money supply. Therefore, when it was converted into a demand deposit, the money supply remained unchanged. The $1,000 in cash became bank reserves, which is not part of the money supply; and a demand deposit of equal amount was established, which is part of the money supply. However, portions of the reserve increase, provided by the initial $1,000 deposit, started moving through the banking system as a result of the lending process. By the end of Bank C's participation in the process, the money supply had increased by $1,440. In loaning out its excess reserves, each bank had contributed to the banking system as a whole, creating money and thereby increasing the money supply. The money creation process, in fact, continues until all reserves have been converted into required reserves.[4] No excess reserves exist at that point and the process stops.

Table 6-4 summarizes the effect of the initial $1,000 inflow of reserves on the entire banking system once the process has reached a conclusion. Bank loans have increased by $4,000 and bank demand deposits by $5,000. However, only $4,000 of $5,000 in demand deposits is new money since the initial increase in deposits was caused by the deposit of $1,000 in cash to Bank A. Furthermore, it is not a coincidence that the increase in the money supply exactly matches

---

[4] This results because of the assumption made in this example that banks do not voluntarily hold any excess reserves. When they have excess reserves, loans are immediately made. It has also been assumed in this example, for ease of presentation, that banks do not hold any securities. However, including securities does not alter the result. If there was insufficient loan demand to enable banks to use all their excess reserves, they would simply buy securities and the example would still be valid.

Table 6-4
Summary for the Entire Banking System
After Full Expansion

Assets		Liabilities	
Reserves	+$1,000	Demand	
Loans	+ 4,000	Deposits	+$5,000

the increase in loans for the banking system, for it is through the lending process that the new money comes into existence.

There is an easier way to calculate the ultimate effects of the initial $1,000 primary deposit into the banking system than working through all the T-accounts. By using the **credit expansion multiplier,** the end result of a primary deposit into the banking system can be determined. This name is appropriate because the money supply increases as a result of the increases in bank credit in the form of loans.

The Credit Expansion Multiplier

The credit expansion multiplier relates a change in reserves in the banking system to the resulting change in deposits. The multiplier makes use of the fact that **leakages** occur at every stage of the credit creation process and lead to a finite expansion of deposits as a result of a reserve increase. The only such leakage that was addressed in our example above was into required reserves. In actuality, there are other leakages as well and the credit expansion multiplier can be modified to take account of these.

The simplest form of the multiplier considers only the leakage into required reserves. The multiplier, therefore, depends on the reserve requirement and is equal to $1/r$, where r is the reserve requirement. The multiplier is employed in the following manner: The multiplier times the change in reserves yields the resulting change in deposits:

$$\Delta \text{ Reserves} \times \frac{1}{r} = \Delta \text{ Deposits}$$

where Δ means "change in." A primary deposit to the banking system of $1,000 with a 20 percent reserve requirement expands deposits by $5,000:

$$\$1,000 \times \frac{1}{.20} = \$5,000$$

which is the same result achieved in our example analyzed above. However, this increase in deposits is not equal to the increase in loans and the money supply under all conditions. Recall that in the example, the $1,000 was already counted in the money supply when the deposit was made at Bank A. Therefore, to determine the resulting increase in loans and the money supply, the original primary deposit into the banking system must be subtracted from the final result. In this case, the $1,000 primary deposit is subtracted from $5,000 to yield an increase in the money supply and loans of $4,000.

There are cases in which a reserve inflow comes about not through a primary deposit to the banking system but through some other mechanism. For example, when a commercial bank borrows from the Federal Reserve System, the funds borrowed are simply credited to the depository institution's account at the Fed. As a result, reserves increase directly without any deposit inflow. Since reserves have increased while deposits have not, the full amount of the reserve increase is initially available for lending. As a consequence, if the reserve increase due to the commercial bank's borrowing at the Fed was $1,000, the resulting $5,000 increase in deposits after the expansion process was completed would be equal to the increase in bank loans and the money supply.[5] Therefore, it is important to know whether an increase in reserves to the banking system is a result of a primary deposit or not, so that the impact on the money supply can be precisely determined.

An additional factor requires attention in discussing the credit expansion multiplier and has been implied in the discussion above. The credit expansion multiplier process only yields the maximum potential credit expansion. It has been assumed for the example that all loans a bank desired to make could be made. In reality, this may not always be the case. If profitable loans are not available to the bank, it could, for example, buy securities. (As noted, in this case the credit expansion process would be the same as it was with lending.) If banks neither make loans nor buy securities up to the level of their excess reserves, full potential credit expansion would not take place. Therefore, it should be kept in mind that under certain situations credit expansion will be less than that indicated by the multiplier process. Many of these factors can be taken into account by modifying the multiplier so that it is capable of handling more complex situations, as we shall do below to analyze the most important factors altering the multiplier. However, while theoretically the multiplier can be expanded to incorporate all possible factors that will alter the amount of credit expansion for a

---

[5] Reserves are not counted as part of the money supply. As the increase in reserves that result from the commercial bank borrowing at the Fed are used to make loans, deposits and, therefore, the money supply grow until the reserves are all utilized as required reserves. This occurs when bank loans and deposits have increased by $5,000 in the example.

given change in reserves, in practice this is often not possible. Therefore, the simple multiplier process discussed above should be regarded
as indicating the maximum amount of credit expansion. Similarly, the
more complex multipliers presented below also yield the maximum
potential increase in deposits for each situation. This maximum may
not be reached in all situations.

Modifications of the Simple Credit Expansion Multiplier

In the example that has been carried through in the discussion thus
far, a number of assumptions were made that need to be relaxed.
By relaxing these assumptions the fundamental analysis is not altered,
but the specific results do change.

Cash Drain It was assumed in the example that after the individual
deposited the $1,000 in cash in Bank A, no cash flowed out of the
banking system throughout the entire credit creation process. That
is, it was assumed that when the $800 loan was made by Bank A,
the entire amount flowed into Bank B and so on. But suppose the
borrower had taken some portion of the loan and had just retained
it in currency. Then the amount flowing into Bank B would have been
reduced. This is simply another way of saying that the public holds
some portion of its money balances in currency instead of in demand
deposits. If the currency–deposit ratio is 10 percent (that is, for every
$10 in demand deposits there is $1 in currency), it is clear that the
loan by Bank A would in all likelihood result in something smaller than
an $800 primary deposit in Bank B.[6] Further, at every stage in the
expansion process a similar drain would occur. Cash drain, then, is
another leakage out of the credit creation process, and the multiplier
must be modified accordingly. If k stands for the currency–deposit
ratio (assumed to be 10 percent), the multiplier becomes $1/(r + k)$
as the leakage into currency is added to the leakage into required
reserves:

$$\Delta \text{ Reserves} \times \frac{1}{r + k} = \Delta \text{ Deposits}$$

or continuing the example from above,

$$\$1,000 \times \frac{1}{.20 + .10} = \$3,333$$

---

[6] On average this would be true given the currency–deposit ratio. For any particular
loan, this result may not hold.

But this result only gives the increase in deposits. In addition, 10 percent of the increase in deposits flowed out of the banking system in the form of currency. Thus the total increase in deposits plus currency was $3,333 + $333.[7] As before, if the original increase in reserves was the result of a primary deposit, that deposit must be subtracted from the resulting increase in deposits and currency in order to obtain the increase in the money supply and loans. The results of the example show that the multiplier and the resulting expansion in the money supply and loans is substantially reduced from that obtained before the consideration of cash drain.

Desired Excess Reserves It was also assumed above that banks seek to lend out all their excess reserves. But some banks may desire to retain a margin of excess reserves at all times to take care of any unforeseen contingencies. Excess reserves thus retained would be another leakage out of the credit creation process and can be accounted for in the multiplier. The excess reserve ratio (excess reserves/deposits), e, is added to the denominator of the multiplier:

$$\Delta \text{ Reserves} \times \frac{1}{r + k + e} = \Delta \text{ Deposits}$$

and, continuing the numerical example, with e at 10 percent:

$$\$1,000 \times \frac{1}{.20 + .10 + .10} = \$2,500$$

Thus the multiplier is reduced by this additional leakage and the existence of cash drain. Once again, the original primary deposit must be subtracted from the increase in deposits and currency (10 percent of the increase in deposits) to yield the increase in the money supply and loans.

The amount held by banks in excess reserves has declined substantially in recent years. With the high rates of interest that have prevailed in the economy almost continuously since the late 1960s and early 1970s, banks became very conscious of the opportunity cost of holding excess reserves. Much effort has been expended by banks in developing techniques to closely manage their reserve position. With this investment in techniques for reserve management, it is unlikely that, even should interest rates move to lower levels for a long period of time, bank behavior would alter substantially. Among other things, this

---

[7] Strictly speaking for this result to hold, it must be assumed that the original deposit is also subject to the cash drain. The reason for making this assumption is that the process of cash drain is continuous throughout the credit creation process. This will be seen clearly when a full model of money supply determination is presented later in the chapter.

alteration in behavior has meant that many banks (particularly large banks) essentially aim at having zero excess reserves and rely much more heavily on the federal funds market—the market where banks borrow and lend excess reserves to each other—to meet any reserve deficiencies that may occur from such a closely managed position.[8] In turn, the federal funds market has grown enormously in the 1970s and early 1980s as will be discussed in detail in the next chapter and in the chapter on the money market.[9] As a result of this behavior alteration, e is currently very low in practice; therefore, excess reserves are not a very large leakage out of the credit creation process.

Time Deposits Thus far, our analysis has ignored time deposits, yet time deposits are of major importance to banks as a source of funds. The various types of time deposits will be discussed in detail in the next chapter. However, for purposes of the discussion below, we will assume that all time deposits are the same.

The major feature of time deposits important to the credit creation process is that the reserve requirement on time deposits is less than that on demand deposits. In fact, reserve requirements on personal time deposits will be zero under the changes currently being phased in. Further, time deposits are generally not considered money.[10] The credit expansion multiplier can be altered to account for time deposits by adding the reserve requirement (r_t) on time deposits multiplied by the ratio of time to demand deposits (t) to the denominator of the multiplier. Assume that the reserve requirement on time deposits is 5 percent and the ratio of time to demand deposits is 2 for purposes of the example, then the multiplier is:

$$\text{Multiplier} = \frac{1}{r + k + e + r_t t}$$

therefore,

$$\Delta \text{ Reserves} \times \frac{1}{r + k + e + r_t t} = \Delta \text{ Deposits}$$

---

[8] See Raymond E. Lombra and Herbert M. Kaufman, "Commercial Banks and the Federal Funds Market: Recent Development and Implications," *Economic Inquiry* (Oct. 1978), pp. 549–62, for a discussion of the issues relating to this change in bank behavior and the impact of the change on the federal funds market.

[9] By utilizing the federal funds market, a bank with excess reserves can earn a return on these funds, even if the reserves are only available overnight.

[10] Automatic transfer accounts are the only type of time deposit that may be considered money since funds are automatically deposited in a demand deposit account when needed. However, these accounts, which are a very small portion of time deposits, have become relatively unimportant with the nationwide spread of interest-earning checking accounts. Automatic transfer accounts are ignored, therefore, in this discussion.

and continuing the example,

$$\$1{,}000 \times \frac{1}{.20 + .10 + .10 + .05(2)} = \$2{,}000$$

To arrive at the amount of new money and loans, the primary deposit (if any) generating the increase in reserves must be subtracted from the resulting increase in demand deposits and currency due to cash drain (10 percent of $2,000).

The multiplier is lower with the existence of time deposits because the reserves against time deposits are another leakage out of the process. However, the example is misleading in a sense. Once time deposits have been taken account of, transfers from demand deposits to time deposits can lead to additional money creation and will almost certainly lead to expansion in total deposits (demand deposits plus time deposits). To see this, remember that the reserve requirement on time deposits is lower than that on demand deposits. Suppose the banking system has the following situation: $1 million in reserves, $4 million in demand deposits and $4 million in time deposits. With a 20 percent reserve requirement on demand deposits and 5 percent on time deposits, the banking system would be all loaned up. Reserves are just sufficient to satisfy the reserve requirement. However, suppose a $1 million shift from demand deposits to time deposits takes place, perhaps because of the action of a large depositor. At first the banking system held $200,000 in reserves on the $1 million in demand deposits; but after the shift occurs, the banking system only needs to hold $50,000 in reserves against the $1 million that has now been shifted to time deposits (.05 × $1 million). Thus, the banking system now has $150,000 in excess reserves where it had none before, and this can lead to additional money creation. Movement of funds from time deposits to demand deposits will have the opposite effect.

Multiple Credit Contraction

The thrust of the discussion so far has been on the credit expansion process. But this process is symmetrical. A loss of reserves to the banking system leads to multiple credit contraction. In our numerical example of multiple credit expansion, an individual deposited $1,000 in cash into the bank. However, if $1,000 in cash is withdrawn from the banking system, this action will set in motion changes in the money supply and bank credit that would exactly cancel out the original credit expansion. The $1,000 loss of reserves, all else being equal, would mean a $5,000 decline in deposits and a $4,000 decline in loans and the money supply, if the simple multiplier is used. The money supply declines by only $4,000 since the cash that has been withdrawn is still included in the money supply. The calculation for this is:

$$-\Delta \text{ Reserves} \times \frac{1}{r} = -\Delta \text{ Deposits}$$

$$-\$1,000 \times \frac{1}{.20} = -\$5,000$$

Multiple credit contraction can also be worked through by using T-accounts and assuming that the banking system is loaned up when the withdrawal of cash takes place. The first bank in the chain experiences the withdrawal and in order to meet it calls in loans. By tracing this process through the banking system, the result will be the same as using the multiplier.

A Full Model of Money Supply Determination[11]

Our preceding discussion focused upon the credit creation process. However, the money supply includes currency in circulation as well as demand deposits as the discussion of cash drain indicated. By developing a complete model of the money supply, we can not only account for currency but reinforce the discussion of credit expansion. The first essential element in money supply determination is the monetary base.

The Monetary Base

The monetary base is sometimes also called "high powered money" because it is a measure of the reserves of the banking system as well as additional potential reserves of the banking system held in the form of currency in circulation.[12] Since these reserves support multiple amounts of demand deposits, the term "high powered money" is appropriate. The monetary base can be measured in two ways. The **source base** is derived from components of a consolidated balance sheet of the Treasury and the Federal Reserve. It is much easier, however, to focus on the base determined from the uses to which it is put—the **use base.** The source base and the use base yield equivalent

---

[11] This section draws heavily on Jerry L. Jordan, "Elements of Money Stock Determination," Federal Reserve Bank of St. Louis *Review* (Oct. 1969), pp. 10–19. The presentation to follow is somewhat simplified in that the ratio of government to private demand deposits is deleted from the model. For their inclusion see Jordan. The money multiplier process is discussed in great detail in Albert Burger, *The Money Supply Process* (Belmont, Calif.: Wadsworth, 1971).

[12] There is a specific reserve measure that is called "high powered money" that differs slightly from the monetary base as defined in this section. Using the phrase high powered money as it is used in this section to denote the fact that reserves support multiple amounts of the money supply should not be confused with the exact measure "high powered money."

values for the monetary base. Monetary base uses consist of the reserves of the banking system and currency outside the banking system in the hands of the nonbank public. By employing the monetary base, we can explain the full money supply process.

The Money Supply Process

In symbols the monetary base is

$$B = R + C \qquad [6\text{-}1]$$

where: B = monetary base
R = bank reserves
C = currency

The money supply (MS) is equal to demand deposits (D) plus currency,

$$MS = D + C \qquad [6\text{-}2]$$

If reserves are defined as fractions of demand deposits and time deposits (T), then

$$R = r(D + T) \qquad [6\text{-}3]$$

where r is equal to a weighted average of reserves held on demand deposits and time deposits. (Notice that r includes both the required reserve ratios and the excess reserve ratio.) If currency is expressed as a proportion of demand deposits, then

$$C = kD \qquad [6\text{-}4]$$

(Recall that $k = C/D$ is how cash drain was defined previously in the credit expansion multiplier). Time deposits can also be expressed as a proportion of demand deposits

$$T = tD \qquad [6\text{-}5]$$

(Again recall $t = T/D$ from the credit expansion multiplier.) If [6-3] and [6-4] are substituted into [6-1] then

$$B = r(D + T) + kD \qquad [6\text{-}6]$$

so that the monetary base is expressed in terms of time and demand deposits. But time deposits can also be expressed in terms of demand deposits by using [6-5] so that

$$B = r(D + tD) + kD \qquad [6\text{-}7]$$

and [6-7] can be rewritten as

$$B = [r(1 + t) + k] \times D \qquad \text{[6-8]}$$

Noticing that

$$D = 1 / [r(1 + t) + k] \times B \qquad \text{[6-9]}$$

and

$$C = k(1 / [r(1 + t) + k]) \times B \qquad \text{[6-10]}$$

since $C = kD$ from equation [6-4], then the complete money supply is

$$MS = (1 + k) / [r(1 + t) + k] \times B \qquad \text{[6-11]}$$

The expression $(1 + k) / [r(1 + t) + k]$ is known as the money multiplier and is usually defined as m, so simplifying

$$MS = mB \qquad \text{[6-12]}$$

A numerical example may be useful at this point to illustrate the money supply process derived above. Suppose that in equation [6-1], $R = \$30$ billion and $C = \$100$ billion. Then B, the monetary base, is equal to $\$130$ billion. Giving hypothetical numerical values to the money multiplier parameters as follows $k = .10$, $r = .15$, and $t = 2$ and substituting these values into equation [6-11] yields the following expression

$$\begin{aligned} MS &= (1 + .10) / [.15(1 + 2) + .10] \times \$130 \text{ billion} \\ &= 1.10 / .55 \times \$130 \text{ billion} \\ &= 2 \times \$130 \text{ billion} \\ &= \$260 \text{ billion} \end{aligned} \qquad \text{[6-11a]}$$

Or substituting in equation [6-12]

$$\begin{aligned} MS &= 2 \times \$130 \text{ billion} \\ &= \$260 \text{ billion} \end{aligned} \qquad \text{[6-12a]}$$

Thus, using this hypothetical data, the money supply equals $\$260$ billion.

The relationship between the money multiplier and the credit expansion multiplier is very close. This can be seen by multiplying the denominator of [6-11] out so that

$$MS = [(1 + k) / (r + rt + k)] \times B$$

Note that the only major differences are the inclusion of the currency–deposit ratio in the numerator of the expression to reflect the fact that currency is part of the money supply and a use of the monetary base and the inclusion of the desired excess reserve ratio in r. The monetary base rather than bank reserves is multiplied by the money multiplier since this model is concerned with the determination of the entire money supply, not only demand deposits.

The money multiplier derived above can be made considerably more complex for analytical purposes. For example, further derivation and disaggregation of the reserve ratio can yield expressions in the denominator of the multiplier to account for changes in the composition of reserves among member and nonmember banks and between banks meeting different reserve requirements. This is not done here for two reasons. First, the increased complexity yields very little additional insight into the overall money supply process for our purposes. Second, once the new system of reserve requirements is fully operable, any expression derived from current practice would have to be altered. Since the multiplier derived above is a general expression, it is equally useful for analysis of the process under the old and new reserve requirement systems.

The money multiplier model is very useful for tracing the causes of changes in the money supply. The monetary policy actions of the Fed that were discussed in the last chapter, for example, have a pronounced effect in this model. Through its open market operations, the Fed influences the monetary base by affecting bank reserves. Some economists argue that the Fed can completely control the monetary base, if it chooses—though this has been disputed by other economists. Nevertheless, there is no dispute that the Fed can exert a great deal of influence on the base and thus through the base on the money supply. Furthermore, since the Fed can alter reserve requirements, it can also affect the reserve ratio in the multiplier.[13]

The remaining parameters of the multiplier are not under the control of the Federal Reserve. The currency–deposit ratio is based on the public's decisions on what proportions of currency and demand deposits they wish to hold. Excess reserves that banks wish to hold, included in this model in the reserve ratio (r), are decided upon by banks. Thus, the money multiplier framework demonstrates the interaction of decisions by the Fed, the public, and the banking system in determining the money supply.

There have been discussions among economists as to whether the money multiplier is stable or predictable. Those who argue that the multiplier is stable or predictable believe that the Federal Reserve can control the money supply very closely by controlling the monetary base. For example, if the multiplier is predicted to be 3 for the next

---

[13] A full discussion using the money multiplier framework of monetary policy effects on the money supply is deferred to a later chapter (Chapter 19).

Table 6-5
Money Supply (M1), Monetary Base, and Money Multiplier, 1980 (Monthly Data, *MS* and *B* in Billions of Dollars)

Month	MS	B	m
January	$388.3	$150.9	2.57
February	391.4	152.1	2.57
March	391.2	153.1	2.55
April	386.3	153.5	2.52
May	386.1	154.2	2.50
June	391.3	155.4	2.52
July	395.5	156.6	2.53
August	402.7	158.2	2.55
September	408.0	159.6	2.56
October	412.0	160.5	2.57
November	415.0	162.6	2.55
December	411.9	162.5	2.53

Source: Federal Reserve Bank of St. Louis *Monetary Trends,* April 24, 1981.

year and the Fed wants the money supply to average $300 billion, the Fed "merely" has to keep the average monetary base at $100 billion. However, many economists argue that the multiplier is not stable or predictable and that the Fed cannot control the base very well anyway; or they reject the money multiplier framework entirely as too mechanical. While these issues will be discussed in more detail in the context of monetary policy later on, it can be noted that there has been a good deal of empirical work attempting to analyze the components of the multiplier and address the issues of stability and predictability.[14] Particularly, the work by Johannes and Rasche[15] has attracted considerable attention. By forecasting the individual components of the money multiplier they argue that the multiplier itself can be forecast reasonably well. But as was noted, the stability and predictability of the money multiplier and the use of this framework for money supply control is still a contentious issue among economists.

For the actual data, Table 6-5 presents the monetary base, the

---

[14] See Jane Anderson and Thomas M. Humphrey, "Determinants of Change in the Money Stock: 1960–1970," Federal Reserve Bank of Richmond *Monthly Review* (March 1972), pp. 3–7; Robert Rasche, "A Review of Empirical Studies of the Money Supply Mechanism," Federal Reserve Bank of St. Louis *Review* (July 1972), pp. 11–19; and Albert E. Burger, "The Relationship Between Monetary Base and Money: How Close?" Federal Reserve Bank of St. Louis *Review* (Oct. 1975), pp. 3–8.

[15] James M. Johannes and Robert H. Rasche, "Predicting the Money Multiplier," *Journal of Monetary Economics* (July 1979), pp. 301–25.

money supply, and the calculated money multiplier (MS/B) monthly for 1980. While the multiplier appears reasonably stable from the data in the table, ranging between 2.52 and 2.57, it is clear from the discussion above that much more extensive analysis is necessary to come to any firm conclusions.

THE MONEY SUPPLY PROCESS

That Strong First Quarter

By Lindley H. Clark Jr.

Last week the Commerce Department told us that the nation's output of goods and services, after adjustment for inflation, exploded at a seasonally adjusted annual rate of 8.4% in this year's first quarter. That was an upward revision from the 6.5% gain reported a month earlier, and even 6.5% had been startling enough. As recently as last February, midway through the quarter, the average economist had been expecting GNP to *decline* in the first three months of the year.

Not only economists were surprised. President Reagan came to office in January saying the country was in the worst economic mess since the Great Depression. So suddenly we have the gross national product growing faster and inflation slowing down. The economic news can and should be qualified, but it can't be transformed into proof that three years of 10% tax cuts are a clear and pressing need.

It is quite likely that the arrival of the Reagan administration has done good things for businessmen's expectations. While rising confidence alone would not have generated the sharp rise in real GNP that occurred in the first quarter, it is possible that a failure to follow up promises with actions could deflate expectations in a hurry.

In any case, slower economic growth seems sure this quarter. When GNP grows at an annual rate of 8.4% in one quarter it has trouble figuring out what to do for an encore. The United Mine Workers are giving the economy a firm downward shove as they appear determined to strike themselves right out of business. And the easing of inflation owes a great deal to food price developments, some of which are likely to be transitory.

One reason that economists were looking for a decline in the first quarter was that they assumed the Federal Reserve System had tightened money sharply late last year and would keep it tight for some time to come. The monetary base, currency plus member bank reserves with Reserve Banks, is the raw material from which money is made. From November through January the base was essentially flat.

M1-B is the most common version of the money supply, consisting of currency plus checking accounts in financial institutions. M1-B, like the base, showed almost no growth from November through January.

But Lacy Hunt, executive vice president of Philadelphia's Fidelity Bank, is one economist who thought the tightness was overstated. He stressed a couple of relatively new money market instruments: repurchase agreements and money market mutual funds.

Under repurchase agreements, funds in corporate checking accounts are used near the end of a banking day to buy short-term securities, which the banks buy back the following day. The agreements in effect result in interest-bearing corporate checking accounts. But since the funds are not in the checking accounts at the end of the day they don't show up in M1-B.

Money market mutual funds increasingly are allowing investors to write personal checks on their fund holdings. The funds can't offer checks directly, so the accounts go through a commercial bank. Investors theoretically have checking accounts in these banks but the balances are kept at zero. So nothing shows up in M1-B, although some portion of money market funds surely is transactions money just like bank checking accounts. Mr. Hunt estimates that portion now is 20%.

Putting M1-B together with repurchase agreements and 20% of money market funds, you get a different picture of money growth in the past few months. Money growth, as measured by Mr. Hunt, did slow briefly at the end of 1980, but growth otherwise has been rapid.

The growth has been rapid enough, in fact, to be consistent with an 8.5% rise in real GNP in the first quarter. Conventional M1-B, on the other hand, can be put together with the first-quarter result only by assuming an unprecedented rise in "velocity," the rate at which money is used.

The importance of the monetary base is to some extent understated because of the money market checking accounts. To the extent that individuals increase their use of such accounts and rely less on other checking accounts, interest-paying or otherwise, a given amount of base is consistent with a larger amount of checking-account money.

This fact leads Mr. Hunt to urge that reserve requirements of some sort be placed on money market funds. The reason is not that he regards the funds as unfair competition for the banks, because he doesn't. It's just to let the Fed get a better grip on the money supply.

Such a grip is of course desirable, but my own feeling is that the same aim can be accomplished without reserve requirements. All that's needed is for the Federal Reserve to recognize that the importance of the base changes as the money market funds expand.

However that may be, the monetary base as reported was flashing danger signals in February and March, as its growth began to accelerate. As usual the Fed waited too long to act, so that when it finally moved it had to step hard on the brake.

Mr. Hunt, for one, is convinced that this time the Fed really means it. If he's right the economy surely will slow from the 8.4% pace of the first quarter. Interest rates still may move a little higher but decreasing inflationary expectations will in time bring them down.

The first quarter was surely a striking performance. The economy would find it hard to live with much more of the same, however, even if it could somehow be arranged.

Key Points

1. Most of the money supply comes into existence through the credit creation process of the commercial banking system.

2. A primary deposit increases bank and possibly banking system reserves

while a derivative deposit results from the lending process and does not add to bank or banking system reserves.

3. Money creation comes about as excess reserves are loaned by banks and transformed through the banking system into required reserves, supporting some multiple amount of demand deposits.

4. The credit expansion multiplier relates a given change in reserves to the resulting change in demand deposits. The total change in the money supply can then be determined.

5. There are various leakages in the credit expansion process, and these can be taken account of in the credit expansion multiplier.

6. The uses of the monetary base consist of reserves plus currency in circulation. Deriving the money multiplier, which relates the monetary base to the money supply, illustrates the interaction between the Federal Reserve, the banks, and the public in determining the money supply.

Questions for Discussion

1. Explain why an increase in bank reserves will lead to a multiple increase in demand deposits and the money supply.

2. A loss of reserves by the banking system will result in multiple credit contraction since the multiplier process is symmetrical. Is there any way that such a loss of reserves can be temporarily covered by the banking system without contracting credit?

3. Why is the money supply process as discussed in the chapter an important analytical device?

4. Will an increase in reserves in the banking system as a result of a primary deposit have any different effect on the resulting money supply increase than an increase in reserves that arise from bank borrowings from the Fed? Explain.

5. Trace the credit expansion process through T-accounts for four banks in a multiple banking system when one bank receives a primary deposit in cash of $500, assuming a 15 percent reserve requirement on demand deposits and no time deposits. Summarize the resulting credit expansion using the credit expansion multiplier. Indicate how much deposits, loans, and the money supply change.

Suggested Readings

Anderson, Leonall, and Jerry L. Jordan. "The Monetary Base—Explanations and Analytical Use." Federal Reserve Bank of St. Louis *Review,* August 1968, pp. 7–11.

Burger, Albert E. *The Money Supply Process.* Belmont, Calif.: Wadsworth, 1971.

Durkin, Thomas A., and Robert O. Edmister. "The Supply of Money and Bank Credit." In *Financial Institutions and Markets.* Murray E. Polakoff et al. 2nd ed. Boston: Houghton Mifflin, 1981, pp. 81–104.

Nichols, Dorothy M. "Modern Money Mechanics: A Workbook on Deposits, Currency, and Bank Reserves." Federal Reserve Bank of Chicago, May 1961. (A copy is available free of charge by writing the Federal Reserve Bank of Chicago.)

Tatom, John A. "Issues in Measuring An Adjusted Monetary Base." Federal Reserve Bank of St. Louis *Review,* Dec. 1980, pp. 11–29.

Commercial Banking: The Bank as a Business Firm

7

he fundamental importance of the commercial banking system to the economy in lending and the resulting money creation was established in the last chapter. The focus of the discussion on the credit creation process—the role of the commercial bank in the overall economy—can, however, overshadow the fact that the commercial bank is in the first instance a business firm. The commercial banker provides services and, in return, maximizes profits subject to certain constraints. These constraints are imposed by competition of other banks and nonbank financial institutions and by governmental regulation. How the commercial bank conducts its business is the subject of this chapter.

An Overview of a Bank's Operation

A bank can be thought of as issuing various liabilities in order to raise funds and using these funds to acquire various income-earning assets. The primary sources of funds for a bank are equity capital (the capital necessary to start and operate a bank), deposits, and borrowings. The bank pays interest, either implicitly or explicitly, on the funds raised through the issuance of liabilities. The bank allocates these funds to acquire assets that yield a return. The difference between the total return on income-earning assets and the total cost of funds to the bank represents the gross profit to the bank before other expenses and taxes are deducted. Once these items are removed from gross profit, the resulting net profit is the return to the bank owners or, put another way, the return on equity. The discussion that follows fills in this sketch of the operation of a bank.

153

The Commercial Bank Portfolio

The income-earning assets that a bank holds are referred to as its portfolio. Three major considerations enter into the construction and management of a commercial bank portfolio. These considerations are liquidity, return, and risk minimization.

Liquidity, Return, and the Minimization of Risk

Liquidity, as defined previously, is the ease with which an asset can be converted into money without substantial loss. The return on an earning asset is the income that the asset is expected to yield. There are two dimensions to risk related to a bank's earning assets that the banker attempts to minimize. Default risk is the likelihood that the issuer of an obligation held in the bank's portfolio will default when the obligation becomes due. Market risk is the possibility that an asset will have to be sold at a loss, due to market fluctuation, if funds must be raised from its sale prior to maturity. Market risk is related to liquidity since for an asset to be liquid it must have relatively little market risk.

Unfortunately for the banker, an asset does not usually possess the three attributes of liquidity, return, and safety to the same degree. In fact, often an asset strong in one or two of these qualities will be considerably weaker in the remainder. For example, the most liquid assets usually yield the lowest return; similarly the highest return is usually found on the most risky assets. Further, the more risky an asset, the less liquid it usually is. Thus, the banker must weigh the attributes of an individual asset that she plans to acquire for the bank's portfolio against the bank's goals and the existing composition of the portfolio before deciding on the acquisition. More generally, the banker will construct the bank's portfolio so that there is a comfortable balance between liquidity, return, and risk. For example, Treasury bills are very safe and highly liquid; yet because of these attributes, Treasury bills usually do not yield as much as many other potential assets that a bank may acquire. A banker will give up some liquidity and safety by only holding a relatively small amount of Treasury bills in the portfolio. Table 7-1 presents the portfolio of income earning assets of a typical bank.

The Portfolio in Detail

Loans Loans constitute the primary portion of commercial banks' portfolios. Until recently the loan portfolio was dominated by business loans. But while business lending remains the largest category of bank loans, it has declined as a share of the total loan portfolio. Beginning after World War II, but accelerating in the 1960s and 1970s, other

---

Table 7-1
Income-Earning Assets of a Typical Commercial Bank

Loans
    Business
    Real Estate
    Consumer
    Brokers and Dealers
    Federal Funds Sold and Security Repurchase Agreements

Securities
    U.S. Government
        Treasury Bills
        Treasury Notes
        Treasury Bonds
    Municipal Securities
    Federal Agency Securities

---

types of loans—particularly residential mortgage loans and consumer installment loans—became a much more important part of bank portfolios. For example, as of March 1981, loans at commercial banks totaled $921.2 billion. Of these, $330.4 billion were commercial and industrial loans, $265 billion were real estate loans, and $172 billion were loans to individuals. The remaining $153.8 billion in loans were accounted for by a number of smaller categories. The historic association of commercial banks with business lending—which led to their being called "commercial" banks—while still of major importance, has been diminished by the movement of banks into these other areas of lending. Yet any examination of bank lending must still begin with business lending.

Business Lending Bank lending to business is divided between **short-term loans** and long-term loans called simply **term loans.** Short-term loans usually have one year or less to maturity from the time they are made, while term loans are over one year to maturity. Originally, almost all commercial bank lending was short term. The rationale for confining lending to the short term was the **real bills doctrine,** which was taken extremely seriously as a tenet of sound banking for many years. The real bills doctrine held that banks should make only short-term self-liquidating loans that would serve business needs and at the same time ensure sound lending matched to the short-term nature of bank deposit liabilities.

A self-liquidating loan finances production or business increases sufficient to redeem the loan. For example, an agricultural loan made to finance crop planting in the spring would be assumed to be self-liquidating because the sale of the resulting crop in the fall would provide sufficient funds to extinguish the debt. Similarly, a loan made to allow a merchant to increase inventories in anticipation of Christmas buying would also be considered self-liquidating since the loan would be redeemed from the proceeds of the merchant's sales.

While many bank loans are indeed self-liquidating, the weakness of the real bills doctrine as an "iron law of banking" can easily be seen. The extent to which a loan is self-liquidating depends on a number of factors, not all under the control of the banker. "Acts of nature" can interfere with agricultural production, and economic fluctuation may prevent individual businesses from reaching production or sales goals, thus preventing the repayment of loans. These disturbances may be beyond the ability of the banker to foresee when making lending decisions.

The banker may also evaluate loans differently depending on the reserve condition of the bank, judging some loans "self-liquidating" when the bank's lendable reserves are plentiful, and others not self-liquidating when reserves are tight, even though the lending opportunities are identical. The state of economic activity also contributes to a banker's lending decisions. In times of economic expansion, many loans are made that may not be made in times of economic contraction. This behavior can exacerbate economic fluctuation.

Despite the shortcomings of the real bills doctrine, it had become so ingrained as sound banking practice that it was incorporated explicitly into the Federal Reserve Charter Act of 1913. However, as its weaknesses became more apparent and as the demands of bank customers increased for longer term financing and for consumer and mortgage loans, and as banks began to view these lending opportunities as profitable, banks gradually abandoned their rigid adherence to this doctrine. Nevertheless, most short-term bank lending still finances projects that are by nature self-liquidating, including inventory and agricultural loans.

Term Loans In the post–World War II period, banks have been willing to grant loans to business for long-term purposes such as financing capital expenditures. Plant and equipment expenditures have typically been financed by larger businesses out of internally generated funds or in the capital markets. While these avenues of financing are still dominant, banks have made inroads into plant and equipment financing, particularly during those times in the 1970s when the capital markets have been inhospitable to new equity issues and long-term interest rates have generally been high. Long-term lending by banks has introduced a degree of diversification into banks' business loan portfolios that has been welcome for the stability it adds to earnings. The importance of long-term business lending by banks in recent years can be judged by the fact that at the end of 1980, over 50 percent of domestic business loans by large commercial banks were term loans.

The Rate of Interest on Business Loans The **prime rate** is the rate charged by banks on short-term loans made to their most credit-worthy business customers. The prime rate is perhaps the best known of bank interest rates. Its prominence in the financial press and in the financial community derives from its role as a benchmark. Short-term bank lending rates are, in general, scaled up from the prime rate. Thus, when the prime rate moves, it is taken by the financial community as symptomatic of short-term bank lending rate movement in general. Further, movement in the prime rate may give an indication of possible movement in long-term lending rates. Figure 7-1 shows

Figure 7-1
Prime Rate and Commercial Paper Rate (Three Month) Quarterly Averages, Third Quarter 1974 to First Quarter 1981

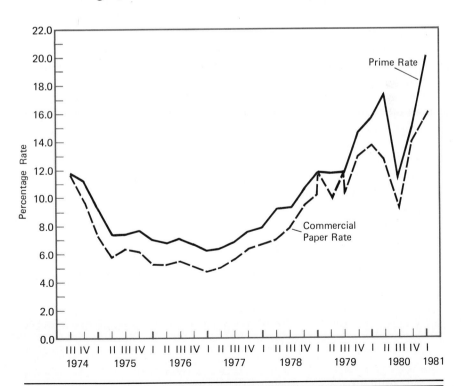

the prime rate from the third quarter of 1974 to the first quarter of 1981 and the three-month commercial paper rate for the same period. Note the close movement of the two short-term rates.

The relationship of the prime rate to short-term open market rates led a number of banks to formally tie the prime rate to open market rates of interest in the late 1970s. When the prime rate is determined by a formula linking it to an open market rate, it is known as a **floating prime rate.**[1] Usually the floating prime is linked to an open market rate such as that on commercial paper or Treasury bills. Often the secondary market rate on negotiable certificates of deposit is used, as it was by Citibank, the largest commercial bank that had at one time employed a floating prime.[2] The rationale behind using the certificate of deposit rate is to link the prime closely to the cost of funds to the bank.

Although the prime rate is thought of as a benchmark rate, the prime has appeared to have lost some of its significance in recent years. Starting in 1979 and accelerating in 1980 and 1981, there have been widespread reports of substantial discounting from the prevailing prime rate for favored customers. These favored customers generally have widespread alternatives for borrowing including the open market. In order for banks to compete for these customers and yet maintain a posted prime rate at a level they believe appropriate, they must offer discounts from the prime. This has led to some interesting situations. When a major commercial bank was asked by a Congressional committee investigating the discounting process to define its prime rate, it said essentially that the prime rate was the rate it periodically posted and called the prime rate.

This rather uninformative definition of the prime rate and the discounting process appears to diminish the importance of the prime. However, the attention paid by the financial community to periodic posted prime rate changes, and its still key role as a cornerstone of bank lending rates to business should not be ignored. Further, at times the prime rate, as well as any quoted business lending rate, can actually understate what the borrower is paying for a loan. This understatement results from possible **compensating balance** requirements. Such requirements can raise the effective cost of funds to a borrower.

Compensating Balances Compensating balances may be required by a bank as a condition of borrowing by a business firm. Com-

---

[1] Even though the prime rate floats, the minimum adjustment made by most banks is a quarter point increment or decrement and in recent years one-half and even one percentage point changes have become common.

[2] However, even banks that use floating primes do not always alter the rate when called for by the formula used. This has been particularly true when open market rates have been particularly volatile, such as in the first half of 1981. In fact, this volatility led Citibank to abandon its floating prime.

pensating balances usually entail the maintenance by the borrower of a specified level, on average, of usually noninterest-earning deposits (demand deposits) over the period for which the loan is outstanding. Compensating balances are often required as well to maintain open lines of credit that are pre-approved loans up to a specified amount. Many corporations keep such lines of credit to ensure ready access to credit on call. It is rare, but not unheard of, for a compensating balance to be in an interest-earning account, but the usual form is noninterest-earning. Compensating balances increase the return to the bank on the loan and may raise the cost to the borrower.[3]

To see why the bank's return and the customer's cost increase with a compensating balance, consider a $1 million loan made by a bank at prime. Compensating balances are usually 10 percent to 20 percent of the value of a loan or of the line of credit. Suppose that the agreed-upon amount is 10 percent. If the firm would have held zero in its demand deposit on balance and now holds $100,000, it has effectively borrowed $900,000 although it is paying the prime rate on $1 million. Suppose the prime rate is 12 percent. The firm is paying $120,000 at an annual rate for $900,000 or an effective rate of interest of 13.3 percent ($120,000/$900,000), not the stated prime of 12 percent. The bank makes use of the $100,000 interest-free demand deposit to acquire additional earning assets, thus raising its return.

However, the example above is extreme. Since compensating balances are calculated on maintaining some average deposit and, further, since the borrower maintains a demand deposit anyway, the borrower's cost is increased only to the extent that the compensating balance requirement requires the borrower to keep a higher average deposit than would otherwise be kept. Also, the compensating balance requirement is negotiable and brings even more variation into the interest rate charged by banks; and this, therefore, makes it more responsive to competitive factors. Banks do face competition for the corporate borrower not only from other commercial banks but from the open market.

Prominent corporations have resorted more and more to short-term financing by going directly to the open market. Commercial paper, which is short-term promissory notes issued by businesses, has become an increasingly important competitor for the business borrower. With the very high interest rates of the 1970s and early 1980s, large, well-known corporations have been increasingly tempted to try to save on bank lending fees by doing their own financing. This option is only open to a very select, well-known group of corporate borrowers, but it has flourished. The amount borrowed in the commercial paper market

---

[3] Compensating balances may also be implicit payments to a bank for services provided independent of any lending. This will be discussed below.

exceeded $132 billion in March 1981, the highest on record and almost double the amount outstanding at the end of 1977. Since corporate borrowings in the commercial paper market are for short periods of time, usually one to six months, and are for inventory and accounts receivable financing, it is likely that almost all of this financing would have come from commercial banks in the absence of the commercial paper market. Instead, credit is now provided by the purchasers of commercial paper—corporations, insurance companies, and other financial institutions.

The corporations issuing prime commercial paper of the highest quality have indeed reduced their borrowing costs.[4] For example, Figure 7-1 p. 157 shows the posted prime rate was above the three-month commercial paper rate during the entire period covered by the figure. This accounts for the popularity of this market and puts additional competitive pressure on the commercial banks. Many corporations, in anticipation of issuing commercial paper, secure back-up lines of credit at banks to facilitate the issuance and hence provide a cushion if the market proves unfavorable to a commercial paper issue at the time other commercial paper of the corporation comes due. The usual compensating balance requirements hold for these lines of credit as well. Even with compensating balance requirements, however, it is still usually cheaper for a highly rated issuer of commercial paper to finance in this market.

Bank Services to Business[5] In return for their loan and deposit business, a bank provides certain services to its business customers. Compensating balances, as we have discussed, are a means by which corporations "pay" for the maintenance of lines of credit with their banks. However, lines of credit are only one service provided to corporations by banks in return for compensating balances. As part of the overall strategy of corporate cash management to ensure maximum return on corporate funds, corporate treasurers have secured a number of services in return for the bank's use of corporate deposits. Table 7-2 lists some of these services provided by banks. As the table shows, these services are diverse. Cash management refers to a number of related services that banks provide, such as lock boxes to which corporate customers send payments that bypass corporate offices and go directly to the bank. The bank is thus able to process the payments

---

[4] Commercial paper is placed into three grades by Moody's Investors Service, Standard and Poor's, and Fitch Investors Services. It is the top grade that receives the best rate. If a corporation is in the lowest grade, it usually does not borrow in this market because it is unlikely to save anything over what it would be charged by a bank.

[5] This section is adapted from the Appendix to "The Market for Federal Funds and RP's," by Thomas D. Simpson of the Division of Research and Statistics, Board of Governors of the Federal Reserve System, typescript (1978). The Appendix entitled "Cash Management Practices" was prepared by Patricia Davis.

Table 7-2
Bank Services to Corporations

1. Lines of Credit
2. Cash Management
3. Payroll Services
4. Credit Investigation
5. Coin and Currency
6. Trust Services
7. Data Processing

quickly saving the corporation both time and money. Payroll services, background credit checks, and computer record keeping and reporting are among the other services provided.

Banks differ widely in determining the amount of corporate deposit balances necessary to compensate them for the provision of these services. The **earnings credit rate** (ECR) is a device banks use to determine the level of required balances a corporation must maintain in compensating balances. For example, suppose that the services used by a corporation are calculated by the bank to cost $50 a month. If the ECR is 8 percent, the customer must keep a monthly average balance of $7,500 ($50 divided by .0066, the monthly ECR, which is 08 divided by 12).

The ECR required is usually determined by comparison with some market rate. It may be tied to the Treasury bill rate or the six-month certificate of deposit rate. Sometimes it is tied to the bank's own yield on its portfolio, which really is a weighted average of various interest rates. A survey done in 1976 by the Federal Reserve Bank of Kansas City[6] shows the 91-day Treasury bill rate is the rate most often used to arrive at the ECR. Additional fees may be added to the ECR by the bank to arrive at the total charge that the customer must meet, such as the passing through to the customer of the cost to the bank in foregone interest of having to hold required reserves on the customer's demand deposits.

Real Estate Loans Prior to World War II, it was unusual for banks to make residential mortgage loans, although commercial mortgage loans had formed a small part of the bank loan portfolio. However, after the war, banks started moving cautiously into the residential market. In part, this attention by banks was stirred by the rapid increase

---

[6] Robert Knight, "Account Analysis Survey," typescript (Jan. 1977).

in housing construction that occurred after the war. However, bank commitment was still modest until the mid-1960s, when the level of interest rates generally rose. Banks then decided to take advantage of the fact that mortgage interest rates had risen substantially. The residential mortgage loan was regarded by banks as a stable source of earnings since mortgages are long-term instruments. Making mortgage loans at what appear to be relatively high rates locks in the return on this portion of the bank portfolio for a long time. Further, banks made many mortgage loans that carried federal government guarantees through such agencies as the Federal Housing Administration (FHA) and the Veterans Administration (VA). In this way, default risk on the overall mortgage portfolio was reduced.

From the mid-1960s on, banks have been major mortgage lenders in the residential market. In most years in the 1970s and early 1980s, banks were the second leading residential mortgage lender after savings and loan associations. While residential mortgage lending has proved beneficial for banks,the benefits have not been all positive for the mortgage market. Table 7-1 (p. 155) shows that banks have a great deal of flexibility in the asset mix in their portfolios. Since short-term rates tend to change more rapidly than long-term rates in general and mortgage rates in particular, during periods of rising interest rates banks have an incentive to cut their mortgage lending in order to make additional loans in other lending areas or to purchase securities. The mortgage market itself is very cyclical. As a result of bank lending behavior, this cycle is intensified as banks come into the market to make substantial amounts of mortgage loans when credit is easily available and shift out of the market during periods of tight credit. Thus, both the cyclical peaks and the cyclical troughs of the mortgage credit cycle are intensified. Since home building follows mortgage credit availability, and mortgate lending rates, the housing market cycle is also intensified. In this way bank behavior no doubt contributed to the severe decline in mortgage lending and housing in 1966, 1969–70, 1973–75, and 1980–81. For example, banks reduced their new mortgage lending from $32 billion in 1979 to $19.4 billion in 1980.

Consumer Installment Lending The introduction of the bank credit card in the mid-1960s marked the beginning of very aggressive growth in bank consumer lending. Banks had increased their share of the consumer installment market significantly in the post-war years, particularly in auto lending, but the introduction of bank credit cards marks a watershed. Since that time, bank consumer lending has burgeoned. In the mid-1970s, with relatively slack business loan demand, banks extended their consumer effort. For example, Citibank, the nation's second largest commercial bank, increased its consumer loan portfolio by 60 percent in 1978 alone. While Citibank has been the most aggressive in consumer lending, many other banks have behaved similarly. These activities have been fueled by national campaigns to enlist credit card holders and grant personal lines of credit. Banks have discovered that consumer lending is a way of overcoming, to some degree, restrictions that prevent banks from branching across state lines.[7] Consumer borrowers have generally been loyal to the banks in which they have deposit accounts. However, by the nationwide attempts to obtain credit card holders, large banks have penetrated this loyalty and have built a potential deposit base on which to build, if the interstate branching restrictions are lifted and banks are permitted to branch nationwide.

The motivation behind consumer lending stems from the profitability inherent in this lending. Consumer demand for credit has been very strong since the mid-1970s, in part due to inflation, which has elicited a "buy now" psychology and made even high lending rates attractive. Banks have actively accommodated the demand and have benefited from the relatively high rates of return that consumer lending commands. From their inception, credit card financing rates have generally been at the upper limit permitted by states, in most cases 18 percent on unpaid balances. These state limits were preempted in 1980 by federal legislation, and in most cases credit card charges now exceed 20 percent. In addition, the merchant who accepts the card also pays a fee for each credit card transaction. Furthermore, some banks have also instituted a small annual fee to be paid by credit card holders. Banks have generally found these arrangements lucrative.

In addition, bank holding companies have made further inroads into the consumer lending market by acquiring personal finance companies. While loans made through these companies do not appear in the portfolio of the commercial bank, the acquisition of finance companies does demonstrate the commitment that commercial banks have to consumer lending.

Loans to Brokers and Dealers The major portion of loans to securities brokers and dealers are made to carry customer margin accounts. Securities can be purchased by making a down payment on the purchase price and borrowing the remainder from a broker. However, since brokers are not depository institutions, the funds that brokers need for loans to margin account customers must in turn be borrowed from banks. To facilitate this borrowing, brokers have prearranged lines of credit with commercial banks that are drawn upon to finance the broker loans to customers. Since the loans are fully collateralized (secured) by the securities that have been purchased and in addition are "call loans" (repayable to the bank on demand),

---

[7] The McFadden Act of 1927 prohibits commercial banks from establishing branches outside their home state; however, it does not prohibit the solicitation of loan and deposit business outside the home state, and large banks have increasingly gone after this national market.

the rate charged by banks to brokers is very favorable, usually under the prime rate.

The margin requirement (the required down payment) is set by the Federal Reserve Board of Governors. In May 1981, it was 50 percent on stocks and convertible bonds. This means that in order to borrow to purchase a stock, the buyer would have to put up 50 percent of the purchase price, borrowing the remainder from the broker. The broker, in turn, borrows from the commercial bank. If the margin requirement was 60 percent, a 60 percent down payment would be required of the buyer, and the buyer would be said to be buying stock on 60 percent margin. While the broker generally charges a higher rate to the customer than the broker pays to the bank in order to cover transactions costs and make a profit, the customer could not in general obtain a better rate by going directly to the bank. Brokers get favorable rates from the bank because of loan volume, the call provision of the loan, and the size of the deposit balances they hold.

In addition to loans to brokers, banks also make loans to securities dealers and other financial institutions. Since securities dealers are continually buying and selling securities in the secondary market, they generally hold securities on hand (in inventory) that exceed their own capital. Thus, they borrow from commercial banks to finance their securities inventories, usually at terms similar to a securities broker borrowing to finance margin account lending. The most interesting of the loans to financial institutions are the loans banks make to each other through the federal funds market.

Federal Funds Federal funds are reserves that one bank lends to another bank for one day (overnight). Though federal funds have nothing to do with the federal government, despite their name, trading in federal funds is accomplished through the Federal Reserve System. If a bank has excess reserves on a particular day and another bank is deficient in reserves, the bank that needs reserves can borrow from the bank that holds excess reserves. The transaction is easily accomplished by a phone call. Funds are transferred from the bank that is lending the federal funds (technically, selling federal funds) to the bank borrowing federal funds (technically, buying federal funds).[8] The transaction is usually facilitated by the Federal Reserve, which transfers reserves from the depository institution account of the selling bank to that of the buying bank and reverses the process the next day.

The selling bank sells federal funds because of the interest return received on its lending. The interest rate on these loans is called the

---

[8] The terms "buying" and "selling" of federal funds rather than "borrowing" or "lending" were introduced to enable banks to avoid various technical limitations on the amount of lending to any one borrower set by regulation.

federal funds rate. It is expressed, as are all interest rates, at an annual rate, even though the loan is made for only one day. Since the amounts loaned in this market are very large, even a one-day loan can yield a substantial return. This is particularly attractive to the selling bank, since excess reserves otherwise would earn no return. For example, if the federal funds rate is 10 percent and a bank sells federal funds of $50 million to another bank, the return is $13,698 in interest ($50 million multiplied by 10 percent divided by 365 days).

Sellers of federal funds are typically smaller commercial banks while buyers are usually larger, more aggressive commercial banks. Later in this chapter liability management will be discussed, and the reasons for the differing behavior of banks in the federal funds market will be explored in detail. However, as pointed out in the last chapter, major banks aim at zero excess reserves when interest rates are high, as in recent years. This behavior on the part of large banks has contributed to the rapid growth of the federal funds market over the last decade. These large banks have used the federal funds market to cover reserve deficiencies that often result from their tightly managed reserve positions.[9] On the other hand, the selling bank finds the opportunity of using its excess reserves profitably in the federal funds market attractive.

The federal funds rate itself is very important. The prime rate, which is a benchmark for short-term bank lending rates, is influenced considerably by the federal funds rate. This stems from the fact that the federal funds rate is a cost of bank funds to the buying bank. Further, in the past the federal funds rate has been used by the Federal Reserve as a key interest rate in its conduct of monetary policy; as a result, at times it has been regarded by the financial community as indicating the direction of the Fed's monetary policy.

Securities

While lending is the primary business of commercial banks, banks also hold substantial amounts of securities in their portfolios. Because liquidity, return, and risk minimization are the governing principles of bank portfolio management, securities—while yielding a return—are held primarily to increase portfolio liquidity and to reduce overall portfolio risk. In addition, when the demand for loans slows, securities provide a readily available earning asset that enables a bank to achieve some rate of return with its excess reserves. Of the three types of securities listed in Table 7-1 (p. 155), U.S. government securities are held by banks primarily for considerations of liquidity and risk minimization. Federal agency securities are held for the same reasons, but both

---

[9] Aggressive banks may also use federal funds to take advantage of attractive lending opportunities rather than exclusively to correct reserve deficiencies.

liquidity and safety are sacrificed somewhat for a small additional return. Municipal securities, however, are included in bank portfolios primarily for return.

Banks are not permitted to hold corporate stock for their own portfolios.[10] Banks may hold corporate bonds of very high quality, but these account for such a small part of their securities holdings that they are omitted from Table 7-1. For example, in 1980 banks purchased only $600 million in corporate securities compared to $25.6 billion in U.S. government securities. Banks can, however, buy, sell, and hold corporate stock for trust accounts that they manage and are active traders in both stocks and corporate bonds for these accounts. These securities, however, are not part of bank portfolio holdings; rather they belong to the individuals whose assets are being managed by the bank. Government securities held by banks for their own portfolios include Treasury bills, Treasury notes, and Treasury bonds. Thus, the entire maturity spectrum of government securities is covered.

Treasury Bills Treasury bills are one of the largest category of securities issued by the U.S. government to finance the federal debt. They are short-term money market securities issued for one year or less. Actual maturities issued are 91-day (three-month) bills, 182-day (six-month) bills and one-year bills. There are also occasional issues of very short-term maturity bills called cash management bills. These bills are designed for corporate cash management purposes as the name implies.

Treasury bills make up a prominent portion of banks' government securities holdings. The attractiveness of Treasury bills to banks is the high degree of liquidity the bills possess. The secondary market for these securities is very broad since the amount of bills outstanding is large and bills are actively traded. The short-term maturities of these securities also make them attractive to banks, since prices do not fluctuate substantially over short periods of time.[11] Further, since they are government securities, default risk is not an issue. Because of these attributes, banks are easily able to dispose of large amounts of these securities on short notice. This is particularly useful for a bank to accommodate increased loan demand quickly. The bills are sold and the funds loaned out. Treasury bills are so liquid in fact that they are sometimes called **secondary reserves** to reflect this liquidity.

Treasury Notes Treasury notes are issued in maturity ranges of two to ten years. Since they are longer-term securities, under usual

---

[10] There are some very minor exceptions to the prohibition of stock holdings by banks. These include Federal Reserve stock that must be held by member commercial banks.

[11] The shorter the term to maturity of a security, the less the fluctuation in price necessary to reflect a change in interest rates.

circumstances they yield somewhat more than Treasury bills. Yet they are also very liquid and possess the same safety attributes as Treasury bills. Banks have tended to favor holdings of government securities in the one to five-year maturity range, and hence Treasury notes are popular bank portfolio holdings. For example, large commercial banks reported for the week ended April 29, 1981, that about 60 percent of the government securities they held had one to five years to maturity. By giving up some small amount of liquidity and accepting the possibility of more market risk—since the price of notes fluctuates more than that of bills—the bank is able to increase its return by holding notes.

Treasury Bonds Treasury bonds are issued in maturities of 10–30 years. They are not as liquid as Treasury bills and Treasury notes because the market is not as large—only about 14 percent of marketable Treasury securities outstanding are Treasury bonds—and the price fluctuations of long-term securities increase market risk. As is the case with all Treasury securities, however, Treasury bonds have no default risk. Because of the lower liquidity of Treasury bonds compared to bills and notes, typically bonds are bought for longer-term investment by banks. Further, since they are not a preferred long-term bank investment, bank holdings of Treasury bonds are rather small.[12] For example, large commercial banks reported that for the week ended April 29, 1981, holdings of government securities over five years to maturity, not all of which are bonds, constituted only about 11 percent of their holdings of government securities.

Municipal Securities Municipal securities—those issued by state and local governmental entities—are held in bank portfolios primarily for the return they offer. Yields on municipal securities, as reported in the financial press for example, appear quite low. However the low yield is deceptive. Returns on municipal securities are exempt from federal income taxes, and as a result, the yield on municipals compares favorably to the after-tax return on other securities.[13] Banks are in the corporate tax bracket of 46 percent if they have income above $50,000. Thus, to achieve the same return on a taxable security after taxes as on a municipal security, the bank would need to earn almost twice as much on the taxable security.

---

[12] There is a potential source of confusion that should be addressed. Treasury bonds are *not* U.S. Savings Bonds. U.S. Savings Bonds are nonnegotiable (they cannot be resold on the open market) saving instruments used to finance the debt, as are all other Treasury securities (including the Treasury bonds), by offering individuals a return in exchange for their funds. However, savings bonds differ from the marketable Treasury securities that have been discussed above because of the nonnegotiability of the instrument and the fixed yield. Savings Bonds make up only about 7 percent of total government securities outstanding.

[13] Returns on Treasury securities are not exempt from federal income taxes, although they are exempt from state income taxes. However, the state exemption is of considerably less importance, since state taxes are much lower.

This tax exempt feature has made municipal securities popular holdings for bank portfolios. Further, rates on municipals have risen substantially (absolutely and relatively) since the New York City fiscal crisis in 1976, when New York came close to defaulting on its obligations. This event shook the entire municipal bond market. As a result, municipal securities have become even more attractive to banks in recent years so that bank holdings of municipal securities currently exceed holdings of Treasury securities by a substantial margin. About 47 percent of the securities holdings of large commercial banks in the week ending April 29, 1981, were municipal securities.

Federal Agency Securities A number of agencies are sponsored by the federal government to serve some public purpose, but operate independently. The largest of these agencies is concerned with providing assistance to the mortgage market. The Federal National Mortgage Association, known as Fannie Mae, buys mortgages that have already been issued in the secondary mortgage market. While a federally sponsored agency, Fannie Mae is privately owned and its stock is traded on the New York Stock Exchange. Since it became a private corporation in 1968 (it had previously been a formal part of the federal government), Fannie Mae has purchased about $57 billion in mortgages in the secondary market. The Federal Home Loan Bank System, another federally sponsored agency, also provides assistance to the mortgage market by making loans, called **advances,** to savings and loan associations, the largest group of mortgage lenders. In addition, there are other federally sponsored agencies such as the Federal Land Banks and the Federal Intermediate Credit Banks. The federally sponsored agencies are not supported by the federal government out of tax revenue or the proceeds of federal borrowing. Rather, the activities of these agencies are financed by the issuance of securities in the open market. These securities are known as "agencies" and over $166 billion were outstanding as of February 1981.

Federally sponsored agency securities are considered to be almost as safe from default as Treasury securities. While not backed by the "full faith and credit" of the United States government, as are Treasury securities, agencies are secured by lines of credit to the Treasury and the moral obligation of the government. As a result, the market regards the risk of default on these securities as very small, and, consequently, agencies yield returns just slightly above those of Treasury securities of the same maturity. Banks hold agencies in their portfolio because they can get a slightly better return than on Treasury securities, without meaningfully sacrificing safety or liquidity. On the latter point, it should be noted that the market for agencies is quite broad because of the large amount of securities outstanding and the safety of the obligations. Hence, banks can sell them easily. Agency securities constituted about 14 percent of security holdings of large commercial banks in April 1981.

Bank Security Holdings: Summary In summary, banks hold securities primarily for reasons of liquidity and safety; the return they yield is secondary. This contrasts with the loan portion of the bank portfolio, which overall may not be as safe or as liquid as the security portion of the portfolio, but which yields a higher rate of return. The typical bank earning asset portfolio consists of approximately 75 percent loans and 25 percent securities.

Bank Liabilities

Major categories of bank liabilities include demand deposits, time and savings deposits, and borrowing, as shown in Table 7-3. Demand deposits require little attention here since they have been explored fully in the last chapter. Demand deposit offerings set commercial banks apart from other financial institutions, although there is a growing amount of other checkable deposit accounts offered by nonbank financial institutions. The other major categories of commercial bank sources of funds do need to be discussed in detail.

Savings and Time Deposits

Although all savings deposits at commercial banks may be called time deposits, it is common to distinguish between passbook accounts and other time deposits at commercial banks. Passbook accounts are referred to as savings deposits and time deposits is used to refer to all other types of savings deposits at commercial banks.

The total of time and savings deposits at commercial banks exceeds the amount of demand deposits. For example, in April 1981, demand deposits totaled $357 billion at commercial banks while time and savings deposits were $795 billion. Until the early 1970s, demand deposits had always been larger than time and savings deposits. How-

**Table 7-3
Major Liabilities of Commercial Banks**

Demand Deposits
Savings Deposits
Time Deposits
Borrowings
    From the Federal Reserve
    From Other Commercial Banks (Federal Funds)
    From Others (Repurchase Agreements)

ever, with the increase in interest rates in the 1970s, the liability composition changed. Most of the growth has in fact taken place in the
time deposit category as commercial banks have become aggressive
in seeking time deposit accounts. This bank aggressiveness has been
aided by regulatory changes that have allowed new types of time deposit accounts to be created and that have relaxed some of the interest
rate restrictions limiting the amount of interest banks can pay on certain
categories of time deposits. Under legislation passed in 1980, all interest rate restrictions on interest payable on savings and time deposits
will be eliminated by 1986 at the latest. Current plans call for such
elimination by 1985.

Savings Deposits

Passbook deposits at commercial banks are easily accessible since
they can be withdrawn on presentation of the passbook. Legally, the
bank can require that thirty days notice of a withdrawal be given,
but, in practice, the notice is waived. As a result of the ready availability
of these funds to the depositor, banks historically have paid low rates
of interest on these deposits. The interest rate that can be offered
is, in addition, limited by regulation. In 1982 the maximum allowable
rate was 5.25 percent.

Because the rate on passbook accounts has been so low in the
late 1970s and early 1980s compared with time deposit and open
market rates, deposits in passbook accounts have declined in recent
years. Time deposit accounts have increased rapidly in this same period
so that the decline in passbook deposits relative to time deposits has
been dramatic. Thus, an inexpensive source of funds has contributed
a smaller percentage of total bank funds while the more expensive
time deposit source has contributed a larger percentage. This rise in
the overall cost of funds to banks has been passed on in higher lending
rates. Once interest rate ceilings are totally eliminated, banks will be
able to compete more aggressively for passbook savings by raising
passbook rates. The convenience of the passbook account may compensate some savers for giving up higher returns on time deposits if
the rate spread between passbook and time deposits is narrowed.
This may once again restore some of the popularity of passbook accounts, although at a higher cost to the banks.

Time Deposits

In order to secure commitments on funds for longer periods of time
from depositors, a device developed earlier, the certificate of deposit
or CD, became important in the 1960s. At first, CDs were geared
only to large depositors—they were issued in denominations of
$100,000 or more. While the $100,000 minimum still holds for negotiable certificates of deposit, there has more recently been a substantial

increase in the holdings of smaller denomination nonnegotiable CDs by consumers. In exchange for the depositors' giving up immediate access to funds, banks are willing to pay a higher rate of interest on these types of deposits. As a result, CDs have been favorably received by corporations and consumers alike. Combining negotiable and nonnegotiable CDs, the total exceeds the amount of savings deposits at commercial banks by a wide margin. In April 1981, time deposits totaled $572.2 billion compared to $223 billion in savings deposits at all commercial banks.

The real breakthrough in the issuance of CDs came in 1961 when the First National City Bank of New York (now Citibank) for the first time issued large CDs that were negotiable. This development of a secondary market for CDs meant that although CDs were issued for specified periods of time, a corporation (CDs were originally designed for corporations) could obtain a CD from a bank; and, if funds were needed by the corporation prior to maturity, the CD could be sold in the open market. As a result, the secondary market for CDs has expanded very rapidly.[14] The success of the large CDs led to the development of the consumer certificate.

Consumer certificates of deposit are issued by banks for much smaller amounts than the $100,000 required for negotiable CDs. These certificates offer a higher rate of return than that payable on passbook accounts. Although consumer certificates are, in general, not negotiable, the funds can be recovered before maturity by the payment of a penalty. Effective July 1, 1979, for certificates issued after that date, the penalty is six months' loss of interest if the certificate matures in more than one year and three months loss of interest if the certificate matures in less than one year.

Consumer CDs vary from six months to eight years in maturity. In general, interest payments tend to increase with the maturity. However, the most popular of consumer certificates of deposit are the six-month market certificates that were first offered in 1978. The rate on these certificates is permitted to vary weekly depending on the latest auction rates on six-month Treasury bills. On new certificates banks may pay one quarter of a percentage point more than the average yield at the previous four auctions. Once a depositor purchases a money market certificate, however, the rate on that certificate is fixed for the six-month holding period. These certificates are sold only for deposits of $10,000 or more. Another relatively recent certificate that has attracted some depositor attention is the two-and-one-half-year certificate. The offering rate on this certificate is determined every two weeks by the rate on new two-and-one-half-year Treasury notes.

---

[14] Another key change took place in 1973 when the Federal Reserve regulation fixing the maximum allowable rate on CDs over $100,000 was suspended, and banks were free to compete by interest rate for CDs.

Originally there was an 11.75 percent interest ceiling on these certificates for commercial banks. This ceiling prevented these certificates from growing very rapidly. However, in August 1981 the ceiling was removed on the two-and-one-half-year certificate. Effective May 1, 1982, ceilings on three-and-one-half-year or longer certificates were also removed, permitting banks to pay competitive rates on these certificates. Also effective on that date, banks were permitted to offer a three-month saving certificate similar to the six-month certificate but tied to the rate on three-month Treasury bills.

In the past the maximum interest payable on all certificates has been set by the Federal Reserve for member banks (however, the regulation on all large CDs has been suspended since 1973) and by agreement with the Federal Deposit Insurance Corporation (FDIC); the maximum rate is the same for nonmember banks. (Virtually all commercial bank deposits are insured by the FDIC; and, therefore, essentially all banks must abide by the regulations of this organization). In addition, other financial intermediaries such as savings and loan associations offer certificates of deposit at rates also fixed by regulation. However, 1980 legislation requires that all rate ceilings be completely eliminated by 1986 at the latest. To handle the phase-out, all ceilings are being decided upon by a committee called the Depository Institutions Deregulation Committee, which includes among others the Chairman of the Federal Reserve Board of Governors.[15] It is this committee that has eliminated the ceilings on the two-and-one-half-year and three-and-one-half-year and over certificates.

Certificates of deposit have been an important innovation by commercial banks. Besides being popular with depositors, the large certificates are important in the aggressive liability management undertaken by commercial banks in recent years. This will be discussed later in this chapter.

Borrowing

Commercial banks can borrow from the Federal Reserve,[16] other commercial banks, or other nonbank institutions, as shown in Table 7-3 (p. 169). Federal Reserve lending was the original manner in which the Fed was expected to provide an "elastic currency." It has always been stressed by the Fed that borrowing at the "discount window"

---

[15] Other voting members are the Secretary of the Treasury, and the chairmen of the Federal Home Loan Bank Board, the Federal Deposit Insurance Corporation, and the National Credit Union Administration.

[16] In the past only member banks could borrow from the Fed unless the Fed declared an emergency in which case borrowing privileges could be extended to nonmember banks. However, with the imposition of reserve requirements on nonmember banks and nonbank depository institutions offering checkable deposits, any institution required to hold reserves may borrow from the Fed. In practice the overwhelming amount of borrowing from the Fed is still done by member banks.

is a privilege, not a right, and could be denied to banks that abused this privilege. This stricture is necessary since the discount rate—the interest rate the Fed charges on bank borrowings—is often below open-market rates and banks would be tempted to borrow large amounts to relend at higher rates. Since the discount window is not expected to enhance bank profitability but to allow banks to meet temporary reserve deficiencies, the Fed closely monitors borrowing by banks. At times, when the discount rate has been substantially below open-market rates, banks have increased their borrowing, but abuse of the discount window has never proved to be a major problem because banks value the discount privilege too much to endanger their access to it. (The Fed has also tried to keep the discount rate in line with open-market rates, raising the rate when open-market rates substantially exceed the discount rate, thus attempting to make abuse of the discount window less tempting.) As a result, other sources of borrowing to acquire additional reserves have proved more popular.

The federal funds market has grown rapidly in recent years, though it has existed since the 1920s. Recall that the federal funds market is where banks borrow and lend reserves overnight at the federal funds rate. A number of changes in the 1960s and 1970s have substantially enhanced the attractiveness of this market. The most important of these changes has been the high level of interest rates in the late 1960s and particularly in the late 1970s and early 1980s. These high rates make it expensive for banks with excess reserves to hold these idle for even a day, and so these reserves have been offered in the federal funds market. On the other hand, the high level of interest rates has meant that banks with lending opportunities are eager to acquire additional reserves, and they have tapped the federal funds market for these reserves.

Bank use of the federal funds market has been at a substantially higher level than borrowing at the discount window in recent years. At the end of April 1981, the Federal Reserve had $2.3 billion in discount loans outstanding, while in the same month the average level of outstanding federal funds loans was well over $50 billion. Thus, the reluctance of banks to borrow at the discount window can be seen in these data, especially when it is realized that the federal funds rate is generally above the discount rate charged by the Fed on borrowing. However, when the funds rate exceeds the discount rate by a substantial margin, there does appear to be some noticeable (though small in dollar amount) increase in discount window borrowing. Usually, however, the Fed will raise the discount rate if these two rates remain too far out of line for very long.

In addition to high interest rates, certain regulatory changes in the 1960s and the 1970s also made the federal funds market more attractive. In 1964, the Fed authorized banks to borrow federal funds from member or nonmember banks even if the borrowing did not involve funds transfer at the Fed. Prior to this ruling, federal funds borrowing had to involve the transfer of funds at the Fed from one member bank account to another. In 1970, the Fed allowed savings and loan associations, some other financial institutions, and some government agencies to be considered "banks" for the purpose of federal funds borrowing. This increased the breadth of the federal funds market considerably.

A regulatory change that was not specifically aimed at the federal funds market, nonetheless, had the indirect effect of further enhancing this market. In 1968, the Federal Reserve changed the way in which reserve requirements are computed. The reserve requirement is met, not on current deposits, but on the average level of deposits at a bank two weeks before.[17] This means that in the week when banks have to meet reserve requirements, they know precisely the level required. Any excess can be immediately lent in the federal funds market and any deficiency made up in the market. Thus, the regulatory changes noted above as well as the interest rates of the 1970s combined to expand the federal funds market considerably. In December 1968, the average daily level of federal funds outstanding was only $7 billion compared to the over $50 billion in the early 1980s.

Another instrument of commercial bank borrowing expanded very rapidly in the 1970s as well, the repurchase agreement or RP. Unlike the federal funds market, which essentially involves transactions between two banks, the RP market involves transactions between borrowing commercial banks and nonbank institutions, including corporations and state and local governments. Under federal law, commercial banks cannot borrow from nonbanks. The RP is essentially a legal subterfuge around these restrictions. It entails the sale of a Treasury or federal agency security to a nonbank institution, such as a corporation, with the agreement to repurchase the security at a later date, perhaps a day or a week. Typically, repurchase agreements of this sort rarely exceed thirty days, although they are renewable. The repurchase price the bank pays is agreed upon at the time of the sale and is higher than what the bank received, thus yielding a return to the lender. Since the loan is fully collateralized by the security, the rate is usually slightly below the federal funds rate.

By 1981, it is estimated that outstanding RPs averaged about $50 billion. The key regulatory change that allowed this market to flourish occurred in 1969 when the Fed exempted RPs from reserve requirements and interest rate ceilings.[18] RPs have become quite attrac-

---

[17] The Federal Reserve announced a change in principle in June 1982 so that reserve requirements would be met on the current level of deposits. However, no effective date for this change had been stipulated as this book goes to press.

[18] In the late 1970s, the Fed had periodically imposed various marginal reserve requirements on "managed liabilities" that include repurchase agreements. However, these have apparently had little effect in discouraging the use of RPs, and in July 1980 they were eliminated entirely.

tive to potential lenders and have become an integral part of corporate cash management. The attractiveness of RPs to a corporate treasurer is due to their maturity flexibility and risk-free return. If a corporate treasurer has some funds available for a short period of time, say a week, he may not be able to find an alternative security that matures at exactly the moment he needs the funds and therefore risks having to sell the security when its price is falling. With an RP, the maturity can be tailored to the corporation's needs, and the return is guaranteed at the time the RP agreement is entered into.

Repurchase agreements have proved especially attractive for the large, aggressive commercial banks that are the main issuers of RPs. Since the funds generated through RPs are nonreservable (that is, no reserve requirement must be met on them) the entire amount is available to acquire income-earning assets. Even if the funds are already in the bank in a corporate demand deposit account, for example, the transfer to an RP releases the required reserves held against the demand deposit, although the bank must pay an interest return on the funds. However, the bank may have otherwise lost these funds to an open-market purchase by the corporation, so RPs may also be considered defensive responses by the bank to retain interest sensitive funds.

In addition, all else being equal, banks are able to pay more for these funds than they can on time deposits because there is no reserve requirement on RPs. For example, suppose the certificate of deposit rate is 10 percent and the reserve requirement on large CDs is 6 percent. Then banks are really paying 10.64 percent for each $1,000 of the CD ($100/[$1,000 − .06($1,000)]) and can pay up to this rate on RPs. The use of RPs by aggressive banks has become an integral part of liability management.

Liability Management

Commercial banks are sometimes popularly regarded as rather passive institutions. They await the arrival of deposits and then use these funds to acquire income-earning assets. However, a key part of modern commercial banking is liability management. Liability management means that banks are actively utilizing liability items to raise funds that will then be profitably reloaned or used to make up reserve requirement deficiencies. In a sense, banks are gaining liquidity from the liability side of their balance sheets.

Managed liabilities include such nondeposit items as federal funds, repurchase agreements, and Eurodollar borrowing as well as large certificates of deposit. These instruments all have in common a market-determined rate of interest. That is, there are no regulations governing the maximum rate payable on managed liabilities, and banks can bid whatever they feel necessary and profitable for funds raised in those categories. The most aggressive liability managers are the large commercial banks, particularly the money center banks in New York. Because they are large and well-known institutions, they can usually obtain funds at rates that, under normal circumstances, allow these funds to be profitably employed. Smaller, less well-known institutions would generally have to pay more to attract substantial amounts of managed liabilities and typically raise a much smaller proportion of their funds in this way. In fact, smaller banks are often on the other side of the market, selling Federal funds to larger banks.

Many banks have become so active in managing their liabilities that they are continuously in the market to raise additional loanable funds and to meet Federal Reserve requirements. No longer do they regard borrowing as a temporary means of coping with reserve deficiencies. Borrowing becomes an integral part of bank management.

Aggressive liability management shows no signs of abating as a technique of bank management. While the high interest rates of the 1970s and early 1980s have spurred this activity, it is not clear whether such behavior would change if interest rates were to return to lower levels. Banks have invested substantially in acquiring the expertise to manage their liabilities aggressively and with this investment behind them, the use of the liability side of the balance sheet for liquidity is unlikely to be abandoned, even in a lower interest rate climate.

The Consolidated Balance Sheet of the Commercial Banking System

The major assets and liabilities of the commercial banking system have now been discussed. Table 7-4 presents the consolidated balance sheet of the commercial banking system for December 1980. By examining the table, we can see the magnitudes involved for the categories of assets and liabilities so far discussed and the percentage of the total each category represents. In addition, some items in the table have not been explained as yet, and a brief mention of these is appropriate.

On the asset side of the balance sheet, the cash category includes vault cash as well as depository institution deposits at the Fed and correspondent balances. This category also includes cash items in the process of collection—checks currently in the clearing process.

Equity capital appears on the right side of the balance sheet. This category includes capital stock as well as any retained earnings (profits not paid out to bank owners). Bank capital requirements are relatively stringent and must be met for either a national or state charter. The requirements for each type of charter differ, and requirements for state charters vary from state to state. The amount of bank capital sets some categorical limits on bank lending, depending on the type of charter. For example, a national bank may not lend more than 10

Table 7-4

Consolidated Balance Sheet of the Commercial Banking System, December 1980
(Billions of Dollars)

Asset Account		Liability and Capital Account	
Cash	$ 194.2 (12.6%)	Total Deposits	$1,187.4 (77.3%)
Total Securities	325.8 (21.2%)	Demand Deposits	$432.2 (28.1%)
U.S. Treasury	$111.2 (7.2%)	Time Deposits	553.8 (36.0%)
Other	214.6 (14.0%)	Savings Deposits	201.3 (13.1%)
Total Loans (Excluding		Borrowings[3]	156.4 (10.2%)
Interbank)	851.4 (55.4%)	Other Liabilities	79.0 (5.1%)
Commercial and		Equity Capital	114.2 (7.4%)
Industrial	281.5 (18.3%)		
Other[1]	569.9 (37.1%)		
Other Assets[2]	165.6 (10.8%)		
Total Assets	$1,537.0 (100%)	Total Liabilities and Capital	$1,537.0 (100%)

[1] Includes mortgage loans and consumer loans.
[2] Includes loans to U.S. commercial banks (federal funds sales).
[3] Includes federal funds purchases and repurchase agreements.

Source: Federal Reserve *Bulletin*, March 1981.

percent of its capital to any single borrower. This provision is intended to limit potential abuse and risk to the bank. The "other" categories in the balance sheet combine items of less economic importance and include such items as the value of bank buildings on the asset side and utility bills outstanding on the liability side of the balance sheet.

WHAT'S IN A NAME?

Lending at Less Than Prime Rates Produces a PR Problem for Banks

By LINDLEY H. CLARK JR.

According to Webster's Dictionary the "prime rate" is supposed to be "the most favorable rate of interest available on loans from banks."

There's only one trouble with that definition: It's wrong.

The prime rate has been a source of growing controversy over the past year. It began 1980 at 15½%, zoomed to 20% in April, plummeted to 11% in August, and then shot up to a record 21½% by the end of the year before edging down to the current level of 18½% to 19%.

Understanding Prices

Highly volatile and just plain high rates were irritating enough for borrowers. Some smaller borrowers, with their rates pegged at levels a percentage point or more above the prime, became even more disturbed when they found that many large companies were getting loans

rates well *below* the prime rate. The extent of this below-prime practice is detailed in the accompanying table.

Fernand J. St Germain (D., R.I.), the new chairman of the House Banking Committee, is no man to ignore a popular financial controversy. Last month he fired off letters to the chief executives of the 10 largest commercial banks in the U.S. demanding that they explain themselves. Responses are due by March 12.

"I would think the banking industry would be most anxious to have its prices known and fully understood by all its customers," Rep. St Germain says.

Indeed the banks are anxious, as well as a little nervous. They're nervous enough about the situation, in fact, that it's difficult to find a banker who will discuss the matter in detail for the record. Some of them may have to go on the record, however, if Rep. St Germain decides to schedule public hearings. He says

Undercutting the Prime Interest Rate

1980 Period	Prime Rate	Percent of Business Loans Made at Rates Below Prime		Spread Between Prime Rate And Average Rate on Loans Made Below Prime (in Percentage Points)	
		48 Largest Banks	Medium and Smaller Banks	48 Largest Banks	Medium and Smaller Banks
Feb. 4–9	15¼%	50.0%	15.2%	1.23	2.11
May 5–10	17½%–18½%	53.0	26.8	4.13	2.47
Aug. 4–8	10¾%–11%	57.9	16.3	1.08	1.20
Nov. 3–8	14½%–15½%	20.3	16.0	.65	1.77

Source: Federal Reserve System Board of Governors

he hasn't decided whether to hold hearings. "It will depend on the responses to the letters," says a spokesman for his office.

In Atlanta, Jackie Kleiner, a lawyer and business professor, has filed suit against the First National Bank of Atlanta charging that the bank violated truth-in-lending laws by tying his loans to a stated prime while it and other banks gave below-prime loans to others. The bank declines to comment on the suit.

First National may have a problem, legal authorities suggest, because Mr. Kleiner's contract specifically defines his interest rate as one percentage point above the rate charged the bank's "best commercial borrowers."

"That was a sloppy contract," says an official of a major New York City bank. "For several years now, we have been careful to explain to our customers just exactly what the prime rate is—and what it isn't."

Jerry L. Jordan, who left his job as senior vice president of Pittsburgh National Bank last year to become dean of the Anderson Schools of Management at the University of New Mexico, suggests that it may be necessary to invent new terminology: "We might call it the basic lending rate or the basic benchmark rate, something like that."

The prime rate got its start in the early 1930s, a period when hardly anyone wanted to borrow and interest rates were rapidly falling toward zero. To put some sort of floor under business loan rates, a major New York bank announced that its "prime" rate was 1%. The prime interest rate didn't get as high as 3% until the 1950s, so, needless to say, it wasn't much of a cause for controversy.

Even then, however, some loans were always made at rates below the prime. "Every big loan has always been a special deal," says A. James Meigs, an economist at the New York investment firm of Oppenheimer & Co.

No Discounts, But . . .

Even if the stated rate wasn't discounted, a bank always could cut the effective cost of a loan by requiring smaller "compensating balances." Banks usually expect a large borrower to keep a portion of a loan on deposit with the lending bank.

As the prime rate moved upward in the 1960s, it often became the target of political attack. Many members of Congress charged that the banks artificially boosted the rate to inflate their profits.

To take the rate out of politics, Citibank of New York City a decade ago pegged its prime to rates in the money market and allowed it to move up or down as market rates moved. Amid the recent increase in rate volatility, however, Citibank abandoned the method.

The current prime problem, bankers say, stems largely from two factors: increased competition from foreign banks in the U.S. market, and high inflation, with the accompanying high interest rates.

"The prime rate today isn't what it was five years ago," says a New York bank executive. "The change was forced by market factors, by competition from foreign banks with a price advantage.

"We don't object to competition, of course, but the foreign banks don't have the reserve and capital requirements that we have. They go after the best credits, and we've had to meet the competition."

Mr. Jordan says interest rates in the international market have been tied either to the prime rate of the London Interbank Offered Rate, "whichever is lower." The London rate, known as Libor, is the rate charged in the market for Eurodollars, deposits held abroad that are denominated in dollars. Libor has usually been at levels below the prime.

The international lending competition involves mainly the largest U.S. banks. That helps to explain why the medium-sized and smaller banks have been less active in the below-prime lending area. But they have been making these loans, too, as the table indicates.

"We have been so liquid that some of our big customers have simply had us over a barrel," says a banker in Philadelphia. "In effect, they've forced us to buy their commercial paper, and this is still going on."

Despite all the controversy, bankers say they have to have some sort of benchmark rate, whatever it's called. A generally rising level of inflation and interest rates in recent years has led most banks to adopt floating rates: The rates on loans float upward (and occasionally downward) as the prime changes.

Former banker Jordan contends that the system doesn't discriminate against smaller borrowers. "When market conditions are the way they've been recently," he says, "smaller borrowers probably pay a smaller premium over the prime than they otherwise would."

However that may be, many bankers realize that they've got a serious public-relations problem. "I believe that we're going to have to be very straightforward with all of our customers, and I'm convinced that most major banks will be, too," says a New York City banker.

"We've got to have a prime rate, and I don't think it has been a phony rate," he says. "But maybe it would help if we started calling it something else."

Key Points

1. The commercial banker is in business to provide services and, in return, maximize profits subject to constraints. These constraints are imposed by competition of other banks and nonbank financial institutions and by governmental regulation.

2. The income earning assets that a bank holds are referred to as its portfolio. There are three major considerations that enter into the construction and management of a commercial bank portfolio—liquidity, return, and risk minimization.

3. Loans constitute the primary portion of a commercial bank portfolio. The largest category of lending is commercial and industrial loans, but these loans have declined as a relative share of bank lending as consumer and real estate lending have increased in recent years.

4. Banks hold substantial amounts of securities in their portfolios. Securities are held in bank portfolios to increase portfolio liquidity and decrease overall portfolio risk, while yielding a return. Major types of securities held by banks are U.S. government securities and municipal

securities. Banks hold U.S. government securities for liquidity, favoring the one-to-five-year maturities, and municipal securities, primarily for return due to their tax exempt status.

5. Major categories of bank liabilities include demand deposits, time deposits, and savings deposits. Time and savings deposits have grown relative to demand deposits, with time deposits accounting for most of this growth. As a result, time and savings deposits exceed demand deposits as sources of bank funds by a wide margin.

6. Borrowing is a major source of commercial bank funds. Commercial banks can borrow from the Federal Reserve, other commercial banks, and other nonbank institutions.

7. Liability management has become an important part of the banking business. Liability management means that banks are actively utilizing liability items to raise funds that will then be profitably reloaned. Managed liabilities include such nondeposit items as federal funds, repurchase agreements, and Eurodollar borrowing, as well as large certificates of deposit. Some large banks have become very aggressive liability managers.

Questions for Discussion

1. Discuss the criteria that enter into the assembly and management of a bank portfolio. How do the portfolio holdings of a typical bank fit these criteria?

2. Aggressive liability management has become an important part of bank management for some large banks. Discuss the meaning of liability management, including the details of how the categories of managed liabilities are utilized in liability management.

3. Time deposits have grown rapidly relative to saving and demand deposits as bank deposit liabilities. What factors account for this growth?

4. Discuss the major types of U.S. government securities held by commercial banks. Distinguish between the motivation(s) for banks holding government securities and municipal securities.

5. How does the way in which banks raise funds influence the use to which these funds are put by banks?

Suggested Readings

Brewer, Elijah. "Bank Funds Management Comes of Age—A Balance Sheet Analysis," Federal Reserve Bank of Chicago *Economic Perspectives,* May/June 1980, pp. 13–18.

Haslem, John A., and George H. Hempel. "Commercial Banking as a Business." In Murray E. Polakoff et al. *Financial Institutions and Markets,* 2nd ed. Boston: Houghton Mifflin, 1981, pp. 57–80.

Hempel, George H., and Jess B. Yawitz. *Financial Management of Financial Institutions.* Englewood Cliffs, N.J.: Prentice-Hall, 1977.

Klein, Michael A. "A Theory of the Banking Firm." *Journal of Money, Credit and Banking,* May 1971, pp. 205–18.

Luckett, Dudley G. "Approaches to Bank Liquidity Management." Federal Reserve Bank of Kansas City *Economic Review,* March 1980, pp. 11–27.

Mason, John M. *Financial Management of Commercial Banks.* Boston: Warren, Gorham, and Lamont, 1979.

Robinson, Roland I. *Management of Bank Funds,* 2nd ed. New York: McGraw-Hill, 1972.

Savings and Loan Associations

8

Savings and loan associations (S&Ls) are among the oldest of the financial intermediaries in the United States. The first S&L was established in 1831. However, these intermediaries became a major factor in the financial system only after World War II. For example, from 1940 to 1950, S&L assets increased by over 200 percent, from $5.6 billion to $16.9 billion. By the end of 1980, the assets of S&Ls had surpassed $600 billion, making S&Ls the second largest depository financial intermediary. Only the commercial banking system is larger.

The rapid growth of S&Ls corresponded to the post–World War II boom in housing. S&Ls are the largest residential mortgage lender. This role in the mortgage market, derived as it is from law and regulation as well as from custom, has meant that S&Ls have generally held over 80 percent of their assets in mortgage loans. Currently, approximately 80 percent of the assets of S&Ls are accounted for by mortgages. The remainder of the S&L portfolio is composed of securities and other loans, many related to housing.

The percentage of mortgage loans in an S&L portfolio is likely to decline in the future. S&Ls are currently evolving into more complete financial institutions. In recent years, as a result of regulatory and legislative changes, they have gained considerably broadened lending authority. Legislative changes in 1980 authorized savings and loans to issue credit cards and granted them wider authority to make construction and other real estate related loans. Up to 20 percent of S&L assets may now be invested in consumer loans and corporate debt, previously not eligible for savings and loan investment. Even the mortgage-lending authority has been expanded to permit them to make second mortgage loans, and S&Ls can now make mortgage loans free of any geographical restrictions. S&Ls are pressing for even more asset flexibility. It appears likely that their lending authority will be expanded further in the near future.

The primary motivations behind the movement toward increased asset flexibility derive from the cyclical nature of mortgage lending, the increased competition for funds between S&Ls and other financial institutions, as well as the increased deposit flexibility that S&Ls have in raising funds. A mortgage loan is a long-term loan, usually with a term of 25 or 30 years, although in practice most loans are paid off in less time. While the development of a secondary market in mortgages—the resale market for already existing mortgage loans—has enhanced the liquidity of the mortgage instrument, it has not solved the problem faced by savings and loans of the mismatch between short-term liabilities and long-term assets. Of all financial intermediaries, S&Ls face the most severe problem of intermediating along the yield curve, borrowing short term and lending long term.

This asset–liability mismatch was further exacerbated in the late 1970s and early 1980s by a combination of high interest rates and enhanced flexibility in raising funds. S&Ls found their cost of funds rising precipitously due to the development of the six-month money market certificates tied to open market interest rates and other certificate accounts. While the popularity of these accounts increased the maturity level of S&L deposits over passbook accounts, it barely closed the time gap between assets and liabilities. Further, 1980 legislation permitting the nationwide offering of NOW accounts has shortened the maturity of S&L liabilities. The combination of rising rates for S&L funds and short maturities placed a severe strain on S&Ls whose portfolio consists of long-term low interest fixed rate mortgages. For many S&Ls, the overall return on their portfolio was less than their overall cost of funds in 1980 and 1981. It was this situation that motivated many of the changes in the laws and regulations governing savings and loan associations in recent years. These regulatory changes in turn are transforming not only S&Ls but nonbank financial intermediaries in general into more diversified financial institutions.

The Organization of S&Ls

A dual system of chartering and supervising S&Ls exists, just as it does for the commercial banking system. Federal associations are chartered under federal law and are subject to Federal Home Loan Bank Board supervision. The Federal Home Loan Bank System (FHLB) was established in 1932 in reaction to the economic difficulties of the Great Depression, which severely affected savings and loan associations. It was believed that the FHLB would provide a solid foundation to the S&L business. Federal associations must be members of the

FHLB. State savings and loan associations are chartered by the state in which they do business and are supervised and examined by the savings and loan regulatory departments of these states and by the FHLB of which most are members.

Table 8-1 shows the number of S&Ls operating under state or federal charter for selected years. There are somewhat more state chartered associations than federally chartered associations. However, it should be noted that as of December 31, 1979, 56 percent of all S&L assets were held by federally chartered associations, so that federal associations are on average somewhat larger than the state associ-

Table 8-1
Number of Savings Associations by Type of Charter

Yearend	Federal Charter[2]	STATE CHARTER			Grand Total
		Total	FSLIC-Insured	Noninsured[3]	
1950	1,526	4,466	1,334	3,132	5,992
1955	1,683	4,388	1,861	2,527	6,071
1960	1,873	4,447	2,225	2,222	6,320
1965	2,011	4,174	2,497	1,677	6,185
1966	2,051	4,061	2,459	1,602	6,112
1967	2,056	3,980	2,431	1,549	6,036
1968	2,063	3,884	2,407	1,477	5,947
1969	2,071	3,764	2,367	1,397	5,835
1970	2,067	3,602	2,298	1,304	5,669
1971	2,049	3,425	2,222	1,203	5,474
1972	2,044	3,254	2,147	1,107	5,298
1973	2,040	3,130	2,123	1,007	5,170
1974	2,060	2,963	2,081	882	5,023
1975	2,048	2,883	2,030	853	4,931
1976	2,019	2,802	2,025	777	4,821
1977	2,012	2,749	2,053	696	4,761
1978	2,000	2,723	2,053	670	4,723
1979[1]	1,989	2,720	2,050	670	4,709

[1] Preliminary.
[2] All federally chartered associations are insured by the Federal Savings and Loan Insurance Corporation.
[3] Includes institutions insured by the Co-operative Central Bank of Massachusetts, the Maryland Savings-Share Insurance Corporation, the North Carolina Savings Guaranty Corporation, and the Ohio Deposit Guarantee Fund.

Source: *Savings and Loan Fact Book*, 1980, United States League of Savings Associations.

ations. Table 8-1 also shows the number of state associations insured by the Federal Savings and Loan Insurance Corporation (FSLIC). All federally chartered associations are required to be insured by the FSLIC. The FSLIC was established in 1934 and is similar to the FDIC, which insures commercial bank deposits. Deposits are insured up to $100,000 just as they are by the FDIC at commercial banks. The table indicates, however, that the overwhelming number of state chartered associations are also insured. Overall, 86 percent of all S&Ls have FSLIC insurance and virtually all other S&Ls have some insurance protection as can be seen by the footnote to the table relating to the "noninsured" category.

The number of savings and loan associations has declined rather steadily since 1960 as Table 8-1 shows. This trend accelerated in the early 1980s as a number of S&Ls merged, many with FSLIC assistance. This assistance generally enabled financially stronger S&Ls to acquire other S&Ls that were experiencing financial difficulties. The alternative would have been for the FSLIC to have permitted the weaker institutions to go out of business, requiring the FSLIC to pay off depositors under its insurance guaranty. This was a less favorable alternative for the FSLIC. It is estimated that by early 1982, there were fewer than 4,000 S&Ls as a result.

A dual system of ownership also exists for savings and loans associations. Most are mutual associations, that is, they are nominally owned by their depositors.[1] A minority of savings and loans, however, are stock associations in which capital stock has been issued to stock holders and may be held by nondepositors. All Federal S&Ls were originally organized as mutual associations. However, some mutual associations converted to stock associations to enable them to sell shares to the public and thereby raise additional capital. The conversion of associations from mutual to stock ownership has not always met with the approval of the regulators. As a result, for much of the period since 1955 the conversion from mutual to stock ownership has not been permitted by regulatory bodies.

There are several reasons that many S&Ls desire to convert to stock ownership. The ability to raise additional capital is perhaps the most important. In addition, the conversion affords some small amount of protection against adverse funds flows during periods of high open-market interest rates because the S&L can potentially raise funds by issuing more stock. Stock issuance nationally also enables S&Ls to raise funds in areas where capital is plentiful and bring it to areas where capital is tight.

The opposition of regulators to conversion and the reasons for the intermittent suspension of the conversion process stems mostly

---

[1] Nominal ownership means that the depositors have no practical control over the association.

from the problem of how to distribute the newly issued capital stock of an association. Particularly, concern by the regulators has focused on the windfall profits that would accrue to existing depositors by the receipt of valuable stock.[2] The "problem" of windfall profits is under continuous study by the FHLB and other groups. Effective May 1979, the Federal Home Loan Bank Board issued new regulations that permit the conversion of federally insured S&Ls from mutual to stock associations, and a number of associations have applied for and been granted permission to convert. However, given the history of the conversion process it cannot be said with certainty that the conversion privilege will not once again be suspended in the future.

Sources of Funds for S&Ls

From the 1950s and into the 1960s, the passbook savings account was the major source of savings funds to S&Ls. As with the commercial bank passbook account, funds can be withdrawn from these accounts at any time. However, starting in the 1960s and accelerating significantly in the 1970s and early 1980s following changes in regulation and practice, other types of savings instruments, mainly certificates of deposit, grew in popularity. S&Ls are permitted to pay higher interest on these certificates of deposit accounts. They differ from each other in term to maturity and the minimum amount that must be held in the account. Despite the increased popularity of certificate accounts and the rapid decline in passbook savings relative to certificates, particularly in 1980 and 1981, passbook savings is still a major category of saving sources of funds. However, certificate accounts are currently a larger source of savings funds for S&Ls. Almost all new savings deposits flowing into S&Ls in 1980 and 1981 have gone into certificate accounts. The remaining deposit source of funds for S&Ls includes checkable deposits called NOW accounts (Negotiable Orders of Withdrawal). S&Ls nationwide have been permitted to offer NOW accounts only since January 1981, and these deposits currently account for only a small but growing source of funds. S&Ls are currently pressing for permission to offer demand deposit accounts. As this is being written permission has not been granted.

Certificates of deposit are issued for a maximum period of eight years and in amounts and maturities fixed at the time of issuance. There was an increasing emphasis during most of the 1970s on longer-term certificates. The two-year certificate was first offered in January 1970, and its success spawned the four-year certificate in 1973, the

---

[2] See Lawrence Conway, "Conversion of FSLIC Insured Institutions from Mutual to Stock under Current Regulations—Some Benefits and Costs," paper presented at the Western Economic Association Meetings, June 1979, for a thorough analysis of the issues involved in the conversion of mutual to stock ownership of S&Ls.

six-year certificate in 1974, and the eight-year certificate in 1978. However, the introduction of the six-month money market certificate in 1978 and its immediate and continuing popularity reversed the trend toward longer maturities.

Certificate savings accounts have rapidly increased in the last decade. For example, in 1966 these accounts made up only 11.7 percent of deposits at insured S&Ls. However, except for 1968, the certificates as a percent of total deposits have increased in every year since. By year-end 1973, more funds were held in certificates than in passbooks, and the trend has continued. By the end of 1979, 74 percent of all deposits were held in certificates.

The distribution in favor of certificate accounts has increased even more rapidly since the introduction of the money market certificate (MMC) in June 1978. The MMC is a six-month certificate tied to the Treasury bill rate. Approximately $127 billion in money market certificates, representing 28 percent of total deposits at S&Ls, were held by S&L depositors as of December 1979. While many of these MMCs represent transfers of funds from other savings accounts at S&Ls, funds have also been attracted that would have gone into other instruments. Figure 8-1 graphically presents the relative breakdown between passbook accounts and certificates and special accounts[3] for the years 1970 through 1979, with 1966 included for comparative purposes. The change in the distribution of deposits in favor of certificates is dramatic.

The detailed breakdown of deposits by maturity, presented in Table 8-2, sheds further light on the emerging pattern of savings deposits. Notice that as of September 1979, the largest single category of certificates, over 30 percent of total deposits, were held in maturities of over two years. While this trend toward longer maturities has been eroded by the MMCs in the period after September 1979, the emphasis on longer maturities is in keeping with the attempt by S&Ls to better match the maturity length of their liabilities to the maturity length of their assets. Notice the change in maturity distribution since March 1973, which is included in Table 8-2 for comparison. Starting in 1973, S&Ls were allowed by regulators to offer better interest incentives on long-term certificate accounts. The sharp decline in passbook deposits as a source of funds for S&Ls is also clearly apparent.

To the extent that S&Ls can lock in savings for longer periods of time and at higher rates, the danger of disintermediation—the flow of funds out of savings and loans to the open market—that has existed in earlier periods of rising open-market interest rates is reduced with beneficial effects on the mortgage market. However, in 1980 and

---

[3] These special accounts include notice passbook and retirement accounts under Individual Retirement and Keough plans. The total amount in these accounts is small, only about 2 percent of total deposits.

Figure 8-1
Savings Accounts by Type at Insured S&Ls

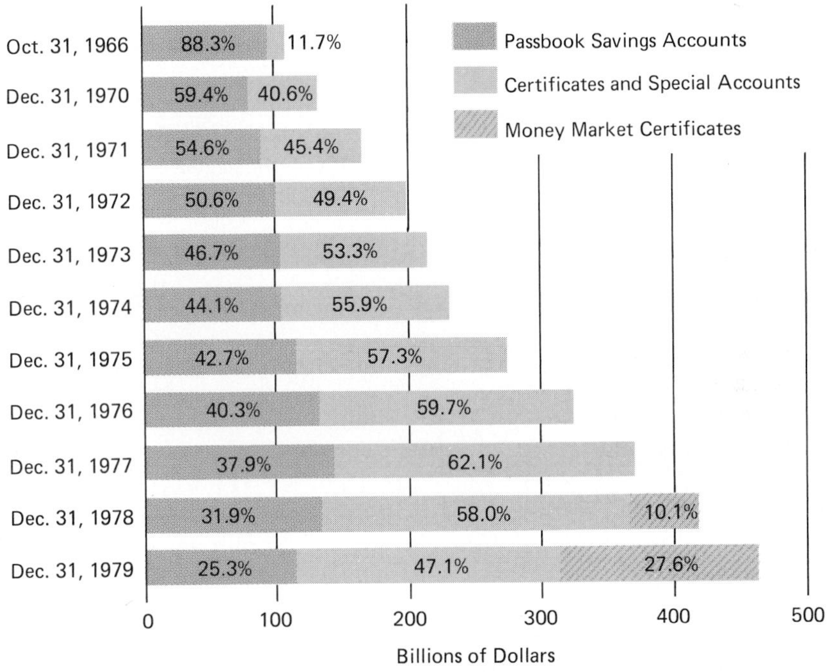

Oct. 31, 1966	88.3%	11.7%	
Dec. 31, 1970	59.4%	40.6%	
Dec. 31, 1971	54.6%	45.4%	
Dec. 31, 1972	50.6%	49.4%	
Dec. 31, 1973	46.7%	53.3%	
Dec. 31, 1974	44.1%	55.9%	
Dec. 31, 1975	42.7%	57.3%	
Dec. 31, 1976	40.3%	59.7%	
Dec. 31, 1977	37.9%	62.1%	
Dec. 31, 1978	31.9%	58.0%	10.1%
Dec. 31, 1979	25.3%	47.1%	27.6%

Passbook Savings Accounts

Certificates and Special Accounts

Money Market Certificates

0   100   200   300   400   500

Billions of Dollars

Source: *Savings and Loan Fact Book,* 1980, United States League of Savings Associations.

1981 as some of the longer-term deposits matured, depositors tended to roll these over into short maturity certificates like MMCs or remove them from S&Ls altogether. The volatility of open-market interest rates made these depositors reluctant to commit their deposits for long periods. Further, the introduction of the six-month money market certificates tied to the Treasury bill rate has altered the inflow mix. The ability of S&Ls to offer high rates that compete with money market rates resulted in much less than usual outflow of funds during the 1978–79 period of high open-market rates and allowed S&Ls to retain funds that otherwise would have been lost. However in 1980 and 1981, despite the continuing popularity of money market certificates, disintermediation became quite severe as depositors took advantage of even higher yields to be found in the open market and at mutual funds specializing in purchasing money market instruments.

The introduction of money market certificates in 1978 led to the rapid introduction of other certificate accounts whose rates were per-

Table 8-2
Maturity Structure of Savings Accounts at Insured Associations
(Millions of Dollars)

Type of Account	MARCH 31, 1973		SEPTEMBER 30, 1979	
	Amount	Percent of Total Savings	Amount	Percent of Total Savings
Passbook	$103,814	49.53%	$126,324	27.87%
Certificate less than $100,000:				
Up to 90 days to maturity	12,908	6.16	64,382	14.20
91 to 180 days to maturity	8,449	4.03	80,229	17.70
181 to 270 days to maturity	7,947	3.79	13,249	2.92
271 to 365 days to maturity	21,224	10.13	11,871	2.62
More than 1 year to maturity	51,756	24.69	152,381	33.62
Other	3,500	1.67	4,863	1.07
Total Savings	$209,598	100.00%	$453,299	100.00%

Note: Components may not add to totals due to rounding.

Source: *Savings and Loan Fact Book*, 1980, United States League of Savings Associations.

mitted to change with open-market rates. In 1979, the four-year certificate was authorized for a brief period and in 1980 the two-and-one-half-year certificate tied to the Treasury note rate was introduced. However, the maximum interest on the certificate was set at 12 percent, even if the Treasury rate was higher. This discouraged depositors from using this certificate account when open-market rates rose significantly above 12 percent, as they did in 1980 and 1981. In August 1981, the maximum was suspended and the rate is now free to move with open-market rates.

The increasing authorization that S&Ls are receiving to offer certificate accounts that may vary with open-market rates is a trend that is likely to continue. For example, a three-month certificate tied to the three-month Treasury bill rate was introduced in May 1982. It can be expected that additional market rate-related certificates will become more common even before the scheduled total removal of all interest rate ceilings by 1985. At that point, S&Ls will be free to pay whatever rates they determine.

Regulatory Ceilings on Interest Payments on Deposits at S&Ls

Rates on savings and time deposits are governed by regulation. However, interest rate ceilings will be completely phased out by 1985 under current schedules. Nevertheless, it is still useful to briefly discuss these ceilings as they have affected the development of S&Ls and until 1985 will continue to do so. Commercial banks also face interest rate ceilings on their time and savings deposits, but Federal Reserve Regulation Q, which sets the maximum ceiling for commercial banks, technically does not apply to S&Ls. However, under the Interest Rate Adjustment Act of 1966, the FHLB was empowered to set maximum rates that could be offered by S&Ls on saving and time deposit accounts. Mutual savings banks were also covered through the FDIC. As a result, following 1966, Regulation Q ceilings were set by an interagency committee composed of the Fed, the FHLB, and the FDIC and applied to all insured commercial banks, savings and loan associations, and mutual savings banks. In 1980, as part of the phase out of the interest rate ceilings, authority to set deposit interest ceilings was given to the Depository Institutions Deregulation Committee (DIDC).

Savings and loan associations can currently pay one-quarter of a percentage point more than banks on many categories of saving and time deposits including passbook accounts. However, there is no differential between what commercial banks and S&Ls may pay on money market certificates when the Treasury bill rate is above 8.75 percent. Below 8.75 percent a differential is permitted. The lack of a differential above 8.75 percent has disturbed S&Ls, which have argued that such a differential is necessary for S&Ls to compete with commercial banks for savings and time deposits. They argue that commercial banks have a competitive advantage as "full service" financial institutions. This competitive advantage was the original rationale behind the creation of an interest rate differential.

The elimination of all interest rate ceilings will soon make such arguments empty. Even now many certificate accounts are free of any ceiling. For example, the ceiling on three-and-one-half-year and over certificates was removed in May 1982. Many economists have long favored the elimination of interest rate ceilings arguing that they not only inhibit competition for funds among institutions and the open market but discriminate against the small saver. The smaller saver does not have the amount necessary to purchase open-market securities or higher yielding certificate accounts because of minimum denomination requirements. While the small saver does face this problem, the major rationale behind the 1980 legislation eliminating interest rate ceilings was that increased competition would lead to a generally more efficient financial system.

The S&L Portfolio

Mortgages are the major asset in the portfolio of S&Ls. Other lending by S&Ls is, for the most part, made up of housing-related loans, with the remainder of the income-earning portfolio in securities. Cash is, of course, also held. S&Ls have recently received approval for other types of lending such as issuing credit cards. Additional asset flexibility is likely to be forthcoming as well, and so the portfolio that is presented here is likely to become increasingly diversified in future years.

Mortgage Lending

The great bulk of S&L mortgage lending goes for single-family loans. At the end of 1980, more than 78 percent of all mortgage loans held by S&Ls were on single-family homes while the remaining mortgage loans were, for the most part, on two- to four-family homes, multifamily (apartment) buildings, and commercial property. Table 8-3 shows the breakdown of the mortgage portfolio for selected years by both dollar amount and percentage distribution. As shown graphically in Figure 8-2, the distribution remained relatively stable throughout the 1970s while the mortgages outstanding have grown.

The mortgage market itself is highly cyclical. S&Ls and the mortgage market have had difficulties during some periods—1966, 1969–70, 1974–75, and 1980–82. Locked in as they are to mortgage lending, S&Ls have been unable to provide financing when their savings inflows have fallen off at times of disintermediation during periods of rising open-market interest rates. The constriction in funds available for mortgage loans and the associated high mortgage interest rates have intensified the cyclical nature of the mortgage market and housing construction. Indeed many economists attribute this mortgage market cyclicality to the problem of mortgage credit availability caused by disintermediation during such periods.[4] The impact of S&Ls on the mortgage market will be explored in greater detail later in this chapter.

A portion of S&L mortgage loans is made for the construction of single- and multi-unit housing. However, construction lending has declined a great deal over the last few decades. In the 1950s more than 30 percent of S&L lending was for construction, while in 1979 only about 18 percent was construction lending. The short-term nature of construction loans has led other financial institutions like commercial banks to enter this market. However, S&Ls are still an important factor.

---

[4] For example, see David Huang, "Effect of Different Credit Policies on Housing Demand," in *Study of the Savings and Loan Industry,* Irwin Friend, Dir., Federal Home Loan Bank Board (Washington, D.C.: FHLBB, July 1969), pp. 1211–239. However for an alternative view, see Francisco Arcelus and Allan H. Meltzer, "The Market for Housing and Housing Services," *Journal of Money, Credit and Banking* (Feb. 1973), pp. 78–98.

Table 8-3
Mortgage Portfolio of Insured Associations by Type
(Billions of Dollars)

Type of Property	1973	1974	1975	1976	1977	1978	1979[1]
Single-family	$168.7	$181.9	$202.9	$237.4	$283.2	$325.3	$367.0
Two- to Four-family	12.6	13.0	13.9	15.6	18.6	21.1	21.7
Multifamily	21.9	23.0	24.6	27.5	31.4	34.9	33.7
Commercial	19.1	21.3	25.3	29.5	32.9	35.1	38.6
Other	3.5	4.0	4.6	5.3	6.3	7.1	6.3
Total	$225.7	$243.1	$271.3	$315.3	$372.4	$423.5	$467.3

Percentage Distribution

Type of Property	1973	1974	1975	1976	1977	1978	1979[1]
Single-family	74.7%	74.8%	74.8%	75.3%	76.0%	76.8%	78.5%
Two- to Four-family	5.6	5.3	5.1	4.9	5.0	5.0	4.6
Multifamily	9.7	9.5	9.1	8.7	8.4	8.2	7.2
Commercial	8.5	8.8	9.3	9.4	8.8	8.3	8.3
Other	1.6	1.6	1.7	1.7	1.7	1.7	1.3
Total	100.0%	100.0%	100.0%	100.0%	100.0%	100.0%	100.0%

Note: Components may not add to totals due to rounding.
[1] Preliminary.

Source: Savings and Loan Fact Book, 1980, United States League of Savings Associations.

In 1980 the S&Ls were granted expanded authority to make construction loans. This authority should put them on a more equal footing with commercial banks, and as a result, construction lending may increase. S&Ls look to increased construction lending as one of the ways to shorten the maturity of their portfolio.

S&Ls in recent years have at times purchased loans in the secondary mortgage market. This is a relatively new development. S&Ls traditionally have been mortgage originators, that is, original mortgage lenders. However, the recent increase in the scope and depth of the secondary mortgage market (the market for already existing mortgages) has made the purchase of loans in blocks attractive to S&Ls for the expansion of their mortgage portfolio.[5]

The Mix of Mortgage Loans

Basically there are two types of mortgage loans, conventional mortgage loans and government-insured mortgage loans. The conventional mortgage loans are preferred by S&Ls, and have become even more attractive since the advent of private mortgage insurance in the early 1970s. Private mortgage insurers (PMIs) insure a portion of the mortgage loan against default.

The government has had two major mortgage insurance programs in operation, FHA (Federal Housing Administration) loans and VA (Veterans Administration) loans. S&Ls have not looked upon the government-insured mortgages with favor because of the fixed interest rate on these loans—which is adjusted only slowly (though charges, called points, can be added to bring the rate close to the conventional rate)—the paperwork involved in the insurance procedure, and the delays in the processing of loans. These delays have sometimes exceeded six weeks when mortgage loan demand was heavy.

Consumer Lending

S&Ls have rapidly expanded their nonmortgage lending in recent years, although consumer loans are still a very small portion of the S&L portfolio. Between the years 1974 and 1979, the consumer loan portfolio of S&Ls insured by the FSLIC (the vast majority of S&Ls) increased from $5.7 billion to $15 billion. The majority of these loans are associated with residential financing; about 15 percent of the consumer loan portfolio of S&Ls are mobile home loans, while 30 percent are home improvement loans.

In addition, S&Ls have always made a significant number of loans secured by savings accounts. For a number of years, about 30 percent of the consumer loan portfolio had been accounted for by this type

---

[5] S&Ls have also made use of the secondary market to sell packages of mortgage loans to raise funds.

Figure 8-2
Mortgage Portfolio by Type of Property at All Associations

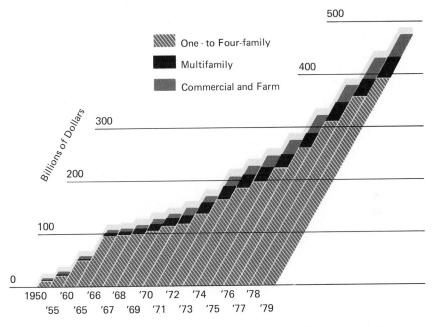

Source: *Savings and Loan Fact Book*, 1980, United States League of Savings Associations.

of lending. In 1978 and 1979 this lending increased dramatically to 40 percent of all consumer lending. In part this was due to the fact that until 1980, the only way S&Ls could offer credit cards was to make them contingent on savings deposit balances.

Savings and loans have been pressing for increased authority to make numerous kinds of consumer loans. This effort for more consumer lending authority is in keeping with their desire to increase the flexibility of their portfolio. Proposals under consideration by Congress and the FHLB may result in broadening the power of S&Ls in this area. Some of this pressure has borne fruit in authority for S&Ls to issue credit cards and make a limited amount of nonhousing-related consumer loans.

Cash and Securities

Much of the remainder of S&L assets are in cash and securities, which constitute the second largest portion of S&L assets. The majority of these holdings are needed to meet liquidity requirements set by the

FHLB. In 1950, liquidity requirements were incorporated into the Federal Home Loan Bank Act. This Act, along with FHLB regulations, determines what constitutes legal liquid investments for S&Ls and the liquidity ratio. The liquidity ratio, although it is satisfied in quite different ways, is analogous to the required reserve ratio imposed on banks by the Federal Reserve System. Since 1972, a certain percentage of the assets necessary to meet the liquidity ratio must be in short-term investments. Table 8-4 presents the S&L liquidity requirements of the FHLB.

Cash, demand deposits, U.S. government securities, and federal agency securities (with maturities of five years or less), commercial

Table 8-4
Minimum Liquidity Requirements
for Members of the Federal
Home Loan Bank System

| Effective Date | MINIMUM PERCENTAGE[1] | |
	Short-Term	Overall
December 1950	—	6.0%
March 1961	—	7.0
August 1968	—	6.5
June 1969	—	6.0
December 1969	—	5.5
April 1971	—	6.5
May 1971	—	7.5
August 1971	—	7.0
January 1972	3.0%	7.0
May 1973	2.5	6.5
August 1973	1.5	5.5
September 1974	1.0	5.0
April 1975	1.5	5.5
June 1975	2.0	6.0
September 1975	2.5	6.5
March 1976	3.0	7.0
May 1978	2.5	6.5
January 1979	2.0	6.0
October 1979	2.5	5.5
April 1980	1.0	5.0

[1] Liquid assets as a percentage of total savings deposits, plus borrowings repayable on demand or within one year

Source: Federal Home Loan Bank Board *Journal*, June 1981.

bank time deposits of under one year to maturity, and some other short-term securities all qualify as liquid assets. Therefore, the requirement is less onerous than that imposed by the Fed because so much of the requirement can be met by the holdings of income-earning assets. The FHLB can vary the liquidity ratio between 4 and 10 percent. It will reduce the requirement to increase funds availability when the mortgage market is tight[6] and increase the requirement when mortgage funds are readily available.

The three main categories of the portfolio of S&Ls are mortgage loans (by far the overwhelming amount), cash and securities, and consumer loans generally related to housing. The S&L portfolio, therefore, is less diverse than that of a commercial bank, and this fact is indicative of the problem of the lack of portfolio flexibility that faces S&Ls. We will address this point by presenting a total picture of S&Ls assets and liabilities in the consolidated balance sheet for all S&Ls.

Consolidated Balance Sheet of the S&Ls

Figure 8-3 graphically depicts the balance sheet of S&Ls for year-end 1980 while Table 8-5 presents a simplified consolidated balance sheet. Two major items that are included and have not already been discussed are FHLB advances and other borrowing. FHLB advances are loans made to S&Ls. They are in some ways similar to Fed discount loans to commercial banks. However, unlike Fed discounts, the FHLB will actively encourage S&Ls to borrow from it by altering the advances rate—the rate of interest the FHLB charges the borrowing association—during periods when the FHLB determines that the mortgage market is in need of assistance. The importance of advances to S&Ls can be appreciated by comparing the size of advances indicated in Table 8-5 to the amount of discount loans usually outstanding. For December 1980 the average level of discount loans outstanding by the Fed was about $1.6 billion. Rarely is this amount much over $2 billion on average. The level of FHLB advances in December 1980 was almost $50 billion. Thus, the ratio of FHLB advances to discount loans can be 20 or 30 to 1. Advances outstanding are repaid when conditions ease and funds flow into S&Ls. The advances rate is adjusted accordingly. In addition, S&Ls occasionally borrow from commercial banks as is reflected in the "other borrowing" category.

"Loans in process" is also an important category of S&L liabilities. This item is the amount of mortgage loans that are recorded on the asset side of the balance sheet but have not yet been disbursed to borrowers. The important categories of the remainder of the balance sheet have been discussed previously with the exception of net worth.

---

[6] Since the bulk of S&L lending goes to mortgages, it is assumed that any funds released will be used for this type of lending.

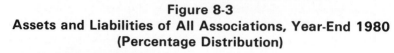

Figure 8-3
Assets and Liabilities of All Associations, Year-End 1980
(Percentage Distribution)

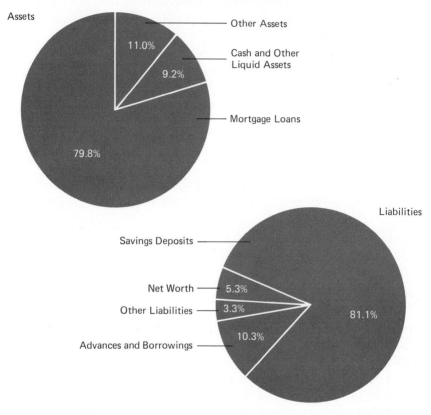

Source: Federal Home Loan Bank Board *Journal,* June 1981.

Net worth includes general reserves, undistributed profits, and the capital stock for a stock association. General reserves are set aside to protect depositors against loss.

The Mortgage Credit Cycle and S&Ls

In order to fully understand the key role played by savings and loan associations in the mortgage market and in housing, we need to examine the housing cycle. Figure 8-4 depicts housing starts from 1970 through 1980. Housing starts are homes on which construction has actually started and is usually taken to be a key indicator of the strength

Table 8-5
Balance Sheet of All Savings and Loan Associations,
December 1980
(Millions of Dollars)

Item	Amount	Percentage of Total
Assets:		
Mortgage Loans Outstanding	$502,812	79.8%
Cash and Investments	57,572	9.2
All Other Assets	69,445	11.0
Total Assets	$629,829	100.0%
Liabilities and Net Worth:		
Savings Deposits	$510,959	81.1%
Federal Home Loan Bank Advances	48,963	7.8
Other Borrowed Money	15,528	2.5
Loans in Process	8,783	1.4
All Other Liabilities	12,277	1.9
Net Worth	33,319	5.3
Total Liabilities and Net Worth	$629,829	100.0%

Source: Federal Home Loan Bank Board *Journal,* June 1981.

or weakness in construction. Notice the extreme cyclical quality, particularly the deep downturn in 1969–70, which can be inferred from the figure, and similar declines in 1974–75 and 1979–80. Table 8-6 presents the number of housing starts for 1965-80 and adds 1960 data for comparison. The year 1966 also showed a substantial constriction in housing starts.

Many economists believe that the cycle in housing is determined by the availability of mortgage credit. When mortgage credit is hard to obtain and at the same time is expensive (that is, the mortgage rate is high and down payment requirements may also be increased), housing will turn down. Since S&Ls are the major mortgage lenders, lack of mortgage credit is traceable in part to lack of available loanable funds at S&Ls.[7] Table 8-7 presents net savings receipts at S&Ls for

[7] The following are just some of the studies that have analyzed mortgage credit availability and its effect on housing: Huang, "Effect of Different Credit Policies"; L. Grebler and S. J. Maisel, "Determinants of Residential Construction: A Review of Present Knowledge," in *Impacts of Monetary Policy,* Commission on Money and Credit, Englewood Cliffs: Prentice-Hall, 1963, pp. 475–620; C. Swan, "The Markets for Housing and Housing Services," *Journal of Money, Credit and Banking* (Nov. 1973), pp. 960–72.

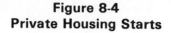

Figure 8-4
Private Housing Starts

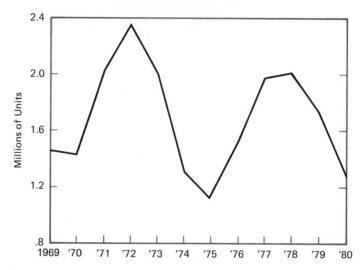

Source: *Savings and Loan Fact Book,* 1980, United States League of Savings Associations.

the same years contained in Table 8-6. Net receipts are simply deposits minus withdrawals. Notice the substantial reduction in net savings receipts at S&Ls in 1966, 1969, and 1974, years that marked severe downturns in housing. The relative decline in savings inflows in 1979 and 1980 was not as great as in the previous periods of housing difficulties, but mortgage rates rose substantially in 1979 and 1980 adding to the effect of the savings inflow declines. This pattern with consequent effects on housing continued in 1981 and 1982. Since the bulk of S&L funds are invested in mortgages, credit for the mortgage market is substantially reduced when the inflow of funds to S&Ls is diminished. Housing downturns continue for some time after savings inflows increase, for example in 1970 and 1975, because of lags between the availability of credit and its full effect on housing. Therefore, the parallels between the S&L deposit situation and the housing market are clear.

What precipitates the downturn in funds available to S&Ls and hence the housing market? When interest rises on open market instruments, such as Treasury bills, relative to what S&Ls can pay for deposits, disintermediation results. As previously noted, **disintermediation** is the outflow of funds from financial intermediaries—including S&Ls—to take advantage of high open-market rates. The introduction of

Table 8-6
Private Housing Starts

Year	Number of Units
1960	1,252,100
1965	1,472,800
1966	1,164,900
1967	1,291,600
1968	1,507,600
1969	1,466,800
1970	1,433,600
1971	2,052,200
1972	2,356,600
1973	2,045,300
1974	1,337,700
1975	1,160,400
1976	1,537,500
1977	1,987,100
1978	2,020,300
1979	1,745,100
1980	1,292,200

Source: *Savings and Loan Fact Book,* 1980, United States League of Savings Associations; and The Federal Home Loan Bank *Journal,* June 1971.

money market certificates (MMCs) tied to the Treasury bill rate has moderated disintermediation only partially. Further, the MMC and other market rate-related certificates have had to compete for funds not only with open-market instruments but with money market mutual funds that allow an investor to acquire a portion of a large portfolio of money market instruments with a much lower initial investment than, for example, the $10,000 required for an MMC. Table 8-8 shows the average annual yield on savings deposits at S&Ls and the three-month Treasury bill rate for the same years. The years in which the Treasury bill rate exceeded the deposit rate generally coincide with years of marked reductions in savings inflows.

The removal of interest rate ceilings by 1985 should allow the S&Ls to compete more actively for funds and thus serve to reduce disintermediation in the future. However, this ability to compete depends in part on the S&L portfolio. The portfolio must provide the S&Ls with a return sufficient to offer competitive rates when open market rates are rising.

Table 8-7
Net Savings at All Savings Associations
(Millions of Dollars)

Year	Net Savings Receipts
1960	$ 7,559
1965	8,513
1966	3,615
1967	10,649
1968	7,478
1969	4,079
1970	11,018
1971	27,974
1972	32,663
1973	20,237
1974	16,068
1975	42,806
1976	50,585
1977	51,016
1978	44,864
1979	39,304
1980	41,417

Source: *Savings and Loan Fact Book,* 1980, United States League of Savings Associations; and the Federal Home Loan Bank *Journal,* June 1971.

The S&L portfolio is dominated by long-term mortgage loans. Although a mortgage loan is generally made for 25 or 30 years, the average life of a mortgage in an S&L portfolio is actually about eight years. The relatively short average life is due to the fact that people sell their houses and repay the mortgage loan. In addition, S&Ls may sell the mortgage loan in the secondary market. Nevertheless, a typical S&L portfolio contains a number of fixed rate loans made over the years at low rates that are only salable in the secondary mortgage market at great loss. Thus, the S&Ls are stuck with them.[8] When open market rates rise, mortgage rates on new loans rise. But the yield on existing fixed rate loans in the S&L portfolio does not change. By comparison when deposit rates rise, almost all deposits are affected. Even long-term certificate holdings may be rolled over into higher yield-

---

[8] There have been recurrent proposals for Congress to appropriate funds to purchase low interest rate mortgage loans from S&Ls. However, none of these proposals have been acted upon.

Table 8-8
Average Annual Yield, Savings Deposits and Three-Month Treasury Bills

Year	Savings Deposits in Savings Associations	Three-Month Treasury Bills
1950	2.52%	1.20%
1955	2.94	1.73
1960	3.86	2.93
1965	4.23	3.98
1966	4.45	4.91
1967	4.67	4.36
1968	4.68	5.37
1969	4.80	6.68
1970	5.06	6.70
1971	5.33	4.39
1972	5.39	4.02
1973	5.55	6.97
1974	5.98	7.95
1975	6.24	5.97
1976	6.32	5.11
1977	6.41	5.27
1978	6.56	7.19
1979	7.29	10.07
1980	8.78	11.43

Sources: *Savings and Loan Fact Book,* 1980, United States League of Savings Associations; Federal Reserve Board of Governors; and the Federal Home Loan Bank *Journal.*

ing saving certificates if the incentive is sufficient. The result is a squeeze on the spread between the portfolio return and the cost of funds. In the second half of 1980 the average cost of funds (including nondeposit items) to the S&L rose to 9.11 percent from 8.70 percent, while the average interest return on mortgages was 9.44 percent. In 1981 the spread actually turned negative.

Obviously this situation is not sustainable in the long run; institutions cannot continuously suffer losses. Further, the relatively low yielding portfolio would prevent the S&Ls from paying market rates on their deposits even if no regulatory constraints existed. Some solution must be found, and part of that solution is already in progress. This is the increasing ability of S&Ls to diversify their portfolio by making other types of loans, such as consumer loans. Another part of the solution is currently transforming the mortgage loan from a fixed rate loan to a variable rate loan.

Variable rate mortgages, or VRMs, are mortgages that are tied to one of several potential open market rates or to the average cost of funds to S&Ls. In 1979 a change in Federal Home Loan Bank regulation permitted federally chartered S&Ls to offer VRMs. Some states had permitted their state chartered S&Ls to offer VRMs prior to 1979.[9] In 1981, many restrictions on VRMs that had limited the extent of permissible interest rate adjustments, as well as the frequency of these adjustments, were lifted by the FHLB, and S&Ls were allowed a great deal of freedom to alter rates. The AML or adjustable mortgage loan, a type of VRM, has resulted. The frequency and extent to which the rate on AMLs can change may lead to a new phenomena in the mortgage market, the negative amortization loan. If the rate on an AML rises substantially, rather than the monthly mortgage payment increasing, the term of the loan may be extended, say from 30 to 32 or 33 years. As a result, the fixed monthly payment may not cover the interest payment and the capital amount owed will increase. It is not clear at this point how negative amortization will be handled. However, if interest rates fall, the AML will be adjusted downward eliminating the problem.

AML and other variable rate mortgages have met widespread consumer resistance since their introduction, even when offered at favorable initial rates compared to fixed rate mortgages. This resistance is motivated by the fear of having rates rise considerably if the cost of S&L funds rise once the borrower agrees to an AML. However, given the need for S&Ls to meet the competition for deposit funds by increasing the deposit rate, it seems clear that over time the fixed rate mortgage will be replaced increasingly by variable rate loans in the S&L portfolio.[10]

AML loans and other variable rate loans have been made possible by changes in FHLB regulation. However, meaningful AMLs would not have been possible without federal legislation in 1980 that preempted state usury ceilings. These ceilings had restricted the rate S&Ls could charge for mortgage loans. Usury ceilings were so low relative to market rates in some cases that mortgage lending in a number of states (New York was an example) would virtually come to a halt when interest rates rose to high levels. Without these usury ceilings, the rate will not be restricted, perhaps ensuring mortgage lending if the borrower is willing to pay the price.[11]

---

[9] For example, California state S&Ls had been allowed to make VRMs for some time before federally chartered S&Ls were given permission.

[10] See Carl Gambs, "Variable Rate Mortgages—Their Potential in the United States," *Journal of Money, Credit and Banking* (May 1975), pp. 245–51.

[11] States, however, may reimpose usury ceilings as long as they act by 1983. It seems doubtful that most states would so act.

Monetary Policy and S&Ls

Federal Reserve monetary policy is directed at influencing open-market interest rates and the money supply by affecting commercial banking system reserves. As open market rates rise, disintermediation occurs and housing suffers. In fact, housing has borne the major burden of the economy's adjustment to tight monetary policy over the years. It is not surprising that the years of housing difficulties, 1966, 1969–70, 1973, and 1979–81, have generally been years of rising interest rates often due to monetary restriction.

Should the S&Ls and the housing industry bear such a large part of this burden of adjustment? Some economists have argued that since housing is an easily postponable expenditure, it is appropriate that it be strongly affected. If housing did not bear such a disproportionate burden, monetary policy would have to be more severe to accomplish the same degree of restriction in the economy. This would affect many sectors of the economy such as services that are less amenable to postponement and recovery later. Housing units can be produced at a later date to ameliorate any shortfall in a period of credit restriction.[12]

However, other economists have argued that it is unfair for one segment of the economy (and the labor and capital in that sector) to bear a disproportionate burden. The cost of credit restriction in terms of a decline in economic activity should be more evenly distributed throughout the economy, these economists maintain. It is also pointed out that many government programs, such as the activity of the FHLB itself, are designed to moderate cyclical impacts upon housing. Thus, the Fed and these government programs are working at cross purposes.[13]

We cannot resolve this issue here. The appropriateness of the disproportionate impact of monetary policy is part of an ongoing debate. However, it is clear that S&Ls are severely affected by monetary policy and that this has severe repercussions on the housing market.

---

[12] See W. L. Smith, "The Role of Government Intermediaries," in *Housing and Monetary Policy,* Conference Series No. 4, The Federal Reserve Bank of Boston (Oct. 1970), pp. 86–101, for a discussion of these issues.

[13] See H. M. Kaufman, "A Study in Conflicting Goals: Federal Stabilization and Mortgage Market Policies," in *The Political Economy of Policymaking,* M. Dooley, H. M. Kaufman, and R. Lombra, eds. (Beverly Hills, Calif.: Sage Publishers, 1979), pp. 129–48, for a discussion of these issues.

THE END OF THE FIXED RATE MORTGAGE?

California S&Ls Signal Impending Demise Of Fixed-Rate, 30-Year Home Mortgage

By G. Christian Hill

The fixed-rate, 30-year mortgage isn't dying in California. It is just about dead and buried.

In the last couple of months, several of the giant, state-chartered savings and loan associations that dominate California's mortgage market decided, quietly and independently, to stop offering long-term, fixed-rate mortgages, except to fulfill existing commitments.

Thrifts and banks across the country, their profits battered by wildly fluctuating interest rates, moved aggressively last year toward shorter-term mortgages—ones with rates renegotiable every one to five years, or with rates indexed to money costs. But the official death knell for the 30-year, fixed-rate home loan was probably tolled when some of the nation's biggest S&Ls decided to end them as a matter of policy.

Last December, Home Savings & Loan Association, the nation's largest S&L and a unit of H. F. Ahmanson & Co., switched almost exclusively to variable-rate mortgages. The rate can be adjusted up to one-half percentage point a year, depending on the cost of funds to Home Savings. Great Western Savings & Loan Association, the second-biggest S&L and a unit of Great Western Financial Corp., decided in January to write only fixed-rate mortgages due and payable in five years. Monthly payments, however, are calculated on a 30-year basis.

"No Longer Viable"

On Jan. 15, Home Federal Savings and Loan Association of San Diego adopted a single mortgage: three years with a renegotiable rate. The long-term, fixed-rate home loan "is no longer a practical and viable instrument in today's inflationary environment," says Richard Christopher, a senior vice president.

The retreat from the traditional mortgage isn't total. Some S&Ls still offer long-term, fixed-rate home loans under tiny minority-lending programs. Some may try to package fixed-rate mortgages for sale to government agencies. And lots of S&Ls haven't yet officially decided to stop making these long-term loans.

But for practical purposes, says an official of the California League of Savings and Loans: "It is dead, whether the consumer knows it yet or not."

Last year's roller-coaster interest rates did most of the damage. Banks and S&Ls were constantly having to adjust the rates they paid to attract savings. Rates rose and fell five percentage points to six percentage points within three months. At the same time, S&Ls were stuck with relatively fixed earnings from huge portfolios of long-term mortgages. As the cost of money skyrocketed, profits were squeezed.

The final blow was the near-demise of the secondary mortgage market, in which S&Ls used to sell off big packets of loans to raise cash for more lending. Now, traditional buyers such as insurance companies, and other S&Ls, want nothing to do with long-term loans.

"We don't know who in hell is going to buy fixed-rate, long-term mortgages," says Louis Anderson, a vice president at Imperial Savings & Loan Association, San Diego. "The purchasers are waking up. They don't want to lock their money up for 30 years any more than we do."

Imperial, a subsidiary of Imperial Corp. of America, along with World Savings & Loan Association, a unit of Golden West Financial Corp. of Oakland, led the movement to exclusively short-term lending last fall when it decided to offer mortgages callable in three to five years. Among California S&Ls, "callable" or "rollover" mortgages such as these are becoming the norm. In San Diego, Point Loma Savings & Loan Association is even writing a few loans at the bank prime rate of about 20%, due in full in one year.

Some Officials Worry

This practice worries state regulators and some thrift executives because unlike a federal or state-authorized renegotiable-rate mortgage, there's no guarantee that the lender will refinance the home when the mortgage comes due. But California S&Ls have been avoiding renegotiable mortgages because their rates can only go up one-half percentage point a year. Rollover mortgage rates, on the other hand, can rise without limit.

What happens if thousands of home buyers facing huge balloon payments in a few years find that mortgage money is tight or real estate prices haven't appreciated much? "The rollover mortgage bothers me," says Anthony Frank, chairman of Citizens Savings and Loan Association in San Francisco. "It puts the borrower in jeopardy."

Others point to Wisconsin, where banks have offered a form of rollover mortgage for 100 years, and thrifts now offer one year to five-year mortgages. Since the credit squeeze began, lenders there have held rate increases to an average 2½ percentage points to three percentage points. Richard Larson, president of West End Savings and Loan Association, West Bend, Wis., says he isn't aware of any recent evictions.

California S&L officials say that even with short-term callable mortgages, their rates haven't kept pace with money costs. They, and S&L executives elsewhere, want authority to copy an ultra-flexible loan sold since last fall by Wachovia Mortgage Co., a unit of Wachovia Bank & Trust Co., Winston-Salem, N.C.

Its interest rate moves quarterly without limits according to an index based on the price of three-month Treasury bills. Monthly payments, however, remain the same for five years. If interest costs exceed monthly payments, the excess is accrued as unpaid interest due at the end of the loan, or when the house is sold. The increase in monthly payments can't exceed 25% of payments in the previous five-year term, and the principal must be paid in 30 years.

Industry sources think some variant of the Wachovia mortgage, probably one tied to a less volatile index, will become the dominant mortgage in the U.S. Dennis Jacobe, an economist for the U.S. League of Savings Associations, says it "assures borrowers of a fixed monthly payment for a number of years, and it assures lenders that the interest rate will keep up with the market cost of money." The plan has been adopted by a number of state banks and S&Ls that don't have mortgage restrictions.

The Wall Street Journal, Feb. 12, 1981, p. 27. Reprinted by permission of *The Wall Street Journal,* © Dow Jones & Company, Inc., 1981. All Rights Reserved.

Key Points

1. Savings and loan associations are among the oldest financial intermediaries in the United States. They are the largest residential mortgage lender and their period of most rapid growth occurred with the boom in housing which followed World War II.

2. A dual system of chartering and supervising S&Ls exist just as it does for the commercial banking system. As a result, there are state chartered S&Ls and federally chartered S&Ls.

3. The basic problem that S&Ls face is the mismatch between their short-term sources of funds and their long-term mortgage lending. S&Ls intermediate along the maturity spectrum to a greater degree than any other depository intermediary. In periods of rapidly increasing interest rates, this mismatch places a serious squeeze on the margin between S&Ls' deposit rates and S&Ls' loan portfolio returns.

4. The major source of funds for S&Ls are savings and time deposits. Certificate accounts have grown rapidly in recent years, and certificates of deposits have surpassed passbook accounts as the largest deposit category. Of this category, six-month money-market certificates have shown the most rapid growth since their introduction in 1978.

5. The portfolio of S&Ls is dominated by mortgage loans. However, in 1980 S&Ls were granted increased authority to make consumer loans and construction loans and to acquire previously ineligible securities. This is just the start of what appears to be an increasing amount of diversification that will occur in the S&L portfolio. The mortgage instrument itself is also changing from the traditional fixed rate mortgage to a variable rate mortgage.

6. Housing is a very cyclical sector of the economy. This cyclical quality depends in part on the flow of funds from S&Ls into mortgages. Mortgage lending by S&Ls in turn depends upon their deposit inflows. These inflows are affected by open market interest rates. When these rates rise relative to deposit rates, disintermediation results leading to a reduction in funds available for S&Ls to lend in the mortgage market.

Questions for Discussion

1. It has been noted in the chapter that S&Ls do more intermediation along the maturity spectrum than any other financial intermediaries. What does this mean and why can this be a problem for S&Ls?

2. Compare and contrast the benefits and drawbacks of a fixed rate versus variable rate mortgage for S&Ls and for the mortgage borrower.

3. How does the S&Ls' role as the largest residential mortgage lender affect the housing cycle? What is disintermediation and how does it contribute to the S&Ls' impact upon the housing cycle? What recent developments can be regarded as attempts to reduce the amount of disintermediation that S&Ls face during periods of rising open-market interest rates?

4. What is the purpose of the FHLB advances program and how important is it as a source of funds to S&Ls?

5. Discuss the reasons that passbook saving accounts have declined relative to certificate of deposit accounts as a primary source of funds for S&Ls. What are some of the major types of certificate accounts?

6. S&Ls appear to be financial intermediaries in transition from very specialized mortgage lenders to more diversified financial intermediaries. What accounts for this change and how might S&Ls appear ten years from now compared to their present asset and liability structure?

Suggested Readings

Berkman, Neil G. "Mortgage Finance and the Housing Cycle." Federal Reserve Bank of Boston *New England Economic Review,* Sept./Oct. 1979, pp. 54–76.

Board of Governors of the Federal Reserve System. *Ways to Moderate Fluctuations in Housing Construction.* Washington, D.C.: FRS, 1972.

Feige, Edgar L., and D. K. Pearce. "The Substitutability of Money and Near Monies: A Survey of the Time Series Evidence." *Journal of Economic Literature,* June 1977, pp. 439–69.

Friend, Irwin, ed. *Study of the Savings and Loan Industry.* Washington, D.C.: Federal Home Loan Bank Board, 1969.

Lucarelli, Alphonse S., and Robert F. Teague, Jr. "Converting Into a Stock Company." Federal Home Loan Bank Board *Journal,* Sept. 1979, pp. 3–9.

Marcis, Richard G., and Dale Riordan. "The Savings and Loan Industry in the 1980s," Federal Home Loan Bank Board *Journal,* May 1980, pp. 2–15.

Winningham, Scott. "The Effects of Removing Regulation Q—A Theoretical Analysis." Federal Reserve Bank of Kansas City *Economic Review,* May 1980, pp. 13–23.

Other Depository Institutions: Mutual Savings Banks and Credit Unions

9

T here are two other major depository institutions in the United States in addition to commercial banks and savings and loan associations. These institutions are mutual savings banks (MSBs) and credit unions (CUs). Like S&Ls, mutual savings banks specialize in residential mortgage lending. Although MSBs are located in relatively few states, the size of the states in which they operate (New York and Massachusetts have the largest number) and their importance in these states make MSBs major financial intermediaries in the United States. Credit unions, by contrast, are located nationwide. Because they specialize in consumer lending, their rapid growth in the 1970s made them a major factor in the provision of consumer credit. These two institutions we will now consider in detail, beginning with mutual savings banks.

Mutual Savings Banks

Mutual savings banks are the third largest depository financial intermediary in the United States after commercial banks and savings and loan associations. Total assets at MSBs exceeded $172 billion as of February 1981. The size of MSBs is particularly noteworthy considering that mutual savings banks operate in only seventeen states, most in the New England and mid-Atlantic states. In fact, about 74 percent of all MSBs are located in Massachusetts, New York, and Connecticut. Table 9-1 lists the mutual savings bank states and the number of banks in each state.

The restriction of MSBs to only a minority of states is due to the fact that, uniquely among deposit institutions, MSBs were exclusively

Table 9-1
Number of Mutual Savings Banks, December 31, 1979

State	MUTUAL SAVINGS BANKS		
	Banks	Branches	Total Offices
Massachusetts	163	474	637
New York	112	1,155	1,267
Connecticut	65	329	394
Maine	29	92	121
New Hampshire	26	53	79
New Jersey	20	182	202
Washington	10	183	193
Pennsylvania	9	201	210
Rhode Island	6	69	75
Vermont	6	27	33
Indiana	4	3	7
Maryland	3	62	65
Wisconsin	3	—	3
Alaska	2	3	5
Delaware	2	24	26
Oregon	2	17	19
Minnesota	1	1	2
Total	463	2,875	3,338

Source: *1980 National Fact Book of Mutual Savings Banking,* National Association of Mutual Savings Banks.

state chartered until 1978. Legislation had been periodically placed before Congress to grant federal charters to mutual savings banks. In 1978, the Financial Institutions Regulatory and Interest Rate Control Act became law. One provision of this act permitted MSBs to convert to federal charter in the states in which they operated, and a number of MSBs have converted since 1978.

All MSBs, whether state or federally chartered, are eligible to join the Federal Home Loan Bank System. By the end of 1979, about 21 percent of MSBs were FHLB members. Furthermore, most deposits at MSBs are insured by the Federal Deposit Insurance Corporation, although the state of Massachusetts has a state insurance fund to which many MSBs in that state belong.

Although MSBs are regulated by the states in which they operate, all insured MSBs were required to abide by the interest rate ceilings set by the interagency coordinating committee composed of the Federal Reserve System, the FDIC, and the FHLB before 1980 and by the Depository Institution Deregulation Committee thereafter. These interest rate ceilings are set at the same level for MSBs as for S&Ls. Therefore, on most categories of time deposits, interest rates that MSBs can pay are one quarter of a point higher than for equivalent categories at commercial banks.[1] As is true for commercial banks and savings and loan associations, these ceilings are currently scheduled to be completely eliminated by 1985.

The Development of MSBs

Mutual savings banks are old institutions. The first mutual savings bank was founded in 1816 in Philadelphia.[2] As the name "mutual" implies, all MSBs are owned by their depositors. There are no stock mutual savings banks.[3] As a result, earnings after expenses, taxes, and additions to reserves are distributed to depositors as interest payments subject to interest rate ceiling restrictions.

Mutual savings banks, like S&Ls, have experienced most of their growth in the post–World War II period. Table 9-2 presents the assets of MSBs for selected years. From 1945 to 1980, assets at MSBs grew from $17 billion to over $170 billion. Until recent years, the increased growth of MSBs was accompanied by an increased association with residential mortgage financing, although MSB participation in the mortgage market has fluctuated a great deal. Figure 9-1 shows the percentage distribution of assets at MSBs through 1979. By the end of 1979, the MSB mortgage portfolio including mortgage-backed bonds[4] had dropped slightly from its 1970 level to about 71 percent of the total earning asset portfolio. This percentage is considerably smaller than that of S&Ls; the smaller commitment to mortgages by MSBs when compared to S&Ls is primarily due to the great degree of portfolio flexibility enjoyed by MSBs. However, mortgage holdings constitute a significantly larger percentage of the MSB portfolio than they do of portfolios of commercial banks and life insurance companies, two other prominent holders of mortgages. Figure 9-2 presents mortgage holdings by MSBs from 1960 to 1979 as a percentage of assets compared to commercial banks, life insurance companies, and S&Ls.

---

[1] There is no interest rate differential on Individual Retirement Accounts (IRAs) and Keough Plans. Further, the differential on money market certificates is suspended when the rate on six-month Treasury bills exceeds 8.75 percent, as noted in the last chapter.

[2] Actually two MSBs were founded in 1816, the Philadelphia Saving Fund Society first and the Provident Institution for Savings in Boston.

[3] There are, however, some stock savings banks, but these are very small in number.

[4] GNMA mortgage-backed bonds, which are pools of government-insured mortgages traded in the secondary mortgage market, are included in Table 9-2 in the "corporate and other" category. They amounted to about $1.2 billion in the MSB portfolio in 1979.

Table 9-2
Assets of Mutual Savings Banks, Selected Years, 1900–80
(Millions of Dollars)

Year	Mortgages	SECURITIES			Nonmortgage Loans	Cash and Other Assets	Total Assets
		U.S. Government	State and Local	Corporate and Other			
1900	$ 858	$ 105	$ 567	$ 462	$ 169	$ 167	$ 2,328
1910	1,500	13	765	906	194	220	3,598
1920	2,291	783	650	1,213	336	313	5,586
1930	5,635	499	920	2,278	312	520	10,164
1940	4,836	3,193	612	1,429	82	1,764	11,916
1945	4,202	10,650	84	1,116	62	849	16,962
1950	8,039	10,877	96	2,260	127	1,047	22,446
1955	17,279	8,463	646	3,364	211	1,382	31,346
1960	26,702	6,243	672	5,076	416	1,463	40,571
1965	44,433	5,485	320	5,170	862	1,962	58,232
1970	57,775	3,151	197	12,876	2,255	2,741	78,995
1971	61,984	3,268	390	18,030	2,810	3,099	89,581
1972	67,563	3,510	873	21,906	2,979	3,762	100,593
1973	73,231	2,958	926	21,382	3,871	4,282	106,650
1974	74,891	2,555	930	22,550	3,812	4,812	109,550
1975	77,221	4,740	1,545	27,993	4,023	5,535	121,056
1976	81,630	5,840	2,417	33,793	5,183	5,948	134,812
1977	88,195	5,895	2,828	37,918	6,210	6,240	147,287
1978	95,157	4,959	3,333	39,732	7,195	7,796	158,174
1979	98,908	7,658	2,930	37,087	9,253	7,568	163,405
1980	99,813	8,947	2,390	39,274	11,730	9,342	171,495

Note: End-of-year data except for 1900 to 1930 which are as of mid-year.

Source: *1980 National Fact Book of Mutual Savings Banking*, National Association of Mutual Savings Banks, and Federal Reserve *Bulletin*, May 1981.

Figure 9-1
Percentage Distribution of Assets of Mutual Savings Banks, Selected Years, 1900–79

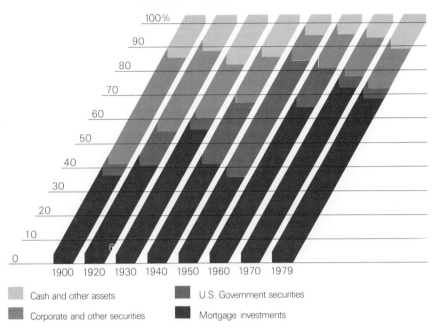

| Cash and other assets | U.S. Government securities |
| Corporate and other securities | Mortgage investments |

Note: End-of-year data except for 1900 to 1930 which are as of mid-year. Asset classifications are comparable to Table 9-2 except for corporate and other securities which include state and municipal obligations for all years shown and cash and other assets which include nonmortgage loans. Mortgage investments for 1979 include mortgage-backed securities, which are included in "Corporate and Other" in Table 9-2.

Source: *1980 National Fact Book of Mutual Savings Banking,* National Association of Mutual Savings Banks.

Returning to Figure 9-1, we can see that changes since 1945 are apparent in other categories of the portfolio. Particularly noticeable is the substantial decline in holdings of U.S. government securities and the increase in corporate and other securities. To explain these changes, let's consider the MSB portfolio in detail.

The MSB Portfolio

Table 9-3 presents the MSB portfolio for December 31, 1979. Although mortgages clearly dominate the MSB portfolio, notice the diversity of income-earning assets when compared to the portfolio holdings of S&Ls. As already noted, the MSBs have a great deal more flexibility

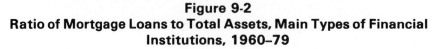

Figure 9-2
Ratio of Mortgage Loans to Total Assets, Main Types of Financial Institutions, 1960–79

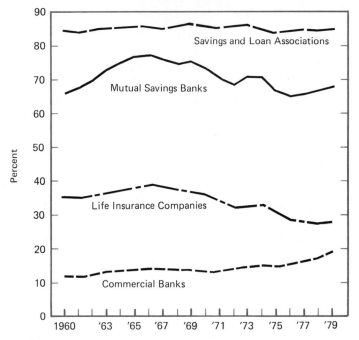

Source: *1980 National Fact Book of Mutual Savings Banking,* National Association of Mutual Savings Banks.

in portfolio selection than do S&Ls. Particularly striking is the inclusion in the securities portfolio of corporate bonds and stock. S&Ls are excluded from owning corporate bonds and stocks.

During and immediately following World War II, as Figure 9-1 made clear, MSBs had invested in federal government securities. In fact, as late as 1950, 48 percent of MSB assets were in federal government securities. But as Figure 9-1 showed, by the 1950s the major movement out of government securities and into mortgages had begun as the funds coming into MSBs grew and the post–World War II housing boom developed. At the same time, corporate securities became a more important part of the MSB portfolio, a trend that has continued in recent years. By February 1981, mortgages and corporate securities constituted 85 percent of total income-earning assets in the portfolio of MSBs.

The attraction to MSBs of both mortgages and corporate securities

Table 9-3
Portfolio of Mutual Savings Banks, December 31, 1979
(Millions of Dollars)

Items	Total
Cash	$ 3,156
U.S. Government and Federal Agency Obligations	7,658
State and Local Obligations	2,930
Mortgage Investments	110,729
Mortgage Loans	98,908
GNMA Mortgage-backed	11,820
Corporate Bonds	16,922
Other Bonds, Notes, and Debentures	3,584
Corporate Stock	4,760
Other Loans	9,253
Guaranteed Education Loans	1,274
Consumer Installment Loans	1,622
Home Improvement Loans	884
Federal Funds	3,076
Passbook Loans	1,340
All Other Loans	1,058
Total Income Earning Portfolio plus Cash	$158,992

Source: *1980 National Fact Book of Mutual Savings Banking,* National Association of Mutual Savings Banks.

was the generally higher returns on these holdings when compared to the return on federal government securities. Table 9-4 shows the rates of return since 1955 for selected years on mortgages, Treasury securities, and prime corporate securities. The differential advantage between the returns on mortgages and corporate securities over Treasury securities for most years is clear. However in 1978, 1979, and 1980, this advantage narrowed or even disappeared. In fact, in 1980 MSBs placed more of their new funds in government securities, including those of federal agencies, than in mortgages.

Mortgages as a percent of total MSB assets peaked in 1965 at about 76 percent and have since declined to about 65 percent. This decline occurred as MSBs directed much of their new funds inflows into corporate securities. With open market interest rates rising, and mortgage interest rates lagging, MSBs found corporate securities increasingly attractive, particularly when the liquidity advantage that corporates possess (there is a large secondary market for corporates) over mortgages is considered. The decline in mortgage loans may

Table 9-4
Rates of Return on Mortgages Held by Mutual Savings Banks
Compared to Open-Market Rates, Selected Years, 1955–77
(Percent)

Year	Mortgages	Corporate Bonds	Treasury Bonds
1955	4.25%	3.38%	2.91%
1960	4.75	4.94	3.88
1961	4.89	4.58	4.06
1962	5.02	4.28	3.87
1963	5.13	4.49	4.14
1964	5.18	4.49	4.14
1965	5.22	4.92	4.43
1966	5.30	5.98	4.65
1967	5.41	6.93	5.36
1968	5.56	7.28	5.66
1969	5.77	9.22	6.81
1970	5.97	8.13	5.97
1971	6.26	7.54	5.62
1972	6.53	7.50	5.63
1973	6.77	8.09	6.35
1974	6.98	9.47	6.77
1975	7.16	9.59	7.17
1976	7.38	7.90	6.38
1977	7.61	8.39	7.24
1978	7.92	9.07	8.49
1979	8.26	10.12	9.29

Note: Data represent operating income as a percentage of average holdings of mortgages. Mortgage income is net. Treasury bond and corporate bond rates are December of the year given until 1977, thereafter yearly average.

Source: *1980 National Fact Book of Mutual Savings Banking,* National Association of Mutual Savings Banks, and the Board of Governors of the Federal Reserve System.

have been even larger had it not been for the increasing purchase by MSBs of GNMA mortgage-backed securities in the 1970s. These securities represent large pools of mortgages. MSBs have found these securities attractive since their introduction in 1970 because they are actively traded in the secondary market and, therefore, more liquid than regular mortgage loans.

Rounding out the MSB portfolio are other loans, municipal securities, and federal agency obligations. Municipals are held because of their tax exempt status. MSBs are taxed at the corporate tax rate of 46 percent on earnings over $50,000. Federal agency securities, particularly those of the Federal National Mortgage Association and the Federal Home Loan Bank System, are held for their slightly higher yield than governments, their high liquidity, and their safety—the same reasons that govern commercial banks including these securities in their portfolios. Other loans are quite diverse, although for the most part consumer oriented. However, notice the federal funds category. MSBs are treated as banks for purposes of federal funds lending. Thus, federal funds loans are those made to commercial banks by MSBs.

Despite the greater portfolio flexibility enjoyed by MSBs when compared to S&Ls, MSBs still have suffered in recent years from the substantial rise of their deposit rates relative to the rates received on their portfolio. Fixed mortgage loans that had been made by MSBs in periods of lower rates and even long-term bonds that had been acquired failed to yield sufficient amounts to cover the increased cost of funds that MSBs faced.

In part to address this problem, 1980 legislation—which has previously been referred to in connection with commercial banks and S&Ls—gave federally chartered MSBs increased lending authority. Federally chartered MSBs may now make commercial, corporate, and business loans, although these may not exceed 5 percent of MSB assets. Lending directly to business augments the flow of funds into business that comes from MSB corporate stock and bond purchases. While this additional lending flexibility is rather small it will no doubt be expanded in time and may serve to substantially alter the MSB portfolio. State regulations are likely to be altered to permit state MSBs to follow suit. If such changes are not made, the incentive for state MSBs to switch to a federal charter will be quite large.

The Sources of MSB Funds

As Table 9-5 shows, the bulk of MSB funds are derived from deposits. However, a rapid change has occurred in the composition of deposits at MSBs. Until recently virtually all deposits at MSBs were passbook accounts. A majority of deposits are now certificate accounts (time deposits) as is clear from Table 9-6. In 1970, for example, about 16.5 percent of deposits were in certificates, while by December 1980 63 percent of regular deposits were in certificates. This change in deposit composition follows the similar trend at S&Ls and commercial banks. As open-market interest rates have risen and new types of certificate accounts paying higher rates have been introduced—such as the money market certificates (MMCs)—depositors have shifted their accounts and new deposits have flowed into certificate accounts.

The remaining sources of funds listed in Table 9-5 are minor and

Table 9-5
Liabilities at Mutual Savings Banks, December 31, 1980
(Millions of Dollars)

Regular Deposits	$151,355
Savings	53,942
Time	97,413
Other Deposits	2,084
Total Deposits	$153,439
Other Liabilities	6,692
Total Liabilities	$160,131

Source: Federal Reserve *Bulletin,* May 1981.

are lumped together in other liabilities, but the major item is borrowing. Recall that some MSBs are members of the FHLB and are eligible for FHLB advances. These advances constitute a major portion of MSB borrowing. MSBs also offer NOW accounts which are included in the "other deposit" category of Table 9-5.

There is one source of funds for MSB activity that is typically overlooked—as it is for savings and loan associations—and that is mortgage repayments. Mortgage repayments are the amount of funds flowing into MSBs in monthly mortgage payments, total mortgage payoffs, and sales of existing mortgages by the MSB in the secondary mortgage market. For example, in 1979 out of $144 billion flowing into MSBs, Table 9-7 shows that about $10 billion was derived from mortgage repayments. Mortgage repayments have been an important source of funds for MSBs for some time. They must be added to deposits in order to determine the funds available to MSBs to meet withdrawal claims and to acquire new income-earning assets. Table 9-7 gives a complete picture of the gross inflows and outflows of funds from MSBs. In addition to mortgage repayments, note the significant amount of interest credited to deposits and the negative sign on state and municipal and corporate security investments—indicating net sales of these securities to raise funds for the acquisition of other assets. MSBs also sold some U.S. government securities to raise funds.

Disintermediation

MSBs, like S&Ls, have faced the severe problem of disintermediation through the years. Table 9-8 presents the percentage change in regular deposits, excluding interest for selected years. (Excluding interest that MSBs credit to depositor accounts yields a more accurate picture of

Table 9-6
Deposits in Mutual Savings Banks by Type of Account,
1930–80
(End of Period, Millions of Dollars)

Year	Total	REGULAR Total	Savings	Time
1930	$ 9,465	n.a.	n.a.	n.a.
1940	10,618	$ 10,584	n.a.	n.a.
1945	15,332	15,287	n.a.	n.a.
1950	20,025	19,893	n.a.	n.a.
1960	36,343	36,086	n.a.	n.a.
1970	71,580	71,157	$59,345	$11,812
1971	81,440	81,082	63,976	17,106
1972	91,613	91,214	68,238	22,976
1973	96,496	96,056	65,221	30,836
1974	98,701	98,221	64,286	33,935
1975	109,873	109,291	69,653	39,639
1976	122,877	121,961	74,535	47,426
1977	134,017	132,744	78,005	54,739
1978	142,701	141,170	71,816	69,354
1979	146,006	144,070	61,123	82,947
1980	153,439	151,355	53,942	97,413

n.a.—not available or not applicable.
Note: Total includes other deposits which are not listed separately. These are primarily checkable deposits.

Source: *1980 National Fact Book of Mutual Savings Banking,* National Association of Mutual Savings Banks, and the Federal Reserve *Bulletin,* May 1981.

depositor decisions.) Notice the outflow of funds (disintermediation) during the years 1969, 1973–74, and 1978–79 and the very slight inflow of 1966. Outflows also occurred in 1980 and 1981. These years correspond to periods of rising open-market rates. The outflow of funds from MSBs has often contributed to difficulty in housing, as noted for these years in the last chapter. Even though MSBs have typically placed whatever funds were available into the mortgage market during these periods, their contribution to the market because of their lack of funds was very slight; in 1979 they acquired only $3.8 billion net in mortgages, and in 1980 they acquired only $900 million in mortgages.

Open-market interest rates rose a great deal in 1978 and 1979.

Table 9-7
Gross Flow of Funds Through Mutual Savings Banks, 1979
(Millions of Dollars)

Item	1979
Inflow:	
Amounts Deposited	$122,026
Interest on Deposits	9,876
Mortgage Repayments	9,992
Retained Earnings	741
U.S. Governments	649
All Other Sources	—
Total Inflow	$143,284
Outflow:	
Withdrawals	$128,987
Mortgage Loans Acquired	14,255
Net Security Investment	
State and Municipal	−623
Corporate and Other	−886
All Other Uses	1,551
Total Outflow	$143,284

Note: Amounts deposited and withdrawn exclude school, club and other special-purpose accounts.

Source: *1980 National Fact Book of Mutual Savings Banking,* National Association of Mutual Savings Banks.

However, until well into 1979, the amount of disintermediation that would normally occur at the levels of prevailing open-market rates did not occur. The reasons are not hard to determine. First, the MSBs' depositors channeled more funds into the higher interest rate CDs that have longer maturities and are subject to early withdrawal penalties. Most importantly, since they were introduced in June 1978, the MMCs have given the MSB depositor the chance to receive open-market rates at MSBs. However, discontinuing the monthly compounding of interest in MMCs (which was allowed from the inception of MMCs until March 1979) lessened the popularity of these deposits somewhat. The pull of higher open-market rates started to induce disintermediation in the middle of 1979, and this continued in 1980 and 1981 as money market mutual funds and open-market securities attracted funds from MSBs despite the MMCs. In an inflationary environment, people are more aware of interest rates and are more interested in securing the highest return possible than when prices are relatively

Table 9-8
Percentage Change in Regular Deposits, Excluding Interest, in Mutual Savings Banks, 1960–79

Year	Total Change
1960	0.4%
1961	1.6
1962	3.9
1963	3.8
1964	5.2
1965	3.1
1966	0.4
1967	4.4
1968	2.0
1969	−1.1
1970	1.4
1971	8.0
1972	6.7
1973	−0.5
1974	−2.9
1975	4.8
1976	4.8
1977	2.4
1978	−0.4
1979	−4.9

Note: Regular deposits include savings and time deposits. Data are based on amounts deposited less amounts withdrawn, excluding interest credited, in regular accounts.

Source: *1980 National Fact Book of Mutual Savings Banking,* National Association of Mutual Savings Banks.

stable and interest rates low. In 1980 and 1981, MSB depositors realized that they could achieve higher liquidity and a somewhat higher rate of return for smaller amounts of funds at money market mutual funds than at MSBs and acted accordingly. While MMCs held their own, other deposits were significantly affected as a result.

Consolidated Balance Sheet of MSBs

An overall picture of MSBs comes from considering the consolidated balance sheet of the savings banks presented in Table 9-9 for December 31, 1979. The balance sheet is a recapitulation to some degree

Table 9-9
Assets and Liabilities of Mutual Savings Banks,
December 31, 1979
(Millions of Dollars)

Item	Total
Assets	
Cash	$ 3,156
U.S. Government and Federal Agency Obligations	7,658
State and Local Obligations	2,930
Mortgage Investments	110,729
Mortgage Loans	98,908
GNMA Mortgage-backed	11,820
Corporate Bonds	16,922
Other Bonds, Notes, and Debentures	3,584
Corporate Stock	4,760
Other Loans	9,253
Guaranteed Education Loans	1,274
Consumer Installment Loans	1,622
Home Improvement Loans	884
Federal Funds	3,076
Passbook Loans	1,340
All Other Loans	1,058
Bank Premises Owned	1,573
Other Real Estate	304
Other Assets	2,535
Total Assets	$163,405
Liabilities	
Regular Deposits	$144,070
Savings	61,123
Time	82,947
School and Club	199
Other Deposits	1,737
Total Deposits	146,006
Borrowings and Mortgage Warehousing	3,653
Other Liabilities	2,220
Total Liabilities	151,879
Capital Notes and Debentures	385
Other General Reserves	11,141
Total General Reserve Accounts	11,525
Total Liabilities and General Reserve Accounts	$163,405

Source: *1980 National Fact Book of Mutual Savings Banking,* National Association of Mutual Savings Banks.

of the information found in Tables 9-3 and 9-5. Therefore, most categories have been discussed previously. However, cash on the asset side and reserves on the liability and capital side of the balance sheet require some attention. Cash is necessary for day-to-day business; it is held for the same reasons commercial banks hold vault cash. General reserves are the equivalent of the capital account for stock institutions. This category consists of retained earnings and reserves against bad loans. One item that appears on the balance sheet that hasn't been examined in detail is other deposits. Other deposits are, for the most part, checking-type deposits which require further discussion.

NOW Accounts and Other Checkable Deposits

The evolutionary changes that are occurring in the financial system are apparent at MSBs. In fact, part of the change toward a more competitive financial system was initiated by MSBs in Massachusetts and New Hampshire, when MSBs in those states found a way around the prohibition on the payment of interest on demand deposits by the simple expedient of calling them something else. In 1972 MSBs in these states began offering NOW accounts (Negotiable Orders of Withdrawal). While initially NOW accounts were only legal in those two states as Congress restricted their spread, subsequent legislation at both the national and state level led to the authorization of checking accounts in 1975 at MSBs in Oregon, Maine, Connecticut, New York, and Delaware; the extension of NOW accounts to all of New England in 1976; the authorization of noninterest-earning NOW accounts (NI-NOWs) in Pennsylvania and New England; and the authorization of NOW accounts in New York in 1978. By these measures, almost all of the 466 MSBs that were doing business in 1978 could offer checkable accounts prior to the nationwide authorization of NOW accounts in 1980. Further, the legislation authorizing NOW accounts nationwide also allowed federally chartered MSBs the authority to accept demand deposits in connection with a commercial, corporate, or business loan relationship.

Aside from the fact that NOW accounts pay interest, the differences between NOW accounts and demand deposits are not significant. Both are checking accounts. However, NOW accounts are only permitted for individuals and nonprofit institutions. The extension of demand deposit authority to federal MSBs, therefore, appears to open the door for both MSBs and S&Ls to gain permission to offer demand deposit accounts in the future much as commercial banks do. If such authority is granted, this will open up an entirely new source of funds to these institutions.

NOW accounts and demand deposits at MSBs represent a very small portion of total deposits at these institutions. In 1979, when 427 out of 463 MSBs were authorized to offer NOW accounts, these deposits totaled only $1.3 billion compared to total deposits of $146 billion at MSBs. By April 1981, when nationwide NOW account authority had existed for four months, all checkable deposits at MSBs, S&Ls, and credit unions only totaled $12 billion. This compared to demand deposits of $250 billion and NOW accounts of $52.6 billion at commercial banks. However, the importance of NOW accounts in general will no doubt grow over time, and MSBs should gain a share of this growth.

Credit Unions

Credit unions (CUs) are the smallest of the depository institutions in the United States, with total assets of just over $70 billion as of March 1981. Credit unions differ from other depository institutions in a number of ways. CUs are cooperative institutions whose members are related by occupation, employer, or, sometimes, residence. Credit unions are also highly specialized in their lending activity, which is restricted to lending to credit union members with loans directed to consumer financing. As Table 9-10 makes clear, CUs are the second largest financial intermediary in the provision of consumer installment credit.[5]

There is a dual system of chartering for CUs as there is for commercial banks and S&Ls. Credit unions can receive a federal charter or a state charter in 46 states. Although credit unions have existed in the United States since 1908, when the first credit union was formed in New Hampshire, it is only since the Federal Credit Union Act of 1934 that federal charters have been available. Nevertheless, total assets of federal credit unions had grown to $36.5 billion by 1979 compared to $29.5 billion for state-chartered credit unions. The National Credit Union Administration (NCUA) regulates federally chartered CUs.

The growth of credit unions has been very rapid in the period since World War II. In the 1950s assets increased sixfold; and, while the rate slowed somewhat in the 1960s, assets of CUs still increased by three times. In the decade of the 1970s, assets increased about fourfold. This rapid asset growth makes credit unions among the fastest growing of financial intermediaries although their growth slowed in 1979, 1980, and 1981 due to disintermediation.

The growth of credit unions has been greatly enhanced since 1970 by the availability of federal insurance for savings at credit unions. All federally chartered credit unions have their member accounts in-

---

[5] If all financial institutions are counted, credit unions trail finance companies, which are not intermediaries, in the provision of consumer credit. In 1979 finance companies had $68.3 billion in consumer credit outstanding.

Table 9-10
Consumer Installment Credit Outstanding for Financial Intermediaries December 31, 1979 and 1978
(Millions of Dollars)

Type of Lender	AMOUNT OUTSTANDING	
	1979	1978
Financial Intermediaries, total	$214,888	$196,455
Commercial banks	$149,604	$136,189
Credit unions	48,186	45,939
Miscellaneous lenders[1]	17,098	14,327

[1] Includes savings and loan associations and mutual savings banks.
Source: National Credit Union Administration, *Annual Report,* 1979.

sured up to $100,000 by the National Credit Union Share Insurance Fund. This is the same limit provided by the FDIC for commercial banks and MSBs and by the FSLIC for savings and loan associations. State-chartered credit unions are also eligible for federal insurance. While only about 50 percent of all state-chartered credit unions were insured by the National Credit Union Insurance Fund as of 1979, 63 percent of the savings at all state-chartered credit unions were covered, indicating that it is the larger of the state credit unions that seek federal insurance.

Consumer lending dominates the credit union portfolio. As Table 9-11 shows, consumer lending has hovered around 90 percent of all credit union lending since 1975. Since credit union loans constituted about 89 percent of the CU income-earning portfolio in 1979, the business of credit unions may well be said to be making consumer loans. However, in 1980 credit union consumer lending actually declined. The reason that this occurred, despite positive deposit inflows, was that credit unions were restricted to charging only 12 percent per year on loans. Since many credit unions were paying higher rates for their new funds, a negative spread between borrowing and lending rates arose. As a result, CUs used new funds to acquire income-earning securities, primarily those of the U.S. government. Legislative changes in 1980, however, now permit a much more flexible CU lending rate. In 1980 this rate was 15 percent per year. In 1981 and early 1982, it was 21 percent. As a result of this increase in permissible loan rates, CUs once again resumed their traditional role as consumer lenders by the end of 1980.

Table 9-11
Credit Union Loans Outstanding, 1975–79
(Millions of Dollars)

| | TOTAL CONSUMER CREDIT | | | TYPE OF CREDIT | | | | |
| | | | | AUTOMOBILE | | OTHER | |
Year	Total Loans	Amount	Percent of Total Loans	Amount	Percent of Total Consumer Credit	Amount	Percent of Total Consumer Credit
1975	$28,168	$25,666	91.1%	$12,741	49.6%	$12,925	50.4%
1976	34,310	31,169	90.8	15,238	48.9	15,931	51.1
1977	41,895	37,605	89.8	18,099	48.1	19,506	51.9
1978	50,269	45,939	91.4	21,967	47.8	23,972	52.2
1979	52,230	48,186	92.3	23,042	47.8	25,144	52.2

Source: National Credit Union Administration. *Annual Report,* 1979.

Table 9-11 shows that the largest single category of credit union lending was for automobiles. Automobile lending accounted for almost one half of credit union lending in 1979. The remainder of the lending was primarily for personal, household, and family expenses. Vacation loans and bill consolidation loans figured prominently in this total. Repair and modernization loans round out the total loan portfolio.

The credit union portfolio contains investments as well as loans. In 1979, investments accounted for about 11 percent of the income-earning portfolio of credit unions. Of this amount the primary investments were U.S. government and U.S. agency securities and deposits at other institutions. Historically these investments were made by CUs for liquidity purposes. However, in 1980, the amount of U.S. government securities increased percipitously due to the low rate on loans obtainable in the first part of the year and the high rates obtainable on these securities. In 1980, CUs purchased $8.3 billion in U.S. government securities compared to a neglible amount in 1979 and 1978. This increase in holding government securities contrasts with a $2.5 billion decline in consumer lending in 1980. Thus, investments are currently a larger portion of the CU portfolio than historically has been the case. With increased lending rates, however, it is likely that the historic position of investments as a relatively small portion of the CU portfolio will be reestablished over time.

Credit unions have proved to be particularly innovative in their lending programs in recent years. Credit unions were the first institutions to move to 60-month auto loans. Further, rules published in November 1977 permit federal credit unions to make residential mortgage loans on one-to-four family houses. However, mortgage lending by CUs is still very limited. Most credit unions have not yet geared up for mortgage lending and do not yet offer mortgage loans. Nevertheless, mortgage lending by CUs may grow into an important source of credit to the mortgage market and an important part of the credit union portfolio over time.

Sources of Credit Union Funds

The bulk of credit union funds comes from member shares. The shares represent ownership in the credit unions since CUs are cooperative associations. Shares are very similar to passbook accounts at other depository institutions. However, CUs have historically paid higher rates on these accounts than has been paid by other intermediaries. This was due to the higher interest rate ceiling permitted by regulators and the fact that as nonprofit institutions CUs were exempt from federal taxation and could pass this saving on to depositors. Some state institutions are permitted to accept other types of savings accounts called deposits. These deposits are advantageous to credit unions in raising funds in that states usually allow higher rates to be paid on these funds. Credit unions are permitted to offer MMCs as well and have done so since 1978. As they have for other depository financial intermediaries, MMCs have become an important source of funds for CUs in recent years. Over 85 percent of credit union funds come from member savings.

In 1978, federal credit unions were permitted to offer share draft accounts. Share draft accounts are checking-type accounts that pay interest, very similar to NOW accounts. As with NOW accounts, legislative changes now permit all CUs to offer share draft accounts. However, share drafts are a very small source of funds to CUs at this time.

In recent years as CUs, like S&Ls and MSBs, have faced disintermediation, they have increased their level of borrowing to raise additional funds. In 1979, federal credit unions raised about 5 percent of their funds in this way, and borrowing has been much higher at some individual credit unions. The CUs typically have to pay market rates for borrowings; and, since their loan portfolio is generally weighted with many loans made at relatively low rates, such borrowing has seriously squeezed margins at some CUs. It is likely, however, that this recourse to borrowed funds will not increase substantially above current levels. Furthermore, the increase in permissible lending rates at CUs should relieve the pressure on margins as old loans at low rates are repaid and new loans at higher rates replace them in the CU portfolio. The CUs have an advantage in this regard over S&Ls and MSBs in that almost all their loans have terms of less than five years. The replacement in credit union portfolios of low yielding loans by higher yielding loans became even more important in 1982. Effective May 1, 1982, the National Credit Union Administration removed all deposit ceilings on federally chartered credit unions. Thus, credit unions became the first depository intermediaries to have their deposit rates totally deregulated.

CREDIT UNIONS IN CRISIS

The Tight Squeeze on Credit Unions

Not so long ago, credit unions—member-owned financial institutions—seemed blessed with a golden opportunity. Able to attract deposits through interest-bearing checking accounts known as share drafts and benefiting from low overhead, they were poised to grab a sizable share of the consumer loan market and thereby make inroads on the traditional turf of their large competitors—commercial banks, thrift institutions, and finance companies.

But rising interest rates, financial reform, federally imposed credit controls, and a wave of credit union failures have changed all that. Now, credit unions will be doing well simply to prevent their competitors from carving away still more of their business.

For credit unions are feeling the pressure not only of high interest rates, but of burgeoning competition in a deregulated financial environment. Because of landmark federal legislation passed last year, commercial banks and savings and loan associations are now paying interest on checking accounts; thrift institutions are expanding their consumer lending activity. And larger credit unions must now post reserves at the Federal Reserve Board. All told, this spells a loss of market share for the financial cooperatives and imperils the health of small credit unions.

Losing advantages. "The credit unions will survive. But as the financial system becomes more homogeneous, they are going to lose their competitive edge," says Jerome I. Baron, analyst with Merrill Lynch & Co. In fact, credit unions have already lost much of that edge. While empowered to pay up to 7% interest on share draft accounts, few can afford to do so, and only the largest offer share drafts at all. And rates on four-year car loans are sometimes the same as rates quoted by banks.

Today, the credit unions' share of the consumer lending market has fallen to 14% from 16.5% at the start of 1977. More distressed even than the savings and loan associations, credit unions were victims last year of record high rates of interest and an anemic economy. A record 326 credit unions entered liquidation in 1980, up from 277 in 1979.

All of this is in marked contrast with the bright future that seemed to lie ahead for credit unions at the start of 1977. Their costs of operation were—and are—minimal because they pay no taxes, make big use of volunteer services, and often have free office space provided by employers of their members. And they were just coming into possession of imposing powers: share draft accounts paying 7%, authority to branch out into mortgage lending, and a hookup with the Visa credit card system.

But all those new features proved expensive for most credit unions because an average-sized union has assets of only $3 million. And when interest rates began running up in late 1977, leading to creation of the six-month money market certificates that permitted banks and savings and loans to pay higher rates on deposits, the credit unions lost "core" deposits. By 1979 they were lending out almost every dollar they could collar, yet their consumer loans outstanding rose only 5% while consumer lending nationwide rose 14%.

Then came 1980. The credit controls imposed in March weighed heaviest on consumer lending. The recession and an increasing number of plant closings in industries such as autos and steel squeezed credit union members' financial positions and dissolved the employment affiliation at the core of scores of these institutions.

'Sense of pride.' Credit union regulators think the pressure may be easing. A federally mandated override of state usury ceilings, recovery from the 1980 recession, and declining interest rates may have staved off a crisis. "There has been considerable improvement in the earnings of credit unions," says Lawrence Connell, chairman of the National Credit Union Administration.

Credit union representatives remain confident there is a place for them in the financial system. "I think our future looks very good," says Jim R. Williams, president of the Credit Union National Assn. "People are not just users of a credit union, they are the owners of a credit union. And there's a great sense of pride in that."

Most analysts think that credit unions will still be the primary lenders for their traditional constituency—young, usually middle-income wage earners with little or no credit history. But it is no longer likely that they can significantly erode the business of banks or thrifts. "That's particularly true when you realize credit unions don't have branches and are not very convenient—convenience being the key for the consumer," says Merrill Lynch's Baron.

Key Points

1. Mutual savings banks (MSBs) specialize in mortgage lending and credit unions (CUs) specialize in consumer lending. Mutual savings banks could only obtain a state charter until 1978, but thereafter they could receive a federal charter. Credit unions can obtain either a state or federal charter.

2. Historically MSBs invested in U.S. government securities. However, following World War II, MSBs started moving out of governments and into mortgages so that mortgage lending came to dominate the MSB portfolio. MSBs, though, have more portfolio flexibility than S&Ls; and, as a result, the percentage of MSB assets held in mortgages was never as great as that of S&Ls and this percentage has declined in recent years. Federal MSBs have recently been permitted to expand their lending into loans to business and as a result over time portfolio diversification at MSBs can be expected to increase. Further, all MSBs can offer NOW accounts, and when associated with lending, federal MSBs can accept demand deposits.

3. The major source of funds for MSBs are savings and time deposits. Certificates of deposit, especially MMCs, grew rapidly in the 1970s and now exceed passbook savings accounts by a wide margin.

4. Credit unions are the smallest of the depository intermediaries. They specialize in consumer loans, which constitute the major portion of their portfolio. CUs became an important source of consumer credit for the economy in the 1970s when they experienced rapid growth. This growth occurred primarily because CUs offered favorable rates on consumer loans relative to alternative lenders.

5. The major source of funds for CUs is savings and time deposits. As is true of all depository institutions, certificate accounts have grown rapidly at CUs in recent years. Credit unions can offer NOW accounts, which are called share draft accounts at credit unions.

Questions for Discussion

1. The depository intermediaries have now been discussed in this and preceding chapters. Each intermediary specializes to some degree in lending to a particular sector of the economy. Compare and contrast commercial bank, S&L, MSB, and CU lending specialization.

2. What changes common to all depository financial intermediaries have taken place in the last decade in the way in which depository financial intermediaries obtain funds?

3. Compare MSBs and S&Ls in their ability to diversify their portfolios and the differences in portfolio composition that have resulted.

4. Credit unions experienced rapid growth in the 1970s. What accounted for this growth?

5. Why have all other depository financial intermediaries argued that CUs have an unfair advantage when it comes to paying interest on savings deposits? (Hint: They are nonprofit institutions.)

Suggested Readings

Berkman, Neil G. "Mortgage Finance and the Housing Cycle." Federal Reserve Bank of Boston *New England Economic Review,* Sept./Oct. 1979, pp. 54–76.

Black, Harold, and Robert H. Dugger. "Credit Union Structure, Growth, and Regulatory Problems." *The Journal of Finance,* May 1981, pp. 529–38.

Brockschmidt, Peggy. "Credit Union Growth in Perspective." Federal Reserve Bank of Kansas City *Monthly Review,* Feb. 1977, pp. 3–13.

Cargill, Thomas F. "Recent Research on Credit Unions: A Survey." *Journal of Economics and Business,* Winter 1977, pp. 155–62.

Flannery, Mark J. "Credit Unions as Consumer Lenders in the United States." Federal Reserve Bank of Boston *New England Economic Review,* July/August 1974, pp. 3–12.

Melvin, Donald J., Raymond N. Davis, and Gerald Fischer. *Credit Unions and the Credit Union Industry.* New York: New York Institute of Finance, 1977.

National Association of Mutual Savings Bank, *Annual Report,* May 1981.

National Credit Union Association, *Annual Reports.*

Nondepository Financial Intermediaries and Institutions

10

A number of important financial intermediaries have not yet been discussed. These intermediaries, while disparate in their operations and goals, can all be characterized as nondepository intermediaries. They do not accept deposits in contrast to the financial intermediaries previously examined. Nondepository financial intermediaries include life insurance companies, pension funds, and mutual funds or investment companies as they are sometimes called.

In addition to the nondepository intermediaries, some important financial institutions are not truly financial intermediaries but have some of the characteristics of financial intermediaries. These include finance companies and casualty insurance companies. Financial intermediaries have been defined in this text as institutions that transfer funds from ultimate savers to ultimate borrowers in the economy. Thus, finance companies, which typically do not obtain funds directly from ultimate savers, and casualty insurance companies, which sell a service, do not meet the strict definition of financial intermediaries. Nevertheless, their similarities to financial intermediaries and their importance requires that they also be discussed.

Finally, the last section of this chapter deals with what may be called the "new financial intermediaries." These intermediaries have been called "financial supermarkets" or "financial department stores." They began to develop in the late 1970s and early 1980s, led by the stock brokerage firm of Merrill Lynch. These new financial intermediaries offer a wide range of financial services including cash management accounts, credit cards, and real estate brokerage. They are typically outside the regulatory framework of traditional financial intermediaries, and this gives them a great deal of flexibility in satisfying

237

customer demands for financial services. Many observers view these financial supermarkets as already incorporating many of the services that will be provided by all financial intermediaries in the future. Their current activities have already put a great deal of pressure on regulatory bodies to allow traditional financial intermediaries more flexibility in offering a larger array of financial services to their customers. Our discussion will point out what these new financial intermediaries are doing now and what their development means to the future of financial intermediaries. First, however, we will examine the nondepository financial intermediaries.

Life Insurance Companies

Life insurance companies are one of the largest financial intermediaries in the United States. They are organized as either mutual or stockholder-owned companies, although this makes little practical difference in their operations. Life insurance company assets exceeded $476 billion at the end of 1980. These companies provide whole life insurance, annuity plans, and endowment policies, which are in part savings programs, as well as term insurance, which has no saving feature. An annuity is a stream of payments to a beneficiary commencing at some prearranged period of time and generally payable until death. An endowment policy pays a lump sum after some agreed upon period of time. Included in the premium paid for a whole life insurance policy is an amount that goes to build up a cash value in the policy. Thus, part of the policyholder's premium is saving while only part goes to pay for protection. Whole life differs from term insurance because of the saving feature. Term insurance premiums are payments only for the insurance protection. That is why term insurance premiums are usually lower than whole life premiums for the same amount of coverage.

The Portfolio of Life Insurance Companies

Table 10-1 shows the distribution of life insurance company assets for selected years through 1979, both in dollars and in percentage terms. Focusing on the latest year, 1979, notice that the largest category of life insurance assets was corporate bonds, accounting for over 39 percent of the portfolio. Mortgages (in recent years mostly nonresidential) were the second largest category representing about 27.4 percent of the portfolio. While still a large percentage, mortgages have declined substantially as a percentage of the life insurance company portfolio from the mid-1960s. The reduction in the commitment of life insurance companies to the residential mortgage market has been even more dramatic than is apparent from the overall mortgage category.

In the 1950s and into the 1960s, life insurance companies concentrated heavily on residential mortgages. However, residential mortgage holdings have declined precipitously in relative terms in recent years. For example, at the end of 1959 almost 70 percent of mortgage loans held by life insurance companies were on residential properties. By 1969, this percentage had declined to less than 60 percent, and by 1979 only 30 percent of life insurance mortgage holdings were residential. Home mortgages defined as those held on one-to-four family houses faired even worse. From 1959, when home mortgages accounted for 60 percent of mortgage holding, these had declined to only 13.5 percent in 1979.

The movement into nonresidential mortgage loans (mostly commercial mortgages), the heavy concentration in corporate bonds, and the acquisition of corporate stock indicate a distinct shift by life insurance companies to business financing. There are a number of reasons for this shift. Among these reasons are higher returns available on alternative investments during much of the last twenty years and their greater liquidity. Furthermore, the rapid growth in nonresidential mortgage financing coincided with the boom in what life insurance companies regarded as attractive mortgage opportunities. These included financing shopping centers and office buildings.

The shift from mortgages, particularly residential mortgages, was not the only dramatic change in portfolio composition that has taken place at life insurance companies. At the end of World War II, 50 percent of life insurance company portfolios were made up of government securities. This percentage declined to 4 to 7 percent of the portfolios by the late 1960s and stayed at that level during the 1970s. The relative increase in government securities holdings that took place in the latter part of the 1970s is almost entirely accounted for by increases in federal agency securities. Federal government securities are held primarily for liquidity purposes.

Municipal securities are not a large holding in life insurance portfolios. These holdings are included in the government securities column of Table 10-1. In 1979, about $6.5 billion in municipals were held by life insurance companies. Because life insurance companies are treated more favorably than most other financial intermediaries under existing tax laws, municipals lack popularity with them. The lower effective tax rate for life insurance companies means that the interest exemption feature of municipals is worth less to them.[1]

---

[1] The after-tax yield on municipal securities relative to other taxable securities is dependent on the tax bracket of the investor, as has previously been discussed.

Table 10-1
Distribution of Assets of Life Insurance Companies
(Millions of Dollars)

Year	Government Securities	Corporate Securities Bonds	Stocks	Mortgages	Real Estate	Policy Loans	Misc. Assets	Total
1917	$ 562	$ 1,975	$ 83	$ 2,021	$ 179	$ 810	$ 311	$ 5,941
1920	1,349	1,949	75	2,442	172	859	474	7,320
1925	1,311	3,022	81	4,808	266	1,446	604	11,538
1930	1,502	4,929	519	7,598	548	2,807	977	18,880
1935	4,727	5,314	583	5,357	1,990	3,540	1,705	23,216
1940	8,447	8,645	605	5,972	2,065	3,091	1,977	30,802
1945	22,545	10,060	998	6,636	857	1,962	1,738	44,797
1950	16,118	23,248	2,103	16,102	1,445	2,413	2,591	64,020
1955	11,829	35,912	3,633	29,445	2,581	3,290	3,742	90,432
1960	11,815	46,740	4,981	41,771	3,765	5,231	5,273	119,576
1965	11,908	58,244	9,126	60,013	4,681	7,678	7,234	158,884
1970	11,068	73,098	15,420	74,375	6,320	16,064	10,909	207,254
1971	11,000	79,198	20,607	75,496	6,904	17,065	11,832	222,102
1972	11,372	86,140	26,845	76,948	7,295	18,003	13,127	239,730
1973	11,403	91,796	25,919	83,369	7,693	20,199	14,057	252,436
1974	11,965	96,652	21,920	86,234	8,331	22,862	15,385	263,349
1975	15,177	105,837	28,061	89,167	9,621	24,467	16,974	289,304
1976	20,260	120,666	34,262	91,552	10,476	25,834	18,502	321,552
1977	23,565	137,889	33,753	96,848	11,060	27,556	21,051	351,722
1978	26,552	156,044	35,518	106,167	11,764	30,146	23,733	389,924
1979	29,719	168,990	39,757	118,421	13,007	34,825	27,563	432,282

Percent

Year								
1917	9.6%	33.2%	1.4%	34.0%	3.0%	13.6%	5.2%	100.0%
1920	18.4	26.7	1.0	33.4	2.3	11.7	6.5	100.0
1925	11.3	26.2	.7	41.7	2.3	12.5	5.3	100.0
1930	8.0	26.0	2.8	40.2	2.9	14.9	5.2	100.0
1935	20.4	22.9	2.5	23.1	8.6	15.2	7.3	100.0
1940	27.5	28.1	2.0	19.4	6.7	10.0	6.3	100.0
1945	50.3	22.5	2.2	14.8	1.9	4.4	3.9	100.0
1950	25.2	36.3	3.3	25.1	2.2	3.8	4.1	100.0
1955	13.1	39.7	4.0	32.6	2.9	3.6	4.1	100.0
1960	9.9	39.1	4.2	34.9	3.1	4.4	4.4	100.0
1965	7.5	36.7	5.7	37.8	3.0	4.8	4.5	100.0
1970	5.3	35.3	7.4	35.9	3.0	7.8	5.3	100.0
1971	4.9	35.7	9.3	34.0	3.1	7.7	5.3	100.0
1972	4.8	35.9	11.2	32.1	3.0	7.5	5.5	100.0
1973	4.5	36.4	10.3	32.2	3.0	8.0	5.6	100.0
1974	4.5	36.7	8.3	32.8	3.2	8.7	5.8	100.0
1975	5.2	36.6	9.7	30.8	3.3	8.5	5.9	100.0
1976	6.3	37.5	10.7	28.5	3.3	8.0	5.7	100.0
1977	6.7	39.2	9.6	27.5	3.2	7.8	6.0	100.0
1978	6.8	40.0	9.1	27.2	3.0	7.8	6.1	100.0
1979	6.9	39.1	9.2	27.4	3.0	8.1	6.3	100.0

Source: American Council of Life Insurance, *Life Insurance Fact Book*, 1980.

Policy loans are the fourth largest category in the portfolio of life insurance companies. These loans constituted about 8 percent of their portfolio in 1979. Policy loans are made to policyholders against the cash value of the holders' whole life policies. These loans are made at favorable rates. Thus, they become attractive when interest rates in general are high. The policyholder can borrow at a relatively low rate to finance current spending or to reinvest at a profit in the open market. Notice, for example, that policy loans represented 8.7 percent of the portfolio in 1974, a year of high interest rates, and fell to 7.8 percent in 1977 when interest rates were lower. (They had returned to their 1974 percentage level in early 1981 as open-market rates soared.) The low rate on policy loans is generally set by state governments. In recent years, most states have increased the permissible rate in the policy loan provision of new policies to take account of the generally higher level of interest rates, but lower rates still apply to existing policies.

Finally, real estate holdings are important in the portfolio of life insurance companies. Even though only about 3 percent of the portfolio is in real estate, the actual dollar amount of insurance company holdings have increased steadily for three decades. Life insurance companies have been an important element in both apartment building construction and shopping center development, a particular favorite for outright ownership by life insurance companies. Downtown office buildings also appear among their real estate holdings.

Table 10-2
Disposition of Funds Inflow of Life Insurance Companies, 1980
(Billions of Dollars)

Real Estate	$ 3.8
Net Acquisition of Financial Assets	35.6
Demand Deposits + Currency	−.1
Corporate Equities	.3
Credit Market Instruments	32.1
U.S. Government Securities	2.5
State + Local Obligations	.2
Corporate Bonds	8.5
Mortgages	12.1
Money Market Securities	2.5
Policy Loans	6.2
Miscellaneous Assets	3.3
Current Surplus	5.7

Source: Federal Reserve Board of Governors, Flow of Funds Accounts.

A picture of what life insurance companies have recently been doing with new funds is presented in Table 10-2, which shows the disposition of funds inflow for 1980. The patterns that have been analyzed above generally continue to hold. However, in 1980, due primarily to higher interest rates and the increasing acquisition of packages of mortgages in the secondary mortgage market, insurance companies committed the largest percentage of their new funds to mortgages. Whether this becomes a trend or is simply a temporary change in behavior remains to be seen. The performance of the equity market in the 1970s discouraged the purchase of equities by insurance companies. In 1980, insurance company net purchases of equities were very small.

The impact of life insurance companies on the financial markets is substantial. Table 10-3 shows the contribution of life insurance companies to funds flowing into the various money and capital markets in selected years. The table demonstrates that in 1979 life insurance companies were the third largest among financial intermediaries in

Table 10-3
Sources of Funds in the Money and Capital Markets
(Billions of Dollars)

	1967	1975	1979[1]
Life Insurance Companies	$ 8.4	$ 19.0	$ 33.8
Private Non-Life Insurance Company Pension Plans	5.5	12.8	22.0
State and Local Retirement Funds	4.0	11.6	18.2
Savings and Loan Associations	9.1	37.3	46.6
Mutual Savings Banks	5.4	10.9	5.2
Commercial Banks	37.4	31.5	120.3
Federal Reserve	4.8	8.5	7.7
Federal Agencies	5.5	33.9	71.1
Nonfinancial Corporations	2.1	13.6	33.1
Fire and Casualty Insurance Companies	1.6	6.6	18.9
Real Estate Investment Trusts	—	−4.9	−0.3
Mutual Funds	1.4	0.3	17.0
Foreigners	2.7	10.9	−6.1
Individuals and Others	−3.3	34.8	82.9
Total	$84.6	$226.8	$470.4

Note: Details may not add to totals due to rounding.
[1] Preliminary.

Source: American Council of Life Insurance, *Life Insurance Fact Book*, 1980.

supplying funds to the financial markets. They have held third place behind commercial bank and savings and loan associations for some time.

Sources of Life Insurance Funds

Thus far our discussion has been concerned with the assets acquired by life insurance companies with the funds at their disposal, but we must also examine the origins of the funds that life insurance companies employ. Table 10-4 presents the sources of funds to life insurance companies for selected years. The table shows that premiums received from policyholders are the largest source of funds. The table includes health insurance premiums for completeness. These premiums do not have the saving feature common to both life insurance and annuity premiums. However, it is interesting to note that this category grew rapidly from almost nothing in 1950 to almost $28 billion in 1979. The decade of the 1970s in particular saw a substantial increase in health insurance premium income as insurance companies became a major supplier of health insurance. Annuities have also gained in popularity among policyholders as more of them have decided that purchasing an assured stream of income payments for retirement was a sensible saving strategy. In contrast, life insurance premiums have not grown at the rate of annuities or health insurance, implying a change of mix in insurance purchases on the part of policyholders. For example, in 1960 the proportion of premium income derived from life insurance was about 70 percent compared to 46 percent in 1979. Nevertheless, life insurance premiums remain the major source of funds for life insurance companies.

The other major source of funds for these companies is investment income. The rise in interest rates in the 1970s is in part responsible for the growth in investment income from 21 percent of insurance company income in 1970 to 25 percent in 1979. Investment income includes interest income on bonds, stock dividends, and rental income on real estate.

Life insurance companies in the early 1980s are striving to become more complete financial institutions so they can offer more services to their customers and remain successful in an increasingly competitive environment. Besides diversifying the type of insurance programs they are offering, they have moved through acquisition of other financial organizations to offer services not traditionally associated with life insurance companies. For example, Prudential Insurance Company, the largest life insurance company, acquired the stock brokerage firm of Bache and Company in 1981. It may be expected that insurance company diversification through both acquisition and internal change will continue.

Table 10-4
Sources of Funds: Life Insurance Companies, Selected Years
(Millions of Dollars)

| Year | Premium Receipts | | | | Net Investment Income | Other Income | Total Income |
	Life Insurance Premiums	Annuities	Health Insurance Premiums[1]	Total Premium Receipts			
1950	$ 6,249	$ 939	$ 1,001	$ 8,189	$ 2,075	$1,073	$ 11,337
1955	8,903	1,288	2,355	12,546	2,801	1,197	16,544
1960	11,998	1,341	4,026	17,365	4,304	1,338	23,007
1965	16,083	2,260	6,261	24,604	6,778	1,785	33,167
1970	21,679	3,721	11,367	36,767	10,144	2,143	49,054
1975	29,336	10,165	19,074	58,575	16,488	2,959	78,022
1976	31,358	13,962	21,059	66,379	18,758	3,421	88,558
1977	33,765	14,974	23,580	72,319	21,713	3,953	97,985
1978	36,592	16,339	25,829	78,760	25,294	4,152	108,206
1979	39,083	17,939	27,894	84,916	29,562	4,661	119,139

[1] Includes some premiums for workers' compensation and auto and other liability insurance.

Source: American Council of Life Insurance. Life Insurance Fact Book. 1980.

Pension Funds

Pension funds fulfill the role of financial intermediaries by receiving funds that are being accumulated by savers for retirement and investing these funds in the open market, primarily in capital market securities. The emphasis of this section is on private pension funds and state and local government retirement plans. Federal retirement plans invest in a very limited range of assets, generally government securities.

Pension funds of all types have expanded very rapidly in the post–World War II period. Combined assets of all forms of pension funds exceed $600 billion. If the assets of all types of pension funds are aggregated in this way, pension funds would be the third largest financial intermediary. Aggregating the assets of pension funds is, however, somewhat misleading because it includes the federal retirement plans such as social security trust funds, which are generally quite restricted in their portfolio holdings. It is more meaningful to concentrate on the major pension funds independently. These are the private retirement systems and the state and local retirement funds. Both types of pension funds have grown rapidly in recent years. For example, total assets of noninsured pension funds increased from $18 billion in 1955 to almost $300 billion by the end of 1980. Private pension funds are of two types. Noninsured pension funds are managed by pension fund trustees, usually commercial banks. Insured pension funds are plans that are set up with insurance companies. These are annuity plans and as such are intertwined with other insurance company assets. Noninsured pension funds are the larger of the two types.

The growth in state and local government retirement plans has also been very dramatic. These are retirement plans set up by government units for their employees. By mid-1979, the assets of these plans had grown to almost $160 billion from only $23 billion in 1962.

The Pension Fund Portfolio

Table 10-5 presents the balance sheet of private noninsured pension funds for selected years. Since pension fund obligations are long term, it is not surprising that, for the most part, their portfolio is composed of capital market securities. As the table shows, the largest holding of pension funds in 1980 was common stock, which comprised 59 percent of their portfolio. However, the relatively poor performance of the stock market during much of the 1970s affected both the market value of the pension funds' common stock holdings and their commitment of new funds to this investment area. This resulted in a reduction in the percentage of the portfolio held in common stocks in the 1970s. In 1971, for example, over 68 percent of the pension fund portfolio was in common stocks. In 1979 and 1980, pension funds, in conjunction with a rising stock market for much of this period, increased their

Table 10-5
Assets of Private Noninsured Pension Funds, Market Value, End of Year
(Millions of Dollars)

	1955	1960	1965	1970	1975	1976	1977	1978	1980
Cash and Deposits	$ 415	$ 546	$ 940	$ 1,804	$ 2,962	$ 2,199	$ 3,721	$ 8,110	$ 9,290
U.S. Government Securities	2,938	2,655	2,913	2,998	11,097	14,918	20,017	18,767	26,334
Corporate and Other Bonds	7,702	14,629	21,949	24,919	34,519	37,858	42,754	48,633	59,987
Preferred Stock	624	718	768	1,631	892	1,212	1,009	1,162	1,367
Common Stock	5,461	15,827	39,986	65,456	87,669	108,483	100,863	106,732	174,437
Mortgages	321	1,304	3,391	3,504	2,139	2,160	2,362	2,554	3,814
Other Assets	592	1,398	2,950	4,422	6,341	7,073	10,838	15,585	21,980
Total Assets	$18,053	$37,077	$72,898	$104,737	$145,622	$173,906	$181,564	$201,545	$297,209

Note: Includes deferred profit sharing funds and pension funds of corporations, unions, multiemployer groups, and nonprofit organizations.

Source: Securities and Exchange Commission. *Monthly Statistical Review,* formerly *Statistical Bulletin,* various issues.

commitment to common stocks. They placed over 60 percent of new funds received into equities in 1979. Corporate bonds and government securities, whose higher yields over the last ten years have attracted more pension fund participation, have tended to grow relative to equities in those years when equity investment was low. As a result, these two categories are the other major holdings by these funds.

In the late 1970s, there was some movement by pension funds to diversify into the precious metals, real estate, and collectables (paintings, sculpture, and so on) markets, all of which outperformed both stocks and bonds during that period. However, such tangible holdings as reflected in the "Other Assets" category are still very small when compared to pension fund financial holdings. Further, some of the incentive to participate in those markets has been reduced by the reduction in inflation in the early 1980s. Even in the late 1970s, investments of these kinds did not prove more popular with pension funds because of their lack of liquidity, their failure to generate any current return, either in interest or dividends, and the effective restriction of some pension funds to financial assets by various pension fund by-laws and rules of prudence. Normal rules of prudence were reinforced by formal federal legislation in the mid-1970s that expanded pension fund trustee responsibility and contributor protection.

The remainder of the pension fund portfolio is made up of cash and deposits, preferred stock, and mortgages. These assets make up a relatively small portion of the portfolio. The deposit category includes large CDs, which pension funds found attractive in the late 1970s and early 1980s when interest rates rose dramatically. Private pension funds hold virtually no municipal securities; since pension fund earnings are exempt from federal taxes, there is no incentive to do so.

The holdings of state and local government retirement plans are quite similar to those of private pension funds. State and local pension funds hold more corporate bonds than corporate stock, the reverse of the situation for private pension plans. Table 10-6 presents the portfolio for all state and local retirement systems, broken into categories for the fiscal year ended June 1979. It can be seen that corporate bonds constitute about 43 percent of portfolio holdings while corporate stock, the second largest category, accounts for 21 percent of the portfolio. State and local funds also hold substantially more municipal securities than private funds. Since state and local pension fund earnings are also not taxed, their motivation for holding municipals must be regarded as a contribution to state and local financing. In addition, some state and local governments require their employee retirement funds to hold a certain amount of the securities they issue.

In 1974, out of some concern over the long term viability of pension plans, Congress passed the Employee Retirement Income Security Act (ERISA). ERISA only applies to private pension plans though there has been some discussion about extending the act to include state

Table 10-6
Portfolio of State and Local Governmentally Administered
Employee Retirement Systems, June 1979
(Millions of Dollars)

Item	All Systems
Cash and Deposits	$ 3,323
Governmental Securities	29,215
Federal	25,347
United States Treasury	13,327
Federal Agency	12,020
State and Local	3,867
Nongovernmental Securities	127,114
Corporate Bonds	68,802
Corporate Stocks	33,682
Mortgages	11,490
Other	13,139
Total Cash and Security Holdings	$159,651

Source: U.S. Bureau of the Census, *Government Finances, 1978–1979.*

and local government plans. This act contained a number of important provisions: formal and strict requirements for trustee management of pension funds, federal insurance for participants in case a pension fund should become insolvent, and more stringent reporting requirements for pension fund trustees. In addition, ERISA also provided for self-employed persons to contribute up to $7,500, not to exceed 15 percent of earned income, tax free to qualified retirement plans and for workers not covered by retirement plans to contribute up to $1,500, not to exceed 15 percent of earned income to individual retirement accounts (IRAs). (These limits were subsequently increased by the tax cut legislation of 1981.)

Contributions are the major source of funds for both private and state and local government pension funds. Table 10-7 presents the percentage breakdowns of sources of funds for 1980 for both types of funds. In both cases it is clear that employer contributions are the largest source of funds.[2] However, notice that these contributions are

---

[2] One might wonder, if the employer pays so large a share of the pension fund contribution, is the pension fund truly a financial intermediary taking from the savers and relending. The common explanation offered to answer this query is that the employer would have paid these funds directly to the employee if the retirement fund did not exist so that it is truly employee savings.

Table 10-7
Sources of Funds in Percentages for Pension Funds, 1980

Item	Private Noninsured	State and Local
Employee Contributions	4.3%	15.4%
Employer Contributions	78.4	49.3
Earnings on Investments	17.3	35.3
	100.0%	100.0%
Benefit Payments as a Percentage of Total Receipts	44.7%	31.5%

Source: Economics Department, Bankers Trust Co., *Credit and Capital Markets, 1981.*

considerably larger for the private funds. This occurs because frequently private pension plans are entirely employer supported, while governmental plans are more often jointly supported by contributions from the employer and the employees. Earnings on investments is also a significant source of funds for pension funds as the table shows, accounting for 17 percent of funds for private plans and 35 percent for state and local plans.

Table 10-7 also presents pension fund benefit payments as a percentage of total receipts. The fact that these benefit payments are substantially below receipts allows the surplus to be invested in income-earning assets. The lower percentage of payments to receipts for government funds may account for the larger contribution that earnings make to their receipts when compared to private funds. The lower the percentage paid out in benefits the more that is available for investment in income-earning assets.

Pension funds are an increasingly important financial intermediary. They are now very substantial participants in the capital markets and are expected to continue to increase their role. Hence, the management of these pension funds—for example bank trustees—control large amounts of financial assets including substantial voting stock in many major U.S. corporations. As a result, pension funds, if they choose to use their increasing financial power, can have a large impact on the financial system and the economy.

Mutual Funds

A mutual fund performs as a financial intermediary by gathering savings—primarily from individuals—by selling shares and by using these funds to purchase securities. Depending on the purpose of the mutual fund, the securities purchased may be common stocks, corporate and government bonds, or money market securities. Further, within general categories of security holdings and depending on the purpose of the fund, a wide variety of securities may be held. For example, some mutual funds are growth oriented and, hence, hold stock in growth companies with major emphasis on capital gains. Growth companies are generally smaller, less well established firms that are expected to show substantial year-to-year earnings increases. However, these companies tend to be more risky investments. Other funds are more income oriented and conservative, and they will hold stocks in well-known companies that pay substantial dividends. By pooling funds from many savers and investing in a diversified portfolio of securities, mutual funds spread risk in a way that an average individual could not hope to do. They also offer the advantage of professional management of investor funds, a service that is unaffordable to the small investor individually.

The first true mutual funds were established in London in 1868. During the latter part of the nineteenth century, a number of mutual funds, then commonly called investment companies, were founded in the United States. A sharp spurt in the growth of these funds took place in the 1920s, but the stock market crash of 1929 and the subsequent decline in the stock market in the 1930s caused a severe contraction in these funds. Mutual funds recovered after World War II and assets grew rapidly, particularly in the decade of the 1960s as Figure 10-1 shows. This rapid growth was due to both a large inflow of funds and the substantial increase in stock prices. Most of the decade of the 1970s witnessed a flattening out of this growth pattern and, in some years, an actual decline as the stock market, particularly in 1974, performed below historical trends.

Two developments served to change this situation in the latter part of the 1970s and early 1980s. The first development was the improvement in stock market performance that resulted in a reversal of the outflow of funds that had taken place through virtually all of the 1970s. In 1980, mutual funds specializing in purchasing stocks and bonds saw their first net increase in share issues since 1971. (The increase in asset values for some years in the 1970s apparent in Figure 10-1 was a result of increased stock prices in these years. Shareholders in these mutual funds were still redeeming more shares than they were buying throughout this period.) The second and most dramatic development was the explosive growth in money market mutual funds in 1979, 1980, and 1981. Money market mutual funds specialize in purchasing money market securities. In 1979, these funds saw inflows of $34.4 billion to purchase their shares. This was followed by $29.2 billion in 1980. In the first quarter of 1981 alone, $37 billion flowed into the money market mutual funds. The growth of money market mutual funds is so important that it will be discussed in detail following an examination of the way mutual funds are organized.

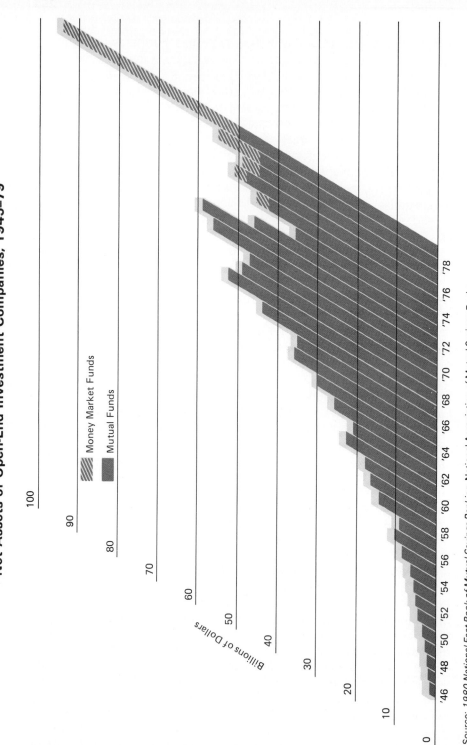

Figure 10-1
Net Assets of Open-End Investment Companies, 1945–79

Money Market Funds

Mutual Funds

Billions of Dollars

0   10   20   30   40   50   60   70   80   90   100

'46 '48 '50 '52 '54 '56 '58 '60 '62 '64 '66 '68 '70 '72 '74 '76 '78

Source: *1980 National Fact Book of Mutual Savings Banking*, National Association of Mutual Savings Banks.

The Organization of Mutual Funds

The vast majority of mutual funds including all money market funds are open-end funds. This means that the fund stands ready to sell as many shares as the public wishes, using the proceeds of the sales to acquire additional securities. The fund also stands ready to redeem any shares that are tendered to it by its investors at the value of the shares prevailing at the time of redemption (determined by taking the value of the mutual fund's portfolio at the date of redemption and dividing by the number of shares outstanding to arrive at a value per share.) There are, however, a few closed-end mutual funds. Closed-end mutual funds issue a fixed number of shares. To acquire shares in such a fund after the fund is established, a potential investor must purchase these shares from another investor in the fund in the open market. (Closed-end funds are similar to equity shares in a company. Some are listed on stock exchanges like the New York Stock Exchange.) Similarly, to liquidate a position in the fund, the investor must sell shares on the open market; the company will not redeem the shares. The price of closed-end fund shares fluctuates, sometimes independently of the value of the securities held in the portfolio. (Closed-end funds typically sell at a discount to the value of their security holdings.) Thus, in a closed-end fund, the risk to the investor from fluctuations in the price of securities in the fund may be compounded by changes in the fund shares reflected in the open market.

Open-end mutual funds may be load or no-load funds. A load fund charges a sales commission to a perspective purchaser. This commission may be as high as 8.5 percent of the fund's asset value per share. A no-load fund charges no sales commission. There are many load and no-load funds spanning the spectrum of investment objectives from growth of capital to income. There has never been a conclusive study to demonstrate that load fund performance, despite the sales charge, is superior to no-load funds. Both types of funds charge a yearly management fee, usually a small percentage of the value of the funds assets, to manage the fund.

Many open-end mutual fund managers operate a family of funds each of which is designed to meet a different investment objective. For example, a typical group may contain a growth stock fund, a more conservative stock fund, a bond fund designed solely for income, a municipal bond fund for higher income investors desiring tax-exempt income, and a money market fund. Often with a phone call, an investor in one of the family of funds may redeem shares in one of the group's funds and automatically reinvest in another of the group's funds if this is prearranged. This has proved to be a very attractive feature for fund shareholders. In this way, shareholders can remain with a particular group when their investment objective changes or when they alter their outlook on the potential return from a particular category of investment.

The earnings of mutual funds are tax exempt as long as 90 percent are distributed to their shareholders. However, shareholders are taxed at normal rates on earnings and capital gains distributions on their mutual fund investments.

Money Market Mutual Funds

Early in the 1970s, as interest rates rose, a new type of mutual fund made its appearance—the money market mutual fund. Money market funds are all no-load. These funds invest only in short-term securities. Their objective is to generate the highest yield possible, consistent with safety. The restriction of their investment to short-term securities ensures that their assets are highly liquid. Certificates of deposit, commercial paper, and Treasury bills are among the most popular holdings of the money market funds. While initially successful, particularly during the period of high interest rates in 1974, as interest rates fell after 1974, the popularity of these funds declined. However, starting in late 1978 and accelerating in 1979, 1980, and 1981, participation in these funds has soared. By mid-1982, money market mutual funds assets exceeded $190 billion. Many times in the first half of 1981, fund assets grew by over $3 billion in a single week, testimony indeed to the attraction to investors of the money market funds.

The attractiveness of money market funds derives from a number of factors. One very important reason is that the money market mutual funds offer small savers a vehicle that enables them to receive a return that cannot be obtained on a saving deposit or small CD. Money market mutual funds usually have minimum initial investment requirements of $1,000 to $2,500, considerably less than that needed to acquire a three-month Treasury bill ($10,000), a money market certificate at a depository institution ($10,000), or a large CD ($100,000). Sometimes these minimums are even lower. Further, once the initial investment is made it can be increased in increments as low as $50 depending on the fund.

Undoubtedly, the increase in money market mutual fund assets has come in part at the expense of saving and time deposits at depository institutions. The rates of return a small depositor can receive in a money market fund compared to the deposit alternatives have been very attractive. Even the larger depositor, including some institutional investors, has often found that the money market funds can pay higher returns than available, for example, on money market certificates because of the mix of money market assets in the mutual fund portfolio.

The resulting large scale flow of funds from depository intermediaries to the money market mutual funds has created problems for these intermediaries similar to that resulting from large scale disintermediation. This has raised wide-ranging protest from the deposit intermediaries. Among other things, they want the Federal Reserve to extend reserve requirements to the money market funds (which would lower the yield the funds could pay), and they want permission in some cases to start their own funds. There has also been some attempt to have the money market funds purchase large CDs from smaller banks and other depository institutions to rechannel the funds to these institutions. Money market funds already purchase large CDs from large money center banks.

Another factor that has led to the growth of money market funds is the "parking" of investment funds at high yields. Money market funds have attracted funds that have been temporarily removed from the stock and bond markets waiting for improvement in these markets. Because of the liquidity of shareholder investment and the attractive return on funds, money market funds have appealed to the financial market investor. In fact, the money market mutual funds sponsored by brokerage houses are the largest grouping of money market funds.

Investors in a money market fund can receive funds at any time. This makes the fund attractive for many investors. Further, most money market mutual funds allow the writing of checks against these funds (usually in $500 denominations). Thus, a shareholder can use this check-writing privilege to pay large bills or write checks to cash. With the check-writing privilege, money market mutual fund shares take on much the same characteristics as NOW accounts, except that they currently yield substantially higher returns. Their return, however, depends on the return on their securities and can fall rapidly if short-term rates decline.

It should be noted that since there is no federal insurance on these accounts, investments in money market mutual funds are not protected as they are in most depository intermediaries. However, the securities held by these funds are of very high quality thus minimizing default risk. Figure 10-1 (p. 252) shows the proportion of mutual funds assets in money market mutual funds through 1979.

Other Financial Institutions

A number of other financial institutions in the United States are not strictly speaking financial intermediaries. These institutions do not raise funds directly from savers in the economy, or they may be selling services that are not saving related. Nevertheless, they resemble financial intermediaries in some key ways. Therefore, it is useful to discuss the most important of these, the finance companies and the casualty insurance companies.

Finance Companies

Finance companies exist to provide credit to consumers and business. Often borrowers from finance companies cannot secure credit elsewhere because they are considered high risk. Borrowers may also be attracted by the increased convenience and personal service available at a finance company. For example, large auto manufacturers have finance company subsidiaries. A car buyer may find it very convenient to borrow from the auto manufacturer's subsidiary when purchasing the car since the financing can usually be arranged at the same time and in the same place. In return for assuming more risk and providing increased convenience, finance companies will usually charge a higher rate than is charged by financial intermediaries for similar credit. Further, finance companies raise funds in the open market and through bank borrowing, and of necessity they must charge higher rates to yield a positive interest rate spread on their lending and thus earn a profit.

Table 10-8 presents a highly aggregated picture of the financial assets and liabilities of finance companies for 1978. The table shows that the major sources of funds are credit market borrowing, and the major uses of funds are loans to consumers and business.

Lending By Finance Companies The major type of consumer loan is the personal loan. Increasingly in recent years these personal loans have been secured by second mortgages on homes. Finance companies have found these second mortgage loans particularly attractive as they have removed much of the risk from granting consumer credit since the loan is secured by real estate. Homeowners have also found finance companies attractive sources for converting the in-

Table 10-8
Financial Assets and Liabilities of Finance Companies, 1978
(Millions of Dollars)

Financial Assets	
Cash	$ 4,444
Consumer Loans	67,120
Loans to Business	63,348
Mortgages	10,837
Total Financial Assets	$145,749
Liabilities	
Corporate Bonds	$ 51,314
Commercial Paper	47,396
Bank Loans	20,843
Total Financial Liabilities	$119,553

Source: Board of Governors of the Federal Reserve, *Flow of Funds Accounts,* 1949–1978.

creased equity they have in their homes into spendable funds. The second major consumer lending category for finance companies has been automobile lending. It was noted above that major car manufacturers have finance company subsidiaries that specialize in financing the purchase of that company's cars; for example, the largest manufacturer has the largest of these subsidiaries, General Motors Acceptance Corporation (GMAC). However, many finance companies not associated with auto manufacturers also make a substantial number of auto loans. Other types of consumer loans made by finance companies are revolving credit loans in which a consumer can obtain credit up to a maximum amount on a continuing basis, and mobile home loans.

Finance companies also make loans to business. As Table 10-8 shows, at the end of 1978 loans to business by finance companies almost equalled the amount of consumer lending. However in 1979, 1980, and 1981, consumer lending substantially exceeded business lending. In the first quarter of 1981, for example, consumer loans increased at a $20 billion annual rate compared to a decline of $2 billion in business lending. Nevertheless, business lending is still an important use of funds for finance companies.

Finance company loans to business generally provide financing for inventories, installment contracts, leasing arrangements, and accounts receivable. A car or major appliance dealer must keep large dollar amounts of inventories on hand. These dealers will often turn to finance companies to provide the necessary financing. The use of installment credit by business often parallels the use of this type of credit by consumers. For example, a business that uses a large fleet of delivery vans may finance these under an installment arrangement with a finance company. Farm equipment is also financed in a similar way. Finance companies also provide financing for companies that lease equipment to other firms. This type of financing has increased as lease arrangements have gained in popularity due to tax and other considerations, such as the ability for a firm to retain ownership over durable equipment. The equipment leaseholder generally finds it advantageous to lease rather than buy equipment since it keeps the initial investment low. Accounts receivable may be used as collateral to borrow from a finance company as well. Alternatively, the finance company may actually buy accounts receivable at a discount to provide a substantial return. This is called factoring. It is clear that finance company lending to business fills a niche in general business financing often not filled by conventional intermediaries or the financial markets. This makes businesses willing to pay the generally higher rates that finance companies charge.

Often finance companies will specialize in a particular type of lending, a fact obscured by considering the group as a whole as was done above. Many finance companies specialize in lending to consumers while others specialize in lending to business. There is even specialization within these categories. Automobile finance companies mentioned before and companies specializing in factoring are but two examples.

Rates on finance company loans have typically been controlled by state usury ceilings on consumer and sometimes on business lending. These ceilings appeared to be quite high in most states and did not present a problem for finance companies. However, with the rise in interest rates in recent years this is no longer the case. That is why finance companies have increased the amount of secured financing they have done. The increase in second mortgage loans are an example. The collateral behind the loan reduces the risk for the finance company and allows it to charge lower rates than would otherwise be possible.

Sources of Finance Company Funds Table 10-8 shows that finance companies raise most of their funds in the credit markets. About 43 percent of funds have come from the issuance of long-term bonds and about 40 percent from commercial paper. The remaining funds came from bank loans. Although not shown in the table, finance companies do have a relatively small amount of capital as well. However, generalizing in this fashion masks a number of differences in finance company behavior both in the manner of financing and the timing of that financing.

Finance companies are most inclined to issue corporate bonds when they believe the rate structure is favorable for doing so. Since most finance company loans are short or intermediate term, they do not wish to finance long term unless they are locking-in what they consider to be low rates. For example, in 1976 when long-term rates were low, finance companies raised more than 60 percent of their funds by issuing bonds and retired a lot of short-term debt with the proceeds. Further, it is only the large finance companies that are able to raise funds in the credit markets at all. Smaller companies tend to use bank borrowing and bank lines of credit to secure funding for their activities. The borrowing by these smaller companies makes up a proportionately greater share of bank borrowing in Table 10-8 than that of large finance company bank borrowing.

The largest of the finance companies have access to the commercial paper market. These companies either borrow in the commercial paper market through dealers or more often place the commercial paper directly with ultimate purchasers. These purchasers are often large financial institutions such as life insurance companies. Many large finance companies have a group of institutions that buy their paper regularly as a matter of course.

When interest rates are high, the amount of commercial paper issued increases. Finance companies expecting lower rates in the near future prefer to borrow short term even at high rates in the hope that they will be able to refinance shortly at lower rates rather than borrowing long term at high rates. For example, in the first quarter of 1981, when interest rates rose rapidly, finance companies issued over $20 billion in commercial paper at an annual rate while reducing their outstanding corporate bonds by over $2 billion at an annual rate.

Casualty Insurance Companies

While life insurance companies are often selling a service (insurance protection) along with a saving program, casualty insurers sell only a service—loss protection against fire, theft, accident, and negligence. There is no saving component to the premium paid. The insured's premium is determined as closely as possible on the basis of expected loss for a particular category of coverage. For example, the probability of loss from a fire on a residence of a particular type of construction in a particular area would determine the premium for that particular homeowner's fire insurance. Casualty companies insure property of all kinds, such as homes and automobiles, for virtually all possible contingencies. They also issue liability insurance which protects individuals and businesses in the event of negligence claims.

The predictability of casualty losses tends to be less accurate than that for life insurance losses. Casualty insurers also do not enjoy the favored tax treatment of life insurance companies. Instead, they pay the full corporate tax rate on their earnings. Both of these factors dictate the composition of their portfolio and account for the differences in their portfolio relative to life insurance companies.

Table 10-9 presents the financial assets of casualty insurers at the end of 1978 and the percentage of the income-earning portfolio accounted for by each asset category. The composition of casualty insurers' portfolios is quite different from that of life insurance companies as can be seen from a comparison of Table 10-9 with Table 10-1 (p. 240). Notice in particular that almost one-half of the portfolio of casualty companies is in municipal securities. This is a direct result of the tax status of casualty companies since earnings on municipals are exempt from federal taxes. In contrast, only a very small amount of life insurance assets are municipal securities as previously discussed. Further, note the relatively high percentage of government securities held by casualty insurers. The reason for this is that these insurers must remain more liquid to enable them to deal with large, sudden, and unexpected losses. If a breakdown of corporate bonds by maturity was presented in Table 10-9, it would be clear that these bonds tended to be short-term obligations held also for liquidity reasons. Thus, tax considerations and the nature of the casualty insurance business clearly dictate the portfolio holdings of these companies.

Since the portfolio composition of casualty issuers is dictated by such basic considerations as tax status and liquidity needs, we would expect that it would remain relatively stable over time. This is confirmed

Table 10-9
Income Earning Portfolio of Casualty Insurance Companies,
1978
(Millions of Dollars)

Item	Amount	Percentage
Corporate Equities	$ 19,400	14.9%
Government Securities	15,841	12.1
Municipal Securities	62,456	47.8
Corporate Bonds	21,358	16.3
Other	11,651	8.9
Total	$130,706	100.0%

Source: Board of Governors of the Federal Reserve System, *Flow of Funds Accounts,* 1949–1978.

by examining more recent data. In the first quarter of 1981, casualty issuers placed 46 percent of their new funds into municipal securities and the next largest percentage into federal government securities.

Casualty companies derive the major amount of their funds from policy premiums. The remainder of their funds comes from the earnings on their portfolio. The largest casualty insurance company is State Farm Mutual closely followed by Allstate Insurance, a subsidiary of Sears.

The "New Financial Intermediaries"

The discussion of financial intermediaries in this portion of the book has emphasized the growth and change that has recently taken place in the activities of these institutions. The dynamic nature of financial intermediation in the United States is clear from our analysis. However, the changes in financial intermediation that have been examined have, for the most part, occurred within the traditional organizational structure of these financial intermediaries. In the late 1970s and early 1980s, however, accompanying the changes going on at traditional financial intermediaries was a development that may have profound effect on what financial intermediaries will be like in the future. This was the movement to what have been called financial "supermarkets" or "department stores."

The names most closely associated with these new financial service organizations are Merrill Lynch, American Express, and Sears—among organizations that were previously not considered financial intermediaries—and Citicorp, the parent company of Citibank (the second largest commercial bank in the United States) and Prudential Insurance Company. The latter are already financial intermediaries but are moving in the direction of full service financial service organizations. Of these, Citibank, much to its displeasure, is the only organization that currently is at a disadvantage in this regard since it is still bound by banking regulation, a matter that is currently receiving considerable attention from Citicorp management in its lobbying activities in Congress. Citicorp is among the leaders in pressing Congress for additional deregulation of commercial banking including repeal of the McFadden Act, which prohibits interstate banking. Because the other organizations mentioned above are not bound by bank regulation, they can engage in a considerable number of activities that are not available to banks. Through the internal development of innovative programs in the case of Merrill Lynch or through acquisition in the case of the others, these firms are now offering a host of services that banks offer and many that banks cannot offer.

Before examining these organizations in detail to see why they have been called financial supermarkets, we need to have some general idea of what a complete full service financial institution might offer. This institution would accept customer funds and pay money market interest rates, offer access to accounts by check, make loans and mortgages, issue credit cards, have branches coast-to-coast, act as securities brokers and underwriters, offer insurance, perhaps even act as real estate brokers, and offer consumers cash management services. Consumers need not look elsewhere for their financial requirements. Interestingly enough, these services are all currently offered by Merrill Lynch. It is no wonder that when Walter Wriston, the Chairman of Citicorp, was asked what a commercial bank should be, he said it exists now and "its called Merrill Lynch." While Merrill Lynch is restricted in the type of lending it can do (it also cannot offer demand deposit or NOW accounts, and offers only specific types of insurance), it has truly developed into a financial supermarket.

Perhaps the first major step in the development of Merrill Lynch from the largest security brokerage firm in the United States to a full service financial institution occurred in 1977 when it established its Cash Management Account (CMA). Prior to 1977, Merrill Lynch had already been innovative. In 1975, it had established its Ready Asset Fund, which allowed its securities customers to "park" the funds they received from the sale of securities in a money market fund located at their brokers. With the success in the late 1970s of money market funds in general, Merrill's fund proved particularly popular and at the end of 1981 was by far the largest of the money market funds with assets of $23 billion. However, the Cash Management Account (CMA) was quite different in design and marked a clear expansion in the financial services Merrill was offering its customers.

The CMA requires a customer to deposit at least $20,000 in cash or securities with Merrill. The customer then has access to a substantial number of financial services. The customer can write checks against the account, receive a monthly statement, borrow against the value of the securities in the account, and have any cash in the account invested in a money market fund to earn money market rates. The customer is even issued a VISA card, which can be used to access the account. The CMA has proved immensely popular and had attracted $13 billion in "deposits" by the end of 1981. Other large brokerage firms have recently begun to offer similar accounts.

Merrill has shown additional willingness to expand beyond its traditional brokerage and investment banking function in other ways as well. Merrill offers mortgage insurance and annuities, for example. Beginning in 1978 Merrill also began to acquire real estate brokerage firms and is now the largest company-owned residential real estate firm in the United States. Further, the expansion of Merrill Lynch's financial service role continues. In 1982, it began test marketing a second mortgage plan in California. Unlike conventional second mortgages, Merrill's plan allows the qualified homeowner to borrow on a revolving charge basis up to 70 percent of the value of the home less any mortgages outstanding. The customer receives a VISA card and checkbook and can borrow funds at any time. The interest rate on the amount borrowed is tied to the prime rate and thus moves when the prime rate does, always exceeding the prime rate by 2.25 percentage points. However, the rate cannot fall below 14 percent. The customer who uses the account only needs to pay the interest if so desired, leaving the principal balance unpaid until the home is sold. If the test marketing turns out successful, Merrill will no doubt offer the plan outside of California.

Given this array of financial services that Merrill can offer, it is not surprising that Mr. Wriston of Citibank is chagrined. As a commercial bank, Citibank cannot match many of the services offered by Merrill to its customers, nor under current banking laws can Citibank engage in the traditional lines of activity of Merrill, such as security brokerage and investment banking. Clearly if the current restrictions on the offering of demand deposits were to be lifted, Merrill would be in an enviable position.

However, Citicorp has also been particularly aggressive in expanding its range of services and would clearly do more if regulations permitted. Perhaps this is why Mr. Wriston has been so vocal in his complaints about the competition from Merrill Lynch. If regulations should be relaxed so that commercial banks are allowed to offer money market funds and particularly if interstate banking becomes permissible, Citicorp is in a particularly strong position to take advantage of these changes. Its national customer base includes six million VISA card holders across the country (there are no interstate restrictions on the extension of credit), and these customers can be solicited as depositors to Citibank branches across the country in the event of interstate banking. Further, in a sense these branches are already in place for Citicorp's finance company subsidiary is already located in 27 states. Citicorp has indicated that, should interstate banking become permissible, these offices will be turned into bank branches. However, at the moment Mr. Wriston and other commercial bankers can only grit their teeth and continue to lobby for further deregulation and interstate banking.[3]

Citibank and other traditional financial intermediaries are concerned not only by what Merrill Lynch is doing but also by what some other organizations are doing in the area of financial services. It may not be surprising that the largest brokerage firm would move the way in which Merrill has. However, when a credit card and travel service firm like American Express, an insurance company like Prudential, and—perhaps most surprising of all to those who have not followed recent developments—a retailer like Sears appear to be moving in the same direction, questions are raised about the nature of future financial intermediaries in the United States.

These firms have all entered the financial services business through acquisitions, unlike Merrill Lynch, which for the most part developed its services internally. In early 1981, Prudential acquired Bache, a major brokerage firm. By doing so, Prudential entered not only the securities business but also the money market mutual fund business and the cash management business. Prudential was already active in real estate. One month later American Express acquired Shearson, the second largest brokerage house and a large securities underwriter. Shearson also had a large money market fund and was developing a cash management account. In October 1981, Sears purchased Dean Witter, another large brokerage house, only one month after having purchased Coldwell Banker, a large real estate brokerage firm. This was not Sears' first entry into the financial services area; for a long while Sears has been in the insurance field with its Allstate insurance subsidiary and it had purchased a number of savings and loan associations in the 1970s.

Perhaps there is a common theme in the acquisitions by all these companies. All three faced problems with their traditional business. American Express's principal businesses, credit cards and traveler's checks, were under competitive pressure. Prudential's main product, life insurance, had not been doing well in an inflationary, high interest rate environment, and Sears' retail sales were under pressure. In contrast, the brokerage businesses had prospered with their money market funds and other investment vehicles that these firms offered were also doing very well. They were in a relatively less regulated environ-

---

[3] It should be noted that such a desire is not shared by all banks. Smaller regional banks are in many cases opposed to repeal of the McFadden Act, which prohibits interstate banking, for fear of increased competition from banking giants such as Citibank.

Table 10-10
"New Financial Intermediaries"

American Express	Household
Merrill Lynch	Equitable Life
Prudential	AVCO
Sears	DANA
Transamerica	RCA
Baldwin Piano	Control Data
Gulf & Western	E.F. Hutton
American General	General Electric
Beneficial	National Steel

Source: *The Wall Street Journal,* Oct. 5, 1981.

ment than banks, and, as Merrill had shown, this meant that they had substantial opportunities in the area of financial services.

There is also a belief on the part of the acquiring firms that a nice match—a synergism—exists between parts of their existing business and the business of the brokerage firms that were acquired. American Express, for example, has a high income group of credit card holders, a natural potential customer base for brokerage and financial services; and Prudential agents are no doubt eager to sell insurance to all those Bache clients. Although the synergisms have not yet borne fruit, it is too early to make any judgment about the future payoff of these operations. Further, each of the acquired brokerage firms has a nationwide office network. If interstate banking and further financial deregulation should occur, these offices are all in place for participation in nationwide banking should the parent firms wish.

Though we have focused on the development of financial supermarkets by four major organizations because they are the leaders, *The Wall Street Journal* in late 1981 listed fourteen more firms that have entered multiple areas of financial service provision, mostly through acquisition. Table 10-10 presents a list of these firms. As can be seen from the table, the list includes such seemingly unlikely names as RCA, General Electric, and National Steel. These firms, through subsidiaries, are active in money management, real estate brokerage, and mortgage lending to name just some of the financial services they offer.[4]

The pressure that the financial supermarkets are generating on traditional financial intermediaries appears to simply add to the argu-

---

[4] See "Bankers Getting Increasingly Upset About Unregulated Status of Rivals," *The Wall Street Journal,* Oct. 5, 1981, p. 29.

ments for additional deregulation of these institutions. The most likely next steps in this process appear to be allowing banks and perhaps thrift institutions as well to offer money market funds. This is, of course, only speculation, but it seems reasonable to suggest that ultimately the financial supermarket approach that we appear to be seeing most clearly at Merrill Lynch but also at other organizations may be a glimpse at what the financial intermediary of the future will resemble.

MONEY MARKET FUNDS AND FINANCIAL INTERMEDIARIES

Money-Market Funds Rose 3% to $101.21 Billion In Latest Week, Setting 10th Consecutive Record

By TOM HERMAN

Money-market funds, continuing their explosive growth this year, pierced the $100 billion mark in assets this week, setting a record for the 10th consecutive week.

The latest big increase comes in the face of rapidly escalating efforts by bankers to persuade Congress and state legislatures to impose restrictions on the funds, which they claim are draining deposits away from them at an alarming rate. If these bankers have their way, funds won't be able to offer regular checking privileges to customers and will have to set aside reserves, as banks must, which would lower their yields.

"We don't want to put the funds out of business but we're at a sore disadvantage," argued Robert W. Renner Sr., chairman of the American Bankers Association's "strike force" on money-market funds and chairman of Citizens State Bank in Hartford City, Ind. "We want to be able to compete with them on a level playing field."

The nation's 103 funds recently have been paying yields of about 15½%. Their assets soared about $3.17 billion, or around 3%, to $101.21 billion in the week ended Wednesday, according to the Investment Company Institute in Washington, D.C. Since the end of last year, their assets have soared about 35%.

"If the funds keep growing at this rate, they'll be about $250 billion by the end of this year," Mr. Renner said.

Bankers' Accusations

Many bankers accuse the funds of undermining the nation's financial health. The funds "have become an engine of inflation," Rollin D. Barnard, president of the U.S. League of Savings Associations, charged. The funds have hurt "small business, home builders, home buyers, auto dealers and all but the largest financial institutions," Mr. Barnard maintained.

Furthermore, fund managers note that banks have actually been gaining deposits, rather than losing them, as the chart shows. The chart indicates that savings deposits have slumped—but this has been more than offset by huge increases in time deposits under $100,000. In short, banks and thrifts have much more money—but cd's are also much more expensive for them.

The funds, however, insist that most of their customers would have pulled their money out of low-yielding bank deposits even if money-market funds had never been invented.

"If money funds didn't exist, many investors would go directly to Treasury bills or other high-yield paper," said Howard M. Stein, chairman of Dreyfus Corp., a large mutual fund organization. "The serious leaders in banking realize that money funds aren't their problem. Their problem is inflation and high interest rates."

In addition, the chart shows that the money funds represent only a small percentage of the total pool of money that they might attract.

Banks, savings institutions and credit unions held about $377 billion in savings deposits during January, on a seasonally adjusted basis, according to the Federal Reserve Board. In addition, they held about $778 billion in time deposits under $100,000.

Fund managers also note that a large portion of the money flowing in lately has been coming from the stock and bond markets, rather than banks. According to the latest Investment Company Institute data, funds managed by brokerage firms recorded a $1.7 billion increase in assets this week, raising their assets to $53.3 billion, or more than half of the total in all funds.

Institutional Participants

Institutional investors, such as insurance companies and pension funds, also have been major participants in money-market funds. Funds designed for institutions showed a $712.3 million increase in assets this week, raising their total to $19.2 billion. General purpose funds reported a $757 million gain, raising their assets to $28.67 billion.

The Wall Street Journal, March 13, 1981, p. 2. Reprinted by permission of The Wall Street Journal, © Dow Jones & Company, Inc., 1981. All Rights Reserved.

Money-Market Funds (Billions of Dollars)

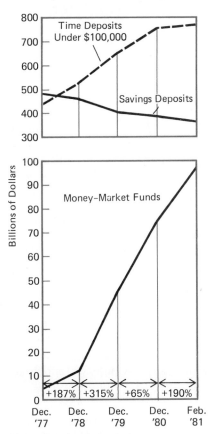

Source: Federal Reserve Board

Money-Market Funds (Weekly)

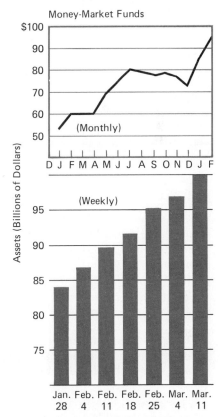

Source: Investment Company Institute.

Key Points

1. This chapter has dealt with a number of nondepository financial intermediaries and other financial institutions. Life insurance companies, pension funds, and mutual funds are important financial intermediaries. Finance companies and casualty insurance companies, while not true financial intermediaries, resemble intermediaries in a number of ways.

2. Life insurance companies are one of the largest types of financial intermediaries in the United States. These companies provide whole life insurance, term life, annuity plans, and endowment policies. Except for term life, all these programs have saving features. Life insurance companies receive most of their funds from premiums and use the proceeds to purchase a wide range of financial assets. Their largest portfolio holding is corporate bonds.

3. Pension funds use funds being accumulated for retirement and purchase primarily capital market securities with these funds. Pension funds include federal retirement funds, private pension plans, and state and local government retirement plans. Federal plans are strictly limited in their portfolio holdings. Private and state and local government plans have much greater portfolio flexibility. These funds purchase primarily corporate bonds and corporate stock.

4. Mutual funds gather savings from individuals and use these funds to purchase securities. There are a wide range of funds specializing in growth stocks, more conservative stocks, bonds, and municipal securities. The most rapidly growing of the mutual funds, however, have been the money market funds, which purchase short-term money market securities.

5. Finance companies and casualty insurance companies are not strictly financial intermediaries. Finance companies do not typically raise funds from ultimate savers in the economy but rather from financial institutions including financial intermediaries. However, they specialize in making loans to businesses and consumers, a business they share with many financial intermediaries. Casualty insurance companies sell a service, insurance protection for property against fire, theft, and accident as well as protection for the insured against negligence claims. Their similarity to intermediaries comes through the securities portfolio which includes many types of securities. Their major investment is municipal securities.

6. The "new financial intermediaries" offer a wide range of financial services to their customers. These include cash management, money market funds, stock and bond trading, credit cards, and real estate brokerage. Their advantage over other financial intermediaries arises from their exclusion from the regulatory framework that governs the traditional financial intermediaries. Many observers view these "financial supermarkets" as the shape of financial intermediaries in the future.

Questions for Discussion

1. Compare and contrast life insurance companies and casualty insurance companies. What major influences result in the difference in portfolio holdings of these types of insurance companies?

2. Why have money market funds grown from virtually nothing to the largest type of mutual fund in ten years? What features of money market mutual funds make them particularly attractive to the relatively small saver?

3. Describe the differences between private pension plans and state and local retirement plans. Pension funds are among the largest and most rapidly growing financial intermediaries. What implications may this have for the economy in future years?

4. Distinguish between (a) an open-end and closed-end mutual fund; and (b) a no-load and load mutual fund.

5. Why are finance companies and casualty insurance companies described in the chapter as not being true financial intermediaries? Is this distinction important in the way in which they have an impact upon the financial system?

6. Why do traditional financial intermediaries regard the "new financial intermediaries" as a serious competitive threat? Are their concerns justified?

Suggested Readings

American Council of Life Insurance. *Life Insurance Fact Book.* Washington, D.C.: American Council of Life Insurance, 1981.

Board of Governors of the Federal Reserve. "Survey of Finance Companies, 1980." Federal Reserve *Bulletin,* May 1981, pp. 398–409.

Cook, Timothy Q., and Jeremy G. Duffield. "Money Market Mutual Funds: A Reaction to Government Regulations or A Lasting Financial Innovation?" Federal Reserve Bank of Richmond *Economic Review,* July/August 1979, pp. 15–31.

Dougall, Herbert E., and Jack E. Gaunitz. *Capital Markets and Institutions* 3rd ed. Englewood Cliffs: Prentice-Hall, 1975.

Loomis, Carol J. "The Fight For Financial Turf." *Fortune.* Dec. 28, 1981, pp. 54–65.

Malca, Edward. *Pension Funds and Other Institutional Investors.* Lexington: Lexington Books, 1975.

Polakoff, Murray E., et al. *Financial Institutions and Markets,* 2nd ed. Boston: Houghton Mifflin, 1981, Readings 7–10.

Financial Intermediaries and Financial Markets

11

The previous six chapters of this text have dealt with the financial intermediaries, one of the major components of the financial system. The next part of the book will analyze another major financial system component, the financial markets. The money market, capital markets, and international financial markets will be discussed in detail. Distinctions between components of the financial system must be drawn sharply for analytical purposes. However, the financial system is a fully integrated system whose parts interact. Therefore, to conclude our study of financial intermediaries and to introduce the financial markets, we must look at some of the ways in which the financial intermediaries and the financial markets are interrelated. Recall from our previous discussion that money market securities are debt instruments that mature in one year or less from the date of issuance. Capital markets securities include debt instruments maturing in more than one year from the date they are issued, as well as equity securities. Trading in these financial markets takes place in both new issues, called primary market securities, and already outstanding issues, called secondary market securities.

The acquisition of financial market securities by financial intermediaries for their portfolios is perhaps the most obvious way in which financial intermediaries interact with financial markets. Reconsidering information already presented on the portfolios of the financial intermediaries, we can clearly see that all intermediaries hold money and capital market securities. For some intermediaries such as mutual funds and pension funds, these securities represent essentially their entire income-earning portfolios. For other intermediaries whose portfolios are dominated by loans, commercial banks and mutual savings banks for example, the primary motivation in holding financial market securities is to achieve diversification and increased liquidity. Whatever the motivations that dictate security holdings by different financial intermediaries, the interaction of the financial intermediaries and the financial markets is a key conduit for the allocation of credit in the economy.

The diversity of financial market securities held by financial intermediaries is substantial. Virtually all major groups of securities are represented in the combined holdings of the intermediaries. Table 11-1 indicates the net amount of securities purchased by selected institutions for their own portfolios in 1980. The table shows that the intermediaries provide substantial amounts of credit to these sectors by their securities acquisitions. For example, the federal government (including federal agencies) issued $127 billion in securities in 1980. In the same year, the financial intermediaries increased their holdings of federal government securities by almost $60 billion or almost 50 percent of the new government issues. The institutions listed in the table, therefore, used the financial markets to channel significant amounts of savers' funds to borrowers in the economy, fulfilling their role as financial intermediaries.

Examining the portfolio holdings of financial intermediaries only scratches the surface of their participation in the financial market. Intermediary portfolios of financial market securities must be assembled and managed. This requires that financial intermediaries have

Table 11-1
Net Open-Market Securities Acquired by Selected Financial Intermediaries, 1980
(Billions of Dollars)

	Security Types		
Institution	Federal Government Securities[1]	State and Local Securities	Corporate Securities[2]
Commercial Banks	$25.0	$13.2	$ 0.5
Savings & Loan Assocs.	12.1	—	1.5
Mutual Savings Banks	3.3	0.5	1.9
Life Insurance Companies	2.6	0.3	12.2
Pension Funds (Private, State and Local)	13.2	0.2	29.6
Mutual Funds	2.9	—	25.2

[1] Includes federal agency securities.
[2] All private open-market securities including bank CDs.

Source: Board of Governors of the Federal Reserve System, Flow of Funds Accounts.

trading departments to buy and sell securities for their portfolios. The management of financial intermediary security portfolios requires considerable expertise and familiarity with the financial markets. But interaction of financial intermediaries with the financial markets extends even beyond holding securities and managing their securities portfolios.

Some large commercial banks have divisions that are dealers in government securities. These dealers buy securities from and sell securities to other institutions and brokers. Furthermore, some financial intermediaries issue securities themselves. For example, stockholder-owned commercial banks issue equity securities while bank holding companies, the parents of many commercial banks, raise funds in the commercial paper market. Finally, the financial intermediaries are in competition for funds with the open market and, even in many cases, in competition with the open market for loan customers. In this chapter all these interactions between financial intermediaries and financial markets will be explored.

Financial Intermediaries as Portfolio Managers

The acquisition and disposal of open-market securities for the financial intermediary portfolios can require extensive trading departments. This is particularly true for large commercial banks but also describes operations at mutual funds, insurance companies, and some pension funds. However, as previously noted, pension funds often hire expert outside financial management companies or utilize trust departments of major commercial banks to manage their portfolios.

The management of bank portfolios and the factors governing the assembly of these portfolios have been previously analyzed. However, in examining the portfolio in the aggregate, we must not overlook the fact that the portfolio encompasses many daily decisions that bank professionals are actively making by adding and deleting securities. While commercial banks, because of their size, present the clearest examples of these operations, other intermediaries either internally or through external assistance are doing much the same thing.

Trading rooms at large commercial banks are areas of constant activity. Portfolio management is a sophisticated art, requiring enormous amounts of information processing and rapid decision making. The computer revolution has been very apparent in this area. Since trades are continually being executed for the bank's portfolio, it is therefore vital that information on price movements in all the financial markets be up-to-the-minute and instantaneously available. Through the use of computer terminals plugged into diverse sources of market information, the necessary price quotations are accessible literally at a touch. News and financial service tickers, as well as extensive tele-phone communication, provide additional relevant data. Foreign ex-change trading (the exchange of one currency for another) also occurs at commercial banks, so information on movements in the value of currencies worldwide is received continuously and trades executed.

The effect of financial institution participation in the money and capital markets from the perspective of the markets is to make these larger and more liquid markets. As buyers and sellers of securities, the financial intermediaries enhance the ability of other buyers and sellers to trade actively. This in turn adds to the marketability of primary security issues—issues marketed for the first time. Primary securities would be considerably less marketable if potential investors were un-sure of an active secondary market—the market for securities that are already outstanding. Financial intermediaries by their active partici-pation thus add considerable depth to these financial markets.

Further, commercial banks, the largest of the financial intermediar-ies, play a considerable role in the money and capital markets indepen-dent of their own portfolios. A number of large New York money center banks have departments that are dealers in government securities. In addition, most large banks manage trust accounts in which trading in the secondary market by the bank is done for the portfolios of the trust accounts being managed. We will turn first to an examination of government securities dealers and investment banking in general and second to the trust activities of commercial banks.

Government Securities Dealers and Investment Banking

Securities dealers buy and sell securities for their own account, unlike brokers who merely match security purchasers with sellers. There are both dealers and brokers for all securities traded in the financial market. Government securities dealers specialize in buying and selling govern-ment securities. Most of these dealers are located in New York City, the center of the money market.

Government securities dealers stand ready to buy government se-curities at a given **bid** price at a moment in time and sell at an **ask** price at the same moment. The ask price always exceeds the bid price on the same security and it is this differential, called the **bid–ask spread,** that generates a return to the dealer. For example, the bid price on a $10,000 face value Treasury bill may be $95.25 meaning that the dealer will pay $9,525.00. The ask price might be $95.35 or $9,535.00. The spread would then be $10 per Treasury bill.

Since prices of securities continuously change during a market day, the level of bid–ask prices may be quite different from one hour to the next even if the bid–ask spread remains the same. Thus, there is substantial room for large profits in being a dealer and substantial risk of large losses. For example, a dealer may purchase a security for his inventory at a particular bid price, and find that the price of that security declines considerably after the purchase. As a result, the ask price may be lower when the dealer sells the security than was the bid price when the dealer purchased the security. Thus, the dealer would realize a loss. Alternatively, the price of the security may rise in the interim between purchase and sale, giving the dealer a profit that exceeds the bid–ask spread that prevailed at the time the security was purchased.

There are two types of government securities dealers. About half of the dealers are departments of large commercial banks, while the other half are private firms. There are approximately 45 dealers in all. The private firms that are government securities dealers are almost all investment bankers. Investment bankers are securities traders, dealers, and underwriters (distributors of primary securities). The Banking Act of 1933, known as the Glass–Steagall Act, separated investment banking—primarily the underwriting of private securities—from commercial banking itself so that no commercial bank can be a complete investment banker. Commercial banks are permitted, however, to act as government securities dealers. The restriction on commercial bank underwriting activities explains why government securities departments of commercial banks focus their activities on government securities, while private government securities dealers are part of larger full-line investment banking organizations.

In underwriting securities, investment bankers usually buy a security issue, often in syndicates with other investment bankers, and then market these securities to institutions and the public in general in smaller packages. Occasionally, if an issue to be underwritten is thought to be very risky—say one issued by a firm that is thought to have financial problems—the investment banker may market this for the issuer on a "best effort" or contingency basis. The securities underwritten by investment bankers include both debt and equity issues of private firms as well as those of state and local governments (municipal securities).[1]

Government securities dealers, including the commercial bank dealers, are also active bidders for federal government securities at auctions periodically held by the Treasury to sell new issues of Treasury securities. Since the amounts bought at these auctions are large and are

---

[1] Commercial banks are permitted to underwrite one category of municipal security, general obligation securities. Interest on these securities and ultimate redemption are paid by the issuing municipality out of general revenues. Commercial banks have been lobbying in Congress for years, thus far unsuccessfully, to be permitted to underwrite municipal revenue bonds, which are the most rapidly growing segment of the municipal market. Revenue bonds' interest and principal are paid out of the revenues generated by the project they fund. An example might be a college dormitory, which generates revenue from the fees charged residents.

then offered by the dealers for resale, in a sense government securities dealers can be considered underwriters of Treasury issues.

The dealer market for government securities ensures that the market is liquid. By standing ready to buy and sell government securities, dealers serve to cushion, but not prevent, rapid price changes in one direction or another, thus providing "orderly markets" that add to the liquidity of the securities. As a result of this willingness to buy and sell, dealers must often stock large inventories of securities, far in excess of the value of their capital. To finance their inventories, they depend on borrowed funds. If the dealer is a department of a bank, the bank will supply the necessary funds. A private dealer has lines of credit to commercial banks that can be drawn upon for needed financing. Loans of this type are included in the category of loans to brokers and dealers on commercial bank balance sheets.

The activities of government securities dealers also include doing business with the Federal Reserve. The Federal Reserve Bank of New York buys and sells government securities in the secondary market for the Federal Reserve System as the primary means of conducting monetary policy. Recall that these purchases and sales of securities are called open-market operations. Federal Reserve open-market operations are accomplished through government securities dealers.

Thus, commercial bank dealers, as a major part of the group of government securities dealers, are important participants in the government securities market. Acting as dealers, they help to ensure the liquidity of this market. This benefits all government securities holders and sellers, including the commercial banks themselves.

Trust Management

Commercial banks participate in the money and capital markets in another important way—through their management of trust accounts. Large banks have trust departments that manage both individual and institutional portfolios. The largest institutional trust department customers are pension funds. The ownership of the trust accounts remains with the individual or institution while the bank manages the portfolio for a fee. Some of the largest trust departments, which are found primarily at the large money center banks,[2] manage assets that exceed the assets of the commercial bank itself. Bankers Trust of New York, which has one of the largest trust departments in the United States, is an example of a bank whose trust assets under management exceed its commercial banking assets. For all commercial banks, trust accounts are approximately one-half of aggregate commercial bank assets.

---

[2] This phrase is generally used to designate the very largest of the commercial banks, most of which (but not all) are located in New York—the center of the money market.

Table 11-2
Trust Assets of Banks and Trust Companies, December 1978[1]
(Millions of Dollars)

Noninterest-Bearing Deposits	$ 3,150
Interest-Bearing Deposits	19,115
U.S. Government and Agency Obligations	49,922
Municipal Securities	28,769
Other Securities	101,727
Preferred Stock	4,008
Common Stock	205,054
Mortgages	5,883
Real Estate	16,082
Miscellaneous	8,088
Total Assets	$441,798

[1] Note: 4,108 banks were surveyed.

Source: Federal Reserve Board of Governors, FDIC, and Office of the Comptroller of the Currency—Trust Assets of Banks and Trust Companies, 1978.

Commercial banks cannot hold corporate equities for their own portfolio and hold only a very small amount of corporate bonds. However, they are permitted to hold equities for their trust accounts, and these accounts contain large amounts of both equities and bonds. In fact, since trust accounts are typically managed for long-term return, most of the assets held by these accounts are capital market securities. Money market securities are used primarily as "resting places" for funds not yet invested in the capital markets. However, in 1979, 1980, and early 1981, the amount of trust funds "resting" in short-term money market assets did substantially increase as interest rates in the money market were very high, and alternative investments appeared less attractive to trust fund managers. However, trust fund accounts generate considerable periodic inflows of investable funds from institutions such as pension funds. As a result, money market instruments can grow in importance in trust fund accounts—this happened in the 1979–81 period—without requiring that trust fund managers liquidate significant amounts of capital market holdings.

Table 11-2 presents the asset holdings in trust fund accounts at commercial banks and trust agencies of commercial banks as of December 1978.[3] Common stock represents the largest component of

[3] Since trust activities of commercial banks are not covered by the McFadden Act—which prohibits interstate branching—many large commercial banks have set up trust agencies outside their home states.

trust fund holdings, accounting for almost 50 percent of assets. The second largest asset component is called "other securities." The majority of these securities are corporate bonds and commercial paper. About 23 percent of trust fund assets are in this category. Government securities and municipals round out the major asset categories.

Trust fund departments of commercial banks generally serve two distinct groups: institutions, such as pension funds and corporations, and individuals. The diverse needs and interests of these groups account in part for the wide range of assets held in trust fund accounts. For example, since pension funds are tax exempt institutions, the municipal securities held in trust fund accounts as shown in Table 11-2 can be assumed to be held primarily in accounts of individuals. Therefore, differences in the needs of trust fund account holders will dictate different portfolio compositions. Further, differing services are provided by trust fund managers depending on the clients.

In recent years, there has been an increased use by corporations of bank trust fund accounts for purposes other than corporate pension fund management. Corporate trust accounts at the trust departments of the large money center banks, where these accounts are concentrated, have been utilized to assist corporations in such matters as stock transfers and registration. Further, with the periodic merger waves that seem to sweep the economy, bank trust fund departments have provided assistance in stock tender offers by one corporation in the attempt to acquire another corporation.

In personal trust management, the bank assists wealthy individuals in the management of their investments, through investment counseling and estate planning. In addition, services such as acting as an executor of a will, preparing taxes, and collecting dividends and interest are often performed by the trust department for their clients. Personal trust departments are found throughout the country at larger commercial banks. Pension fund management and other corporate trust services discussed above tend to be confined to the major money center commercial banks.

Because there is considerable potential for abuse of trust fund accounts or collusion between the trust fund department of a bank and the commercial banking division of the bank, rigid rules exist that limit contact between these divisions. For example, the exchange of investment information is severely circumscribed. However, the existence of trust departments at commercial banks increases the importance of the commercial banking system's role in the financial markets.

Nonbank Intermediaries' Participation in the Financial Markets

Much of the discussion thus far in this chapter has focused on the interaction of the commercial banking system and the financial markets. The reason for this is the large size of the banking system. Nevertheless, nonbank financial institutions clearly are significant participants in the money and capital markets. Mutual funds hold large amounts of money and capital market securities, for example. These intermediaries were, in fact, formed with this purpose in mind. They gather funds from shareholders and pool these funds to acquire money and capital market securities. Life insurance companies are also heavily involved with investing funds in the capital markets as are pension funds whether managed by a bank trust department or independently.

Other nonbank financial intermediaries such as savings and loan associations, mutual savings banks, and credit unions, also include money and capital market securities in their portfolios. The amounts held by these institutions are considerably smaller in absolute as well as percentage terms compared to commercial banks' holdings and the other nonbank intermediaries' holdings mentioned above, but they are still substantial.

The participation of financial intermediaries in the money and capital markets considerably broadens the markets for these securities. This increased breadth enhances the liquidity of money and capital market securities thus adding to their attractiveness. Furthermore, the regularity of funds flowing through many of the financial intermediaries, such as pension funds, into the financial markets provides a stability that these markets might otherwise lack. Such stability enhances the usefulness of the financial markets by more smoothly allocating credit in the economy. Finally, the goals of these large investors may be different from those of other market participants. For example, life insurance companies emphasize long-term return and thus long-term investment. This adds to the diversity of the types of securities that can, under normal conditions, be marketed.

The interaction between financial intermediaries and the financial markets goes well beyond the inclusion and management of open-market securities in financial intermediary portfolios and their associated activities. These institutions also compete with the open market for investors (depositors) and for borrowers as we have seen in previous chapters. This aspect of financial intermediary association with the financial markets we will now discuss.

Financial Intermediaries and the Open Market: Competitors

The financial intermediaries are in continuous competition with the financial markets for investors (depositors). This competition exists because the potential investor always retains the option of participating directly in the open market by purchasing securities. This competition becomes particularly intense, as previously explained, during periods of high and rising interest rates. During such periods in the past, substantial disintermediation—the movement of funds out of intermediaries directly into the open market—has occurred. Disintermediation diminishes the flow of funds to the mortgage market and small businesses as well as reducing the profitability of the financial intermediaries themselves. The thrift institutions (S&Ls and MSBs) have been particularly affected during such periods. The introduction of certificate accounts at depository intermediaries whose rates are tied to open-market rates has not eliminated this problem. For example, the money market certificate introduced in 1978 certainly aided depository institutions in retaining deposits. However, when the incentives provided in the open market became quite large in 1980 and 1981, the existence of money market certificates did not prevent funds flowing out of intermediaries.

Our discussion of financial intermediation has pointed out that depositors are willing to accept a lower return from financial intermediaries in order to take advantage of the protection offered through the spreading of risk over a large portfolio of income-earning assets and many depositors. In addition, the existence of government insurance on deposits adds to the safety of these deposits. However, when the rate on government securities, which are backed by the full faith and credit of the United States, exceeds the rate obtainable on deposits at thrifts by a sufficient amount, funds do move to the open market. Further, it should be noted that even MMCs have a disadvantage compared to many open-market instruments, even Treasury bills. MMCs are fixed at six months to maturity, while Treasury securities can be sold in the secondary market. In addition, MMCs are tied to the rate on only one type of government security, the six-month Treasury bill. Moreover, Treasury interest returns are exempt from state and local income taxes, a fact which can be an important consideration for the high income investor as the tax deduction can significantly increase the after-tax yield on actual Treasury bills compared to MMCs. Other deposit accounts that don't require the $10,000 minimum of MMCs have even larger disadvantages over alternative investment possibilities, such as money market mutual funds.

The removal of interest rate ceilings by 1986 should help depository financial intermediaries compete for funds more effectively in the open market. The accompanying increase in asset flexibility for thrift institutions contained in the legislation mandating the removal of ceilings should make this competition more feasible for the thrifts, particularly S&Ls. Recent steps that have been taken by the Depository Institution Deregulation Committee have already provided depository intermediaries some additional freedom to offer higher market rates on some certificate accounts. Nevertheless, only when the adjustment to this new competitive environment is completed sometime after 1986, will it become clear whether disintermediation can be eliminated.

The competition for deposits is only one side of the competition between financial intermediaries and the open market. There is also competition for borrowers as well during most periods. The best example of this competition is between banks and the money market for the large corporate borrower. Large corporations can use the commercial paper market, the market for short-term business securities, to meet their short-term borrowing requirements rather than turning to banks. Thus, if large corporations find the terms on bank loans unattractive, they will issue commercial paper. Banks are clearly aware of this competition but are often limited in meeting it because of the cost of their own funds. The difficulty faced by banks is that banks are raising funds in the money market themselves by issuing negotiable certificates of deposit. Therefore, while banks have made concessions to the large business borrower who has a commercial paper alternative[4] by discounting the posted prime rate and adjusting compensating balance requirements, nevertheless, the amount of commercial paper issued has soared in recent years as the bank prime rate has risen. By the middle of 1981, commercial paper outstanding was approaching $150 billion compared with just $65 billion at the end of 1977. This rapid growth in the commercial paper market reflects the seriousness of the competitive problem facing commercial banks.

Competition for the long-term business borrower between banks and the open market has also increased in recent years as banks have made some inroads into a traditional capital market area—the long-term financing of business. Remember that the real bills doctrine under which commercial banking developed held that banks should concentrate on short-term lending. However in the 1970s, banks became increasingly willing and even eager to attract more long-term borrowers. For example, a survey of selected commercial banks made by the Federal Reserve Board of Governors in February 1980 indicated that about 16 percent of commercial and industrial loans at these banks had original maturities greater than one year. Term lending accelerated sharply in 1980 so that by May 1981 over 50 percent of the loans on the books of the same sample of banks had an original maturity of more than one year. To attract such borrowers, a bank must make it clear that the borrower can do better at a bank than by issuing capital market securities. Banks have been particularly successful in this regard when the stock market has been inhospitable to new issues of stock, as it was during much of the 1970s, and when bond market rates have been high, as they were in 1980 and 1981. Thus, for banks, the competition with the open market covers the spectrum from competition for long-term borrowers to competition for short-term borrowers.

Competition between financial intermediaries and financial mar-

---

[4] Recall that only large well-known corporations can raise funds in the open market at attractive rates relative to the rates on bank loans.

kets for mortgage borrowers also takes place, though on a smaller scale than for the corporate customer. The development of the secondary mortgage market and particularly passthrough securities, which are simply pools of mortgages sold in the open market, has meant that the open market is being increasingly utilized to raise funds directly for mortgages. The typical mortgage packagers are mortgage bankers, nondepository institutions that serve as brokers in the mortgage market making mortgages and then placing them with "final" mortgage investors, like commercial banks and thrifts. Selling a group of mortgages as a package in the open market is one way in which the mortgage banker may place mortgages with final investors. These packages of mortgages are usually sold through the auspices of the Government National Mortgage Association, a government agency. The ability to sell mortgage packages in the capital markets enhances the liquidity of the mortgage instrument. It does not, however, eliminate direct mortgage lending by the financial intermediaries. The secondary mortgage market is the name given to the part of the capital markets in which mortgages and mortgage pools are sold. Since this is a rapidly expanding part of the capital markets, the secondary mortgage market will be discussed in detail in Chapter 13.

Mutual funds and life insurance companies also compete with the open market. Mutual funds are essentially selling a management service. That is, funds could be directly invested by the mutual fund shareholder in securities in the open market. Thus, to attract investors, mutual funds must prove that their financial management and ability to pool funds works to the customers' advantage. If they cannot, customers will directly participate in the financial markets. The recent popularity of money market mutual funds illustrates the potential when mutual funds are successful in demonstrating the benefits of participation in their funds.

Life insurance companies are basically selling a savings program along with insurance protection. Since insurance protection can be achieved by purchasing term insurance, they must convince policyholders and prospective policyholders that they are better off buying a whole life policy or an annuity than managing their own savings. Thus, competition with the open market as well as with other intermediaries exists here too. The competition by life insurance companies with the open market can manifest itself during periods of high interest rates in an interesting way through the existence of policy loans. Policy loans, as indicated in Chapter 10, increase when interest rates rise in the open market. Since policy loans are made at rates considerably below those in the open market, when open-market rates move higher, there tends to be a lot of borrowing on policies to take advantage of this spread. Policyholders simply borrow on the cash value of their policies and reinvest these funds in the open market. For example, in March 1981, policy loans exceeded $43 billion. In the first three months of 1981, they increased by over $6 billion at an annual rate. It is likely that the proceeds of most of these policy loans were reinvested in the money and capital markets by policyholders to profit from the spread between what they received on these investments and what they were paying to borrow the funds.

Thus, it is clear that there is active competition between financial intermediaries and the open market for both investors and borrowers. Movements between the open market and the financial intermediaries can have a significant impact on the way in which credit is allocated in the economy. It is important, therefore, to realize in studying the money and capital markets and their relation to the financial intermediaries that the instruments discussed not only are important components of the financial intermediary portfolio but can also affect the level of financial intermediation in the economy.

Financial Intermediaries as Demanders of Funds in the Financial Markets

The previous sections have focused upon financial intermediaries as suppliers of funds to the financial markets and as competitors with the markets for savers' funds and for lending opportunities. The role of financial intermediaries as direct demanders of funds in the financial markets typically receives little attention. The only aspect of financial intermediaries' role as demanders of funds in the financial markets that is often fully explored in considering financial intermediary–financial market interaction is the large negotiable certificate of deposit. Financial intermediaries use large CDs to tap available investment funds in the money market. However, financial intermediaries depend upon the financial markets as direct sources of funds in a number of ways besides the issuance of large CDs.

The equity markets are utilized by intermediaries that are stockholder-owned to raise additional funds through equity issuance. Further, the existing shares of these intermediaries are in many cases actively traded in the secondary equity markets, thus aiding the placement of new issues of equities by the financial institutions. For example, commercial banks raised $1.3 billion in this way in 1979 and another $400 million in 1980. Commercial banks and their bank holding company parents are the largest equity-owned intermediaries, but some life insurance companies and a small proportion of savings and loan associations are also stockholder owned.

The capital market is also increasingly used by savings and loan associations and by commercial banks to sell off mortgage holdings in packages called passthroughs. While mortgage bankers, usually working through the Government National Mortgage Association (GNMA), are the most significant factor in this market, the use of pass-throughs by financial intermediaries to gain access to the general capital markets is of growing importance.

The money market is utilized as well as the capital markets, primarily by commercial banks, to raise funds. Both negotiable CDs and the federal funds and RP markets have been previously discussed. This discussion will be carried further in the next chapter on the money market. Therefore, little need be added here about this aspect of financial intermediary direct access to the money market. However, the use of the money market as an indirect source of funds for commercial banks does require some explanation. Issues of commercial paper by bank holding companies occur frequently. Often the funds raised are deposited in the commercial bank owned by the holding company. The nonbank affiliates of holding companies (like personal finance companies) also raise funds in the commercial paper market. These funds are deposited in accounts at the finance company's parent bank until they are disbursed by the finance company. Thus, the bank has some of the advantages of commercial paper issuance even though it is not itself permitted to issue commercial paper.

Increasingly, commercial banks, in particular, and more recently savings and loan associations are making use not only of the domestic financial markets but also of the international money and capital markets to raise funds. The international markets grew tremendously important in the decade of the 1970s. In Chapter 5, international banking aspects of this growth were discussed, and Chapter 13 will examine the international markets in detail. Without the terminology of the international markets, we cannot easily indicate the nature and extent of financial intermediary use of these markets. Nevertheless, it will be useful to recall the considerable current utilization of these markets by financial institutions in Chapter 13. This interaction is likely to grow additionally in the future.

Finally, in discussing the use of the money and capital markets by financial intermediaries as demanders of funds, we should recall that the primary motivation behind the holding of short-term government securities by commercial banks and other financial intermediaries is liquidity. In fact, it has previously been noted that short-term government securiites in commercial bank portfolios are sometimes referred to as secondary reserves to indicate the motivation behind their inclusion in the bank portfolio. The ability to gain access to the secondary money and capital markets to raise funds by liquidating portfolio security holdings is vital to sound portfolio management on the part of the financial intermediaries. The intermediaries can at times be substantial sellers of securities to take advantage of what are considered to be more profitable portfolio opportunities. To take a dramatic example, in the final three months of 1978, commercial banks sold over $30 billion in Treasury securities at an annual rate. Banks were motivated to sell these securities primarily to take advantage of increased business loan demand at profitable rates. This was an unusually large amount of net securities sales for such a short period. However, the example serves to illustrate the manner in which financial intermediaries rely on the financial markets for readily available funds through liquidating securities holdings.

The fact that financial intermediaries are both suppliers and demanders of funds in the financial markets and that their activity can be significant on both sides of the market should be kept in mind as we study the financial markets in the next few chapters. The integration of the financial system, the recurrent theme of this book, should be increasingly clear. This chapter has attempted to serve as the bridge between two important elements of the financial system—the financial intermediaries and the financial markets. We now turn to a detailed examination of the financial markets in Chapter 12.

COMPETITION FOR BORROWERS

A Prime Challenge to the Banks

Banks are losing business to the commercial paper market at a fast clip, but they continue to hold the prime lending rate at uncompetitive levels. Repelled by a prime that has not dropped below 19½% from a December peak of 21½%, corporations issued $7 billion in commercial paper during the first five weeks of 1981. Now the banks will have to lower the prime or peddle below-prime loans more aggressively if they hope to put more business loans on their books.

The dramatic shift by corporate borrowers from the banks to the commercial paper market is consistent with seasonal patterns—businesses frequently borrow heavily from the banks in December and pay down those loans early in January. And it is being fueled by a huge spread between commercial paper rates at around 16% and the prime at 19½%. But some new entrants in the commercial paper market are giving it greater breadth and also contributing to its recent growth. Commercial paper outstanding reached a record $130.5 billion at the end of January.

Among the new issuers are foreign banks and corporations. There has been a steady stream of the foreign banks into the commercial paper market, and "some of the biggies are just getting started," says George M. Van Cleave, partner at Goldman, Sachs & Co. Also issuing paper are special-project firms, mostly for energy financing. Pacific Energy Trust, established in early February, will issue up to $300 million in commercial paper to buy nuclear fuel for lease to Pacific Gas & Electric Co.

No competition. So far this year the banks have shown little desire to match declines in market rates of interest. Citi-bank held its prime lending rate at 19½% on Feb. 17, despite the fact that a few major institutions had posted a prime of 19%. And the banks have been slow to push below-prime loans.

If the banks bring the prime rate down over the next few weeks and the spread between the prime and the paper rate narrows, some moderation in commercial paper issuance could occur as corporations move to restore their relationships with banks. A modest decline of $400 million in total paper outstanding occurred during the first week in February. But a small decline in the prime may be insufficient to buoy loan demand at the banks significantly, and a pickup in below-prime lending may well result. "It normally takes the banks a month or so to judge what has happened to loan demand," says Donald T. Maude, senior financial economist at Merril Lynch & Co. But corporations, having brought inventories "amazingly well under control," may have a reduced need for short-term funds if the economy slows, says Roger M. Vasey, president of Merrill Lynch Money Markets Inc.

Major banks in New York are in a bind, having "purchased" money by issuing certificates of deposit at close to 20% late last year, anticipating continued strong loan demand and the possibility of still

**Commercial Paper Grows Faster
Than Bank Loans**

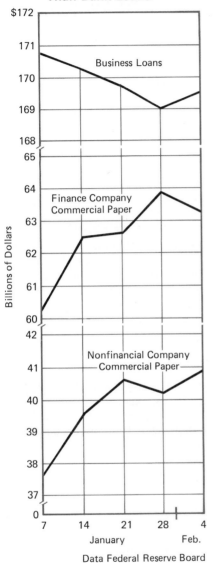

Data Federal Reserve Board

earnings at some major banks during the final quarter of the year. Net interest margins—the difference between what the banks charge borrowers and what they must pay to obtain lendable funds—narrowed to 2.22% at money center banks during the fourth quarter, according to Salomon Bros. Adjusted for loan loss provisions, the margin amounted to 1.97%. During the third quarter, the adjusted net interest margin was 2.29%. And during the second quarter—a banner three months for the banking industry—the adjusted net interest margin was 2.32% at money center banks. One of the hardest-hit banks during the final quarter of the year was Citicorp, which suffered a decline in net interest revenue of $116 million, or 18%, compared with the same period a year earlier. For the year as a whole, the giant bank holding company registered a minuscule $36 million increase in net interest revenue.

For these reasons, major banks are loath to start slashing lending rates. "There's a strong effort on the part of the banks to restore their spreads," says William V. Sullivan, senior vice-president and economist at Bank of New York. But lending may have to occur at the expense of spreads, especially at the New York banks. By and large, regional banks posted better earnings than New York banks for the fourth quarter, and they are better positioned to offer corporate borrowers favorable rates. The competition could foster rate slashing by major banks and this will come as the long-simmering brouhaha over below-prime lending and the definition of the prime rate is again coming to a boil. Representative Fernand St Germain (D-R. I.), chairman of the House Banking Committee, on Feb. 12 wrote chair-

higher rates of interest. Business loan demand is now slack and short-term interest rates lower, but the banks average cost of funds remains high.

Interest errors. Furthermore, miscalculations earlier in 1980 slashed men of the nation's top banks asking that they define the prime lending rate and its use at their institutions. "I am concerned," he said, "about the widening credibility gap between the public announcement of changes in commercial banks' prime lending rates and actual day-to-day lending practices."

Key Points

1. The interaction between the financial markets and financial intermediaries is an important aspect of the manner in which the financial system serves to allocate credit in the economy. This interaction comes about through financial intermediaries' securities holdings; through direct participation in the financial markets as buyers, sellers, and issuers of securities; and through competition for funds and borrowers with the markets.

2. The assembly and management of the portfolios of large financial intermediaries, especially commercial banks, require extensive trading departments. Further, the active participation of large commercial banks in the markets extends to their activities as government securities dealers and trust account managers.

3. The participation of financial intermediaries in the money and capital markets considerably broadens the markets for these securities. This fact enhances liquidity in these markets and hence increases the attractiveness of financial market securities.

4. The financial intermediaries compete with the financial market in raising funds and in the disbursement of these funds. Savers can always bypass financial intermediaries and invest directly in the financial markets. Many large borrowers have an alternative of borrowing from financial intermediaries or directly in the markets.

5. Finally, financial intermediaries utilize the financial markets to raise funds by issuing stock and debt securities.

Questions for Discussion

1. It was pointed out in the chapter that financial intermediaries' participation in the financial markets increases the liquidity of financial market securities. Why is this the case and how does this increased liquidity actually aid the financial intermediaries themselves?

2. What is investment banking and what limitations apply to commercial banks in underwriting securities?

3. Competition with financial markets in attracting funds is an important fact of life for commercial banks and other financial intermediaries. Explain why the financial intermediaries are in competition for funds with the markets in general and the specific ways they attempt to meet this competition.

4. The commercial paper market has grown rapidly in recent years. This growth has affected the way in which commercial banks deal with large corporate customers. How has commercial bank behavior been altered?
5. The financial markets are not equally important to all financial intermediaries. How would you assess the differences in the relationship between the major financial intermediaries and the financial markets?

Suggested Readings

Baumol, W.J. *Portfolio Theory: The Selection of Asset Combinations.* Morristown: General Learning Press, 1970.

Brill, Daniel H., and Ann P. Ulrey. "The Role of Financial Intermediaries in U.S. Capital Markets." Federal Reserve *Bulletin,* Jan. 1967, pp. 18–31.

Ehrlich, Edna E. "The Functions and Investment Policies of Personal Trust Departments." Federal Reserve Bank of New York *Monthly Review,* Oct. 1972, pp. 255–70.

Havrilesky, Thomas M. *Current Perspectives in Banking,* 2nd Ed. North Arlington: Alter Publishers, 1980, Parts I and II.

McCurdy, C.J. "The Dealer Market for United States Government Securities." Federal Reserve Bank of New York *Quarterly Review,* Winter 1977–78, pp. 35–47.

PART 3

The Financial Markets

12

The Money Market

Money market securities have been previously defined as those that have one year or less to maturity at time of issuance. The money market is the market in which the federal government, federal agencies, corporations, and commercial banks among other institutions raise short-term funds. The funds are raised by issuing primary securities. However, much of the trading in the money market takes place in the secondary market, the market for already existing securities. Activity in this secondary market runs into the billions of dollars every trading day. Many of the money market securities have been discussed in previous chapters as it became necessary in connection with commercial bank and other intermediary balance sheets. However, it is now time to examine these securities and the operation of the money market in detail.

The money market itself is a "telephone market"; trades are arranged over the phone. They usually involve the money center banks (almost synonymous with the 25 or so largest banks in the United States) located primarily in New York; commercial bank government securities dealer departments; investment bankers (who may also be government securities dealers) who deal in many of the money market securities; and a group of small specialized money market brokers. Brokers differ from dealers: brokers match buyers and sellers (lenders and borrowers) while dealers buy for their own inventory and sell from this inventory. These brokers deal primarily in the commercial paper market, the market for bankers acceptances, and the federal funds and repurchase markets. The Federal Reserve Bank of New York in implementing monetary policy is also involved in the money market as previously noted, but a detailed discussion of their involvement is deferred until the chapters on monetary policy.

Table 12-1
Money Market Securities Outstanding, 1980
(End of Period, Billions of Dollars)

Treasury Bills	$216.1
Commercial Paper	125.1
Bankers Acceptances	54.7
Repurchase Agreements and Federal Funds	108.0
Negotiable Certificates of Deposit	116.4

Source: Federal Reserve *Bulletin,* May 1981.

The largest of the money markets is the Treasury bill market. The large secondary market in Treasury bills ensures their liquidity. Other important markets also discussed in this chapter are the commercial paper market, the federal funds and repurchase markets, the markets for bankers acceptances and for negotiable certificates of deposit, and the market for federal agency money market securities. Table 12-1 presents the money market securities outstanding by category as of the end of 1980. This gives some picture of the relative size of these markets.

The Treasury Bill Market

More Treasury bills are outstanding than any other money market security—over $216 billion in bills at the end of 1980. The largest market is for six-month bills, although bills also come in maturities of three months and one year and there are cash management bills as well. As of December 1980, there were approximately $103 billion of the six-month bills outstanding, $52 billion in three-month bills outstanding and $53 billion of one-year bills outstanding. Three- and six-month bills are sold at weekly auctions and one-year bills at monthly auctions. Cash management bills of varying maturity have been sold at auction only at infrequent intervals in the 1970s and early 1980s. Often the cash management bills have maturities of less than three months, although there have been some issues of longer maturity.

The auctions work in the same way for all maturities and are a variant of the Dutch auction in which bids start high and are moved lower until someone buys. However, in the Treasury bill auction all the bids are entered before the auction results are determined and each successful bidder (there are a number) pays the price bid. The auction works as follows. On the day of the auction, the Treasury accepts bids on the amount of bills it has decided to sell. The bids are ranked from high price to low price. (Recall the higher the price the lower the yield, therefore, the lower the interest cost to the Treasury). The lowest price accepted is called the stop out price and determines the highest yield the Treasury is accepting for that auction. The highest bid determines the lowest yield. By weighting the bid prices by amounts, the average auction price and hence the average auction yield is determined. This is very important for bids may be entered by the Federal Reserve acting for individuals and institutions. These are called noncompetitive bids. Any one can bid noncompetitively for up to $500,000 of bills. By bidding noncompetitively, the holder agrees to accept the average auction yield and is guaranteed receiving the securities that are requested.

As an example, Table 12-2 presents a hypothetical auction that is simplified in a number of ways. The number of bidders is much larger, and the bids are much closer together in price at the actual auction than the example makes it appear. However, in the example, all the relevant information needed to understand the actual auction is presented. The Treasury has offered $3 billion in three-month bills. Prices are expressed based on $100 being par so that a $10,000 face value Treasury bill is indicated as $100. Thus the highest price paid at the auction in the example is $97.67 meaning the bidder pays $9,767 for each $10,000 in Treasury bills purchased. The stop out price is $97.45 and the stop out yield 10.2 percent. Notice that

Table 12-2
Hypothetical Bids at Auction
Ranked from Highest to Lowest Price

	Price	Amount	Yield-Discount Basis (Annual Rate)
	$97.67	$ 1 billion	9.32%
	97.60	$500 million	9.60%
	97.53	$250 million	9.88%
	97.50	$ 1 billion	10.00%
	97.48	$200 million	10.08%
Stop Out Price	97.45	$ 50 million	10.20%
	97.35	$ 1 billion	10.60%
	96.00	$ 1 billion	16.00%

Average Auction Yield = 9.72%

among the unsuccessful bidders, one of the bidders had entered a bid of $96.00, substantially below the price bid by the others. This bid is called a throwaway bid; it is bid in hopes that there will be an insufficient number of bidders, and the bidder will be able to get a bargain. In practice, auctions in the past have always been oversubscribed and the throwaway bid never has been accepted. The average auction price and yield is also calculated; weighted by the amount bid, the average auction price is $97.57 and the average auction yield is 9.72 percent.

The average auction yield determines the price to be paid by noncompetitive bidders so that in this case they would pay $9,757 for each Treasury bill. In the example, the Treasury is shown to have sold $3 billion in bills. However, this excludes the noncompetitive bids. In fact, what would occur is that the Treasury would announce how much in bills of a particular maturity it was selling at this auction. The Federal Reserve would inform the Treasury of the amount of noncompetitive bids. Thus, the Treasury knows before it determines the auction results how much in noncompetitive bids have been entered. If these noncompetitive bids totaled $1 billion, for example, the bidders at the auction would only receive $2 billion of the bills, the average auction yield would be calculated and the noncompetitive bidders would receive the final $1 billion since they are guaranteed successful purchase of these bills. Often these noncompetitive bids are as large as 20 or 30 percent of the total bills being sold. In addition, the average auction yield on six-month bills has taken on added importance in recent years because of money market certificates. The rate on MMCs is tied to the rate on a discount basis on six-month bills.

The Treasury bills are all sold at discount. That is, the bills are sold below face value and the interest obtained comes from receiving the face value of the bill at maturity, which is higher than the price paid. For example, a three-month bill sold at $9,700 will pay $10,000 at maturity; hence the interest return is $300 over three months. On a discount basis this means that the interest return is 12 percent at an annual rate. On a coupon equivalent basis the rate is 12.3 percent. The difference between calculating the interest on a discount basis, the usual way in which bill yields are expressed, and on a coupon equivalent basis depends mainly upon what is used in the denominator of the return calculation. The discount basis utilizes the face value of the security, in this case $10,000, and this number is divided into the $300 in the example to determine the discount yield. The coupon equivalent yield is determined by calculating the interest return by dividing by $9,700, the actual funds invested. The coupon equivalent will always be higher than the discount return. The term "coupon equivalent" is derived from the fact that this is how rates are calculated on bonds that have stated interest returns attached. Both rates are expressed at annual rates so that a three-month rate, however calculated, must be multiplied by four to obtain the annual rate. (For a six-month bill the rate must be multiplied by two to obtain the annual rate.)[1]

Treasury bills have not always been sold in denominations of $10,000. Until the late 1960s, they had been sold in $1,000 denominations, but disintermediation, when rates were high, led to raising this minimum. The higher minimum made it more difficult for average savers to purchase bills. However, there is continuous pressure to lower the denomination to enable small savers to take advantage of a safe money market investment. Although there has been no reduction in the minimum denomination on bills, some longer-term note issues (2–10 years in maturity) have been issued in denominations of $1,000. These issues have proved quite popular with smaller investors. Further, the introduction of money market funds has given smaller savers some ability to take advantage of money market rates with lower initial investments.

Once the bills have been issued, they are actively traded in the secondary market. While the rates on newly issued and outstanding bills tend to move together, they are not exact replicas of each other. The primary reason is the differing lengths of time to maturity on the outstanding bills versus newly issued bills.

The volume moving in the secondary Treasury bill market on a

---

[1] There is an additional slight difference between the rate on Treasury bills calculated on a discount basis and on a coupon equivalent basis. The rate on a Treasury bill at discount is calculated for a 360-day "financial year," while for a bond the 365-day year is used; technically, in the example above, the interest return should be multiplied by 360 divided by the number of days to maturity. (In the case of a newly issued three-month Treasury bill that would be 91 days). This would give the yield at an annual rate on a discount basis. The yield on a coupon equivalent basis would be multiplied by 365 days divided by the days to maturity to get the annual rate. Multiplying each yield by four, as was done in the above example, generates sufficient accuracy for most purposes. However, on an outstanding bill, it is best to follow the procedure outlined in this footnote.

In symbols, the formula for calculating the discount rate is

$$d.r. = \frac{360}{m}\left(\frac{100-P}{100}\right)$$

where $d.r.$ is the discount rate, m is the number of days to maturity, and P is the price paid. In the example, P is 97, meaning that $9,700 was paid for the $10,000 face value bill.

The formula for the coupon equivalent rate is:

$$c.e.r. = \frac{365}{m}\left(\frac{100-P}{P}\right)$$

where $c.e.r.$ is the coupon equivalent rate and the other symbols are defined in the same way as in the discount rate formula. Although the discount rate is the one utilized by the Treasury, the coupon equivalent rate is a more accurate measure of the investor's return from purchasing a Treasury bill.

It is interesting to note that the rate on MMCs is tied to the discount rate on Treasury bills, not the higher coupon equivalent rate. This explains the reluctance of some larger investors to purchase MMCs. They receive a higher actual rate on their investment by buying the Treasury bills themselves rather than MMCs.

Table 12–3
**Treasury Bill Transactions of Government Securities Dealers
(Averages of Daily Figures, Billions of Dollars)**

1974	$ 2.55
1975	3.89
1976	6.68
1977	6.75
1978	6.17
1979	7.91
1980	13.77
May 1981	12.36

Source: Federal Reserve *Bulletin,* July 1981.

given day is often in the billions of dollars. Table 12-3 shows the average daily Treasury bill transactions at government securities dealers for 1974–80 and May 1981. (Not all trades in Treasury bills move through the dealers.) It is clear from the amount traded why the liquidity

Figure 12-1
Supply and Demand for Securities in Two Different Markets

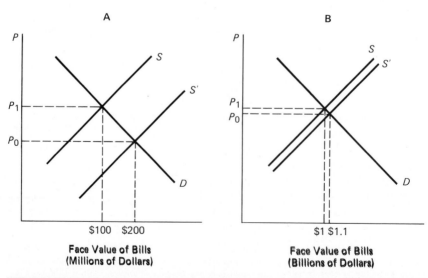

A

B

Face Value of Bills
(Millions of Dollars)

Face Value of Bills
(Billions of Dollars)

of Treasury bills is so good. It is easy for a large holder, like a commercial bank, to sell large amounts of bills very quickly without significantly driving down the price it receives for the bills. To see how the large market serves to moderate fluctuations in price, consider Figure 12-1. Figure 12-1A depicts the supply and demand for a market in which the average daily trading is $200 million. Suppose a bank needs to sell $100 million in securities in this market. The supply curve shifts from S to S'. That is, in order for the bank to sell the $100 million, the price has to drop significantly with a fixed demand curve. However, suppose the market is trading $1 billion a day. Then the $100 million is only a 10 percent addition to supply and the price has to drop much less to absorb the additional supply as shown in Figure 12-1B. These figures demonstrate the importance of the depth and breadth of the Treasury bill market to the liquidity of Treasury bills.

Short-Term Federal Agency Securities

The two large federally sponsored agencies, the Federal National Mortgage Association (FNMA) and the Federal Home Loan Bank System (FHLB), as well as other federally sponsored agencies, issue short-term securities that very much resemble Treasury bills.[2] These securities are issued at discount and have grown to a significant amount in the last decade. As of December 1980, $165 billion in agency securities were outstanding, over $96 billion issued by FNMA and FHLB. Of these, a substantial portion were short-term money market securities. The yields on these securities are usually somewhat higher but still quite close to those on Treasury bills. However, the difference between these yields and Treasury bill yields do fluctuate a good deal. For example, Table 12-4 shows the average yield and the yield spreads (in basis points)[3] between agency securities with three months to maturity and three-month Treasury bills for the years 1970–80.

The major reason that agency securities usually yield more than Treasury securities is that these securities are viewed as slightly more risky than Treasury bills since they do not carry the "full faith and credit" guarantee of the government. Adding to the higher return is the fact that the market is not as large as for Treasury bills, and these securities are therefore regarded as slightly less liquid. (Recall Figure 12-1A and 12-1B).

Active dealers in the secondary market for agency securities are for the most part the same organizations that deal in government securi-

---

[2] The federally sponsored agencies are discussed in detail in Chapter 15.

[3] A basis point is equal to one one-hundredth of a percentage point.

Table 12-4
Average Yields and Yield Spreads on Three-Month Treasury Bills and Three-Month Federal Agency Securities, 1970–80
(Coupon Equivalent Basis)

Year	Three-Month Treasury Bill Rate	Three-Month Agency Rate	Yield Spread in Basis Points
1970	6.85	6.94	9
1971	4.55	4.56	1
1972	4.18	4.22	4
1973	7.15	7.40	25
1974	8.11	8.73	62
1975	6.06	6.03	−3
1976	5.23	5.15	−8
1977	5.37	5.38	1
1978	7.44	7.68	24
1979	10.32	10.34	2
1980	11.88	12.09	21

Note: 1 basis point = .01 of a percentage point.

Source: Salomon Brothers, *An Analytical Record of Yields and Yield Spreads.*

ties. More dealers have become interested in agencies as the amount outstanding has grown. This fact has added further to the liquidity of these securities. Banks and other financial intermediaries are among the largest holders of these agency securities.

The Commercial Paper Market

The commercial paper market is the market for short-term business debt. Once dominated by finance company issues, the commercial paper market has, in recent years, become a major source of short-term financing for major corporations as well as for commercial bank holding companies. Commercial paper is issued for maturities of three days to 270 days (nine months). However, most commercial paper has a relatively short maturity. The average maturity of commercial paper outstanding is less than 30 days. Commercial paper generally comes in denominations of $25,000 to $100,000, with denominations of $100,000 being the most common. However, denominations can range up to $1 million and the average purchase in the commercial paper market is $2 million.[4] Because of the large amount of money necessary to purchase commercial paper, major purchasers are financial and nonfinancial institutions. The growth of the commercial paper market has been almost incredible in the past few years. From December 1977 to April 1981, the amount of commercial paper outstanding increased from $65 billion to $134 billion.

Commercial paper issued by finance companies is usually directly placed, primarily with institutional investors. Often the finance company has on-going relationships with its commercial paper purchasers and will tailor the maturity of its issue to the needs of the purchaser. In recent years, however, the amount of commercial paper issued by finance companies placed through dealers has grown. Dealers buy the paper and resell it in the open market. By the end of 1980, of the $88 billion in commercial paper outstanding that had been issued by financial institutions, mostly finance companies, $68 billion had been directly placed and $20 billion dealer placed.

Nonfinancial corporation commercial paper is almost entirely dealer placed. To issue commercial paper, business firms must be quite large and have good credit standing as their securities are rated by various agencies including Standard and Poors and Moody's. Only for those firms receiving a top category rating does it usually pay for them to issue commercial paper in preference to securing a bank loan. That is, only in the case of top rated commercial paper will the rate the market demands to purchase the commercial paper be less than the rate the corporation will pay at a bank to borrow.

The recent increase in commercial paper issued by nonfinancial corporations has been dramatic. In December 1977, commercial paper outstanding that had been issued by these firms totaled $15.6 billion. This had almost tripled to $40.5 billion by April 1981. This marks a return in force by corporations to the commercial paper market after a hiatus in the early 1970s. The commercial paper market had been severely shaken by the bankruptcy of Penn Central, one of the largest corporations in the United States, in 1970 and its consequent default on its commercial paper. The subsequent uncertainty in the market regarding the credit worthiness of commercial paper issues made it difficult and expensive for even high quality paper to be placed. However, the growth in the commercial paper market in the late 1970s and the new records recorded in commercial paper outstanding on a monthly basis in 1980 and 1981 demonstrated that the combination of careful rating and back-up lines of credit at commercial banks have restored investor confidence in the market. The legacy of Penn Central can be seen, however, in the rapid closure of the commercial paper

---

[4] Peter A. Abken, "Commercial Paper," Federal Reserve Bank of Richmond *Economic Review* (March/April 1981), pp. 9–11.

market to the Chrysler Corporation in 1979, when it suffered serious business losses, until government guarantees of its securities were granted.

Because large firms can go directly to the open market to borrow short-term funds, the commercial paper market is a competitor for borrowers with commercial banks, as was pointed out in Chapter 11. Recall that short-term business lending is a true specialty of the commercial banks, so the burgeoning of the commercial paper market in recent years is truly a competitive challenge for banks. Among other things, banks now must be more cognizant of the interest charges they make on loans to those corporations that have access to the commercial paper market. Furthermore, during periods of tight credit, commercial banks are likely to accommodate loan demand first by those firms that have recourse not only to other banks but to the commercial paper market because of their size. The converse of this proposition is that commercial banks can be less accommodating to small firms since these firms do not have market access.

Commercial paper rates are above those on Treasury bills of comparable maturity. Table 12-5 shows the Treasury bill rate and the rate on prime commercial paper. They yield spread between the two fluctuates, but as can be seen commercial paper rates exceed the Treasury bill rates over the entire period by a substantial amount. The positive

Table 12-5
Commercial Paper and Treasury Bill Rates Compared 1970–80
(Coupon Equivalent)

Year	Average Yield on Three-Month Treasury Bills	Average Yield on Three-Month Commercial Paper	Yield Spread in Basis Points
1970	6.85	8.22	137
1971	4.55	5.32	77
1972	4.18	4.80	62
1973	7.15	8.51	136
1974	8.11	10.61	250
1975	6.06	6.68	62
1976	5.23	5.49	26
1977	5.37	5.66	29
1978	7.44	8.06	62
1979	10.32	11.27	95
1980	11.88	13.10	122

Source: Salomon Brothers, *An Analytical Record of Yields and Yield Spreads.*

spread reflects the premium for the increased default risk of commercial paper over the risk-free Treasury bill and the lower liquidity of the commercial paper.

Commercial paper has proved a popular holding among a number of institutions including corporations that buy commercial paper as part of their cash management programs. Most commercial paper is bought by corporations in anticipation of some payment, such as taxes, and is held to maturity. Commercial paper has also proved particularly attractive to many money market mutual funds. These mutual funds also tend to hold the commercial paper to maturity. Since most holders do hold commercial paper to maturity, the secondary market is very small, especially in comparison to the volume of outstanding paper.

The acceptance of commercial paper by the investment community has meant that the rates paid by prime issuers of commercial paper have been lower than they otherwise would have paid at banks, especially when bank rates are high. For example, in March 1981 when the prime rate averaged 18.05 percent, the rate on three-month commercial paper averaged 14.56 percent. It is rather ironic to recall that one of the major reasons that commercial paper enjoys this rate advantage over bank loans is the back-up lines of credit that commercial paper issuers secure from commercial banks. These credit lines ensure that funds will be available, should they be needed, to pay off the commercial paper issue at maturity.

Negotiable Certificates of Deposit

It has been fully explained in Chapter 7 how commercial banks issue large certificates of deposit (CDs) and how CDs have grown enormously since the establishment of a secondary market in 1961 and particularly since the suspension of Regulation Q ceilings on large certificates in 1973.[5] While the amount of negotiable CDs outstanding does fluctuate considerably from year to year, they have become a significant factor as a source of funds for banks. Negotiable CDs outstanding exceeded $120 billion in May 1981.

Negotiable certificates of deposit are issued aggressively by large commercial banks to raise funds as part of their liability management. Although virtually all major commercial banks issue large CDs, those issued by large commercial banks account for most of the market. For example, banks with over $1 billion of assets had issued $114

---

[5] Ceilings were first suspended on large CDs (over $100,000) for maturities of 30–89 days in June 1970 and on remaining longer maturities in May 1973. The Fed did impose an 8 percent supplemental reserve requirement on large CDs above a certain level in October 1979 increasing to 10 percent in April 1980 as on other "managed liabilities," such as repurchase agreements. A smaller supplemental reserve requirement of 2 percent had been imposed on large CDs in November 1978. These supplemental requirements were eliminated in July 1980.

billion in negotiable CDs as of May 1981 or about 95 percent of the total outstanding at that date. Large banks in New York City alone accounted for more than 23 percent of negotiable CDs outstanding.

Certificates of deposit have proved particularly popular for corporate cash management purposes. They are also widely held by money market mutual funds. The acquisition of CDs by money market mutual funds has resulted in an interesting situation concerning the manner in which funds are channeled in the financial system. Money market mutual funds compete with financial intermediaries for depositors, and there is a good deal of evidence that funds flowing to the money market funds in many cases come from small time and savings accounts at banks and financial intermediaries throughout the country. The large amount of CDs acquired by money market funds has meant that deposits have been reallocated from all financial intermediaries to the larger commercial banks—particularly the money center banks—through this channel. This in turn has led the smaller financial intermediaries to put additional pressure on Congress to regulate the money market mutual funds. Deposit reallocation has also altered the lending pattern in the economy to the extent that large money center banks make loans to different categories of borrowers than do smaller commercial banks and nonbank financial intermediaries. For example, deposit reallocation has resulted in some restriction in agricultural credit that is often provided by small regional commercial banks.

The rate on large CDs varies with other money market rates. The secondary market, while substantial, is considerably smaller than that for Treasury bills. As with commercial paper, many purchasers of CDs, particularly the money market mutual funds, hold them to maturity. The CD rate exceeds the Treasury bill rate as Table 12-6 shows by a considerable amount on average. However, what the table does not show is the decided rate advantage for CDs issued by the large well known money center banks over those of their less well known competitors. There are a number of factors that are responsible for the divergence of rates, including simply name recognition and the uninsured nature of the major proportion of large CDs since they are often issued in denominations considerably above $100,000—often $1 million. Thus, there is potential risk for the purchaser if the bank should fail. This fact enhances the purchaser's propensity to purchase CDs of the better known banks and ensures greater liquidity in the secondary market for issues of these larger banks.

The interest rate on CDs is a key component of the cost of funds for banks. Banks, such as Citibank, formally tied their prime rate to their cost of funds. Many other banks that have no such formal scheme also pay considerable attention to the cost of their funds when setting their lending rates. In fact, since prime rates move together and banks are influenced by the prime rate at other banks, particularly large banks, the cost of funds to the larger banks that issue most of the CDs is

Table 12-6
Negotiable CDs and Treasury Bill Rates Compared, 1970–80
(Coupon Equivalent Basis)

Year	Yield on Three-Month Treasury Bills	Yield on Three-Month Negotiable CDs	Yield Spread in Basis Points
1970	6.85	7.79	94
1971	4.55	5.14	59
1972	4.18	4.67	49
1973	7.15	8.32	117
1974	8.11	10.42	231
1975	6.06	6.70	64
1976	5.23	5.38	15
1977	5.37	5.63	26
1978	7.44	8.16	72
1979	10.32	11.17	85
1980	11.88	13.15	127

Source: Salomon Brothers, *An Analytical Record of Yields and Yield Spreads.*

clearly reflected in the prime rate. Further, CDs are among the most expensive ways for banks to raise funds since the rate on these instruments is usually the highest of the time deposit rates due to the lack of interest rate ceilings and intense competition for large deposits. Therefore, CD rate changes contribute explicitly to prime rate moves.

Bankers Acceptances

The market for bankers acceptances, while relatively small when compared to the Treasury bill or commercial paper markets ($55 billion in acceptances were outstanding at the end of 1980, compared to over $125 billion in commercial paper, for example), is of considerable interest because of the importance of this instrument for international trade between the United States and the rest of the world. A bankers acceptance is accurately described by its name. A bank, called the accepting bank, accepts responsibility for payment of a bill by one of its customers, usually (but not exclusively) for international trade purposes. A simple example will illustrate the nature of bankers acceptances.

Suppose a U.S. importer decides to import televisions from a Japanese manufacturer. The TV manufacturer, the exporter, agrees to have a bank accept the importer's obligation for the televisions. There are two reasons why this may be desirable from the exporter's point of view. First, it ensures the Japanese exporter that the bill will indeed be paid. Second, it allows the Japanese exporter to raise funds at once by selling the acceptance. In the latter case, often the accepting bank will retain the acceptance and pay the Japanese exporter straight away. However, the accepting bank, if it retains the acceptance, will only pay a discounted price so that the bank receives a yield on the acceptance. The same thing would happen if the exporter sold the acceptance in the secondary market. Since the acceptance carries no rate of interest, the exporter must offer it at a discount to induce buyers to purchase the acceptance. The interest return to the purchaser of the bankers acceptance is determined by the difference between its face value at maturity and the purchase price.

The importer for whom the bank is accepting the obligation is, of course, responsible for the payment of the acceptance at maturity. The bank charges the importer a fee for this service, which is generally a flat rate. Thus, in periods of rising open-market rates, the use of the bankers acceptance may increase because the fee may be less than the importer would pay for equivalent short-term financing to pay the bill immediately. Further, during tight credit periods, the bankers acceptance is a popular instrument for a bank since the bank does not employ any of its own funds in guaranteeing payment. Therefore, the bank can earn the fees without diverting funds from other profitable lending opportunities.

The market for bankers acceptances grew rapidly in the 1970s and early 1980s owing to increased trade between countries and the increasing sophistication of exporters and importers. The use of bankers acceptances in the importation of oil has been a particularly important factor in the growth of this market. For example, in December 1975, about $19 billion in acceptances were outstanding while, as noted above, almost $55 billion were outstanding at the end of 1980. Thus the market almost tripled in six years.

Corporations as well as a number of financial intermediaries hold bankers acceptances in their portfolios. The short and staggered maturities of the acceptances make them particularly attractive for corporate cash management purposes. Interestingly, the Federal Reserve itself buys bankers acceptances from time to time and holds them for its own account. This stems from the importance that bankers acceptances have in international trade. Only acceptances that are issued to finance international trade are eligible for Federal Reserve purchase in order to encourage such trade.

The rates on bankers acceptances tend to move with other short-term rates. In general, the rate is somewhat higher than that on Treasury bills and about the same as the rate on negotiable CDs. The similarity of the bankers acceptance and CD rates is not coincidental. Most bankers acceptances are issued by the same large commercial banks

Table 12-7
Yields on Bankers Acceptances and Negotiable CDs Compared,
1970–80
(Coupon Equivalent Basis)

Year	Yield on Three-Month Negotiable CDs	Yield on Three-Month Bankers Acceptances	Yield Spread in Basis Points
1970	7.79	7.82	3
1971	5.14	5.11	−3
1972	4.67	4.68	1
1973	8.32	8.43	11
1974	10.42	10.33	−9
1975	6.70	6.55	−15
1976	5.38	5.38	0
1977	5.63	5.66	3
1978	8.16	8.24	8
1979	11.17	11.32	15
1980	13.15	13.35	20

Source: Salomon Brothers, *An Analytical Record of Yields and Yield Spreads.*

that issue most of the negotiable CDs. In both cases it is the credit standing of these banks that stands behind the instrument. Table 12-7 presents the average rate on bankers acceptances for the years 1970 to 1980 and the comparable CD rate.

Federal Funds and Repurchase Agreements

The market for federal funds and repurchase agreements between banks and nonbanks was covered extensively in Chapter 7, and therefore that discussion will not be repeated here. However, a review and amplification of some aspects touched on previously will prove useful in rounding out the coverage of the money market.

The federal funds market is the market in which banks buy (borrow) and sell (loan) excess reserves. The rate on federal funds depends on the amount of excess reserves in the banking system and Federal Reserve policy. Repurchase agreements are arrangements in which banks sell securities to nonbank investors—usually corporations or state and local governments—and agree to repurchase them later. The difference between the selling price of the securities and the repurchase price of the securities provides the return to the investor.

Federal funds and funds raised through repurchase agreements are immediately available. For this reason funds raised through repurchase agreements are often called "term federal funds." There is no clearing process for the banks to go through, and the borrowing bank has the funds available as soon as the loan takes place. This occurs through the assistance of the Federal Reserve system, which transfers funds from one depository institution account to another immediately, and then automatically reverses the transaction at some agreed-upon time. If a repurchase agreement is between a bank and a nonbank that is not the bank's customer, the same process occurs. The purchaser (a corporation, for example) informs its bank and the transaction is handled as any federal funds transaction. Usually the actual securities that are used for the repurchase transaction never leave the selling bank. However, if the term of the agreement is relatively long or the purchaser desires to hold the securities during the period of the repurchase agreement, regardless of its length, they can be transferred.

The federal funds rate (to which the repurchase agreement rate is related, though the funds rate is usually slightly higher) is a very important interest rate. It represents one of the key marginal costs of bank funds and hence affects the whole level of rates including the prime rate. It also has been used as a guide as well as a target (something the Fed tries to control) of Federal Reserve policy.

The rate on federal funds can fluctuate substantially over short periods of time, particularly on Wednesdays, the last day of the statement week for meeting reserve requirements on deposits. However, the federal funds rate can be controlled on a daily basis by the Fed within relatively narrow limits by injecting or removing reserves from the banking system. (However, even the Fed can have difficulties on Wednesdays.) Since October 1979, the federal funds rate has been subject to less control by the Fed as we will see in the discussion of monetary policy later in this book.

The Relationship Between Money Market Rates

The relationship between interest rates was discussed extensively in Chapter 4. Despite that discussion, it is useful to reiterate what has been apparent throughout this chapter, that the money market rates tend to move together. Previous tables have indicated this fact, but perhaps it is best summarized in Figure 12-2. This figure presents the average interest rates on many of the securities that have been discussed in this chapter as well as the bank prime rate. The securities all have three months to maturity.

While Figure 12-2 makes the co-movement of the rates clear, it

Figure 12-2
Average Quarterly Yields on Selected Money Market
Instruments and the Bank Prime Rate, First Quarter 1976 to
Second Quarter 1980

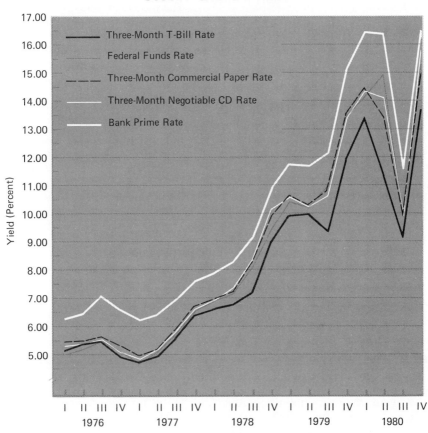

Source: Salomon Brothers and Federal Reserve *Bulletin*.

also shows that the yield spreads between the securities are not constant. The movements in rates are not simply exact images of each other at higher or lower levels. Further, while rates on a type of security are normally higher or lower than that on another type, even this may not hold for short periods. For example, the figure shows periods when the three-month CD rate exceeded that on three-month commercial paper. Figure 12-2 also demonstrates that short-term rates can change rapidly. For example, look at the rapid rise in interest rates in 1978 and 1979, the peak in early 1980, the rapid fall in the middle of the year and the upward spurt in late 1980.

TREASURY BILL PRICES

The T-Bill, When You Need to Sell

By MICHAEL QUINT

Investors, lured by high interest rates, have been trooping by droves into Treasury bills. The bills pay far more than a savings account, the interest is exempt from New York State and New York City income taxes and the nearness of maturity—three months to a year—protects the investor against loss of principal. No matter how high interest rates go, and how much Treasury bill prices might then decline, the United States Government guarantees that at the bill's maturity the investor will be paid the full face value of the bill.

As comforting as all that may seem, not everyone wants to hold a bill to maturity, nor does everyone get in on the ground floor of a bill sale. When faced with a need for cash, an investor may want to sell. When suddenly blessed with cash, an investor may want to quickly lock into an issue that is already on the market. But how does one find out the value of one's holdings or the price of an outstanding bill?

The question has been posed in many letters and phone calls to The Times. The answer is not easy.

Unlike the stock market, where the results of each day's trading are widely published, there is no exchange for trading of Treasury bills. Once these bills have come out, the only market is over-the-counter, where a few dozen dealers connected by telephone buy and sell Treasury bills and other Government securities. Among dealers, the price is a matter of bargaining between the buyer and the seller.

The individual does not deal directly with those traders, but the price he pays or sells at is closely linked to the over-the-counter market. Typically, the individual gives instructions to a salesman or registered representative who then confers with the Government securities department to tell the investor the going rate.

At weekly auctions of three- and six-month bills, and the monthly auction of one-year bills, the price an individual pays is set at the average of the competitive bids submitted by securities firms.

When the Treasury is selling $4 billion of six-month bills, for example, it first sets aside an amount of

How to Compute What a T-Bill Is Worth

First, calculate the discount, which is the return not yet earned.

Discount

$= $ Face value $\times$

$$= \$10,000 \times \frac{(\text{days to maturity} \times \text{T-bill rate*})}{360}$$

$$= \$10,000 \times \frac{(67 \times .144)}{360}$$

$$= \$10,000 \times \frac{9.648}{360}$$

$$= \$10,000 \times .0268$$

$$= \$268$$

Then, market value is the face value less the discount.

Market value $= \$10,000 - \$268$
$$= \$9,732$$

* The "bid," expressed as a decimal

bills equal to the "noncompetitive" tenders—which includes the vast majority of individual buyers—that it received.

Then it awards the bills that are remaining to the competitive bids, starting first with the highest prices offered and working its way down until it gets the full $4 billion, including the portion set aside. The rate for the noncompetitive tenders is the average of the competitive bids accepted by the Treasury.

After buying a Treasury bill, the investor can follow the discount rate for the issue in many newspapers, which publish daily a bid and asked price expressed as a percentage interest rate. The bid price is the first number printed, and the asked, or offered, price is the second. For example, bills due July 9 carried a bid of 14.40 recently and an ask of 14.32, meaning someone was willing to buy that bill at a discount rate of 14.40 percent and someone was willing to sell at a rate of 14.32 percent.

But the discount rates do not tell the investor the dollar value of his Treasury bill. To compute the dollar price, the investor must use the discount rate and the maturity of the bill to figure the dollar value of the discount. The value of his bill is then equal to the face value less the discount.

To figure the dollar value of the discount, the investor who wants to sell multiplies the bid discount rate published in the paper by the number of days to maturity, then divide by 360. Multiply the result by the face amount of the bills, and the result will be the dollar value of the discount. Assume for example, that on May 4, the Treasury bill due July 9 was bid at a rate of 14.4 percent. For a $10,000 bill, the discount is $268 and the bid indicates that someone out there is willing to pay a price of $9,732 for the bill.

At least, that would be the price if the bid holds. But the bid will change depending on the latest developments in the credit markets, and at times, these changes have been dramatic enough to raise or lower the discount rate a full percentage point between weekly auctions.

Once the investor has figured roughly what the bill should bring, then checked to see if rates have changed much, there is another little hurdle to be faced. The standard fee among securities firms and banks in New York for Treasury bill orders of less than $100,000 is $25. That is applied to each transaction, so the total would be $50 if one bought and sold one bill. Of course, by purchasing a Treasury bill directly at a Federal Reserve Bank or from the Treasury, the investor can avoid the purchase fee. Similarly, the fee can be avoided if one holds the bill until maturity.

If all this sounds like more trouble than it is worth, that may well be the case. The popularity of money market mutual funds, which now exceed $100 billion in assets, lies partly in the ease of transactions. Prices and interest paid are computed daily, and making a withdrawal is as convenient as writing a check at many funds.

The drawback is that interest paid on the money market mutual fund is taxed by New York State and New York City, and the investor pays about half a percentage point as a management fee. Then too, there is no Washington guarantee that you'll get all your money back in the end.

Key Points

1. Money market securities are defined as those securities that have one year or less to maturity at time of issuance. The money market is a telephone market in which trades are arranged over the phone. Usually trades will involve government securities dealers, investment bankers, or money market brokers.

2. The largest of the money markets in terms of both the amount of securities outstanding and daily trading volume is the Treasury bill market. Treasury bills are sold in denominations of $10,000 at periodic auctions. Treasury bills are issued in three-month, six-month, and one-year maturities. Cash management bills of varying maturities are also offered.

3. In addition to Treasury bills, federal agency securities, commercial paper, negotiable CDs, federal funds and repurchase agreements, and bankers acceptances are all considered part of the money market. Federal agency money market securities are short-term securities issued by federally sponsored agencies, primarily the Federal National Mortgage Association and the Federal Home Loan Bank Board, that resemble Treasury bills. Commercial paper is issued by both financial and nonfinancial business to raise short-term funds. Negotiable CDs are large CDs primarily issued by major commercial banks. Federal funds and repurchase agreements are used by banks to raise immediately available funds while bankers acceptances are bank guarantees of payment used primarily in international trade.

4. Money market rates tend to move together. However, yield spreads between money market securities do fluctuate a great deal.

Questions for Discussion

1. Explain the operation of the Treasury bill auction. The auction yields are expressed on a discount basis. However, most market participants feel that the coupon equivalent basis of expressing yields is a more accurate measure of return. Why? What distinguishes these two ways of calculating yields?

2. Why do large corporations find the commercial paper market attractive for raising short-term funds? Distinguish between dealer and directly placed commercial paper.

3. Why do many observers believe that the OPEC-induced increases in oil prices are an important factor in explaining the increase in the market for bankers acceptances? Why do banks like to issue acceptances during periods when credit is tight?

4. What does it mean to say that federal funds and repurchase agreement transactions are conducted in immediately available funds?

5. Differentiate between a broker and a dealer.

Suggested Readings

Abken, Peter A. "Commercial Paper." Federal Reserve Bank of Richmond *Economic Review,* March/April 1981, pp. 11–21.

Banks, Lois. "The Market for Agency Securities." Federal Reserve Bank of New York *Quarterly Review,* Spring 1978, pp. 7–21.

Bowsher, Norman N. "Repurchase Agreements." Federal Reserve Bank of St. Louis *Review,* Sept. 1979, pp. 17–22.

Hervey, Jack L. "Bankers' Acceptances." Federal Reserve Bank of Chicago *Business Conditions,* May 1976, pp. 3–11.

Judd, John P. "Competition Between the Commercial Paper Market and Commercial Banks." Federal Reserve Bank of San Francisco *Economic Review,* Winter 1979, pp. 39–53.

Lucas, Charles M., Marcos T. Jones, and Thom B. Thurston. "Federal Funds and Repurchase Agreements." Federal Reserve Bank of New York *Quarterly Review,* Summer 1977, pp. 33–48.

Melton, William C. "The Market for Large Negotiable CDs." Federal Reserve Bank of New York *Quarterly Review,* Winter 1977–78, pp. 22–34.

McCurdy, Christopher J. "The Dealer Market for United States Government Securities." Federal Reserve Bank of New York *Quarterly Review,* Winter 1977–78, pp. 35–47.

Stigum, Marcia. *The Money Market: Myth, Reality and Practice.* Homewood, Ill.: Dow Jones–Irwin, 1978.

Summers, Bruce J. "Negotiable Certificates of Deposit." Federal Reserve Bank of Richmond *Economic Review,* July/August 1980, pp. 8–19.

13

The Capital Markets

This chapter is concerned with the markets for intermediate and long-term debt and equities. These markets are known as the capital markets due to their historical association with the financing of capital spending—the purchase of plant and equipment. While much capital market financing, such as that by the government, is no longer tied directly to capital spending, nevertheless the designation of capital market securities has come to be applied to any security having a maturity of more than one year from date of issuance. Therefore, the markets for intermediate and long-term government debt, mortgages, intermediate and long-term corporate debt, intermediate and long-term federal agency debt, municipal securities, and equities all compose the capital markets.

There is a distinction between the primary and secondary markets for capital market securities as there is in the money market. At issuance, capital market securities are primary market securities. However, most of the activity in the capital market takes place in the secondary market for already issued securities. Indeed, it is the large volume of secondary market activity in many capital market securities that contributes to their liquidity and hence adds to their desirability as holdings in investor portfolios. As the discussion progresses in this chapter, the various procedures by which securities are initially issued and subsequently traded will be explained.

Long-Term Government Securities

The government, as we saw in the last chapter, issues substantial amounts of money market securities—Treasury bills. However, it also finances over a wide range of maturities running from notes with two

Table 13-1
Marketable U.S. Government Securities Outstanding, April 1981
(Billions of Dollars)

Treasury Bills	$225.8
Treasury Notes	341.1
Treasury Bonds	91.0

Source: Federal Reserve *Bulletin*, July 1981.

to ten years to maturity to government bonds with 30 years to maturity. Table 13-1 presents the outstanding amount of marketable government debt by type as of April 1981.[1] Treasury bills outstanding are included for comparison.

The overall government debt stood at $964.0 billion as of April 1981. While this represents an increase from $389.2 billion in 1970, as a percentage of GNP, which can be used to put this debt into perspective, government debt has actually fallen throughout the post–World War II period. As Table 13-2 shows, government debt represented about 39.6 percent of GNP in 1970 and had fallen to 35.4 percent of GNP by December 1980. For comparison, 1946, the first year after WW II, government debt outstanding was 110 percent of GNP. In absolute amount, however, government debt grew rapidly in the latter part of the 1970s and early 1980s in coincidence with the large budget deficits of these years. Although there are congressionally mandated limits on the amount of government debt that can be issued, these ceilings are periodically raised as the need for further issuance becomes apparent.[2]

The usefulness of the ceilings can be questioned because they are always raised when approached. However, while the ceilings have proved ineffective in limiting the expansion in federal debt, it perhaps can be argued by defenders of such ceilings that their existence gives Congress a chance during deliberation leading to the ceiling increases to question budgetary policy that would not routinely come into question. However, such questioning has not appeared to alter behavior in any meaningful way. Since Congress appropriates funds for federal

---

[1] In addition to marketable debt, a large amount of nonmarketable debt has been issued by the Treasury. Of the $304.9 billion in nonmarketable debt outstanding as of April 1981, the largest portion ($193.9 billion) was held by government trust funds such as the social security trust fund. The total of nonmarketable debt also included $69.8 billion U.S. savings bonds, which are redeemable but not negotiable. In addition, $24.4 billion in foreign issues either denominated in dollars or in foreign currency were outstanding, the large majority held by foreign governments.

[2] For example, the ceiling stood at $985 billion on March 31, 1981.

Table 13-2
Government Debt[1] and Gross National Product, 1970–1980
(Billions of Dollars)

Year	Government Debt	Gross National Product	Government Debt as a Percentage of GNP
1970	$389.2	$ 982.4	39.6%
1971	424.1	1,063.4	39.9
1972	449.3	1,171.1	38.4
1973	469.9	1,306.6	36.0
1974	492.7	1,412.9	34.9
1975	576.6	1,528.8	37.7
1976	653.5	1,702.2	38.4
1977	718.9	1,899.5	37.8
1978	789.2	2,156.1	36.6
1979	845.1	2,413.9	35.0
1980	930.2	2,626.1	35.4

[1] Outstanding at end of year.

Source: Federal Reserve *Bulletin,* various issues.

expenditures and these expenditures must be financed, perhaps it is not surprising that only rhetorical opposition to rises in the debt ceiling are heard.

The Government Budget Constraint

To understand the process that requires additional debt to be issued to finance budget deficits, an examination of the government budget constraint is very useful.[3] The government budget constraint is at once a very simple but compelling picture of how changes in the federal debt are necessitated by spending and taxing decisions taken by government. In other words, the budget constraint simply says that government expenditures and transfer payments (social security, welfare payments, and so forth) that exceed tax receipts must be financed either by issuing debt or by increasing the money supply. This can be seen most clearly if put into equation form:

---

[3] Although his work is quite technical, Carl Christ, "A Simple Macroeconomic Model with a Government Budget Constraint," *Journal of Political Economy* (Jan. 1968), pp. 53–57, was one of the first economists to focus on the importance of the government budget constraint. Stephen J. Turnovsky discusses the government budget constraint extensively in *Macroeconomic Analysis and Stabilization Policy* (Cambridge: at the University Press, 1977).

$$G + T = t + dD + dM \qquad\qquad [13\text{-}1]$$

where

    G = government expenditures on newly produced goods or ser-
          vices over a year
    T = transfer payments over a year
    t = tax receipts for the year
  dD = the change in debt
  dM = the change in the money supply

Simple algebraic manipulation makes the meaning of the constraint clear. Rearranging equation [13-1] we have:

$$(G + T) - t = dD + dM \qquad\qquad [13\text{-}2]$$

If $G + T$ exceeds t, then the constraint shows that either the debt or the money supply must increase to pay for the excess of expenditures over taxes. Since dM is not directly under the control of the government but under the control of the Federal Reserve when $G + T$ exceeds t, the Treasury must increase the amount of its debt.[4] The constraint is also symmetrical in that in periods when tax receipts exceed expenditures, the Treasury can reduce the debt accordingly by redeeming some portion of it. (However, concentration in this section is on the deficit case not only because government debt and its issuance is of central concern in this chapter, but also because only twice since 1960 has the government budget been in surplus, 1960 and 1969, and these surpluses have been small.)

The Fed can buy the newly created debt in the open market and has frequently done this to keep interest rates down (this process is called monetizing the debt). However, debt held by the Fed is still considered to be outstanding—the Fed's balance sheet is not consolidated with that of the government.[5] The debt that must be issued is determined as a result of spending and taxing decisions taken by the government.

The Issuance of Government Debt

In the last chapter, we saw how Treasury bills, which are short-term government debt, are sold at auction. Long-term government debt has been marketed in various ways. Sometimes, the Federal Reserve, serv-

---

    [4] Technically, the Treasury can directly borrow $5 billion from the Fed, thus directly increasing M by that amount. Since this is relatively a rather small amount, it is ignored in the analysis.

    [5] However, the Fed does return the bulk of interest received on its holdings of the federal debt to the Treasury, as will be explained in Chapter 17.

ing as the fiscal agent for the Treasury, accepts subscriptions to an issue that has been announced. If the issue is oversubscribed, proportions are allotted, or the issue is sold on a first-come-first-served basis. Increasingly, however, both notes and bonds are being sold at auction. One factor that has previously constrained auctions for long-term securities (particularly bonds) is that there is a ceiling on the note rate that can be attached to long-term government securities. The ceiling was established by Congress in the belief that it would keep Treasury financing costs low; selling at auction implies discounts from the note rate. However, in recent years because the note rate ceiling has been so low (4.5%), the Treasury has periodically obtained exemptions from the ceiling from Congress. This became mostly routine in the 1970s and early 1980s because the high open-market interest rates would have made it impossible for the Treasury to sell any securities at par with the low mandated rate. This routine exemption from the note rate ceiling has made it possible for the Treasury to increase its use of the auction process for bond sales. Certain Treasury bond issues have been placed directly with large investors—sometimes the governments of foreign countries—as well.

The Market for Government Securities

Treasury notes are the largest category of government securities (see Table 13-1 p. 316). However, the liquidity of both Treasury notes and Treasury bonds is less than that of Treasury bills.[6] Despite the less liquid nature of these securities, holdings of notes and bonds are widespread. For example, Treasury notes have proved popular holdings for commercial banks. Individuals have also favored Treasury notes, especially when they have been issued in $1,000 denominations as has often been the case in the 1970s and early 1980s. Table 13-3 shows the distribution of marketable U.S. government securities among private holders for 1980, with bonds of 20 years or more to maturity shown separately. Bonds outstanding are not very large relative to bills and notes but are widely held as Table 13-3 shows, particularly by state and local governments, and by individuals.[7]

As was true of Treasury bills, Treasury bonds and notes are traded by government securities dealers. These dealers, individual firms or

---

[6] The secondary market in Treasury bills is much larger than that for notes and bonds. Further, it is useful to recall at this point that liquidity is defined as the ability to convert an asset into money without substantial capital loss. Since price fluctuates more on long-term than on short-term securities for a given yield change, longer-term securities are by definition less liquid than shorter-term securities.

[7] One type of bond, known popularly as "flower bonds," is of particular interest. These bonds are no longer issued, but issues that have not yet expired are still available in the market although they are gradually disappearing. Flower bonds are bonds that were issued at discount but are accepted by the Treasury at par in payment of inheritance or estate taxes. Their name derives from this use.

Table 13-3
Private Ownership of Government Marketable Securities, 1980
(End of Period, Millions of Dollars)

Holders	All Maturities	Bonds with 20 Years or More to Maturity
Commercial Banks	$ 77,868	$ 1,325
Mutual Savings Banks	3,917	110
Insurance Companies	11,930	730
Nonfinancial Corporations	7,758	476
Savings and Loan Associations	4,225	21
State and Local Governments	21,058	3,086
All Others (Including Individuals)	365,539	18,838
Total	$492,295	$24,587

Source: Federal Reserve *Bulletin*, July 1981.

divisions of large money center banks, make markets in these securities and stand ready to buy and sell. They not only buy in the secondary market, but, as with the Treasury bill auctions, participate in the purchase of primary securities issues.

Refunding the Debt

Large amounts of Treasury bills, as well as smaller amounts of notes and bonds, come due frequently and have to be refunded. As a result, the Treasury is not always increasing the size of the debt when it issues new securities. In fact, a substantial portion of the proceeds of most weekly Treasury bill auctions goes to retire maturing Treasury bills. Similarly, new note and bond issues are often utilized, at least in part, to retire maturing debt. In retiring longer-term debt, the Treasury has often engaged in what is known as "advanced refunding." Using this technique, the Treasury offers to exchange a new securities issue for securities maturing at some future time. By offering an interest rate incentive—that is, paying something above the current yield on the securities—the Treasury can induce holders to take part in the swap. The Treasury can, if it wishes, extend the maturity of the debt somewhat by this practice. However, the higher interest rates of the 1970s and early 1980s have reduced the attraction of advance refundings, and they have not been pursued aggressively in recent years.

Debt Management

The Treasury has in the past issued securities of particular maturities for fiscal policy impact. This impact was expected to occur through the effect of the securities issues on the term structure of interest rates in the economy. For example, concentrating issues in shorter maturities would, it was presumed, put upward pressure on short-term interest rates while essentially leaving long-term rates unaffected. This would be desirable as long-term rates are an important determinant of investment spending.

There has always been controversy over whether debt management policies by the Treasury can be useful in influencing the economy in a desired direction or for such other potential policy aims as affecting the international balance of payments. As explained in Chapter 4 on interest rates, whether Treasury debt management policies can be an effective policy tool in influencing the economy depends very much on how interest rates are related. To the extent that markets are segmented—that is, supply and demand in the bond market has little to do with supply and demand in the money market, for example—debt management policy may work. However, if markets are extensively related so that all interest rates essentially move together, debt management policies may have little impact on the structure of interest rates.

There has been a great deal of research, particularly in the 1960s and early 1970s, that has attempted to evaluate the importance of Treasury debt management. While much of this research has tended to minimize the importance of debt management as part of active economic policy, it is clear that the Treasury remains conscious of the potential effects on the economy of how it manages its debt.[8] In recent years, the issue of the Treasury's debt management policies and the effect of these policies have received attention in another context: the "crowding out" of private financing by Treasury financing.

The Treasury can always find buyers for its securities. This result is assured by the liquidity of these securities, their safety, and the fact that the Treasury is unconstrained in the rate of interest it can pay. "Crowding out" refers to the question of whether the impact of Treasury debt financing reduces the availability of funds or raises interest rates through increasing the supply of securities such that some private projects are not financed. The answer to this question depends in part on the impact of the Treasury's financing on wealth

---

[8] There is an excellent compendium of papers and comments on these papers entitled *Issues in Federal Debt Management* published by the Federal Reserve Bank of Boston (June 1973), which discusses many of the issues in managing the federal debt and reviews previous research in the field. See particularly the paper by William D. Nordhaus and Henry C. Wallich in this volume for a survey of the issues in Treasury debt management.

in the economy. Debt management has been one of the factors that has been analyzed in this context.[9] It appears, therefore, that the manner in which the Treasury debt is managed will continue to receive attention by researchers.

Debt Issuance and Policy

For most of the post–World War II years, government fiscal policy has been theoretically governed by Keynesian economics. That is to say, the government is essentially supposed to run a deficit to stimulate aggregate demand in times of recession. This deficit must be financed and leads to increased government debt issuance. To a large extent the increase in the deficit is automatic: as income declines during a recession, taxes are reduced and transfer payments—for instance, unemployment insurance payments—are increased. Alternatively, the government is supposed to run a surplus when the economy is rapidly expanding and to retire some government debt. However, the failure to generate surpluses undermines the traditional Keynesian macroeconomic prescriptions and leads to ever increasing amounts of government debt.

The failure to generate a surplus during economic expansion must be due either to increased government expenditures and transfer payments or to reduced taxes. Using the government budget constraint presented as equation [13-1] on p. 318, we can clearly see the accuracy of our statement. With M (money supply) unchanged, only increases in G (government expenditures) or T (transfer payments) or reductions in t (taxes) lead to an increase in D (debt). Because T should fall as the need for transfer payments programs is reduced during an economic expansion and t should increase as income increases, decisions that increase G and T or reduce t are political determinations made by Congress and the President. Increased debt issuance, then, is clearly a result of political as well as economic considerations.

The Market for Long-Term Corporate Bonds

Traditionally corporations borrow in the long-term market to finance capital expenditures for plant and equipment. The short-term market and bank borrowing have traditionally been utilized for inventory and accounts receivable financing. Sometimes, short-term financing has

---

[9] See Benjamin M. Friedman, "Crowding Out or Crowding In? Economic Consequences of Financing Government Deficits," *Brookings Papers on Economic Activity,* No. 3 (1978), pp. 593–641.

been used to secure "temporary" plant and equipment financing when long-term rates were high and were expected to fall, as occurred in both 1980 and 1981. However, as soon as long rates did fall, corporations moved back to the long-term market for "permanent" financing for plant and equipment. While corporations have in recent years increased the amount of long-term bank borrowing, corporations still use the long-term bond market to secure most of their outside plant and equipment financing.

Despite corporate utilization of the bond market for financing capital spending, debt financing is not the major way in which corporations finance such long-term spending. Funds generated internally through capital consumption allowances and retained earnings are the primary source of funds for capital spending. However, with the acceleration in inflation beginning in the late 1960s, internal funds have increasingly proven insufficient to supply the corporation with enough funds to undertake major projects. Thus, corporations have utilized the bond markets with increasing frequency.

The equity markets, the traditional alternative to the bond market for long-term financing, were relatively sluggish through much of the 1970s. As a result, corporations did not issue a great deal of new corporate stock since the prices per share that would have been received in most years did not appear favorable. For example, the ratio of a firm's market value to the replacement value of its plant and equipment was often below one.[10] This meant that $1 of additional investment in capital was valued by the stock market at less than $1, not a desirable situation for corporate new stock issues. There was some increase in new equity issues in 1979 and 1980 when the market improved, but equity issues still remained far behind bonds as a source of funds. In 1980 nonfinancial corporations raised $9.5 billion by issuing stock compared to $28 billion by issuing corporate bonds.

There is an additional consideration in the bond versus equity financing decision of corporations that would be expected to lead corporations to favor bond financing. Dividends paid out to stockholders come out of after-tax profits, while interest paid to debt holders is tax deductible. Interestingly enough, this consideration does not appear to be important according to various studies. Because corporations and potential bond investors are cognizant of the ratio of corporate debt to equity, if this debt-to-equity ratio is too high relative to

---

[10] This ratio is known as "q" and is due to James Tobin. See, for example, James Tobin, "A General Equilibrium Approach to Monetary Theory," *Journal of Money, Credit, and Banking* (Feb. 1969), pp. 15–29. For an extensive discussion of "q" and the investment decision, see George M. Von Furstenberg, "Corporate Investment: Does Market Valuation Matter in the Aggregate?" *Brookings Papers on Economic Activity,* No. 2 (1977), pp. 347–97 and Tobin's "Discussion" of this paper in the same issue, pp. 401–405.

what is considered "reasonable," corporate debt may be hard to place. Thus, corporations appear constrained to some degree by this consideration in issuing debt.

The External Deficit

The necessity for corporations to finance can be analyzed by examining the corporate financing constraint. The corporate financing constraint is in some ways analogous to the government budget constraint. If a corporation decides to undertake a capital project or projects, it must decide how to finance that project. If internal funds are insufficient, it must, if it is to proceed with the project, either borrow those funds it needs or raise equity capital. For all corporations taken together,

$$CE = IF + dD + dE \qquad [13\text{-}3]$$

where
  CE = capital expenditures
  IF = internally generated funds (through retained earnings and capital consumption allowances)
  dD = change in debt
  dE = change in equity

With a little algebraic manipulation, then, equation [13-3] becomes:

$$CE - IF = dD + dE \qquad [13\text{-}4]$$

That is, the difference between capital expenditures and internally generated funds, if positive, must be financed through borrowing or the issuance of additional stock. Realistically, most of the **external deficit**, which is the name given to the $CE - IF$ difference, is financed through bond issuance. As Table 13-4 makes clear, the external deficit has risen over the past years as capital consumption allowances particularly have not kept pace with the increased replacement costs of capital, which have risen substantially due to inflation. This was explicitly recognized in the tax reductions enacted in 1981. Among other provisions dealing with such items as income tax rates, this legislation provided for accelerated depreciation schedules. Over time, this may enlarge internally generated funds for corporations relative to their capital expenditure needs.

Capital Spending Decisions

The external deficit is the amount of financing required to finance capital expenditures. However, we have not yet discussed the decision to undertake capital expenditures. At its most basic level, the decision

Table 13-4
Capital Expenditures, Internal Funds, and the External Deficit, 1975–81
(Billions of Dollars)

Year	Capital Expenditures	Internal Funds	External Deficits
1975	$115.8	$104.6	$11.2
1976	154.0	132.5	21.5
1977	186.7	139.6	47.1
1978	212.7	152.1	60.6
1979	239.8	160.1	79.7
1980 (estimate)	249.0	158.0	91.0
1981 (projection)	282.5	186.5	96.0

Source: Salomon Brothers, *1981 Prospects for Financial Markets.*

for a firm to undertake capital expenditures depends upon the expected return on that investment relative to the cost of financing that expenditure. If the expected return exceeds the cost of financing, the project will be undertaken. If the expected return is less than its cost, it will not be undertaken.

Expectations of future return on an investment are estimates made at the time the project is being considered and are strongly influenced by the current perceptions of the business firm as to the state of the economy and the state of its business in particular. By considering these factors and more specific needs of the business, the firm arrives at an expected rate on return on the investment project over its life. This expected return is then compared to the rate that the firm expects to pay to finance the project. The rate relevant for comparison is the market rate of interest. (Theoretically, even if the business firm finances the project out of internal funds, the market rate of interest represents the opportunity cost of using these internal funds to finance the investment project rather than in an alternative use. Therefore, the expected return will still be compared to the market rate of interest because the internal funds can always be invested in the open market rather than be used for the capital expenditure.) However, both the expected rate of return on the project and the market rate of interest can alter in very short periods of time. New information that will affect the business firm's expectations could become suddenly available, and market rates can change dramatically in short periods of time.

Nevertheless, proceeding on its best estimate, the business firm can use the expected return to determine the present value of the project. This present value is the discounted future stream of earnings.

Figure 13-1
Marginal Efficiency of Investment

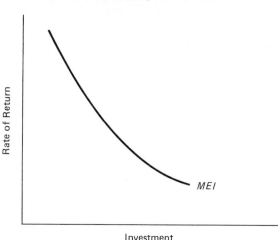

MEI

Rate of Return

Investment

Similarly, the business firm can calculate the present cost of the project, which is the discounted future stream of payments.[11] If the present value of the project exceeds the present cost of the project, the business firm should go ahead. If not, the project will be shelved either permanently, or perhaps temporarily, until either the return calculation is altered by new information or the market interest rate becomes more favorable. (Economists are fond of saying that investment will take place to the point where the rate of return on the investment project just equals the market rate of interest. The business firm is, however, unsure of the accuracy of its estimate of the expected rate of return. Therefore, for it to be assumed that the firm invests to the point where the expected return on the project equals the market rate implies that the firm's rate of return estimate includes some allowance for uncertainty.)

If the economy as a whole is considered, investment projects can be ranked from high to low rates of return. This gives the marginal efficiency of investment (MEI) schedule as indicated in Figure 13-1. The lower the rate of return that is examined, the more investment projects qualify for consideration. Investment will occur in this analysis at the point where the marginal efficiency of investment equals the market rate of interest. Thus, if the market rate of interest is 8 percent,

---

[11] See the appendix to Chapter 4 for a formal explanation of this process.

only those investment projects that yield at least 8 percent will be undertaken. It is easy to see that if the market rate of interest increases, less investment will occur; and if the market interest rate falls, more investment will occur. That is, an inverse relationship exists between the amount of investment and the market rate of interest. The investment level determined by this analysis then leads directly to the value of the *CE* term in the external deficit discussed above. The value of *CE* when related to *IF* then determines the amount of financing done by corporations in the open market.

In a sense, the process discussed above is somewhat simultaneous in that the external deficit will influence the market rate of interest as it results in changes in the amount of securities coming to market. For example, increases in the deficit will lead to additional securities being issued which, in turn, will put upward pressure on interest rates and perhaps lead to revisions in investment plans.

The Amount and Ownership of Long-Term Corporate Debt

The total of corporate bonds outstanding as of December 31, 1980, was $478.2 billion. The comparable figure for 1969 was $147 billion. Bonds outstanding quite clearly have grown very rapidly over this period of time. Previous discussions of the financial intermediaries have made clear that corporate securities are widely held. Long-term corporate bonds are held in portfolios of mutual savings banks, life insurance companies, trust accounts at banks (as has been noted, commercial banks hold very little corporate debt for their own portfolios), mutual funds that specialize in bond holdings, and individuals. Individuals find corporate bonds attractive because corporates typically come in denominations of $1,000 at par and many sell at discounts from par.

The debt of corporations is rated by a number of rating services such as Moody's and Standard and Poors. Ratings categories run from A, the highest category, through C, the lowest or speculative category. These categories are further divided. If a security has an AAA (the highest rating), AA, or A rating, it is regarded as high quality while ratings beginning with B have more risk attached to the security. The ratings are for risk of default only, not market risk. Therefore, ratings do not directly relate to fluctuations in the price of a security as interest rates change. However, the price volatility of lower rated securities, because they are more speculative, is usually greater than that of higher rated securities.

The rating given to a corporate security affects its marketability and the yield the corporation must pay in order to secure financing. The spreads between equivalent maturity securities of different risk characteristics is dramatic. Figure 13-2 plots these yield spreads in basis points between AA and Baa bonds for the years 1971–80. The

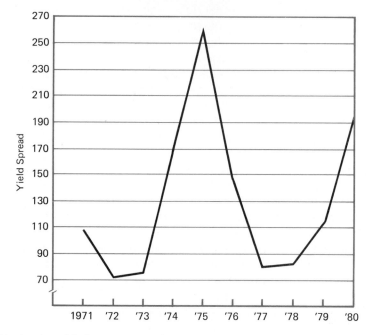

Figure 13-2
Yield Spreads Between AAA and Baa-Rated Bonds,
From 1971–80
(in Basis Points)

Note: 1 basis point = .01 of a percentage point.
Source: Salomon Brothers, *An Analytical Record of Yields and Yield Spreads.*

spread fluctuates, but it is always significant with the Baa securities paying a higher interest rate to compensate for the perceived greater risk of these securities. The risk premiums on lower rated securities tend to increase in periods of economic recession when the danger of business failure increases. Note, for example, the sharp increase in the spread in 1974 and 1975, recession years in the economy, and the subsequent reduction in 1976 as economic recovery was well underway.

Deep Discount Bonds

Some bonds are known as deep discount bonds because they sell at very substantial discounts from par to yield very high rates. Often these bonds are in the lowest C category. Rates of return on C-rated securities are as much as 30 percent or more. These bonds are usually obligations of companies that are in trouble and are viewed as likely to default with some probability or are already in receivership. They are, as a consequence, very speculative because they may never be redeemed, interest payments may be suspended, or interest payments may already be suspended and may not be resumed. However, some speculators make a practice of buying deep discount bonds for, if the bonds purchased are ultimately redeemed or some favorable change in their status occurs, the profits can be substantial. But they are not for the faint of heart.

However, the high rates of interest experienced in the late 1970s and early 1980s have resulted in many highly rated bonds selling at deep discounts from par. If a bond yields a very low rate of interest at par because it was issued during a lower interest rate period, the rise in interest rates will cause its price to fall to a deep discount in secondary market trading. Bond investors may be attracted to such bonds, for when interest rates fall the price of the bonds will rise and capital gains can be obtained. Since capital gains are taxed at more favorable rates than interest income, this can be a real advantage. In 1981, some highly rated corporations decided to issue intentionally bonds with low coupons (low interest rates at par) or zero coupons and market these bonds at deep discount. These bonds were well received by the market (they are particularly attractive to certain institutional investors like pension funds) and, as a consequence, underwriters sold these issues quickly.

The Call Provision

Most corporate bonds are issued with call provisions. This is particularly the case for bonds issued during periods of relatively high interest rates. Call provisions entitle the issuer to call in the bonds for redemption at par after a specified period, called the **call protection period** (in many cases five years). This allows the corporation to refinance the issue at a lower rate should interest rates drop substantially during the life of the issue.[12] Differing call provisions are noted by potential bond investors and can account in part for different yields on securities that are seemingly the same.

New Issues

New issues of corporate bonds come to market through investment banking syndicates, or they can be directly placed with ultimate investors. A syndicate of investment bankers usually with one or two invest-

---

[12] The drop in interest rate usually must be substantial because the transactions costs of calling bonds would not make it feasible to do so if rates had not dropped by significant amounts. Also there may be a loss of investor goodwill if a company is too "trigger-happy" in calling bonds.

ment bankers acting as the managing partner or partners may underwrite the issue in which case the syndicate has actually purchased
the securities from the corporation for resale to bond investors. Alternatively the syndicate may simply broker the securities for the corporation. The latter process is often followed for security issues of less
well known corporations or of lower rated corporations. The investment banking syndicate is unwilling to take the risk of not being able
to resell the securities at a price to insure it a profit.

Private placement of corporate bond issues is also utilized to raise
funds from new issues. Often these are arranged with large financial
institutions like insurance companies, and investment bankers are often
instrumental in arranging private placements. Usually the private placement securities are somewhat less liquid than regular issues of securities because they may contain special provisions that have been negoti-
ated between the bond issuer and the bond purchaser. In 1980, about
22 percent of all corporate bonds issued were directly placed.

Corporate Equities

In the previous section, our discussion on the corporate financing constraint showed that the external deficit ($CE - IF$) has to be financed
either by the issue of debt or equity. Corporate equities are ownership
shares in publicly held business enterprises. The secondary markets
for these shares are broad and very active, although the primary issuance of equities has been much less than for corporate bonds and
notes in the 1970s and early 1980s. Table 13-5 compares the
amounts of new equity issues coming to the market over the years
1970–80 with those of corporate bond and note financing.

Activity on the stock exchanges—that is, in the secondary market—
has been substantial in the 1970s as indicated by the volume of trades.
The largest of the exchanges is the New York Stock Exchange. Most
of the major corporations in the United States are traded (or listed)
on the New York Stock Exchange, and the value of the combined
securities represented on the New York Exchange is huge, totaling
about $1 trillion as of June 1980. The American Stock Exchange is
the second largest of the organized exchanges; usually smaller companies are traded on this exchange. Smaller exchanges are the Philadelphia, the Pacific, and the Mid-West Stock Exchanges, and there are
a number of even smaller, regional exchanges. The largest "exchange"
in number of companies is the over-the-counter market because it represents all publicly traded corporations not listed on an organized exchange. (In some cases, securities listed on the major exchanges are
traded over the counter as well.) Most small companies are traded
"over-the-counter," but in some industries even when companies grow
large because of a historic association with the over-the-counter market

Table 13-5
New Issues of Corporate Common Stock and Corporate Bonds
and Notes, 1970–80
(Billions of Dollars)

Year	Stock	Bonds and Notes
1970	$ 7.0	$29.0
1971	9.5	30.1
1972	10.7	25.6
1973	7.6	20.7
1974	4.0	31.5
1975	7.4	42.8
1976	8.3	42.2
1977	8.0	42.3
1978	7.9	37.4
1979	8.7	40.8
1980	19.0	56.3

Source: *Economic Report of the President,* 1982.

they may not seek listing on one of the major exchanges even when qualified to do so. These firms include many financial institutions like banks, savings and loan associations, and insurance companies.

The over-the-counter market is a telephone market with one or more dealers; usually they are also brokers who make markets in certain of the stocks traded. The stocks, unlike those on the listed exchanges, are quoted at bid–ask prices. The bid is the price at which the dealer will buy the stock, while the ask is the price at which the dealer will sell the stock. The bid–ask price spread increases the return to the dealer over any brokerage fee that might be received. As the efficiency of the over-the-counter market increases, with more securities listed in electronic quotation devices as some are currently, it may be expected that bid–ask spreads will narrow. The spreads are actually quite small in absolute amount for lower priced securities, and they increase for higher priced securities in absolute amount. In percentage terms, the spread is usually about 1 or 2 percent of the value of the securities or less.

There is an important difference between the two types of stocks, common and preferred, traded in the equities markets. Common stocks represent actual ownership shares in business. Holders share the good fortune of the corporation in increased dividends and capital appreciation as the market takes account of corporate success and values the securities upward. Unfortunately, the holder of common stock also

shares in the misfortunes of corporations as well when earnings decrease or the corporation suffers a loss. Preferred stock, on the other
hand, is much like a bond specifying a fixed return with no additional
distribution based upon comparable earnings success. In failure, however, preferred stockholders have a claim on corporate assets in liquidation ahead of holders of common stock. As yields fluctuate, so does
the price of preferred stock to reflect yield changes. The determination
of common stock prices is, however, more complicated. Basically it
depends on the supply and demand for the stock; however, this in
turn is supposed to depend on what are thought of as fundamental
factors.

The Determination of Stock Prices

Earnings, dividends, and expected future growth and profitability of
a company are all supposed to be factors that determine stock prices
as reflected in the supply and demand for the stock of the company.
This is often called the fundamental view of stock price determination.
However, sometimes the value of a particular stock appears to have
little relation to fundamental factors. There are those who argue that
stock prices are essentially a random walk and it is not possible to
systematically predict the future movement of the price of a stock.
This theory is associated with what is known as the efficient markets
view of financial markets.

The efficient markets view states that current stock prices reflect
the compilation of all known information that would affect the value
of a stock. Unless there is inside information known only to a few—
for example, a pending merger—all public knowledge is reflected in
the current price of the stock. Thus, in this view a stock cannot be
undervalued or overvalued at any moment in time, and it is impossible
to predict the future course of its price. Most market participants don't
agree with this view; they prefer to analyze the stock market as is
clear from the various stock advisory services that profitably sell their
analyses. Note that the efficient markets theory does not suggest that
prices won't change, but merely that information currently available
is reflected in the stock price and an investor cannot use such information to systematically profit from stock movements. The controversy
between those who hold the efficient markets view and the market
analysts is not easily settled.

Yet a third view of stock market price movements states that examining earnings, dividends, and other "fundamental" factors in trying
to determine stock price movements is useless. Only a careful analysis
of the supply and demand situation of a particular stock as reflected
in the price movements is needed to determine buy and sell decisions.
This process of evaluating stocks is called "technical analysis" and
can be quite sophisticated in employing charting techniques and a

language all its own.[13] Thus, while stock prices seemingly reflect the underlying value of the company, deciding on how and when stock prices will change can be a very difficult process indeed and is the concern of technical analysis.

Stock Options

In the 1970s, listed stock options were traded for the first time. Both put and call options on a small but increasing number of listed securities are traded on the Chicago Board of Options Exchange, the American Options Exchange, the Philadelphia Options Exchange, and the Pacific Options Exchange. The New York Stock Exchange has also from time to time expressed interest in forming an options exchange. A stock does not have to be traded on the exchange on which its option is listed. An **option** grants the purchaser the right to buy and sell 100 shares of a stock at a specified price, called the strike or striking price, before an expiration date. A **put** is an option to sell the stock, while a **call** is an option to purchase the stock. Typically the price paid for the option depends on the current price of the stock in relation to the strike price and the length of time to expiration of the option. The longer the option has until its expiration, the higher is the price that the option can command, everything else being constant. Options are listed for three, six, and nine months for each stock and follow the same cycle. That is, when the three-month option expires, a new nine-month option is added. Notice that as time passes the three-month option expires, the six-month option becomes a three-month option, and the nine-month becomes a six-month option. At this point the new nine-month option is added.

Buyers of put options are usually speculators betting on a fall in the price of the stock, while buyers of call options are betting on a rise in the price of the stock. The purchase of a call option gives the purchaser substantial leverage because it is much cheaper to buy the option than to purchase the 100 shares of stock the option represents. Therefore, if the stock should rise significantly over the period of the option, the percentage gain on the option will significantly surpass the percentage gain on the actual holding of the stock. For example, imagine a call option that allows the purchase of 100 shares of Pear Computer Company at $50 per share. Currently Pear is selling at exactly $50 per share and the option is selling at $1. This means that to purchase the option, the speculator will pay $100 ($1 for each share the option represents). The $1 price for the option is called the option premium; the purchaser is willing to pay a $1 premium to obtain the option. Suppose the stock now rises in price to $55

---

[13] Technical analysts are often heard talking about "base building," "double bottoms," and "trend breakouts," for example.

per share, a 10 percent gain. The option, assuming the premium remains constant at $1, will now rise to $6, representing the $5 value
of the option and its premium. Thus, the option has increased sixfold in value while the stock went up only 10 percent. However, note
that the option, unlike the stock itself, will expire in time. If Pear stock
doesn't increase in price but stays fixed at $50 over the life of the
option, the option will expire worthlessly and the holder will lose the
$100 plus any commission paid for the option. Similar leverage exists
on a put option.

Along with leverage, speculators like stock options because the
potential loss is limited to the cost of the option. The most the speculator can lose is the purchase price of the option if it expires worthlessly.
(It will be worthless at expiration if the strike price is not exceeded
as indicated in the example above.) Issuers or writers of call options
are usually owners of the stock who use options to increase their
returns and are willing to risk having to yield the stock to the option
holder. Put writers are undertaking more speculation because the put
writer may have to purchase the stock offered. Many buyers of puts
are actually owners of the stock who are buying puts as a hedge
against a market fall in the value of the stock. In practice, very few
options are exercised. Rather they are simply traded.[14]

The Market for Federal Agency Securities

We noted previously that federally sponsored agencies such as the
Federal National Mortgage Association (FNMA) and the Federal Home
Loan Bank System (FHLB) finance their operations by issuing securities.
A good deal of these securities are long term. Indeed, in recent years
it has been a goal of some agencies, particularly FNMA, to lengthen
the maturity of their outstanding securities to match more closely the
long-term maturities of their assets. As the activities of the federal
agencies have grown, so have their securities issues. As of December
31, 1980, over $172 billion dollars in agency securities were out-
standing.[15] In 1980, alone, federal agencies issued over $26 billion
in new securities. The increasing size of the amount of agency securities outstanding and their widespread holdings among financial institutions have meant that the secondary market in agencies has become

---

[14] For an informative introduction to stock options see the *Prospectus: The Options
Clearing Corporation,* available from any brokerage firm. Further, there are a number
of books on options trading available, for example, Jarrott T. Miller, *Creative Options
Trading* (Chicago: Contemporary Books, 1979).

[15] This excludes over $100 billion in mortgage pool securities. See the discussion
of the mortgage market below.

increasingly broad, and hence the degree of liquidity of these securities increased significantly in the 1970s and early 1980s.

The long-term securities of these agencies are placed through underwriters and coordinated through the agencies' fiscal agents. Smaller federal agencies like the Export–Import Bank can borrow through the Federal Financing Bank (FFB), created in 1974. The Federal Financing Bank essentially borrows from the Treasury, and, therefore, the Treasury is actually doing the borrowing. The private federally sponsored agencies like FNMA and the FHLB cannot borrow through the FFB.[16] However, the marketability of the federally sponsored securities is so great that it is not necessary for them to borrow through the FFB as shown by the small yield spreads between these securities and equivalent maturity government securities. Even though sponsored agency securities are not guaranteed by the government, it is inconceivable that the government would allow agencies to default. As a result the securities of these agencies yield considerably less than those of even the top-rated corporations.[17]

In fact, sponsored agency securities are treated so much like government securities in the market place that they are handled in the secondary market by many government securities dealers and government securities departments of commercial banks. Since 1971, they have been eligible for purchase by the Federal Reserve in its conduct of open-market operations.

Municipal Securities

There are basically two types of municipal securities—general obligation bonds and revenue bonds. The interest on both types of bonds is exempt from federal taxation. The general obligation bonds are backed by the full taxing authority of the state and local entity issuing the security, while revenue bonds are paid out of the proceeds of the project they finance, such as a bridge or a sports stadium. Revenue bonds have been the most rapidly growing category of municipal bonds in recent years. Municipalities issued $45 billion in new bonds in 1980 compared to $29 billion in 1975; much of this increase is accounted for by revenue bonds.

The tax exempt feature of municipal bonds makes them very popular with higher income individuals who generally hold them directly

---

[16] The only federally sponsored agency that can borrow from the FFB is the Student Loan Marketing Association. Thus, all other borrowers from the FFB are federal agencies that are part of the U.S. government, not federally sponsored agencies.

[17] Yield spreads between securities of different issuers were discussed in Chapter 4. Table 12-3 showed the small yield spread between short-term agencies and Treasury bills.

Table 13-6
Ownership of Municipal Securities, December 31, 1980
(Billions of Dollars)

Holder	Amount
Mutual Savings Banks	$ 2.4
Savings and Loan Associations	1.2
Life Insurance Companies	6.5
Property Insurance Companies	84.5
State and Local Pension Funds	2.9
Municipal Bond Funds	25.4
Security Brokers and Dealers	0.9
Commercial Banks	149.7
Business Corporations	3.4
Individuals	82.7

Source: Salomon Brothers, *1981 Prospects for Financial Markets.*

or hold shares in municipal bond mutual funds. Institutions are also holders, with commercial banks the largest holders. Besides the attractiveness to commercial banks of the tax exemption feature, commercial banks sometimes have to hold municipal securities as a condition of being able to underwrite general obligation issues of that governmental unit or as a condition of deposit business.[18] Table 13-6 shows the distribution of ownership of municipal securities for those outstanding as of December 31, 1980. The New York fiscal crisis of 1974 in which New York almost defaulted on its obligations[19] and the subsequent Cleveland fiscal crisis made many potential municipal bond purchasers more aware of the risk in some municipal issues. The increase in perceived risk combined with the limited market for municipals arising from their attractiveness only to individuals and institutions in high tax categories has led to relatively large fluctuations in the yields on municipals compared to those of other securities, such as Treasury securities. There is some concern about this among municipalities in finding holders for the securities at prices attractive to the issuer. However, as inflation has pushed individuals into higher tax brackets, the attractiveness of municipals has increased as evidenced by the growth

---

[18] Commercial banks are prohibited under the Glass–Stegal Act (which separated investment and commercial banking) from underwriting revenue bonds, something that commercial banks are trying to have changed by legislation, as noted in Chapter 7.

[19] Technically New York did default because payment on a number of obligations was postponed.

of municipal bond mutual funds in the 1970s. Nevertheless, the still limited market for municipals and the continued expansion in municipal financing seems to ensure continued large yield fluctuations in this market in future years.

The Mortgage Market

The mortgage market is truly enormous. Table 13-7 gives a total picture of mortgages outstanding and where these mortgages are held. If mortgages of all types are included, over 1.45 trillion were outstanding as of December 31, 1980. Of these, home mortgages were by far the largest category. Unlike many of the other markets that have been discussed in the last chapter and this chapter, the primary market for mortgages is very large relative to the secondary market. However, the secondary market has grown substantially in recent years.

The Primary Market for Mortgages

We have seen that the major mortgage investors are savings and loan associations, mutual savings banks, and commercial banks. These institutions are all mortgage orginators; they make mortgage loans to residential home buyers. However, they also buy mortgages from mortgage bankers (sometimes called mortgage companies) who are mortgage originators fulfilling a brokerage function between ultimate mortgage investors and borrowers. Mortgage bankers originate mortgages but place the loans with ultimate mortgage investors, such as commercial banks and savings and loan associations. Life insurance companies do not originate mortgages themselves but rather rely on mortgage

Table 13-7
Mortgages Outstanding, December 31, 1980
(Billions of Dollars)

Type	Amount
One-to-Four Family Nonfarm	
Home Mortgages	$ 952.1
Multifamily Mortgages	137.0
Commercial Mortgages	255.4
Farm Mortgages	106.4
Total	$1,450.9

Source: Salomon Brothers, *1981 Prospects for Financial Markets.*

bankers a great deal to sell them mortgage packages—groups of mortgages.

Mortgage bankers are not depository institutions. Rather, they finance their activity through short-term loans. Thus, in order to continue to make new mortgage loans, they must sell what they have. The amount of mortgages they hold are said to be warehoused—that is, waiting for a buyer. When short-term rates exceed the mortgage rate, mortgage bankers cannot hold warehoused mortgages for long. However, when the mortgage rate exceeds short-term rates, mortgage bankers will warehouse mortgages for longer periods of time because they make a profit on the spread between the mortgage rate and the short-term rate.

Mortgage rates themselves are of interest in connection with the financial intermediaries that have previously been discussed. Mortgage rates tend to lag behind other long-term rates when these latter rates are moving up or down, although this lag has diminished in recent years. However, since long-term rates, in turn, usually lag behind short-term rate adjustments, the problem of disintermediation for the institutions is traceable in part to the lag in the adjustment of mortgage rates to short-term rates. This is especially true in terms of the effect on the profitability of institutions as they are permitted more flexibility in paying money market rates on deposits.[20] However, the lag in mortgage rates should be substantially reduced or eliminated over time as variable rate mortgages replace fixed rate mortgages in mortgage lender portfolios.

There are two basic types of mortgages, conventional mortgages and government-insured mortgages. The two federal agencies that insure mortgages are the Federal Housing Administration (FHA) and the Veterans Administration (VA). The conventional market is much larger than that for government-insured mortgages and has grown even more rapidly since the development of private mortgage insurance (PMI). PMI was introduced by the Mortgage Guaranty Investment Company (MGIC and often in the industry called "Magic"). MGIC was soon followed by a number of other companies. With private mortgage insurance insuring a portion of the principal, conventional mortgages have proved more attractive to life insurance companies and other mortgage holders. Savings and loan associations have always specialized in conventional mortgages because of their basic distaste for the large amount of paperwork associated with the FHA–VA programs and the S&Ls' emphasis on local lending. However, the introduction of PMI has made the conventional mortgage even more attractive to S&Ls.

Table 13-8 presents the breakdown between conventional and

---

[20] See Sanford Rose, "How Savings Banks Can Save Themselves," *Fortune* (Jan. 28, 1980), pp. 76–81, for a discussion of the problem and squeezes between mortgages and deposit rates.

Table 13-8
Mortgages Outstanding by Type, 1973–80
(End of Year, Billions of Dollars)

Year	FHA/VA	Conventional
1973	$135	$ 547
1974	140	602
1975	146	654
1976	154	735
1977	162	862
1978	176	996
1979	199	1,135
1980	225	1,227

Source: Federal Home Loan Bank Board *Journal,* July 1981.

government-insured mortgages for selected years. The growth in the conventional sector in the 1970s is clear from the table. The success of PMI and other changes in the mortgage market has also spurred the large-scale development of the secondary mortgage market.

The Secondary Mortgage Market

The secondary mortgage market essentially began with the establishment of the Federal National Mortgage Association (FNMA) in 1938 by the federal government to provide liquidity for government-insured mortgages. FNMA was made a private agency in 1968 and soon thereafter had developed a very large secondary market. Table 13-9 shows the growth of FNMA from 1974 to 1980 compared to 1960 levels. The nonsecondary market functions of FNMA, particularly mortgage assistance, remained in government hands in the newly created Government National Mortgage Association (GNMA) when FNMA became private in 1968. In 1971 FNMA was joined in the secondary market by the Federal Home Loan Mortgage Corporation (FHLMC), a subsidiary of the Federal Home Loan Bank System, to provide S&Ls an outlet for conventional mortgages because FNMA was initially only allowed to purchase government-insured mortgages. In 1972, after securing congressional approval, FNMA began to purchase conventional mortgages. FNMA's main customers, however, are mortgage bankers; and, since mortgage bankers specialize in government-insured mortgages, FNMA conventional mortgage holdings are considerably smaller than its holdings of government-insured mortgages as Table 13-9 shows.

Table 13-9
FNMA Mortgage Holdings, 1960, 1974–80
(Billions of Dollars)

Year	FHA/VA	Conventional	Total
1960	$ 2.9	—	$ 2.9
1974	27.5	$ 2.1	29.6
1975	29.3	2.5	31.8
1976	28.1	4.8	32.9
1977	27.8	6.6	34.4
1978	31.8	11.5	43.3
1979	35.0	16.1	51.1
1980	39.0	18.4	57.4

Source: Federal Reserve *Bulletin*, various issues, and FNMA.

It should be noted, however, that conventional holdings have grown very rapidly in recent years.

The rationale behind the purchases of mortgages by FNMA and FHLMC is to inject funds into the mortgage market. The purchase of mortgages from traditional mortgage lenders makes available additional funds that they can then use to make more mortgage loans. It is hoped that in this way the cyclical nature of the mortgage and housing markets can be moderated.

In addition to the growth of federal mortgage market agencies in the 1970s, another important development in the secondary mortgage market was the growth of mortgage pools. These pools became particularly popular in the late 1970s, and their popularity has continued in the early 1980s. These mortgage pools are groupings of mortgages on which the interest and principal is "passed through" to the purchasers of certificates that represent the mortgage pools as payments are received by the servicer of the mortgage. The servicer collects mortgage payments, pays taxes, and so forth on the mortgages even though it doesn't own the mortgage.

Mortgage "pass-throughs" were originated by the Government National Mortgage Association (GNMA), and they represent government-insured mortgages typically packaged by a mortgage banker who continues to service the mortgages, collecting a fee for the service. The insured mortgages in the pool are reinsured by GNMA when the pass-throughs are sold to investors. Thus, the pass-throughs are very secure because the mortgages that the pass-through represents are insured mortgages and the pass-through itself is insured by GNMA.

The success of the GNMA pass-throughs led the Federal Home Loan Mortgage Corporation (FHLMC) to issue their own pass-through securities. Since FHLMC purchases conventional mortgages, the FHLMC pass-throughs represent pools of conventional loans in contrast to the GNMA pass-through securities, which contain pools of government-insured loans. Almost all mortgages purchased by FHLMC are converted into pass-through securities.

The popularity of the government agency pass-through programs has enticed commercial banks and other institutions to begin to package their own pass-throughs as well as to issue mortgage-backed bonds. Mortgage-backed bonds differ somewhat from pass-throughs because they do not provide ownership interest in mortgage pools. Rather, the principal repayment on a mortgage-backed bond is secured by mortgage collateral, and the interest on the mortgages is used to pay the interest on the mortgage-backed bond.

Pass-throughs and mortgage-backed bonds have proved an ingenious way of enhancing the liquidity of government-insured and conventional mortgage loans. These securities have enabled the capital markets to be directly accessible for mortgage financing. This was the aim of the original GNMA pass-through program. As investors gain more experience with these securities, the popularity of private pass-throughs and mortgage-backed bonds should further enhance the ability to channel funds that might otherwise not flow to the mortgage market into mortgage financing. Insurance companies and pension funds are among the major holders of pass-throughs and mortgage backed bonds. In fact, the return of insurance companies to the mortgage market in the late 1970s was due in great part to the development of pass-through securities.

In 1981 the FHLMC expanded its pass-through program in an attempt to deal with the problem that S&Ls have in holding a large amount of low interest fixed rate mortgage loans. S&Ls may swap a limited amount of these mortgage loans for FHLMC-issued mortgage-backed securities. Because these mortgage-backed securities are liquid, S&Ls are then able to sell them in the open market to raise cash. In a related development, FNMA also agreed to purchase low interest loans as well. While participants, such as S&Ls, will suffer losses in either the FHLMC or FNMA programs, the ability to raise funds by swapping or selling these low yielding, nonliquid mortgage loans should prove attractive. In 1982, FNMA also began issuing pass-through securities.

The activities of the federal mortgage market agencies and the increasing importance of mortgage pass-through securities and mortgage-backed bonds in the mortgage market have resulted in a substantial broadening of the secondary market in mortgages in the 1970s and early 1980s. Increased efficiency of this secondary market has enhanced the liquidity of mortgages and increased the pool of funds that can be drawn into the motgage market. However, as the housing recession of 1980–82 shows, these developments have not yet eliminated the cycle in housing.

DEEP DISCOUNTING

Bonds That Carry Minicoupons

The stunningly low 7% coupon that Northwest Industries Inc. tacked on a $125 million, 30-year bond offering on Mar. 18 does not signal a drastic decline in long-term interest rates. The bonds carrying that minicoupon were issued at a 47% discount from par—that is, at $527.50 apiece—which works out to an effective 13.5% yield to maturity. Further, Northwest was following the lead of Martin Marietta Corp., which sold $175 million worth of bonds at a deep 46% discount on Mar. 10.

Transamerica Financial Corp. has a deep-discount issue in registration, and several other deals are being done privately, including one rumored to have no coupon at all but a very big discount. The really unusual thing about these new deep-discount bonds is that they are rated A or better and are appearing for the first time in a public market formerly relegated to bonds of lesser quality—often dubbed junk.

Savings. Higher-rated creditors are now willing to move into this new neighborhood because they can get impressive interest-cost savings. Thanks to the discount, Martin Marietta and Northwest, for instance, are paying about 100 basis points less for their money than they would have paid if the debt had been sold at par. Moreover, their bonds have no sinking funds, which means that the companies do not have to set aside or repay anything until maturity, in 2011.

Significant cash savings result, as well, from the discount's tax ben-efits. A company must charge a portion of the discount against income each year as though it were interest expense, even though it actually involves no cash outlay. For tax purposes, that noncash charge would amount to $\frac{1}{30}$ of the discount. (For reporting purposes, by contrast, companies can follow a different schedule, where charges are minuscule in early years and escalate toward maturity.) Deducting that charge from taxes results in a bigger cash flow for the company. In Martin Marietta's case, for instance, the tax savings arising from that amortization charge knock $7.08 per bond off the company's annual aftertax dollar outlay for interest—to $30.72 from the $37.80 it would otherwise cost, considering only the 7% coupon and assuming a 46% tax rate. Of course, Martin Marietta will have to come up with $175 million in cash in 2011, when the issue matures, even though it took in just $94.2 million in proceeds. In essence, the company is deferring a big part of its interest payment until maturity.

The first half. The cement and aerospace company, which earned $188 million on $2.6 billion in sales last year, is funding a big capital expansion program. The company plans to borrow a total of $200 million this year and next. This issue takes care of roughly the first half.

Martin Marietta's preliminary filing consisted of $150 million in long-term bonds and $50 million in 10-year notes. Charles H. Leithauser, chief financial officer, notes that this was his way of testing the waters. When he learned how eager institutional investors were for discount bonds, he decided to scratch the intermediate-term portion and increase the long-term part. The bonds are callable only at par. Since it would be pretty expensive for the company to pay $1,000 before maturity for a bond that it sold at $538, an early call is unlikely.

These discount bonds are tailor-made for such tax-exempt investors as pension funds, foundations, and life insurance companies. They hold little appeal for taxpaying investors because the difference between the discounted issue price and the $1,000 the investor gets at maturity does not act like a capital gain for tax purposes, even though it looks like one. These "original issue discounts" (as distinct from those that occur when a bond price drops in market trading) get special tax treatment. Each year the taxpayer must count a portion of the bond discount as gross income and must pay income—not capital gains—taxes on it, although he gets no cash consideration for it. Tax-exempt buyers do not have such problems.

The lure for investors. These bonds help protect investors against "reinvestment risk" and are useful in portfolio management. Buyers of the Martin Marietta bonds can lock in a 13.25% return for the next 30 years without too big a danger of having the bonds called back by the company. Investors who lack that guarantee typically fear that they will get their cash from investments back sooner than they want it and

will have trouble reinvesting the proceeds at equally attractive rates. The discount-bond buyers, then, have essentially paid for that protection by allowing Martin Marietta to get away with a lower interest cost.

These bonds are also helpful in liability management. Insurance companies, for instance, have been offering their pension accounts "guaranteed income contracts" (GICs), which essentially promise a rate of return no matter how well or poorly an insurance company's investment portfolio performs. Now they can use the discount bonds, which lock in a return for 30 years, to match a GIC liability. One other way these bonds are used is for swapping. Some investors have been exchanging old, even lower-coupon debt, which is selling at embarrassing discounts in the market, for the new deep-discount issues that have slightly higher coupons. Here, a portfolio manager picks up a little more income for his fund, without having to show a horrendous loss of principal on the books.

At the moment, no one knows the exact depth of the market. But not all potential buyers are diving for the stuff. The chief investment officer at one large insurance company wrinkles his brow at one aspect: "It piles up a big payment at the end," he says. "If a lot of companies do that, you will have huge balloon payments coming due at once. Can the market stand all that money-raising again?"

Key Points

1. The capital markets are the markets for debt that mature in more than one year from date of issuance as well as the equity markets. Capital markets include those for corporate securities, U.S. government securities, federal agency securities, and municipal securities.

2. Most marketable U.S. government debt is intermediate term notes. Long-term bonds are the smallest category of government debt. The government budget constraint indicates that if government expenditures and transfer payments exceed tax revenues, with the money supply unchanged, the government must finance the difference by issuing debt. Most governmental marketable debt is issued at auction.

3. Long-term debt and equities are issued by corporations primarily to finance capital expenditures. Similar to the government budget constraint, the corporate financing constraint indicates that, to the extent capital expenditures exeed internal funds, the corporation must issue either debt or equity. In practice, corporations raise most external funds for capital expenditures in the bond market. Most of this debt is issued through investment banking syndicates.

4. Federally sponsored agencies finance much of their activity through the issuance of intermediate and long-term debt. Municipal securities issued by state and local governments can be either general obligation or revenue bonds. General obligation bonds are repaid out of municipal tax revenue, while revenue bonds are refinanced from the proceeds of the project that is financed.

5. The mortgage market is truly staggering in size. The primary mortgage market is very large relative to the secondary market. However, rapid growth has taken place in the latter market in recent years. This growth has occurred through the activities of the federally sponsored agencies, particularly FNMA, and the development of pass-through securities and mortgage-backed bonds. These securities have allowed mortgage funds to be raised directly in the general capital markets.

Questions for Discussion

1. Distinguish between the primary and secondary markets for mortgages. Explain the difference between mortgage pass-through securities and mortgage-backed bonds. What accounts for the growth of these securities in recent years?

2. Explain the government budget constraint and how it demonstrates the need for government financing. What factors may influence the types of securities that the government may issue in financing its deficit?

3. The yield on municipal securities increased rapidly in 1981. Many observers at that time suggested it was because traditional purchasers of these securities, such as commercial banks and casualty insurance companies, had had bad years in terms of profit. How are these factors

related? Why do municipal security yields fluctuate a good deal in general?

4. Why has bond financing exceeded equity financing through the 1970s and early 1980s by such a substantial amount? The secondary markets in equities have been relatively active nevertheless. Explain the differing views on the determination of stock prices.

5. How does perceived risk affect the yield on corporate issues of the same maturity?

Suggested Readings

Arak, Marcelle, and Christopher J. McCurdy. "Interest Rate Futures." Federal Reserve Bank of New York *Quarterly Review,* Winter 1979–80, pp. 33–46.

Browne, Lynn E., and Richard F. Syron. "The Municipal Market Since the New York City Crisis." Federal Reserve Bank of Boston *New England Economic Review,* July/August 1979, pp. 11–26.

Federal Home Loan Bank Board. "The Impact of Financial Innovations and Reforms on the Housing and Mortgage Markets." Federal Home Loan Bank Board *Journal,* May 1981, pp. 4–13.

Melton, William C. "Corporate Equities and the National Market System." Federal Reserve Bank of New York *Quarterly Review,* Winter 1978–79, pp. 13–25.

Melton, William C. "Recent Behavior of the Risk Structure of Bond Yields." Federal Reserve Bank of New York *Quarterly Review,* Summer 1977, pp. 21–26.

Sivesind, Charles M. "Mortgage-Backed Securities: The Revolution in Real Estate Finance." Federal Reserve Bank of New York *Quarterly Review,* Autumn 1979, pp. 1–10.

Stevens, Neil A. "Government Debt Financing—Its Effects in View of Tax Discounting." Federal Reserve Bank of St. Louis *Review,* July 1979, pp. 11–19.

Zwick, Burton. "The Market for Corporate Bonds." Federal Reserve Bank of New York *Quarterly Review,* Autumn 1977, pp. 27–36.

International Financial Markets

14

The importance of the relationship between the U.S. economy and financial system and the rest of the world became increasingly evident in the 1970s and early 1980s. U.S. participation in overseas markets, foreign participation in U.S. markets, the growth of the Eurodollar markets, and international banking have been enormous. The vital nature of international trade financed by international financial flows is most dramatically demonstrated in the energy field. The reemergence of gold internationally has also drawn headlines and consequent attention. These developments and numerous others demonstrate the necessity for analyzing international finance. This chapter will discuss foreign exchange rate determination and the international financial markets in detail.

Foreign Exchange Rate Determination

Foreign exchange for a particular country is the currency of any other country. Thus, for an American, anything but U.S. dollars is foreign exchange—for example, German marks or British pounds. The importance of foreign exchange derives from its use in international trade and financial transactions. For example, if a German firm sells goods to the United States, it will most likely want German marks in return. The firm's workers will wish to be paid in the currency that is the medium of exchange in their country. The firm's stockholders will also wish to receive their dividends in marks and the firm's suppliers to be paid in marks. Similarly, an American firm selling goods abroad

347

wishes to receive payment in dollars. Thus, a desire for foreign goods is really, in turn, a desire for the foreign exchange to pay for these goods. To understand why this is the case, consider the bare essentials of an international trade transaction.

How Trade Takes Place

Suppose that an American importer of British cars wishes to order a hundred cars. To import the cars, the importer first needs to know the price of the cars and the exchange rate between the British pound and the U.S. dollar. The **exchange rate** is the rate at which one currency converts into another currency. Thus, unlike a purely domestic transaction in which only one price is involved, in an international transaction there are two prices, the price of the goods and the exchange rate, which is the price of the currency. The importer finds that the exchange rate is one British pound to two U.S. dollars.[1] The price of each car is £3,000. Thus, the importer knows that each car will cost $6,000 to purchase, and 100 cars will cost $600,000. How will the importer go about paying the car manufacturer for the cars? The car importer has $600,000, but the car manufacturer wants to be paid in pounds. At this point, the importer goes to the bank and asks for help. Suppose that the importer's bank is one of the large New York banks with branches all over the world, such as Chase Manhattan.[2] The importer turns over the $600,000 to Chase in New York. Chase, in turn, informs its London branch that it should issue a draft to the British car manufacturer for £300,000. The London branch does this and the cars are shipped. Notice that the demand by the importer for British cars has, in turn, increased the demand for British pounds, that is, for foreign exchange.

This example is very simplified; transactions, in fact, tend to be more complex. However, it is important to note that the essentials of a trade transaction are all included in the example. To reemphasize, notice that in the example the demand for British goods is in turn a demand for British currency. That is, the demand for British currency is derived from the demand for British goods. Also notice that actual conversion takes place. That is, the dollars are actually converted into pounds. The reason for this is that most of the British manufacturer's costs must be paid in pounds, not in dollars. (Dollars are the most widely held internationally of all currencies. This will be explained more fully below. Nevertheless, most dollars traded internationally are converted into the home, or domestic, currency.)

---

[1] Later it will be explained how this exchange rate is determined.

[2] This need not be the case but it makes the example easier without changing its applicability.

Exchange Rate Determination

The example of an international transaction presented above demonstrated that the demand for a country's currency is derived from the demand for its goods. This example can be generalized by saying that the demand for a country's currency is derived from the demand for its goods and services and its financial instruments. As the chapter progresses, this will become clearer. For convenience, at this point let us continue to use the term "goods" to refer to all that a country may sell or market internationally, including financial instruments.

Determination of the rate at which one currency exchanges for another can be seen with the help of supply and demand analysis. Figure 14-1 shows both the supply and demand curves for British pounds.[3] (Ignore the supply curve for the moment). Notice that like all demand curves the demand for British pounds is downward sloping. The reason for this is clear to see. The higher one moves along the vertical axis, the more dollars it costs to buy £1. British goods are priced in terms of pounds; therefore, the higher the cost in dollars, the higher the cost of British goods in dollars. For example, a British book is priced at £10. If £1 can be bought for $2, then the British book will cost $20. However, if it takes $3 to buy £1 then the book will cost a holder of dollars $30. As with all normal goods, the lower the price, the larger the quantity of the good demanded. Thus, at a lower price in dollars for pounds—that is, the fewer dollars it takes to purchase pounds—people having dollars will want to buy more British goods. But to buy more British goods, they need to acquire more British pounds so that at a lower dollar price for pounds—in other words, a higher exchange rate[4]—the quantity of pounds demanded will be larger; thus, the downward-sloping demand curve results.

Turning to the supply curve in Figure 14-1, notice that it is upward sloping like any other conventional supply curve. That is, the higher the price for pounds, the more pounds holders of pounds are willing to supply. From the point of view of the suppliers of pounds, the higher the pound price in dollars, the more dollars each of their pounds commands. Who are the holders of pounds? For the most part, these holders are the British. But why do they desire to acquire dollars? The answer to this question is that they wish to acquire dollars to buy American goods. In other words, from their point of view, the

---

[3] The British pound will be used to discuss exchange rate determination. However, any currency could be utilized for the analysis. Further, if desired, the reader can think of the British pound in this discussion as some composite world currency representative of all currencies except the dollar.

[4] The fewer dollars it takes to buy a British pound the *higher* is the exchange rate for dollars since each dollar is worth more in terms of pounds. Similarly, the more dollars it takes to buy a British pound the *lower* is the exchange rate.

Figure 14-1
Market for British Pounds

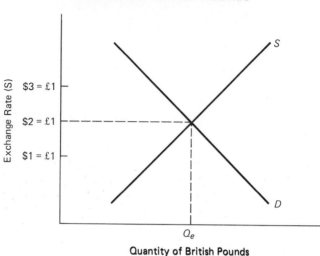

Quantity of British Pounds

desire to supply pounds is really a demand on their part for dollars to buy American goods. Further, the more dollars they receive for their pounds, the cheaper American goods become. Thus, the upward slope to the supply curve of pounds indicates that the cheaper the dollar is for a holder of pounds, the greater the quantity of dollars they will want. The exchange rate is determined at the intersection of the supply and demand curves. Thus, the equilibrium exchange rate depicted in Figure 14-1 is at $2 for £1. The horizontal axis determines the equilibrium quantity (Q_e) of pounds exchanged for dollars.

To investigate how the exchange rate can change, take the following example. Suppose that there is an increase in the desire of Americans to own British cars. That is, a change in tastes in favor of British goods takes place. What would this do in the analysis of Figure 14-1? Figure 14-2 depicts the result. The supply and demand curves from Figure 14-1 are reproduced. The increase in the demand for British goods is reflected in an increase in the demand for British pounds. The demand curve shifts to the right to D'. The new exchange rate is $2.50 for each pound. Thus, the price of pounds has risen in dollars—that is, the exchange rate of dollars for pounds has fallen. The price of dollars has fallen in terms of pounds—the exchange rate for pounds has risen. At this higher exchange rate, more pounds are then supplied to meet this demand. But notice that the change in the exchange

Figure 14-2
Market for British Pounds: Increased Demand

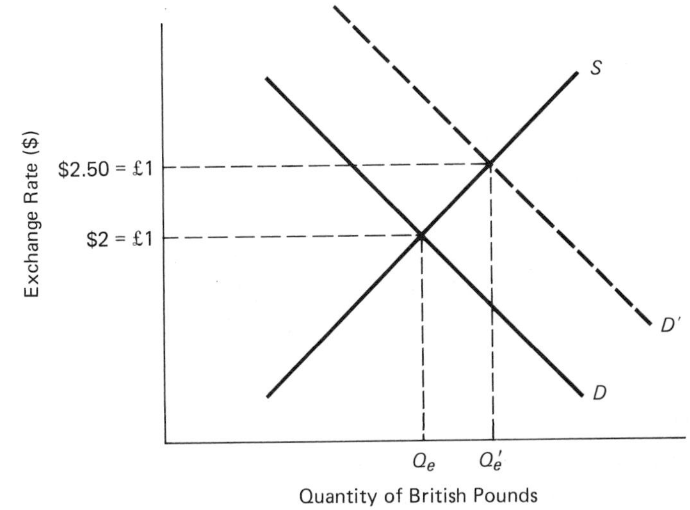

Quantity of British Pounds

rate results in a change in British prices for Americans, and American prices for the British. British prices have risen for Americans, and U.S. prices have fallen for the British. The British will now buy more American goods because of the fall in price. That is why they are willing to supply a larger quantity of pounds.

The alteration in the exchange rate discussed above has implications for the balance of payments, a summary of the nation's transactions with the rest of the world, and its adjustment. It is clear that the exchange rate move will be determined by supply and demand. However, there are currently and have been in the past exchange rate systems in the world that in some ways have interfered with changes in exchange rates depicted in the above example. Before discussing these exchange rate systems, it is useful to examine specific recent exchange rates between currencies.

Exchange Rates

Table 14-1 presents the exchange rates in terms of dollars per unit of foreign currency for July 1981 compared to the previous year. The diversity of exchange rates is clear from the table. Note, for example, that a Japanese yen in July 1981 was worth approximately .004 of a dollar or that there were 250 yen to a dollar. Similarly there

Table 14-1
Foreign Exchange Rates, July 1981 and July 1980

Country	Monetary Unit	Dollars Per Unit of Foreign Currency	
		July 1981	July 1980
Australia	Dollar	1.143	1.159
Austria	Schilling	0.058	0.081
Belgium	Franc	0.025	0.036
Canada	Dollar	0.826	0.868
Denmark	Krone	0.131	0.185
Finland	Markka	0.220	0.277
France	Franc	0.173	0.247
Germany, W.	D Mark	0.410	0.572
India	Rupee	0.112	0.129
Ireland	Pound	1.494	2.148
Italy	Lira	0.008	0.012
Japan	Yen	0.004	0.005
Malaysia	Dollar	0.425	0.467
Mexico	Peso	0.041	0.044
Netherlands	Guilder	0.368	0.523
New Zealand	Dollar	0.838	0.986
Norway	Krone	0.164	0.208
Portugal	Escudo	0.015	0.020
South Africa	Rand	1.085	1.308
Spain	Peseta	0.010	0.014
Sri Lanka	Rupee	0.053	0.063
Sweden	Krona	0.193	0.242
Switzerland	Franc	0.477	0.622
United Kingdom	Pound	1.874	2.373

Source: Federal Reserve Board of Governors.

was .410 of a dollar to a German mark or 2.44 marks to a dollar and 1.87 dollars to a British pound. Listing exchange rates in this way brings up a common misconception. It is not relevant how many units of a particular currency trades for $1 in evaluating the strength or weakness of a particular currency; only its change in value over time against another currency can establish its strength or weakness.[5] The basic unit in a country depends on how that country defines that unit. For example, if the basic unit of U.S. currency was cents rather

---

[5] In fact, a currency is considered strong if it takes increasingly less of that currency to buy another. The currency that is falling in value is considered weak.

than dollars, the exchange rate would be defined in terms of cents, and, clearly, then it would take only 2.5 yen to buy one cent. Thus, the fact that it takes 250 yen to buy one dollar doesn't make the Japanese currency a weak currency. If a year ago it took 275 yen to buy one dollar and this year it takes 250 yen to buy one dollar, then the Japanese yen has strengthened against the dollar, while, if last year it took 200 yen to buy one dollar, the Japanese yen has weakened against the dollar. In Table 14-1 it is clear that the Japanese yen has weakened somewhat against the dollar between July 1980 and July 1981. In fact, from July 1980 to July 1981, the dollar strengthened against all currencies listed. However, the year before, the dollar had weakened against many currencies. For example, in June 1979 one dollar would buy 1.89 marks. By July 1980 the dollar bought only 1.75 marks, a decline in value. By July 1981, the dollar had strengthened considerably. Thus, the exchange rate will change frequently, and the direction of that change tells us whether the currency is strengthening or weakening against other currencies.

Exchange Rate Systems

The International Monetary Fund and Fixed Exchange Rates

As it became clear that the allies were going to win World War II, a meeting was held at Bretton Woods, New Hampshire, in 1944 to discuss the international financial arrangements that were to prevail after the peace came. The international financial system had been torn apart by the worldwide depression of the 1930s. (In fact, the collapse of the international financial system was at the same time a result and a cause of the depression.) The participants at the Bretton Woods meeting felt that planning was advisable if the postwar international financial system was to be successful.

Out of the meeting came the International Monetary Fund (IMF) to oversee a system of fixed exchange rates that was decided upon. The system was underpinned by the convertibility of the dollar into gold. This convertibility was to be the centerpiece of the system. Since the dollar was convertible into gold at a fixed price of $35 per ounce and all currencies were convertible into dollars, in a sense currencies were tied to gold. This was called the **gold exchange standard.** While the tie of other currencies to gold was mostly illusion, it did add stability to the system. The IMF, which had started with 30 member countries, had grown to 141 countries by November 1980.[6]

---

[6] The role has changed somewhat as the world system has moved from the fixed exchange rate system to a flexible exchange rate system as will be seen below. Of the 141 countries in the IMF, only Rumania was a member of the Warsaw Pact, although Hungary was likely to be admitted in 1982.

It is relatively easy to understand the operation of a fixed exchange rate system. Assume that there are only two countries in the world, Britain and the United States. If both countries define their currency in terms of a fixed quantity of gold, say one ounce, then that automatically fixes the exchange rate between the two countries. For example, if Britain says that £17.5 is equal to 1 ounce of gold and the United States states that $35 is equal to 1 ounce of gold, then £1 is equal to $2. Presumably the initial fixing is related in some way to the purchasing power of the currency in each country. This system applied to all member countries of the IMF. The participants to the IMF articles agreed to abide by the fixed exchange rate except for "fundamental disequilibrium" when, with the approval of the IMF countries, the exchange rate could be changed. Barring such a change, the currency could only fluctuate between +1 percent or −1 percent of the fixed rate. That is, in the case of the example above, the dollar could fluctuate against the pound only between $1.98 and $2.02. Similarly the dollar could fluctuate only within the same percentage limits against other currencies. This, in turn, meant that the countries involved would intervene in the market if the currency approached these limits.

Recall Figure 14-2, which is here reproduced as Figure 14-3 with additions. Suppose that, as in the example of Figure 14-2, there was

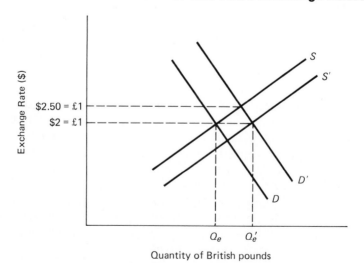

Figure 14-3
The Market for British Pounds: Fixed Exchange Rates

an increased demand for British goods and consequently for British pounds to buy the goods. Similar to that in Figure 14-2, the demand curve of Figure 14-3 would shift to D'. However, under a fixed rate system the exchange rate would move out of the accepted range, and this was not permitted. Therefore, the supply curve would have to be shifted to keep the exchange rate fixed. This could only be accomplished by the Bank of England buying American dollars for British pounds (or the Federal Reserve selling holdings of pounds it might possess, although in practice the United States did not intervene regularly in the markets), thus shifting the supply curve of pounds to S'. Notice, however, that in this case the price of British goods does not rise for Americans, as it did in the previous analysis, nor for that matter does the price of American goods fall for the British. Thus, there is nothing to discourage the continued purchase of British goods by Americans nor encourage the British purchase of American goods— no adjustment automatically takes place to discourage purchases by Americans of British goods or to encourage purchases of American goods by the British. This means that if there is an imbalance in the funds flowing between two countries it will not be corrected by a change in exchange rates. Countries will continue to maintain deficits or surpluses in their balances of payments.[7] This lack of automatic adjustment in the balance of payments through exchange rate changes was the fatal flaw in the fixed exchange rate system, which ultimately led to its collapse.

Before turning to the system that replaced the fixed exchange rate system in 1973, we must note that the fixed exchange rate system has one striking advantage: It provides a certain knowledge of the exchange rate. If an importer of British cars is charged £100,000 for the cars and given three months to pay, except for extraordinary circumstances, she knows at the time of the contract what amount of dollars will be needed to be paid at the end of the three-month period. If the exchange rate is $2.00 to £1, the importer knows that in three months she will owe $200,000. However, if the exchange rate is allowed to fluctuate as in Figure 14-2, the amount is not certain. A rise in the exchange rate, say, to $1.50 to £1 means that the importer pays $150,000. However, a fall in the exchange rate to $3 to £1 means the importer pays $300,000, quite a variation. Many importers and exporters favored a fixed exchange rate system (and many still do) because it removes uncertainty in international trade that can exist under a flexible or floating exchange rate system.[8]

---

[7] The balance of payments is a summary of international trade and finance between one country and the rest of the world. The meaning of deficits and surpluses in the balance of payments will be fully explored in a later section of this chapter.

[8] Actually under flexible exchange rates, the risk can be hedged in what is known as the futures market, discussed later in the chapter.

The Post-1973 System of Floating Exchange Rates

In August 1971, President Nixon declared that the United States would no longer redeem dollars for gold.[9] The action Nixon took had been necessitated by the large number of dollars held abroad, much more than could be redeemed, and the inability of foreigners to absorb much more without the danger of mass conversion into gold. Foreigners held so many dollars because the dollar was the central currency utilized in international trade; and, because of its key role in the fixed exchange rate system as a reserve currency, a currency used to settle international transactions between countries. By running continuous deficits in the balance of payments, the United States had sent many dollars abroad. However, an ever increasing number of these dollars were being converted into gold despite two separate increases in the number of dollars it took to purchase an ounce of gold, called devaluations of the dollar.[10] It became clear that this conversion could not continue without soon exhausting the stock of gold in the United States; therefore, Nixon acted.[11] Once the dollar became nonconvertible into gold, however, the fixed exchange rate system was untenable, and the construction of a new system of international exchange rates became necessary. It should be clear, however, that the nonconvertibility of the dollar became necessary because the system was no longer working. That is, nonconvertibility essentially was a recognition that change in the system was required. The new system, finally agreed upon formally in 1973, had at its core a floating—also known as a flexible or fluctuating—exchange rate system.

Floating Exchange Rates and the Current System

A floating exchange rate system is supposed to work exactly as depicted in Figure 14-2 (p. 351). That is, the exchange rate is determined exclusively by supply and demand for the currency without interference by countries in movements of exchange rates. However, the system that emerged in 1973 and still applies is best called a "managed" floating exchange rate system. Countries intervene in the markets in

---

[9] The United States had permitted conversion since the IMF agreements, although only for foreign, not American, organizations and individuals. Americans were not permitted to hold gold except in jewelry, for industrial uses, and for similar purposes.

[10] Devaluation of the dollar, which had the effect of formally lowering the exchange rate under a fixed exchange rate system, had been resisted despite the continuous balance of payments deficits until 1971. The role of the dollar as the key currency in the system was thought to necessitate an unchanging relationship to gold.

[11] There were other fundamental actions that Nixon could have taken to combat the conversion problem; however, these would have been painful for the U.S. economy and Nixon chose to "close the gold window."

a similar manner to that under the fixed exchange rate system by buying and selling their currency. The aim of this intervention is not necessarily to fix their currency's exchange rate as under the old system, but to prevent it from changing too rapidly in value or too much in value. By intervening, however, they interfere to a degree with the automatic adjustment that changing exchange rates are presumed to bring about in the balance of payments. Thus, the full function of the system is not carried through.[12] Further, the intervention often appears to be less effective in stabilizing exchange rates than the intervening countries desire. It is very difficult for a country's central bank to prevent speculative pressures on a currency from moving it substantially in one direction or another even with substantial intervention.

Despite the initial fears and objections of exporters and importers that a floating exchange rate system would lead to uncertainty and, therefore, be disruptive to international trade, trade has, in fact, grown rapidly since the advent of the floating system. One reason for this is that the uncertainty caused by exchange rate changes can be hedged by the traders in the foreign exchange futures market. This market allows an exporter or importer to lock-in an exchange rate for several months in advance by buying a contract for future sale or future purchase of one currency or another at a fixed rate. Speculators keep the futures market orderly for the most part,[13] and the trader is assured of an exchange rate at the time he receives payment for goods or is required to pay for goods. Futures markets have become increasingly important not only in foreign exchange but in financial assets and precious metals as well.[14]

Though world trade has expanded rapidly under the "managed float," the assumed great strength of floating exchange rates in automatic adjustments of the balance of payments has not been realized by the current system. The failure of the system to bring about automatic adjustments in the balance of payments derives from a number of factors including the "management of the float." In addition, however, economists who have been strong supporters of floating ex-

---

[12] In addition, it should be pointed out that not every member country in the IMF allows their currency to float at all. Most small countries tie their currencies to the currency of a large country, primarily the dollar, in a fixed relationship. Over 95 countries in October 1980 had their currencies tied to another currency that floated or to special drawing rights (SDRs) of the IMF which, in turn, floats with a basket of other currencies. Further, in January 1979 the European Economic Community (EEC), except for Great Britain, agreed on a fixed exchange rate system between them, the European Monetary System (EMS). The currencies in the EMS float against other currencies, however.

[13] The role of speculators in the futures market is to accept risk in hopes of large gains. That is, the futures market is supposed to transfer risk of exchange rate movements from the exporter or importer to the speculator.

[14] For a discussion of futures markets in foreign exchange, see Miltiades Chacholiades, *International Monetary Theory and Policy* (New York: McGraw-Hill, 1978), Chapter 6.

change rates did not realize the substantial lags involved in adjustment—it takes time for the adjustment to exchange rate changes to
be reflected in changes in the components of the balance of payments.
Further, the fall in a country's exchange rate means not only that its
exports are cheaper, encouraging their purchase, but that their imports
are more expensive. If the demand for one of these imports—oil, for
example—is relatively price inelastic, at least in the short run, funds
flowing out of the country increase to pay for the increased cost of
the imported item. If the imported item is an important input in the
production process, as oil is, the country's cost of production will
rise and contribute to inflation in the country. This, in turn, may lead
to decreases in the value of the country's currency internationally and
still more increases in the cost of imports. Thus, rather than moving
to adjustment, the country may move away from it if it still must purchase imports even at a higher price. Any ultimate adjustment then
will be painful for the domestic economy in terms of lost output, employment, and so forth. To understand the adjustment process more
completely, we must discuss the balance of payments in some detail.

The Balance of Payments

The balance of payments is a summary of the economic and financial
transactions between the country for which it is prepared and the
rest of the world. The name balance of payments implies that it must
balance; however, this is true only in an accounting sense. How the
balance of payments comes into balance is the interesting question.
Table 14-2 presents the balance of payments for 1980 for the United
States. The major components are the merchandise balance, the current account balance, the balance on goods and services, and the
capital account balance, which are taken up in turn.

The Merchandise Trade Balance

The merchandise trade balance (sometimes called the balance of trade)
is a summary of goods exports and imports. Exports are goods sold
abroad while imports are goods that are purchased from abroad. Exports result in inflows of funds to the United States as the merchandise
is paid for by foreigners, and imports result in outflows of funds from
the United States as the country pays for these goods. If the United
States buys more from abroad than it sells, which has been the case
for most years since 1971, the United States is said to have a **trade
deficit**. A **trade surplus** occurs when the United States buys less
from abroad than it sells. As the table indicates, the trade deficit was
over $25 billion in 1980.

Table 14-2
Balance of Payments of the United States, 1980
(Billions of Dollars)

Item	Amount	Category Summary
Merchandise Exports	+$224.0[1]	
Merchandise Imports	− 249.3	
Merchandise Trade Balance		−$25.3
Military Transactions (net)	− 2.5	
Investment Income (net)	+ 32.8	
Other Service Transactions (net)	+ 5.9	
Balance on Goods and Services		+ 10.9
Remittances, Pensions and Other Transfers	− 2.4	
U.S. Government Grants (Excluding Military)	− 4.7	
Balance on Current Account		+ 3.8
Changes in U.S. Private Assets Abroad	− 71.5	
Changes in Foreign Private Assets in U.S.	+ 34.8	
Changes in U.S. Government Assets (Including Official Reserves; a negative sign indicates an increase)	− 13.3	
Changes in Foreign Official Assets in the U.S. (a positive sign indicates an increase)	+ 15.5	
Balance on Capital Account		− 34.5
Allocation of SDRs		+ 1.1
Statistical Discrepancy		+ 29.6
Total		−0−

[1] A positive sign indicates that the item results in an inflow of funds into the United States while a negative sign indicates that the item results in an outflow of funds from the United States.

Source: Federal Reserve *Bulletin*, July 1981.

The trade deficits in the mid-to-late 1970s and the early 1980s reflected to a large degree the significant amounts of imported oil brought into the United States, as well as autos and other manufactured goods from countries such as Japan and West Germany. U.S. exports grew rapidly, however, in the late 1970s and 1980, for the most part through increased agricultural sales and sales of high technology products, such as computers and electrical components; but these gains were not sufficient to extinguish the deficit.

The United States has the largest trading economy in the world

Table 14-3
Imports and Exports as a Percent of GNP for Selected Countries

Country	Imports as a Percent of GNP	Exports as a Percent of GNP
Austria (1980)	41.4%	39.5%
France (1979)	20.7	20.6
W. Germany (1980)	28.7	28.6
Italy (1979)	26.2	25.5
Japan (1980)	16.1	15.1
United Kingdom (1979)	28.5	28.6
United States (1980)	10.9	9.9

Source: International Monetary Fund, *International Financial Transactions,* June 1981.

in absolute amount. However, because of the size of the U.S. economy, exports and imports represent a much smaller portion of U.S. goods and services production (GNP) than they do for most other major western countries. Table 14-3 shows imports and exports as a percent of GNP for various countries for recent years. Imports and exports when compared to GNP for the United States are about 10 percent compared with about 30 percent for Britain and 30 percent for West Germany.

In many ways, the trade balance is of great importance in showing U.S. competitiveness in world trade. Most other items in the balance of payments relate to financial elements. It is the trade balance that deals explicitly with the purchase of goods from the rest of the world and the sale of goods to the rest of the world. The trade deficit decreased in 1980 from its 1979 level of $29.4 billion. This was aided by a decline in oil demand occasioned by the rise in oil prices and the slow economic growth in the United States in 1980. These trends continued in 1981 and early 1982.

The Balance on Goods and Services and the Current Account

The next summary item in Table 14-2 is the balance on goods and services. To arrive at this item, military transactions, investment income, and other service transactions are added to the trade balance. Of these items, investment income is clearly the largest. This item records the net income received by the United States from investments abroad, which include both real and financial investments. The earnings returned to the parent company by a foreign subsidiary, as well as interest or dividend income received by American holders of foreign securities, are included in this item. The size of this item depends upon the amount and manner in which U.S. institutions and individuals have invested abroad in the past. To arrive at the net figure, earnings by foreigners from investment in the United States is subtracted. The fact that this item is positive indicates that Americans receive considerably more from investments abroad than foreigners receive from investments in the United States. This item has always been positive in the post–World War II period and has grown steadily throughout the period reflecting the growth and extent of U.S. investments abroad during this period, a subject that we will return to in discussing the capital account. Because of the substantial amount of net investment income, the overall balance on goods and services was in surplus in 1980.

When the goods and services balance is coupled with both private and government transfers to foreigners and receipts from foreigners, the balance on current account is the result. Transfers from the United States result in outflows of funds while transfers to the United States are inflows of funds. In 1980, the net amount of private and government transfers was negative, typical of the post–World War II period. Despite the negative transfers, the balance on current account was in surplus in 1980 after a small deficit in 1979 and deficits of about $14 billion in 1977 and 1978. However, the overall balance of payments was substantially in deficit in 1980 because of the capital account.

The Capital Account

The capital account reflects real and financial investment by the United States. Thus, direct investment, like the construction of a car plant by General Motors in West Germany, leads to an outflow of funds, and this is a negative item in the capital account. Similarly, the construction of a Volkswagen plant in the United States is a direct foreign investment, and an inflow of funds into the U.S. economy. Foreign direct investment has been growing rapidly in recent years. This increase stems from a number of factors: the expansion of the U.S. economy in this period, the fall in the dollar during most of the 1970s (though this was reversed in 1980 and 1981) making it cheaper for foreigners to invest in the United States and to hire U.S. labor, and fear that the U.S. would construct barriers to trade such as quotas or tariffs. The Japanese are particularly sensitive to this last possibility. As pointed out previously, however, there has been substantially more direct U.S. investment abroad in the post–World War II period than foreign investment in the United States.

Financial transactions—such as the purchase of stock, bonds, and direct lending—are also included in the capital account. The purchase of foreign securities and loans to foreigners are an outflow of funds, while foreign purchases of U.S. securities are an inflow. The purchase and sale of foreign financial assets depends on such things as the perceived business climate and future earnings prospects (for equities) and the relative interest rates on securities in different countries. Funds flows into short-term securities are particularly sensitive to differentials in rates of return between different countries. Funds moving from country to country in response to changes in short-term interest rates are sometimes called "hot money" to reflect the fact that they move rapidly in response to interest rate changes. For example, large institutions, such as multinational corporations as part of their aggressive management of cash balances, are quite willing to move funds from one country to another to seek higher returns. These substantial funds movements for short periods of time can significantly affect exchange rates between currencies in a floating exchange rate system.

While real and financial investment abroad leads to an outflow of funds from the United States, it should be recalled from the previous discussion of the current account that the earnings generated from this investment are an inflow of funds. Similarly, while foreign investment in the United States leads to an inflow of funds, the earnings generated from this investment become an outflow in later years. Therefore, as is really true of all components of the balance of payments, we cannot draw a conclusion that because an item may be a negative entry in the accounts, it is automatically to be regarded as unfavorable. Under purely floating exchange rates, the only impact of an overall positive or negative balance in the items of Table 14-2 should be on exchange rates. However, since the current system is not pure, included in the accounts are government official transactions that are often thought of as balancing transactions so that the balance of payments is always technically in balance. These items relate to a government's borrowing foreign currency or selling reserves to support its currency. In 1980, the U.S. government increased its holdings of reserves, while foreign official assets and allocation of special drawing rights—the IMF unit of account that is based on a basket of currencies—also increased.

Overall, there was a substantial deficit on capital account. Usually it would be expected that if the current account is in deficit, the capital account, as long as it includes changes in official assets, will substantially offset the current account deficit. (Theoretically, this offset must be precise.) However, the result in 1980 was that both the current account and capital account were in deficit according to the recorded numbers. Because the balance of payments must balance, the U.S. Commerce Department, which compiles the balance of payments, assumed its data were considerably inaccurate and thus the large statistical discrepancy was recorded to bring the total to zero. The statistical discrepancy, which is usually considerably smaller than it was in 1980, means that commerce simply didn't know why the balance of payments didn't balance in a technical sense.[15]

Balance of Payments Adjustment

In discussing exchange rate determination previously, we noted the balance of payments adjustment process. When a country is experiencing a balance of payments deficit—that is, except for changes in official reserve holdings and borrowings necessary to bring it into balance—more funds are moving abroad than coming into the country. There are a number of ways in which the balance of payments can be brought from deficit to balance. (Remember in an accounting sense the balance of payments is always in balance. This balance occurs due to changes in official reserve holdings and from borrowing. Under pure floating exchange rates, these activities should not be necessary if adjustments take place rapidly.) The easiest way to see how the balance of payments would be brought into balance is by focusing on the U.S. trade balance. If U.S. goods become cheaper and foreign goods more expensive, this would encourage the purchase of U.S. goods and discourage the purchase of foreign goods. To accomplish this task, the exchange rate must fall. Under fully floating exchange rates, this fall is expected to be automatic. As we noted previously in discussing the floating exchange rate system, this system leads to automatic adjustment in the balance of payments. Under the old fixed exchange rate system, currencies would have to be formally devalued, that is, the exchange rate reduced. However, the procedure to accomplish a **devaluation** was cumbersome; therefore, in practice it was employed relatively infrequently. As a result, countries facing chronic balance of payments deficits often had to resort to depressing their economies to slow import demand. This clearly was unpalatable. Under floating exchange rate systems, the domestic economy is expected to be insulated from these problems, as the exchange rate takes care of the adjustment.

However, the present experience with a modified floating system has not worked well in bringing about automatic adjustment. Besides the interference with the floating system by countries attempting to prevent their exchange rates from changing, adjustment problems are also related to financial flows that occur because of interest rate changes and speculation. Further, to the extent important world commodities like oil face an inelastic price demand, at least in the short run, this problem may interfere with the adjustment process. Despite

---

[15] In recent years the statistical discrepancy has grown rather large implying that the Commerce Department is missing a number of significant items in their data collection. There has been some suggestion that this "miss" may reflect an increase in illicit transactions.

price increases, countries do not cut back significantly on imports very quickly. Thus, adjustment is delayed until the impact of higher import prices results in substantial conservation and product substitution. The 1974 oil price rises (which occurred almost immediately after the move to the floating rate system) and those that have followed put a heavy burden on the system. So the adjustment process is clearly not automatic, at least in the short run, under the managed floating exchange rate system. The world is still struggling with the problem.[16]

The Euromarkets

The term Euromarkets refers to the markets that trade securities and make loans in currencies that are not the currencies of the country in which the financial transaction is taking place. The markets for short-term securities, bank loans, and bank deposits are known as the Euro-currency markets, while long-term securities are issued and traded in the Eurobond markets. By far the largest of the Euromarkets is the Eurodollar market. However, there are Euromark, Euroswissfranc, and Euroyen markets as well. The major trading center of the Eurocurrency markets is London. However, significant activity takes place in the Caribbean, particularly in Nassau and the Cayman Islands.[17] A decision in 1981 by the Federal Reserve to allow Eurocurrency business through international banking facilities (IBFs) set up in the United States has brought some Euromarket trading directly to this country.

To understand the Euromarkets, we must concentrate on an example. A bank deposit is made in London by a British exporter. Suppose that the exporter plans to purchase materials shortly in the United States. The exporter receives payment in dollars for some finished goods that he sells. Instead of converting the dollars into pounds, the exporter deposits them in a London bank as a dollar-denominated deposit, knowing that at some point this deposit will be used to pay for materials. The term dollar-denominated deposits means that the deposit is actually carried on the books of the bank in dollars even though the currency of the country is pounds. Thus, a Eurodollar deposit now exists.

It is interesting to note that the actual dollars involved in this deposit may very well stay in the United States. Suppose, for example, that the check the exporter deposits is drawn on Chase Manhattan Bank

---

[16] There are numerous textbooks on international trade and finance that discuss the balance of payments and the adjustment process. See the suggested readings at the end of this chapter.

[17] Even though these areas are not part of Europe, the term Euromarket encompasses Eurocurrency activity in these areas.

in New York and is deposited in Lloyds Bank in London. Lloyds may hold the funds at Chase—not bring the dollars to London—and use its account at Chase to make its loans, holding some in reserve as it would against any deposit. Even though it is estimated that more than one-half the funds that Eurodollar deposits represent are in the United States, they are, nevertheless, still considered Eurodollars because of their ownership.

Eurodollar deposits are interest-earning deposits.[18] They range from overnight deposits to time deposits that can have maturities of a number of years. However, most deposits are short term; almost 90 percent have maturities of six months or less and a substantial fraction (nearly one-third) have maturities of a week or less. Some London banks have also issued negotiable CDs that are then traded in the secondary market. The major source of deposit funds comes from corporations and other institutions in the major industrial countries. However, as will be noted below, the oil exporting countries have become an important source of funds to the Euromarkets in the last decade.

Eurobanks, banks that deal in the Euromarkets, use the funds that they receive in deposits to make loans in the Eurodollar market. Borrowers include governments, central banks, government-owned corporations, financial institutions, and multinational corporations. In recent years, less developed countries and Eastern block countries have become large Euromarket borrowers. Poland is a fairly dramatic example of a country that has made extensive use of the Eurodollar market as a borrower.

The most common financing by Eurobanks is short-term loans, often extended through lines of credit. Longer-term loans of three to five years are also common, but these are renewed, or rolled over, on a three to six month basis so that rate adjustments can be made. Large loans are often made by syndicates or groups of banks rather than by a single bank. Since these large loans are often to governments of developing or eastern block countries, the syndicates permit the spreading of risk over a number of banks, usually located in different countries. These large loans are often for fixed maturities as long as ten years, but the interest rate is revised, commonly every six months.

Interest rates on Eurodollar loans are usually expressed as some mark-up over the London Interbank Offer Rate, which is known as LIBOR.[19] This rate is somewhat analogous to the federal funds rate

---

[18] Much of the information in this paragraph and the succeeding six paragraphs is drawn from Edward J. Frydl, "The Debate Over Regulating the Eurocurrency Markets," Federal Reserve Bank of New York *Quarterly Review* (Winter 1979–80), pp. 11–20.

[19] Since late 1980, some large loans granted by international syndicates of banks have been pegged to the prime rate in the United States and Canada rather than to LIBOR as a way of increasing the interest return on these loans. It is estimated that approximately one in five syndicated loans have been so pegged since late 1980.

in the United States because it is the rate at which Eurobanks loan funds to each other. The amount of the mark-up over LIBOR depends on the assessment of how risky the loan is likely to be and the degree of competition for a particular loan customer. If funds are plentiful in the Eurodollar market, a potentially risky loan customer may still be able to obtain a very favorable rate, as low as one-quarter or one-half percentage point above LIBOR. The same customer may have to pay several percentage points above LIBOR when funds are tight. The establishment of international banking facilities (IBFs) in the United States means that U.S. banks, which operate in the Euromarkets through their foreign branches and subsidiaries, are also able to accept Eurodollar deposits and make Eurodollar loans at their U.S. offices.

In addition to bank loans made in the Eurodollar market, short-term and long-term securities are also sold in the Eurodollar market. Long-term Eurodollar securities are known as Eurobonds. Both short- and long-term securities are issued by public borrowers, such as governments, and by private corporations, usually large multinational corporations. These multinational corporations are very sophisticated borrowers and will often shift their securities offerings between the domestic and the Eurodollar market to take advantage of favorable interest rates in one market or the other.

Much of what has been discussed above in connection with the Eurodollar market is equally applicable to trading in the Eurocurrency and Eurobond markets in currencies other than the dollar. Trading takes place in Euromarks, Euroswissfrancs, as well as Euroyens. However, dollars account for more than 70 percent of Euromarket activity. It was estimated that in 1980 all types of Eurodollar claims totaled about $1 trillion.

The development of the Eurodollar market has important effects on domestic financial markets in the United States as borrowers and depositors shift funds and credit demands between domestic markets and financial institutions and the Euromarkets. Further, multinational corporations and other institutions use overnight Eurodollar deposits to earn a return on otherwise noninterest-earning demand deposits. The next day these funds are brought back to the United States and redeposited into demand deposit accounts. The use of overnight Eurodollar deposits, particularly at branches of U.S. banks in the Caribbean, has become common practice.

As a result of these and other Euromarket activities, the growth and development of the Euromarkets have presented challenges to central banks and governments in managing their domestic economies and exchange rates. To gain further insight into these issues it is useful to explore the development of the Euromarkets. The starting place for this exploration is the key role played by the dollar in international trade.

The Development and Growth of the Eurodollar Market

The dollar became the major currency in international trade following World War II and the establishment of the IMF under the Bretton Woods agreements. In the 1950s, the Soviet Union, concerned about the security of its dollar holdings in the United States because of the cold war, sought a safe haven for these dollars and found it in the major London banks in dollar-denominated deposits. These dollar-denominated deposits grew rapidly outside the United States and particularly in London, the center of the Eurodollar market. Rules changes by the United States, such as the Interest Equalization Tax, which became effective as of 1963, and the existence of Regulation Q ceilings on time deposits in the United States in the early 1960s, encouraged the growth of the Eurodollar market. The Interest Equalization Tax made it more expensive for Americans to buy foreign bonds, and thus encouraged foreign issuers of bonds to issue dollar-denominated bonds abroad. Regulation Q ceilings limited the rate of return that could be offered in the United States on dollar time deposits.

In the late 1960s, large U.S. banks started using the Eurodollar market through their European branches and subsidiaries for raising funds through aggressive liability management and returning the funds to the United States when the Federal Reserve became restrictive in its domestic credit policies. In this way banks attempted to circumvent the intent of the Fed's restrictive policy. The Fed tried to halt bank use of the Eurodollar market by placing reserve requirements on such repatriated Eurodollars in the late 1960s. While this checked U.S. bank repatriation of funds for a while, the Euromarkets as a whole were firmly entrenched, spreading in the 1970s to other non-European areas. A big boost to this market came from the 1974 increase in oil prices. Since oil was priced and paid for in dollars, literally billions of dollars flowed into the OPEC coffers. These "petrodollars" (the only difference between a "petrodollar" and a Eurodollar is in its ownership) in turn found their way back into the international banking system and into the Eurodollar market in substantial amounts.

The extraordinary growth of the Eurodollar market in the 1970s— it had literally more than quadrupled from 1974 to 1980—has posed interesting challenges to the international financial system. Among these challenges are the huge amount of dollars abroad that can lead to rapid and substantial swings in the exchange value of the dollar when Eurodollar holders switch from dollars to other currencies or into dollars from other currencies. For example, multinational corporations make extensive use of the Euromarkets. Corporate treasurers of these corporations, as part of their cash management programs, have the ability to shift massive amounts of funds from the United

States abroad to take advantage of interest rate differentials that may exist between Eurodollar deposits and Euromarket securities, and their domestic equivalents. Further, these treasurers are also comfortable in moving from dollars entirely into other currencies either for interest rate or exchange rate advantages. In an era of floating exchange rates, these movements can have important impacts upon exchange rates between the dollar and other currencies as they significantly alter the demand for, or supply of, one currency relative to another.

There is also concern that because no central bank has control over the amount of Eurodollars, their expansion will continue to feed worldwide inflationary pressure. (In fact, the reason the statistics that have been given on the amount of Eurodollars above are so imprecise is that nobody has any clear notion of the exact size of the Eurodollar market.) Similar to domestic deposits, there may be a Eurodollar multiplier. That is, an increase in Eurodollar deposits may lead to a further increase in these deposits. While there are numerous leakages in such a process that serve to make this multiplier relatively small, the multiplier may be greater than one. The major central banks' concern stems basically from the fact that no central bank can set reserve requirements on these Eurodollar deposits in order to influence the multiplier. There have been attempts of late by central bankers, particularly led by the Federal Reserve System, to develop a system to control these markets. However, because such control requires international cooperation of all major central banks, such attempts are likely to fail.

The case for regulatory control of the Euromarkets—even if it could be effectively implemented—is not open and shut. Much of the basic information and analysis that is needed to make reasonable judgments concerning the arguments for or against regulation are simply lacking. While research and debate continue, it is likely that the Euromarkets will remain essentially unfettered by regulation for some time to come.[20] As a result, they will continue to be of international importance and play a significant role in the world financial system.

Gold

Gold has been considered valuable for millenia and has frequently served as money in the past. The major nations remained essentially on a full gold standard well into the twentieth century. Under a gold standard, currency is fully convertible into gold by all holders. A gold exchange standard existed until 1971 in which the convertibility of the dollar into gold was assumed to provide a bedrock to the fixed exchange rate system. Since currency of all IMF countries could be

---

[20] See Edward J. Frydl's previously cited article for a thorough discussion of the debate surrounding regulation of the Euromarkets.

converted into the dollars, essentially this implied some gold backing for currency. In fact, such convertibility was a fiction. For many years, prior to Nixon's eliminating convertibility in 1971, the United States was incapable of redeeming even a small portion of dollars held abroad at the official price of $35 per ounce. U.S. gold reserves were completely inadequate, and the United States had to rely on the "goodwill" of foreign official holders of dollars, that is, foreign central banks, not to ask for conversion. After 1971, gold was supposed to be "demonetized"[21] and treated like any other commodity. The demise of convertibility was expected to lead to recognition that gold was a "barbarous relic," as John Maynard Keynes called it many years ago, as far as international exchange was concerned.

On January 1, 1975, Americans were permitted to own gold bullion for the first time since the early 1930s. After rising in value to over $200 per ounce in 1974 in anticipation of this change, gold's price in 1975 got as low as about $100. However, in 1979 and early 1980 with an unsettled political and economic climate, gold rose rapidly. Figure 14-4 traces the price of gold from 1972 to August 1981. Gold hit its all time high of $850 per ounce on February 21, 1980, before declining. By August 1981, gold was trading at about $420 per ounce and was below $350 in May 1982. As we noted previously, prior to the 1970s, gold had been fixed officially at only $35 per ounce.

The increases in the price of gold in the 1970s took place despite periodic auctions of gold by both the U.S. Treasury and the IMF, which were undertaken not only to put downward pressure on gold's price but to indicate that it had no future role in the world monetary system. These auctions were halted in 1980. Interestingly, however, while the auctions were proceeding some "remonetization" of gold had taken place as early as January 1979 with the formation of the European Monetary System (EMS) composed of the members of the European Economic Community (the Common Market) except Great Britain.[22] Gold was to account for 20 percent of the reserves of the EMS. There have periodically been calls to more generally remonetize gold, but whether it will be fully remonetized remains to be seen. In 1981, the Reagan administration formed a committee, the U.S. Gold Commission, of business people, government officials, and economists to study the impact of restoring a gold standard. This was the first serious attempt under U.S. government auspices to study the restoration of the gold standard in recent decades. However, the report released early in 1982 recommended that the gold standard not be restored.

---

[21] Demonetization meant that gold was no longer to be considered reserves against currencies.

[22] There were nine members of the EEC at the time of the formation of the EMS: Belgium, Denmark, France, West Germany, Ireland, Italy, Luxembourg, The Netherlands and Great Britain. Greece became the tenth member of the EEC in 1981.

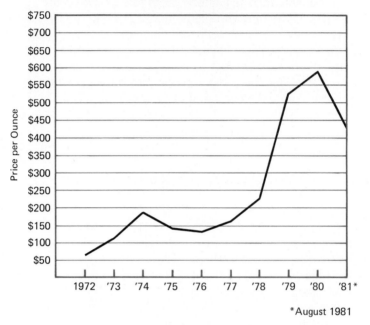

Figure 14-4
The Price of Gold,
(London, End of Period, Dollars per Ounce)

*August 1981

Source: International Monetary Fund, *International Financial Statistics*, various issues.

Ironically, if gold should ever be remonetized, the United States is in a strong position with 264 million ounces of gold in its official holdings as of April 1981, by far the largest in the world as can be seen from Table 14-4. At $350 per ounce the U.S. gold reserves would be $92 billion, for example. This is equal to about 75 percent of the currency portion of the U.S. money supply and by far the highest proportion of gold to currency in U.S. history. Nevertheless, many economists argue strenuously against the remonetization of gold. These economists are particularly concerned that the rapid price movements in gold and the control of new supply by essentially two countries, South Africa and the Soviet Union, make any remonetization of gold ill-advised because under a gold standard the U.S. money supply would change as the amount and value of the gold stock changed. These and other reasons entered into the majority decision by the U.S. Gold Commission to recommend against the restoration of the gold standard.

Table 14-4
Official Holdings of Gold, Selected Countries, April 1981

Country	Gold Held in Millions of Troy Ounces	Gold Value at $350 per Ounce in Billions of Dollars
Austria	21.11	$ 7.38
France	81.85	28.64
W. Germany	95.18	33.31
Italy	66.67	23.33
Japan	24.23	8.48
United Kingdom	18.89	6.61
United States	264.17	92.45

Source: Gold holdings from the International Monetary Fund, *International Financial Statistics,* Sept. 1981.

An Additional Word on the Role of U.S. Banks Internationally

The growth of U.S. banking internationally and foreign banking in the United States has been discussed in Chapter 5. However, we can now fill in some of the gaps that were left in our discussion by the lack of background on the Eurodollar market and exchange rates.

From the foregoing discussion in this chapter, it is apparent that by facilitating exchange between currencies, the large multinational banks play an important role in making exchange rate changes smoother. Further, the role of the banks in financing international trade is of great importance. Their Eurodollar lending and general international trade financing provides the needed liquidity for international trade. U.S. banks, among the world's largest, are crucial in this provision of liquidity.

As noted, however, problems are created for the Federal Reserve in conducting monetary policy because of the growth of "offshore" banking (branches of American banks outside the U.S.) and the commensurate growth of the Eurodollar market. As banks move funds between the United States and foreign countries, reserve positions of banks change. This is equally true even with on-shore IBFs because they are considered separate entities from the domestic U.S. banks in which they are housed. To the extent that these changes cannot be foreseen by the Federal Reserve and thus offset, the ability of the Fed to control the money supply domestically is affected. Further, the Fed and other central banks have no control over the expansion of the Eurodollar market and, therefore, in an important respect, expansion in the world's money supply and credit. During a period of world-wide inflation, these concerns are clearly genuine. However, even if additional regulation could be obtained through international central bank cooperation, it is doubtful that this would effectively solve these problems. The Euromarkets have thus far demonstrated a substantial ability to circumvent the few regulations that have been thrown in their path.

THE PRIME RATE'S NEW ROLE INTERNATIONALLY

A New Peg for Eurolending

Banks operating in the syndication market in London are quietly pricing their loans on the basis of the prime rates in the U.S. and Canada to increase their profits on international loans by as much as 40%. By pegging their loans to the North American rates instead of the London interbank offered rate (LIBOR), the banks can achieve a higher return, while their customers—mostly sovereign governments—can please their local politicians with what appears to be a lower rate.

One of every five international syndications has been wholly or partly based on the prime since late 1980. Once the lead banks and a borrower agree on the prime/LIBOR option, individual banks in the syndicate decide which of the two will be the peg for the interest rate, and how much the borrower will pay.

In the past, when differences in U.S. prime and LIBOR rates were negligible, banks hardly bothered with prime-based syndications. But as interest rates became more volatile, the relationship between the prime and LIBOR changed sharply. At times the prime has soared above LIBOR—as high as 4.9% in May, 1980—but has seldom sunk much below it.

Factoring in politics. Euromarket borrowers are not protesting, even though the prime-based loans are currently costing them 2% more in additional interest charges. For example, Belgium is paying ¼% above the U.S. prime for the first four years of a $500 million seven-year loan managed by Chase Manhattan Ltd., and ⅜% over prime for the last three years. With Chase's prime rate at 17½%, that means that Belgium is now paying 17¾% for its cash. But for Belgium and other borrowers, prime-based credits are cosmetically appealing because the borrower appears to be paying less. Belgium, for example, would have had to pay an eye-opening 3⅛% over LIBOR for the same funds if the loan had been priced in the LIBOR manner.

Political factors and matters of national ego often play an important role in determining spreads. Even though government finance ministry officials understand the true cost of prime-pegged loans, some politicians and the public may not. Nations are constantly trying to negotiate the narrowest spreads on their loans. "It looks good to the uninitiated," remarks one U.S. banker.

Prime-based deals also provide much-needed cash to some borrowers who might otherwise be left out in the cold because of their insistence on low spreads. Recently, Italy set out to raise $2 billion with a low-priced loan pegged to both LIBOR and the U.S. prime rate. Banks complained that the deal was unprofitable, and eventually Rome had to settle for only $1 billion, with almost all of that pegged to the prime.

Dissatisfied with ⅜%. At the same time, borrowers such as Sweden, Mexico, and Venezuela have taken out loans with prime/LIBOR options to attract a broader base of lenders, including U.S. regional banks that have become less active in the Euro-market as spreads over LIBOR have narrowed. "U.S. regionals are not satisfied with spreads of ⅜% over LIBOR," notes one New York banker. "They just won't do it." Adds Donald R. Marsh, senior vice-president at Rainier National Bank in Seattle: "We have more worthwhile things to do than participate in seven- or eight-year loans at a spread of ½% or ⅜% [over LIBOR].

The large U.S. money markets also offer U.S. banks a secure supply of short-term funds whose costs are nearly always below the U.S. prime rate. The same holds true for Canadian banks in loans where there is an option of borrowing in Canadian currency. Explains one U.S. banker: "Lending out of their own base, Canadian banks have no exposure to international funding risk."

U.S. banks provide themselves with a "safety net" in prime-pegged deals by mandating that the borrower pay the higher of either the prime rate or the secondary 90-day certificate of deposit rate adjusted for reserve requirements and insurance premiums.

European banks with U.S. branches have likewise jumped on the bandwagon. Robert C. French, manager of the loan syndication department of Lloyds Bank International Ltd. in London, says his bank sees better margins on prime-based loans than LIBOR-based ones. But he adds: "These aren't the answer to a banker's dream. What we would really most like to see is a return to LIBOR with a healthy spread."

The U.S. Prime Rate's Advantage over LIBOR

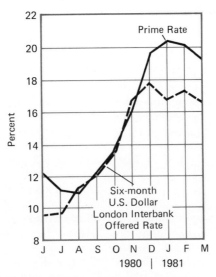

Data: Bank of America International Ltd.

Key Points

1. Foreign exchange for a particular country is the currency of any other country. The exchange rate is the rate at which one currency converts into another currency. As a result, an international transaction always involves two prices, the price of the good, service, or financial asset being traded and the exchange rate.

2. The current exchange rate system is called a managed float. This means that while exchange rates change in response to currency supplies and demands, countries intervene in the market to attempt to prevent too rapid and too dramatic exchange rate changes. This contrasts with a pure floating exchange rate system in which no intervention takes place and a fixed exchange rate system in which intervention is designed to prevent exchange rates from changing at all.

3. The balance of payments is a summary of the economic and financial transactions between the country for which it is prepared and the rest of the world. The major components of the balance of payments are the merchandise trade balance, the current account, and the capital account.

4. The Euromarket is the name given to the markets that trade securities and make loans in currencies that are not the currencies of the country in which the financial transaction is taking place. The markets for short-term securities, interest-earning bank deposits, and bank loans are known as the Eurocurrency markets, while those for long-term securities are known as the Eurobond market. The market for Eurodollars is the largest of the Eurocurrency markets. The Euromarkets are utilized by governments, public institutions, and large multinational corporations. The major reference interest rate in the Euromarkets is LIBOR, the London Interbank Offer Rate. Most Euromarket loans carry interest rates that are scaled up from this rate.

Questions for Discussion

1. Differentiate in detail between a floating exchange rate system, a managed floating exchange rate system, and a fixed exchange rate system. What are the implications for balance of payments adjustment in these systems?

2. How can Euromarket transactions affect exchange rates under a managed floating exchange rate system? What factors are responsible for the rapid growth of the Euromarkets in recent years? Are those factors transitory such that they may be expected to diminish over time, in which case the Euromarkets may stabilize or contract or can they be expected to underpin further Euromarket growth? Explain.

3. What is LIBOR and why is it important?

4. Why has the syndication of large Euroloans become much more common in the last few years? What are the advantages of syndication for the lending banks?
5. Explain the balance of payments and the major categories that compose it.

Suggested Readings

Batten, Dallas S. "Foreign Exchange Markets: The Dollar in 1980." Federal Reserve Bank of St. Louis *Review,* April 1981, pp. 22–30.

Federal Reserve Bank of Boston. There are three issues of their conference series that are particularly relevant to the discussion in this chapter.
  1. *International Aspects of Stabilization Policy.* Federal Reserve Bank of Boston Conference Series No. 12, June 1974.
  2. *Key Issues in International Banking.* Federal Reserve Bank of Boston Conference Series No. 18, Oct. 1977.
  3. *Managed Exchange Rate Flexibility: The Recent Experience.* Federal Reserve Bank of Boston, Conference Series No. 20, Oct. 1978.

Federal Reserve Bank of San Francisco. "Responses to International Inflation." *Economic Review,* Summer 1980.

Frenkel, Jacob A., and Harry G. Johnson, eds. *The Economics of Exchange Rates.* Reading, Mass.: Addison Wesley, 1978.

Frydl, Edward J. "The Debate Over Regulating the Eurocurrency Markets." Federal Reserve Bank of New York *Quarterly Review,* Winter 1979–80, pp. 11–20.

Goodman, Laurie S. "The Pricing of Syndicated Eurocurrency Credits." Federal Reserve Bank of New York *Quarterly Review,* Summer 1980, pp. 39–49.

Keran, Michael W. "Money and Exchange Rates—1974–1979." Federal Reserve Bank of San Francisco *Economic Review,* Spring 1979, pp. 19–34.

Keran, Michael W., and Stephen Zeldes. "Effects of Monetary Disturbances on Exchange Rates, Inflation and Interest Rates." Federal Reserve Bank of San Francisco *Economic Review,* Spring 1980, pp. 7–29.

Little, Jane Sneddon. "Liquidity Creation by Eurobanks: 1973–1978. Federal Reserve Bank of Boston *New England Economic Review* Jan./Feb. 1979, pp. 62–72.

Westerfield, Janice M. "How U.S. Multinationals Manage Currency Risk." Federal Reserve Bank of Philadelphia *Business Review,* March/April 1980, pp. 19–27.

PART 4

Government in the Financial System

Federally Sponsored Agencies and the Financial Markets

15

Federally sponsored agencies are organizations chartered by the federal government to serve a public purpose such as assisting the mortgage market. They are called **sponsored** agencies because, although these agencies retain some relationship to the federal government, they are privately owned. They fulfill their public purpose by extending credit in various forms to particular sectors of the economy. The two largest of these agencies, both concerned with the mortgage market, are the Federal National Mortgage Association and the Federal Home Loan Bank System, which have both been mentioned previously. Other sponsored agencies exist to provide agricultural credit and student loan assistance.

In this chapter, the sponsored agencies will be examined in detail and their purpose and operations described. Further, the impact that these agencies have on the financial markets will be analyzed. The provision of credit by federally sponsored agencies is only one of two major ways the federal government aids in providing credit to the economy. Federal guarantees of private borrowing is the other and will also be discussed briefly in this chapter.

The Federally Sponsored Agencies

Almost all sponsored agencies raise funds in the open market; and, therefore, they not only have an impact upon the sectors of the economy that they are designed to assist but on the allocation of credit in the economy in general. As their activities have grown, so has their open market financing and therefore their impact on the credit markets. The growth of federally sponsored agencies was particularly dramatic

379

in the decade of the 1970s. In 1971, total credit extended by these agencies, including mortgage purchases by the Federal National Mortgage Association, totaled about $39 billion. By mid-1981, this figure was in excess of $170 billion. The financing of such a large amount of activity can affect interest rates and credit flows in the economy significantly.

The federally sponsored agencies designed to provide direct and indirect assistance to the mortgage market are discussed first. These agencies are the largest of the federally sponsored agencies and have grown most rapidly in recent years. These agencies are generally called the mortgage market agencies. The largest of these is the Federal National Mortgage Association.

The Federal National Mortgage Association

The Federal National Mortgage Association (FNMA, called Fannie Mae) was established in the late 1930s to contribute to the marketing of the then fledgling Federal Housing Administration (FHA) mortgages. The FHA program was the first government-insured mortgage program, and FNMA's role was to provide a secondary market for these mortgages. (Recall that a secondary market is a market in which already issued financial instruments, in this case mortgages, are bought and sold). The operations of FNMA were very small, however, until 1966 when it essentially doubled its mortgage holdings from $2 billion to $4 billion in an attempt to deal with the very severe housing recession of 1966. The recession had been brought on by then record high interest rates.

Later, in assessing FNMA's activity in 1966, it was believed that FNMA could have done even more to moderate the decline in housing. But, FNMA was constrained in its mortgage purchases because it was a formal part of the federal government and its activities counted in the federal budget. Therefore, the larger FNMA's purchases of mortgages, the greater its contribution to the federal deficit. Thus, it was prevented from doing all it could by this concern. (This was also the case with the Federal Home Loan Bank System, the FHLB.) For this reason, the President proposed that FNMA (and the FHLB) should become private. This change was implemented in the Housing Act of 1968. This act transferred the secondary market function of FNMA (the buying and occasionally selling of already existing mortgages) to the newly constituted FNMA, which became a government-sponsored federal agency. The special assistance function consisting of subsidy programs that before 1968 had also been under FNMA auspices was transferred to the newly created Government National Mortgage Association (GNMA), which was to remain a part of the government. (GNMA will be discussed below.)

Although FNMA is a private corporation (its stock is traded on the New York and Pacific Stock Exchanges), it is still expected to serve a public purpose by providing a secondary market for mortgages and thus assisting the mortgage market through its mortgage purchases. In 1971, FNMA's authority was expanded to allow it to provide a secondary market for conventional mortgage loans in addition to the market it was already providing for government-insured mortgages of FHA and VA loans. FNMA began purchasing conventional mortgages in 1972. All funds utilized by FNMA to acquire mortgages, except for the relatively small amount it receives in repayments on mortgages it already holds and through certain fees, are raised by FNMA in the open market through the issuance of securities. There is also a relatively small back-up line of credit to the Treasury, but this has never been used.

Since 1968, FNMA has increased its activity tremendously. From $4.3 billion in mortgages in 1966 and $7.1 in 1968, by May 1981 FNMA held $39.0 billion in government-insured mortgages and $18.6 billion in conventional mortgages.[1] The bulk of FNMA mortgages are on one-to-four-family homes and are acquired at biweekly auctions.

The FNMA auction is conducted in a fashion similar to the Treasury bill auction discussed in Chapter 12. The major difference is that in this auction FNMA is the buyer and the bidders are the sellers. On the day of the auction,[2] FNMA customers, mostly mortgage bankers, bid to secure a commitment to sell mortgages at various prices—and therefore various yields—to FNMA. The bids are ranked from lowest price to highest price, and FNMA then moves from the lowest price to the last bid it will accept. (Notice that the reason FNMA ranks bids from the lowest to the highest price is FNMA is buying mortgages; the less it pays for these mortgages the more they yield to FNMA.) Once it decides on the highest price, FNMA issues four-month commitments on these mortgages providing that for four months from the date of the auction, the successful bidder may deliver the mortgages for purchase to FNMA at the price bid. Whether the holder of a FNMA commitment will actually deliver these mortgages to FNMA for purchase depends upon whether the holder can find someone else to purchase the mortgages at a more attractive price. During periods of tight credit, many mortgages will be delivered to FNMA when alter-

---

[1] A subsidiary of the FHLB, the Federal Home Loan Mortgage Corporation (FHLMC)—usually referred to as Freddie Mac—specializes in buying conventional loans from S&Ls (the largest conventional loan originator) and reselling them. Since FNMA customers are mostly mortgage bankers making FHA–VA loans, this explains the weight in the FNMA portfolio of government-insured loans. However, conventional mortgage purchases by FNMA have increased substantially in recent years.

[2] Actually there are three auctions—for government-insured mortgages, for conventional loans, and for graduated payment mortgages begun in 1980. However, since all are conducted in exactly the same way, the auction process is discussed as if only one takes place. In addition, FNMA began a commitment to purchase adjustable rate mortgages at the end of July 1981, whereas until that time only fixed rate mortgages had been eligible for commitment and purchase.

native outlets for sales are not available.[3] However, it is unlikely even during such periods that all mortgages on which commitments are held will be delivered to FNMA.

In addition to the auction, FNMA has a number of other purchase programs that relate to multifamily (apartment) housing and subsidized housing. Furthermore, in August 1981, FNMA announced a new program to purchase low-yielding mortgages from S&Ls at market prices. This is designed to help S&Ls holding these mortgages to liquidate them, take their loss, and relend at higher rates. In addition, FNMA has begun packaging mortgage passthroughs and selling them in the open market, as the Federal Home Loan Mortgage Corporation (FHLMC), a division of the FHLB, has been doing for years. GNMA also sells passthrough securities. Nevertheless, the auction remains the centerpiece of the FNMA program of assistance to the mortgage market.

Financing FNMA Purchases Purchases of mortgages committed to FNMA must be financed in the open market. It is interesting to note that since FNMA's activity is dictated by the needs of the mortgage market as expressed in the bids it receives in the market, it typically is purchasing most mortgages when the credit markets are already tight. Table 15-1 shows FNMA purchases by year from 1968 to 1980. Notice the increase in FNMA purchases in 1969–70, 1973–74, and 1978–79, all periods of credit tightness in the mortgage market and the financial markets in general. Thus, FNMA financing puts substantial additional demands for funds on the credit markets, particularly during periods when funds demand is high relative to supply, and this, in turn, may increase the upward pressure on interest rates in the credit markets.[4] Table 15-1 also presents FNMA securities outstanding for 1968–80. Notice the upsurge in borrowing in the years 1969–70,

---

[3] Recall that most FNMA customers are mortgage bankers. Since these organizations are not depository institutions but really brokers, they are not able to hold mortgages themselves for long; they must sell to someone.

[4] To the extent that there is additional upward pressure on interest rates from FNMA financing, the assistance that FNMA is actually providing to the mortgage market may be less than the purchases of mortgages would lead one to believe. This results because upward pressure on open-market rates may induce additional funds to leave (that is, disintermediation) traditional mortgage lenders, such as S&Ls, thereby reducing their ability to make mortgage loans. See, for example, L. Grebler, "Broadening the Sources of Funds for Residential Mortgages," *Ways to Moderate Fluctuations in Housing Construction,* Board of Governors of the Federal Reserve System (1972), pp. 177–252; Craig Swan, "The Impact of Residential Construction of Federal Home Loan Bank Policy," *Journal of Monetary Economics,* Supplement, Vol. 4 (1976), pp. 205–29; Herbert M. Kaufman, "An Analysis of Federal Mortgage Market Agency Behavior," *Journal of Money, Credit, and Banking* (May 1977), pp. 349–55, for a fuller explanation of this problem. There is a general question of how effective federally sponsored agencies are in providing assistance to their particular sectors because of their need to finance their assistance and what this means to the allocation of credit in the economy that will be discussed more fully below.

Table 15-1
Purchases of Mortgages and Securities Outstanding by FNMA, 1968–80
(End of Period, Millions of Dollars)

Year	Purchases	Securities Outstanding
1968	$ 1,944	$ 6,376
1969	4,120	10,511
1970	5,079	15,206
1971	3,574	17,701
1972	3,699	19,238
1973	6,127	24,175
1974	6,953	28,167
1975	4,263	29,963
1976	3,606	30,565
1977	4,780	31,890
1978	12,303	41,080
1979	10,806	48,486
1980	8,100	55,185

Source: Federal Reserve *Bulletin,* various issues.

1973–74, and 1978–79, corresponding to the years of increased mortgage purchases when FNMA is called upon for most assistance.[5] FNMA securities are issued across the whole maturity spectrum from short-term discount notes through long-term bonds. Being a federally sponsored agency, FNMA has preference in the financial markets. As has been explained in previous discussions of federal agency securities, FNMA securities are regarded to be almost as default free as Treasury securities, and FNMA will always find buyers for its securities at interest rates that are usually only slightly above Treasury rates for the same security maturity. Thus, it is not constrained by funds availability in providing mortgage market assistance.

However, as a privately owned corporation, it cannot ignore, for any extended period of time, the need to be profitable; therefore, it may be constrained by profit considerations. FNMA's profitability comes in major part through holding mortgages in its portfolio that yield more than it is paying to finance these mortgages. During the

---

[5] In addition to borrowing, FNMA also purchases mortgages with funds it receives through repayments of mortgages it already holds. This is the major reason that the increase in outstanding securities does not correspond precisely to the mortgages purchased.

early 1980s, as financing rates have increased substantially, profitability has not always been possible despite the favorable financing rates. FNMA's portfolio is composed of long-term mortgages while its financing is mostly short and intermediate term. Thus, it is continually refinancing. When rates are rising, this refinancing takes place at higher rates, unfavorably affecting its financing–mortgage rate spread. Because of its unique role as a private corporation with a public purpose, however, FNMA has continued and even increased its mortgage purchase programs, something it might not have been able to do if it weren't a federally sponsored agency. As such, the ultimate result of the lack of profitability, namely bankruptcy, need not be a concern. This is not to suggest, however, that FNMA does not desire to restore its profitability. In a lower interest rate environment, it will be in a very favorable spread position as it refinances high interest debt and continues to hold the relatively high mortgage rate loans purchased in 1979–82.

The Federal Home Loan Bank System

The Federal Home Loan Bank System (FHLB) was a product of the Great Depression of the 1930s. It was established when the then small savings and loan industry was in difficulty because of the deteriorating financial climate. By aiding S&Ls, the FHLB could indirectly aid the mortgage market since S&Ls hold most of their assets in mortgages. The FHLB provides its assistance by making loans, called **advances,** to S&Ls. However, unlike discount loans at the Fed, the FHLB encourages S&Ls to borrow when they need funds to continue mortgage lending and adjusts the interest rate charged on this borrowing, called the **advances rate,** accordingly. As pointed out, the result has been that on average the level of advances from the FHLB exceeds the amount of discount loans to commercial banks from the Fed by many times. Under legislation passed in 1980, S&Ls offering transactions accounts are permitted to borrow from the Federal Reserve at the discount window. However, they also retain their ability to borrow from the FHLB and are expected to use the discount window only as a last resort.

Unlike commercial bank membership in the Fed, most S&Ls belong to the FHLB. Federally chartered S&Ls must belong to the FHLB, while most state chartered S&Ls do so voluntarily. (Table 8-1 in Chapter 8 p. 187 reported FHLB membership of S&Ls.) While the FHLB sets a liquidity requirement similar to the Fed's reserve requirement, it is usually kept low (about 5 percent or less) and is met by the holding of short-term government securities and cash. As a result, it is not considered a hinderance to FHLB membership. This liquidity ratio is adjusted up and down as needed to encourage or discourage mortgage lending. When the ratio is reduced, for example, additional funds are freed to be used by S&Ls to make mortgage loans if they desire.

The FHLB is organized in the following way. There is a Federal Home Loan Bank Board located in Washington, D.C., which is the governing authority of the system. The Federal Home Loan Bank Board is composed of three members appointed by the President and confirmed by the Senate. The President also designates one of the members to serve as chairman, and this appointment must also be confirmed by the Senate. The advances rate and the liquidity ratio are determined by the Bank Board. There are also twelve district Federal Home Loan Banks. S&Ls do their advances borrowing and other local business with the Federal Home Loan Bank for their district. Figure 15-1 shows the Federal Home Loan Bank Districts and lists the office for each district.

Table 15-2 depicts the spread between the advances rate and the rate on large CDs, savings inflows to S&Ls, the advances rate, and the amount of advances for the period 1972–80. With the CD

Figure 15-1
Federal Home Loan Bank Districts

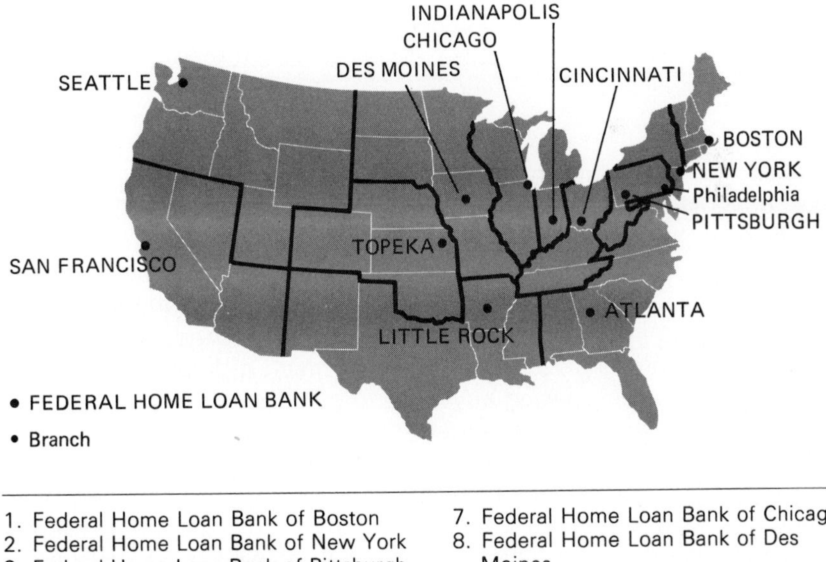

• FEDERAL HOME LOAN BANK

• Branch

1. Federal Home Loan Bank of Boston	7. Federal Home Loan Bank of Chicago
2. Federal Home Loan Bank of New York	8. Federal Home Loan Bank of Des Moines
3. Federal Home Loan Bank of Pittsburgh (Philadelphia Branch Office)	9. Federal Home Loan Bank of Little Rock
4. Federal Home Loan Bank of Atlanta	10. Federal Home Loan Bank of Topeka
5. Federal Home Loan Bank of Cincinnati	11. Federal Home Loan Bank of San Francisco
6. Federal Home Loan Bank of Indianapolis	12. Federal Home Loan Bank of Seattle

Source: Federal Home Loan Bank Board *Journal.*

Table 15-2
Net Savings Inflows to S&Ls, the FHLB Advances Rate,
the Advances Rate–CD Rate Spread, and
FHLB Advances Outstanding, 1972–80
(Millions of Dollars)

Year	Net Savings Inflows	Average Advances Rate (Percent)	Spread (in Basis Points) Between Advances Rate and Large CD Rate (Three-Month Rate)	Advances Outstanding
1972	$32,663	6.41%	+180	$ 7,979
1973	20,237	7.68	− 53	15,147
1974	16,068	8.33	−195	21,804
1975	43,121	7.81	+120	17,845
1976	50,703	7.63	+232	15,862
1977	51,016	7.64	+209	20,173
1978	44,864	8.56	+ 51	32,670
1979	39,304	9.91	−111	41,838
1980	41,417	11.23	−174	48,963

Source: Federal Home Loan Bank Board *Journal*, various issues.

rate as indicative of open-market interest rates, the table demonstrates that generally the spread between the advances rate and the CD rate declines, or becomes negative, when savings flows slow encouraging S&Ls to borrow. S&Ls typically take advantage of this by increasing their indebtedness to the FHLB accordingly. Savings inflows—as was fully discussed in Chapter 8—turn down during periods of high open-market rates, and this decrease tends to mean difficulty in mortgage lending. Thus by increasing advances, the FHLB hopes to insulate the mortgage market to some degree from the impact of tight credit, as does FNMA when it increases its purchases in the secondary market.

The FHLB must finance its advances by issuing securities in the open market. The FHLB's lending thus differs from the Fed's discount lending in that the Fed is able to make discount loans simply by increasing depository institution accounts and, therefore, bank reserves. The FHLB, like FNMA, is financing much of its activity when credit is tight, and this act puts additional pressure on the financial markets. Such an effect as raising open-market rates implies that the full extent of the assistance to the mortgage market may be less than the assistance appears. Funds that would have flowed into the S&Ls and would have been used to make mortgage loans are directed to the open market. Also similarly to FNMA, the FHLB offers securities covering the full maturity spectrum from very short maturity notes to long-term bonds and is able to finance at favorable rates as a federally sponsored agency.

The Federal Home Loan Mortgage Corporation

The Federal Home Loan Mortgage Corporation (FHLMC, often called Freddie Mac) is a subsidiary of the FHLB. The FHLMC was established in 1970 primarily to purchase conventional mortgages from S&Ls. It was pointed out above that until 1972 FNMA did not purchase conventional mortgage loans. Since S&Ls specialize in making conventional mortgage loans, this meant that there was no effective secondary market for S&Ls before the FHLMC was established. The FHLMC developed as a natural outgrowth of the FHLB's association with S&Ls. The FHLMC finances the purchase of mortgage loans by issuing securities. However, unlike FNMA (but like the Government National Mortgage Association), most mortgage purchases are not held by the FHLMC but rather pooled and sold off. These pools are purchased by large institutional investors such as life insurance companies.

Table 15-3 shows the mortgage holdings of the FHLMC from 1972 to 1980 as well as FHLMC purchases and sales for those years. FHLMC

Table 15-3
FHLMC Mortgage Holdings, Purchases, and Sales, 1972–80
(Millions of Dollars)

Year	FHLMC Mortgage Holdings (End of Period)	Purchases	Sales
1972	$1,788	$1,297	$ 407
1973	2,604	1,334	409
1974	4,586	2,190	53
1975	4,987	1,713	1,521
1976	4,269	1,127	1,797
1977	3,267	4,160	4,640
1978	3,091	6,525	6,211
1979	4,052	5,717	4,544
1980	5,056	3,722	2,526

Source: Federal Home Loan Bank Board *Journal*, July 1981.

mortgage holdings are small when compared to FNMA's holdings, but this is somewhat deceptive in assessing the importance of the FHLMC in the mortgage market. As the table shows, the FHLMC has purchased and sold substantial amounts of mortgages especially during the latter part of the 1970s and in 1980. For example, in 1980 the FHLMC purchased $3.7 billion in conventional mortgages and sold $2.5 billion.

The FHLMC announced in August 1981 that it will allow S&Ls to swap low-yielding mortgages for FHLMC participation certificates in the form of mortgage passthrough securities. The S&Ls could then take their losses on the mortgages by selling the participation certificates in the open market and thus raise funds to make higher yielding mortgage loans. These certificates are highly marketable. Until this program was announced, S&Ls were inhibited from trying to sell these mortgages because the loss that they would take would seriously reduce their net worth. However, the FHLB ruled that the loss that the S&Ls would sustain under the swap would not have to be recorded on the books of the S&Ls. Although this ruling in no way changes the fact that S&Ls will suffer losses on the swap, the FHLB ruling does allow the S&Ls to put a brighter face on the needed liquidation of some of their low-yielding mortgages because the net worth of the S&Ls would not fall. The FHLMC was expected to make $10 to $20 billion swaps in 1982. Coupled with the FNMA's purchase of low-yielding loans, this would enable S&Ls to liquidate large amounts of low-yielding mortgage loans.

The Government National Mortgage Association

In 1968, when FNMA was made a private corporation by Congress, the new FNMA was constituted to provide a secondary market for government-insured mortgages. Left behind in the newly established Government National Mortgage Association (GNMA, often called Ginnie Mae), which remained a part of the government, was the special assistance function of the old FNMA. This special assistance function relates to various government programs that are designed to aid primarily low-income individuals through mortgage and rent subsidies. The retention of this function by the federal government recognizes the exclusively public purpose presumed to be served by such subsidy programs. FNMA was expected to be self-supporting and profitable; clearly if it had to administer government subsidies, its profitability would be reduced or eliminated. Therefore GNMA was needed. GNMA's special assistance function comes in paying the difference between market rates of interest and the interest received on subsidized mortgages it has purchased and resold.

GNMA is located in the Department of Housing and Urban Development (HUD). Its formal inclusion in the federal government has given it scope to innovate in the field of home financing. GNMA was the first organization involved in the packaging of pools of mortgages for resale. This was initially done through FNMA but has now evolved into a substantial program in which mortgages packaged by GNMA are sold to institutional investors. As discussed in the section on the mortgage market in Chapter 13, the idea of mortgage pools being resold to institutional investors has grown rapidly as has the amount sold. By the end of 1980, $94 billion in GNMA-guaranteed mortgage-backed securities were outstanding. Many private mortgage issuers, like commercial banks and S&Ls, are now also packaging their own mortgages for resale. All GNMA packages consist of federally insured mortgages. This is not the case, however, with those packages issued by private institutions. They primarily contain conventional loans, as do the mortgage participation certificates issued by the FHLMC.

Table 15-4 shows the mortgage debt outstanding in the mortgage pools issued by GNMA, the FHLMC, and the Farmers Home Administration, another federal agency which deals with farm mortgages. The growth of these pools has been phenomenal. As the table shows, pools totaled $13.6 billion in 1973, virtually all GNMAs, and they had grown to $122 billion by the end of 1980, increasing by about 20 percent in 1980 alone.

The rationale behind the development of mortgage pools was to tap the national capital markets directly for mortgage funds by creating a desirable and liquid asset out of relatively illiquid mortgages. The response of private financial institutions as mortgage-backed security purchasers, reflected in the growth of these pools, shows that GNMA has been successful in accomplishing this goal. Once again, however, it should be noted that the increase in credit demands in the economy from these pools places upward pressure on interest rates, perhaps

Table 15-4
Mortgage Pools Outstanding, 1973–80
(End of Period, Millions of Dollars)

1973	$ 13,636
1974	18,639
1975	28,081
1976	42,084
1977	60,573
1978	75,789
1979	101,579
1980	121,756

Source: Federal Home Loan Bank *Journal,* various issues.

pulling funds into these pools that otherwise would have flowed into mortgages anyway. Therefore, as in the case of FHLB and FNMA assistance to the mortgage market, it is difficult to arrive at the net assistance provided by GNMA to the mortgage market in general. Nevertheless, it is clear that GNMA is directing funds into the low-income housing market that might otherwise not be available.

Other Federally Sponsored Agencies

The focus of the discussion to this point has been on the federal agencies designed to assist the mortgage market. These are the largest of the federal agencies and hence get the most attention. However, there are many other agencies that attempt to channel funds into particular sectors of the economy. Table 15-5 shows all the federally sponsored agencies and the amounts of their outstanding securities as of April 1981. (Notice that GNMA is not included because it is not a federally sponsored agency; it is an agency of the federal government.)[6] The names of the agencies themselves give a good picture of their roles and their outstanding debt is a good representation of their importance. Most of the nonmortgage market agencies[7]—the Federal Land Banks, the Federal Intermediate Credit Banks, the Bank for Cooperatives, and the Farm Credit Banks—direct their activities to channelling credit to the agricultural sector. The Federal Land Banks extend credit to farmers which is collateralized by mortgages on agricultural property. Thus, this lending is for long-term agricultural needs. Short-term agricultural credit is provided by the other agricultural credit agencies; for example, the Federal Intermediate Credit Bank provides credit to farmers to finance current production. In January 1979, the Farm Credit Banks began issuing consolidated bonds on a regular basis to replace the financing activities of the Federal Land Banks, the Federal Intermediate Credit Banks, and the Banks for Cooperatives. This issuance accounts for the substantial amount of debt outstanding for this one agency, because it is really raising funds not only for itself but for the other agricultural agencies as well. The Student Loan Marketing Association (Sallie Mae) assists lending to college students.

The total amount of debt outstanding by the federally sponsored agencies taken together has become substantially significant in the marketplace. As Table 15-5 shows, by April 1981, the debt of federally sponsored agencies exceeded $170 billion. For comparison, at the

---

[6] Another agency that is also part of the federal government is often included in analyzing federally sponsored agencies because of its similarity to sponsored agencies. This is the Export–Import Bank. The Export–Import bank provides financing for international trade.

[7] Actually designating these agencies as "nonmortgage market," while commonly done, is somewhat misleading since farms are often used as collateral for the loans made.

Table 15-5
Debt Outstanding of Federally Sponsored Agencies, April 1981
(End of Period, Millions of Dollars)

Agency	Amount
Federal Home Loan Banks	$ 44,357
Federal Home Loan Mortgage Corporation	2,409
Federal National Mortgage Association	54,183
Federal Land Banks	10,583
Federal Intermediate Credit Banks	1,388
Banks for Cooperatives	220
Farm Credit Banks	54,345
Student Loan Marketing Association	3,445
Total	$170,930

Source: Federal Reserve *Bulletin*, July 1981.

end of 1976 debt was about $81 billion. The large increase in outstanding agency securities in recent years has had a substantial impact upon the financial markets as has been suggested throughout the discussion of this chapter. Before turning to an examination of that impact, however, it is necessary for completeness to discuss the Federal Financing Bank.

The Federal Financing Bank

The focus of this chapter has been on the **federally sponsored** agencies with the exception of GNMA, which is a **federal agency,** part of the U.S. government. The sponsored agencies have important impacts upon the sectors of the economy that they are designed to assist as well as on the financial markets. However, there are a large number of federal agencies spread throughout the federal government, such as the Rural Electrification Administration and the Export–Import Bank, which also have in the past borrowed directly in the financial markets. In 1973, the Federal Financing Bank (FFB) was established to coordinate and assist federal agency borrowing. The FFB is wholly owned by the government and housed in the Treasury department. Federally sponsored agencies are excluded from borrowing from the FFB (with the exception of the Student Loan Marketing Association). The intention in establishing the FFB was to have federal agencies borrow from the FFB and the FFB borrow in the open market to finance the loans to the agencies. Thus, instead of a large number of small agencies borrowing, only periodic financing by the FFB would be necessary. However, the FFB was also permitted to borrow from the Treasury. After selling one security issue in the open market in the early days of the FFB and receiving a rate the FFB considered too high, the FFB has borrowed exclusively from the U.S. Treasury. In 1975, this became a formal policy of the FFB. The Treasury in turn must issue additional debt to finance FFB borrowing.

While the FFB, therefore, has brought coordination to small agency borrowing, it has added substantially to the Treasury's financing requirements, something that was not expected when the FFB was created. The agencies borrowing from the FFB have benefitted by lower rates; the FFB charges the agencies only one-eighth of a percent above what it pays the Treasury, and it pays the Treasury only slightly more than the Treasury is paying for its funds. Besides the lower rates the FFB pays the Treasury, another advantage of borrowing from the Treasury rather than going directly to the market is that the amount the FFB can borrow from the Treasury is practically unlimited. As a result, the Federal Financing Bank had total debt of $96.5 billion outstanding in April 1981, almost all borrowed from the Treasury. The rapid growth of FFB debt is apparent when it is compared to the $28.7 billion in FFB debt at the end of 1976, less than five years before. The growth in FFB debt would not have been possible, under present law, if it had borrowed directly from the public, since the limit on FFB direct public borrowing is $15 billion.[8]

The Impact of Federally Sponsored Agency Financing on the Financial Markets

Federally sponsored agencies finance their activities across all maturity categories as has been pointed out. Their securities are held by many financial institutions including commercial banks. Prior to the 1970s, agency debt was a relatively small factor in the financial markets. However, the rapid acceleration in the 1970s in agency financing—particularly in the last half of the decade—and its continuation in the 1980s has meant that large amounts of securities of these agencies have been offered in the open market with consequent important effects. As was indicated previously, there is likely to have been an impact on interest rates, especially when the fact is recalled that the mortgage

---

[8] The activities of the FFB have raised a number of important issues concerning the provision of credit by the government. For a complete analysis of the FFB, see "The Federal Financing Bank: A Primer," in *Loan Guarantees: Current Concerns and Alternatives for Control,* the Congressional Budget Office of the Congress of the United States (Washington, D.C.: GPO, 1979), pp. 111–40.

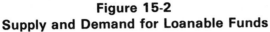

Figure 15-2
Supply and Demand for Loanable Funds

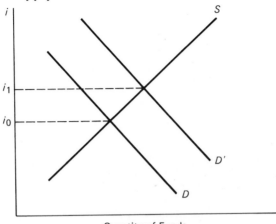

Quantity of Funds

agencies are issuing most of their securities during periods when the mortgage market is most in need of assistance. Such periods typically coincide with tight credit conditions that are associated with high and rising interest rates and excess demands for credit. The impact on interest rates of agency financing can be analyzed in the very simple supply and demand framework shown in Figure 15-2. The demand curve is demand for loanable funds, while the supply curve is the supply of loanable funds. The interest rate is the market rate of interest. All else being equal, the increase in the demand for funds by agencies, indicated by the shift in the demand for funds to D', as occurred in the 1970s and early 1980s, will raise the rate of interest.[9]

Throughout the discussion of federal mortgage market agencies such as FNMA, we noted that the impact of their operations in channel-

---

[9] The use of the term "the interest rate" follows the explanation presented in Chapter 4. If the rate used was the rate on agency securities, however, through the relationship among rates explained in Chapter 4, it is easy to see that the entire level of interest rates would rise. Thus nothing is lost by the simplifying assumption. There is also an implicit assumption made in the analysis that agency financing is a net addition to the demand for funds. However, it is certainly possible that some financing currently done by agencies would be done by private borrowers in the absence of agency assistance. For example, if FNMA did not purchase mortgages from mortgage bankers, financed in the open market, mortgage bankers would still attempt to sell mortgages in the open market, perhaps in pools. Consideration of this fact does not negate the analysis of Figure 15-2, but it may modify the extent to which interest rates are affected by agency financing. In terms of Figure 15-2, the demand curve may not shift out as far if agencies did not finance in the open market, but it still would be likely to shift outward.

ling funds to the mortgage market may be less than that indicated by the gross amount of their activity. The reason for this comes from considering the result of Figure 15-2 and recalling the previous discussion of disintermediation. In that discussion it was pointed out that deposits at traditional mortgage lenders, such as S&Ls, are sensitive to open-market rates. When the open-market rate rises above deposit rates, savings flow out and reduce the amount of funds these institutions have available for possible mortgage lending. Therefore, to the extent agency financing puts upward pressure on interest rates, this may *induce* additional disintermediation from traditional mortgage lenders. The agencies then take the funds raised and channel these funds back to the mortgage market. However, the increase in disintermediation that results from the impact on interest rates of agency financing of their activities must be deducted from the gross assistance that the agencies provide to the mortgage market. What the resulting net amount is has been the subject of dispute. For example, one analyst argues that for every billion dollars in mortgages purchased FNMA provides net assistance of $600 million.[10] Others have come up with different results.[11] To arrive at a definite answer is quite complicated and has not been accomplished. Recognition that this problem exists, however, is important. Further, although most attention has been focused on the mortgage market, similar arguments may be advanced for the agencies providing agricultural assistance. However, the possible channels in which the gross amount of their assistance may be reduced by the impact of their financing on the financial markets is not as clear as it is in the case of the mortgage market agencies.

Additionally, it should be noted, there is no guarantee that all funds provided to the mortgage market by federal mortgage market agencies will be utilized to make new mortgage loans. For example, although S&Ls have had limited options for the use of their funds in ways other than mortgage lending, that is changing. To the extent that the S&Ls sell mortgages in the secondary market to FNMA or to the FHLMC or increase the amount of their advances borrowing from the FHLB and then use these funds to acquire income-earning assets other than mortgages, the purpose of the federally sponsored agency assistance is circumvented. This possibility may further reduce the net assistance that the federally sponsored mortgage agencies provide to the mortgage market.

Federal Agencies as Financial Intermediaries

There has been some controversy among economists about whether federally sponsored agencies are financial intermediaries and thus federally sponsored competitors to private financial intermediaries. It has

---

[10] See the article by Craig Swan cited earlier.
[11] For example, see the article by Leo Grebler cited earlier.

been discussed before that a financial intermediary acquires obligation against ultimate borrowers and issues obligation to ultimate savers. From the discussion of federal agencies it is clear that depending on how literally this definition is interpreted, it could be stretched to include institutions like FNMA. FNMA acquires obligation indirectly against ultimate borrowers since it buys mortgages from mortgage originators. However, unlike financial intermediaries dealing in the mortgage market, it does not make mortgage loans directly. Further, it issues obligations against itself that are not purchased for the most part by ultimate savers in the economy but by institutions, in many cases financial intermediaries. Thus, FNMA's intermediary role is an indirect one. This is equally true of the FHLMC and other federally sponsored agencies.

The importance of the debate over whether federally sponsored agencies are intermediaries stems from the fact that these agencies have been established by the federal government. If they are financial intermediaries, then they are presumably competing against other financial intermediaries that they are designed to help. Further, these agencies would enjoy an unfair competitive advantage because their status as federally sponsored agencies allows them to raise funds in the open market at favorable rates.

The argument that federally sponsored agencies are financial intermediaries is related to the discussion in the last section. If federally sponsored agencies are intermediaries that compete with private financial intermediaries, their complete role in the financial system requires extensive analysis to determine their full impact in the financial markets and on financial intermediaries. Only when the complete role of the federally sponsored agencies is understood, can an assessment of their effectiveness be made. Because the federally sponsored agencies are a major way that the federal government has chosen to channel credit to particular sectors of the economy, this assessment is very important. However, a complete assessment cannot be made on strictly theoretical grounds. Additional empirical analysis to better evaluate the impact of Federally sponsored agencies on the financial system is required.

Federal Loan Guarantees

To this point, the chapter has been concerned primarily with the activities and impact of federally sponsored agencies. Their operations are generally categorized as composing part of a wider subject of study, the provision of credit by the federal government; and, the other major aspect of this subject is the providing of loan and security guarantees. Federal guarantees that change the characteristics of loans and securities have an impact upon the credit markets and the allocation of credit in the economy. Thus, it is useful to explore this growing area of federal credit.

Federal government guarantees of private obligations make them more attractive for lenders and enable borrowers to obtain credit that they otherwise might be unable to obtain. Lenders are attracted to guaranteed obligations, despite their generally lower yields, because the guarantees ensure their safety. Borrowers obtain credit at lower rates than they otherwise would have had to pay assuming they could have obtained credit at all. The most dramatic recent examples of major guarantee programs are the guarantees by the government of the securities of New York City and the Chrysler Corporation. While the decisions to guarantee securities of these issuers were dramatic, loan guarantees have existed since the 1930s. Billions of dollars in home mortgage loans (FHA and VA), farm mortgage loans, and other loans in specific areas have been guaranteed. However, in the 1970s, there was a rapid acceleration in the amount and type of obligations guaranteed. By the end of 1980, government loan and security guarantees exceeded $300 billion. Further, the composition of loan and security guarantees altered in the 1970s. Until then, the overwhelming amount of guarantees were utilized for housing. For example, in 1950, 97 percent of guarantees made in that year were for housing (principally FHA loans). By 1979, however, housing guarantees—while they had grown in absolute amount—had declined as a percentage of new federal guarantees to about 66 percent, with the remaining guarantees spread among numerous programs including the Chrysler programs, as well as programs designed to aid international trade, small business, and agriculture.

There are a number of concerns raised by the rapid acceleration of federal guarantees. First, the government is technically responsible, in the event of default, for these obligations. Some guarantee programs are actuarially sound, which means that the insurance premium the borrower pays is supposed to allow for some default. The FHA mortgage program is an example of an actuarially sound guarantee program; fees charged by the FHA are expected to cover an anticipated number of defaults. However, many guarantee programs are not actuarially sound. In any case, the federal government is ultimately responsible in the event of any defaults. Guarantees, exceeding $300 billion and still growing, are a significant contingent liability for the government. Second, and perhaps more important from the perspective of this book, the government guarantees—particularly of securities sold in the open market—alter the characteristics of these securities and therefore the allocation of credit in the economy. By guaranteeing securities, the federal government is ensuring funding to areas that funds may not have flowed to without the guarantees. Thus, decisions that would have been made by the market not to grant credit to particular activities are subverted. For example, it is clear that the Chrysler Corporation would not have been able to borrow funds in 1979 and 1980 without government guarantees. Because economists assume that the market will make decisions to fund the most economically viable of undertakings, thus ensuring that the most economically efficient projects are pursued, the existence of guarantees may draw funds away from these projects to those that might be considered less desirable to the economy as a whole. Further, potentially increasing the demand for funds in the market (as when a guaranteed borrower who may not have even tried to borrow without the guarantee now comes to the market) may raise interest rates significantly in the market, forcing what would otherwise be economically viable borrowers out or raising their cost of borrowing substantially.

These economic consequences of the large growth of government guaranteed loans and securities are just now being considered by government officials. Until now the attractiveness of guarantees to Congress and various administrations tended to overshadow general financial and economic factors, even when these were considered. The attractiveness of guarantees to the government arises since no funds need to be appropriated by the federal government in providing guarantees. The guaranteed loans and securities are financed in the financial markets. Thus, the government can support politically popular areas with guarantees without altering the federal budget. Only in the event of default on the guaranteed obligations will the federal budget be affected.[12] However, recently the government has begun to address the economic consequences of the guarantee programs and additional study is likely in the future.[13]

---

[12] There is, however, some small amount of administrative costs for some programs. Furthermore, it should be recalled that the Federal Financing Bank has been purchasing substantial amounts of guaranteed loans and securities. Since the FFB borrows its funds from the U.S. Treasury, which in turn issues securities to raise these funds, guarantees may serve to increase the amount of Treasury debt outstanding even though they don't affect the size of the Treasury deficit.

[13] See the previously cited study by the Congressional Budget Office "Loan Guarantees: Current Concerns and Alternatives for Control," and Congressional Budget Office, Proceedings of a *Conference on the Economics of Federal Credit Activity* (Washington, D.C.: GPO, 1981).

MORTGAGE AGENCIES EXPAND THEIR ACTIVITIES

Freddie Mac and Fannie Mae Each Offer To Pick Up S&L's Low-Yield Mortgages

WASHINGTON—Used mortgages, anyone?

Freddie Mac and Fannie Mae are both offering to take old, low-yielding loans off the hands of savings and loan associations.

Freddie Mac—the Federal Home Loan Mortgage Corp.—said it will allow S&Ls to swap such mortgages for mortgage-backed securities that can be more readily converted into cash.

Fannie Mae—the Federal National Mortgage Association—said that if proposed regulatory changes go through it will pay cash for old mortgages.

For both Fannie Mae and Freddie Mac, the old mortgages represent potential profits.

Freddie Mac is practically guaranteed a profit on each old mortgage it swaps, because it will pay the S&L slightly less principal and interest than it receives from the person paying off the old mortgages.

Fannie Mae would use the old mortgages to upgrade its portfolio, which currently is yielding much less than current market rates.

Freddie Mac, a government-run corporation owned by the S&L industry, already has swapped $461 million of its pass-through certificates for old mortgages. Officials said its test marketing of the program showed a strong demand for the swaps, even though S&Ls must accept yields that are ¼ percentage point to ⅜ percentage point below the yields on the mortgages.

S&Ls find the pass-through certificates attractive because of their liquidity. Also, Freddie Mac said it had obtained a regulatory interpretation from the Federal Home Loan Bank Board that allows many S&Ls to make such swaps without recording the loss on their books, even though the new securities have a much lower market value than the face amount of the exchanged mortgages.

Last week, the bank board proposed to go even further and let many S&Ls sell old mortgages for cash and spread the resulting loss over many years. Generally accepted accounting principles require that such losses be accounted for immediately. Fannie Mae, the financial giant that already owns one mortgage in every 20, said that if that proposal takes effect the company will offer to buy unlimited quantities of old mortgages at market prices.

Currently, S&Ls are inhibited from cashing in old, low-yielding mortgages because recording the full loss would seriously deplete their net worth at a time when the industry is already suffering record losses on current operations.

Fannie Mae's chief executive officer, David Maxwell, said the company already is developing procedures for purchasing old mortgages, although it will be at least a month before the regulatory change becomes final.

Freddie Mac's swap program will move from the test phase to a full-scale national program sometime next month, corporation officials said. It expects to swap $2 billion more in mortgages this year and will have the capability to swap $10 billion to $20 billion next year, officials said.

Freddie Mac's swaps are mainly for S&Ls, the corporation's principal customers, but officials said other qualified lenders could participate.

Key Points

1. Federally sponsored agencies are organizations that are chartered by the federal government to serve a public purpose, such as assisting the mortgage market. These agencies are privately owned but retain a relationship to the federal government in a number of ways including the availability of lines of credit at the U.S. Treasury. The most important of these agencies are The Federal National Mortgage Association and the Federal Home Loan Bank System.

2. The Federal National Mortgage Association provides assistance to the mortgage market by purchasing government-insured and conventional mortgages after making purchase commitments through an auction process. FNMA currently owns almost 5 percent of all mortgages outstanding. The Federal Home Loan Bank System provides assistance to the mortgage market through its advances programs, which provide funds to the largest mortgage lenders, savings and loan associations. A subsidiary of the FHLB, the Federal Home Loan Mortgage Corporation purchases mortgages from S&Ls, pools these mortgages, and resells them in the capital markets. Other federally sponsored agencies provide agricultural credit and student loan assistance.

3. The Government National Mortgage Association, which is a federal agency, a part of the government, originated the passthrough mortgage security. It has sponsored most of the passthrough mortgage securities currently outstanding. The Federal Financing Bank, part of the Treasury, coordinates borrowing by federal agencies and provides funding for these agencies through borrowing from the Treasury. Federally sponsored agencies are generally not permitted to borrow at the FFB.

4. There is a question about the net assistance provided by federally sponsored agencies, particularly the mortgage market agencies. Since virtually all agency assistance must be financed in the open market, upward pressure is put on interest rates, which induces disintermediation from traditional mortgage lenders. To the extent this happens, the gross amount of agency assistance to the market will be reduced.

5. Federal loan and securities guarantees are a growing part of the provision of federal credit to the economy. The U.S. Congress and President have found guarantees an attractive way of providing credit to various sectors of the economy since, for the most part, guarantees have no impact upon the federal budget. However, they do have an impact on the financial markets, altering the allocation of credit in the economy.

Questions for Discussion

1. Some economists argue that the amount of assistance provided by federally sponsored agencies is less than the gross amount of their activities. How can this be the case? Analyze.

2. Distinguish between a federally sponsored agency and a federal agency. The Government National Mortgage Association, a federal agency, and the Federal Home Loan Mortgage Corporation, a federally sponsored agency, both issue passthrough mortgage securities. What then distinguishes the operations of these two agencies?

3. Why have loan and securities guarantees proved so popular with various administrations and the U.S. Congress in recent years? What is the impact of the growth of federal guarantees on the financial markets?

4. Why do some argue that federally sponsored agencies are simply financial intermediaries and thus are unfairly competing with private financial intermediaries?

5. The Federal Home Loan Bank System provides indirect assistance to the mortgage market. Why is this assistance considered indirect and what can interfere with the assistance provided from actually reaching the market?

6. The Federal National Mortgage Association makes commitments to purchase mortgages through an auction process. How does this auction process work?

Suggested Readings

Congressional Budget Office of the U.S. Congress. *Federal Credit Activities: An Analysis of the President's Credit Budget for 1981.* Staff Working Paper, Feb. 1980.

Congressional Budget Office of the U.S. Congress. Proceedings of the *Conference on the Economics of Federal Credit Activity.* Washington, D.C.: GPO, 1981.

Pollock, Stephen H. "Off-Budget Federal Outlays." Federal Reserve Bank of Kansas City *Economic Review,* March 1981, pp. 3–15.

Schwartz, Harry S. "The Role of Government-Sponsored Intermediaries in the Mortgage Market." Federal Reserve Bank of Boston, Conference on *Housing and Monetary Policy,* Conference Series No. 4, Oct. 1970, pp. 68–85.

Sivesind, Charles M. "Mortgage-Backed Securities: The Revolution in Real Estate Financing." Federal Reserve Bank of New York *Quarterly Review,* Autumn 1979, pp. 1–10.

U.S. Office of Management and Budget. Special Analysis *Federal Credit Programs,* issued yearly as part of the U.S. Budget. Washington, D.C.: GPO.

The Role of Regulation and Innovation in the Financial System

16

The process of development for the financial system has involved the interplay of regulatory and legislative changes, economic changes, and financial innovation. We have discussed how the financial system has responded to particular regulatory changes or to existing regulation when the economic environment has changed. In this chapter, this process will be investigated in detail.

Innovation is defined as (1) "the introduction of something new" and (2) "a new idea, method, or device."[1] In the financial context, one observer has defined innovation as "changes in techniques, institutions, or operating policies that have the effect of altering the way the industry functions."[2] Many of these changes have occurred in response to regulations that have been placed on the system by regulatory bodies or through legislative changes. Regulation imposes constraints on the financial institutions and financial institutions respond as other firms do to constraints by attempting to reduce the impact of these constraints on their profitability.[3] Thus financial institutions innovate. The financial institution maximizes some objective, such as profit, subject to constraints imposed by regulation and the economic environment. Despite the straightforward statement of the problem, however, the actual process through which innovation occurs is rather complex.

The interaction between regulations, the economic environment,

---

[1] *Webster's New Collegiate Dictionary,* 1977 ed.

[2] Tilford C. Gaines, "Financial Innovations and the Efficiency of Federal Reserve Policy," in *Monetary Process and Policy,* George Horwich, ed. (Homewood, Ill.: Richard D. Irwin, 1967), pp. 99–118.

[3] William L. Silber, "Towards a Theory of Financial Innovation," in his *Financial Innovation* (Lexington, Mass.: Lexington Books, 1975), pp. 64–65.

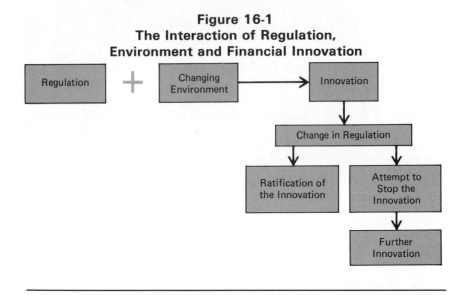

Figure 16-1
The Interaction of Regulation,
Environment and Financial Innovation

and financial innovation may be summarized by the schematic diagram of Figure 16-1. The diagram shows that when a regulation that is in place is coupled with the catalyst of a changing economic environment—for example, higher interest rates—financial innovation may occur. This innovation is often met by regulatory changes that may be of one of two types. Regulatory change may take place that ratifies the innovation. On the other hand, regulation may be changed to attempt to control or extinguish the financial innovation. Such a regulatory response may simply lead to further financial system innovation if the incentive is sufficient. Examples of both types of regulatory change in response to financial innovation and their results will be presented below.

The Development of the Financial System and Regulation

The development of the financial system over the past few decades has been substantial. Savings and loan associations have grown rapidly in the post–World War II period; credit unions, a very small part of financial intermediaries in 1950, are now a substantial force in consumer lending. New financial instruments, such as negotiable certificates of deposit and Eurodollar loans, are a product of the 1960s and 1970s. Much of this financial system development was a response to the changing financial needs of the economy. However, much change and innovation in the financial system was a response to existing regulations when economic conditions changed. For example, prior to 1966, Regulation Q ceilings, which have existed since the early 1930s, did not affect time deposit rates because these rates were generally well below Regulation Q ceilings. However, following 1966, these ceilings did affect time deposits and banks, and thrift institutions gradually evolved new instruments to avoid these ceilings. Such innovation was, in fact, sometimes aided by the regulators who recognized the necessity for changes. For example, the 1973 suspension of Regulation Q on all large certificates of deposit allowed banks to offer competitive open-market rates to retain existing large deposits as well as to attract additional funds.[4] Sometimes new financial instruments simply grew up around existing regulations despite attempts by regulatory agencies to circumscribe such development. An example of such an innovation is offshore banking and its contribution to the growth in the Eurodollar market. The imposition by the Federal Reserve of reserve requirements on Eurodollar borrowings by banks in 1969 temporarily limited domestic bank use of this market. Banks, however, rapidly developed other sources of funds as a result. For example, the imposition of reserve requirements on Eurodollars along with the prohibition of interest payments on demand deposits contributed to the rapid expansion in the market for bank repurchase agreements (RPs) as banks sought additional sources of funds.

The contribution to the development of the market for RPs provided by a regulatory change that was imposed on another instrument demonstrates very well the interaction of regulation and innovation in the financial system. Regulation in as fluid a system as the financial system acts in the same way as attempts to plug holes in a weakened dike. If one hole is plugged, increased pressure is placed on other parts of the dike leading to additional holes that are in turn plugged and so on. The financial system has the capability to innovate successfully around most regulation when changed economic conditions makes such innovation profitable. The question then becomes why place additional regulations on the system since resources are then expanded to circumvent these regulations. Presumably these regulations are imposed because it is believed they will be of overall benefit to the financial system and the economy. Often, however, the implications of these regulations are not fully appreciated at the time of their imposition.

Many economists have argued that various existing regulations should be eliminated. For example, it has been pointed out previously

---

[4] Ceilings on large CDs between 30–89 days to maturity had been suspended in 1970. All maturity large CDs were included in the 1973 suspension.

that many economists consider Regulation Q ceilings to be discriminatory against small savers. Further, the original rationale behind Regulation Q ceilings, which was to prevent financial institutions from "recklessly" competing against each other, has ceased to have much credibility as new ways to compete have been found. In fact, many of the financial reforms recommended by study commissions in the 1970s favored increased competition. In the case of Regulation Q ceilings, regulators implicitly recognized the desirability of reducing the effect of this regulation by authorizing money market and note rate certificates that move with open-market interest rates and by suspending Regulation Q ceilings on large CDs. This is but one example in which the movement toward less regulation has occurred in recent years.

In 1980, the Depository Institutions Deregulation and Monetary Control Act (DIDMCA) was signed into law. This legislation mandates sweeping changes in the regulations governing the financial system, including the elimination of Regulation Q ceilings. These changes will be completed in the first half of the 1980s; however, additional changes are likely even before DIDMCA fully takes effect. The process of regulatory change has accelerated and the momentum appears well established. To place the most recent changes in perspective, however, it is useful to examine in detail the interplay of financial system development and regulation by focusing on bank and nonbank financial intermediaries. DIDMCA will be explicitly discussed later in the chapter.

Bank Innovation in Response to Regulation

Many of the major changes in bank behavior can be traced to an attempt by banks to circumvent regulations issued either by Congress or the Federal Reserve System. When these regulations become hindersome to banks in particular periods because of changes in the economic environment or intensified competition from other parts of the financial system, banks have acted. Table 16-1 lists some selective bank innovations from 1960 to 1981 and attempts to assign the major reason or reasons for the innovation as examples of innovative response to regulation.[5] To fully understand this table, we must also understand the economic context, not just the regulation or regulations that are credited with bringing about the innovation. For example, in Table 16-1 the reason ascribed for the development of bank RPs is

---

[5] The idea and some elements of this table come from a similar table in William Silber, "Towards a Theory of Financial Innovation," in his *Financial Innovation* (Lexington, Mass.: Lexington Books, 1975), pp. 53–85. Note that there may be other reasons why an innovation took place. This table merely suggests the main regulatory reasons.

Table 16-1
Selected Bank Innovations and the Major Regulatory Impetus, 1960–81

Innovation	Regulatory Contributions to the Development of the Innovation
1. Negotiable CDs (1961)	Rate regulation
2. Eurodollars (1966)	Rate regulation, reserve requirements
3. Repurchase agreements (1969)	Rate regulation, reserve requirements, ban on banks borrowing directly from business
4. Loan production offices, finance company subsidiaries of major banks (1970s)	McFadden Act ban on interstate banking
5. Money market certificates (1978)	Rate regulation, assisted by change in regulation
6. Automatic transfer accounts (1978)	Rate regulation, assisted by change in regulation
7. NOW accounts, nationwide interest-earning transactions accounts (1981)	Rate regulation (DIDMCA permitted change)

rate regulation, in this case the prohibition on interest payments on demand deposits. But interest had been prohibited since the Banking Act of 1933. Why did RPs not develop before? The basic reason was that as interest rates rose in the 1960s and 1970s and corporate cash managers became more sophisticated, these cash managers recognized the increasing opportunity cost of holding noninterest-earning demand deposits. For banks to retain these deposits, it was necessary for them to innovate a solution. One solution was the RP. When interest rates were low, cash managers focused less attention on these lost earnings since the opportunity cost simply was not high enough to be significant (and also sophisticated tools of cash management employing computer technology were not fully developed).[6] The economic context of innovation will be discussed further below.

Most of the innovations indicated in Table 16-1 resulted from rate regulation, either Regulation Q ceilings or the prohibition of interest

---

[6] Theoretically the return from an activity should at least equal its costs. In this context, the low opportunity cost (potential return) from minimizing cash balances was not sufficient to compensate for the cost involved in managing these balances carefully at the margin. This does not imply that the cash manager was oblivious to potential profit opportunities when cash balance holdings were large.

payments on demand deposits. Further, reserve requirements set by the Fed have been responsible for much of the changes in bank behavior. Finally, other restrictions, such as the prohibition of banks borrowing directly from corporations and the ban on interstate banking, have also caused the development of a number of changes in bank behavior. It is interesting to note that many of these changes could not have taken place without the explicit or tacit permission of the regulators themselves. The limited spread of NOW accounts prior to the passage of DIDMCA in 1980 would not have been possible without regulator and legislative approval. Thus in a curious way, the regulators have shown considerable ambivalence about some of the consequences of their regulations.

The other major point to note is that many major bank innovations have occurred in the 1960s and 1970s, the time frame of the table. This is certainly not coincidental and has occurred in large part because of the changing nature of the economic environment.

The Economic Context of Bank Innovation

It was pointed out above that to be fully understood bank innovation in response to regulation must be placed in the context of what was occurring in the economy at the time. That is, it is not only the case that banks may respond to a new regulation by innovation, but they may also respond to an existing regulation that had not previously induced any alteration in bank behavior because the environment had changed. For example, as was noted above, the context in which bank innovation took place in the 1960s and 1970s was one of high interest rates. Robert Eisenbeis, a researcher in the field, has put this into perspective in discussing Regulation Q ceilings: "Whenever interest rates have risen above the ceiling rates, depository institutions have innovated new instruments and institutions or have developed new sources of funds in an attempt to pay market rates and keep their deposits."[7]

The rise in interest rates in the 1960s and 1970s increased the opportunity cost of funds both to the banks and to the nonbank public. This meant not only that Regulation Q ceilings became a problem to the banking system but that reserve requirements, which forced banks to keep funds in noninterest-earning accounts at the Fed, and the inability to pay explicit interest on demand deposit accounts also interfered with bank activities. One response to the joint set of regulations has been that banks turned to raising funds through borrowings and time deposits as opposed to demand deposits. The data clearly demonstrate this behavior. In 1950, about 70 percent of bank liabilities and

---

[7] Robert A. Eisenbeis, "Financial Innovation and the Growth of Bank Holding Companies," in *Bank Structure and Regulation,* Federal Reserve Bank of Chicago, Proceedings from a Conference (April 27–28, 1978), p. 14.

capital were in the form of demand deposits; by July 1981, this percentage had declined to almost 20 percent. From the banks' point of view, time deposits allow more active competition for funds against open-market instruments, especially since the suspension of Regulation Q ceilings on large certificates of deposit (CDs over $100,000) in 1973. Further, the reserve requirement on time deposits is considerably lower than on demand deposits. Borrowings usually carry no reserve requirement[8] and, with the widespread development of the nonbank repurchase market since 1970, allow the bank to retain funds of large depositors by converting demand deposits into RPs. Thus the bank is able to pay a return on what are, for all intents and purposes, transaction accounts. Maturities of RPs are usually overnight or if longer are tailored explicitly to the transactions needs of the depositor.

The RP market illustrates an important aspect of bank innovative behavior. Some of this behavior is a response by banks to the demands of bank customers for additional returns on their funds. The alternative to the bank of not meeting this demand is the loss of deposits because corporate cash managers have become extremely conscious of their interest-earning alternatives. Further, the fact that banks are aggressive liability managers under conditions of high interest rates complements their desire to service their customers. The response of banks in issuing RPs can be traced to the implicit prohibition of interest payments on demand deposits, which has necessitated this type of innovation.[9]

Banks have acted as well to avoid the McFadden Act of 1927, which prohibited interstate banking. In part this response was induced by the higher interest rate environment and in part by the competitive advantage enjoyed by U.S. branches of foreign banks. This advantage was reduced but not eliminated by the International Banking Act of 1978, which was discussed in detail in Chapter 5.

The International Banking Act (IBA), however, is evidence that the regulatory process does respond to new situations. The decline in the value of the dollar in the late 1970s and the perceived good business climate in the United States led to rapid expansion by foreign banks in the United States. As a result, pressures mounted to restrict foreign bank activity by additional regulation. These pressures led to passage of the International Banking Act. But the act did not go all the way to remove the competitive advantage enjoyed by foreign banks. For example, foreign banks can still retain offices in more than

---

[8] The Fed temporarily imposed a reserve requirement on "managed liabilities" in March 1980, but this was removed three months later.

[9] The Depository Institutions Deregulation and Monetary Control Act, by continuing the prohibition on the payment of interest on demand deposits and allowing only individuals and nonprofit corporations to hold interest-earning transactions accounts, will not alter the attempt by banks to pay corporations and others a competitive rate on their demand deposit accounts through such devices as RPs and the provision of bank services.

one state. One of the reasons the act was less than complete in eliminating foreign bank competitive advantages was that large U.S. banks with international interests argued for some restraint in the act for fear of retaliatory action by foreign countries against U.S. bank subsidiaries. However, additional action has been taken to bring foreign banks in line with domestic U.S. banks since the IBA was enacted. Foreign banks, like all depository institutions, now have to maintain reserves on their deposits.

Another response to high reserve requirements and interest rate ceilings as well as to high federal and state tax rates has been the development of offshore banking, a part of the Eurodollar market. It is estimated that in 1981 Eurodollar deposits exceeded $1 trillion. The rapid growth of the Eurodollar market has prompted proposals to extend reserve requirements internationally in an attempt to control this market. Because the proposals require a great deal of international cooperation (and not all major countries are in favor of such implementation)[10] it is unlikely that they will be implemented any time soon.

The discussion in this chapter to this point has only touched upon a few aspects of bank innovative behavior in the context of economic changes. From this discussion, however, and the preceding discussion of bank innovation in response to regulation, it should be clear that regulation itself may not lead to innovation, but the combination of regulation and changes in the economic environment can and often has led to important changes in the banking system. Further, this combination is also apparent in considering changes in the behavior of other financial institutions.

Nonbank Financial Institutions, Regulation, and Innovation

Table 16-2 lists some selected major changes in nonbank financial institution behavior in response to regulation and to changes in the economic environment for the period 1970–81. This period was one of extraordinary change for the nonbank financial intermediaries. This table and Table 16-1 (p. 405) overlap to some degree because a number of changes that affected commercial banks also affected the nonbanks. For example, the advent of money market certificates was an important development for both bank and nonbank institutions. However, a number of changes occurred that had the most impact upon nonbanks. The development of NOW accounts, for example, was initiated by mutual savings banks; NOW accounts were invented in re-

---

[10] Great Britain and Switzerland, whose financial institutions play a large role in the Eurodollar market, have expressed opposition.

Table 16-2
Selected Nonbank Innovations and the Major Regulatory Impetus, 1970–81

Innovation	Regulatory Contributions to the Development of the Innovation
1. Preauthorized transfers from savings accounts to third parties (1970)	Rate regulation
2. NOW accounts offered in Massachusetts and New Hampshire (1972)	Prohibition on the offering of demand deposits by thrift institutions; rate regulation
3. Selected Extension of NOW accounts and similar transactions accounts to certain states and institutions (1970s)	Rate regulation
4. Money market mutual funds (1974)	Rate regulation effect on thrift institutions
5. California state-chartered S&Ls permitted to offer VRMs (1975)	Change in regulation due to pressure from institutions to offer a new instrument
6. Money market certificate (1978)	Rate regulation, assisted by change in regulation
7. Nationwide extension of VRMs at federally chartered S&Ls (1979)	Rate regulation, assisted by change in regulation
8. Nationwide permission for federally chartered S&Ls to offer renegotiable or rollover mortgages (RRMs) without also offering a fixed rate option (1980)	Rate regulation, assisted by change in regulation
9. Nationwide NOW accounts, etc. (1981)	Rate Regulation (DIDMCA permitted change)

sponse to the prohibition on thrift institutions issuing demand deposits and the prohibition of the payment of interest on demand deposits. With the passage of DIDMCA in 1980, NOW accounts were extended nationwide beginning in 1981. If the thrift institutions had not introduced NOW accounts, it is possible that regulators would not have responded and that nationwide payment of interest on transactions accounts could have taken even longer to develop.

The dramatic changes in thrift institution liabilities are being matched on the asset side of thrift institution balance sheets. An environment of rising open-market interest rates and increasing costs of raising funds for thrift institutions made it increasingly hard to justify fixed rate mortgages, traditionally the largest thrift institution asset. Pressure for variable rate mortgages (VRMs) intensified as money market certificates, which were tied to open-market rates, began to represent a very significant portion of thrift institution funds. In the mid-1970s, some state-chartered savings and loans, most notably in California, sought and received permission to offer VRMs. The Federal Home Loan Bank System extended VRM authority to federally chartered institutions in the latter part of the 1970s and has continued to widen the authority of S&Ls to offer VRMs. For example, in 1980 the FHLB authorized the issuance of "rollover mortgages," a type of VRM in which interest changes are renegotiated at periodic intervals without the necessity, as existed with previous VRMs, for S&Ls to also make available a fixed rate mortgage as an alternative. While it is too early to predict the demise of the fixed rate mortgage, it does appear that there is now a considered and well established trend toward the VRM.

The allowance by the FHLB of rollover mortgages demonstrates another aspect of the interplay between the regulator, regulations, and the financial system. Innovation in response to regulation may induce the regulator not only to accede to the change but, with recognition of the changed nature of the environment, to alter regulations to allow the innovation to advance even further. Rollover mortgages are a clear example of such an interplay, as are the allowance of NOW accounts nationally.

A substantial change in the regulatory environment for all financial institutions came about with the passage of the Depository Institutions Deregulation and Monetary Control Act of 1980. The context presented above should allow a fuller appreciation of this landmark legislation to which we now turn.

The Depository Institutions Deregulation and Monetary Control Act of 1980

Economists have generally regarded competition as a favorable aspect in an economy, leading as it does to a more efficient allocation of resources. Many of the changes discussed in the previous sections of this chapter have led to increased competition among financial intermediaries. However, passage of the Depository Institutions Deregulation and Monetary Control Act of 1980 (DIDMCA), which was signed into law on March 31, 1980, represents a substantial leap forward in removing the impediments to financial intermediary competition. These intermediaries will increasingly come to resemble each other, and the importance of the specialist institution as we now know it— business lending by commercial banks, mortgage lending by thrift institutions—may become a thing of the past.

DIDMCA and the resulting changes it will bring about did not occur in a vacuum as our previous discussion has indicated. Therefore, prior to discussing DIDMCA in detail it is useful to explore the evolutionary process leading up to its passage. In part, this discussion of the evolutionary process is a recapitulation of some of the changes previously discussed. This is intentional, for by understanding the flow of these changes, the context of DIDMCA can be fully appreciated.

The Beginnings of the Evolutionary Process

It is true that in a sense all financial intermediaries have traditionally competed against each other for depositor funds. Especially following World War II, when S&Ls and MSBs grew into major financial intermediaries, this competition has been fierce. However, because of the existence of Regulation Q ceilings on commercial banks (and the extension of these ceilings to S&Ls and MSBs in 1966) and the prohibition on the payment of interest on demand deposits, this competition has often taken the form of customer services like free checking accounts and advertising the various presumed advantages of one type of institution over another. (Commercial banks proclaim themselves full service institutions offering checking accounts, savings accounts, and a full range of lending services, while S&Ls and MSBs have emphasized the fact that under interest rate ceilings they are able to offer the saver a one-quarter percentage point interest rate advantage.) However, even before the disintermediation experienced by all financial intermediaries in 1966 when interest rates rose sharply, financial intermediaries were beginning to recognize that in a higher interest rate environment, the ability to attract and keep funds necessitated new savings instruments. These instruments allowed for the payment of higher interest rates. In order to pay these higher rates, increased diversification of assets was necessary.

The large negotiable certificate of deposit, which was introduced in 1961as a way of attracting substantial funds, especially from business, led the way to fixed maturity certificates of deposit for smaller amounts at commercial banks and thrift institutions. This enabled these institutions to pay a higher rate to savers and attract savings for longer periods of time. The regulatory agencies in turn cooperated by placing higher interest rate ceilings on these types of time deposit accounts.

By the early 1970s a number of different accounts existed. In addition, as a result of the disintermediation experienced in the 1969–70 period, Regulation Q ceilings were suspended on large certificates of deposit, thereby setting a precedent that gradually led to the raising of ceilings or the exemption from ceilings of certain types of accounts. Additional certificate authority was granted financial intermediaries in 1973. (This was, in fact, done by allowing higher interest rate ceilings than had previously been permitted to be put into place.) The movement to ease interest rate ceiling restrictions temporarily culminated in the "wild card experiment" of 1973 in which financial intermediaries were given virtually free rein (ceilings were suspended) to compete for certificates maturing in four years or more with a minimum denomination of $1,000.[11] While this experiment lasted only a short time (from July 1, 1973, to October 31, 1973, when ceilings were reimposed) the authority to allow financial intermediaries to compete for funds through interest rate changes made it clear to the regulators and the institutions that such competition was desirable and manageable. A direct result of this was that during the next upward move in the interest rate cycle, the money market certificate was introduced in June 1978. The introduction of the MMCs has had a profound influence on the entire savings structure of society; MMCs, other "small" certificates of deposit (less than $100,000 in denomination as defined by the Fed), and large CDs currently dominate passbook savings accounts in dollar value. In July 1981, time deposits at commercial banks, S&Ls, MSBs, and credit unions exceeded $1 trillion compared to about $400 billion in passbook savings. Ten years earlier almost all small savings at these institutions were held in passbook-type accounts. These changes have permitted more active competition for funds among financial intermediaries and between financial intermediaries and the open market.

As regulations were being relaxed on some certificate accounts and additional new certificate accounts were being offered, regulations were also being altered to allow thrift institutions to offer transactions or payment accounts (checking-type accounts). Most of these changes have been discussed in detail previously. Table 16-3 summarizes the major changes in the ability of thrift institutions to offer checking-type accounts in the 1970s and early 1980s.

Paying more competitive rates on deposits has led to some problems for thrift institutions. Since S&Ls and to a lesser extent MSBs are primarily mortgage lenders, they are in many cases locked into a fixed yield, long-maturing portfolio of assets. When open-market rates rise and thrifts have to pay more for deposits like money market certificates, the fixed return on their assets makes it difficult for them to do so. This has led to pressure to allow more asset flexibility for thrift institutions. Some changes along these lines are contained in the 1980 legislation.

---

[11] However, the amount of these certificates an institution could issue could not exceed 5 percent of its total time and savings deposits.

Table 16-3
New Payments Powers for Thrifts[1]

September 1970	Federally chartered S&Ls are permitted to make preauthorized nonnegotiable transfers from savings accounts to third parties for household-related expenditures.
January 1974	Federal legislation permits all banks and thrifts (except CUs) in Massachusetts and New Hampshire to offer negotiable order of withdrawal (NOW) accounts. NOW accounts are functionally equivalent to interest-bearing checking accounts.
January 1974	Federal S&Ls authorized to establish remote service units (RSUs) on experimental basis. RSUs are electronic terminals located in retail establishments. They enable S&L customers to make deposits, withdrawals, and transfers of funds between accounts without going to the S&L office in person.
August 1974	Three federally chartered CUs permitted to offer share drafts, which are functionally equivalent to interest-bearing checking accounts. These three federal CUs and two state CUs began six-month pilot program in October 1974. By year-end 1978, 740 federal CUs had share draft service in operation.
April 1975	Federally chartered S&Ls are permitted to make preauthorized transfers from savings accounts to third parties for any purpose.
July 1975	Banks, MSBs, and with the approval of the Commissioner of Banking, state chartered S&Ls in New Jersey are authorized to establish manned RSUs and off-premise automated teller machines (ATMs). Such units permit customers to make deposits, withdrawals, and transfers between accounts without making a trip to the bank, MSB, or S&L office.
February 1976	Congress extends NOW account authority to all New England states.
March 1977	MSBs in Pennsylvania are granted authority to offer noninterest-bearing negotiable order of withdrawal accounts (NINOWs). NINOWs are functionally equivalent to checking accounts.

[1] The developments listed in this table do not necessarily give the complete picture of new powers for thrifts. In some cases, state chartered institutions have begun to offer the same services as their federal counterparts without any express enabling legislation.

Table 16-3 (cont.)

October 1978	Federal legislation extends NOW account authority to New York State.
November 1978	Federally insured banks and MSBs are authorized to offer automatic transfers from a savings account to a checking account or other type of transaction account.
March 1980	Congress passes and the President signs into law the Depository Institutions Deregulation and Monetary Control Act of 1980, among other things extending NOW accounts nationwide.

Source: Adapted from "Thrifts Compete With Banks," *Business Review*, Federal Reserve Bank of Philadelphia, Sept./Oct. 1979, pp. 14–15.

As early as 1970, the pressure from the financial intermediaries, especially the thrift institutions, led to the establishment of a commission to study the financial structure of the economy and to make recommendations for changes. The President's Commission on Financial Structure and Regulation was charged with the following mandate: ". . . review and study the structure, operation, and regulation of the private financial institutions in the United States, for the purpose of formulating recommendations that would improve the functioning of the private financial system."[12] The study by the President's Commission on Financial Structure and Regulation, known as the Hunt Commission, was the first of two major studies in the 1970s. The other was the FINE study in 1974–76; FINE stood for Financial Institutions and the Nation's Economy. Both studies led to legislative proposals that were not approved at the time. Many of these proposals, however, were incorporated in DIDMCA, so a brief review of their recommendations is useful.

The Hunt Commission recommended the abolition of interest rate ceilings over a period of years on time deposits while retaining the prohibition of interest payments on demand deposits. The most sweeping recommendations of the Hunt Commission concerned the asset and liability structure of savings and loan associations and mutual savings banks. Broader asset powers would be granted thrift institutions allowing them to make consumer loans and acquire a wide range of securities of all issuers. Thrifts would be able to offer demand deposit accounts but in exchange for this would be required to become mem-

---

[12] *Report,* Washington, D.C.: GPO, Dec. 1971, p. 1.

bers of the Federal Reserve System and meet reserve requirements. No action was taken on these recommendations, though legislation was introduced.

Starting in 1974, however, extensive study was undertaken by Congress consisting of gathering position and study papers, hearings, and the formulation of discussion principles. These activities constituted the FINE study and culminated in the Financial Reform Act of 1976. This act did not pass Congress. The FINE study recommended abolition of interest ceilings on time deposits and the granting of demand deposit authority to thrift institutions. Consumer lending by S&Ls and MSBs would be allowed and the securities acquisition powers of thrifts would be enhanced. All federally insured institutions would be required to meet Federal Reserve requirements that would be phased in.

The Major Provisions of DIDMCA

While the legislative recommendations of the Hunt Commission and the FINE study were not accepted at the time, DIDMCA was a direct outgrowth of these recommendations. Table 16-4 presents the major provisions of DIDMCA. DIDMCA goes far in thoroughly transforming depository financial institutions into intermediaries that will be more alike and hence more competitive. The result is a major step toward the evolution of similar, nonspecialized financial institutions.

The act allows NOW accounts to be offered nationwide. It also provides for nationwide automatic transfer accounts. All depository institutions can now offer interest-bearing checking accounts to individuals and nonprofit organizations. Corporations and other business organizations still must utilize regular demand deposit accounts generally restricted to commercial banks, thus for the time being limiting the market from which thrift institutions can draw for checking deposits. The offering of checking accounts by thrifts has implications for the entire payments system of the economy and for the control of the money supply by the Fed because the institutions lie outside control by the Fed. In recognizing these implications, the act requires the introduction of reserve requirements over an eight-year period against both transactions accounts and some time deposits at institutions that are not currently members of the Federal Reserve System. Since the reserve requirement on checking accounts contained in the bill is lower than the existing reserve requirements for many member banks, a four-year period is allowed to lower the reserve requirements for current member banks.[13] The movement to a uniform reserve requirement has

---

[13] The lower reserve requirement and the imposition of reserve requirements on nonmember banks should halt the erosion in Fed membership and perhaps reverse this trend.

Table 16-4
Summary of the Depository Institutions Deregulation and Monetary Control Act of 1980

Permits nationwide NOW accounts	All depository institutions (after December 31, 1980) may offer NOW accounts (interest-earning checking accounts) to individuals and nonprofit organizations. The act also allows banks to provide automatic transfer services from savings to checking accounts, permits S&Ls to use remote service units, and authorizes all federally insured credit unions to offer share draft accounts, effective immediately.
Phases out deposit interest rate ceilings	Congress declares that interest rate ceilings on deposits discourage saving and create inequities for depositors, especially those with modest savings. The act therefore sets up machinery to phase out interest rate ceilings on deposits over a six-year period.
Eliminates usury ceilings	State usury ceilings on first residential mortgage loans are eliminated (as of March 31, 1980) unless a state adopts a new ceiling before April 1, 1983. Credit unions may increase their loan rate ceiling from 12 percent to 15 percent and may raise the ceiling higher for periods up to 18 months. The act also preempts state usury ceilings on business and agricultural loans above $25,000 and permits an interest rate of not more than 5 percent above the Federal Reserve discount rate, including any surcharge, on 90-day commercial paper. This provision expires on April 1, 1983, or earlier if the state reinstitutes its ceiling.
Increases level of federally insured deposits	The act increases federal deposit insurance at commercial banks, savings banks, S&Ls, and credit unions from $40,000 to $100,000, effective immediately.
Requires reserves on all transactions accounts at depository institutions	The act specifies that any reserve requirement will now be uniformly applied to all transactions accounts at all depository institutions. Transactions accounts include demand deposits, NOW

Table 16-4 (cont.)

accounts, telephone transfers, automatic transfers, and share drafts. Specifically, all banks, savings banks, S&Ls, and credit unions will have to maintain reserves in the ratio of 3 percent for that portion of their transactions accounts below $25 million and 12 percent (the Board can vary this between 8 and 14 percent) for the portion above $25 million. They also must maintain reserves of 3 percent (or within a range of 0 to 9 percent) against their nonpersonal time deposits and must report (directly or indirectly) their liabilities and assets to the Federal Reserve.

The act provides for an eight-year phase in of reserve requirements for depository institutions which are not Federal Reserve members and a four-year phase down of previous reserve requirements for member banks.

Permits board to impose supplemental reserves	The act permits the Federal Reserve Board, in "extraordinary circumstances," to impose an additional reserve requirement on any depository institution of up to 4 percent of its transactions accounts. If it were imposed, this supplemental reserve would earn interest.
Provides access to discount window	Any depository institution issuing transactions accounts or nonpersonal time deposits will have the same discount and borrowing privilege at the Federal Reserve as member banks, effective immediately.
Establishes fees for Fed services	The Federal Reserve is required to establish fees for its services, such as currency and coin services, check clearing and collection, wire transfers, and automated clearing house services. The fees will take effect by October 1, 1981, and the Board must publish a proposed fee schedule by October 1, 1980.
Expands power of thrift institutions	The act authorizes federal credit unions to make residential real estate loans. It also gives S&Ls greater lending flexibility and higher loan ceilings, expands their investing authority, permits them to issue credit cards, and gives them trust powers.

Table 16-4 (cont.)

Simplifies truth in lending disclosures and financial regulations	The act reduces the number of disclosures that must be made under truth in lending (TIL) requirements and eliminates agricultural credit from TIL coverage. It also requires the use of "simple English phrases" to describe key terms in such disclosures, effective March 31, 1982.

Source: Federal Reserve Bank of Atlanta *Economic Review* (March/April 1980), pp. 4–5.

long been advocated by economists as a way of enhancing monetary control by the Fed, because it eliminates shifts in funds between different size banks eliminating a source of fluctuation in required reserves. In addition, with the signing of the act, all member and nonmember intermediaries offering transactions accounts can now borrow from the Fed.

Interest rate ceilings on time and savings deposits are to be phased out over a six-year period under the provisions of the act. The result of abolishing interest rate ceilings will be to eliminate the one-quarter point interest rate advantage on most time and savings deposits that thrift institutions currently enjoy over commercial banks. Commercial banks had long lobbied for the abolition of this differential while thrift institutions resisted any change in order to keep their competitive advantage. It is not clear that thrift institutions will be at any disadvantage in attracting deposits when NOW accounts and other changes that have been made in the rules affecting thrifts are considered.

While less sweeping, other provisions of the act are also of significance. Additional asset flexibility is allowed to thrift institutions. For example, savings and loans can now make consumer loans up to 20 percent of their assets, and they are allowed to do some construction lending. Commercial banks were considerably upset by the latter provision, arguing that it allows thrifts a foot in the door to business lending—the exclusive territory of commercial banks. Bankers clearly regard the trend as one which will turn thrift institutions into commercial banks.[14] Indeed, bank fears appear justified as thrift institutions are already lobbying Congress for increased lending authority for business loans.

DIDMCA established a committee called the Depository Institutions

---

[14] See "Are We On The Way to 19,000 Banks?" *American Bankers Association Journal* (May 1980), p. 99. The number 19,000 is composed of the approximately 14,000 commercial banks and the 5,000 thrift institutions.

Deregulation Committee (DIDC) to oversee the implementation of the changes mandated by the act. The committee consists of the Secretary of the Treasury, the chairman of the Board of Governors of the Federal Reserve System, the chairman of the Board of Directors of the Federal Deposit Insurance Corporation, the chairman of the Federal Home Loan Bank Board, and the chairman of the National Credit Union Administration, all voting members, as well as the Comptroller of the Currency, a nonvoting member. The committee has already issued a number of rulings implementing the provision of the act, including phasing out many interest rate ceilings more rapidly than the act requires.

The 1980 act means fundamental alteration in the activities of depository institutions. While it is likely that in the future there will be additional movement toward ever more similar depository institutions, the act is clearly the culmination of the process first begun formally with the Hunt Commission study. The speed of future changes will depend on the evaluation of the 1980 changes after they have been in force for some time, the condition of the financial system, and further study.

Technological Innovation: Electronic Funds Transfer

In discussing the evolution of the financial institutions in this chapter, we have given little attention to the impact that technological change has had on the financial system. The introduction of widespread computer technology has transformed the entire accounting process within financial institutions, bringing increased speed and efficiency to the daily accounting tasks of the institutions. However, more dramatically and with substantial implications for the future has been the development of extensive electronically assisted changes that relate to both interfinancial institution activity and customer–financial institution activity. These developments are all classified under the title electronic funds transfer or EFT.

The Federal Reserve's Role in Electronic Funds Transfer

The Fedwire, as the Federal Reserve Communications System is known, was begun in 1917. But it was only in the last decade with the advanced techniques of corporate cash management and high speed computers that the wire has become significant in the payments system. The Fedwire allows Federal Reserve member banks, as well as other organizations holding reserve balances at the Fed, such as the

U.S. government and certain international organizations, to transfer reserve account balances held at the Fed to other users on the same day. For example, a New York member bank, such as Chase Manhattan, can transfer funds to a member bank in San Francisco, say, the Bank of America, in a matter of minutes using the Fedwire and computers. Some large member banks actually have terminals directly linking them to the Fedwire. With others, the transfers are concluded at the district Federal Reserve Bank and the member bank is notified. Similarly, U.S. government securities can be transferred between member banks the same way, since under current procedures member bank holdings of securities exist only as bookkeeping entries at the Federal Reserve Banks. Further, transfers may be made by member banks for third parties such as nonmember banks that are correspondents of the members or for individuals or firms. For example, a member bank can transfer funds from a firm's account it holds to an account of another firm at another member bank when directed, thus materially eliminating the traditional lags associated with payments by check. Speed can become crucial in a period of high interest rates when the sums are large. The existence of the Fedwire and its current use in many instances make traditional check transfers obsolete. This has implications for the nation's payment system as will be noted below.

To understand the Fedwire and how it is employed, consider the following example. A corporate treasurer has $100 million in a demand deposit account that she is going to use to purchase a certificate of deposit at a large money center bank. The demand deposit is not at that bank. The treasurer instructs the bank holding the deposit to utilize the Fedwire, and the funds are put to use that day and receive a return without delay. Delay in such a situation would mean several thousand dollars in lost interest. Similarly, large individual investors in money market funds often transfer funds to, say, a money market mutual fund's bank by wire so that the investors' balances can immediately start earning a return. A check might take a week or more to reach the fund with consequent loss of interest. These investors may have no idea that they are using the Fedwire when they instruct their bank to "wire" the funds.[15]

The Fedwire is also used to transmit payment orders in another operation sponsored by the Federal Reserve, the Automated Clearing Houses (ACHs) operated, for the most part, at the Federal Reserve Banks. With automatic clearing houses, payments are made by computer tape rather than with checks. For example, a large business may use a computer tape to pay employees who have signed up to have their pay automatically deposited to their bank account. (Some ACHs

---

[15] For a discussion of the Fedwire and its implication for the U.S. payments system, see Ralph C. Kimball, "Wire Transfer and the Demand for Money," Federal Reserve Bank of Boston, *New England Economic Review* (March/April 1980), pp. 5–22.

include thrift institutions as participants as well.) The employer sends a tape with the complete payroll information for the employees to the ACH, which transfers the information to other computer tapes that are sent to the employer's bank and to the banks of the employees for credit to their accounts. Similarly, social security payments are made to the accounts of social security recipients who have signed up for automatic deposits. The potential increases in efficiency and the reduction in costs generated by ACHs (the elimination of the need to process paper saves both time and expense) are yet to be fully realized. These benefits will increase with greater participation as more payments are made in this way.

Financial Transfer by Computer Terminal

Perhaps of even more long-range significance than the utilization of electronics for interfinancial institution transfers is the development of electronic means for transfers between customers and the financial institution directly. Computer terminals, called remote service units (RSUs), that handle routine financial institution chores like deposits, withdrawals, and loan payments are growing rapidly, particularly at commercial banks, after a rather slow start in the early 1970s. These terminals may be located at the bank or at a location such as at a shopping center where there is no regular bank office. They can be accessible 24 hours a day, thus servicing customers when the institution is closed and saving bank personnel considerable time during banking hours in handling routine chores. A user of the terminal, for example, can directly withdraw funds from a demand deposit account, thus not taking teller time with check cashing. RSUs are also being put into service by thrift institutions for servicing customer accounts.

Similarly, although spreading much less rapidly than RSUs, are point of sale computer terminals. A point of sale terminal at, for example, a supermarket in conjunction with what is known as a "debit card" can be utilized to directly access the customer's demand deposit account. Thus, the items to be purchased are totaled, the customer, rather than writing a check, presents the debit card to the clerk and the funds representing the total purchases are automatically transferred from the customer's account at the financial institution, in most cases a bank, to the merchant's account. Banks are very keen on this aspect of electronic funds transfer, for it is potentially much cheaper for the bank per transaction than processing checks. However, this aspect of EFT has grown relatively slowly, due basically to customer resistance. By using point of sale terminals, the delay between the time a customer writes a check and when the check is cleared, known as the float, is eliminated because the customer's account is accessed at the moment of purchase and the transfer made at that moment. Many people are reluctant to lose the few days "free ride" they currently enjoy through the slower speed of the conventional check-clearing process. Nevertheless, it appears that the impetus over time is in the direction of more electronic funds transfer, including point of sale terminals, and customers will sooner or later adapt to the new processes. It is clearly a goal of the financial institutions to move to a "checkless" system in the interests of lower costs and more efficiency. In an electronic age, it is likely that this goal will ultimately be achieved.[16]

Ongoing Innovation and Change

As this book goes to press, rapid changes in the economic and regulatory environment continue to take place. While interest rates are falling, they continue to be historically high and extremely volatile. As a result, thrift institutions continue to seek additional regulatory changes and direct congressional help in assisting them to cope with their low-yielding mortgage portfolios. Proposals have been made to Congress for direct federal purchases of low-yielding mortgages, subsidies for borrowers on new mortgage interest rates, and for federal legislation allowing enforcement by state-chartered institutions of due-on-sale clauses in existing mortgages. A buyer would no longer be permitted to take over a low interest mortgage when buying a house. Federally chartered thrifts already have this power.

Proposals also are being considered to allow thrift institutions to expand their liability powers beyond those envisioned by DIDMCA. The Federal Home Loan Bank Board is proposing that federally chartered savings and loans be allowed to offer demand deposits. Similar legislation for all thrift institutions is pending in Congress.

These are but a few examples of the continuing evolution going on in the financial system. The pace of change highlighted in this chapter shows no signs of slowing. The electronic revolution in funds transfer continues to accelerate. Indeed, the financial system should look very different at the end of the decade of the 1980s from its appearance at the beginning of the decade.

---

[16] However, note that the elimination of the check does not mean the elimination of checking accounts. The only thing that would change is how the funds in checking accounts are transferred, by electronics rather than by paper. The medium of exchange—checking accounts—will remain unchanged.

FINANCIAL REFORM DOES NOT STAND STILL
Instant Replay of Financial Reform

Having passed the most sweeping financial legislation in a half-century last year, Congress, with new chairmen in both of the banking committees, is loath to rush into new legislation this year. Yet the elements are falling into place for a replay of the 96th Congress, when a court decision helped break a four-year logjam and led to passage last March of the landmark legislation phasing out interest-rate ceilings and easing involvement of thrift institutions in home lending.

The hottest issue is the raging fight between depository institutions and money market mutual funds, but that is far from the only issue. The new Congress may have to deal with a bailout of thrift institutions—crisis legislation that would amount to a limited start on interstate banking—and federal preemption of state laws limiting interest rates on consumer loans.

With a Republican in the White House, Republican control of the Senate, and a slimmer Democratic majority in the House of Representatives, leadership of financial legislation probably will fall to Senate Banking Committee Chairman Jake Garn of Utah. Garn, a former Salt Lake City mayor who shares President Reagan's passion for deregulation, succeeds Democratic Senator William Proxmire of Wisconsin in the post. And Garn says he feels strongly about what his committee should—and should not—do. "I would not see any bold, new initiatives," he says. "I am so tired of that kind of rhetoric."

Setting priorities. Indeed, Garn's first goal is merely to review consumer protection laws already passed, with an eye to determining how the regulatory burden on financial institutions might be eased. "Congress could take two years and not pass another law and just do oversight on the monstrosities we have passed," says Garn.

Yet there is a good chance that events may force Garn to shed this seemingly relaxed attitude, much as events forced the last Congress to pass the sweeping Depository Institutions Deregulation & Monetary Control Act of 1980. For openers, Garn may find himself quickly shifting priorities to deal with near-crisis conditions at the thrift institutions.

Mutual savings banks and savings and loan associations are hemorrhaging from paying out unprecedentedly high rates on six-month money market certificates—dubbed the "suicide sixes" by bankers—while receiving low, fixed rates on their mortgage portfolios. Burgeoning money market mutual funds, meanwhile, continue to draw money away from financial institutions, and the thrifts are hurting most as a result. "If there's a wave of savings and loan failures, then there's going to have to be some sort of crisis legislation," says W. Lee Hoskins, chief economist at Pittsburgh National Bank.

The thrifts, for instance, want the government to bail them out by buying old, low-yielding, low-profit mortgages—an issue that easily could come before Congress. Further, federal banking regulators last year proposed legislation that would permit commercial banks to buy failing thrift institutions, in some cases in neighboring states. But that legislation, which could be a first step toward interstate banking, as well as a turn away from the current taboo against bank ownership of thrifts, went nowhere. House Banking Committee Chairman Fernand St Germain (D-R.I.), who assumed the chairmanship when Representative Henry Reuss (D-Wis.) moved to chair the Joint Economic Committee, says he still regards the failing institution legislation as "at best a Band-Aid." But he says it might make sense as a last resort. Garn is similarly cautious.

A push for Congress. The money market mutual funds, whose growth helped prompt the 1980 Monetary Control Act, are growing strongly again, and Garn has said that he believes the checking privileges offered by the funds give the banks unfair competition. Just as a 1979 U.S. Appeals Court decision on interest-bearing checking accounts propelled Congress to legalize NOW accounts in 1980 banking legislation, legislation pending in Utah to curb the Merrill Lynch Cash Management Account may force Congress' hand again.

Indeed, the Cash Management Account touches raw nerves all over the place. Merrill Lynch customers can deposit their credit balances in a money fund, and they can obtain certain banking services. If Congress tackles this one, it would get into the middle of not only the clash between the money funds and the banks but also the touchy relationship between banks and brokerage houses.

The pressures would be to impose new regulations—such as reserve requirements—on the money funds or to provide the financial institutions with new instruments to meet the competition. St Germain says he would lean toward the new instruments, while Garn says he would expect Congress to "come down somewhere in the middle." One way or another, Garn plans hearings on the money funds.

Garn hopes events permit him some time to launch a congressional study of what financial institutions will look like five or ten years from now—a period that is likely to see a massive shakeout among financial institutions.

Finally, Congress this year will almost certainly tackle:

- State usury ceilings. Chances of federal pre-emption are "pretty good," says Garn, who would give states three years or so to revoke the federal override.
- Export finance. Passage of legislation permitting banks to participate in the formation of export trading companies is the best bet for early passage of any banking legislation. Such legislation passed both Houses last year but got snagged on technical differences as time ran out in the old Congress. A new round of hearings is set for Feb. 17.

Key Points

1. The process of financial system development has involved the interplay of regulatory and legislative changes, economic changes, and financial innovation. Innovation in response to regulation has occurred as financial institutions have attempted to reduce the impact of regulatory constraints on their profitability, particularly when the change in the economic environment has made this advantageous.

2. Many changes in bank and nonbank institution behavior, particularly in the decade of the 1970s, are traceable to particular regulations that became particularly burdensome when interest rates rose. These regulations included Regulation Q ceilings and the prohibition of interest payments on demand deposits, which led to such innovations as repurchase agreements, negotiable CDs, and NOW accounts.

3. The Depository Institutions Deregulation and Monetary Control Act of 1980 has been considered a landmark in financial legislation. Among its many provisions, it extends NOW accounts nationwide, phases out Regulation Q ceilings, requires all institutions offering transaction accounts to meet Federal Reserve System reserve requirements, and increases asset flexibility for thrift institutions. Its passage came after a decade of extraordinary evolutionary change in the financial system and on the basis of two major governmentally sponsored study commissions during the 1970s.

4. DIDMCA means a fundamental alteration in the activities of depository institutions. It is likely that the near future will see additional changes that may result in the gradual disappearance of distinct financial institutions.

5. Computer technology has also resulted in innovative activity on the part of the financial system. Electronic funds transfer, automated clearing houses, and remote service computer terminals among other developments have increased substantially in recent years, and further development appears inevitable.

Questions for Discussion

1. There has been substantial emphasis in this chapter on the interaction of regulation and financial innovation. Why may regulation lead to financial innovation? What role is played by the economic environment in the interaction between regulation and financial innovation?

2. Briefly explain the major provisions of DIDMCA. Why is this legislation regarded as so significant by economists?

3. It was asserted in the chapter that financial institutions are becoming increasingly alike and this development is likely to continue. What similarities are there now between commercial banks and thrift institutions that didn't exist in, say, 1970? How has DIDMCA contributed to this development?

4. How is the Fedwire utilized in electronic funds transfer?

5. Pick one major regulation (Regulation Q, prohibition of interest payments on demand deposits, and so on) and trace its influence on financial system innovation.

Suggested Readings

Board of Governors of the Federal Reserve System. "The Depository Institutions Deregulation and Monetary Control Act of 1980." Federal Reserve *Bulletin,* June 1980, pp. 444–53.

Cacy, J. A., and Scott Winningham. "Reserve Requirements Under the Depository Institutions Deregulation and Monetary Control Act of 1980." Federal Reserve Bank of Kansas City *Economic Review,* Sept./Oct. 1980, pp. 3–16.

Federal Reserve Bank of Chicago. "The Depository Institutions Deregulation and Monetary Control Act of 1980." *Economic Perspectives,* Sept./Oct. 1980, (entire issue).

Gaines, Tilford C. "Financial Innovations and the Efficiency of Federal Reserve Policy." In *Monetary Process and Policy,* George Horwich, ed. Homewood, Ill.: Richard D. Irwin, 1967, pp. 99–118.

Niblack, William C. "Development of Electronic Funds Transfer Systems." Federal Reserve Bank of St. Louis *Review,* Sept. 1976, pp. 10–18.

Shull, Bernard. "Economic Efficiency, Public Regulation, and Financial Reform: Depository Institutions." In *Financial Institutions and Markets,* 2nd ed., Murray F. Polakoff et al. eds. Boston: Houghton Mifflin, 1981, pp. 671–702.

Silber, William L. *Financial Innovation.* Lexington, Mass.: Lexington Books, 1975.

The President's Commission on Financial Structure and Regulation. *Report.* Washington, D.C.: GPO, Dec. 1971.

U.S. House of Representatives, Committee on Banking, Currency and Housing, Papers presented for the FINE Study. Washington, D.C.: GPO, 1976.

Central Banking and the Federal Reserve System

17

A major portion of this book has been devoted to an examination of the principal components of the financial system. The financial intermediaries and the financial markets have been explored. The Federal Reserve System, the central bank for the United States, whose influence is reflected in the activities and operations of the intermediaries and markets was briefly introduced in Chapter 5 but thereafter has not figured prominently in the discussion. However, the role of the Fed in the financial system is of such importance that this chapter and the two that follow will analyze the Federal Reserve System in detail.

Central Banking

The interactions between the Fed and the financial system occur through a number of channels. The Fed, as the U.S. central bank, influences the level of money and credit in the economy as well as the level of interest rates through its conduct of monetary policy. It uses the financial markets to implement its monetary policy. The Fed has regulatory responsibility for the major portion of the commercial banking system. Since the passage of the Depository Institutions Deregulation and Monetary Control Act of 1980, it has explicit responsibility for all commercial banks and many thrift institutions in the areas of reserve requirements and discount lending. As the Federal Reserve System is analyzed, the interactions of the Fed, the financial system, and the economy will become apparent. The Fed is inextricably intertwined with the financial system. To begin to understand the Federal

Reserve System and its role, it is useful to first develop some insight into what a central bank does. We begin with the origins of central banking.

What Is a Central Bank?

Central banks have existed in many Western European countries far longer than in the United States. The Bank of England was established in the seventeenth century. In many ways the development of the Bank of England and the functions it assumed over the years shed light on what a central bank does because modern central banking resulted from an evolutionary process. It is worthwhile to briefly discuss the Bank of England and its early role in the British financial system.[1]

The Bank of England was for centuries a private bank. It grew into its role as a central bank while still private. It was not until 1946 when it was officially nationalized that it became part of the government although it had been recognized as the British central bank for decades. As is true of all central banks, the major purpose of the Bank of England was to be a banker's bank. The Bank of England kept reserves of other British banks and on the basis of these reserves, commercial banks in Britain issued bank notes. Bank notes, which were also issued by the Bank of England, were an early form of currency in Britain. (Bank notes were also an early form of currency in the United States.) Over time, the Bank of England gained a monopoly over the issuance of bank notes similar to the Fed's current monopoly on the issuance of currency in the United States. Commercial bank deposits at the Bank of England also served as reserves for bank demand deposits as these developed into the most important component of the money supply in Britain in the nineteenth century. By holding commercial bank reserves, the Bank of England also became the lender of last resort to the British banking system. It was noted in Chapter 5 that the establishment of the Fed in the United States resulted in part from the need of some institution to be a lender of last resort to the banking system. The Bank of England had served this role in Britain over the centuries.

The Bank of England gradually took on additional duties associated with a central bank. It became the bank for the government and acted as its fiscal agent in distributing securities issued by the government. Further, its regulatory authority over other banks grew and its responsibility for the conduct of monetary policy—influencing interest rates and the money supply in the economy and therefore economic activity—evolved. These activities of the Bank of England are the major functions of central banks today including the Federal Reserve System.

---

[1] For a classic account of the Bank of England, its role in the financial system, and indeed the origins of the money market, see Walter Bagehot, *Lombard Street* (New York: Scribner, Armstrong & Co., 1873; rpt. Homewood, Ill.: Richard D. Irwin, 1962).

The Federal Reserve System, like the Bank of England, has regulatory responsibility for commercial banks. Federal Reserve member banks account for the majority of commercial bank assets and liabilities. As was pointed out in Chapter 5, while only a minority of commercial banks are members of the Fed, these banks are generally large. Although the percentage of commercial bank assets held by member banks has fallen, these banks still hold over 70 percent of commercial bank assets. Through its operation of the discount window where it makes loans to banks, it serves as lender of last resort to the banking system. Under the provisions of the Depository Institutions Deregulation and Monetary Control Act of 1980 the Fed assumed this role for all financial institutions offering transaction accounts including nonmember banks and nonbank financial intermediaries. These institutions are in turn required to meet Federal Reserve reserve requirements. Through its powers to set reserve requirements, the Fed can influence the amount of money in the economy. However, reserve requirement changes are only one of the tools available to the Fed in performing one of the most important functions of a central bank, the execution of monetary policy. The formulation and execution of monetary policy is such an important aspect of the Fed's activity that it will be discussed extensively in this and later chapters.

The Fed also performs many other functions traditionally associated with a central bank. Among these, it acts as the fiscal agent for the U.S. Treasury in distributing newly issued Treasury securities, holds Treasury deposits on which the Treasury writes checks, assists in the check-clearing process nationally, and passes judgment on such issues as bank acquisition and interpretation of various aspects of banking legislation. Further, it is consulted by both the President and the Congress on matters relating to banking, the conduct of monetary policy, and the financial system in general. For example, Federal Reserve officials are frequently called to testify before congressional committees.

The Fed was not the first central bank in the United States. The First Bank of the United States (1791–1811) and the Second Bank (1816–36) were central banks. After the demise of the Second Bank in 1836, no central bank existed until 1914, although some of the functions of a central bank were performed by the U.S. Treasury. The Panic of 1907, which culminated a series of financial panics that took place in the latter part of the nineteenth century and early twentieth century, finally provided sufficient motivation to Congress for the establishment of a central bank. The Federal Reserve Charter Act was passed in 1913 and the Fed began operations in 1914. With the exception of the establishment of the Federal Open Market Committee in 1935, the Fed has retained the basic organization provided for in the 1913 Charter Act. However, the Fed's operations have evolved considerably over time, including the development of its responsibility for conducting monetary policy.

The Organization of the Federal Reserve System

The debate over the establishment of the Federal Reserve System made clear a divergence of views between those who wished to see the central bank as a single entity in the Northeast, the center of the financial system, and others who were concerned that such a concentration of power would be harmful to the financial health of the national economy, not to mention possibly being unsympathetic to their interests. Similar regional disagreements had led to the demise of both the First and Second Banks of the United States. As a result, a compromise was agreed upon, which is still reflected in the organization of the Federal Reserve System.

The Federal Reserve System is composed of a seven-member Board of Governors, headquartered in Washington, D.C., and twelve Federal Reserve Banks spread throughout the country in twelve Federal Reserve Districts. As the map in Figure 17-1 shows, the geographic districts for which each bank is responsible are quite diverse. Changing population and economic patterns since 1913 are responsible for the oddity of having the Federal Reserve Bank of San Francisco, for example, responsible for an area containing over 30 million people while the Federal Reserve Bank of Boston is responsible for an area containing perhaps 15 million people. Only minor alterations in Federal Reserve district boundaries have been made since the system's founding.

The Board of Governors is responsible for setting basic policy of the Federal Reserve including setting reserve requirements on deposits within ranges stipulated by Congress[2] and approving discount rate changes. The initiation of discount rate changes, however, must come from the Federal Reserve Banks. Further, the most important tool of monetary policy, the buying and selling of securities, called open-market operations, are decided by a twelve-person joint committee, the Federal Open Market Committee (FOMC), whose members are the Board of Governors and the presidents of the Federal Reserve Banks. To ensure majority representation on the Federal Open Market Committee by the Board of Governors, only the president of the Federal Reserve Bank of New York is a permanent member of the FOMC, with the remaining Federal Reserve Bank presidents rotating on and off the committee.

The Federal Reserve Banks are responsible for holding depository institution accounts (before DIDMCA these were only member bank accounts), conducting the majority of the day-to-day business of the Federal Reserve such as check-clearing, and making discount loans.

---

[2] Prior to DIDMCA the ranges set by Congress were 7 to 22 percent on demand deposits and 3 to 10 percent on time deposits. DIDMCA set the range at 8 to 14 percent on demand deposits and 0 to 9 percent on time deposits.

Figure 17-1
Boundaries of the Federal Reserve Districts and their Branch Territories

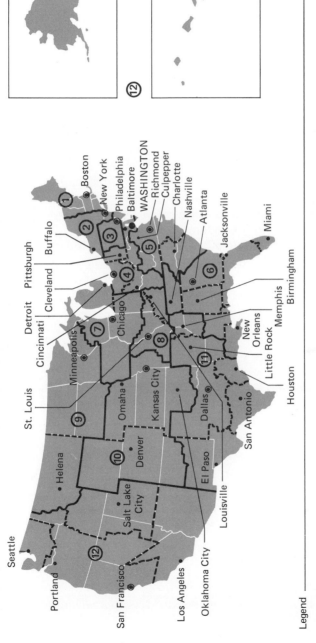

Legend

—— Boundaries of Federal Reserve Districts

---- Boundaries of Federal Reserve Branch Territories

● Board of Governors of the Federal Reserve System

◉ Federal Reserve Bank Cities

• Federal Reserve Branch Cities

• Federal Reserve Bank Facility

Source: Federal Reserve *Bulletin*.

Depository institutions within a particular Federal Reserve district deal directly with the Federal Reserve Bank for that district.

While the disputes concerning regional interests resulted in the present organization of the Fed, there was also concern during the debate over the Fed's charter that it be constituted independently of the executive branch of the federal government. If the Fed was under the control of the executive, many feared that it would not always be able to operate objectively for the best interests of the financial system and the economy.[3] Thus, the Fed was created as an independent unit of government responsible to Congress and nominally owned by the commercial banks that were its members (although they have no formal influence on the operation of the Fed).[4] The members of the Board of Governors are appointed by the President and must be confirmed by the Senate. To further enhance the independence of the Fed, terms of office for the seven members of the Board of Governors were made to run for 14 years, with terms staggered every two years. Thus, at most, if every member of the Board of Governors, known as a governor, served for a full term, a President could only appoint four members during a two-term period in office.[5]

The President appoints one member of the Board of Governors as chairman, subject to Senate confirmation. The chairman serves a four-year term, which does not coincide with that of the President, and the chairman can be reappointed. Since the chairman also serves as one of the seven governors, even if he (thus far there has not been a woman chairman of the Board of Governors) is not reappointed after his four-year term as chairman expires, he may serve out the unexpired portion of his term as a governor. However, in practice most chairmen who have not been reappointed have resigned from the Board of Governors. Most recently Arthur Burns resigned after he was not reappointed as chairman by President Carter in 1977, although he could have remained a member of the Board of Governors until 1984.[6]

The chairman has important, although for the most part informal, power in the Federal Reserve well beyond the notion of "first among equals."[7] This power derives from the chairman's role as chief spokes-

---

[3] Later in this chapter, political influence on the Fed will be discussed.

[4] The formal influence of the commercial bank stockholders is even less than that of a stockholder holding a small number of shares in General Motors Corporation on the operation of General Motors.

[5] In practice, because of illness, retirement, and death, Presidents serving two terms have generally been able to appoint more than four governors.

[6] An interesting exception to the usual resignation of a nonreappointed chairman from the Board of Governors occurred in 1948 when Harry Truman failed to reappoint Marriner Eccles as chairman. Because of Eccles' strong disagreement with Truman's economic policy, he remained on the Board of Governors for three years after his term as chairman expired.

[7] In *Animal Farm*, George Orwell, the British author most famous for his novel *1984*, talked about the organization of the animal society in his novel. He said in this society, "All animals are equal, but some animals are more equal than others." Without carrying the analogy too far, the chairman of the Board of Governors is much more equal (more important) than the other governors.

man for the Fed before the public and Congress, frequent contact with the President of the United States, and his chairmanship of both the Board of Governors and the Federal Open Market Committee. As chairman of these two bodies, he is in the important position of steering the meetings by establishing agenda and generally summarizing the results of the meetings. This means his interpretations are reflected in these summaries and the operational instructions that result from these meetings.

Sherman Maisel, the first former member of the Federal Reserve Board to write a book about the Board, says that the chairman has overwhelming authority in the Federal Reserve System and in its most important function, the conduct of monetary policy, relative to the governors. Maisel estimates that the chairman has 45 percent of the power within the system compared to about 3 percent for each governor. The remaining power is mostly concentrated in the staffs of the Federal Reserve Board of Governors and the Federal Open Market Committee. The Federal Reserve Banks, in Maisel's judgment, have very little power in influencing monetary policy formulation.[8]

The Federal Open Market Committee

The Federal Open Market Committee (FOMC) sets policy for open-market operations in the buying and selling of securities by the Fed, the major tool of monetary policy. It is the most important standing committee of the Federal Reserve System.[9] This committee was not established in its present form until 1935 when congressional action formally recognized the need for a standing committee to oversee the management of the Federal Reserve's securities portfolio. The FOMC is made up of twelve members—the seven members of the

---

[8] Sherman Maisel, *Managing the Dollar* (New York: Norton, 1973). Although this book appeared in 1973, there has been no significant development that would lead one to believe that anything has changed. The table below is drawn from Maisel.

Power Within the Federal Reserve System

The Chairman	45%
The Staff	25%
The Other Governors Combined	20%
Federal Reserve Banks	10%
Total	100%

Reprinted by permission of W. W. Norton and Company, Inc.

[9] There are other committees such as the Federal Reserve Advisory Committee. This committee, which is mandated in the Federal Reserve Charter Act, is made up of bankers who advise the Fed periodically. The Advisory Committee is of relatively minor importance. In addition to the Advisory Committee, meetings and conferences of various Federal Reserve officials outside the FOMC context take place relatively frequently. Furthermore, the Fed often appoints committees with members drawn from either inside the Federal Reserve System or outside the system or both to study or advise on particular matters of concern to the system.

Board of Governors, with the chairman of the Board of Governors serving as the chairman of the FOMC; the president of the Federal Reserve Bank of New York, who serves as vice-chairman of the FOMC; and the four other places held by presidents of the other eleven Federal Reserve Banks on a rotating-term basis of one year. At any one time, four of the presidents and the president of the Federal Reserve Bank of New York are voting members of the committee, seven are not. However, all Fed presidents attend the FOMC meetings, even if they are not currently members. The reason that the president of the Federal Reserve Bank of New York has permanent membership is that open-market operations are conducted by the New York Fed and a vice-president of the New York Fed is in charge of the open-market trading desk and responsible for executing FOMC policy. Technically, however, the vice-president in charge of the open market trading desk (the Manager for Domestic Operations) is responsible to the FOMC, not to the New York Federal Reserve Bank president.

The FOMC meets eight times a year to decide on the course of monetary policy for the immediate period ahead and to review and change longer term monetary policy over the next year. As a result of their meeting, a directive is issued to the manager of the open-market trading desk to guide open-market operations. The directive summarizes the discussion of the FOMC concerning the economy and monetary policy and then instructs the trading desk manager on open-market operations. The operative paragraphs in the directive for the meeting held February 1–2, 1982, are excerpted below as an example. While at this junction much of the excerpt may be confusing, it will become much clearer as the conduct of the Fed's monetary policy is discussed in further chapters. However, it is clear at this point from the directive that the manager has some latitude in interpreting the instructions on a day-to-day basis.

> The Federal Open Market Committee seeks to foster monetary and financial conditions that will help to reduce inflation, promote a resumption of growth in output on a sustainable basis, and contribute to a sustainable pattern of international transactions. The Committee agreed that its objectives would be furthered by growth of M1, M2, and M3 from the fourth quarter of 1981 to the fourth quarter of 1982 within ranges of 2½ to 5½ percent, 6 to 9 percent, and 6½ to 9½ percent respectively. The associated range for bank credit was 6 to 9 percent.
>
> The Committee seeks behavior of reserve aggregates over the balance of the quarter consistent with bringing M1 and M2 over time into their longer-run target ranges for the year. Taking account of the recent surge in growth of M1, the Committee seeks no further growth in M1 for the January-to-March period and growth in M2 at an annual rate of around 8 percent. Some decline in M1 would be associated with more rapid attainment of the longer-run range and

would be acceptable in the context of reduced pressure in the money market. The Chairman may call for Committee consultation if it appears to the Manager for Domestic Operations that pursuit of the monetary objectives and related reserve paths during the period before the next meeting is likely to be associated with a federal funds rate persistently outside a range of 12 to 16 percent.

As the excerpt implies, it is common for the FOMC or a subgroup of the FOMC, which always includes the chairman, to have telephone meetings between scheduled meetings as events warrant. The manager for domestic operations is not only a part of these conference calls but in addition attends all the regular FOMC meetings.

The Role of the Staff of the FOMC and the Federal Reserve Board

It was noted above that former Federal Reserve Board Governor, Sherman Maisel, assigned considerable power to the Federal Reserve Board and FOMC staffs.[10] The professionals on the Federal Reserve Board staff are economists whose role is to provide information to the Board and to the FOMC. There is also a large legal staff that advises the Board on legislative interpretation and rule implementation.

The Board staff is continuously generating materials that are useful to the Board in making its decisions. To gain an appreciation of the kind of analysis done by the staff, it is most useful, however, to focus on the staff preparations for the FOMC meetings at which monetary policy decisions are made. The staff provides to the FOMC two basic sets of information. The "Greenbook," or as it is formally known "Current Economic and Financial Conditions," presents staff forecasts of critical economic variables, such as GNP and inflation, and contains current economic and financial data. The economic forecast contained in the Greenbook is generated by the staff through the use of econometric models (representations by equations of how the economy operates). The results of the econometric analysis are combined with staff judgment to yield the economic forecast. The major econometric model used by the staff to forecast the course of the economy is the MPS quarterly econometric model. The initials stand for the model developers, researchers at the Massachusetts Institute of Technology, the University of Pennsylvania, and the Social Science Research Council.

The second set of information provided by the staff is contained in "Monetary Aggregates and Money Market Conditions," called the "Bluebook." The Bluebook contains data on recent changes in financial

---

[10] The FOMC staff is chosen from the staff of the Board of Governors and is supplemented for meetings and advice by officers of the Federal Reserve Banks.

variables, such as interest rates and credit market conditions in general, and analyzes the conduct of monetary policy since the last FOMC meeting. Future alternative monetary policy courses are also presented in the Bluebook for the FOMC to consider. The FOMC may adopt one of these alternatives, modify and adopt an alternative, or decide to adopt a monetary policy course not presented by the staff. The senior members of the staff are present at FOMC meetings to answer questions about both the Greenbook and the Bluebook.

The discussion above makes the policy-making process sound very scientific and well defined. However, in practice, there is much room for disagreement by the FOMC with the staff assumptions, with suggested policy alternatives offered by the staff, and with staff analysis. The FOMC frequently formulates alternative scenarios at its meetings and acts on these. These alternative scenarios may not coincide significantly with any of the alternatives put forward by the staff. Nevertheless, staff input of factual information is crucial and staff policy alternatives are regarded as very useful even if these alternatives only serve to narrow the scope of the FOMC deliberations.

The Federal Reserve Banks

The twelve Federal Reserve Banks provide most of the daily contact between depository institutions and the Fed. They hold depository institution accounts, handle check-clearing, facilitate federal funds transactions, and make loans to depository institutions. Each Federal Reserve Bank has a board of directors composed of nine members. Three Class A and three Class B directors are elected by member banks, while three Class C directors are appointed by the Board of Governors and are drawn from the public at large. The Class A directors are drawn from banking, while the Class B directors are business people. The Board of Directors selects the president and first vice-president of the bank, subject to the approval of the Board of Governors. This means that the Board of Governors effectively has veto power over the appointment of the top two officers of each bank. The bank president is the chief executive officer of the bank.

The Federal Reserve Banks have relatively little influence on monetary policy. Sherman Maisel places their power at only 10 percent in the formation of monetary policy. Their influence comes in part from the membership of Federal Reserve Bank presidents on the FOMC, the conduct of open-market operations through the New York Federal Reserve Bank, and the necessity according to the Federal Reserve Charter for one or more Fed banks to petition for a change in the discount rate. (We will see in the next chapter that changes in the discount rate at which the Fed makes loans is considered a tool of monetary policy.) Since at any one time only five Federal Reserve Bank presidents are voting members of the FOMC, their minority membership status does not allow them to effectively control monetary policy, even if they should all be in agreement. Further, the manager of the open-market trading desk is technically an employee of the FOMC, not the New York Federal Reserve Bank and thus responsible to the FOMC. Finally, the Board of Governors must approve any discount rate change, and in practice the change is coordinated by the Board. Thus, the Federal Reserve Bank's influence in monetary policy formulation formally is indeed probably as small as Maisel indicates. However, the number of informal contacts among the bank officers, bank staffs, the Board, and the Fed staff can, at times, mean that through persuasion perhaps the banks can have more influence than the formal assessment would imply.

We should point out that at the formation of the Fed, member bank borrowing at the discount window was regarded as the Fed's main avenue to providing an "elastic currency." Therefore, it was believed that requiring discount rate changes to be initiated by the Federal Reserve Banks would give these banks real power relative to the Board of Governors. However, the rise of open-market operations as a major policy tool in the 1930s diminished the importance of the power of the Federal Reserve Banks. Indeed, one could argue that the evolution of the Federal Reserve System to the present has seen a shift in power to the Board from the regional Federal Reserve Banks. At one time the banks, particularly when the New York Federal Reserve Bank had a strong president, could be a major factor in Fed decisions. When individual bank presidents do influence Fed policy currently, it is due more to the stature of the individual president himself.[11] To summarize the organization of the Federal Reserve System discussed in this section, Figure 17-2 depicts the relationships of the key elements of the system.

Outside Influences on the Federal Reserve System

The Federal Reserve System was set up as an independent part of the government, and the appointments to the Board of Governors were staggered so as to insulate the Fed from political influences. There are a number of countries in which the central bank is under governmental control, including Britain. However, it was believed at the founding of the Fed, and is still believed by many, that independence of the Fed is vital for a truly effective monetary policy. Yet, how much is the Fed actually insulated from politics? The chairman of the Board

---

[11] For example, Paul Volcker, the Chairman of the Federal Reserve Board as this book goes to press, was President of the Federal Reserve Bank of New York from August 1975 to August 1979 and his standing through his years of experience in monetary matters made him a strong voice in policy formulation when he was president.

Figure 17-2
Organization of the Federal Reserve System

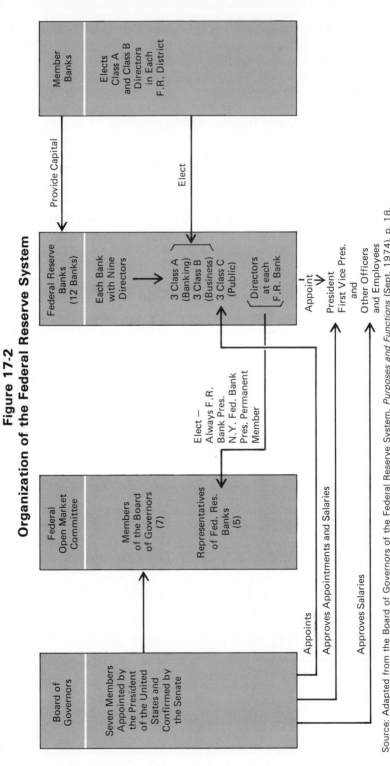

Source: Adapted from the Board of Governors of the Federal Reserve System, *Purposes and Functions* (Sept. 1974), p. 18.

of Governors is in frequent contact with the President and all members of the Board of Governors testify often before Congress and hear congressional views. Further, the Fed is not unaware that its independence stems from congressional legislation and can be rescinded by congressional action. In addition, the Fed is continuously exposed to the views of the public, the financial community, and the press; and such views may influence the governors' thinking.

Maisel notes that political and economic influences outside the Federal Reserve System have an impact on the Fed's decision making. Table 17-1 presents his view of how outside influence on the Fed is divided among various groups in and out of government. The administration and the Congress have the most influence on the Fed, with the White House being most important in recent years. The influence of Congress derives mostly from the key congressional committees that directly oversee the Fed, such as the House and Senate Banking Committees. The public through the press, economists outside the Fed, and lobbyists for business and labor command the attention of the Fed to their views and also influence the Fed through the impact such discussion has on the Congress and the administration. Finally, the financial community that is affected by the Fed's actions has some voice as do the regulatory agencies that share some supervisory authority with the Fed.

Maisel's comments suggest that while the Fed is independent it does not ignore the views of the government of which it is a part nor the opinions of groups outside the government. Indeed, it has long been believed that if the Fed did ignore these outside groups, the independence that it cherishes would not long be maintained. Thus, the Fed, while conducting monetary policy as it sees fit, does not do so oblivious to the opinion, advice, and demands of other groups in and out of government. It must carefully balance competing pressures both within and outside the system in order to pursue a monetary policy that it believes to be in the economy's best interests.

The Balance Sheet of the Federal Reserve System

A good overview of the specific activities of the Federal Reserve is provided by examining the consolidated balance sheet of the Federal Reserve System. The balance sheet presented for July 1981 is shown in Table 17-2. The items listed are taken up in turn.

Gold Certificates

Every time the U.S. Treasury purchased gold in the past, it issued a gold certificate to the Federal Reserve for the price that was paid.

Table 17-1
Outside Influences on the Federal Reserve System

The Administration	35%
The President	
The Treasury	
The Council of Economic Advisors	
The Office of Management and Budget	
All Other Nonfinancial	
The Congress	25%
House and Senate Committees on Banking	
Joint Economic Committee	
Senate Finance Committee	
House Ways and Means Committee	
The Public Directly	20%
Unorganized	
The Press	
Economists	
Lobbyists	
The Financial Interests	10%
Banks	
Savings and Loans	
Stockbrokers	
Etc.	
Foreign Interests	5%
Other Regulatory Agencies	5%
FDIC	
Comptroller	
FHLBB	
SEC	

Source: Sherman J. Maisel, *Managing the Dollar* (New York: Norton, 1973). Reprinted by permission of W. W. Norton and Company, Inc.

This price was fixed from the end of World War II to the early 1970s under the fixed exchange rate system. When the Treasury redeemed foreign holdings of dollars with gold, it retired the equivalent amount

Table 17-2
Consolidated Balance Sheet of Federal Reserve Banks, July 1981
(End of Period, Millions of Dollars)

Assets		Liabilities	
Gold Certificates	$ 11,154	Federal Reserve Notes	$124,765
Loans (Discounts	1,027	Deposits	
and Advances)		Depository Institutions	26,011
Securities		U.S. Treasury	2,922
U.S. Government	123,172	Foreign	285
Acceptances	453	Other	472
Federal Agency	9,054	Deferred Availability	5,834
Cash Items	7,085	Other Liabilities	1,992
Other Assets	13,142	Capital	2,806
Total Assets	$165,087	Total Liabilities	$165,087
		and Capital	

Source: Federal Reserve *Bulletin,* Sept. 1981.

of gold certificates. The Treasury ceased buying and selling gold (except for occasional gold auctions) in August 1971.[12] The gold certificates on the books of the Fed represent the value of the U.S. gold stock at $42.22 per ounce, the last official price of gold prior to the formal abandonment of the fixed exchange rate system in 1973. (Obviously at current market prices, the value of the gold stock is substantially more than indicated by the $11.15 billion of gold certificates.)

Gold certificates were utilized in the past as reserves against the amount of Federal Reserve Notes outstanding and member bank deposits. However, in 1968, the final link between gold certificates and Federal Reserve Notes was removed. It had been previously eliminated on member bank deposits and increased finally to a ratio of Federal Reserve Notes to gold certificates of $4 to $1. When that limit was approached in 1968, President Johnson requested of Congress and was granted authority to sever the link entirely. Thus, gold certificates serve no function at all presently other than corresponding to the U.S. gold stock at outdated prices.

---

[12] Still, when the gold was sold at auction, equivalent gold certificates were retired as they will be for the gold utilized in the minting of the annual Treasury gold medallions.

Loans

When the Federal Reserve System was established, the primary manner through which it was expected to meet its obligations of providing an elastic currency and acting as lender of last resort to the banking system was through the loans made to member banks through the "discount window." At least from the 1930s, however, open-market operations have overshadowed discount lending as a means of providing needed reserves to the banking system and conducting monetary policy. Nevertheless, the Federal Reserve does make loans to member banks and, under DIDMCA, to nonmembers banks and nonbank financial intermediaries that are required to meet Federal Reserve requirements.[13] In the next chapter, the use of changes in the discount rate—the rate charged for such borrowing—in executing monetary policy will be discussed.

The amount of discount loans actually outstanding at any moment in time usually is relatively small. As the table indicates, such loans totaled only a little over $1 billion as of July 1981, although the amount outstanding can vary considerably from month to month. The full name for Federal Reserve lending is discounts and advances. Banks can "discount" (sell) eligible commercial paper to the Federal Reserve Banks, or they can borrow (receive an advance) collateralized by government securities. In practice, Federal Reserve loans for many years have been almost completely in the form of advances collateralized by Fed holdings of commercial bank–owned government securities. Even though these loans are advances, the loan category is usually still called discounts as it has been throughout this book, and the rate on these loans is called the discount rate.

Securities

Table 17-2 shows that the major asset of the Federal Reserve System is government securities. It is by the buying and selling of these securities that the Fed conducts open-market operations and in turn open-market operations are the major way in which the Fed affects the reserves of the banking system. From previous analysis we know that when bank reserves are affected so is bank lending and the money supply. The Federal Reserve's massive holdings of U.S. government securities, which makes it a very important direct participant in the financial markets, can be put into perspective if it is realized that these holdings represented over 12 percent of the entire U.S. government debt in July 1981. The Fed, after expenses and a 6 percent return

---

[13] In practice, however, nonbank financial intermediaries such as savings and loan associations are supposed to exhaust their borrowing possibilities before turning to the Fed for a discount loan.

to member commercial banks on their holdings of Federal Reserve stock[14] must remit the full amount of its earnings to the Treasury. As a result, the holding by the Fed of U.S. government securities significantly reduces the amount of interest the Treasury actually pays on the debt. The Fed also holds some banker's acceptances and since 1971 has been permitted to purchase federal agency securities such as those issued by FNMA. Both of these latter moves were made to make these securities more liquid than they otherwise might be without Fed participation in these markets and are a rather small part of Federal Reserve securities holdings.

Cash Items in the Process of Collection

Cash items in the process of collection are checks that have been submitted by depository institutions to the Fed for clearing but have not yet been subtracted from the depository institution account on which they are drawn. That is, the depository institution on which the checks are drawn still has that amount represented by the checks in reserves. The full meaning of the asset item "Cash Items in the Process of Collection" is only apparent when combined with the liability item "Deferred Availability of Cash Items." Deferred availability are checks that have been presented to the Fed for clearing but have not yet been credited to depository institution accounts. That is, the amount has not yet been added to these accounts, thus increasing reserves. The difference between cash items and deferred availability is known as **Federal Reserve float.** In July 1981, Federal Reserve float totalled about $1.25 billion.

A little reflection will make the meaning of the float clear. Cash items mean bank reserves have not yet been reduced by this amount, while deferred availability means bank reserves have not been increased by that amount. The positive float means that banks had $1.25 billion more in reserves in July 1981 than they actually would have if all checks were cleared instantaneously.

Since float, which is always positive, adds reserves to the banking system and reserves support some multiple in deposits, the impact of changes in float on the money supply can be substantial and must be considered by the Fed in the conduct of monetary policy. The problem for the Fed is that float can fluctuate a great deal and these changes cannot be predicted with any accuracy. While schedules in crediting and debiting checks to member bank accounts are followed by the Fed, unexpected developments, in the weather, for example, which affect the transfer by air of batches of checks from one Federal Reserve Bank to another, can significantly affect float. The large in-

---

[14] Recall that the Fed is nominally owned by its member banks.

crease in float in January and February 1979 was ascribed to the terrible weather that winter which grounded or delayed a number of check transfer flights. Table 17-3 shows float from May 1978 to July 1981. The large changes in float seen in the table demonstrate the difficulties that float can present to the Fed's attempts to control the money supply. The Federal Reserve announced in August 1980, as mandated by DIDMCA, that it would take steps to substantially elimi-nate float by mid-1982. These steps would include stepped up trans-port of checks and electronic clearing of some large checks. In addition, the Fed will begin to charge banks interest on float to further spur its reduction. It remains to be seen whether float will actually be elimi-nated. After some changes designed to reduce float were instituted by the Fed in the early 1970s, float actually increased. However, the situation has changed considerably since then, particularly with the imposition of interest charges, and it is likely that the Fed will be more successful this time around.

Table 17-3
Federal Reserve Float, May 1978 to July 1981
(Monthly Averages of Daily Figures, Millions of Dollars)

May 1978	$4,119	January 1980	$5,825
June 1978	5,399	February 1980	5,617
July 1978	4,826	March 1980	4,658
August 1978	5,316	April 1980	3,902
September 1978	5,220	May 1980	3,642
October 1978	5,742	June 1980	4,167
November 1978	6,588	July 1980	2,808
December 1978	7,521	August 1980	3,467
January 1979	9,882	September 1980	3,192
February 1979	8,955	October 1980	2,194
March 1979	5,933	November 1980	6,792
April 1979	6,635	December 1980	4,467
May 1979	6,652	January 1981	2,280
June 1979	6,383	February 1981	1,545
July 1979	5,758	March 1981	3,261
August 1979	4,884	April 1981	2,156
September 1979	5,906	May 1981	2,542
October 1979	6,116	June 1981	2,506
November 1979	6,119	July 1981	1,251
December 1979	6,499		

Source: Federal Reserve *Bulletin,* various issues.

Other Assets

This category includes Federal Reserve holdings of foreign currencies which it uses for foreign exchange intervention. It also includes such economically unimportant assets as the value of bank premises.

Federal Reserve Notes

Turning to the liability side of the balance sheet, the largest Federal Reserve liability is Federal Reserve Notes. All currency in the United States is Federal Reserve Notes. Until the 1960s, there was some one-dollar-denomination Treasury currency in circulation called silver certificates. Now, however, silver certificates that remain are in collectors' hands and only Federal Reserve Notes circulate. It was indicated above that the last remaining tie between Federal Reserve Notes and gold certificates was eliminated in 1968. Since the gold certificate requirement had never inhibited the Fed from issuing notes when banks required more, the elimination of this tie as it was utilized in practice has not been significant. It is important to understand that currency comes into circulation as banks request it from the Fed to meet customer needs. The issuance of currency by itself does not increase bank reserves and, therefore, potential money supply growth, since at the time that a bank receives additional currency its depository institution account at the Fed is reduced accordingly. The Fed, as mandated by DIDMCA, has started to charge for the distribution of coin and currency to banks.

Deposits

Depository institution accounts at the Fed (which are still primarily member bank accounts) constitute the major portion of bank reserves. Changes in this item reflect changes in banks' ability to expand or contract their deposits and, therefore, Fed activities aimed at influencing the money supply are directed at influencing bank reserves.

It was noted above that one of the functions of a central bank is to act as the banker to the Treasury. The U.S. Treasury holds funds at the Federal Reserve on which it issues checks. As it is going to issue checks, it transfers needed funds from its tax and loan accounts at commercial banks to the Fed. The commercial banks are notified in advance of these transfers and therefore of the potential loss of reserves as the Fed moves deposits from depository institution accounts to the Treasury account. The Fed is aware of this (temporary) drain of bank reserves and can offset any such change if it wishes through open-market operations.

Foreign deposits are those of foreign central banks that keep deposits at the Fed primarily for foreign exchange transactions. These transactions are usually interventions in the foreign exchange market to "stabilize" exchange rates as explained in Chapter 14. The Fed maintains similar deposit accounts for similar reasons at foreign central banks.

Other Liabilities

There is little economic importance attached to this category. It reflects items such as unpaid bills.

Capital

The capital of the Federal Reserve and any surplus it hasn't distributed to stockholders or repaid to the Treasury is included in this item. The stockholders are the member commercial banks that hold stock as a condition of membership. They receive an annual dividend of 6 percent on this paid-in capital. This category has little economic significance. The only benefits that stockholders derive from their holdings aside from the general benefits of membership are the dividend (which is well under market rates) and the right to elect the Class A and B directors of their district Federal Reserve Bank.

The discussion of the Federal Reserve balance sheet yields a beginning insight into the varied activities of the Federal Reserve System. For example, changes in the securities portfolio, member bank borrowing, and Federal Reserve float directly affect member bank deposits and therefore the reserves of the banking system. As the discussion of the Federal Reserve System continues in the next two chapters these insights will be substantially expanded. Before proceeding, however, it is interesting in rounding out this introductory chapter on central banking and the Federal Reserve System to briefly note the relationship of the major central banks in the western world.

International Cooperation of Central Banks

The last decade has seen an unprecedented degree of international consultation and much cooperation among the major central banks of the West. The primary motivation for the increased level of consultation stems from the floating exchange rate system, the increasing importance of international financial flows, and the not unrelated increase in oil prices, which have resulted in substantial transfers of funds to the Middle East. These funds are then recycled through the financial system of Western Europe and the United States.

Some international consultation among central bankers takes place in formal settings such as the periodic meeting of the International

Monetary Fund (IMF) and the Bank for International Settlements (BIS), which is located in Basle, Switzerland. The IMF has previously been discussed. The Bank for International Settlements, little known outside international financial circles, has often been described as a central bankers' club. It is much more than that, having as its function the exchange of international financial information, but it does provide a forum for central bankers to meet and discuss international financial matters and central banking policy.

Interestingly, the BIS is a much older institution than the IMF. It was established in the wake of World War I, primarily to aid in the German reparations payments that resulted from that war. However, not since the interwar period between World War I and World War II has it achieved the notoriety of recent years. This increased attention to the BIS derives primarily from the seriousness of international financial matters and the much greater international financial interrelationships that were a product of the 1970s.

Perhaps even more important than the formal organizations that allow central bankers to meet and confer, are the informal exchanges that go on all the time between central bankers. Much of these consultations relates to foreign exchange market intervention. It was explained in Chapter 14 that the world currently is operating under what is known as a managed floating system. To some degree, central bank intervention in foreign exchange markets is currently coordinated by the central banks so that they are not working at cross purposes. Central banks such as the Fed, the Bank of England, and the German Central Bank (the Bundesbank), typically have the job of foreign exchange intervention for their governments. Whether foreign exchange intervention is in the long-run interests of the international financial system is hard to determine. Yet it is clear that if intervention is going to occur, it seems logical that it should be consistent among the countries involved, and this requires discussions between central bankers. On a more practical level, foreign exchange intervention often requires one central bank to obtain foreign currencies from other central banks through so-called swap operations. Swap operations are essentially short-term exchanges of currencies and are carried out frequently between central banks. It is easy to foresee that close consultations on internationally important financial matters will continue between the major central banks.

THIS IS THE FED

A Look Inside Paul Volcker's Fed

By STEVEN RATTNER

WASHINGTON On the morning of March 30, Topic A for most Americans was still the shooting of President Reagan the day before. At the Federal Reserve, the nation's seemingly cloistered central bank, the buzzing in the corridors concerned monetary policy. A gathering of the Federal Open Market Committee was getting under way, just as it does every 45 days or so.

Sipping coffee from plastic cups, the Fed governors and reserve bank presidents who are members of the committee mingled in the halls and anterooms adjoining the cavernous board room with its view of Washington's Mall. While a nearby television set sat blank, they chatted among themselves and with senior staff members about economic news, doings at the Fed, and the still-stunning news of the shooting.

By tradition, as they filtered into the cream-colored room, the governors arrayed themselves by seniority, just as they do when they meet twice weekly as the Federal Reserve Board, the Fed's ruling body. Each of the 12 presidents takes the seat belonging—again by tradition and with no particular logic—to his bank. And at the end of the long table, opposite Paul A. Volcker, the chairman, sit key staff members at a small table pushed up to the main table.

When the doors to the board room hiss shut precisely at 9 A.M., the deliberations of the committee— the body charged with charting the monetary course for the world's largest economy—become secret.

They take on a confidentiality as precious as that of the Supreme Court and almost as closely guarded.

But members of the committee are a touch more forthcoming than Supreme Court Justices, and from extensive conversations and interviews, a more textured picture emerges. In sharper focus, it principally concerns the extraordinary influence of by Mr. Volcker, but it extends to other senior officials as well.

Once a little-noticed agency with a coolly impersonal image, the Federal Reserve has taken center stage. Its role as the leading instrument of the nation's anti-inflation effort—and the high interest rates that necessarily flow from that effort— have brought the Fed, more than a little reluctantly, into the national limelight.

On the surface, all is calm at the Fed. The 1,520 bureaucrats bustle through the imposing building on Constitution Avenue and the delicately modern annex across the street, connected by underground tunnel. Freed by law from executive branch control over even its budget, the Fed essentially runs itself, drawing its money from interest on Treasury securities it holds. Oversight by Congress is nominal.

Senior Fed officials enjoy such amenities as tennis and squash courts. The Fed's art curator regularly changes the art exhibits in the halls, and brasswork is never allowed to tarnish. Much like the Supreme Court and unlike almost any other Government agency, reverence and tradition permeate the Fed. Luncheon in the governors' dining room, with its panoramic view of south Washington, is always at 1 P.M. The practice dates from the era of William McChesney Martin, chairman from 1951 to 1970, whose unvarying routine was to end board meetings at noon, play an hour's tennis, and then lunch.

Underneath the placid exterior, the Federal Reserve today is an institution in flux, trying to respond—without complete success—to the new demands of an inflationary and faster-changing present. In the policy arena, the Federal Open Market Committee, which sets monetary policy, has taken tougher action to restrain monetary growth than ever before, even as it delegates to the staff far more authority for conducting that policy.

Among the new experiences for the Fed is the severity of the current attack from conservatives—including a number of key Reagan Administration officials. The Fed has long been used to criticisms from Administrations that money and credit were being too tightly restrained. But, more papist than the Pope, ranking members of the Reagan team contend the Fed has still not shown the necessary backbone—in particular, the will to accept even greater interest-rate fluctuations and perhaps higher average rates as the price of holding tight to its targets.

In late 1979, the Fed adopted new monetary procedures, partly from a reluctance to directly vote large increases in interest rates, only to find itself with record high rates and the prospect that a collision between monetary restraint and an inflationary economy could force rates still higher. Meanwhile, the Fed has moved toward a less dogmatic approach to the money supply and interest rates, less tied to the most recent movements in M-1B, which consists of currency and interest-bearing and noninterest-bearing checking accounts.

And there are new complexities in the governing of the Fed, as well. While extraordinary agreement exists on the need for monetary restraint to fight inflation, more dissents have come in the last two years than in memory.

These days, the Fed, like other institutions, has become less the fiefdom of its chairman, giving a somewhat larger role to the six men and one woman who currently constitute the board of governors of the Federal Reserve System and the 12 men who preside over the system's regional banks.

But at the same time, in the tall and ungainly Mr. Volcker, the Fed has a chairman with unusual ability to provide intellectual leadership—so much so that the Fed's tougher stance on growth of money and credit would have been unlikely without a Volcker.

The Federal Reserve, protector of the dollar, is now known best as the custodian of the nation's money supply. It exercises that responsibility mainly by buying Treasury securities when it believes that the money supply should increase and reversing the process when it wants an opposite effect. But the Fed has an array of other responsibilities as well, burdens that claim the bulk of most Fed governors' time.

The Federal Reserve regulates the banks that are members of its system, approving mergers. Its host of regulations touches every aspect of American financial life—from truth-in-lending to borrowing for stock purchases. At the Federal Reserve in New York, where Treasury securities and foreign exchange are traded, gold is stored for foreign nations in a steel-encased vault on bedrock five stories below ground.

Volcker

The dawning realization of the importance of the Fed and monetary policy brought more prominence to the Fed chairman. It is a development that apparently gives Mr. Volcker genuine discomfort. Often appearing shy or ill at ease, he can be awkward in conversation.

In his endless appearances before Congress, reporters and conventions, Mr. Volcker, now 53, leaves the distinct impression of a man more comfortable with less prominence. His principal passion often seems to be frugality; with one recent visitor, he displayed great excitement over discovering a cigar that costs only 8 cents.

Mr. Volcker's tastes are modest, extending to a matchbox apartment a few blocks from the Fed for his Washington weekdays and occasional dinners at a modest Washington restaurant called Marrocco's. There Mr. Volcker, who earns $60,663, will usually have a single beer—domestic—and frown on those who splurge on imported brands.

The chairman's principal residence remains in Manhattan, where his wife mostly stays to continue her job as a bookkeeper and take care of a handicapped son. Mr. Volcker received $110,000 a year while president of the New York Fed and his constrained financial circumstances, together with obvious discomfort with the pressure, particularly from the Reagan Administration, have led to rumors that he might leave before his term as chairman expires, in August 1983, a prospect Mr. Volcker denies.

What is perhaps most impressive about Mr. Volcker is his extraor-

dinary open-mindedness and penchant for intellectual debate; he is constantly questioning and probing. But he sometimes seems indecisive. He seems able to see so many sides to a question that he sometimes is not sure which side he is on. "Paul has usually argued both sides of every issue," a governor said.

While his rhetoric on reducing the growth of money has been unswerving, he has sometimes gone astray in the implementation. Perhaps the most stunning example came in the fall of 1980, when he failed to move quickly against sharp increases in the money supply until near-panic developed in the financial markets.

"I wasn't too happy with our policy in September," said Frank E. Morris, president of the Boston Fed, who was a voting member of the committee at the time. "By October, it was clear we weren't moving fast enough."

Such mistakes and Mr. Volcker's tinge of indecisiveness have also contributed to the difficulty that Mr. Volcker and the other Fed officials have had in convincing markets and the public of their dedication to reducing monetary growth.

Similarly, Mr. Volcker has avoided confrontations in his relations with both the Carter and Reagan Administrations, in part because he views himself as a team player. Although he argued with Carter officials against the imposition of credit controls in March 1980, he went along—and found his original view ultimately proved correct.

Just a few weeks ago, Mr. Volcker complained privately to Treasury Secretary Donald T. Regan about what he considered carping criticism from Beryl Sprinkel, the Under Secretary for Monetary Affairs, but declined publicly to discuss the matter. Such performances have raised questions both inside and outside the Fed about whether Mr. Volcker is tough enough.

The Morning Call

Since the Federal Reserve adopted its new policy of controlling the supply of money directly, the most important daily meeting in the world of finance and the economy takes place each business morning precisely at 11:15 by telephone conference call. The key participants in the 15-minute session are two slight, gray-haired men each in their mid-50's who wield great influence.

In his airy office on the second floor of the Fed building in Washington sits Stephen H. Axilrod, the staff director for monetary and fiscal policy; in a similar room in New York, Peter D. Sternlight, the manager for domestic operations and senior vice president of the New York Reserve Bank. Although others participate in the conversation, the expertise that Mr. Axilrod and Mr. Sternlight have amassed in more than 60 years of combined service at the Fed assure little questioning of their technical pronouncements.

Before Oct. 6, 1979, the open market committee set limits as narrow as a half percentage point on interest rates, principally on Federal funds, which is money lent by one bank to another. Whenever the economy or the money supply figures appeared to be going awry, a meeting of the committee was required to make a change and 13 or more were held each year. For the staff, the responsibility was to buy and sell securities to achieve the interest-rate targets.

Now the committee focuses on the money supply and sets only broad ranges for interest rates. To Mr. Axilrod, Mr. Sternlight and their respective staffs is left the primary responsibility for determining how much money the Fed should pump into the system in order to achieve those goals.

The morning call ends with an agreement on what adjustments need to be made in the rate at which the Fed allows reserves to flow to the banking system. Then the execution of monetary policy is left to a dozen or so young market experts, working in an unadorned conference room at the New York Federal Reserve Bank, who trade millions of dollars of securities each day with the major Wall Street firms.

Accordingly, Mr. Volcker's role is augmented by his control of the staff and by the high quality of the staff, which prizes longevity and professionalism. It is the staff—in close consultation with Mr. Volcker—that prepares the policy recommendations that doubtless guide the committee. "It's the best permanent staff in town," said Nancy H. Teeters, a Fed governor.

"When we first began the new procedures," a Fed official said, "the committee members were inclined to come in here, vote a 5 percent money target and go away with a warm feeling in their stomachs. Volcker made them at least discuss the reserve path so they would have a sense of the consequences of their actions."

The Governors

The life of a Fed governor is a pleasant one. A gracefully proportioned, high-ceilinged office complete with working fireplace comes with the $55,388-a-year job. There are chauffeurs and ample staff assistance. A sense of contemplation drifts through the governors' corridor and although the workload has been increasing and although most are dedicated, the office hours are hardly overwhelming.

"They all think they should be getting as much attention as the chairman," said a long-time aide. One governor, Henry C. Wallich, mails copies of his speeches to journalists, duplicating the Federal Reserve public affairs office distribution.

Until the reign of Arthur F. Burns (1970 to 1978), the Fed chairman traditionally voted last at open market committee meetings. Dr. Burns changed that, because he didn't want his members to have any doubt of where he stood on an issue—and he was never defeated on a vote. When Dr. Burns sensed opposition, he would allow the discussion to drag on until the opponents were worn down or he would postpone the issue.

"The interaction at the Fed is now very different than it was under Arthur F. Burns," a governor said. "He was such a domineering figure."

Mr. Volcker is by all accounts more willing to delegate responsibility and authority, such as on routine bank mergers. And while Dr. Burns most often knew precisely what result he sought, Mr. Volcker is more openminded and more flexible, holding the view that whether the money supply target is precisely 4 or 4½ percent hardly matters.

"One has to be realistic," said E. Gerald Corrigan, president of the Mineapolis bank and Mr. Volcker's special assistant for the first part of his Washington stay. "This is not quite the science we delude ourselves into thinking it is."

Those at the Fed who enjoy guessing surmise that Mr. Volcker's true inclinations would be in favor of tighter money. It was Mr. Volcker who sided with the conservatives in

early 1979 and dissented twice because he felt insufficient restraint was being applied. Many of those same members of the open market committee have been dissenting on and off in recent months. Indeed, the only evidence of any substantial challenge to Mr. Volcker's performance came last fall when for two successive meetings, four of the 12 committee members dissented on the side of additional tightening.

Marshaling a consensus is made somewhat easier for Mr. Volcker by the fact that members of the open market committee accord the chairman great deference. "It's not like a committee of Congress voting something up or down," said J. Charles Partee, a governor.

By contrast, votes within the board on bank mergers and other nonmonetary matters are a free-for-all, with Mr. Volcker at times on the losing side.

"I don't like to dissent particularly," said Mr. Morris, president of the Boston Fed. "I'm not sure it's healthy for the system to have an awful lot of dissents."

Most members agree with Mr. Morris and withhold dissents except on rare occasions. The views of such members as Mr. Wallich and Mrs. Teeters, who dissent with great regularity, are said to be taken less seriously by their colleagues. Others who dissent only rarely or not at all—such as Mr. Solomon, Lyle E. Gramley and Mr. Partee—are among the most respected participants.

Not that Mr. Wallich, a courtly cigar-smoking former economics professor who looks younger than his 66 years isn't respected. His habits are the source of great amusement at the Fed—his dark, lair-like office, the green eyeshade he sometimes sports. Mr. Wallich has stopped buying breakfast coffee in the dining room because the cost is up to 40 cents a cup.

But Mr. Wallich's warnings about the dangers of fast money growth are listened to, particularly when he relates to other Fed members stories of his early years in Germany, such as going to a swimming pool in 1923 carrying 150 billion marks to pay for admission. If Mr. Wallich continually repeats himself, as when he talks on and on about how seemingly double-digit interest rates are almost always in reality negative, he is quietly tolerated.

Mrs. Teeters—bright, articulate and 50—is less warmly regarded within the Fed, no doubt partly because she is a woman in an institution still overwhelmingly male but more important because she is seen as representing an economic point of view whose time is past. The view, that interest rates can be brought down by faster monetary growth, is dismissed by other Fed members.

Less has been heard of late from the other liberal and the Fed's only black member, Emmett J. Rice, 61, who is widely regarded as the least effective and least dedicated governor but the most frequent user of the Fed's tennis court. Grumbling is heard in the halls of the Fed about Mr. Rice's rule about not attending more than one meeting a day. Mr. Rice declined to return calls requesting interviews.

For Fed watchers, a particularly pleasant surprise was the performance of Frederick Schultz, the 52-year-old vice chairman, who arrived with the image of having been chosen principally for his political connections. Mr. Schultz, a former banker and speaker of the Florida House of Representatives, is a friend of Patrick Caddell, President Carter's pollster.

Mr. Schultz, a tall man with sandy-colored hair who is partial to plaid suits and aviator glasses, has emerged as Mr. Volcker's right-hand man in administering the Fed and in communicating with the outside world. Mr. Schultz frankly admits his lack of background in monetary policy and defers to Mr. Volcker.

"Fred is concerned about what the world out there is thinking," a governor said.

Mr. Schultz says he concluded at the outset that he should never vote against the chairman on monetary policy matters, helping to create the solid base of support with which Mr. Volcker begins.

"I do everything I can to try to take care of the nuts and bolts," said Mr. Schultz.

One fear at the Fed these days is what happens when Mr. Schultz's term expires a year from now—both the prospective loss of a key figure and the prospective appointment of an antagonistic monetarist. One Washington rumor, doubtlessly disturbing to the Fed, has Mr. Schultz being succeeded by the Treasury's Mr. Sprinkel, who would then become chairman when Mr. Volcker's term expires.

As never before, the board of governors today is dominated by former staff members and by economists—qualifications that appear impressive in comparison with a past tendency to more political appointments. Of the seven, all but Mr. Schultz served at either the Washington headquarters or the New York bank. For most, the stay at the Fed was relatively brief, but two—Mr. Partee and Mr. Gramley—have devoted their careers to Fed posts.

Of the two, Mr. Gramley is probably the more influential these days, in large part because he is seen to take the job more seriously. Each Fed member is given a particular area of supervision and Mr. Gramley is regarded as having worked diligently at supervising the Reserve banks, a particularly tedious occupation.

Mr. Gramley has also been accorded substantial respect because of the thought he has devoted to economic policy and because of his intellectual openness, not unlike Mr. Volcker's.

"Lyle's more conservative than most people think," said one governor approvingly. In personality, the 54-year old former Carter Administration economist, a fox hunter and tennis player, is soft-spoken and courteous.

To some Fed officials, Mr. Partee, an easygoing mustached man who wears bow ties, possesses many of these same qualities. "He knows an enormous amount about how the economy works," Mr. Gramley said. "When he has something to say you listen."

The Hand on the Tiller in Money Supply
THE FED STRUCTURE

Board of Governors
7 members, 14-year terms
12 regional Federal Reserve banks
5,426 member banks (as of Aug., 1980)

THE FED PROCESS
The Federal Open Market Committee decides monetary policy.
Voting members are the seven governors, the president of the New York Fed, and presidents of four other regional banks, who serve rotating, one-year terms. The seven other presidents attend but do not vote.

The "Morning Call"
The daily conference call links staff specialists in Washington with their counterparts at the New York Fed, which handles trading for all the regional banks and the system itself. The Federal Reserve chairman and the New York Fed president often take part. The daily instructions to the Fed's trading desk come out of this meeting.

Federal Reserve Bank of New York
Its System Account, or trading desk, handles day-to-day buying and selling of securities. The department also prepares frequent estimates of commercial banks' reserves, a key indicator in carrying out monetary policy.

The Federal Reserve affects the supply of money by buying and selling Government securities. It trades with about three dozen "primary" dealers. When the Fed buys securities, it pays the seller by adding to the seller's checking account at a commercial bank, thus increasing demand deposits, the largest component of the money supply. When the Fed sells, the buyer's payment comes from its bank account, thus reducing this component of the money supply.

But to a lesser extent than Mrs. Teeters, Mr. Partee has disappointed a number of Fed officials with a pronounced tendency to dissent on the side of faster expansion of the money supply. And Mr. Partee has slowed down a bit, Fed insiders say, performing his tasks but not striving to make additional contributions.

To both a casual glance and a more detailed examination, these six men and one woman represent the Federal Reserve, even though they constitute only seven of 12 votes on the open market committee.

For another thing, the governors, whose personal staff consists of only a secretary and special assistant, can avail themselves of a larger and more talented headquarters staff—and do. Every Monday morning, a briefing on the economic and financial situation is provided. Brief written reports on market conditions are circulated.

Interested bank presidents can obtain much of this information by other means. But for a president reposing in Cleveland, burdened with managerial and local responsibilities, the inclination is to devote less time to monetary policy.

"To some extent, we're able to spend more time with monetary policy," said one governor. "To some extent, we have more information."

Barring a monetary crisis, meetings of the open market committee end in time for a 1 P.M. lunch. At roughly four hours per meeting, a total of 32 hours a year—special meetings excepted—are devoted to the committee's role in formulating monetary policy. To some extent, the committee is like a corporate board of directors.

Staff briefings are conducted. Extensive debate goes on. Policy guidance is provided. Votes are taken. But although the governors, in particular, are more involved than most corporate directors, the real power mostly remains with management, Paul Volcker and his staff.

"When you get right down to it, this place is Volcker, Volcker, Volcker," a staff member said.

From *The New York Times*, May 3, 1981. © 1981 by The New York Times Company. Reprinted by permission.

Key Points

1. The Federal Reserve System is the central bank for the United States. As such, it has regulatory responsibility for commercial banks, executes monetary policy, and acts as fiscal agent for the U.S. Treasury. The Fed is independent of the executive branch of government but responsible to Congress.

2. The Federal Reserve System is administered by a Board of Governors composed of seven members who are appointed by the President of the United States and confirmed by the Senate. Governors serve staggered 14-year terms, and one member is appointed by the President as chairman for a four-year term. The system includes twelve Federal Reserve Banks, which handle most of the day-to-day business between the Fed and its member banks.

3. The major monetary policy-making body of the Federal Reserve is the Federal Open Market Committee. Membership on the FOMC consists of the seven members of the Board of Governors and the president of

the Federal Reserve Bank of New York as permanent members. The remaining four members of the FOMC are drawn from the presidents of the eleven other Federal Reserve Banks on a rotating basis. The FOMC oversees the open-market operations that are conducted by the manager of domestic operations (the manager of the open-market trading desk) in New York, who is responsible to the FOMC.

4. While the Fed is constituted as an independent agency considerable indirect influence can be exerted on the Fed by the President and the Congress as well as by outside constituency groups. In order to preserve its independence, the Fed cannot be wholly oblivious to the opinions of these various entities in its conduct of monetary policy.

5. The balance sheet of the Fed is dominated on the asset side by its holdings of U.S. government securities and on the liability side by Federal Reserve Notes, which constitute the currency of the United States.

Questions for Discussion

1. Briefly sketch the organization of the Federal Reserve System. How was this organization a result of regional compromise when the Fed was founded? In practice, how important has the regionalism represented by the Federal Reserve Banks been in influencing the Federal Reserve System?

2. The Fed is an independent agency of government free from all political pressures. True or False? Discuss.

3. The FOMC is said to be the most important standing committee in the Fed. Why is the FOMC regarded as so important?

4. Explain Federal Reserve float. Why are changes in Federal Reserve float considered important?

5. The Fed was established to be a lender of last resort to the banking system through the operation of its "discount window." How has the Federal Reserve's role in the financial system evolved from this initial conception?

Suggested Readings

Board of Governors of the Federal Reserve System. *Purposes and Functions.* Washington, D.C.: Board of Governors, 1974.

Burns, Arthur F. *Reflections of an Economic Policy Maker.* Washington, D.C.: American Enterprise Institute, 1978.

Burns, Arthur F. "The Independence of the Federal Reserve System." *Challenge,* July/August 1976, pp. 21–24.

Kane, Edward J. "New Congressional Restraints and Federal Reserve Independence." *Challenge,* Nov./Dec. 1975, pp. 37–44.

Kane, Edward J. "The Re-Politicization of the Fed." *Journal of Financial and Quantitative Analysis,* Nov. 1974, pp. 743–52.

Maisel, Sherman J. *Managing the Dollar.* New York: Norton, 1973.

The Federal Reserve System and Monetary Policy

18

This chapter deals with monetary policy: What monetary policy means, what the Fed is expected to accomplish by conducting monetary policy, and the tools available to the Fed for this purpose. The details of the day-to-day operation of monetary policy are taken up in the next chapter. Monetary policy may be defined as the attempt by the Federal Reserve to influence the money supply and interest rates in order to affect economic activity. The phrase economic activity encompasses many important economic variables such as economic output, employment, and the rate of inflation. Operating mainly through the financial markets, the Fed implements monetary policy in hopes of achieving desirable levels in these and other variables. This is the goal of monetary policy specifically and of economic policy generally.

Goals of Economic Policy

Economists and policy makers are agreed that the two major goals of economic policy are full employment and price stability. Full employment has actually been a stated goal of economic policy since 1946 when it was incorporated as a mandated requirement of government in the Employment Act of that year. In 1978, this goal and further goals including relative price stability were reaffirmed by the Full Employment and Balanced Growth Act, known as the Humphrey–Hawkins Act. Stating these goals is unambiguous, but achieving the goals is another question to which we will return.

The list of policy goals can be extended beyond full employment and price stability to include economic growth and international economic stability in the balance of payments and exchange rates. Some economists and policy makers may add further to this list by including equitable distribution of income or increasing productivity as other policy goals. Monetary policy cannot hope to accomplish all these goals by itself. Fiscal policy, the use of tax and expenditure changes by the federal government to influence economic activity, is the other major component of economic policy. Before examining monetary policy and its relationship to the achievement of economic goals, we should clarify the meanings of the economic goals.

Price Stability

Price stability refers to little or no inflation in the economy. Inflation has been a continuing problem through the 1970s and early 1980s. Some economists believe that the Fed is most responsible for inflation in the economy. Others argue that it is incorrect to place primary responsibility on the Fed for causing or being able to prevent inflation and rely instead on such alternative explanations of inflation as the increasing federal deficit, energy price increases, and lagging productivity growth. During 1981, for example, many economists suggested that the Reagan economic program of tax and expenditure reductions relied too heavily on monetary policy to control inflation while ignoring the inflationary impact of the large deficits that would be generated by the program. Those differing views of the inflationary process will be explored in detail in Chapter 20. However, no analyst disagrees that the Fed has a major influence on the rate of inflation in the economy through money supply changes. Therefore, restoring and maintaining price stability is one of the major goals of Federal Reserve policy. At times such as in 1980, 1981, and early 1982, Fed policy appeared to be focused entirely on the restoration of price stability.

Full Employment

Although full employment is typically thought of in terms of a fully employed labor force, it implies considerably more than that. It implies a fully utilized resource base, including the labor force but also including other productive resources such as capital (factories, machinery, and so on) and land. Full employment has been a stated goal of national economic policy since the Full Employment Act of 1946 and more recently the Humphrey–Hawkins Act of 1978. Humphrey–Hawkins added price stability as an additional policy goal.

For many years it was argued that there was a tradeoff between inflation and full employment. This hypothesis maintained that lower levels of unemployment were associated with a higher rate of inflation and vice versa. This was known as the Phillips curve tradeoff after A. W. Phillips, who in 1958 demonstrated a statistical relationship between these variables for Great Britain. This relationship became known as the Phillips curve.[1] The experience of the 1970s and early 1980s when often both unemployment and inflation were high has led many economists to doubt that such a tradeoff exists, at least in the very straightforward manner indicated by simple Phillips curves. Others argue that the Phillips curve has simply shifted so that the tradeoff between inflation and unemployment has become very unfavorable. The alternative views of the Phillips curve will be discussed extensively in Chapter 20. However, mentioning the Phillips curve at this point calls attention to the fact that policy goals may be unachievable simultaneously. The potential conflicts between the achievement of goals will become even more apparent as the discussion proceeds.

International Balance

The goal of balance in external payment relations and exchange rates has always been important but has demanded increasing attention from policy makers in the 1970s and 1980s. Policy makers must formulate policy giving considerable attention to the external effects of these policies. This is true even with regard to economic policies that were once considered purely internal. For example, interest rates in the United States have an impact on the balance of payments and the exchange rate because of capital flows in the international economy. Therefore, a policy that is directed at stimulating employment in the United States through lower interest rates can have deleterious consequences for both the balance of payments and the value of the dollar internationally as funds flow out of the United States and into other countries and their currencies.

Furthermore, the Fed, under the managed float, intervenes directly in the foreign exchange markets to influence the dollar exchange rate.[2] Such intervention can have direct impact on the money supply and interest rates in the U.S. economy similar to open-market operations. For example, when the Fed buys foreign currencies with dollars, the reserves of the banking system increase. If this is not offset by open-market sales, the money supply will expand, all else being equal.

Economic Growth

Economic growth is an increase in aggregate output and output per capita over time. Increases in output per capita are used as a measure of an economy's standard of living. Economic growth is a goal of

---

[1] Following Phillips' work, a "Phillips" curve was also generated almost immediately for the United States.

[2] The Reagan administration announced in 1981 that it was suspending intervention in the foreign exchange markets except for emergencies. Since the Fed acts in the foreign exchange markets at the direction of the Treasury, temporarily at least, the Fed no longer attempts to stabilize the dollar internationally.

economic policy. Policies that encourage investment and saving in the economy and increase productivity are desirable. Furthermore, it is desirable that policies implemented to combat inflation have as small an impact upon economic growth as possible. Experience in the 1970s and 1980s has shown the difficulty of achieving this balance.

Income Distribution

Some economists argue that one of the goals of policy is to ensure an "equitable" distribution of income, although "equity" is often defined differently by various people. Others argue that equality is not desirable but some minimum standard of living needs to be achieved for all. Still others believe that if sound policy is followed to achieve other goals, the standard of living over time will rise for all, and thus income redistribution need not be a formal policy goal.

That economic policy does affect the distribution of income is undeniable. Income taxes are progressive (a higher percentage of income is paid in taxes as income rises) and, therefore, changes in income taxes have redistribution effects that may not be fully considered when Congress changes tax rates for purposes of fiscal policy. Similarly, monetary policy affects some sectors of the economy differently than others. For example, both housing and small business are severely affected by tight monetary policy, which may also have an impact on income distribution.

Productivity Growth

Implicit in a number of goals discussed above are increases in economic productivity or, as it is usually measured, output per worker in the economy. Economic policy makers must be aware of the impact on productivity of policies designed to achieve other economic goals. The higher productivity is, the more each worker can produce and the lower inflation is, all else being equal. This follows because a worker who gets a 10 percent wage increase but produces 10 percent more is producing at a constant cost per unit, and the price of the product need not be increased to reflect higher labor costs. Since productivity increases depend importantly on investment by business in additional capital, the impact on capital investment of economic policy must always be considered. Further, policies that encourage increased capital investment can complement policies designed to reduce inflation. This is the notion behind part of the Reagan tax cut program of 1981.

Interdependence of Goals

It should be clear from the discussion of the goals that they are not independent. The achievement of one has implications for others, and the failure to achieve a particular goal may also have implications for other goals. Because the Fed has responsibility for one of the two major types of economic policy in the United States, it is useful to see how the Fed does affect the economy and, therefore, the economic goals discussed above.

The Influence of Changes in the Money Supply and Interest Rates on the Economy

There is no longer any serious disagreement over the issue of whether changes in the supply of money are important in influencing economic activity. However, disagreement continues over the degree of importance of money supply changes and over the channels through which money supply changes affect economic activity and, therefore, the achievement of monetary policy goals. Indeed, a relatively new and decidedly minority view held by some economists is that while changes in the money supply are important, monetary policy cannot influence the economy in a desired manner and therefore should be executed by the Fed in a very mechanical way. The channels through which monetary policy works need to be explored.

The Neo-Keynesian View

The Neo-Keynesian view, also called the portfolio approach, emphasizes, as did Keynes, the role of the interest rate in transmitting changes in the money supply to the economy. However, the Neo-Keynesians have added to Keynes' work consideration of the spectrum of financial assets in the economy and the importance of financial wealth (the value of people's holdings of securities) in influencing spending decisions in the economy. To these Neo-Keynesian economists, monetary policy initially affects the rate of interest on short-term securities like Treasury bills. As asset holders shift between short-term and long-term securities to restore the equilibrium in their portfolios that has been disturbed by the monetary policy change, real spending in the economy is affected. For example, suppose Treasury bill rates fall as a result of monetary policy actions. Asset holders substitute relatively higher yielding long-term securities for the now lower yielding short-term securities. However, by purchasing long-term securities, long-term securities prices are bid up, lowering long-term yields. Since investment spending is particularly influenced by changes in long-term rates, investment spending in the economy may increase. Depending upon whether monetary policy is expansionary (which means lower interest rates to the Neo-Keynesians) or restrictive (higher interest rates) determines the direction in which spending will change. These changes in spending in turn will either stimulate or retard economic activity. At the same time, since bank reserves are influenced by monetary policy, bank loan rates will also change depending on the banks' reserve positions, also encouraging or discouraging economic activity.

There is also an impact on wealth as interest rates change in response to monetary policy changes. For example, restrictive monetary policy implies increases in interest rates that reduce the value of asset-holder portfolios (as the prices of the securities they are holding decline), and this reduces spending. This wealth effect may be reinforced by a reduction in asset-holder liquidity because of the fall in value of securities holdings that occurs with the rise in interest rates. The asset holder may be reluctant to sell securities to raise funds for spending because of the seriousness of a capital loss. On the other hand, expansionary policy that reduces interest rates raises the value of financial assets, thus stimulating spending. Further, this effect is reinforced by the positive impact that declines in interest rates have on liquidity so that the asset holder can more easily and profitably convert securities holdings into money.

To the Neo-Keynesians the importance of monetary policy stems from its impact on interest rates and, through interest rate changes, on financial wealth and liquidity in the economy. Anything that interferes with the change in interest rates or the resulting changes in spending in the economy will blunt the impact of monetary policy. For example, if a change in the money supply simply results in a corresponding change in money demand, interest rates would not change very much. If interest rates don't change, neither will expenditures. Or if interest rates do change but spending is not particularly sensitive to movements in the interest rate, then spending won't change very much in response to monetary policy. Similarly, if the response of spending to increases in financial wealth and liquidity is not pronounced, the economy will not respond significantly to monetary policy changes.

All these factors are possible impediments to a significant impact of monetary policy on the economy. These impediments may be of greater or lesser importance depending upon where the economy is in the business cycle. For example, in a recession if businessmen are basically pessimistic about the economic outlook, lower interest rates may not generate much additional spending according to this view. Thus, Neo-Keynesians feel that monetary policy alone is not always sufficient to induce changes and in order to ensure that spending is directly affected economic policy makers must resort to fiscal policy.

Thus, changes in the money supply in the Neo-Keynesian analysis work on the economy indirectly through the channels discussed above. If changes in the money supply resulting from monetary policy directly affected spending under any economic conditions, the impact of monetary policy would not be blunted, irrespective of what happened to interest rates. Neo-Keynesians do not believe that changes in the money supply have a direct effect on spending. However, monetarists do believe that changes in money supply directly affects spending and economic activity.

Monetarists

Monetarists view changes in the money supply as the most important determinant of economic activity. The monetarist views are most often associated with Milton Friedman, but the number of academic and nonacademic economists sharing his belief in the crucial importance of changes in the money supply in influencing economic activity has increased rapidly, particularly in the last decade.

Monetarists, like Neo-Keynesians, begin with a portfolio framework that includes real goods as well as money and securities in the portfolio. A change in the money supply results in a disturbance to equilibrium rates of return on assets. However, whereas in the Neo-Keynesian view adjustments to restore equilibrium take place among financial assets, in the monetarist view adjustments take place in both financial assets and goods. The public, put out of equilibrium by the money supply change, alters their holdings of both financial assets and real assets. The process of changing real asset holdings means that spending is directly affected by a change in the money supply. There is thus no short circuit possible between money supply changes and spending changes as there is in the Neo-Keynesian model. Thus, in this view, monetary policy is very powerful, and control of the money supply by the Fed is essential.

In addition to the direct effect that money supply changes have on spending, monetarists also emphasize the Fisher effect in their discussion of interest rates. Recall from the chapter on interest rate determination that the Fisher effect refers to the influence of price expectations on interest rates. If money supply increases are perceived as excessive, expectations of increased inflation can result. If this occurs, money supply increases may lead to higher rather than lower interest rates, as they do in the Neo-Keynesian model.

The Rational Expectations View

A relatively new view of the policy effects on economic activity comes from the rational expectationists.[3] These economists hold that people are rational in the sense that they use all information available in making economic decisions. Indeed, they use the same information that policy makers have available in formulating monetary policy. Therefore, the public can anticipate what policy makers will do and include policy

---

[3] The most prominent exemplars of the rational expectations view are Robert Lucas of the University of Chicago and Thomas Sargent of the University of Minnesota.

in their economic decisions. Thus, for these economists policy makers cannot systematically affect economic activity as long as policy itself is conducted systematically. Only if policy makers are willing to continually "surprise" the economy can policy have an effect, and in this case policy will destabilize the economy. Therefore, the Fed's main role in the rationalists' view is to ensure a steady increase in the money supply to prevent unneeded instability in the economy and to supply sufficient money supply growth to ensure smooth economic growth.[4]

To summarize this section, Figure 18-1 presents in schematic fashion a simple view of the manner in which the three approaches discussed above view the transmission process from a change in the money supply to a change in output (and hence employment) and prices.[5] For the Keynesians and Neo-Keynesians, the impact of money supply changes operates through interest rate effects on spending. Output and prices can be affected in both the short run and long run. Monetarists believe the impact on spending of a money supply change is direct, although there can also be some effect from interest rate changes. The change in the money supply can affect output and prices in the short run although in the long run the impact will only be on prices. Real economic factors will be the major determinant of output in the long run. Rational expectationists argue that since changes in the money supply are anticipated by the public, such changes can only affect prices not output in the short run and the long run. Economic participants, anticipating Fed policy, will by their actions cause price changes to occur quickly. Therefore, it is useless for the Fed to attempt to influence output in the economy in any systematic fashion even in the short run. The best policy is a stable and predictable one.

The rational expectations approach is, as pointed out above, held by a small minority of economists. Despite disagreements between monetarist and Neo-Keynesian economists over the degree of importance of monetary policy and the channels by which it influences the economy, most economists believe that monetary policy is significant

---

[4] Interestingly, the widest known monetarist, Milton Friedman, has long recommended a steady growth in money supply, but for quite different reasons from the rational expectationists'. His argument is that the Fed policy has been so mismanaged over the decades since its inception and money supply changes have such a pronounced effect on the economy that monetary policy has caused more economic fluctuations rather than less. This "mismanagement" by the Fed has been compounded by the variability of the lag between a monetary policy change and its impact upon the economy, according to Friedman. Hence, the economy would be better off if the Fed simply provided a steady increase in the money supply. It should be noted, however, that any plan whether inspired by the rational expectationists' views or Friedman's views assumes the Fed can control the money supply sufficiently to generate a constant increase. This assumption is disputed by many Neo-Keynesian economists.

[5] In order to simplify the diagram, any influences on the money supply running from spending and output changes (that is, in a reverse direction) are ignored. However, many Neo-Keynesians believe such "reverse causation" is important.

Figure 18-1
Transmission Process of a Change in the Money Supply

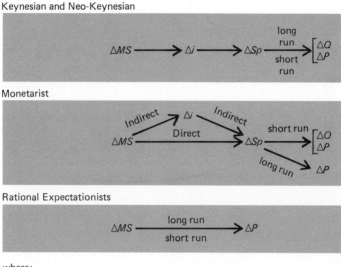

where:

ΔMS = change in the money supply

Δi = change in the interest rate (opposite change from that of the money supply—for example, MS increases, i decreases)

ΔSp = change in spending

ΔQ = change in output (and employment)

ΔP = change in the price level

in achieving economic goals. Therefore, it is useful to examine in detail the tools available to the Fed to conduct monetary policy. The way in which the Fed actually implements monetary policy on an ongoing basis using these tools (the implementation of monetary policy is known as the "strategy") will be discussed in the next chapter.

The Tools of Monetary Policy

The tools available to the Fed in its conduct of monetary policy are usually divided into major tools of monetary policy (also called general tools or quantitative tools) and selective (or qualitative) tools of monetary policy. The major tools of monetary policy are reserve requirement changes, discount rate changes, and open-market operations. Of these, by far the most important is open-market operations.

Reserve Requirement Changes

In discussing commercial banking, we mentioned that the Federal Reserve sets reserve requirements on time and demand deposits for member banks.[6] Under the Depository Institutions Deregulation and Monetary Control Act of 1980, the Fed sets reserve requirements on transactions accounts and time deposits at nonmember banks and nonbank financial intermediaries as well. However, it is simpler to just discuss banks although the effects will be similar on nonbanks.

Because reserves determine the amount of lending that banks can do and the lending process is the process by which the money supply changes, setting of reserve requirements by the Fed is an important factor influencing the supply of money and credit in the economy. By increasing or reducing the reserve requirements, the Fed can dramatically affect the potential expansion of the money supply.

Reserve requirement changes are an infrequently used tool of monetary policy. Changes in reserve requirements lead to rather dramatic changes in the excess reserve position of the banking system, though total reserves are not altered. To see this, assume that the banking system must meet a uniform reserve requirement of 20 percent on demand deposits and that there are no time deposits. If deposits total $100 billion and reserves $20 billion, the banking system has no excess reserves with which to expand loans or purchase securities. If the reserve requirement is lowered to 15 percent, the banking system still has $20 billion in total reserves but now $5 billion of these reserves are excess. Thus, new loans and securities purchases can be made, expanding the money supply. Another way of indicating the effect of a reserve requirement change is to say that reserve requirement changes affect the money multiplier but leave the monetary base unchanged (see Chapter 19).

Reserve requirement changes have also been used infrequently because, until the passage of DIDMCA, Federal Reserve membership had been decreasing. As pointed out previously, banks increasingly left the Federal Reserve System during the 1970s because of the burden of reserve requirements. Thus, raising reserve requirements would surely have induced further membership declines, something the Fed was anxious to prevent. Thus, at least with respect to raising reserve requirements, the Fed was limited in flexibility, and this problem contributed to the infrequency of reserve requirement changes. DIDMCA, by authorizing the Fed to impose reserve requirements on all depository institutions, has removed this incentive to leave Federal Reserve membership. It remains to be seen whether the changes put in place by the 1980 legislation will lead to more frequent use of

---

[6] In fact, the Fed has set reserve requirements at various times in the past on managed liabilities.

reserve requirement changes for policy purposes. The fact that any but marginal changes in reserve requirement changes would still have powerful and sudden effects upon the reserve position of the banking system may still inhibit the Fed from frequently using this tool.

Discount Rate Changes

At the inception of the Fed, the discount rate, the rate the Fed charges depository institutions for borrowing, was supposed to be the major way in which the Fed influenced bank reserves. The provision of an elastic currency and the lender of last resort function that the Fed was supposed to fulfill was to be accomplished through the discount window. A higher discount rate would discourage bank borrowings while a lower rate would encourage banks to borrow. However, in the 1930s, changes in the discount rate was superceded as the primary tool of monetary policy by open-market operations. Further, it turns out that the discount rate does not really have much of an impact on bank borrowings from the Fed.

The reason for the relative ineffectiveness of discount rate changes on bank decisions to borrow from the Fed is that the discount rate is almost always below the prevailing interest rate in the open market. This means that banks can almost always borrow from the Fed and relend at a profit. The only factor discouraging commercial banks from borrowing at will from the Fed is that the Fed stresses that borrowing from it is a privilege not a right and monitors bank borrowings carefully. Banks are, therefore, careful in not abusing their borrowing privilege at the Fed and so police themselves to a large extent. Nevertheless, when the spread between open-market rates and the discount rate gets too wide, it is easy to notice an upswing in bank borrowing at the discount window. Figure 18-2 charts the spread between the prime rate (as a monthly average) and the basic discount rate (at the New York Fed) and, on the same diagram, the amount of borrowing at the Fed from July 1978 to June 1981. Notice that there is some relationship between the spread and the amount of bank borrowing. Particularly, note the large upswing in bank borrowing in the latter part of the period as the spread widened considerably.

The Fed does adjust the discount rate to reflect changes in open-market rates, but in a period of rapidly changing open-market rates such as early 1980 these discount rate adjustments can substantially lag behind actual changes in open-market rates. Many economists have argued that the discount rate would be more effective if it was a penalty rate, that is, above open-market rates. However, the Fed has felt that this would not be appropriate as it would interfere with the lender of last resort function of the discount window. Furthermore, any such move would face widespread opposition from the banking industry. There has been serious consideration given, however, to tying

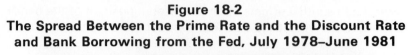

Figure 18-2
**The Spread Between the Prime Rate and the Discount Rate
and Bank Borrowing from the Fed, July 1978–June 1981**

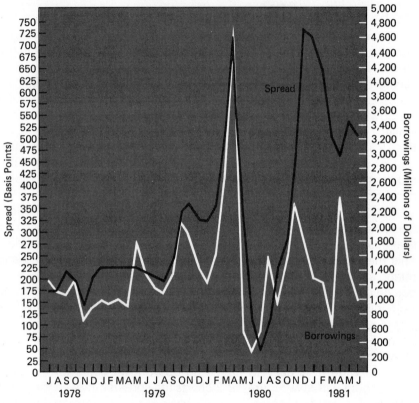

Source: Federal Reserve *Bulletin,* various issues.

the discount rate to open-market rates through a formula. The rate would still not be a penalty rate, but it would move much more quickly in response to open-market rates, thus keeping the spread from widening dramatically as it did in early 1980.

Even though the formula rate has not yet been accepted by the Fed, an attempt has been made by the Fed to tie the discount rate more closely to open-market rates. Beginning in 1980, the Fed imposed a surcharge on its basic discount rate in order to discourage more frequent borrowers at the discount window from taking advantage of particularly favorable spreads between open-market rates and the discount rate. Banks with $500 million or more in deposits that borrow in successive weeks or more than four weeks in a quarter were subject to this surcharge. The surcharge was 3 percent from March to May 1980, 2 percent from November to December 1980, 3 percent from December 1980 to May 1981, 4 percent from May to September 1981, 3 percent in September 1981, and 2 percent in October 1981. The surcharge was eliminated in November 1981, but can be reimposed at the option of the Fed. Frequent alterations in the surcharge can be expected in future years if open-market interest rates continue to be as volatile as they were in 1980 and 1981. The surcharge does seem to have affected the pattern of borrowing observed in Figure 18-2 somewhat. Further, it can be argued that the surcharge has maintained borrowings at levels similar to those in the past, rather than allowing borrowing to increase substantially as the spread between open-market rates and the basic discount rate would have suggested. For example, compare the surge in borrowing in March and April 1980, when the surcharge really hadn't had time to have much effect, with borrowing in December 1980 and the first part of 1981, when the spread once again widened precipitously once the surcharge was well in place.

Although Figure 18-2 showed that borrowing can be influenced to some degree by changes in the discount rate that alter the spread between open-market rates and the discount rate, the most significant monetary policy impact of discount rate changes is thought to result from the "announcement effect." The Fed does have a powerful monetary policy tool at its command, open-market operations, and does use this tool continuously to affect bank reserves. Open-market operations, however, are not announced in advance, and, therefore, the thrust of Federal Reserve policy may be unclear to financial market observers. However, discount rate changes are announced and may be utilized, if consistent with other evidence of the Fed's policy movements, to confirm policy changes.[7] For example, if financial market observers feel that the Fed is tightening up on credit or will be shortly, a significant rise in the discount rate would tend to confirm that such policy is in fact in effect.

However, it may be misleading to consider a discount rate change in isolation from other evidence of Fed policy. The Fed could alter the discount rate merely as a technical adjustment to keep the rate in line with open-market rates as noted above, not necessarily to reflect a fundamental change in policy. But when changes in the discount rate are used in conjunction with other evidence, such as statements by the Fed and indications of open-market operations, discount rate changes can be quite useful to the observer in confirming changes

---

[7] We will see in the next chapter that there are ways in which financial market observers do get some indication of Fed policy from open-market operations, but that this information has to be discerned from patterns of Fed behavior that may be difficult to interpret.

in monetary policy. Further, the effect of announcing discount rate changes seems particularly potent in affecting the foreign exchange markets. This is perhaps due to the failure of foreign exchange traders outside the United States to monitor the thrust of open-market operations on a day-to-day basis or their lack of familiarity with Federal Reserve policy nuances.

Open-Market Operations

It has been noted many times that open-market operations are the major tool of monetary policy. The buying and selling primarily of U.S. government securities by the Federal Reserve Bank of New York through the government securities dealers on instructions of the FOMC is the major way by which the Fed influences the reserves of the banking system. When the Fed buys securities, reserves are injected into the banking system as the proceeds of the purchase are credited to sellers' demand or time deposit accounts at commercial banks and are paid by the Fed through crediting depository institution accounts at the Fed. Therefore, bank total reserves increase by the amount of the purchase, and excess reserves by the amount of the purchase less the required reserves that must be held against the initial deposit. If commercial banks are sellers of securities to the Fed, the increase in excess reserves as a result of the sale is equal to the increase in total reserves because there is no initial deposit against which reserves must be held. Both cases are illustrated by t-accounts in Table 18-1. Panel A shows the effect on the balance sheets of the Fed, the commercial banks, and the nonbank public of the Fed's purchase of $100 million in U.S. government securities in the open market. Notice that since commercial banks have received additional reserves through a deposit, not all those reserves are excess. Some must be held as required reserves against the deposit. On the other hand, when commercial banks are sellers, as in Panel B, the entire increase in reserves is excess reserves since there is no increase in deposits.

Conversely when the Fed sells securities, the buyers pay with checks drawn on their commercial banks, and these checks are cleared by the Fed by reducing depository institution accounts at the Fed, thus decreasing bank reserves. Assuming that banks have excess reserves, the resulting reduction in total reserves will be in part a reduction in required reserves as the deposit represented by the purchase is extinguished and in part a reduction in excess reserves. If the purchaser of the securities is a bank, the commercial bank issues a check on itself, and in this case the full reduction in total reserves is accounted for by a reduction in excess reserves. T-accounts similar to those in Table 18-1 can be used to trace the effect of an open-market sale.

Thus, by buying and selling securities, the Fed can significantly affect the level of bank reserves and through the money supply process

Table 18-1
Federal Reserve Purchase of $100 Million in U.S. Government Securities

A. FED PURCHASE FROM THE PUBLIC

Federal Reserve		Commercial Banks	
U.S. Government Securities +$100	Depository Institution Account +$100	Reserves +$100	Deposit +$100

Nonbank Public	
U.S. Government Securities −$100 Deposit at Commercial Bank +$100	

B. FED PURCHASE FROM THE COMMERCIAL BANKS

Federal Reserve		Commercial Banks	
U.S. Government Securities +$100	Depository Institution Account +$100	U.S. Government Securities −$100 Reserves +$100	

influence the course of the money supply. If banks have additional excess reserves as a result of open-market purchases, they will make loans or buy securities, thus increasing the money supply through the credit creation process discussed in Chapter 6. If reserves are reduced because of open-market sales by the Fed, banks will slow their loan increases or actually contract loans, thus slowing the growth in the money supply.

The increases or decreases in the money supply that result from open-market operations may affect interest rates. In a Keynesian framework, best represented by the liquidity preference theory of interest rate determination discussed in Chapter 4, increases in the money supply lead to lower interest rates, while decreases in the money supply lead to higher interest rates. In liquidity preference theory, if the demand for money remains unchanged, a reduction of money in the economy implies that securities prices would fall and interest rates rise as people sold securities to acquire additional money. The rate on bank loans would also rise as banks have less funds available with which to meet loan demand. Conversely, if the money supply increases, securities prices rise as people use their additional money balances to purchase securities, driving down the interest rate. The rate on bank loans also falls.

Monetarist economists, on the other hand, argue that if money supply increases generate higher inflationary expectations, interest rates would not fall but would rise through the Fisher effect. The higher inflationary expectations lead to lenders that demand higher nominal interest rates to compensate them for the effect of expected inflation on the funds they have loaned. Borrowers also expecting higher inflation in the future are willing to pay the higher nominal rates. Conversely, for monetarists, a deceleration in money growth may lead to a decline in inflationary expectations leading to a fall in interest rates. Expectations may take time to form, however, and even most monetarists agree that initially (during the expectations formation period which may be quite short) interest rates are affected by open-market operations in the way that liquidity preference theory suggests.

The initial impact upon interest rates of open-market operations is easily seen with the aid of demand and supply analysis. Figure 18-3 depicts the demand and supply for Treasury bills, the usual type

Figure 18-3
The Interest Rate Effect of an Open-Market Purchase

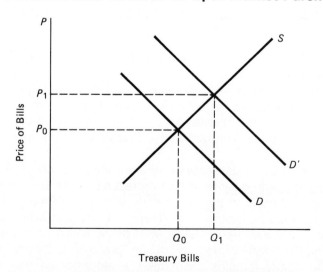

Treasury Bills

of security bought and sold by the Fed in conducting open-market operations. The supply of Treasury bills is positively related to the price of Treasury bills showing that at higher prices (and lower interest rates) more Treasury bills will be supplied. (Remember the Fed is operating in the secondary market so the potential suppliers of Treasury bills are those asset holders with bills in their portfolios.) The demand for Treasury bills is negatively related to the price of Treasury bills; therefore, the higher the price for Treasury bills, the less the quantity demanded. Suppose that the market is in equilibrium at P_0 and Q_0. An open-market purchase by the Fed shifts the demand curve to D' raising the price of bills to P_1 and thus lowering the interest rate. What happens to the interest rate thereafter depends on the effect the resulting change in the money supply has, as discussed above, but it is clear that the direct effect of a purchase must be to lower interest rates. (Conversely, an open-market sale can be depicted in Figure 18-3 by shifting the supply curve to the right resulting in a fall in price and a rise in the interest rate.)[8]

There are two types of purchases and sales that the Fed utilizes in the conduct of open-market operations, outright purchases and sales, and repurchase and reverse repurchase agreements. Outright purchases and sales of securities by the Fed imply no obligation on the part of the Fed to reverse the transaction. However, the Fed often buys securities from and sells securities to government securities dealers under repurchase agreements. The reason for this is that the Fed may only temporarily want to inject reserves into the system or withdraw reserves. When it sells securities with the stipulation that it will buy these back at a specified time and higher price (giving the securities dealer a profit), it is called a repurchase agreement. When it buys securities and the dealer agrees to repurchase the securities at a later date (at a lower price thus giving the dealer a profit in this case as well), the transaction is known as a reverse repurchase agreement.[9]

The Fed often operates through repurchase and reverse repurchase agreements rather than through outright purchases and sales. By utilizing these temporary purchases and sales, it can more closely manage the reserve position of the banking system. For example, prior to tax

---

[8] How long an open-market purchase may keep interest rates lower in a period of rapid inflation depends upon the speed at which inflationary expectations adjust, as noted above, and the extent to which these expectations are incorporated into the interest rate. At times, particularly when inflation has been accelerating rapidly, the direct effect of the open-market purchase may be almost instantaneously reversed, according to monetarists.

[9] The repurchase agreements discussed here are similar to the repurchase agreements between commercial banks and nonfinancial institutions in the sense that the transaction when undertaken results at that time in an obligation on the part of the seller to buy back the securities sold. However, obviously Federal Reserve repurchase and reverse repurchase agreements are undertaken for quite different purposes than is the case for bank repurchase agreements. Thus, these two kinds of repurchase transactions should not be confused.

due dates, the Fed may believe that the banking system needs additional reserves to meet the demand for funds by taxpayers. It may supply these reserves through a reverse repurchase agreement because it doesn't want to increase the reserves of the system "permanently" (it may in fact be in the midst of a tight monetary policy, thus implying open-market sales over a longer period of time) but feels the situation calls for a temporary reserve injection. (Recall the elastic currency rationale behind the establishment of the Fed.) Government securities dealers agree to these activities by the Fed because they are always assured a profit on the transaction. Open-market operations on a day-to-day basis will be fully discussed in the next chapter in connection with the strategy of monetary policy, and then the use of repurchase and reverse repurchase agreements in the overall strategy should become clearer.

Selective Tools of Monetary Policy

The major tools of monetary policy discussed above are supplemented by what are usually called selective (or qualitative) tools. These tools consist of Regulation Q ceilings, margin requirements on stock and convertible bond purchases, moral suasion, and selective credit controls. The importance of selective tools, the frequency of their use, and the consideration of a particular selective tool as a tool of monetary policy varies among the tools. The primary purpose of Regulation Q ceilings is not directly related to monetary policy. Further, the ceilings are being phased out under DIDMCA. Margin requirements have only a peripheral relation to monetary policy, moral suasion is usually ineffective, and selective credit controls are rarely used. Nevertheless, the Fed can utilize these tools and it is appropriate that they be discussed.

Regulation Q Ceilings

Regulation Q ceilings set the maximum interest rate payable on time and savings deposits at commercial banks. As has been discussed previously, the Depository Institution Deregulation and Monetary Control Act of 1980 phases out interest rate ceilings over a six-year period. Under current plans, most, if not all, ceilings will be phased out even before 1986. Regulation Q ceilings are already suspended for large CDs, and money market and note rate certificates have ceilings that vary depending upon the rate on the open-market securities to which they are tied.

Regulation Q ceilings were originally established in the 1930s as a legacy of the Great Depression to prevent banks from engaging in what was considered injurious competition for deposits. In 1966, through the interagency coordinating committee composed of the Fed, the Comptroller of the Currency, the Federal Deposit Insurance Corporation, and the Federal Home Loan Bank Board, they were extended to other nonbank financial institutions. Their connection to monetary policy arises from the fact that failure to raise Regulation Q ceilings when open-market interest rates are rising may exacerbate disintermediation, thus reinforcing restrictive monetary policy. There is little question that in the past the existence of ceilings contributed to disintermediation. This impact was moderated to some degree in 1978 and 1979 with the introduction of money market certificates and note rate certificates, although disintermediation did intensify in late 1979 and continued to be a problem through 1980 and 1981.

The use of Regulation Q ceilings as a monetary policy tool is clearly unnecessary. By using open-market operations, the Fed can accomplish any monetary policy result it desires more effectively and without placing as severe a burden on those sectors of the economy that rely heavily for financing on depository institutions. Therefore, the elimination of Regulation Q ceilings by 1986 should not seriously reduce the Fed's ability to conduct monetary policy.

Margin Requirements on Stock and Bond Purchases

The margin requirement sets the down payment requirement for credit purchases of stocks and convertible bonds. The amount above the margin required can be borrowed by the securities purchaser from the broker. For example, if the margin requirement on stock is 60 percent, this means that the purchaser must pay 60 percent of the amount in cash but that the remainder can be borrowed. In early 1982, the margin requirement was 50 percent, where it had been for most of the 1970s.

The authority for the Fed to set the margin requirement arose out of the legacy of the stock market crash of 1929. No government body prior to that time had the authority to fix margin requirements. As a result, the margin needed to purchase stock was very low in the 1920s, usually around 10 percent. Therefore, very small movements in the price of the stock would wipe out the investor's down payment, sometimes leading to the forced sale of the stock. Such forced sales were automatic if the stockholder did not deposit additional funds to compensate for the fall in the value of the stock that collateralized the margin loan. The failure by many investors to meet "margin calls" resulted in additional declines in the value of stock as the forced sales dumped additional shares of stock on the market. This in turn led to additional margin calls and so on. There is no question that the severity of the crash was due in part to these forced sales. Clearly, with margin requirements of 50 percent or more, the extent and frequency of margin calls is less severe even in market declines than with the lower margin requirements that prevailed in the 1920s.

Margin requirements are used primarily as a safeguard against undue speculation, not as a tool of monetary policy. The Fed will adjust margin requirements upward when it feels there is undue speculation in the market. This was not a problem in the 1970s and early 1980s and the margin requirement stayed very steady. The relation of margin requirement changes to monetary policy comes about if speculation in the stock market can be connected with rapid expansion in the economy that the Fed believes can contribute to inflation. Furthermore, excessive speculation is often regarded as endangering the financial stability of the economy and therefore economic activity. If this is the case, an increase in the margin requirement may be used along with general tools of monetary policy as part of an overall restrictive monetary policy. However, there is no convincing evidence that stock market speculation contributes to inflationary pressures in the economy or economic instability. Indeed, in the inflationary years of the 1970s and early 1980s, stock prices hardly changed at all from the beginning to the end of the period, although they fluctuated considerably during the decade.

Moral Suasion

Moral suasion denotes persuading somebody to do the right thing. In the present context, it means attempts by the Fed to persuade banks to do what the Fed considers appropriate for the economy. For example, the Fed may feel that banks are making too many loans. While the Fed may effectively prevent the banks from doing this through open-market sales that drain reserves from the banking system, for one reason or another the Fed may not wish to do this. Instead, the Fed contacts the banks and asks the bankers to reduce their lending. While the Fed is listened to attentively, moral suasion is usually not effective in general because banks are going to make their decisions on the basis of what they view is in their own best interests. However, the "persuasive" power of the Fed can be effective when directed at the activities of an individual bank that the Fed thinks inappropriate. In the latter case, the use of moral suasion by the Fed falls more into the category of bank regulation than monetary policy.

Selective Credit Controls

The Federal Reserve System has had the power to implement selective credit controls over lending by the banking system at the direction of the President. During the Korean War (1950–53), the Fed did implement credit controls which fixed, for example, the down payment requirements on mortgage loans and severely restricted consumer lending. Selective credit controls were utilized on these borrowing channels so that credit would be directed away from the consumer sector and be available for other lending. They were also used to discourage particular types of spending for fear of inflation during a war situation.

Selective credit controls had been thought to be something of a historical anachronism until discussion of selective credit controls were revived in late 1979 and early 1980. The President of the United States under the 1969 Credit Control Act could request (though not compel) the Fed to impose selective credit controls. The act granted the Fed this authority. On March 14, 1980, the Fed, at the request of the President, did place selective controls on various categories of financial institution sources and uses of funds. These controls were removed completely by July 1980.

The actual program put in place by the Fed in March 1980 had selective credit controls as its main feature but also contained elements of moral suasion and introduced the discount rate surcharge that has been discussed previously. The highlights of what was called the Fed's Special Credit Restraint Program are as follows:[10]

> Banks were advised to hold loan growth within the 6 percent to 9 percent range previously targeted for total bank credit by the Fed.
>
> Banks were also encouraged to hold back on lending considered to be nonproductive, inflationary, or of low social priority. Included were unsecured consumer lending, financing of corporate takeovers or mergers, and financing of speculative holdings of commodities.
>
> Lenders were urged to make "special efforts" to maintain credit flows for farmers, home buyers, and small businesses.
>
> Marginal reserve requirements were increased from 8 percent to 10 percent on the managed liabilities (large time deposits, Eurodollar borrowings, repurchase agreements against U.S. government and federal agency securities) of large banks.
>
> Restraint on the amount of credit raised by large nonmember banks was sought through a special deposit requirement of 10 percent on increases in their managed liabilities.
>
> Rapid expansion of money market mutual funds was to be restrained by a special deposit requirement of 15 percent on increases in their total assets above the level of March 14, 1980.
>
> To discourage use of the discount window and to speed bank adjustments in response to restraint on bank reserves, a sur-

---

[10] This highlight summary is taken from "Looking Back on Credit Controls," *The Morgan Guaranty Survey* (Sept. 1980), p. 5.

charge of 3 percentage points was applied to borrowings by large banks.

There had been debate about the merits of control programs, their effectiveness, and the effects of interference in the credit allocation process of the economy even prior to their brief imposition from March 14, 1980, to July 3, 1980. Their imposition, of course, increased this discussion considerably. The debate following their removal centered on the role controls played in exacerbating the recession of 1980 and in reducing the inflation rate by reducing inflationary expectations. The evidence at this time is unclear as to whether controls had any important effect in either intensifying the recession or moderating inflation, though many observers believe that their impact on consumer spending was substantial. Nevertheless, it is clear that the Fed found the use of controls distasteful because of their interference in the manner in which the financial system allocates credit. The fact that the Fed was uncomfortable with such interference accounts in part for their very brief life.

Despite their brief life, credit controls do illustrate how specific Fed policies affect financial institutions, financial markets, and individual behavior. Financial institutions behaved differently in their lending patterns because of the credit control program. Consumer borrowing was considerably affected because of both the lending guidelines and some consumer misunderstanding concerning the nature of the credit controls. Many consumers believed that banks could no longer make consumer loans, such as credit card loans, which was not correct. Furthermore, the profitability of large commercial banks, which raise a considerable amount of funds using managed liabilities, was affected adversely because of the rise in reserve requirements on these liabilities. As a result, the markets for managed liabilities were influenced by the credit controls program. The Credit Control Act itself, which authorized the program, was allowed to expire in June 1982. However, new legislation was immediately introduced in Congress to reinstate the act. As this text goes to press, it is unclear whether this legislation will become law.

The Impact of Monetary Policy

The tools of monetary policy that have been discussed are at the command of the Fed. Open-market operations, the most important tool of monetary policy, are utilized on a daily basis not only for implementation of monetary policy decisions but also for various technical reasons. The next chapter will examine the strategy of monetary policy, which is implemented by using open-market operations. Before proceeding, however, it is useful to discuss two aspects of monetary policy that are often overlooked, the geographic impact of the tools of monetary policy and the time lags that exist before a change in monetary policy affects the economy.

Reserve requirement changes and discount rate changes affect depository institutions offering transactions accounts at the same time throughout the country.[11] Open-market operations, on the other hand, are conducted in New York, and the first major effects of these operations fall on the large New York banks. But studies have shown that the effect of a change in bank reserves brought about through open-market operations spreads very rapidly throughout the country. Studies vary, but most show that the majority of banks feel the effect of systematic open-market operations designed to implement a change or intensification of monetary policy in less than a month.[12] The rapid effectiveness of open-market operations derives from the fact that the financial system and the banking system in particular are closely interrelated through the check-clearing process, borrower flexibility in moving from bank to bank for loans, and correspondent relationships. Thus, there is really no "regionalism" to open-market operations.

Since policy changes are felt in the banking system very rapidly, is there any lag before the policy actually has an impact upon the economy? This question is usually answered affirmatively. Most economists consider the lag to be relatively long, and most econometric models support this conclusion. Milton Friedman, the well-known monetarist economist and Nobel Prize winner, has estimated the lag to be from six months to two years, implying that changes induced by the Fed in the money supply cannot be counted on to affect the economy when the Fed desires. Friedman has emphasized the variability of this lag as an argument for his recommendation that the money supply should be allowed to grow at a constant rate. Other economists and econometric models have placed the lag in monetary policy at intervals similar to those of Friedman. However, the lag that Friedman and others are referring to occurs between the time a change in monetary policy is actually put into place and the time that the monetary policy change has its full, or nearly full, impact upon the economy. This lag is usually called the impact lag. There are, however, additional lags in monetary policy effects that add to the impact lag and these

---

[11] Technically, discount rates can be different at the various Federal Reserve Banks because a change in the discount rate is proposed by the Federal Reserve Banks and all might not propose a given discount rate change. However, since discount rate changes are really coordinated by the Board of Governors, Federal Reserve Banks are seldom out of line for more than a few days.

[12] See, for example, Vittorio Bonomo and Charles Schotta, "Patterns of Regional Adjustments of Member Bank Reserves to Federal Open Market Operations," *Proceedings of the American Statistical Association,* Business and Economic Statistics Section (1967), pp. 481–87; and Timothy Hogan and Herbert Kaufman, "Lags in Regional Adjustment to Changes in Monetary Policy," *The Quarterly Review of Economics and Business* (Winter 1977), pp. 77–89.

should be noted. These lags are the recognition lag and the implementation lag.

The recognition lag measures the time between a change in economic activity, which may require a change in monetary policy, and the actual recognition of the economic change. Because data are slow to collect and first data are often revised, economic policy makers must be careful about changing policy hastily. By the time, however, that they feel some certainty that a monetary policy change is called for, considerable time may have passed.

Further, once the problem is recognized, policy has to be decided upon and implemented. For example, the FOMC may gradually recognize that policy implemented by open-market operations should be altered, but they still need to meet and confer over the change in policy. Thus, adding the recognition and implementation lags to the impact lag means that a considerable period has passed from the time a monetary policy change is needed to its actual economic effect.

DIFFERING VIEWS ON THE IMPORTANCE OF MONEY
Reagan's Interest-Rate Dilemma

Despite the incantations of economists and the assurances of the Administration, interest rates have doggedly refused to decline. Although two major banks cut the prime rate a half point, to 20%, on Aug. 31, the financial markets were left in a shambles as some bond prices tumbled as much as $30. Interest rates on long-term government bonds reached 14.9%, tax-free yields on municipals touched the astronomical level of 15%, Indiana Bell Telephone Co. sold 39-year debentures at a record 17.1%, and the stock market hit its lowest point in almost 14 months.

The Administration feels that continued tight money is the only way to cut inflationary expectations and bring down interest rates permanently. Yet it is becoming clear that the success of the Reagan supply-side revolution hangs on whether rates can be brought down soon. The Administration is worried.

While the Administration is increasingly nervous about the political and economic effects of continued high rates and the collapse in the markets, officials feel there is nothing they can do about monetary policy except to cheer the Fed. "The markets are worried about the implications of the deficit for monetary policy, and I don't know how to challenge that thinking," says Treasury Under Secretary Norman B. Ture. "I wish I had a quick answer because I would become a hero by suggesting it to the White House."

Economists are offering four major options to get interest rates down: hang tough with tight money, slash the deficit, back off from the tax cut, and return to the gold standard. All are fraught with difficulties, however.

So far the Administration is bolstering its tight-money policy with further budget-cutting. It is accelerating its efforts to come up with the additional federal budget cuts, especially in defense spending, for fiscal 1983 and 1984 that it had promised but not specified.

The markets remain unimpressed. It may be that Wall Street is aware that the two major intellectual groups on which Reagan now depends for advice—the pure monetarists and the supply-siders—do not really believe that curing the deficit is necessary to reduce interest rates. Their views on the deficit contrast sharply with those of mainstream economists, who hold that the deficit matters a lot. It is on this question that the debate on how to lower interest rates will focus. Here is how the key schools of economic thought view the issue:

THE PURE MONETARISTS. This group maintains that rates have been pushed up because the Federal Reserve is not financing the deficit by monetizing the debt. The pure monetarists have championed this approach because it is not the size of the deficit that affects the inflation rate, they say, but how that deficit is financed. As long as the Fed does not monetize the deficit by buying bonds, inflation can remain relatively low. Even though this policy pushes up interest rates in the short run, eventually it will translate into lower inflation and thus lower interest rates. This means that monetary policy must stay tight, say the pure monetarists. "There is no painless way of getting inflation under control," says Treasury Under Secretary Beryl W. Sprinkel. Adds Robert Rasche of Michigan State University: "I think the underlying conditions are in place for rates to begin a gradual decline. All we need is patience with the current policy."

THE SUPPLY-SIDERS. They believe that interest rates are high now because the market has lost faith in currency, and the only way to restore that faith is to back currency with a commitment to redeem it with gold. If that is done, this group maintains, the size of the deficit does not matter. Arther B. Laffer, the supply-side guru, has said that monetary policy is 100 times more important than spending policy. But the supply-siders argue that it is impossible for anyone to manage the money supply. "[Fed Chairman] Paul Volcker cannot control monetary growth, and neither can Ronald Reagan. You have to fight inflationary expectations by bringing Fort Knox into the battle," says Jude Wanniski, president of Polyconomics Inc. and a leading supply-side spokesman. Although it would obviously take time for the U.S. to return to the gold standard, Wanniski believes that interest rates would plummet almost immediately. "All you have to do is have a public flogging of Beryl Sprinkel," he says.

THE PRAGMATIC MONETARISTS. This school maintains that rates are high because the government, when it announces a new debt issue, is really telling the financial markets that there will be growth in the money supply. This increases inflationary expectations and raises the inflation premiums in the interest rate. This group also believes that the pure monetarists have oversold the idea that the deficit does

not matter. Says Robert Lucas Jr., economist at the University of Chicago and heir apparent to Nobelist Milton Friedman: "Milton is putting too much emphasis on money and not enough on the deficit."

Long-term rates are sky-high, in Lucas' view, because the public expects that the Federal Reserve will, as it has done so often in the past, print money to meet those obligations. Chiding the pure monetarists, he says: "Serious inflations are not caused by central bankers who run amok. They are caused by a government that can't cover its expenditures through taxation." In order to get interest rates down, Lucas, like most pragmatic monetarists, wants the Administration to cut spending even further. But if that does not work, he says, "they should rethink the tax cut."

THE KEYNESIANS. Like the pragmatic monetarists, this group is zeroing in on the deficit as the cause of high interest rates. Charles L. Schultze, chairman of the CEA under President Carter, argues that the Administration has to "scrounge around" for $50 billion to $70 billion more in cuts in 1983 and 1984 to get closer to balancing the budget. "It's not all that necessary to get the deficit down to zero, but you should be heading that way," he says. Schultze believes that more budget cuts would allow the Fed's grasp to ease slightly. "You could maintain the money growth targets and move to the upper range of those targets," he says.

Stephen M. Goldfeld of Princeton, a CEA member in the last year of the Carter Administration, also believes in knocking down the deficit. "Right now the Fed is in a straitjacket. Monetary policy is hostage to fiscal policy." Yet he says nothing can be gained by hastily abandoning the monetary growth rule. "If you flooded the market with reserves, you might drive down interest rates for a week, but they would bounce right back. You would cause a major dislocation in the financial markets if you tried to bring rates down quickly. For better or worse, we've become tied to monetary targets because of the effect of monetary policy on expectations."

THE WALL STREETERS. This group also focuses on the deficit as the main culprit for high interest rates, and it has been sharply critical of the Administration's economic policies. Salomon Bros.' Henry Kaufman and First Boston's Albert M. Wojnilower have correctly forecast that rates would go higher rather than lower. They have emphasized the huge borrowings that the Treasury will have to undertake to finance the higher-than-expected deficit that has put such pressure on the money markets. In addition, the Wall Streeters claim that elimination of regulations in the financial markets has left interest rates with the entire burden of rationing credit.

Wojnilower says that the elimi-

nation of credit restrictions means that for each given level of business activity, interest rates will be higher than they would have been in past years. His prescription for lowering interest rates is to impose direct quantitative restraints on credit. He suggests marginal capital requirements on banks, prohibition of floating-rate credit contracts, punitive margin requirements on futures contracts, and rigid downpayments and maturity limits on mortgage and installment debt.

Sharply cutting back the budget or reinstating credit restraints as a way of lowering interest rates may prove to be politically difficult. And unless it wants to scale back the tax cuts, the Administration may be tempted to opt for a return to the gold standard. Says supply-sider Paul Craig Roberts, Assistant Treasury Secretary for economic policy: "Monetarism must be given its chance but if it can't be made to work, there will be a case for gold."

Key Points

1. Monetary policy is the attempt by the Federal Reserve to influence the money supply and interest rates in order to affect economic activity. Monetary policy is one of the two major components of economic policy, the other being fiscal policy. The goals of economic policy include price stability, full employment, and economic growth.

2. Neo-Keynesian economists view monetary policy as affecting economic activity through interest rates and the wealth and liquidity of the economy. Monetarists believe changes in the money supply directly affect economic activity, while rational expectationists believe that monetary policy can have no systematic effect on real economic activity in the economy, influencing only prices in the short and long runs.

3. The major tools of monetary policy are reserve requirement changes, discount rate changes, and open-market operations. Most monetary pol-

icy is implemented through open-market operations, the buying and selling primarily of U.S. government securities. Reserve requirement changes are used relatively infrequently, in part because of the substantial and immediate impact reserve requirement changes have on the reserve position of the banking system. Discount rate changes are regarded as important in part because they may signal changes in monetary policy. A major change in the administration of the discount rate took place in early 1980 when the Fed adopted a surcharge to the basic discount rate to be applied to frequent borrowers.

4. Qualitative or selective tools of monetary policy include Regulation Q, margin requirements, moral suasion, and selective credit controls. There is some question whether any of these tools should actually be considered specific tools of monetary policy. However, the imposition of selective credit controls for a brief period in the first half of 1980 does appear to have had a significant impact on credit expansion during the time they were in place.

Questions for Discussion

1. Open-market operations directly affect interest rates at the time they are conducted. However, monetarists and Neo-Keynesians disagree on the direction of this impact on interest rates after an initial period under certain economic conditions. Explain this disagreement.

2. Why are discount rate changes said to have "announcement effects"? Evaluate the importance of discount rate changes in influencing bank decisions to borrow from the Fed.

3. What are the generally accepted goals of economic policy? Are these goals necessarily all simultaneously achievable? Discuss.

4. Many economists opposed the imposition of selective credit controls in early 1980 because controls interfere with market allocation of credit. Why does this occur?

5. Evaluate the usefulness of the selective tools of monetary policy in implementing monetary policy.

Suggested Readings

Bedford, Margaret. "The Federal Reserve and the Government Securities Market." Federal Reserve Bank of Kansas City *Economic Review,* April 1978, pp. 15–31.

Carlson, Keith M. "The Lag From Money to Prices." Federal Reserve Bank of St. Louis *Review,* Oct. 1980, pp. 3–10.

Eastburn, David P., and W. Lee Haskins. "The Influence of Monetary Policy on Commercial Banking." Federal Reserve Bank of Philadelphia *Business Review,* July/August 1978, pp. 3–17.

Federal Reserve Bank of Philadelphia. *Business Review* Issue on Monetary Policy, Nov./Dec. 1979.

Hetzel, Robert L. "A Primer on the Importance of the Money Supply." Federal Reserve Bank of Richmond *Economic Review,* Sept./Oct. 1977, pp. 3–13.

Lucas, Robert E., Jr., and Thomas J. Sargent. "After Keynesian Macroeconomics." Federal Reserve Bank of Minneapolis *Quarterly Review,* Spring 1979, pp. 1–16.

Morgan Guaranty Trust Company. "Looking Back on Credit Controls." *The Morgan Guaranty Survey,* Sept. 1980, pp. 4–6.

Snellings, Aubrey N. "Stabilization Policy: Time for a Reappraisal?" Federal Reserve Bank of Richmond *Economic Review,* March/April 1976, pp. 3–9.

The Money Supply Process and the Strategy of Monetary Policy

19

The money supply process was first discussed in Chapter 6. In that chapter, it was shown that the product of the monetary base (that is, all currency in circulation plus all bank reserves) and the money multiplier yielded the money supply. Using this framework, we can see the Federal Reserve's influence on the money supply. Through its open-market operations, the Fed can alter the monetary base and, therefore, through the base, the money supply. In addition, by setting reserve requirements, the Fed also affects the size of the money multiplier. This chapter is concerned with the money supply process and the Fed's role in that process. Economists call the Fed's conduct of monetary policy the strategy of monetary policy. Before discussing the strategy of monetary policy, however, we should review and elaborate upon the money supply process.

The Money Supply Process Revisited

The money supply (currency plus checkable deposits)[1] is determined by the interaction of the monetary base and the money multiplier

$$MS = m \cdot MB \qquad\qquad [19\text{-}1]$$

---

[1] Transaction account authority was extended nationwide to nonbank financial intermediaries as a result of the Depository Institutions Deregulation and Monetary Control Act of 1980 (DIDMCA). The term demand deposits should be interpreted in a general way in this chapter to encompass all transactions accounts (checkable deposits), and the money supply includes all transactions accounts at banks and nonbanks. In the terminology of Chapter 3, MS can be interpreted as M1.

where MS = the money supply
                   m = the money multiplier
                   MB = the monetary base

The money multiplier in its simplest formulation is determined by the reserve requirement ratio (r), the currency to deposit ratio (c), and the excess reserve ratio (e):

$$m = \frac{1 + c}{c + r + e} \qquad \text{[19-2]}$$

This formulation can be expanded by taking account of differential reserve requirements on demand and time deposits. Prior to the Depository Institutions Deregulation and Monetary Control Act of 1980, different reserve requirements on deposits at different size banks and the nonmember–member bank distribution of deposits would also have been a factor. These considerations complicate the task of forecasting the money multiplier and conducting monetary policy. The almost complete elimination of differential reserve requirements and the application of reserve requirements to nonmember banks under DIDMCA will reduce sources of instability in the money supply process once these changes are fully in place. However, movements of funds from time to demand deposits and vice versa will still affect the money multiplier. For present purposes, though, it is sufficient to use the simple formulation given above to explore the money supply process.[2]

The money multiplier and its determinants are the first component of the money supply process that we need to address. Reserve requirements are set by the Fed and changes in the reserve requirement (r) will alter the multiplier. Since r appears in the denominator of the multiplier, it is inversely related to the size of the multiplier. If reserve requirements are raised, banks have less excess reserves available to make loans. If reserve requirements are lowered, they have more excess reserves available. Thus, increases in reserve requirements reduce the size of the multiplier, and decreases in reserve requirements increase the size of the multiplier. Reserve requirement changes, within the limits set by Congress,[3] are strictly under the control of the Fed. A smaller money multiplier for a given monetary base will result in a smaller money supply, all else being equal. Analogously, an increase in the size of the money multiplier, everything being equal, will result in a larger money supply for a given monetary base. But are other things equal? Specifically, what about the other parameters of the money multiplier?

---

[2] See Albert Burger, *The Money Supply Process* (Belmont, Calif.: Wadsworth, 1971), for a thorough discussion of the money multiplier.

[3] These limits under DIDMCA are 8 to 14 percent for transactions accounts and 0 to 9 percent for nonpersonal time deposits.

Currency to Deposit Ratio

The ratio of currency to demand deposits (c) in the economy depends upon the preferences of the public with respect to how they hold their money balances. The more that the public decides to hold their money in currency, the larger is c. Since c appears in both the numerator and the denominator of the multiplier, it may seem that a change in c would not affect the size of the multiplier. However, with a little thought we can understand that a change in c affects the denominator more than the numerator of the expression. This is the case because a change in c leads to a larger relative change in the denominator of the multiplier than in the numerator. Thus, an increase in c reduces the multiplier, while a reduction in c increases the multiplier.[4]

The currency–deposit ratio, like all parameters of the multiplier, is less than one. In December 1980 it was over .43. This means that the money supply contained $43 in currency for every $100 in demand deposits. What determines how much of the money supply is held in currency? There are numerous answers that can be given to this question. Currency is convenient for small transactions. People also keep currency for contingencies. Some have even argued that the increase in the currency–deposit ratio in recent years is a result of an upsurge in illegal and tax avoidance activities on the part of the public.[5] Whatever the motivations for holding currency relative to demand deposits, the essential fact is that this is determined exclusively by the public. Table 19-1 shows the average currency–deposit ratio yearly from 1972 to 1980. As can be seen, the ratio increased considerably over that period.

The Excess Reserve Ratio

The excess reserve ratio (e) gives the relationship between bank excess reserves and deposits. Since the ratio appears in the denominator of the multiplier, the larger it is the smaller is the multiplier. The original rationale behind bank holdings of excess reserves was to guard against unforeseen reserve drains or to take advantage of attractive lending opportunities. However, it was always assumed that the excess reserve ratio was dependent upon the interest rate. When rates were high, banks would manage their reserve position more closely, reducing excess reserves accordingly. When rates were low, excess reserves would

---

[4] It may appear equally confusing as to why c appears in the numerator of the multiplier at all. However, since currency is part of both the money supply and the monetary base, the monetary base must be multiplied by c in order to add currency to demand deposits and yield the money supply.

[5] For example, see Peter M. Gutmann, "The Subterranean Economy," *Financial Analysts Journal* (Nov./Dec. 1977), pp. 26–34. To the extent that people want to avoid detection of their economic activities either by the police or the Internal Revenue Service, they tend to deal in cash.

Table 19-1
Average Currency–Deposit Ratio, 1972–80
(End of Year)

1972	.2861
1973	.2935
1974	.3149
1975	.3335
1976	.3471
1977	.3696
1978	.3836
1979	.4037
1980	.4342

Source: Federal Reserve *Bulletin,* various issues.

increase. Such sensitivity of the excess reserve ratio to the rate of interest would impart an interest sensitivity to the money supply itself. This would occur because an increase in interest rates would lower the excess reserve ratio, increasing the money multiplier, and therefore the money supply for a given monetary base.

The excess reserve ratio has been very small for most of the 1970s and early 1980s as banks have carefully managed their reserve positions. Banks with excess reserves have sold (loaned) federal funds when no other alternatives for their use appeared. The basic reason for the close management of excess reserves has been the high interest rates of the 1970s and 1980s. However, it seems likely that a basic change in bank behavior has occurred as a result of the experience gained by banks in closely managing their reserve positions during this period. Even if there should be a return to a lower interest rate environment in the United States, it is unlikely that banks, having invested heavily in developing the expertise to manage their reserve positions so effectively, will cease doing so. This judgment is reinforced by considering that with the expertise now in place the additional cost of reserve management is quite low.

This alteration in bank behavior is but one more example of the interaction between monetary policy and financial institution behavior. Without the impetus of the high interest rates of the 1970s and early 1980s, which are traceable to monetary policy, banks would not likely have developed their expertise in managing their reserves so closely. Furthermore, the markets that allow such close reserve management would not have developed so dramatically. These markets are likely to retain their importance in the future whatever the interest rate environment.

The discussion above implies a reduced or nonexistent relationship between excess reserves and interest rates, at least for relevant interest rate levels. This, in turn, implies a much lower or nonexistent sensitivity of the money supply to interest rates through the channel of a changed excess reserve ratio. Support for this argument comes from realizing that excess reserves in July 1981 were only $350 million, an average of only about $65,000 per Federal Reserve member bank. This average did not change substantially over most of the 1970s and early 1980s. The above analysis implies that the reason for the small amount of excess reserves when compared to the hundreds of billions of dollars in deposits and the relatively small variation in this amount is due to the reduction of excess reserves very close to their minimum. Thus, positive levels of excess reserves are merely transitory results of deposit inflows, soon used to acquire income-earning assets.

If this argument is accepted, any significant dependence of the money supply on movements in interest rates would stem only from changes in the monetary base, in response to interest rate changes, not from a money multiplier response. However, whether the monetary base changes in response to interest rate changes depends in large part on whether the Fed reacts to interest rate changes by altering the monetary base. Consideration of this possibility relates to the strategy of monetary policy to which we will return later in this chapter.

The Importance of the Money Multiplier

The money multiplier is clearly important because it indicates the amount of money supply a given monetary base will support and how changes in the monetary base translate into changes in the money supply. Yet the money multiplier process is not accepted as useful by all economists. It is an important element in the argument between the monetarists and the Neo-Keynesians on how much control the Fed has over the money supply. The argument revolves around the stability and predictability of the multiplier. After a particular period of time has passed, it is easy to calculate the size of the multiplier since all that is needed is the money supply and monetary base for the period. The multiplier is simply the result of dividing the money supply by the monetary base. However, if the multiplier is not stable or predictable, the usefulness of the money multiplier framework for executing monetary policy is minimal. Monetarists maintain that the money multiplier is predictable. Thus, changes in the monetary base will translate into predictable changes in the money supply. Further, they argue that the Fed can control the monetary base and, therefore, the Fed can control the money supply accurately by controlling the monetary base.

To the Neo-Keynesians, the money multiplier framework is too mechanical to be useful for analysis. Further, even if it is utilized, they argue that the money multiplier is not predictable and, therefore, the

Table 19-2
The Money Multiplier—Money Supply (M1) Divided by the Mone-
tary Base

August 1980	2.572
September 1980	2.580
October 1980	2.594
November 1980	2.576
December 1980	2.554
January 1981	2.575
February 1981	2.576
March 1981	2.592
April 1981	2.614
May 1981	2.590
June 1981	2.565
July 1981	2.567
August 1981	2.564

Source: Federal Reserve Bank of St. Louis, *Monetary Trends,* Dec. 23, 1981.

Fed cannot control the money supply very precisely by controlling the monetary base. Even the control of the monetary base may be difficult; at best the Fed may be able to control only a portion of the base. Further, even if the Fed can control the monetary base, the way in which it conducts monetary policy, its strategy, may make the monetary base a function of economic variables that are not under the control of the Fed. This latter argument, called reverse causation, will be discussed in the context of the Fed's strategy below. Finally, the problem is compounded further by the interaction between the base and the multiplier, an interaction that monetarists say is minimal.[6]

Table 19-2 presents the money multiplier on a monthly basis from August 1980 to August 1981. Examining the data in the table, we see that the movement in the multiplier is quite apparent. Monetarists, particularly associated with the Federal Reserve Bank of St. Louis, have argued that such changes can be predicted and the Fed can adjust the monetary base accordingly. For example, if the money multiplier changes by 2 percent, the monetary base can be changed by the Fed by 2 percent in the opposite direction to compensate.[7] However, relatively small changes in the multiplier can result in large

---

[6] See Robert H. Rasche, "A Review of Empirical Studies of the Money Supply Mechanism," Federal Reserve Bank of St. Louis *Review* (July 1972), pp. 11–19.

[7] James Johannes and Robert Rasche, "Predicting the Money Multiplier," *Journal of Monetary Economics* (July 1979), pp. 301–25.

changes in the money supply. For example, a 2 percent movement in the multiplier from, say 2.50 to 2.55, will alter the money supply by $7.5 billion for a given monetary base of $150 billion. Many economists dispute the notion that the money multiplier can be predicted accurately enough to allow the Fed to compensate for the change by altering the base.

Monetary Base

The monetary base is the other major factor in the money supply process. The base has been previously defined as bank reserves plus currency in circulation. This is the most convenient way of calculating the base and is known as **uses** of the base. However, the monetary base can also be computed by examining the **sources** of the base. As in any sources and uses statement, both approaches yield identical measures of the base. Nevertheless, to fully understand the manner in which the Fed influences the monetary base, we must discuss some of the sources of the base. The major source of the monetary base is Federal Reserve holdings of U.S. government securities. Recall from the discussion of the Federal Reserve balance sheet in Chapter 17 that this is by far the largest Federal Reserve asset. The Fed alters its holdings of government securities as it conducts open-market operations, and as it does so, the monetary base changes. Discount loans as well as Federal Reserve float are also sources of the monetary base as are Fed holdings of agency securities and bankers acceptances. Thus, it can be said that the base is determined in major part by decisions of the Federal Reserve to provide or restrict credit to the financial system. Financial market analysts often examine the week-to-week changes in Federal Reserve credit (securities holdings, discount loans, and float) to determine the direction of Federal Reserve policy, knowing that changes in Federal Reserve credit mean changes in the monetary base. Since it is more convenient and more complete to measure the base from its uses (a number of less important items that have not been discussed are also part of the source base), this will be done in the remaining discussion.

The controllability of the base by the Fed in purely technical terms (that is, independent of the strategy of monetary policy) depends upon a number of factors. Perhaps most important is the fact that as the monetary base is defined it includes total bank reserves. Bank reserves can be borrowed and non-borrowed. Borrowed reserves are those borrowed from the Fed at the discount window. While only a small fraction of total reserves are borrowed (usually well below 5 percent) the decision to borrow at the discount window is made by the borrowing banks, not the Fed. The Fed can influence this decision only through the discount rate (assuming banks are not abusing their borrowing privilege). Therefore, as long as the discount rate is not automatically a penalty rate, the Fed can control only the non-borrowed portion of reserves through its open-market operations. Even here the Fed may be limited in perfectly controlling the non-borrowed portion of the base by such things as unpredictable changes in Federal Reserve float.

Further, though in theory the Fed may be able to control the non-borrowed base, there is still a problem of data availability. Data on bank reserves are not available instantaneously. Thus the Fed has a hard time keeping complete tabs on the reserve position of the banking system. Although most monetarists argue that this is not a severe impediment since reserve control is not necessary on a day-to-day basis, it does add to the Fed's problems in attempting to control the monetary base.

However, beginning October 6, 1979, the Fed announced that it would conduct monetary policy with reference to non-borrowed reserves. Because non-borrowed reserves are an important portion of the monetary base, this action by the Fed was widely interpreted as a victory for the monetarists and the way of looking at the money supply process through the money multiplier framework depicted above. To understand this current strategy of monetary policy, we should examine the monetary policy strategies that preceded it in the post–World War II era.

Monetary Strategy Since World War II

The strategy of monetary policy has gone through a number of changes in the postwar period. These changes reflected the perception of how monetary policy affected the economy, its importance, and political and research influences. The effect of influences outside the Fed in determining its policy was never clearer than during the period immediately following World War II. During this period the Fed was under irresistible pressure from both the U.S. Treasury and the U.S. Congress to continue its World War II practice of pegging interest rates. We begin our discussion of Federal Reserve strategy with this period.

Pegging Interest Rates and the Accord

During World War II, in the interest of helping the Treasury finance the war effort, the Federal Reserve had agreed to peg interest rates on Treasury securities at very low rates. The Fed was able to prevent rates from rising by standing ready to buy any securities offered at a price equivalent to the yield it wanted to maintain. Thus, any time the price of Treasury securities started to fall below the price the Fed wished to maintain, the Fed would buy. Because a seller of Treasury securities would never sell at a lower price, there was a floor under prices and therefore a ceiling on yields. However, pegging rates entailed giving up control over monetary policy. In supplying reserves anytime the interest rate started to rise above a very low level, the Fed provided essentially all the reserves that the economy demanded in order to finance whatever level of spending desired in the economy. This inability to conduct monetary policy troubled the Fed but was adhered to as part of the war effort. In addition, because of controls and rationing associated with the war, inflation was bottled up to a large degree. Nevertheless, by 1945 consumer prices were 31 percent higher than they had been in 1939.

However, as soon as the war was over and the economy started adjusting to a peace-time position, inflation exploded. For 1946 and 1947 combined, the consumer price index increased by almost 23 percent. The Fed wished to resume active monetary policy to fight this inflation. However, the Treasury had gotten quite used to low rates on its borrowing and fought successfully against the Fed's unpegging interest rates. In fact, for much of the period until 1951 not only did the Fed still peg rates, but it pegged them at the same very low levels as prevailed during the war.

In early 1951, the Fed and the Treasury finally agreed (after a rather acrimonious struggle) in what was known as the "accord" that the Fed need not peg interest rates any longer. The Fed, for its part, did agree to provide "orderly markets" during Treasury financing to assure the Treasury success in the financing of its debt. This in essence meant that when the Treasury was financing, the Fed would not allow this financing to significantly affect interest rates the Treasury paid, but at other times the Fed was free to allow interest rates to change and thus free to conduct monetary policy.

The Bills Only Policy

Following the accord, the Fed was still concerned that if interest rates were to rise too rapidly, such a rise would be blamed upon the Fed and it would once more be pressured into pegging interest rates. Thus it decided that the "safest" way to conduct monetary policy was to minimize the impact of that policy on interest rates. To accomplish this, open-market operations were restricted to the Treasury bill market, which was the largest of the markets in which the Fed could operate. The large size of this market meant that the Fed's purchases and sales would have minimal direct impact on rates in this market. The Fed followed this policy through the 1950s with only a few exceptions. However, in the early 1960s, it moved away from the bills only policy to conduct what was called "operation twist." After operation twist, while most open-market operations were still conducted in the Treasury bill market, as they are today, the Fed no longer confined its activity exclusively to the Treasury bill market.

Operation Twist

By the early 1960s, large deficits in the U.S. balance of payments were appearing. One of the main contributors to the deficits was funds flowing out of the United States to take advantage of higher short-term rates of interest abroad. The Fed, cognizant of the balance of payments difficulty and feeling that it was important to attempt to eliminate the deficit (recall that stability in the balance of payments is a goal of economic policy), felt that an increase in interest rates was appropriate. As often happens, however, two economic policy goals can conflict. This was the situation in this period.

In the early 1960s, the U.S. economy was in a period of slow economic growth having recovered only slightly from the recession in 1957–58. Such a situation called for stimulative monetary policy, which at the time meant low interest rates. Thus, the Fed faced a dilemma. Balance of payments considerations indicated high interest rates were appropriate in order to keep funds from flowing abroad. However, low interest rates were considered desirable for domestic economic reasons. The Fed attempted to meet both goals by making use of the term structure of the interest rates, that is, the relationship between short-term and long-term rates.

Seeking higher interest rates, funds flowing between countries are typically responsive to short-term rates. Speculators do not like to lock up their funds in long-term assets. Investment spending on plant and equipment, on the other hand, is the kind of spending that low interest rates is expected to encourage. Investment spending is thought to be most responsive to long-term interest rates since such spending is usually financed in the bond market. Given this situation, the Fed decided that it would attempt to "twist" the yield curve so that short-term rates would rise and long-term rates remain relatively low or fall. Notice that such a negative yield curve was thought very unusual in the early 1960s, although it has been pointed out that such yield curves have been more prevalent in the 1970s and 1980s.

In order to twist the yield curve, the Fed abandoned its bills only policy. It sold Treasury bills, thus bidding the price of bills down and increasing short-term rates, while at the same time it bought long-term bonds, bidding the price of bonds up and long-term rates down. It was initially assisted in these activities by the Treasury, which put its financing emphasis on short-term borrowing, thus putting further upward pressure on short-term rates.

Any assessment of operation twist is difficult. It may have succeeded in at least preventing long-term rates from rising. It is hard to be sure for a lot of economic changes were occurring in the early 1960s, including the beginnings of an economic expansion that was accelerated by the 1964 income tax cut. Further, the amount of Federal Reserve open-market operations during operation twist were not substantial enough relative to the activity in the financial markets to dominate those markets. In any event, operation twist did not last very long and had no lasting impact on the balance of payments.

Money Market Strategy

The money market strategy was the name given to the overall framework that governed the execution of monetary policy in the 1950s and 1960s. The bills only policy, operation twist, and monetary policy following the abandonment of operation twist after 1963 were conducted with reference to a whole host of interest rates and the level of free reserves in the banking system. **Free reserves** are the difference between excess reserves and borrowings from the Fed. These reserves are called free reserves because they are assumed to reflect the ability of the banking system to utilize unencumbered reserves to expand bank credit, which consists of loans and securities purchases. Free reserves are not committed for repayment to the Fed or as reserves held against deposits. It was presumed that banks having excess reserves would first desire to repay their borrowing from the Fed. If the amounts of free reserves were large, banks could easily expand bank credit, while if free reserves were small or negative, bank credit was tight. However, the free reserve concept is flawed. The same level of free reserves is compatible with considerably different levels of total and excess reserves depending on how much banks borrow from the Fed. Thus, considerably different levels of bank credit can result. Nevertheless, the Fed in the 1950s and 1960s paid a great deal of attention to the level of free reserves in addition to interest rates in issuing its directives to the manager of the open-market account.

However, besides the failure of the money market strategy to pay any explicit attention to the money supply (in a modern light this seems a gross omission, but it was quite consistent with the prevailing view in the 1950s and 1960s) while concentrating on interest rates and free reserves, the money market strategy was deficient in its failure to **quantify** targets for the variables the Fed considered important. This was true even of interest rates.[8] This lack of quantification led to FOMC directives to the manager of the Fed open market trading desk that were very vague and therefore gave a good deal of latitude to the manager in executing policy decisions. For example, the following quotation comes from the directive of February 6, 1968: ". . . system open market operations until the next meeting of the committee shall be conducted with a view to maintaining firm conditions in the

---

[8] This was pointed out forcefully in a very important paper published in 1966 by Professor Jack Guttentag of the University of Pennsylvania entitled "The Strategy of Open Market Operations," *Quarterly Journal of Economics* (Feb. 1966), pp. 1–30.

money market and operations shall be modified . . . if bank credit appears to be expanding as rapidly as is currently projected."

Clearly the meaning of "firm," the operative word in the above excerpt, was subject to some interpretation by the open-market account manager. Notice, however, the last phrase of the excerpt. In 1966, the Fed had decided to insert a proviso clause in terms of bank credit (bank loans and investments) into the directive. This clause, as can be seen in the excerpt above, required the manager to pay attention to the bank credit in the economy. But to reiterate, a nonquantative guideline was given. By 1970, the Fed had moved to pay increasing attention, at least in its discussions, to money supply measures, that is, the monetary aggregates. It was not, however, until 1972 that quantitative targets for bank reserves were introduced into the directive.

The changes starting in 1970 reflected the Fed's increasing recognition of the importance of reserves and the money supply in the economy. But its basic strategy, which continued until October 6, 1979, was still executed in terms of the interest rate, at least on a day-to-day basis. The interest rate used was the federal funds rate. However, increasingly in the 1970s, quantitative statements for the variables the Fed wished to influence were stated in the directive; and beginning in 1975, the Fed's goals for money supply growth in quantitative terms were communicated to Congress periodically by the Chairman of the Board of Governors. This reporting requirement was formalized by the Humphrey–Hawkins Full Employment and Balanced Growth Act of 1978. The strategy of monetary policy through the 1970s and the current strategy are intertwined and therefore will be examined in detail. The current strategy, which is dated from October 6, 1979, marks a potential movement to a true reserve aggregate strategy—one which focuses directly on bank reserves—from an interest rate strategy.

The Strategy of Monetary Policy

The strategy of monetary policy may be thought of as composed of a long-run strategy and a short-run strategy. The long-run strategy is designed to achieve some goal of Federal Reserve policy such as the restoration of price stability in a period of inflation, while the short-run strategy is the actual day-to-day and week-to-week execution of monetary policy.[9] Clearly the short-run strategy must be consistent

---

[9] For a formal discussion of the long-run and short-run strategies of monetary policy prior to October 1979, see Raymond Lombra and Raymond Torto, "The Strategy of Monetary Policy," Federal Reserve Bank of Richmond *Monthly Review* (Sept./Oct. 1975), pp. 3–14. Much of the discussion of the pre-October 1979 Fed strategy is based on their analysis.

with the long-run strategy for the long-run policy goal to be achieved. To understand short-run Fed strategy and its importance to achieving long-run Fed goals, we begin our discussion with an explanation of the terminology in which the strategy of monetary policy is cast.

Instruments and Targets and the Strategy of Monetary Policy

A monetary policy instrument is something over which the Fed has complete control. Instruments include all the tools of monetary policy. In practice, however, open-market operations are the major monetary policy instrument. There are three types of targets—proximate targets, intermediate targets, and the goal variables of monetary policy, which are known as ultimate targets. Proximate targets are variables that the Fed can control on virtually a daily basis. There are two proximate targets, the federal funds rate and non-borrowed reserves. Intermediate targets are variables that the Fed can control or influence significantly over longer periods of time. Intermediate targets are the money supply and the level of interest rates in the economy. Ultimate targets or goals may be price stability, full employment, and economic growth, for example. The strategy of monetary policy may be thought of as flowing from instruments to proximate targets. Proximate targets are controlled by the Fed in order to influence intermediate targets which, in turn, are ultimately related to the goal variables. This process is shown in Figure 19-1.

The manner in which Fed policy was conducted in the 1970s until October 6, 1979, can be explained as one that focused on a day-to-day basis on the federal funds rate, the rate on reserves that banks borrow and lend to each other. The Fed kept that rate within a narrow range (usually one-half of a percentage point or so) that it assumed to be compatible with a particular level of bank reserve growth and money supply growth. (The federal funds rate was chosen by the Fed not only because it could be controlled on a day-to-day basis but also because it was believed to give a good indication of the

Figure 19-1
The Monetary Policy Strategy Flow

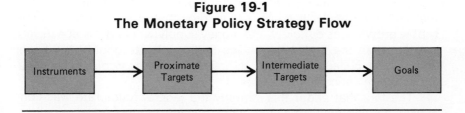

reserve position of the banking system, reflecting as it did the supply and demand for reserves.) When the federal funds rate moved above or below the specified limits on a daily basis, the Fed would buy or sell securities. For example, suppose that the Fed from its econometric analysis and judgment felt that a federal funds rate between 11 and 11.5 percent was consistent with reserve growth of 6 percent. Reserve growth of 6 percent was, in turn, thought to be consistent with money stock growth of 5 to 6 percent, and this level of money supply growth the Fed believed to be desirable in achieving its long-run money supply growth target. The FOMC, in its directive to the open-market trading desk, issued instructions to keep the federal funds rate within such limitations. The manager of the trading desk did so by selling securities (draining reserves from the banking system) anytime the federal funds rate started to move below 11 percent and buying securities (injecting reserves into the banking system) anytime the rate moved above 11.5 percent.

While it was very easy for the manager to accomplish this task, there was no guarantee that the Fed's assumption that such a federal funds rate band was consistent with the expected reserve growth rate and money supply growth rate. If, for example, after a couple of weeks or a month had passed and evidence indicated that the money supply was growing too fast, then the FOMC would likely raise its federal funds rate band. On the other hand, if after some time had passed the money supply appeared to be growing too slowly, the Fed would lower its band. The problem, as should be clear from the discussion, was that the Fed didn't know how fast the money supply was growing at the moment in time it established a particular range on the funds rate, only how fast it had grown some weeks previously. Thus, a situation could occur in which the money supply had grown faster than the Fed desired over, say, the previous month. As a result, the Fed raised the funds rate band but circumstances had changed in the interim which caused the money supply to grow faster than the Fed wished, despite the rise in the funds rate. This indeed seemed to have occurred prior to the strategy change of October 6, 1979, and is often thought of as one of the reasons for this change. Notice that the Fed's decision to control the federal funds rate means that it did not control reserves directly. Reserves were injected and removed from the banking system in response to changes in the federal funds rate. Thus, if the Fed's estimate of the federal funds rate range consistent with a particular level of reserve growth and a particular money supply growth was deficient, the money supply would grow at a different rate than the Fed desired. The Fed's estimate could have been wrong either because their models or judgment were wrong or because economic relationships had altered.

The fact that under this strategy the federal funds rate was controlled directly while reserves were not led monetarist economists, concerned as they are with growth in the money supply, to argue that the Fed should not attempt to directly control the funds rate but instead should seek direct control over bank reserves. In this way the Fed would be able to control the money supply. Despite the increased attention that the Fed paid to the reserves and the money supply in the 1970s, however, the strategy was still to control the funds rate, until the strategy change on October 6, 1979. The October 1979 change has been regarded as recognition of the monetarist argument.

Before examining the October 1979 change in strategy, let us briefly recap the strategy discussed above and the link between the short-run and long-run strategies. The federal funds rate depends upon the supply and demand for reserves in the banking system. If reserves are tight, the funds rate will move up. On the other hand, if reserves are plentiful, it should move down. The Fed picks the funds rate range that it believes is consistent with the reserves needed to achieve some money supply growth rate that it desires in the short run. By controlling the supply of reserves in the banking system through open-market operations, the Fed can keep the funds rate within the range it has decided upon. The short-run money supply target it hopes to attain by this process will be consistent with the long-run money supply growth target that it wishes to achieve in order to accomplish its policy goal, for example, price stability. It is quite possible that the short-run money supply target will not be equal to the long-run target. For example, suppose that the money supply had grown too rapidly (above the Fed's desired long-run money supply growth rate) over the previous month. The Fed may then attempt to slow that growth rate considerably this month in order to get back on track in terms of the money supply growth rate.

The problem with this strategy can be understood by focusing on the demand for total reserves. The Fed has picked its federal funds rate range by assuming a particular level of demand for reserves, setting the supply of reserves, and determining the funds rate it needs to attain in order to achieve that supply. Figure 19-2 illustrates this process. R_D is the demand for reserves, R_S the supply of reserves, and R_0 the reserve level the Fed wishes to maintain. It sets the federal funds rate at FFR^* (where FFR^* can be considered a very narrow range, say 11 to 11.25 percent) to achieve this. However, if the demand for reserves increases to R_D' because, let us say, loan demand at banks increases, the funds rate will rise to FFR_1 and the Fed will increase the supply of reserves to R_S' to hold the funds rate down, increasing the level of reserves to R_1. Similarly the Fed would drain reserves if there should be a fall in the demand for reserves. In fact, the supply of reserves becomes perfectly elastic at FFR^* until the Fed changes the funds rate range. This is reflected by the line labeled R_{SACT} in Figure 19-2, which shows that the supply of reserves will adjust to changes in reserve demand so as to keep the funds rate

Figure 19-2
The Supply and Demand for Reserves Under a Federal Funds Strategy

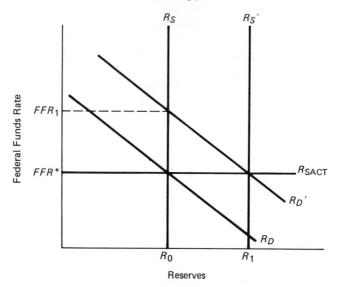

Reserves

fixed at *FFR**. *FFR** will be changed by the Fed only after evidence accumulates that the reserve growth and money supply targets are not being achieved. This may take several weeks or longer. Thus, by the Fed's following the federal funds strategy, the level of reserves is determined by demand. The economy, not the Fed, sets the level of reserves, at least in the short run; this is known as reverse causation. The Fed is responding to the economy, supplying the reserves that the economy demands and, hence, the money supply that the economy demands, at least in the short run. However, the long run is made up of a series of short runs, and the Fed can find that it may not achieve its money supply goals as a result. It is exactly this problem that the monetarists had pointed out in urging the Fed to adopt a reserve target directly, setting reserves at the level via the money multiplier framework consistent with the money supply they want to attain. The Fed had resisted this, arguing that reserves were too hard to control on a day-to-day basis.[10] However, on October 6, 1979, in response

---

[10] The rate on federal funds is available minute to minute while non-borrowed reserves must be estimated. This is one reason why the Fed had resisted a reserve target.

to accelerating inflation, a declining dollar internationally, and rapid increases in the money supply, the Fed announced that it was going to follow a reserve aggregate strategy.

The Change to a Reserve Aggregate Strategy

On October 6, 1979, the Fed announced that it was henceforth going to control non-borrowed reserves rather than the federal funds rate. A reserve aggregate strategy is one whereby the Fed attempts to directly control some measure of bank reserves. Non-borrowed reserves, the total reserves of the banking system less any reserves borrowed from the Fed, was the reserve aggregate that the Fed decided upon in implementing its new strategy. In practice the change has not meant totally abandoning the federal funds rate. However, the federal funds rate range is set so wide (often four to five percentage points compared to one-quarter to one-half of a percentage point before the strategy change) that it merely serves as a secondary guide to short-term policy, and the focus of the strategy is clearly on controlling reserves.

To understand the difference between a reserve aggregate strategy and the previous federal funds strategy, consider Figure 19-3 and compare it to Figure 19-2. Figure 19-3 depicts initial equilibrium at a federal funds rate FFR_0. The demand for reserves increases to R_D'. In contrast to the situation in Figure 19-2, however, the increase in the demand for reserves to R_D' does not induce the Fed to supply additional reserves. R_S is fixed at R_0 because the Fed has decided to control reserves rather than the funds rate. So the funds rate rises to FFR_1 and remains there. In practice, as demand rises or falls, the funds rate can move around considerably but as long as the Fed sticks to its targeted reserve level, reserves will remain at R_0. If R_0 is set so that it is consistent with the Fed's desired growth rate of the money supply, all else being equal, that money supply target should be attained.

However, all else may not be equal and so some potential problems that may interfere with the Fed's achievement of its money supply goals should be noted. The Fed is controlling only non-borrowed reserves, yet total reserves are equal to non-borrowed plus borrowed reserves. If borrowed reserves change in a way that the Fed has not forecasted, the Fed cannot compensate in advance for this alteration in the level of total reserves through a change in non-borrowed reserves. Recall that borrowing at the discount window is done at the discretion of the banking system. The only influence that the Fed can exert in the short run over the level of borrowing comes through changes in the discount rate. Since the discount rate is not a penalty rate, one that exceeds open-market rates, and furthermore does not automatically change with open-market rates, banks can use the discount window to temporarily increase reserves. Thus, the Fed must

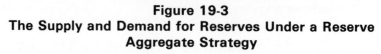

Figure 19-3
The Supply and Demand for Reserves Under a Reserve Aggregate Strategy

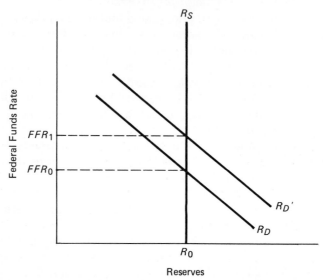

forecast the level of borrowed reserves in deciding on how much in non-borrowed reserves to supply. This is very difficult to do and is the reason that many monetarists continue to argue for a penalty discount rate to discourage all but emergency borrowing. Further, unanticipated fluctuations in the money multiplier through which changes in reserves translate into changes in the money supply may also interfere with the achievement of the Fed's money supply objective. These potential problems demonstrate that even with a reserve aggregate strategy, the Fed may still have difficulties in achieving its precise policy goals.

Furthermore, it was pointed out above that the manner in which the Fed has pursued the reserve aggregate strategy since October 1979 has not led them to completely abandon the federal funds rate as a strategy guide. The Fed has allowed the funds rate to fluctuate within much wider limits than had been the case under the federal funds rate strategy. Nevertheless, the Fed may still find itself increasing or decreasing reserves in response to a funds rate movement if that rate movement should be very dramatic. The fact that the Fed is still paying any attention to the federal funds rate has troubled some monetarists and has left the assessment of how committed the Fed is to the new strategy to the accumulation of evidence on policy implementation over the course of some years.

To summarize the change in strategy, it is clear that under a reserve aggregate strategy interest rates will fluctuate substantially, while under an interest rate strategy reserves will fluctuate considerably. This means that the Fed in pursuing the reserve strategy will necessarily allow more volatility in the federal funds rate and as a result in interest rates in general. The record since October 1979 bears this out. Interest rate fluctuations have been substantial. For example, in the year from October 1978 to September 1979, the monthly average rate on three-month Treasury bills varied between 7.98 and 9.78 percent. From October 1979 to August 1981 the rate varied between 7.07 and 16.30 percent. While the Fed cannot be considered completely responsible for the relative stability prior to October 1979, and all the instability after October 1979, nevertheless, it seems the evidence is consistent with what would be expected given the change in strategy.

THE NEW STRATEGY IN OPERATION

Hard-Nosed Monetarism Takes Over at the Fed

"You guys are in the driver's seat now, and we want to give you what you want." This remark to a top Administration official by a governor of the Federal Reserve System with a reputation as a liberal signals a fundamental change in Federal Reserve policy. For the first time in history, the Fed is practicing hard-nosed monetarism. And monetarist economists inside and outside the Administration believe that this switch in policy explains why interest rates have risen sharply since April and why they may soon begin a sustained decline.

The Administration wants the same thing from the Fed that everyone else in the industrialized world wants: lower U.S. interest rates. But its formula for getting lower rates is specifically monetarist. "If money growth accelerates, interest rates will go up, but if it slows down, rates will decline," says Beryl Sprinkel, Under Secretary of the Treasury and the Administration's top monetarist. A slowdown in money growth will lower rates because it will lessen inflationary expectations, in the monetarist view.

Trade-off. Nothing is more obvious than the fact that the Federal Reserve has not given the Administration the interest rate levels that it wants. Since early April, rates have soared; in the case of Treasury bills, for example, the rise has been from 12¾% to about 17% in late May. But as far as the monetarists and the Fed are concerned, that rise in rates is the price that has to be paid for getting the monetary growth rate down and keeping it down.

In the past two months the Fed has fought to rein in money growth with an unprecedented vigor. The battle has been difficult because of a sharp surge in credit demand that resulted in a $10 billion increase in the money supply in April. Earlier the Fed would have responded to that surge by allowing interest rates to rise gradually in the hope that the rate of growth of money would come down gradually. But this time the Fed risked financial instability by allowing rates to rise sharply. The result was a sharp deceleration in money growth from a 19% growth rate for M1-B in April to a 1.1% rate in May.

In a sense, the Fed's determination to fight rapid money growth was even more impressive in May than it was in the earlier months. In the past a slowdown in money growth would have induced the Fed to relax its policy, allowing rates to fall. This is what the market expected to happen in the wake of the $4 billion decline in money between the week ending on May 6 and the week ending on May 20. After the May 20 number was announced, prices rose and rates fell in the money markets. Traders obviously expected the Fed to return to its old ways and relent.

Unprecedented. But, in a move that caused money market veterans to grind their teeth, the Fed promptly acted to pour water on the market, and June 2 was particularly traumatic. On that day, the Federal Reserve drained reserves from the banking system by selling securities even though the interest rate that it watches most closely, the federal funds rate, stood at 19½%, toward the high end of its recent range. In the past, an upward move in the federal funds rate in the wake of a decline in the money supply would have caused the Fed to add reserves to the system.

Because hard-nosed monetarism is a new policy, there is no experience for telling where interest rates will go in the short run. Many private analysts believe that the money supply will jump, possibly sharply, in the two-week period ending on June 10. That is how they interpreted the Fed's June 2 action. And if that happens, it is quite possible that short-term interest rates will hit new peaks over the next couple of weeks.

No alternative. It should not be imagined that the Fed or the Administration will buckle under political pressure. Much of Wall Street is unhappy with the new Fed policy. The nation's savings institutions are hurting. The public generally is howling over high rates. But so far there is no sign that the White House has abandoned its monetary strategy. It sees no alternative to a slowdown in money growth as a way of getting interest rates down.

Administration economists continue to hope that once it comes, the fall in interest rates will be substantial. In the monetarist world, the main long-run determinant of high interest rates is the inflation rate. Administration economists therefore view the recent rise in rates as a fundamental aberration. They believe that when the financial world wakes up to the news that the inflation rate has dropped from a 12% to 13% range in 1980 to an 8% to 9% range in 1981 and that the Fed will not let money growth soar, a sustained fall in interest rates will be the inevitable consequence.

Key Points

1. The money supply is determined by the interaction of the money multiplier and the monetary base. The money multiplier is determined by reserve requirements, the currency–deposit ratio and the excess reserve ratio. The monetary base may be measured from its uses, which are currency in circulation and bank reserves, or from its sources, which include Federal Reserve holdings of securities and Fed discount lending.

2. Since the monetary base includes total reserves that may be borrowed or non-borrowed, only the portion that is non-borrowed is directly under the control of the Fed. The borrowed portion comes into existence through bank borrowings at the Fed. The level of discount borrowing reflects essentially bank decisions, especially considering the lack of a penalty discount rate. Further, there may be other technical impediments to completely controlling even the non-borrowed portion of the monetary base such as changes in float and data availability.

3. The strategy of monetary policy is the name economists give to the manner in which the Fed implements monetary policy to achieve short-run and long-run policy goals. The governing strategy for much of the period after the 1951 Treasury–Federal Reserve accord, which freed

the Fed from pegging interest rates, until 1970 was called the money market strategy. The Fed focused on interest rates and the free reserves of the banking system under this strategy, though policy was conducted differently through these years. After 1970, the Fed paid much more attention to reserve and monetary aggregates in its strategy, but the Fed still utilized an interest rate, the federal funds rate, in its strategy implementation. Following October 1979, the Fed adopted a reserve aggregate strategy, which focuses on non-borrowed reserves.

4. The federal funds rate strategy as it was implemented meant that a narrow federal funds rate range was chosen by the Fed that was believed consistent with a desired level of reserve and money supply growth. While the range could be and was frequently changed, the result of this strategy was that the level of reserves was determined by demand.

5. The non-borrowed reserve aggregate strategy adopted in October 1979 means that the Fed has much tighter control over the level of reserves in the banking system than under the federal funds strategy. However, the "cost" of this control is substantially more interest rate volatility.

Questions for Discussion

1. Compare and contrast an interest rate strategy such as the federal funds rate strategy with a reserve aggregate strategy such as controlling non-borrowed reserves in their impact on interest rate stability, reserve growth, and money supply control.

2. Why did the Fed decide after the Federal Reserve–Treasury accord to follow a bills only policy? Why was this policy finally abandoned?

3. Why was it stated in the text that the Fed could only control a portion of the monetary base under present procedures? Explain.

4. Discuss the importance of the money multiplier in the money supply process and in monetary policy implementation under a reserve aggregate strategy.

5. What is the rationale behind the argument that the money multiplier imparts an interest rate sensitivity to the money supply? Evaluate this argument.

Suggested Readings

Balbach, Anatol B. "How Controllable is Money Growth?" Federal Reserve Bank of St. Louis *Review,* April 1981, pp. 3–12.

Berkman, Neil G. "Bank Reserves, Money, and Some Problems for the New Monetary Policy." Federal Reserve Bank of Boston *New England Economic Review,* July/August 1980, pp. 52–64.

Board of Governors of the Federal Reserve System. "Monetary Policy Report to Congress." Federal Reserve *Bulletin,* August 1981, pp. 595–606. (This is one of the periodic reports presented by the Chairman of the Federal Reserve Board of Governors to the Congress under the Humphrey–Hawkins Full Employment and Balanced Growth Act of 1978.)

Carlson, John B. "The Monetary Base, the Economy, and Monetary Policy." Federal Reserve Bank of Cleveland *Economic Review,* Spring 1981, pp. 2–13.

Davis, Richard G. "The Monetary Base as an Intermediate Target for Monetary Policy." Federal Reserve Bank of New York *Quarterly Review,* Winter 1979–80, pp. 1–10.

Lombra, Raymond, and Raymond Torto. "The Strategy of Monetary Policy." Federal Reserve Bank of Richmond *Monthly Review,* Sept./Oct. 1975, pp. 3–14.

Sellon, Gordon H., Jr., and Ronald L. Teigen. "The Choice of Short-Run Targets for Monetary Policy, Part I: A Theoretical Analysis." Federal Reserve Bank of Kansas City *Economic Review,* April 1981, pp. 3–16 and "Part II: An Historical Analysis." Federal Reserve Bank of Kansas City *Economic Review,* May 1981, pp. 3–12.

20

Inflation

nflation is defined as a continuous and general rise in prices. However, inflation can also be defined as a continuous fall in the value of money in terms of goods and services. Inflation is a monetary phenomena; and, therefore, in a text about the financial system and money, it is appropriate to analyze inflation. Since the late 1960s, the United States, as well as much of the western world, has been troubled by a serious problem of inflation, which intensified in the 1970s and the early 1980s. Inflation was particularly virulent in the 1973–75 and 1979–81 periods. This chapter will examine inflation from a number of perspectives.

Before turning to an analysis of inflation, it is useful to understand how inflation is measured. While the definition of inflation implies that simply examining a price index is sufficient, the price indices available for the U.S. economy do not always tell the same story about the rate of inflation. They generally indicate that an inflation is underway, but, due to the manner in which they are constructed, they sometimes differ as to the intensity of the inflation.

The Price Indices: Measuring Inflation

Figure 20-1 presents the rate of inflation for the years from 1970 to 1980 as measured by the three most well known of the price indices, the consumer price index (CPI), the producer price index (PPI), and the GNP price deflator (GNPD). Of these, the CPI receives the most attention in the media and by the public and is the index most often utilized in labor contracts containing "cost of living" clauses. It is also

Figure 20-1
**The Rate of Inflation as Measured by the Consumer (CPI) and
Producer (PPI) Price Indices and the GNP Price Deflator (GNPD),
1970–80**

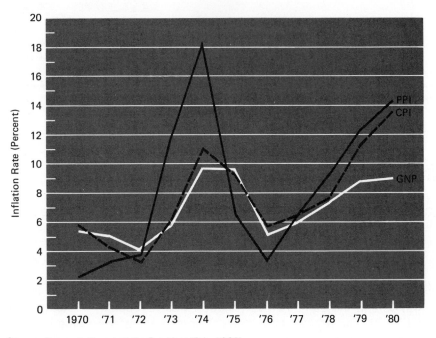

Source: *Economic Report of the President* (Feb. 1982).

used in adjusting social security benefits for inflation.[1] It is quite certain
that when a commentator in the newspapers or on television talks
about the "cost of living," the commentator is referring to the latest
CPI number.

However, an examination of Figure 20-1 indicates that significantly
different pictures of the rate of inflation can be formed depending
upon the price index utilized. In 1980, to take an extreme example,
the inflation rate measured by the CPI differed from that measured
by the GNPD by 4.5 percentage points, a difference in the inflation
rate of 50 percent. Further, the fact that the CPI is often used in
references to the cost of living can be misleading. To the extent the

---

[1] The use of the CPI as a measure of the "cost of living" can be inappropriate as
will be explained below.

CPI is utilized for automatic increases in wages, salaries, and retirement income, it can actually contribute to inflationary pressures if it is not an accurate measure of the cost of living. This occurs because increases in costs, such as wages in excess of actual inflation, can serve to intensify inflation. To understand the differences in the measures of inflation, let us briefly discuss the indices.

The Consumer Price Index

The consumer price index is a measure of the prices of a market "basket" of goods and services that the typical consumer might buy. It is not a measure of all consumer prices in the economy. Further, it need not be a measure of the prices of goods and services that an individual consumer might buy. To the extent that a consumer doesn't purchase all items in the CPI, that consumer's "cost of living" is not indicated by the CPI. For example, considerable weight in the CPI (23 percent) is given to housing and housing-related expenditures. Such things as the price of new houses and mortgage interest rates are included. If a consumer in a particular month or year does not buy a new house, the CPI will be distorted for that consumer for that period. Further, it will be distorted for all consumers that don't purchase housing in that month or year—the large majority. (Only about 6 percent of the population on average purchase and finance a house in a given year.) For example, in early 1980, the CPI was rising at an annual rate of 18 percent. Yet, over three percentage points of this 18 percent increase were traceable to the increased mortgage interest rates of early 1980. If a consumer did not purchase a house and acquire a new mortgage, that consumer would not have been directly affected by that category.

Recognition that housing costs distort the CPI as a measure of inflation has led the Bureau of Labor Statistics (BLS), the organization that compiles the CPI, to propose a change in composition of the CPI effective January 1983. In the BLS plan, many housing cost items will be deleted and they will be replaced by the rental price of housing. Many economists have argued that this change is desirable as it more accurately measures increases in the housing component of the cost of living. The CPI will be significantly affected by this change. For example, if the rental price of housing had been used for the period from October 1980 to September 1981, the CPI would have shown an increase of 9.2 percent rather than the 11 percent reported.

Besides the distortion in the CPI introduced by the way in which housing has been included in the CPI, there are other problems that make the CPI a less-than-perfect measure of the current cost of living. The latest survey of the market basket of goods that is measured by the CPI took place over the period 1972–73. To the extent consumer buying patterns have changed after that period the CPI would not reflect these changes. There has been much argument that the CPI thus overstates inflation since consumers substitute goods whose prices have risen less for goods whose prices have risen more, yet such substitution isn't reflected in the CPI because the market basket and weighting remains unchanged. The CPI also does not reflect any changes in item quality. Because of these problems, many economists argue that the GNP price deflator is a better measure of inflation in the economy.

The GNP Price Deflator

The GNP price deflator (GNPD) measures increases in prices of all items included in the GNP. Since GNP measures the dollar value of all goods and services produced in the economy for the year, economists argue that the GNPD is a much more general measure of inflation than is the CPI. Yet GNPD has not been widely accepted by the public as the best measure of inflation. The reason is that many people argue that the CPI, which focuses only on consumer goods, gives a truer picture of inflation for the consumer.[2] The GNP deflator is a measure of prices of all goods and services in the GNP. Therefore, not only are prices of consumer goods and services included but so are prices of investment goods, goods and services purchased by the government, and net exports.

The GNP deflator is known as an implicit price deflator. That is, measured GNP in current prices is converted to GNP in base period prices (currently the base year is 1972) to yield a measure of "real" (inflation-adjusted) GNP. The difference between these two measures of GNP is the GNP price deflator. The deflator exclusively reflects the weights of the various items in GNP. The general nature of the deflator does have much to commend it as a measure of inflation particularly in a period like 1980 when the CPI was clearly distorted by housing. In 1980 as a result, the rates of inflation as measured by the CPI and the deflator diverged by substantial amounts, with the CPI showing much higher rates. As Figure 20-1 indicates the GNPD increased 9 percent while the CPI showed prices rising at 13.5 percent.

It is unlikely that as a practical matter the GNPD will replace the CPI very soon as the generally accepted measure of inflation for the public. In part this is due to custom. However, in addition, many people benefit from having their income tied to the higher measure of inflation as the CPI has been in recent years and thus have a vested interest in retaining the CPI as a measure of the cost of living. Nevertheless,

---

[2] An alternative recommendation by economists to deal with this problem has been to utilize the GNP deflator for the consumption sector alone, which is available separately.

the change in how housing costs are included in the CPI that begins in January 1983 may reduce the divergence between the CPI and the GNPD substantially.

The Producer Price Index

The producer price index (PPI), which used to be called the wholesale price index, is the most volatile of the price indices as Figure 20-1 shows. It measures the prices of finished goods at wholesale and is said to presage what will occur in the consumer price index by a few months. Figure 20-2 graphs the producer and consumer price indices for 1978 through 1980 monthly at annual rates. While it is clear that there is a strong relationship, the match is not perfect with, as noted above, the PPI showing much more volatility. Nevertheless, the PPI remains a useful measure of the trend of consumer prices in the near future.

Figure 20-2
Percentage Changes in CPI and PPI, Monthly at Simple (Noncom-pounded) Annual Rates, 1978–80

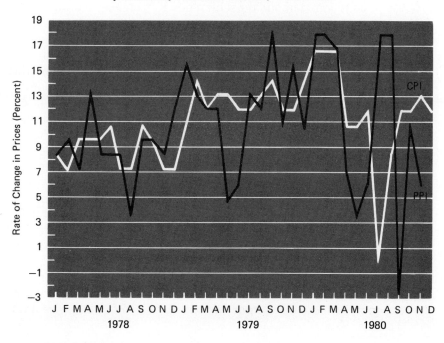

Source: Federal Reserve *Bulletin,* various issues.

The Inflationary Process

The discussion of the measurement of inflation in the previous section provides the necessary background for the analysis of the inflationary process of this section. Throughout the 1950s and 1960s, discussion about the causes of inflation centered on whether inflation was primarily demand–pull or cost–push inflation. Demand–pull inflation (or aggregate demand inflation) ascribes inflation to increases in aggregate demand causing prices to rise, especially when the economy is at or near full employment. Demand–pull inflation has often been summarized in the phrase "too much money chasing too few goods." However, there were inflationary episodes in the late 1950s and early 1960s and again in the early 1970s that appeared not to be capable of explanation by excessive aggregate demand. To explain these episodes, economists looked to the cost side of the economy as reflected in aggregate supply. Cost–push inflation was explained by increases in costs of production such as wages, profit margins, and natural resource prices being passed on by businesses in the form of higher prices in the economy.

However, in retrospect, it seems clear that these distinctions are artificial. Inflation is a continuous rise in prices rather than a once-and-for-all increase in the price level. Therefore, for the inflationary process to continue, demand must continue to increase to bring about price increases in the aggregate even if the initial stimulus for the price rise comes from the supply side. Examine Figure 20-3, which depicts aggregate demand (A_D) in the economy and aggregate supply (A_S) in the economy. (The schedules are drawn as straight lines for simplicity.) Simply, aggregate demand is the demand for all output taken together in the economy. It is negatively related to the price level, indicated on the vertical axis. Aggregate supply is the supply of output in the economy and is positively related to price level.[3] Figure 20-3 initially shows the price level and output at the intersection of aggregate supply and demand at Y_0 and P_0. Suppose that costs rise in the economy. This would imply a leftward and upward shift in the aggregate supply schedule to A_S'. A particularly relevant example of such cost increases that would shift the aggregate supply curve leftwards is a rise in oil prices. Prices rise to P_1 and output falls to Y_1. However, the one-time rise in the price level does not constitute inflation. Inflation is a continuous rise in prices. Therefore, if the situation remained at P_1 and Y_1, inflation would not occur. However, suppose the government finds Y_1 an unacceptable level of unemployment in the economy. (Reduced output implies increased unemployment.)

---

[3] For a complete treatment and derivation of the aggregate supply–aggregate demand model, see, for example, Robert J. Gordon, *Macroeconomics* (Boston: Little, Brown, 1978).

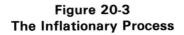

Figure 20-3
The Inflationary Process

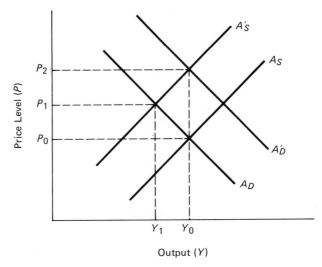

Output (Y)

Thus, through monetary or fiscal policy, it increases aggregate demand to A'_D, restoring output to Y_0 but causing prices to rise to P_2—the inflationary process has started. The process can continue if, for example, wages rise to keep pace with inflation (through automatic cost of living adjustments, for example) further shifting the A_S curve upward and the government attempts to maintain employment at Y_0 by increases in aggregate demand. Thus, it is clear that government policy is necessary to validate inflation. We can even be more specific. Increases in the money supply through the Federal Reserve's providing sufficient reserves to the banking system are necessary at some point to keep the inflationary process going because inflation cannot long continue without sufficient money supply growth. In turn, money supply growth cannot long continue without sufficient growth in banking system reserves, which only the Fed can provide.

In the example given above, the inflationary process began with a leftward shift in aggregate supply. However, it could just as easily have begun with a rightward shift in aggregate demand. This could result from an excessive expansion of the money supply to achieve increases in employment in the economy. The Federal Reserve, in the interest of reducing the unemployment rate, attempts to stimulate the economy but does so at too rapid a rate. Monetarists, like Milton Friedman, argue that only with "excessive" increases in the money supply can inflation continue. They argue that the supply of money is the fundamental determinant of changes in economic activity and inflation in the short-run. In the long run, changes in the money supply are solely responsible for inflation. Excessive increases in the money supply are increases that exceed the long-run production potential of the economy.

Historically, the United States economy has grown at a rate of about 3 percent a year in real terms. Monetarists argue that growth in the money supply should be held a little above this long-run potential. This would provide sufficient money to finance economic growth without any substantial inflation resulting. As evidence of the relationship between money supply growth and inflation, monetarists often present a graph such as Figure 20-4. This figure traces the rate of increase in the money supply (M1) and inflation as measured by the GNP price deflator in the 1970s. If the lags between a change in the money supply and the change in prices are allowed for, the relationship between the two series seems to be close, though far from exact.

Neo-Keynesians reject the monetarist explanation. They argue that the increases in the money supply result from the forces that are driving

Figure 20-4
The Rate of Change Annually in M1 and GNPD, 1970–80

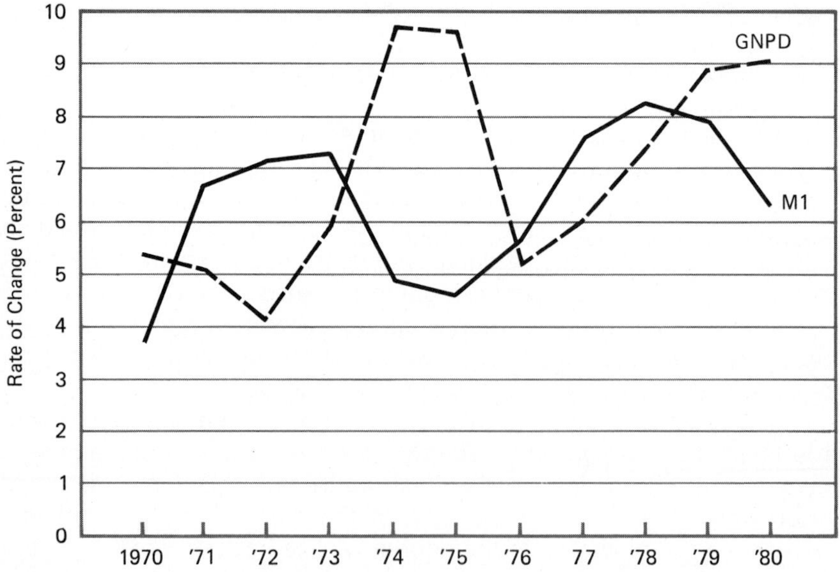

Source: Federal Reserve *Bulletin*, various issues.

up prices anyway—for example, increased economic activity. Their argument is that increased economic activity leads to increases in bank loan demand. The increase in bank lending, in turn, leads to an expansion in the money supply. Which explanation for the inflation is most compelling is less important than the central fact that without the increase in the money supply, inflation could not long continue. For the money supply to continue to grow, the Federal Reserve must increase banking system reserves. This implies that the government makes a decision (perhaps implicitly) that the continued high output in the economy is necessary even at the cost of additional inflation.

For many years in the post–World War II period, it was believed that there was a clear tradeoff between unemployment and inflation. As was mentioned previously, this was known as the Phillips curve tradeoff. The Phillips curve was an important part of the analytical framework that governed economic policy through much of this period. Before examining this relationship, however, it is useful to examine the connection between oil price rises in the 1970s and inflation because many people regard the oil price increases as one of the major causes of the inflation during that decade. However, the necessity of governmental policy validating inflation becomes clear even when the rise in costs is as dramatic as it was in the case of oil price increases.

Oil Prices and Inflation

In 1974, when the Organization of Petroleum Exporting Countries (OPEC) quadrupled oil prices, the effect was to raise prices of many commodities because oil is such an important input into so many products. In terms of aggregate supply and demand, what occurred was a large upward shift in the aggregate supply curve as shown in Figure 20-5 so that prices rose to P_1. But the fall in output (accompanied by increased unemployment), which in the United States characterized the recession of 1973–75,[4] was considered unsatisfactory from the point of view of government economic policy. As a result, both monetary and fiscal policy became highly stimulative, particularly after 1974. Further, expansionary policy continued well after the recession was over. But such stimulation meant substantial increases in aggregate demand and rapid acceleration in inflation. This is shown in Figure 20-5 by the series of rightward shifts in the AD curves.[5] The price level rises from P_1 and output rises from Y_1. When further oil price increases took place in 1979, inflation was already quite serious. It

---

[4] This recession actually began prior to the 1973 oil embargo. Subsequent oil price increases perhaps added to the intensity and the length of the recession but were not responsible for the recession.

[5] Since the aggregate supply and demand curves determine the price level, the only way the acceleration in inflation can be depicted is by increasing differences between price levels. This is not done in the figure for simplicity.

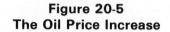

Figure 20-5
The Oil Price Increase

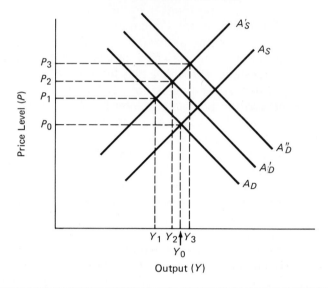

was not until late in 1979 that economic policy became restrictive. This policy tightening had two effects. First the recession of 1980 became more severe (recall the discussion of lags in monetary policy in Chapter 18) and second, inflation, which as measured by the CPI had accelerated in early 1980 to an annual rate of 18 percent, declined substantially but still continued at a high rate. It was not until early in 1982 that inflation decelerated sharply.

The point of presenting the foregoing discussion is to demonstrate that a policy choice was involved in the inflation that took place in the wake of the 1974 oil price increase. Had policy in 1976, 1977, and 1978 not been as expansionary as it was, the economy surely would have grown more slowly, but inflation, which had fallen to less than 5 percent in 1976, would not have accelerated the way it did. It is clear from the example of oil price increases that governmental policy directed at keeping the economy expanding really led to the full inflationary increases. Oil price rises were only the catalyst.

In summary, therefore, it is governmental policy that determines inflation. If governmental policy is too expansionary, while the policy motivation may be admirable—recovery from recession and a continuation of the ensuing expansion—the consequences of this policy should be recognized. Much of the impetus for governmental policy in the

1960s and 1970s is traceable to the widespread acceptance during this period of the Phillips curve, which posited a relatively precise relationship between inflation and unemployment.

The Phillips Curve

In 1958, Professor Phillips of the London School of Economics using British data on wages and unemployment from 1861 to 1957 found that a curve fitted to these data indicated an inverse relation between the rate of wage changes and unemployment.[6] The Phillips curve is shown in Figure 20-6. Thus, lower wage increases could be traded off for higher unemployment and vice versa. This tradeoff was quickly generalized to one between inflation and unemployment. Thus, the policy maker was told that it was a simple choice—more unemployment or more inflation. Both price stability and low unemployment were not possible at the same time; but if more inflation was tolerable, less unemployment was possible. Less inflation could only be achieved at the cost of higher unemployment. This simple device was taken up by economists and policy makers with a vengeance. However, by the 1970s, the simultaneous occurrence of high inflation and high unemployment led to a reevaluation of the Phillips curve tradeoff. The reevaluation gradually evolved into a disagreement between the monetarists and the Neo-Keynesians. The monetarists led by Milton Friedman argued that while there may be a short-term tradeoff between unemployment and inflation, no long-term tradeoff was possible, that is, the Phillips curve was vertical in the long run at what is called the natural rate of unemployment. The natural rate of unemployment is the level of unemployment at which the economy will settle. It is an equilibrium unemployment rate determined by such basic economic factors as the frequency with which people change jobs (and hence are unemployed for brief periods of time) and the match between the skills of the labor force and the jobs available. Presumably the worse the match, the more unemployment. There is nothing necessarily desirable about the natural rate of unemployment. It need not, for example, coincide with some socially desirable level called full employment. But only fundamental economic factors can change it over time.

The only way that the unemployment level could be maintained below the natural rate is for inflation to continuously accelerate. Once inflation stopped accelerating, the unemployment rate would return to the natural rate. The argument of this group became known as the accelerationist argument. The Neo-Keynesians or nonaccelerationists argued that while the tradeoff in the short run is more favorable

---

[6] A. W. Phillips, "The Relation Between Unemployment and the Rate of Change of Money Wage Rates in the United Kingdom, 1861–1957," *Economica* (Nov. 1958), pp. 283–99.

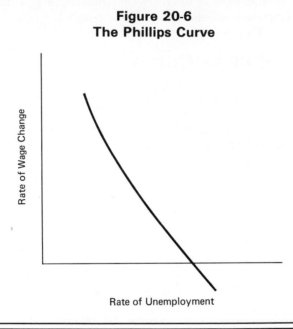

**Figure 20-6
The Phillips Curve**

than in the long run (the Phillips curve is flatter in the short run than in the long run), it still retains its negative slope even in the long run, thus giving a long-run tradeoff between inflation and unemployment. The assumption of a natural rate of unemployment was rejected. The tradeoff may, however, be very unfavorable. It is necessary to examine these arguments in some detail.

The Accelerationist Argument[7]

The accelerationist argument, sometimes also called the natural rate hypothesis, is best explained by making reference to Figure 20-7. U_n indicates the natural rate of unemployment. At the natural rate, the long-run Phillips curve (*LR*) is vertical, showing that any maintained inflation rate is compatible with the natural unemployment rate. In the short run, the government, through stimulative fiscal and monetary policy, can temporarily reduce the unemployment rate along the short-

---

[7] This section draws heavily on Thomas M. Humphrey, "Changing Views of the Phillips Curve," Federal Reserve Bank of Richmond *Monthly Review* (July 1973), pp. 2–13.

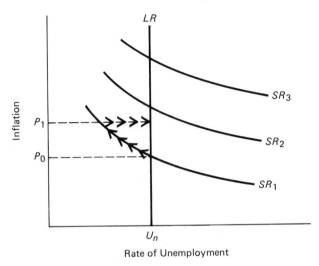

Figure 20-7
The Accelerationist Phillips Curve

run Phillips curve S_1. The arrows show that the price of the reduced unemployment is increased inflation. But if the government then stops stimulating the economy so that the inflation rate stabilizes, the economy will move back toward the natural rate of unemployment as shown by the arrows pointing right. However, this will now coincide with a higher rate of inflation than existed before government policy changed. Only by continually shifting the short-run Phillips curve upward through additional governmental stimulation (as shown by the short-run Phillips curves S_2 and S_3), that is, by continuously accelerating inflation, can the economy be kept below the natural rate of unemployment. Eventually when this stimulation ceases, the economy will return to the long-run curve at the natural unemployment rate and a high inflation rate. Thus, according to the accelerationists, the government should not attempt to reduce unemployment below the natural rate because this will be impossible in the long run and all that will result is even higher inflation.

The Nonaccelerationist Argument

The nonaccelerationist position is depicted in Figure 20-8. The nonaccelerationists reject the notion of a natural rate of unemployment. They believe that if the economy is at unemployment rate U_1, an unac-

Figure 20-8
The Nonaccelerationist Phillips Curve

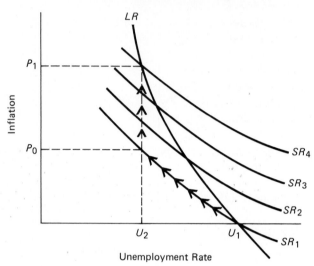

ceptable rate in the government's view, the government starts stimulating the economy which moves along the short-run Phillips curve S_1, showing a fall in the unemployment rate. If the government wishes to achieve the U_2 level of unemployment, it can do so by continuous stimulation (shown by upward shifts in the short-run Phillips curves SR_1, SR_2, and so on) until it hits the long-run, nonvertical Phillips curve (LR). This means that there is a rate of inflation that is compatible with the unemployment level U_2 although that rate of inflation may be quite high. Once, however, that rate of inflation is obtained, the economy will remain at unemployment rate U_2.

Which view is correct? All the evidence is not yet in but the experience for the 1970s appears to be more nearly consistent with the accelerationist view. Allowing for appropriate lags, inflation clearly accelerated throughout much of that decade for given levels of unemployment. Some Neo-Keynesians argue that this merely reflected a deteriorating inflation–unemployment tradeoff over the decade. The worsening tradeoff can be depicted by shifts in LR to the right, which show a higher inflation rate associated with each level of unemployment. Whichever argument is correct, it is clear that the simple view of the Phillips curve as one which gives a clear tradeoff between inflation and unemployment can no longer serve as a basis of economic policy.

An additional feature of the accelerationist argument is worth noting. The accelerationist argument focuses attention on the role of expectations in the economy. The return of the economy to the natural rate of unemployment occurs once inflation stops accelerating because inflation expectations catch up to actual inflation. In fact, technically accelerationists define the natural rate of unemployment as that rate at which inflation expectations equal actual inflation. While inflation is accelerating, business is willing to hire additional workers because prices are rising more rapidly than wages. However, as time passes workers realize that their real wages (their wage rate adjusted for price increases) have declined and demand wage increases to catch up with inflation. If inflation has stopped accelerating over time because the government has stopped stimulating the economy, they will receive wage increases sufficient to compensate them for inflation. Since prices have stopped accelerating, there is no incentive for business to hire workers sufficiently to hold the unemployment rate below the natural rate; price expectations have caught up with actual inflation. There are a number of additional implications for inflation and government stabilization policy when expectations are considered. These are taken up in the next section.

The Role of Expectations in Inflation

In discussing the Fisher effect in Chapter 4 and its relationship to the nominal rate of interest, we pointed out that expectations of future prices are clearly of considerable importance in influencing economic activity. In a chapter on inflation, however, it is useful to discuss expectations as factors serving to make inflation better or worse. For example, the acceleration in inflation that took place in 1979 and early 1980 was in many ways due to the widespread expectation that inflation was going to get worse. As a result, it was sensible for consumers and business to "buy now." If purchases were postponed, buyers assumed they would have to pay considerably more for the goods they desired. But this kind of philosophy serves to intensify inflationary pressures in the economy by adding to aggregate demand. Rapid deceleration in the rate of inflation occurred in the middle part of 1980 in part because the recession and perceived stringency of monetary policy convinced consumers that inflation was going to be of considerably smaller dimensions. This belief can also be self-fulfilling. If consumers believe this and moderate their "buy now" philosophy, inflation may indeed moderate. However, expectations of lower inflation appeared short-lived and by December 1980 the *Wall Street Journal* was blaming inflationary expectations as one reason for the interest rate surge of late November and December 1980.[8]

---

[8] See "Corporate Consumer Expectations Seen as Cause of Interest-Rate Surge," *Wall Street Journal,* Dec. 4, 1980.

The role of expectations has received considerable attention in recent years due to the research of the "rational expectationists," whose work was discussed in Chapter 18. These economists, including such prominent proponents of rational expectations as Robert Lucas of the University of Chicago and Thomas Sargent of the University of Minnesota, hold that the public forms expectations of the future on the basis of all information currently available and acts accordingly. Further, information available to policy makers is also available to the public including the responses of policy makers to changes in economic variables.

The implications of the ideas of the rational expectationists are powerful. If they are correct, policy pursued in a systematic manner by the Federal Reserve System will be anticipated by the public and, therefore, will have no impact on real economic activity. Prices would simply adjust to reflect the Fed's policy. Since the Federal Reserve, therefore, cannot affect real economic activity, the rational expectationists argue that the Fed should give up attempts to follow counter-cyclical policy. For example, the Fed should not attempt to stimulate the economy out of a recession. Rather, the rational expectationists recommend that the Fed keep the money supply growing at a constant rate. This growth will lead to less variability in the economy and ensure a sufficient money supply to keep pace with economic growth while preventing rapid inflation. However, the assumptions underlying rational expectations are very strong, requiring that substantial information be acquired and assimilated by the public in forming its expectations.[9]

A more moderate view of the role of expectations and the impact of expectations on policy effectiveness, which shares some of the same characteristics as that of the rational expectations but requires considerably weaker assumptions, is the credibility hypothesis of William Fellner of the American Enterprise Institute for Public Policy.[10] Fellner has argued that the requirements of the rational expectations are too strong, assuming among other things that individuals are economically sophisticated enough to acquire and process large amounts of information. However, he argues that the strength of the assumptions of rational expectations are unnecessary to make the point that expectations can be very important in affecting the level of inflation. He argues that over time the public forms an impression of how policy

---

[9] See Neil Berkman, "A Rational View of Rational Expectations," Federal Reserve Bank of Boston *New England Economic Review* (Jan./Feb. 1980), pp. 18–29; and Thomas J. Sargent and Neil Wallace, "Rational Expectations and the Theory of Economic Policy, I and II," Federal Reserve Bank of Minneapolis *Studies in Monetary Economics* (June 1975 and June 1976), for summaries of the rational expectations views. The Berkman reference also critiques rational expectations.

[10] William Fellner, *Towards a Reconstruction of Macroeconomics* (Washington, D.C.: American Enterprise Institute, 1976).

will be conducted and that this impression, once it becomes ingrained, is very hard to dislodge. For example, once people become convinced that an inflationary policy is being followed by the Federal Reserve, they will act in a pro-inflationary manner such as taking the "buy now" actions discussed above. Unlike the strictest form of the rational expectationist position, the credibility hypothesis does not require that the public understand the actual policy process itself. The public only needs to observe inflation occurring over a protracted period of time to conclude that a policy is inflationary. Once this view of policy becomes accepted, it takes severe and continuous counteraction by the Fed to convince the public that it is now following a credible anti-inflationary policy. The cost of such severe action may be very high in terms of resulting unemployment and lost output in the economy. However, once the public accepts the notion that the Fed is following a true anti-inflationary policy, it will act so as to reinforce the policy. For example, it appeared that such a conviction became more widespread in the latter part of 1981 and early 1982 but at a cost of a severe recession.

The arguments about the credibility hypothesis and the rational expectations hypothesis focused on the public at large. This focus can be narrowed even further in assessing the role of expectations. Based on our study in this text, it is clear that there are many sophisticated "players" in the financial system who make a considerable effort to gather information in order to anticipate the course of the financial markets and the economy. Financial intermediaries and large corporations are particularly active in this regard. The actions that these institutions undertake based on their expectations have a considerable impact on the markets and the economy.

The discussion above demonstrates that expectations in a dynamic economy may translate into meaningful economic behavior that can substantially affect the course of the economy. Much of the rhetoric surrounding the Reagan economic program and the Fed's recent policy decisions demonstrate an awareness of the importance of public expectations in the economy for achieving policy. It would appear that policy makers have become convinced that they cannot be indifferent to public perceptions of what policy is really trying to accomplish.

Wage and Price Controls

A chapter on inflation would be incomplete without mention of one method that is put forward often as a temporary cure for inflation—mandatory wage and price controls. In recent years, wage and price controls have been implemented once in the United States by President Nixon in 1971 and retained in various forms until 1973. Interestingly, the most frequently heard argument for mandatory wage and price controls is that they would serve to reduce or eliminate inflationary expectations. Virtually no one who proposes these controls argues that they would eliminate inflation. All they can do is temporarily eliminate the price rises that are symptoms of something wrong in the economy. Unfortunately, they also tend to lead to substantial distortions in the economy. Recall that in a market economy prices are important signaling devices, and the elimination of such devices means that in some ways the economy is "running blind." Thus, pressures build up in the economy that will ultimately force the elimination of controls and result in a rapid acceleration in inflation after their removal. This is what occurred after controls were finally removed in 1973. For example, in 1970, the year preceding wage and price controls, the CPI had increased by 5.9 percent. In 1971, the CPI rose 4.3 percent, although prices were frozen for part of that year. In 1974, the first full year after the complete removal of virtually all remaining controls, the CPI shot up at an 11 percent rate. Other price indices such as the GNP deflator showed a similar pattern.

Despite the experience of the Nixon wage and price controls and their aftermath, recommendations for their reimposition have surfaced in recent years. During the Carter administration some voluntary wage–price guidelines were utilized, but these seemed to have little impact and were eliminated by President Reagan. There have also been a number of other plans advanced that rely on tax incentives to reward appropriate labor and management behavior with regard to wages and prices rather than on mandatory wage and price controls. As yet none of these tax incentive plans have been put into effect.

Economic Policy in the 1980s

A major portion of this last part of the text has dealt with economic and regulatory policy, so it may be appropriate to end not only this part but the text with a brief view of economic policy and trends for the remainder of the 1980s. As this book goes to press (mid-1982), the economy is in recession, inflation is falling rapidly, interest rates are falling, and financial innovation continues to proceed at a rapid pace.

Economic policy has been put in place that appears designed to restore price stability even at the price of a severe recession. Monetary policy is tight and easy fiscal policy (tax cuts and increased spending) has not yet reversed the recession. The hope of policy makers is that once price stability is restored, the fall in interest rates that will accompany the fall in inflation and slack economic activity will serve as a catalyst for a new round of noninflationary economic growth. The Fed will, in a noninflationary environment, be able to encourage this growth with a suitable monetary policy. Only time will tell if the goal of noninflationary economic growth will ultimately be achieved. However, both the administration and the Federal Reserve appear to be sticking to their programs. It seems that, whether these programs are the appropriate ones or not, the lessons on the need for policy credibility have been learned.

Further deregulation of financial intermediaries appears to be continuing. Perhaps it is easier to see ahead in this respect than it is with regard to the overall course of the economy. As the 1980s progress, continued movement to financial supermarkets appears almost certain. This movement will put substantial pressure on Congress to continue to relax restrictions on existing financial intermediaries. The services they offer customers both in borrowing and in depositing funds will expand considerably. For example, perhaps even before the publication date of this book, S&Ls will gain permission to offer demand deposit accounts. There will no doubt continue to be mergers among financial institutions (a considerable number of S&Ls and MSBs have merged thus far in 1982) reducing the number of thrift institutions and perhaps commercial banks as well and increasing their size. Increased size in financial intermediaries is necessary for it is not too risky to predict that the specialized financial intermediary will grow into the full service financial center by the end of the decade.

Finally, financial markets will continue to grow and change. As needed by the financial system and the economy, new financial instruments will be developed, much as the bank RP market, to give but one example, developed and became important in the 1970s. One thing that can be stated with certainty at the close of this book is that the financial system will continue to be dynamic and will change to reflect the needs of the economy. This will ensure the continued efficient allocation of credit in the U.S. economy that has served it so well throughout its history.

THE NEW CPI

How the New CPI Will Alter Inflation Readings

In response to growing pressure from both politicians and academic economists, the Bureau of Labor Statistics is making a dramatic change in the consumer price index, the government's most closely watched indicator of inflation. The revision, which is coming at least two years earlier than planned, will insulate the CPI from the widest swings in interest rates. But there is no reason to believe that, over time, the new index will produce consistently lower rates of reported inflation than would be arrived at using the old CPI.

After a decade of internal debate, the BLS has decided to drop a measure of home-ownership costs that its own professional staff has come to consider an embarrassment. Instead of trying to compute the purchase and financing costs for the fraction of the population—about 6%—that buys a house in any given year, the new index will try to measure what it would cost home-owners to rent their own residences. **A quickened pace.** Such a change had been planned for the next regular major revision of the CPI in 1985, but political and economic realities forced the BLS to move with uncommon speed. The decision to use the CPI for all urban consumers (CPI-U) to index individual income tax rates beginning in 1985 made urgent the need for a more stable index that would protect government receipts from oscillations in interest rates. Since interest rate changes are incorporated into rents over a relatively long period, the revised index fills the bill.

The revised CPI-U will first be issued in 1983, giving the required two years of data before the first tax indexing in December, 1984. The corresponding CPI for wage and clerical workers (CPI-W), which is used to index both private wage contracts and most government benefit programs, including Social Security, will not be switched over until 1985. This delay is designed to avoid affecting existing three-year labor contracts, but it did not mollify organized labor. AFL-CIO President Lane Kirkland promptly charged that the change was designed "to undercut our most important measure of inflation."

BLS economists argue that, even without the pressure of tax indexation, they had no choice but to move quickly. They claim that events have rendered the current home-ownership component, which accounts for 22.8% of the total CPI, an embarrassing irrelevancy: BLS house-price estimates are based on data supplied by the Federal Housing Administration that cover a small and shrinking share of the housing market. Interest charges are based on fixed-rate, 30-year mortgages, an endangered species. **Lower rates.** There is no question that had the new treatment of home ownership been in effect during the past two years, reported inflation would have been much lower. For example, in the 12 months ending in September, the CPI-U rose 11%, whereas an experimental index similar to the new CPI was up only 9.2% in the same period. And there is little doubt that if mortgage rates drop over the next 18 months or so, the revised CPI would rise more quickly than would the present index.

The crucial question is how quickly rents will rise relative to the cost of buying and financing a house. Says BLS Commissioner Janet L. Norwood: "We did look at the possible effects of the change [in making the decision] because we don't know what they are."

Over the past decade, rents have not kept pace with house prices, in part because hefty capital gains on property reduced landlords' need to recover costs through rents. In the 12 months ended in September, however, the CPI rent index rose by 8.6%, while home purchase costs were up 5%. (The total home-ownership component was up 15.8%, largely because of rising financing costs.)

Although Kirkland and others charge that the BLS is making the change to lower the reported rate of inflation, the success of the Reagan program could actually cause the new index to rise faster than the old one would have. Declining inflation and tax law changes would reduce the attractiveness of buying relative to renting and put price pressure on rentals. At the same time, an end to soaring real estate appreciation could drive up rents.

Key Points

1. Inflation is defined as a continuous and general rise in prices. Alternatively, inflation can be defined as a continuous fall in the value of money in terms of goods and services.

2. Inflation is measured by changes in price indices. The three major price indices are the consumer price index (CPI), the producer price index (PPI), and the GNP price deflator (GNPD). While economists usually favor the GNPD, the CPI is the best known of the indices and is usually popularly considered to measure the "cost of living." The shortcomings of the CPI as an inflation measure were examined in the text. The major distortion in the CPI caused by the way in which housing costs are included is to be rectified by the substitution of the rental price of housing for housing cost in 1983.

3. The inflationary process takes place through the interaction of economic changes and policy actions. Inflation cannot long continue, whatever its initial impetus, if it is not validated by increases in the money supply. Such increases may be motivated by a desire to keep an economic expansion on track.

4. For many years there was believed to be a simple relationship between inflation and unemployment. This relationship was captured in the Phillips curve, which showed a tradeoff between inflation and unemployment. The economy could have less unemployment only if it was willing to accept more inflation and vice versa. However, the simultaneous oc-

currence of high inflation and high unemployment in the 1970s led to more complicated Phillips curve analyses.

5. Monetarists argue that in the long run the Phillips curve is vertical and that ever accelerating inflation as a result of economic policy decisions is the only way to hold unemployment below its natural rate. The natural rate need not coincide with an "optimal" level of employment. Neo-Keynesians argue that the long-run Phillips curve, while much steeper than this short-run Phillips curve, is nonvertical, thus ensuring that some level of inflation is consistent with full employment although that level of inflation might be undesirable. Neo-Keynesians accounted for the simultaneous high levels of inflation and unemployment experienced throughout much of the 1970s by arguing that the long-run Phillips curve had shifted to the right.

6. The role of expectations in the inflationary process has also received considerable attention in recent years. Both the rational expectations hypothesis and the credibility hypothesis attempt to show how expectations formed about policy can contribute to inflation.

Questions for Discussion

1. Compare and contrast the three major price indices in terms of what they measure. Explain why they do not yield identical measures of inflation.

2. What are the differences between the accelerationist and nonaccelerationist views of the Phillips curve?

3. How would you analyze a sudden and substantial rise in the price of food due, say, to a devastating drought causing a massive reduction in supply? Would this be inflationary if nothing else happened? Explain.

4. What is demand–pull inflation? Cost–push inflation? Explain the inflationary process for demand–pull and cost–push. Are the processes different?

5. Why is a once-and-for-all increase in the price level not inflation?

Suggested Readings

Arak, Marcelle V. "Indexation of Wages and Retirement Income in the United States." Federal Reserve Bank of New York *Quarterly Review*, Autumn 1978, pp. 16–23.

Carlson, Keith M. "Money, Inflation, and Economic Growth." Federal Reserve Bank of St. Louis *Review*, April 1980, pp. 13–19.

Carlson, Keith M. "The Lag from Money to Prices." Federal Reserve Bank of St. Louis *Review*, Oct. 1980, pp. 3–10.

The following three issues of the Federal Reserve Bank of San Francisco *Economic Review* were devoted to discussing issues in inflation:

1. "Alternative Strategies Toward Inflation." *Economic Review*, Fall 1979.
2. "Aspects of Inflation." *Economic Review*, Spring 1980.

3. "Responses to International Inflation." *Economic Review,* Summer 1980.

Gittings, Thomas A. "The Inflation–Unemployment Tradeoff." Federal Reserve Bank of Chicago *Economic Perspectives,* Sept./Oct. 1979, pp. 3–9.

McNees, Stephen K. "The 1979 Consumer Spending Spree: New Era or Last Gasp?" Federal Reserve Bank of Boston *New England Economic Review,* May/June 1980, pp. 5–21.

Resler, David H. "The Formation of Inflation Expectations." Federal Reserve Bank of St. Louis *Review,* April 1980, pp. 2–12.

Willes, Mark H. "The Future of Monetary Policy: The Rational Expectations Perspective." Federal Reserve Bank of Minneapolis *Quarterly Review,* Spring 1980, pp. 1–7.

Index

A 3
B 4
C 5
D 6
E 7
F 8
G 9
H 0
I 1
J 2